MEDIEVAL ENGLISH LYRICS AND CAROLS

MEDIEVAL ENGLISH LYRICS AND CAROLS

Edited by
Thomas G. Duncan

D. S. BREWER

First published 2013
D. S. Brewer, Cambridge

ISBN 978-1-84384-341-2

D. S. Brewer is an imprint of Boydell & Brewer Ltd
PO Box 9, Woodbridge, Suffolk IP12 3DF, UK
and of Boydell & Brewer Inc.
668 Mt Hope Avenue, Rochester, NY 14620-2731, USA
website: www.boydellandbrewer.com

A CIP catalogue record for this book is available from the British Library

The publisher has no responsibility for the continued existence
or accuracy of URLs for external or third-party internet websites
referred to in this book, and does not guarantee that any content
on such websites is, or will remain, accurate or appropriate.

Papers used by Boydell & Brewer Ltd are natural, recyclable
products made from wood grown in sustainable forests

Designed and typeset in Adobe Arno Pro by
David Roberts, Pershore, Worcestershire

Printed and bound in Great Britain by
TJ International Ltd, Padstow, Cornwall.

To
Julie and Hazel
Douglas, Edgar, Irina, Chloe and Roger

Contents

Preface

THIS ANTHOLOGY offers a wide and representative range of medieval English lyrics and carols. A comprehensive selection of 13th- and 14th-century texts, including all pre-Chaucerian love lyrics (other than a few brief snatches), is found in Part I. The lyrics in Part II are mostly from the 15th and early 16th centuries. Within each Part the lyrics and carols are ordered according to theme, arrangements which are fully explained in the Introduction.

At first sight it may seem odd to include lyrics from the Tudor period in an anthology of medieval lyrics. However, the early 16th-century lyrics in Part II are indeed characteristically 'late medieval'. Whatever the importance of the Battle of Bosworth Field (1485) as a turning point in English political history, significant changes in English culture were not to emerge before the second quarter of the 16th century. The music and poetry of England remained 'medieval' as long as French rather than Italian influences still prevailed, and the impact of Renaissance humanism and the Reformation had yet to be felt. In courtly poetry of the period 1370–1530, 'Chaucer and Wyatt, Charles d'Orléans and Henry VIII can be said to have been playing the same game and obeying the same rules.'[1] A similar claim regarding the continuity of what is characteristically late medieval may also be made for the religious and non-courtly lyrics in this volume.

Although many more English lyrics survive from the period 1400–1530 than from the 13th and 14th centuries, the earlier lyrics have hitherto tended to predominate in anthologies. Editors, consciously or unconsciously, seem to have shared the view that 'in artistic terms, one line of verse from the 14th century is worth ten from the 15th century'.[2] The present volume offers a fuller representation of later lyrics than is found in other general anthologies, and amply demonstrates that there are many excellent late medieval English lyrics which are at least as good as their early Middle English counterparts. As with the earlier lyrics, many of these poems are anonymous. Some, however, are by named writers, sometimes little known, such as John Audelay, an early 15th-century priest, Humfrey Newton (1466–1536), a country gentleman, and the late 15th-century Franciscan, James Ryman. Poetic merit could have justified the inclusion of more than the ten poems by Charles d'Orléans (1394–1465); one seemed sufficient representation for the Monk of Bury, John Lydgate (1370?–1452), notwithstanding his prominence in his own time. Poetry at the Tudor court is represented here by lyrics from Henry VIII's manuscript rather than by the early lyrics of Sir Thomas Wyatt (1503–42), who is found in many other anthologies. The excellence of the Scottish poet William Dunbar (c. 1460–c. 1513) made the inclusion of some of his lyrics essential.

Every effort has been made to present these texts in a readily readable form. The language of the lyrics in Part I has been normalized in accordance with the grammar

---

[1] *M&P*, p. 156.

[2] Stemmler (1970), p. v, rephrasing R. H. Robbin's dictum that 'historically, one line of verse from the 14th century is worth a hundred from the 15th century'.

and spelling of the Middle English of late 14th-century London. As the language of Chaucer, this is the form of Middle English most familiar to modern readers.[3] The lyrics in Part II are printed largely as found in the surviving sources. However, spellings which might prove difficult or misleading to readers unfamiliar with late Middle English have been replaced by more familiar spellings equally current in manuscripts of the period. The changes made are detailed in the Introduction.[4] In addition, generous glossing is provided to meet the needs of readers who have little or no acquaintance with Middle English. The glosses usually keep as close as possible to the literal sense and word order of the texts; they are not meant to serve as a translation but as an aid to a fuller understanding of the poems in their original language.

Metre, a subject so frequently passed over with little or no attention in editions of Middle English lyrics, is considered at length in the Introduction and in two Appendices. Of particular metrical significance is the treatment of the vowel 'e' in unstressed syllables where sometimes in Middle English, for various reasons, it may or may not have been pronounced. In the texts it is printed as 'ë' where it was probably pronounced. An outline description of the pronunciation of Middle English is also offered in the Introduction.[5] Where required, further explanation of scansion, sense, grammar or syntax is provided in the Commentary.

In establishing the lyric texts many manuscripts, facsimiles and microfilms were consulted; for only a few lyrics were standard scholarly editions relied upon. My debt to previous editors will be evident from references in the Commentary. The editorial approach followed has been eclectic. Where a poem survives in more than one manuscript, the text of the base manuscript has usually been followed; but where that manuscript fails in sense or rhyme, or is metrically suspect, superior readings have been adopted from other manuscripts or (when numerous) a selection of these manuscripts. Emendation has also been attempted whenever possible to restore metre, rhyme and sense in lyrics surviving in sole copies. Efforts by earlier editors to rescue these poems from obvious scribal corruption have often been sporadic at best. In the Introduction to *Medieval English Songs*, E. J. Dobson gave the following bold statement of his editorial aim: 'It has not been my object to reproduce the texts given by the scribes, but to recover as far as might be the text written by the original author.'[6] Though more conservative in practice, I salute this principle. In every case where an emendation has been adopted the original reading of the base manuscript is recorded in the Commentary along with relevant readings from other manuscripts where such exist.

The critical appraisal offered in the Introduction seeks to place these lyrics in the context of the development of English literature from Old English to the early 16th century, and through them to represent the main currents in literature and culture, sensibility and life, in the Middle English period. Further textual, contextual and linguistic information is provided in the Commentary.

---

[3] See p. 48.   [4] See pp. 48–9.   [5] See pp. 50–1.

[6] *MES*, p. 27. For further discussion of scribal corruption and the editorial aims and approach adopted in this volume, see Duncan (1981), (1992), (1994), and *Companion*, pp. 26–38.

Acknowledgements

My gratitude to those who made invaluable contributions to *Medieval English Lyrics, 1200–1400* and *Late Medieval English Lyrics and Carols, 1400–1530* was acknowledged in these volumes. In the preparation of this single-volume, revised edition I now offer my grateful thanks for valuable help in various ways to the following St Andrews friends and colleagues: Dr Margaret Connolly, Miss Andrea Givan, Mrs Ann Hargreaves, Dr Ian Johnson, Miss Jennifer Key, Professor Tony Lodge and Professor Karla Pollman. My thanks also go to Dr David Roberts who designed this volume and to Rohais Haughton and Anna Robinette of Boydell & Brewer. Finally, for her support, patience and good cheer from first to last in bringing this edition to publication I wish warmly to thank Boydell & Brewer's Editorial Director, Caroline Palmer.

Abbreviations and References

Books and Editions

AND — *Anglo-Norman Dictionary,* ed. L. W. Stone and W. Rothwell (London, 1977–92)

AV — The Holy Bible, Authorised King James Version

Benson — *The Riverside Chaucer,* ed. L. D. Benson, 3rd edn (Oxford, 1988)

Brook — *The Harley Lyrics,* ed. G. L. Brook, 4th edn (Manchester, 1968)

Brown XIII — *English Lyrics of the XIIIth Century,* ed. C. Brown (Oxford, 1932)

Brown XIV — *Religious Lyrics of the XIVth Century,* ed. C. Brown, 2nd edn rev. G. V. Smithers (Oxford, 1952)

Brown XV — *Religious Lyrics of the XVth Century,* ed. C. Brown (Oxford, 1939)

Champion — *Charles d'Orléans: Poésies,* vol. 1, ed. P. Champion (Paris, 1923)

Companion — *A Companion to the Middle English Lyric,* ed. T. G. Duncan (Cambridge, 2005)

CT — *The Canterbury Tales,* quoted from *The Riverside Chaucer,* ed. L. D. Benson, 3rd edn (Oxford, 1988)

EMEVP — *Early Middle English Verse and Prose,* ed. J. A. W. Bennett and G. V. Smithers, with a glossary by N. Davis, 2nd edn (Oxford, 1968)

Fasc. Mor. — *Fasciculus Morum,* with translation, ed. S. Wenzel (University Park, PA, 1989)

Godefroy — *Dictionnaire de l'ancienne langue française,* F. Godefroy (Paris, 1880–1902)

Gray, *Selection* — *A Selection of Religious Lyrics,* ed. D. Gray (Oxford, 1975)

Greene — *The Early English Carols,* ed. R. L. Greene, 2nd edn (Oxford, 1977)

LMELC — *Late Medieval English Lyrics and Carols, 1400–1530,* ed. T. G. Duncan (Harmondsworth, 2000)

LMVP — *The Oxford Book of Late Medieval Verse and Prose,* ed. D. Gray, paperback edn (Oxford, 1988)

M&P — J. Stevens, *Music and Poetry in the Early Tudor Court* (London, 1961)

MC — *Medieval Carols,* ed. J. Stevens, Musica Britannica 4 (London, 1952)

MED — *Middle English Dictionary*

Meditations — *Meditations on the Life of Christ,* ed. I. Ragusa and R. B. Green (Princeton, 1961; reprinted 1977)

MEL — *Medieval English Lyrics, 1200–1400,* ed. T. G. Duncan (Harmondsworth, 1995)

MES — *Medieval English Songs,* ed. E. J. Dobson and F. Ll. Harrison (London, 1979)

MEV	*The Oxford Book of Medieval English Verse,* ed. C. and K. Sisam (Oxford, 1970)
Mustanoja	T. F. Mustanoja, *A Middle English Syntax* (Helsinki, 1960)
NIMEV	*A New Index of Middle English Verse,* ed. J. Boffey and A. S. G. Edwards (London, 2005)
OED	*Oxford English Dictionary*
OLD	*Oxford Latin Dictionary* (Oxford, 1968–82)
Pat. Lat.	*Patrologiae cursus completus … series latina,* ed. J. P. Migne, 221 vols (Paris, 1844–64)
Robbins, *Hist.*	*Historical Poems of the XIVth and XVth Centuries,* ed. R. H. Robbins (Oxford, 1959)
Robbins, *Sec.*	*Secular Lyrics of the XIVth and XVth Centuries,* ed. R. H. Robbins, rev. edn (Oxford, 1955)
Whiting, *Proverbs*	*Proverbs, Sentences and Proverbial Phrases from English Writings Mainly before 1500,* ed. B. J. and H. W. Whiting (Cambridge, MA, 1968)
Woolf	R. Woolf, *The English Religious Lyric in the Middle Ages* (Oxford, 1968)

Other editions, books and articles referred to in this volume are to be found in the Select Bibliography; they are cited by the author's surname and the date of publication.

Biblical References

The names of the Books of the Old Testament (OT), the New Testament (NT), and the Apocrypha are abbreviated as follows:

Acts	Acts of the Apostles
Cor.	Corinthians
Eccles.	Ecclesiastes
Ecclus.	Ecclesiasticus
Eph.	Ephesians
Gen.	Genesis
Heb.	Hebrews
Lam.	Lamentations
Mal.	Malachi
Matt.	Matthew
Rev.	Revelation
Rom.	Romans
2 Sam.	2 Samuel
S. of S.	Song of Solomon
2 Tim.	2 Timothy

Unless stated otherwise, quotations in English from OT and NT are taken from the King James Authorized Version, those from the Apocrypha from the Douay Version.

Other Abbreviations

Add.	Additional
adj.	adjective
adv.	adverb
AN	Anglo-Norman
BL	British Library
Bodl.	Bodleian Library
c.	*circa*
cf.	compare
conj.	conjunction
d.	died
EETS	Early English Text Society
ES	Extra Series
interj.	interjection
lit.	literally
ME	Middle English
MS	manuscript
MSS	manuscripts
n.	noun
NLS	National Library of Scotland
NLW	National Library of Wales
NS	New Series
OE	Old English
OF	Old French
om.	omitted
ON	Old Norse
OS	Original Series
p.	page
p.p.	past participle
pl.	plural
pp.	pages
refl.	reflexive
sc.	*scilicet*, 'understand' or 'supply'
sg.	singular
v.	verb

This anthology is a single-volume, revised edition of two previous lyric anthologies, *Medieval English Lyrics, 1200–1400* (*MEL*) and *Late Medieval English Lyrics and Carols, 1400–1530* (*LMELC*), first published in 1995 and 2000 respectively. In order to preserve a system of reference to the lyrics and carols compatible with the earlier volumes already widely quoted in scholarly literature and, not least, in *A Companion to the Middle English Lyric* (Cambridge, 2005), the texts here are presented in two sections, Parts I and II, corresponding to the two volumes of the earlier editions. Thus, for example, in this volume, *MEL* **30** and *LMELC* **30** are to be located as **I, 30** and **II, 30**.

Introduction

Medieval English Lyrics and Carols

> With longing I am lad,   *I go* (lit. *am led*)
> On molde I waxë mad,   *on earth I am going mad*
> A maidë marrëth me.   *distresses*
>
> **I, 1**, 1–3

WITH WORDS LIKE THESE Middle English poets expressed their love. This love-longing was something new; it was certainly foreign to Old English literature. Occasionally a cry of love is heard in Old English, as in the following lines from the enigmatic poem *Wulf and Eadwacer*:

> Wulf, O my Wulf, my yearning for you
> Has made me ill; the rareness of your visits,
> My sorrowing spirit, not a lack of food.

Here, however, the speaker is not a man but a woman. In the heroic world of Old English poetry, a man's concern centred on his duty to his lord; his supreme values were those of loyalty and courage in battle. The ideal of love as unqualified devotion to a lady was as yet unknown.

The 12th century was the watershed between the heroic and the romantic worlds of the earlier and later Middle Ages. This period was not only remarkable for pilgrimages and crusades, commercial expansion and social change, ecclesiastical reform and the revitalization of the Church, the flourishing of the cathedral schools and the emergence of the universities; it was also a time of momentous developments in art and architecture, in literature and learning, and, above all, in modes of thought and feeling. It was in the 12th century in the south of France that there emerged, in the poetry of the troubadours, a new concept of love, one which has dominated western literature ever since.

The idea that love was noble and ennobling was, of course, nothing new; viewed in one way or another, such a notion would not have surprised Plato, Virgil, St Paul or St Augustine. But the belief that the proper object of love was a woman, and that unqualified devotion to a woman was the true inspiration of refined and noble conduct, would have astonished them. This, however, was the troubadours' creed. For them, the feudal concept of service to a lord was transformed, in the name of love, to become the service of a lady. Devotion to a lady was the only thing which made life worth living; such love was the ultimate joy. In the words of the 12th-century troubadour Bernart de Ventadorn, 'A man is really dead when he does not feel some sweet taste of love in his heart.'[1]

So important was this new concept of love in the later Middle Ages that it seems appropriate to begin this anthology with its portrayal in Middle English lyrics. Most of the love lyrics before Chaucer survive in one manuscript – MS Harley

---

[1] Goldin (1973), p. 127.

2253 in the British Library. In many of these (**1, 1–5** and **17–20**) urgent and repeated appeals are made to a lady for her 'pity', her 'mercy'.

Lady, thou rewë me,	*have pity on me*
To routhe thou hast me rad,	*to grief; brought*
Be bote of that I bad,	*be the remedy for which I have prayed*
My lyf is long on thee.	*my life is dependent*

I, 1, 7–10

The poet's very life may depend upon her, but the main focus of attention is not primarily on the lady; it is on the lover and his sufferings for *derne love*, 'secret love'.

Nis no fire so hot in helle	
Al to mon	*as a man*
That lovëth derne and dar not telle	*in secret; dares*
What him is on.	*what is wrong with him*

I, 2, 9–12

There is, however, little here of the intensity of devotion and the analysis of love characteristic of the troubadours. Nor are these personal lyrics of private, intimate love. On the contrary, they are public poems operating within and through well-recognized conventions.[2] The lover sighs, lies awake, feels condemned to death, and pleads for mercy; the lady shines, her hair is golden, her neck long, her waist slender, and, not infrequently, she is described as prudent and wise. There is even a common currency in the vocabulary of these lyrics, not least in the frequent use of alliterative tags; the lady is a *byrde in a bour, brightest under bis, geynest under gore* and *beste among the bolde* – all phrases used as much as anything for their alliteration.

Literary convention here, however, does not make for lifeless verse. Quite the reverse. What a reader may sense is the relish with which these poets make play with a range of conventions. Thus, the *reverdie*, the description of springtime with which several of the lyrics begin (e.g. **1, 17–20**), can be more than a conventional opening. In *Lenten ys come with love to toune* (**1, 20**), an entire poem is devoted to the *wynnë wele*, the 'wealth of joys', of spring. A profusion of blossoms and flowers, with the singing of nightingales and song thrushes, and with animals of all kinds mating on hillside and riverside, culminates in an ironic contrast of worms and women:

Wormës wowen under cloude,	*worms make love under ground*
Wommen waxen wonder proude,	*amazingly haughty*
So wel it wol hem seme.	*it becomes them*

I, 20, 31–3

In springtime nature rejoices and even worms make love; but women become difficult and men suffer. With understated brevity, the excellent little song *Foulës in the frith* (**1, 16**), presents the same contrast understood within the same convention. Ladies are sometimes described through a series of comparisons – most frequently with flowers or precious stones. The elaboration of this convention

² See further *Companion*, pp. xx–xxiii.

in *Ichot a byrde in a bour* (**1, 5**) is nothing less than a *tour de force*. Again, in *Moste I ryde by Rybbësdale* (**1, 25**), the detailed description of a lady from head to foot (as advocated in medieval Latin treatises on poetic style) is skilfully elaborated within the flow of the verse without any sense of artificiality or stiff formality. Allegory is effectively used at the end of *Ichot a byrde in bourë bryght* (**1, 3**) where the lover appeals to Love against the activities of the lady's knights, Sighing, Sorrowing and Perplexity.

A significant part of the appeal of these lyrics lies in their song-like qualities. These are not poems in which the poet tries to argue his lady into love; nor does he philosophize. These poems celebrate love in motifs and conventions which are pleasing because they are familiar, and in language which finds its music in a harmony of rhyme and alliteration. As the poet laments and pleads in familiar form, there is nothing tough or intellectually challenging to impede the rhythm and flow of the verse. This poetry, as it were, 'sings' of love – with a parade of suffering, indeed, but without personal *angst*. Nowhere, perhaps, do these qualities make for a more effective expression of the joy of love than in:

An hendy hap Ichave y-hent,	*good fortune I have received*
Ichot from hevene it is me sent,	*I know; sent to me*
From allë wommen my love is lent	*has gone*
And light on Alysoun.	*and alighted*

1, 18, 9–12

This *hendy hap*, a 'good fortune' no less than heaven-sent, dances in these lines. Yet the very mention of all the women in whom the poet's interest ceases with the advent of Alison's love (unusually, the poet's beloved is named here) brings with it a sense of the world at large and of other relationships which would be alien to the singular devotion and claustrophobic atmosphere of many a troubadour lyric. The ecstasy of this refrain runs in counterpoint to the content of the stanzas: the lover's love-longing of stanza 1, the description of the beloved and the poet's despair of stanza 2, his nightly anguish of stanza 3, and his final plea in the concluding stanza.

Some of the lyrics reflect a genre typical of the 13th-century trouvère poets of northern France, the *chanson d'aventure*. Characteristically these poems open with lines like:

As I me rode this endrë dai	*went riding the other day*
On mi playinge.	*for my pleasure*

1, 21, 4–5

In the French *pastourelle* (one form of the *chanson d'aventure*) the poet rides out (riding marks his aristocratic status) to seek pleasure in a pastoral landscape where he comes upon a girl, often a shepherdess under a tree or in a sweet arbour, lamenting lost love. Usually he offers to 'comfort' her, and usually his offer is accepted. However graceful and charming the French poems may be, the protagonist is scarcely more than a high-born seducer; the abject devotion of a troubadour to his lady is totally reversed. Again, unlike the troubadour *chansons d'amour*, these are dialogue poems in which the woman's voice is heard. Of a handful of Middle English poems reflecting this genre (**1, 21–24**), the earliest, *As I me rode this endrë dai* (**1, 21**), is nearest to the manner and pastoral setting of the French *pastourelles*. As in French poems, the poet indeed 'rides' out for pleasure and meets a maiden singing 'in a sweet arbour'. But here, the bitter and vengeful tone of the girl's words – *'The clot him clinge!'* (8) and *'If I mai, it shal him rewe'* (25) – stand in marked contrast to the pastoral setting and the elegance of the verse. There is an Old French poem which closely resembles this lyric.[3] In the French, however, the maiden's tone, though distressed, is not harsh. The French poem also has an extra stanza in which the maiden accepts the poet's love. One may wonder if, perhaps, an equivalent final stanza of the English poem has been lost, or if the girl's tone precluded further overtures on the part of the English poet.

Even further from the style and tone of French *pastourelles* is *In a fryth as I gan farë fremëde* (**1, 22**). It opens with the poet walking (not riding) as a stranger in a wood (rather than in a familiar pastoral setting) and finding not a shepherdess but a *fair fenge* (2) – a 'fair prize'. This poet proves to be a man of guile, but the girl is a match for him in the cut and thrust of sexual politics. The alliterative verse of this poem matches the weightier moral debate which ensues, in the course of which various poetic genres (the 'complaint of the betrayed maiden', the *chanson de mal mariée*[4] and the *chanson des transformations*[5]) are skilfully exploited.[6] Different again is *As I stod on a day* (**1, 23**): the maiden here is of quite another stamp, well dressed and sophisticated. After a rather arch response to the poet's flattering greeting, she wittily dismisses his subsequent advances. Rather in the manner of the lover of the *chanson d'amour* he begs to become 'her man', only to be accused of raving, humbug and folly in her reply:

'Wher gospellëth	*what is the message of*
al thy speche?	*(pious) talk*
Thou findëst her noght here	*her not here*
the sot that thou seche.'	*idiot; seek*

1, 23, 20–21

The poet's further protestations are met with irony ('there must be some other girl who might choose you as chaste!', lines 27–8) and an ignominious dismissal. The 'clerk' of *My deth I love, my lyf Ich hate* (**1, 24**) suffers in a typically love-lorn manner, and makes his appeal to his *swete lemman* (15); her response is, to say the least, curt: *'Do wey, thou clerk, thou art a fol'* (17). The contrast of this brusque girl and the plaintive lover is comical to the point of farce. Yet, three stanzas later, with a sudden *volte face*, and echoing the clerk's first pathetic rejoinder – *'Welawei, why seist thou so?'* (25) – she succumbs to his entreaties. Can this extraordinary poem be anything other than a burlesque by a poet merrily exploiting the ludicrous extremes of different traditions of love poetry?

Love is also the theme of a scattering of short Middle English lyrics in a more popular vein (**1, 7–15** and **26**). The shortest are by turn intriguingly suggestive (**1, 10** and **12**), plaintive (**1, 11**), and rueful (**1, 13**), and, in the case of a couplet found in the same manuscript as **1, 12** and **13** –

---

[3] See Bartsch (1870), no. II. 7.
[4] See Commentary, **1, 22**, 36.
[5] See Commentary, **1, 22**, 45.
[6] See Commentary, **1, 22**, and Woolf (1969), pp. 56–8.

> Ne shaltou never, levedi,
> Twynklen wyth thin eyen

– sinister. In **1, 14** appears the splendid image of a lover so patient in his cold vigil outside his beloved's house that his foot has frozen to the gate-post. Both **1, 7** and **8** witness to the heart-ache of lost love. The poet of **1, 7** may have lost his beloved to some local lord (5–7); and perhaps there may be detected in **1, 8** a whiff of class or even nationalistic antagonism on the part of a jilted lover who would have avenged hurt to his erstwhile beloved from any quarter – even from the son of the king of Normandy. These verses invite endless speculation: they survive without local habitation, name or context.

Chaucerian love lyrics (**1, 32–35** probably, but not certainly by Chaucer) are of an entirely different order. It is in Chaucer that the Middle English love lyric first emerges as fully courtly in character. Though not without glimpses of courtly settings – of castle and hall, of tower and bower – the world of earlier Middle English lyrics was more typically that of nature in springtime, with the blossoming of tree and flower, the song of birds, and the joy of animals in their love-making all presenting an ironic contrast to the misery of the love-lorn poet. Now in Chaucer, as in *at a revel whan I see you daunce* (**1, 29**, 6), the courtly ambience is immediately felt.

This courtliness is not only an evocation of a world of courtly manners; it is also a matter of form and style. Chaucer's poems stand directly in the tradition of the French verse of the courtly milieu in which he was educated. He was probably the first poet to introduce into English two of the fixed forms of French courtly poetry, the roundel and the ballade, both favoured by his French contemporaries Machaut, Deschamps and Froissart. His fluency and skill in the roundel form – a short lyric in which the opening line or lines recur in the middle and at the end – are immediately evident in the lively flowing lines of *Now welcome, somer, with thy sonnë softe* (**1, 28**). The ballade, particularly complex and sophisticated in its versification, would appear, from the short poems which survive, to have been Chaucer's preferred form. Except that it lacks a concluding envoy, *To Rosëmounde* (**1, 29**) follows classical ballade structure – three eight-line stanzas, each ending with the same line as a refrain, and each following not only the same rhyme scheme, a b a b b c b c, but also with identical rhyming sounds in each stanza. In other ballades (including the moral ballades *Truth* (**1, 63**) and *Gentilesse* (**1, 64**), and his *Complaint* to his purse (**1, 120**)) Chaucer uses rhyme royal (a seven-line stanza rhyming a b a b b c c), a form already used in ballades by Machaut and Deschamps. *Fortune* (**1, 62**) is a triple ballade, that is, three consecutive ballades in eight-line form concluding with an envoy. It is also to be noted that Chaucer's ballades are the first English lyrics composed throughout in decasyllabic lines as distinct from the shorter lines of earlier lyrics.

Chaucer's are also the first Middle English love lyrics written in what his contemporaries would have recognized as a 'high' style, a more urbane manner of writing than that of earlier lyrics, with a richer, partly French-derived vocabulary, a more complex syntax, and a more elaborate play of rhetorical devices. In his treatise on the art of poetry, *L'art de dictier et de fere chançons, balades, virelais et rondeaux*, Chaucer's friend Deschamps distinguished between the song lyric (which was sung) and the literary lyric (which was recited rather than sung). Chaucer's ballades are of the latter type, a poetry of complexity and sophistication unsuited to singing. This fundamental contrast with many of the earlier Middle English lyrics is immediately apparent in the involved syntax of Chaucer's speculations about love and his attempts to persuade or excuse by argument. His poetry is also more intimate. Rosemounde, whoever she was, is addressed directly: *Madame, ye ben of al beauté shryne* (**1, 29**, 1). Unlike the earlier nameless poets, with Chaucer we find not only a name but a personality. The humorous exaggeration of weeping a barrel full of tears (**1, 29**, 9) or the witty image of the poet in love like a pike steeped in galantine sauce (**1, 29**, 17–18) are typically Chaucerian, as are the opening lines of the third part of *Merciles Beauté*:

> Sin I fro Love escapëd am so fat,
> I never thenk to ben in his prison lene.   *lean*
>
> **1, 34**, 27–8

Elsewhere Chaucer alludes to his portly figure (e.g. in the *Envoy a Scogan*, line 31, and *The House of Fame*, line 574); here, echoing the line 'Puiz qu' à Amours suis si gras eschappé', from a ballade by his contemporary, the Duc de Berry, he jokingly asserts that as a fat man – pining lovers are supposed to be lean! – his escape from the prison of love is guaranteed.

Whereas Continental influences in the earlier lyrics are French, the cultural context within which Chaucer wrote was both French and Italian. Among Chaucer's lyrics an especially noteworthy instance of Italian influence is found in the *Canticus Troili* (**1, 31**), where a Petrarchan sonnet, eloquently rendered in rhyme royal, makes its first appearance in English.[7]

U NLIKE THE LOVE LYRICS, Middle English penitential and moral lyrics stand in a tradition of themes already well represented in Old English, both in homiletic prose and in poetry. In an age of faith when life expectancy was often short, it is not surprising that such themes as the Day of Judgement, the terrors of hell, death and the transience of this world's joys should have figured so prominently. Man's soul was constantly threatened by three powerful enemies – the world, the flesh and the devil; salvation was to be attained only by sincere and thorough repentance. A considerable proportion of Middle English literature also dwells on such concerns; and it was evidently considered a valid and important function of poetry to stimulate moral reflection and penitential contrition. This may seem alien to present-day taste; yet, at their best, lyrics reflecting such characteristically medieval preoccupations can readily engage the imagination of a modern reader with their urgency and sense of conviction.

Middle English moral verse tended to be more popular in style than Old English 'gnomic' poetry; it also reflected significant cultural differences.

> Where is the horse? Where is the young hero? Where is the generous lord?
> Where are the places of banqueting? Where are the joys of the hall?
> Alas, the bright cup! Alas the mail-clad warrior!
> Alas the glory of the prince!

---

[7] See Gray (1983), pp. 97–8.

In these lines from *The Wanderer*, an Old English poem well known through modern English translations (including a version by Ezra Pound), the poet speaks of the inevitable transience of the things of this world, but with a sense of overwhelming regret at the passing of an aristocratic, heroic culture which the horse, the hero, the banqueting halls, the golden cup, the warrior and the prince represent. The same *ubi sunt* topos is used in a very different manner in a Middle English penitential poem. 'Where are those who were before us?', asks the poet of **I, 47**. The following description of lords with their hawks and hounds, of ladies with gold in their hair and their splendid robes, of their banqueting, their revelry, their courtly dalliance and their pride, climaxes suddenly with:

> And in a twinkling of an eye
> Here soulës weren forloren.   *their souls were lost*
>
> **I, 47**, 11–12

They had their paradise here: now they pay for it in hellfire, where:

> Long is 'ay!' and long is 'o!',   *ah! / ever; oh! / always*
> Long is 'wy!' and long is 'wo!'.   *alas!; woe!*
>
> **I, 47**, 22–3

The tone is unmistakably that of a popular preacher contemptuously revelling in the fate of aristocratic pomp and pleasure.

Typical of the Middle English penitential lyric is the manner in which traditional homiletic exhortations find direct and personal expression. In *Lavedy seynte Marie* (**I, 37**), the poet speaks in the first person. He dreads the consequences of a misspent youth – his sins in word and deed, in bed and at board; his excessive indulgence in food, wine and sumptuous clothing; his neglect of alms-giving and the needs of the poor – and beseeches Mary to intercede with Christ on his behalf for protection from the pains of hell. Often, as in this poem, urgent though the sense of contrition may be, the penitent is not individualized; he speaks, in effect, not only for himself but for every contrite reader. Likewise, the reluctant penitent of *Lord, thou clepedest me* (**I, 49**) – a deft but ominous rendering in Middle English verse of famous words of St Augustine[8] – speaks for any sinner. However, in *Hye Loverd, thou here my bone* (**I, 51**), one of the best of the penitential lyrics, the speaker, again lamenting a misspent life and the miseries of old age, emerges vividly and poignantly. Enduring insults – he is a mere 'floor filler', a 'good-for-nothing fire-gazer' – he sits forlornly lodged by the fire like a social outcast. The romantic dalliance of youth is now a mere memory barely to be hinted at: *Nou I may no finger folde* (21, and similarly, 40). His days of accomplished horsemanship and splendid robes are gone (30–31); now the sight of strong steeds only accentuates his pathetic limping and his despair. Once he cut a dashing figure; now, in words reminiscent of Donne or Hopkins, he can only urge Death not to delay:

> Dredful Deth, why wilt thou dare?   *tarry*
> Bring this body that is so bare   *take*
> And in bale y-bounde.   *torment*
>
> **I, 51**, 86–8

[8] See Commentary, **I, 49**.

Other prominent themes find exceptional expression in the form of a lullaby in **I, 50**. However tender the tone of the refrain, *Lullay, lullay, litel child, child, lullay, lullow,* the mother's song is far from one of joy and expectation for her child. Here the bitter weeping of the child reflects its unhappy lot in this hostile world where it is not even a pilgrim but merely an alien guest. Other creatures may prosper, but not the 'wretched brat of Adam's blood' (19–20). The mother bids the child reflect on the three last things (29–32), the theme of **I, 41** and **42**; the child's foot is already on Fortune's wheel (45–8), an omnipresent medieval moral theme (cf. **I, 58** and **59**); the bitter pain of death is inescapable (67–8).

A rather different manner of writing, more discursive and philosophical, is encountered in **I, 60** and **61**, two of the refrain lyrics found in the Vernon manuscript, a late 14th-century compilation, largely of religious and didactic works. The theme of each poem is anchored in a key-word repeated in the refrain, the final line of each stanza. In **I, 60** the reader is constantly bidden to heed the lessons of 'yesterday' – to recognize the transient nature of existence in the light of past experience. Illustrations are presented and arguments persuasively advanced within the flow of the verse, and sometimes with some imaginative flair, as in stanza 11, where the image of children chasing by candle-light shadows which, inevitably, they cannot catch is used to express the futility of human endeavour. *This world fareth as a fantasy* is the refrain of **I, 61**, a poem which draws heavily on the Book of Ecclesiastes. After earnest reflection on the mutability of all things and all creatures and on the futility of all theology and philosophy, the poet surprisingly concludes: 'But make we merry and slay care' (123). This advice is, indeed, immediately followed by 'And worship God while we are here' (124) and a plea for God's mercy: but the devout conclusion comes as something of an afterthought; the inspiration of both Vernon lyrics is wisdom rather than faith.

In Chaucer's moral lyrics there is none of the insistent and sometimes rather wearing didacticism of the Vernon poems. Chaucer's manner is urbane. His Boethian themes – fortune, truth and *gentilesse* (nobility) – are those central to all medieval literature of any philosophical pretension; in his lyrics they are handled with poise, imagination and control hitherto unequalled in English moral verse. This world is not man's true home, as the mother of *Lullay, lullay litel child, why wepëstou so sore?* (**I, 50**) had recognized; but only in Chaucer's hands could this familiar Boethian theme find expression as:

Here is non home, here nys but wyldernesse:	*no home; is nothing but*
Forthe, pylgryme, forthe! Forthe, beste, out of thy stal!	*onwards pilgrim; beast*
Knowe thy contré, loke up, thank God of al;	*look up*
Holde the heye wey and lat thy gost thee lede,	*keep to the main; let*
And trouthe thee shal delyvere it is no drede.	*[your spirit*

I, 63, 17–21

I F THE PENITENTIAL AND MORAL LYRICS continue themes and traditions already present in Old English literature, many of the devotional lyrics, like the love lyrics, reflect the thought and feeling of a new age. In the finest of Old English religious poems, *The Dream of the Rood*, Christ is depicted as a young warrior in the heroic tradition. Yet, however exceptional the depth of feeling with which the experience of the crucifixion is related by the personified cross in this poem, it is not an emotion akin to such direct expressions of tenderness as:

> Swetë Jhesu, king of blisse,
> Min hertë love, min hertë lisse,   *heart's love, my heart's joy*
> Thou art swetë mid y-wisse,   *sweet indeed*
> Wo is him that thee shal misse.   *who will lose you*
>
> **I, 67,** 1–4

It is to the 11th century rather than to the 12th that one may look for the sources of this later medieval sensibility. One important new departure emerged in St Anselm's fundamental reappraisal of the Doctrine of the Atonement. Previously the doctrine of salvation had been conceived of in heroic terms. God and the Devil were like two feudal lords. Man had withdrawn his service from God and had given himself into the service of the Devil. But because man had done so of his own free will, the Devil had thereby gained 'rights' over man. In justice, therefore, God could not simply use his omnipotence to defeat the Devil. He had to turn to strategy. The master plan was that in Christ God should become man. The Devil, not recognizing Christ's divinity, subjected Him to death. But this he did illegally – for he had no rights over Christ – and Christ was then able to defeat the Devil and thus to rescue man. In this version, salvation was a cosmic struggle between God and the Devil with man as a passive pawn and Christ as a rather impersonal hero. For Anselm, the very notion of the Devil having any 'rights' was unacceptable. He presented a new account of salvation. Man by his sin had incurred the penalty of death. Christ, out of love for man, became a man, and by suffering death paid for man that penalty which man alone could not pay. A cosmic view thus changed to a personal vision – a vision of Christ as a man, suffering for his fellow man out of love. This new doctrinal emphasis on Christ's love for man and on love as man's appropriate response to Christ contributed to a fundamental change in later medieval piety already to be seen emerging in forms of monastic devotion in the 11th century, new modes of meditation dwelling with love and compassion on the humanity of Christ, on his earthly life, and on his agony on the cross, especially characteristic of the Cistercian order and its leading 12th-century figure, St Bernard of Clairvaulx. 'It was the Cistercians,' claims R. W. Southern, 'who were the chief agents in turning the thin stream of compassion and tenderness which comes from the 11th century into the flood which, in the later centuries of the Middle Ages, obliterated the traces of an older severity and reticence.'[9]

Middle English devotional lyrics reflect this tenderness and compassion. The theme of the first group here (**I, 67–73**) is love, the mode and language of love characteristic of later medieval devotional poetry expressing man's love for Jesus and His love for man. The sweetness of the very name of Jesus, Jesus as a 'sweet lover', Jesus who freely but so dearly 'bought' us with *Woundës sore and peynës strong* (**I, 68,** 14), with His very heart's blood, Jesus 'my love', 'my God', 'my kyng', 'my light', Jesus 'all my thought' – such are the characteristically new expressions of love as seen in *Jhesù, swete is the love of thee* (**I, 68**), a lyric which was inspired by and which echoes the famous Cistercian poem *Jesu dulcis*

---

[9] Southern (1959), p. 242.

memoria.[10] Here is the source of much that is familiar in later English devotional verse as, for example, in the work of the great 17th-century poet George Herbert. In the lyrics concerning Mary, the Annunciation, and the Virgin and child (**1, 74–83**), the same tenderness prevails. Sometimes it is matched by joy, as in the superb lullaby *Lullay, myn lyking* (**1, 80**), a Christmas carol still popular today; sometimes it merges with mystery, as in *I syng of a mayden* (**1, 79**), a simple but unique expression of the paradox of the Virgin birth; and sometimes with sorrow, as at the nativity, pictured here in the later medieval manner with manger, ox and ass:

Jhesu, swetë sonë dere,	*dear*
In porful bed thou list now here,	*on a pitiful bed you lie*
And that me grevëth sore;	*grieves me bitterly*
For thi cradel is as a bere,	*byre*
Ox and assë ben thi fere,	*are your companions*
Wepe may I therfore.	*weep*

I, 83, 7–12

Wholly unlike the Old English *Dream of the Rood*, the crucifixion lyrics focus directly on Christ's suffering and humanity, often expressed through the intimate human relationships of mother and child, son and mother. In one lullaby, the Virgin is reluctant to sing 'as do mothers all' (**1, 81**, 16) as the misery of a cold, weeping baby prompts her to think of suffering in store:

Lullay, lullay, litel grom,	*lad*
king of allë thinge,	*things*
Whan I thenke of thy mischeef,	*misfortune*
me list wel litel singe.	*I have very little wish to sing*

I, 82, 13–16

Mary, at the foot of the cross, pleads not only with her son (**1, 91**); with dramatic force she directs her mother's grief at his persecutors:

Why have ye no routhe on my child?	*no pity*
Have routhe on me ful of mourning;	
Tak doun o rode my derworth child,	*from the cross my precious child*
Or prik me o rode with my derling!	*or nail me on the cross; darling*

I, 92, 1–4

Yet, though the emphasis of the crucifixion lyrics is on Christ's suffering, Middle English lyrics do not characteristically make this theme an occasion for excessive detail and lurid description. It is their restraint in this regard which makes for the finest poetry. The power of the burden of **1, 93** (possibly inspired by a painting or a crucifix) derives from its restricted focus – the evocation of Christ's suffering in terms of a single tear:

Lovely ter of lovely eye,	*lovely tear*
Why dost thou me so wo?	*do you cause me such grief*
Sorful ter of sorful eye,	*sorrowful*
Thou brekst myn herte a-two.	*you are breaking; in two*

I, 93, 1–4

---

[10] See Commentary, **1, 68**.

The concentration in this burden on Christ's tear, at once lovely and sorrowful, controls the poem as the stanzas widen to embrace first Christ as man of sorrows and mighty redeemer, then the pride of the sinner, *I proud and kene / Thou meke and clene* (11–12), then the sorrowing mother, and finally the paradox of the cross – Christ crucified as Christ victorious:

> Thin herte is rent,
> Thi body is bent,
>   Upon the rodë tre;
> The weder is went,   *storm is past*
> The devel is shent,   *destroyed*
>   Crist, thurgh the might of Thee.

I, 93, 23–8

Similarly, images generic and particular (the setting sun and the grief-darkened face of Mary), images of immediate effect and deeper biblical and liturgical resonance,[11] can combine with an absolute simplicity of language to create evocative strength in a mere quatrain:

> Now goth sonnë under wode,   *goes the sun under the wood*
> Me reweth, Marie, thi fairë rode. *I grieve, Mary, for your fair face*
> Now goth sonnë under tre,   *the tree*
> Me reweth, Marie, thi sone and thee. *son*

I, 84

This simplicity is not, however, that of unlettered poets. Rather, it reflects an awareness that in devotional poetry the appropriate level of style was what was known as the *sermo humilis*, the 'humble style'. Nor do these poems lack literary skill. In *Love me broughte* (**I, 70**), for instance, the diction could not be more simple. However, the use of anaphora (the rhetorical device of beginning successive lines or sequences of lines with the same words) and the handling of rhythmic effect are masterly. The sequence *Love / And love / Man* (A) and *Love / And love / And love* (B) of the initial words of the two three-line groups of stanza 1 is almost mirrored in reverse by *Love / And love / And love* (B) and *Love / For love / Man* (A) of stanza 2. The rhythmic pattern is, of course, exactly maintained. The repeated pronoun of these stanzas is 'me'. The emphasis and balance of this arrangement – *Love / me / man* – changes in the final stanza. Without anaphora, the rhetorical emphasis is partly on the pronouns, now of both first and second person – *thee / I / thee / thee / me / I / thee*. There is also a significant change in rhythm. The initial lines of stanzas 1 and 2 both began with a stressed syllable; the first line of stanza 3 now breaks this pattern by beginning with an unstressed syllable. But the crucial change arrives with the rhetorical and dramatic effect of the initial stress on *Wel* of *Wel is me* in line 17, the only middle line of any of the three-line groups to have initial stress. The joyous effect here – a joyous conclusion to the perplexing paradox of love[12] – is similar to the sudden and triumphant stress on *Modor* and *Wel* at the beginning of lines 17 and 19 of *I syng of a mayden* (**I, 79**).

---

[11] See Commentary, **I, 84**.
[12] See Commentary, **I, 70** and **I, 97**; see also Woolf, pp. 166–8.

Simplicity of language in these lyrics is matched by the absence of any display of ecstasy or agony. There is nothing to compromise the direct sincerity of the speaking voice, whether it be that of Christ or the sinner.

> Levëdie, Ich thonkë thee,   *Lady, I thank you*
> With hertë swithë milde,   *very humble*
> That god that thou hast i-don me   *for that good which*
> With thine swetë childe.

I, **74**, 1–4

This is a personal voice, but it is not self-absorbed: it speaks for all, for every sinner, for 'Everyman'. It is appropriate to a uniquely shared context, that of Christian devotion. Likewise, the address of Christ to his people is equally direct and personal:

> My folk, now answerë me,
> And sey what is my gilt;   *say; guilt*
> What might I mor ha don for thee,   *have done*
> That I ne have fulfilt?   *fulfilled*

I, **100**, 1–4

Echoing such familiar texts as *'Popule meus'* or *'O vos omnes'* from the Easter Liturgy, Christ's voice came to medieval readers with an immediacy and intimacy unknown to those of post-Reformation, non-liturgical traditions.

Sometimes the language and conventions of secular love poetry are used in the devotional lyrics, but to very different effect. *Now I se blosmë sprynge* (**1**, **69**) opens with the conventional *reverdie*; the poet speaks of a *swetë love-longinge* (3) which *gladëth al* [*his*] *song* (7) and upon which his life and joy depend. The poet's beloved is not, however, a lady, but Jesus. The situation of the secular lyric is reversed. The true lover and sufferer of love's anguish is here the beloved, the crucified Christ. The poet, for all his 'love-longing', fails in his love – *Of love ne can I nought!* (37) – and in his service of his *lemman softe*, his 'gentle beloved':

> Jhesu, lemman softe,   *gentle lover*
> Thou yif me strengthe and might,   *give me*
> Longinge sore and ofte   *yearning sore and often*
> To servë thee aright.

I, **69**, 41–4

The lover poet of this devotional lyric is humble and contrite; he has nothing of the secular lover's self-indulgent anguish. Nor is Christ, his beloved, at a distance like the typical lady of a secular lyric.

There is also to be found in some of the devotional lyrics a sophistication of style and play of wit. *In the vaile of restles mynd* (**1**, **73**) opens in the manner of a *chanson d'aventure*, with the poet seeking to find true love in the landscape of his troubled mind. On a hill he hears a voice lamenting:

> 'See, dere soule, my sidës blede,   *bleed*
> *Quia amore langueo'*   *because I languish for love*

I, **73**, 7–8

the voice of Christ suffering for love. Images of Christ as king, knight, lover, mother and husband emerge and merge within the poem. In particular, the poet draws on the romantic theme of Christ as the Lover Knight searching for and ready to sacrifice himself in the service of his beloved, man's soul. As king or knight, the lover's care for and generosity towards his beloved bring but ironic recompense:

> My faire love, and my spousë bryght,
>   I saved hyr fro betyng, and she hath me bet;   *beating; beaten*
> I clothed hyr in grace and hevenly lyght,
>   This blody surcote she hath on me set   *surcoat*
>
> I, 73, 25–8

and not only a 'bloody surcoat', but gloves, not white but red and stained, gloves which will not come off (41–5), and nails to buckle his feet (49–52). (An ironic contrast between items of clothing – this time those of a courtly dandy – and Christ's 'garments' is again exploited in **I, 101**.) The Song of Songs was one of the most important biblical sources of allusion and echo both in secular and devotional lyrics. Here it is the source not only of the refrain, *Quia amore langueo* (because I languish for love) itself, but also of the evocative associations in lines such as the following:

> My swetë spouse, will we go play?
>   Apples ben rype in my gardine;   *are ripe; garden*
> I shall clothe thee in new array,
>   Thy mete shall be mylk, honye, and wyne.   *your food*
>
> I, 73, 81–4

T HE MISCELLANEOUS LYRICS which conclude Part I of this volume are in some ways those most readily accessible to the modern reader. Stable-boys and lackeys, bailiffs and haywards, blacksmiths and pedlars, amorous clerics and ubiquitous friars may not be part of our lives today, but the concerns of these lyrics – unjust imprisonment, exploitation and impoverishment, bribery and corruption, and even noise pollution – are. Along with poems of moving complaint and biting satire which suggest a world far from the Merry England of popular fancy, this selection also offers others which in their zest, wit, humour, *double entendre*, roguery and sheer fun witness to a lighter side of medieval life.

Er ne couthe Ich sorwë non (**I, 109**) dates from the first half of the 13th century and is probably the earliest of these lyrics. Though the speaker, a prisoner, gives few details of his plight beyond the fact that he is an innocent victim of the misdeeds of others, his complaint in the form of a prayer is movingly personal. This lyric is in fact a song, written not to be read but to be sung to the tune of a French poem of which it is a translation. Indeed, it can only be properly appreciated when sung, for some of its lines are slightly awkward to read, reflecting, perhaps, some difficulty on the part of the English adapter in matching the verse form of the French. Of a considerable body of Middle English verse of social complaint and satire concerning the sufferings of the rural poor, *Ich herde men upon molde* (**I, 113**) is one of the most telling and specific. The expense of foreign wars from the reign of Edward I (d. 1307) on through the 14th century added considerably to the burden of taxation on the English peasantry. Here the plight of the small peasant farmer is vividly depicted: exposed to the tyranny of petty officials – the hayward, the bailiff, the wood-keeper, and most of all, tax gatherers – he is stripped of his savings, his seed-corn and his farm animals; his land is bare, or crops lie ruined by storms and flooding. The effectiveness of the poem in conveying its harsh picture derives partly from the force of its alliterative lines, partly from its colloquial language ('the green wax' for 'tax' has something of the smack of Cockney slang), partly from the oppressive sense of all-pervading social corruption as Will and Falsehood personified stalk the land, and partly from the use of direct speech to recreate the callous, overbearing arrogance with which tax collectors dealt with the peasantry.

Alliterative verse is used in several other poems here, in each to different effect. Its potential for linking of words in two-beat alliterative phrases is exploited to the full in a forceful and fast-moving tirade of invective directed against idle attendants, lackeys, stable-boys, and menials in general in *Of rybaudz I rhyme and rede o my rolle* (**I, 115**), a poem in which personal polemic enhances the impact of social satire. The élan of this lyric lies in a relish of sustained abuse, sometimes crude, sometimes ironic, akin to that found in the later Scottish poet Dunbar; and, as in some of Dunbar's poems, the popular, racy, idiomatic style here involves the use of words and phrases the exact sense of which is difficult to determine even if the gist is usually clear enough. Indeed, a straining of sense is by no means uncommon where, in the rhetoric of invective, the choice of words is mainly determined by the demands of alliteration. *Swarte smekëd smithes smatered with smoke* (**I, 132**) is another poem of invective in alliterative form, this time against blacksmiths by a poet deprived of sleep on account of their nightly din. This shorter poem is no less forceful, but it is more tightly wrought; the poet's exasperation provokes more than a flood of abuse. Here the zest is as much that of composition, the joy of a wordsmith, expertly fashioning in sustained alliteration a vivid and detailed presentation of blacksmiths at work both in sight and, with skilful onomatopoeia, in sound:

The mayster longëth a litel	*the master smith lengthens a small piece*
and lashëth a lesse,	*and hammers out a smaller bit*
Twynëth hem twayn	*twists the two together*
and touchëth a treble.	*and strikes a treble note*
Tik, tak! hic, hac!	
tiket, taket! tik, tak!	
Lus, bus! lus, das! –	
swych lyf they leden!	

I, 132, 17–20

Here the plosive 't's and 'k's with differing vowels evoke the anvil's response to various kinds of hammer strokes; the 's' consonants register the splutter and hiss of red-hot iron plunged into water.

It is mainly in song that a lighter side of life finds expression in these lyrics. In the famous Cuckoo Song, *Somer is y-comen in* (**I, 110**), with cuckoos singing loudly and merrily, meadows and woods blossoming, ewes bleating, cows lowing, bullocks and bucks leaping and cavorting, the vitality of nature is absolute, uncomplicated by the agonizing of pining lovers. Sung with the lively merriment of a round, the joy of this lyric is complete. Though no music survives with any of the other lyrics in this section, it seems virtually certain that *Ich am of Irlande* (**1, 117**) and *Maiden in the morë lay* (**1, 118**) were dance songs; *D … dronken* (**1, 119**), also from MS Oxford, Bodl. Rawlinson D.913, may have been a drinking song, but is more likely to have been a dance song too. MS London, BL Sloane 2593 is a small, pocket-sized manuscript with all the appearance of a minstrel's song book, and although lacking musical notation, many of its lyrics seem eminently singable. Some, like *I have a gentil cok* (**1, 122**) and *I have a newe garden* (**1, 125**), excel in subtle sexual innuendo. In a masterpiece of parody and welcome seduction (**1, 129**), the jolly, twinkling priest Jankin sings merrily and treads suggestively on a girl's foot during the mass – and all to her pleasure – *And yet me thinketh it dos me good* (21) – even if – *Deo gratias* (36) – she, alas, ends up pregnant. The variety runs on: poets on their purses (**1, 120** and **121**), another drinking song (**1, 123**), a warning against older wives (**1, 127**), a rogue peddling sex (**1, 128**), ballad-like poems about Judas (**1, 112**) and St Steven (**1, 126**), and satirical accounts of the doings of friars.

It has to be admitted that of all the Part I lyrics Chaucer's are among the finest – at least if one's taste runs to urbanity, a quality again evident in his humorous complaint to his purse (**1, 120**). Parodying the relationship of the courtly lover and his mistress, he addresses his purse as his 'lady dear'. To her alone he complains, punning adroitly on the words 'light' and 'heavy'. He will die unless she is 'heavy again' – i.e. 'serious' in affection, 'heavy' with cash. Chaucer's art is witty and sophisticated. Nevertheless, the Sloane lyric *Whan I have in myn purs y-now* (**1, 121**), however different, also has its own excellence – the ease, the immediate appeal, the lighter rhythms of the simpler song lyric – qualities characteristic of so many of the best Middle English lyrics. But by no means all these poems are songs. *Man in the moone stont and strit* (**1, 114**), a Harley lyric as far removed from the cosmopolitan Chaucer as alliterative from decasyllabic verse, is a poem of subtle wit, humour and imagination which, in its own manner, is without equal.

As one turns to the lyrics of Part II of this anthology it will immediately be evident how marked was Chaucer's influence on his immediate successors, especially in lyrics of a courtly character. Life at the royal and princely courts of late medieval western Europe is vividly portrayed not only in literature but also in late medieval manuscript illuminations, paintings and tapestries: reading, dancing, singing, instrumental music-making, intimate dalliance in garden alleys, bathing in fountains, tournaments, hunting, hawking, and other such activities are depicted in detail. The settings – refined, often lavish, and doubtless idealized – present a kind of paradise on earth. Love, to judge from late medieval literature, played a prominent part in court life, especially a version of love which was, at least in part, a kind of game, an imitation of the manners, conventions and values of a tradition of courtly love literature which originated in the poetry of the troubadours of 12th-century Provence and which found its most influential expression in the first part of the *Romance of the Rose* written in 1230 by Guillaume de Lorris. This idealized form of love 'showed how life in "middeleard", which orthodox theology taught men to despise, could be made a beautiful and worshipful thing'; and whereas the Bible spoke of salvation, courtly love

> was a gospel of leisure and pleasure. It taught you how to behave to your peers when you all had time on your hands; ... how to 'commune', especially in mixed company, and how to please.[13]

Although versions of troubadour conceptions of love were first found in English in love lyrics of the 13th and 14th centuries in a poetry of languishing lovers and idealized mistresses, it was in Chaucer that the Middle English love lyric first emerged as fully courtly in character, with its evocation of a world of courtly manners expressed in the sophisticated courtly versification of the roundel and the ballade.

Remarkably, Chaucer's legacy in the early 15th century is found at its best in the English poetry of a Frenchman, Charles, Duke of Orléans. Captured at the Battle of Agincourt at the age of 20, Charles remained in England as a hostage for 25 years before his release in 1440. While in England, he wrote poems, some in English, some in English and French.[14] His English poems in this volume (II, 1–10) show his mastery of the courtly ballade and roundel. Despite the formal demands of the ballade, Charles writes with Chaucer-like fluency. He also shows great skill and imagination in exploiting the potential of his imagery. In *Tofornë Love have y pleyd at the chesse* (II, 3), Danger (aided by Fortune) takes the poet's *lady* (7). The poet laments being checkmated, *Without so be y make a lady newe* (9). This refrain line unpicks the conventional equation of the poet's lady and the queen in chess. In chess it would indeed be possible to 'make a new lady' (i.e. gain a new queen) if one of the pawns reached the opposite end of the chess-board.[15] But what is possible in chess is impossible – or, at least, unthinkable – in life for a sorrowing lover. In the envoy, the poet passes from the chess metaphor to speak directly of his dead beloved and of grieving for her until his dying day. Yet, ironically, even as he abruptly dismisses any possibility of recovery, this refrain with its underlying implication is repeated yet again:

> For shulde y thenke rekevre me now – nay, nay,   *to recover now*
> Without so be y make a lady newe.
>
>   II, 3, 30–31

In less serious mode, Charles develops the unlikely comparison of a lover and an anchorite in *O sely ankir, that in thi selle* (II, 5), playing wittily on the ambiguities in *wanton* (4) and *helthe* (12). The anchorite is obliged by his monastic rule to remain within the confines of his cell: the poet, governed by no such rule, is free to indulge in *wanton wandryng* – to wander, that is, as he pleases, without restriction. However, as in modern English, *wanton* in Middle English also meant 'amorous', 'unchaste': accordingly, the contrast here is also between the poet in search of love and the anchorite bound by his vow of chastity. Further comparison with the anchorite leads the poet to complain:

---

[13] *M&P*, p. 155.
[14] See Commentary, II, 1.
[15] See Commentary, II, 3, 9.

But, welaway, y stonde in more myscheef,	*but, alas; in greater misfortune*
For he hath helthe and y of helthe am bare.	*salvation; am lacking*

II, 5, 11–12

The *helthe* the anchorite is said to possess is, of course, Christian 'salvation'. It was a commonplace of medieval poetry that this religious concept was metaphorically transferred to the religion of love in which it was the lady who alone could bring about the lover's 'redemption'. This is the rather different version of *helthe* which the poet lacks here.

Probably the best known of Charles's roundels is *My gostly fadir y me confesse* (**II, 7**). Other medieval poems portray lovers making their 'confessions', but this poem is exceptional in its unabashed and casually flippant tone, not least in the poet's aside, 'do you know how?' (3) – to his 'spiritual father', no less – as he admits that, allegedly 'without thinking' (5), he stole a kiss at a window. This 'confession' wittily exploits one of the crucial elements of a good confession – namely, the requirement of restitution, of returning, in a case of theft, what has been stolen. Here the theft has been a kiss; this penitent airily observes he will 'doubtless' restore it if he can – and this he vows to God.

Late Middle English love lyrics were seldom, if ever, purely literary distillations of moments of intense, private emotion: often as not, they were poems which served a practical purpose. Charles d'Orléans conducted an amorous correspondence in a sequence of ballades. The writing of verse epistles was an essential part of the ritual of paying court to a lady. Not surprisingly, petitions from lovers to their mistresses with formulae such as 'Go little bill' are not infrequent among late Middle English courtly lyrics. As in Charles d'Orléans's *Go forth myn hert wyth my lady* (**II, 9**), the convention of sending one's heart as messenger is adopted in:

Go hert, hurt with adversité,	*heart*
And let my lady thi wondes see,	*wounds*
And sey hir this, as y say the:	*say this to her; to thee*
'Farwel my joy, and welcom peyne,	*pain*
Til y se my lady agayne.'	*until*

II, 23

In this brief versified message, the anonymous poet's appeal to his lady centres on the notion of displaying to her his wounded heart. Some medieval readers (or listeners) may have detected here a daring parody of Christ's appeal to mankind in the same terms.[16]

If such elegant exchanges between lovers as *A celuy que pluys eyme en mounde* and the reply (**II, 12** and **13**) served the purpose of private communication, they also functioned as public entertainment. The lover in Gower's *Confessio Amantis* describes himself as having

ofte assaied	
Rondeal, balade and virelai	
For hire on whom myn hertë lai	
To make, and also for to peinte	*compose; embellish*
Caroles with my wordës qweinte	

[16] See p. 27, and Commentary, **II, 70**.

To settë my purpos alofte;	*express; aloud*
And thus I sang hem forth ful ofte	*sang them*
In halle and ek in chambre aboute.[17]	*and also*

He writes 'for her on whom [his] heart lay'. The lady is, of course, unnamed: the conventions of courtly love demanded no less. The fact that these very poems in which he 'sets [his] purpose aloft' were also poems he performed frequently in hall and in chamber made this requirement of secrecy all the more crucial. T. S. Eliot observed that 'a good love poem, though it may be addressed to one person, is always meant to be overheard by other people'.[18] This was certainly true of these courtly lyrics.

Though restricted in range, the themes of these love poems are, in the best lyrics, handled with poise and elegance. The pain of parting and of separation is a frequent complaint, and the blame is often laid on Fortune.

A! mercy, Fortune, have pitye on me,	
And thynke that thu hast done gretely amysse	
To parte asondre them whiche ought to be	
Alwey in on. Why hast thu doo this?	*always united*
Have I offended the? I? Nay, y-wysse!	*offended thee; indeed*
Then torne thy whele and be my frende agayn,	*turn thy wheel*
And sende me joy where I am nowe in payn.	

II, 27, 1–7

Charles d'Orléans was by no means the only poet to feel that *For dedy liif, my lyvy deth y wite* (**II, 2**). This living death, this 'endless sorrow past all despair' is also effectively expressed in **II, 28**:

This ys no lyf, alas, that y do lede,	*lead*
It is but deth as yn lyves lyckënesse,	*in life's likeness*
Endeles sorow assurëd owte of drede,	*guaranteed without doubt*
Past all despeyre and owte of all gladenesse.	*beyond all despair; devoid of all*
Thus well y wote y am remedylesse,	*I know I am without remedy*
For me nothyng may comforte nor amende	
Tyl deith come forthe and make of me an ende.	*death*

Of a good number of lyrics in which poets appeal for or lament the lack of their mistresses' 'mercy', the finest is Dunbar's *Sweit rois of vertew and of gentilnes* (**II, 29**). Sometimes, as in one of the brief songs in MS Oxford, Bodl. Ashmole 191, poets asked why ladies of outstanding beauty should lack mercy:

Thus I complayn my grevous hevynesse	*lament*
To you that knoweth the trewth of myn entent.	
Alas, why shuld ye be mersyles –	*merciless*
So moch beuty as God hath you sent!	*so much beauty*
Ye may my peyn reles.	*pain relieve*
Do as ye list – I hold me content!	*do as you wish*

II, 24

---

[17] Macaulay (1900) vol. 1, p. 110, lines 2726–33.
[18] Eliot (1971), p. 90.

In this case, however, the poet's 'grievous heaviness' seems to give way in the final line to an outburst of ironic exasperation reminiscent of Wyatt.

Beside lyrics in the 'high' style – poems especially characteristic of the Chaucerian legacy – the song lyric typical of earlier Middle English lyric poetry continued to flourish on into the early 16th century. Unadorned simplicity of language and the easy flow of short lines characterize such lyrics. The themes of these later songs (some of which survive with music) are those familiar from the early 14th-century Harley lyrics. Poets still die unless their ladies take pity on them:

Gracius and gay,	*and merry*
On hyr lyyth all my thoght;	*rests (lit. lies); thought*
Butt sche rew on me today,	*unless she has pity*
To deth sche hath me broght.	*death; brought*

II, 17, 1–4

Ladies are still described much as they had been in earlier lyrics:

Hyr eyne byth feyr and gray,	*are fair and gray*
Hyr brues byth well y-bent,	*eyebrows are well arched*
Hyr rode as rede as roose yn May,	*her complexion as red as a rose*
Hyr medyll small and gent.	*waist slender and elegant*

II, 17, 9–12

It is easy to be dismissive of verse of this kind: these later song lyrics have been condemned as being little more than a tissue of conventional phrases.

> When ye be mery than am I glad,
> When ye be sory than am I sad,
> Such grace or fortune I wold I had
> Yow for to plese howeuer I were bestad.

One critic quotes these lines from a lyric attributed to Sir Thomas Wyatt in the Devonshire manuscript – a collection of poems compiled by or for noble ladies of the court in the reign of Henry VIII – noting that the first two lines had already appeared in virtually the same form in *Now wolde y fayne sum merthës mak*,[19] and that even the rhyme words *glad-had-bestad* could be paralleled in an earlier 15th-century lyric and in Gower. Indeed, these features are already to be found in one of the Harley lyrics:

While I may glewe, when she is glad,	*sing, when she is gracious*
Of al this world namore I bad	*would ask*
Than be with hire myn one bistad ...	*alone; settled*

I, 2, 25–7

Verses like these, it is claimed, 'can hardly be said to have an author, since they are put together conventionally from conventional materials, without transcending art'.[20] However, the appeal of such lyrics – and they were much to early

---

[19] Mason (1959), pp. 169–70. See **II, 22**, 11–12: Mason quotes from the Findern text.
[20] Mason (1959), p. 173.

16th-century taste, to judge from the Devonshire and Henry VIII manuscripts – had little, perhaps, to do with anything so grand as 'transcending art'. These are song lyrics, whether originally written to be sung or not, and must be appreciated as such. Far from seeking the surprisingly new or the intellectually challenging, they deal in motifs and conventions which are pleasing partly because they are familiar. Aiming at the musical effects of rhythm, rhyme and cadence, this verse, elegant in manner, makes a virtue of immediacy of comprehension and simplicity in language, form and style.

> Now wolde y fayne sum merthës mak,   *would I gladly make merry*
> Al only for my ladys sak   *entirely on account of my lady*
>   When y her se;   *see*
> But nowe y am so far fro hir   *from her*
>   It wil not be.
>
> II, 22, 1–5

There is, indeed, neither challenge nor novelty here. A reader who fails to appreciate and respond to the flow of these lines – who, in effect, has no taste for the song lyric – will hardly find much pleasure in reading on through this poem, or in reading the two carols, *Myn owne dere ladi fair and fre* (**II, 18**) and *I saw never joy lyk to that sight* (**II, 19**), or King Henry VIII's *Whereto shuld I expresse* (**II, 33**).

Many lyrics express devotion to ladies who may be unresponsive – may 'lack mercy'. In some, however, especially those dealing with the recurrent theme of inconstancy and constancy (love with and without 'variance'), relationships between the sexes are viewed in a critical, sometimes bitter light. 'Be true, lady, for I you trust' runs the refrain of *Thayr ys no myrth under the sky* (**II, 20**); but the very request to be true belies the assertion of trust. Far from trusting his lady, this poet finds himself trying to argue her into constancy. The dove, he points out, albeit lacking the power of reason, is (unlike the fickle hind) true by nature: since irrational creatures can love *withoutyne varryance* (without inconstancy) (26), he urges his lady to do likewise (stanzas 2 and 3). But the hind is not easily forgotten, and this poet is all too well aware of love's instability:

> Love ys strange in all degré,   *in every respect*
> Summtyme hoyt and sumtyme colde,   *sometimes hot*
> Tharfor to dowt, yt caussis me,   *therefore to fear*
> Leyff, that yie shuld fro me foyld.   *beloved, that you should turn from me*
>
> II, 20, 33–6

Despite all his conventional protestations in the last stanza – his lady is the 'ointment' of his wounds, she is beautiful beyond his telling, the thought of her love can expel every sorrow – the poet's anxiety lingers on in the final refrain. The poet of **II, 37** may seek to occupy the moral high ground by espousing constancy, 'love without variance', as an ideal of *triste and gentilnesse* (loyalty and courtesy) (3), but his sceptical brother of **II, 38** argues for the opposite stance: since slavish devotion is a recipe for grief, he will love prudently 'with variance'. An outcast from his lady's favour in *O mestres, whye* (**II, 36**) chides her vigorously for her coldness towards him and peevishly concludes:

But sythe that ye	*since*
So strange wyl be	*distant*
As toward me,	*towards me*
And wyll not melle,	*associate (with me)*
I truste, percase,	*perhaps*
To fynde some grace	
To have free chayse,	*free hunting (i.e. in love)*
And spede as welle!	*succeed*

II, 36, 25–32

In his resentment he makes her hostility a justification for seeking 'free chase' (31) in the hunt of love, and in expressing his hope to 'succeed as well' (32) bitterly hints at inconstancy on her part. After a virulent attack on men for their hypocrisy and duplicity, the speaker of **II, 39** (presumably a woman) waspishly concludes:

Then semëth me	*it seems to me*
Ye may well se	
They be so fre	*are so free*
In every plase,	*place*
Hitt were peté	*it would be a pity*
Butt they shold be	*if they were not*
Begeled, pardé,	*beguiled, by God*
Withowtyn grase.	*without mercy*

II, 39, 25–32

A laconic acerbity in both poems seems to be accentuated by their verse form[21] in which tension is generated by spinning out sentences (some fairly long and complex) in a series of short staccato phrases marked by the rapid repetition of rhymes. In **II, 39** this also has the effect of giving prominence to key-words in the tirade: *varians* (4), *displesauns* (8), *dowbilnys* (12), *Newfangellnys* (16), *shame* (20), and *game* (24). By contrast, in the carol *Care away, away!* (**II, 40**), another forsaken lover merrily, ironically and mockingly asserts his indifference: such is *his* pain that, unlike the lovelorn stereotype of courtly love poetry, he eats well, drinks well, sleeps well and rises to a hearty meal with good wine rather than ale.

I am brought in suche a pyne,	*I am brought to such grief*
Y-brought in suche a bale,	*torment*
Whanne yc havë ryghte god wyne,	*when I*
Me listë drynke non ale.	*I have no inclination to drink any ale*

II, 40, 16–19

With good wine, who needs ale? This may suggest a preference for the wine of freedom to the ale of love-service – the general theme of the poem; it may also suggest that he prefers a new love – a final insult to his former mistress.

   How many of these lyrics actually circulated in courtly settings? Some doubtless did – those, for example, by Charles d'Orléans and the Duke of Suffolk and those in the Devonshire and Henry VIII manuscripts. And, as the contents of these manuscripts show, lyrics associated with the court numbered not only poems in a

---

[21] See Commentary, **II, 36**, and Commentary, **II, 21**.

'high' style: song lyrics and others of a more popular stamp also figured in courtly entertainment. However, the writing of lyrics in the courtly manner spread beyond the confines of aristocratic courts. The Findern manuscript and Humfrey Newton's commonplace book[22] testify to the vogue for such lyrics from the mid-15th century in well-to-do provincial households of Derbyshire and Cheshire. As for many lyrics surviving anonymously in manuscripts of this period, their provenance can only be guessed at.

Only a small selection of the late Middle English lyrics which might in some sense be described as 'courtly' is included here. Many other poems, however pleasant in themselves, are scarcely more than reiterations of conventional themes and language, some, perhaps, the modest products of lesser talents who, unlike the 'squire that served in love's court', had no Lydgate to write on their behalf.[23] However, as the love lyrics of the mid-16th-century Scottish Bannatyne manuscript testify, verse in this late medieval courtly idiom continued to find favour a century and a half after Chaucer's death.

E ARLY MIDDLE ENGLISH devotional lyrics were usually written in a simple, humble style.[24] This style continued to be used in later devotional lyrics, as in the first seven poems of the second part of this anthology. Perhaps the finest of these is *Ther is no rose of swych vertù* (**II, 46**), a carol which is familiar today from the setting by Benjamin Britten in his *Ceremony of Carols*.

The perfection of this shapely little poem is immediately felt in the ease and poise of its faultless metre – a rhythmic counterpoint of octosyllabic English couplets and shorter four-syllable Latin lines. A sense of delicacy and purity arises from the absolute simplicity of its language. Even the Latin lines – familiar phrases from liturgy and Scripture – are far from being learned embellishments; indeed, the Latin words *Gloria in excelcis Deo* of the second line of the fourth stanza seem to run as naturally there as the English words of the second lines of the other stanzas. Likewise, the paradox of the Incarnation, far from being a matter of doctrinal exposition, is here simply the wondrous 'containing of heaven and earth in little space' (7–8) – a mystery enhanced and yet more intimately conveyed by an economy and simplicity of expression. A modern reader will have no difficulty in appreciating how the natural beauty of the rose made it a particularly appropriate symbol for the Virgin; however, other associations (especially religious) of the rose[25] made for a richer response to this lyric on the part of medieval readers.

The structure of the poem is two-fold: the first three stanzas focus on the rose; the final two turn to what this rose signifies to the world and to ourselves. The Latin lines support this structure. The first three (all from the *Laetabundus* sequence)[26] link the first three stanzas by the same final rhyme (just as these stanzas are initially linked by the repetition of the word 'rose' in each first line); similarly

---

[22] See Commentary, **II, 27**, and Commentary, **II, 15**, respectively.
[23] See Commentary, **II, 14**.
[24] See p. 11.
[25] See Commentary, **II, 46**, 1.
[26] See Commentary, **II, 46**, 5.

Gaudeamus and *Transeamus* link stanzas 4 and 5 by both rhyme and grammatical form. Moreover, these lines conclude each stanza most effectively as the import of the poem unfolds. The first stanza (repeating the burden) emphasizes the theme – the rose, unsurpassed in virtue, that bore Jesus – and fittingly ends with *Alleluya*. The second presents that mystery of mysteries – heaven and earth (i.e. God and man) 'contained' in the 'little space' of that rose: *Res miranda* – truly a thing to be wondered at. The third, pointing to the truth of what by this rose 'we may well see' – the very Trinity of Father, Son and (implicitly at Mary's conception) Holy Ghost – appropriately ends with a doctrinal formula, *Pari forma* (in like form). Stanza 4 turns away from the mystery of this rose to the response of the outside world. *Gaudeamus!* – what other reaction could we have than to rejoice at the familiar message of peace and good will, the unexpressed but understood continuation (see Luke 2:14) of the angels' song: *Gloria in excelsis Deo*? But this 'worldly mirth' must lead on to something more – all, in fact, that is entailed in following 'this joyful birth': *Transeamus [usque Bethlehem]* – 'let us go [even unto Bethlehem]'.

Yet there is also, in this poem, a subtle ambiguity of mood, for the joy here is not merely to be felt as jubilant celebration but also as hushed wonder. Indeed, in the final stanza, the poet bids us leave 'worldly mirth' to focus again on the miraculous birth. This quality has been brilliantly caught by Benjamin Britten: in his setting, the words *Alleluya* and *Res miranda* are alike sung quietly, as with awe, on one repeated low note – and so too the final lines of the other stanzas.

The Coronation of the Virgin was a theme which came to prominence in 15th-century Marian lyrics.

'Com, my swetë, com my flour,	
Com my culver, myn owne boure,	*dove; bower*
Com my modyr, now wyth me,	*mother*
For hevyn qwene I makë the!'	*queen of heaven*

II, 53, 1–4

This short poem shows how effectively this theme could be expressed in the simplest language – though, in this case, a language charged with tender resonances from the Song of Solomon. However, Coronation lyrics were more frequently written in a 'high' style: e.g.

The infinite power essenciall,	*absolute*
Me thoght I sawë verrement,	*truly*
Procedyng from his trone celestiall	*throne*
To a dere damsell that was gent.	*dear; noble / beautiful*
Songes melodious was in their tent,	*were the concern*
Of angells synging with gret solemnyté	
Before a quene whiche was present –	
Ecce Virgo, radix Jessé.	*behold the Virgin, the root of Jesse*

II, 54, 1–8

This 'high' or 'aureate' style, often associated with the 15th-century poet Lydgate, was characterized by a copious use of words derived from Latin, many recently or even (in some poems) newly adopted into English. This kind of 'poetic' vocabulary may seem at first sight alien and even bizarre. What was its appeal to 15th-century poets and readers? In the first place, it was the sound of long Latinate words – their sonority and rhythm. Such words normally carried at least two stresses, ending with the rhythmic pattern / × /. When they occurred in rhymes, the combination of weight of stressing with the repetition of like sounds maximized sonority. The same quest for sonority is seen in Chaucer's use of polysyllabic words of French derivation ending in '-aunce' in the rhyme-words *remembraunce* (1), *governaunce* (2), *contenaunce* (5) and *perseveraunce* (8) in *Womanly Noblesse* (**1, 30**). Resonance was sometimes enhanced by alliteration which was often used to link Latinate words in aureate verse. If this kind of writing is read with sympathy, confidence and rhythm, the original appeal of these Latinisms as part of the music of poetry may still be enjoyed.

Medieval writers were greatly concerned with style, and in particular with the classically derived distinctions of the levels of style: high, medium and low. Even Chaucer's Host was conversant with the function of 'high' style, as is evident from his words to the Clerk:

> Youre termës, youre colours, and youre figures,
> Keepe hem in stoor til so be ye endite
> Heigh style, as whan that men to kyngës write.[27]

If appropriate for kings, what style could be more suitable for poems addressed to the Virgin or to Christ? For 15th-century poets aureate diction was a prominent feature of 'high' style, and it is not difficult to understand the appeal of an elevated Latinate vocabulary as, in poems on the Coronation of the Virgin, they attempted to express the almost baroque splendour of ornate celestial settings, with Mary, suffused with resplendent light, enthroned as Queen of Heaven and surrounded by angelic hosts. Admittedly, some 15th-century poems to the Virgin in this manner are rather artificial and heavy-going; but others, like *The infinite power essenciall* (**1, 54**), read in the light of medieval poetic taste, are representative of a higher level of imaginative and technical achievement. However, for the aureate style handled with exuberant and compelling virtuosity one turns to the Scottish makar Dunbar's masterly hymn to the Virgin, *Hale, sterne superne, hale, in eterne*:

Hale, sterne superne, hale, in eterne,	*hail, star on high; in eternity*
In Godis sicht to schyne;	*in God's sight to shine*
Lucerne in derne for to discerne	*lamp in darkness by which to see*
Be glory and grace devyne.	*by; divine*
Hodiern, modern, sempitern,	*for this day, this age, for ever*
Angelicall regyne,	*queen of angels*
Our tern inferne for to dispern	*gloom infernal to disperse*
Helpe, rialest rosyne.	*most royal rose*
Ave Maria, gracia plena,	*Hail Mary, full of grace*
Haile, fresche floure femynyne,	*fresh flower of femininity*
Yerne us guberne, virgin matern,	*diligently us govern, virgin mother*
Of reuth baith rute and ryne.	*of compassion both root and bark*

II, 55, 1–12

---

[27] *CT*, IV, 16–18.

The 'golden' diction here, with words such as *superne, hodiern, regyne* (only slightly altered from Latin *superna, hodierna, regina*), is manifestly an elevated and specifically poetic vocabulary remote from the language of common usage.

N O P O E T I C F O R M is more characteristic of the 15th century than the carol. Of about 500 surviving Middle English carols only a dozen or so date from before 1400. The potential of the carol form,[28] with its repeated burden and characteristically simple style, for expressing joy and celebration is evident in the Nativity carols in this volume (**11, 56**–62). *A kyng ys comen to save kynde* (**11, 58**, 13)! With the joy of the Nativity rather than the agony of the Passion in mind, the poet of *Owt of your slepe aryse and wake* (**11, 56**) offers an exceptionally buoyant account of this salvation. The joyous repetitions of 'nowel' in the burden and refrain of this carol are linked with the equally emphatic and exultant repetitions of 'now' in each stanza. What is celebrated 'now', however, is not only the joy of Christ's Incarnation at the Nativity (the beginning of *this game* (17) – the process of salvation), but also, in anticipation, the triumphant outcome of the Crucifixion and Resurrection, an outcome seen here in exceptionally optimistic terms for mankind: not only is man now free who formerly was captive (21), now, with Christ in human form, man has also become 'of great worth' (10) with angels kneeling before him (11) and heaven and earth bowing to him (28). The exalted status man now achieves through Christ is most strikingly expressed in 'Now is man brighter than the sun' (15), an image usually used of Christ alone. In the excitement and elation of this carol, not only has Christ become man's human brother, but man, in his redeemed state, has virtually become Christ's divine brother. Reflecting this, it is with a sense of confidence (rather than the more usual contrition) that the poet asks his 'blessed brother' (33) for a place for us on the Day of Judgement in the court of heaven, so 'that we may sing nowel there' (36).

While this and other carols celebrate the significance of the Nativity in the scheme of salvation, one exceptional 15th-century carol tells of a shepherd-boy, Wat, who, on hearing the angels' song, runs to Bethlehem to find Jesus and Mary (**11, 59**). This carol, reminiscent of and no doubt inspired by shepherd scenes in medieval mystery plays, is remarkable for its homely realism and vivid detail. Wat's adventure is dramatically presented: it is related scene by scene, reaching its climax as Wat arrives 'sweating' at the very Nativity itself. His voice is heard in direct speech and in brief dialogue with Mary. His affectionate concern for his sheep, Mall and Will, his uninhibited enthusiasm in making his simple offerings – pipe, kilt, tar-box and bag – to the infant Jesus, and his naive astonishment that Mary should actually know his name, reveal the happy, innocent nature which allows him so spontaneous a response to the joy of Christ's birth. The contrast between Wat's open, happy nature, reflected in his piping, and the sense of the inadequacy and inhibition of the narrator – the 'I' of the burden who can scarcely even echo the shepherd-boy's joyful music – lends an unusual poignancy to this carol.

---

[28] For a definition and brief history of the carol form, see Commentary, **11, 44**. For an excellent and comprehensive account of the Middle English carol, by Karl Reichl, see *Companion*, pp. 150–70.

The conventions of the *chanson d'aventure*[29] are frequently adopted in late Middle English religious lyrics. Among the earliest English religious lyrics to do so is *As I lay upon a night* (**1, 81**), a lullaby from the Franciscan friar John of Grimestone's commonplace book of 1372, in which the poet comes upon the Virgin and the infant Jesus. In a slightly later lyric, *In the vaile of restles mynd* (**1, 73**), the lamenting voice the poet encounters is that of Christ. Several of the moral refrain poems of the late 14th-century Vernon manuscript are framed as *chansons d'aventure*, as are the moral refrain lyrics **11, 94** and **95**. In later religious lyrics, *chanson d'aventure* openings sometimes introduce scenes which are far removed from the settings of the original French genre. As the poet of **11, 73** stood musing on the moon he had a spiritual vision in which he encountered the Virgin Mary and overheard her making her complaint to mankind; in **11, 74** – another nocturnal experience – a poet, 'half waking, half sleeping' (1), encounters a distressed woman who turns out to be the Virgin of the late medieval pietà.

The pastoral setting of the French *chanson d'aventure* seems to re-emerge in *I passëd thoru a garden grene* (**11, 63**) with a green garden, an arbour, trees, singing turtle-doves and a maiden 'bright of hue' (5). However, this maiden is no shepherdess but, once again, the Virgin Mary, here singing of the Incarnation and announcing the birth of 'a peerless prince' (13). This scene – obviously not the Nativity – recalls medieval depictions of the Annunciation in which the angel Gabriel greets Mary in a garden. Great excitement attends the poet as he travels on through the landscape of this poem. He hears the song of 'three gracious shepherds' (19) and hastens after them *full fast* (22); he meets 'three comely kings' (34) and 'speeds him forth' (35) to speak with them. The shepherds' message here is not, however, only of glory to God and peace on earth but also of the Nativity, of a spotless maiden who has borne a child between ox and ass (29–30). The kings, likewise, tell not only of witnessing 'God become flesh' (41), but especially of a maid whose womb harboured, succoured and held him (44–6). Throughout, this poem focuses on the Virgin: the beautiful *mayden bryght off hew* in the garden of the first stanza, the spotless mother of stanza 4, the Virgin whose womb was Christ's dwelling (stanza 6), and, finally, 'that princess' (49), gentle mother and maiden, to whom we pray (stanza 7). This lyric is a joyous but gentle celebration, romantic and doctrinal, of the Virgin in her several roles throughout the Annunciation–Incarnation–Epiphany sequence and in her subsequent role as Intercessor, presented in a manner which is wholly in harmony with the conventions adopted from the *chanson d'aventure*.

Fifteenth-century lullaby lyrics and carols continue the style and conventions of the Virgin-and-Child lullabies in John of Grimestone's commonplace book. Some, like **11, 65** and **67**, take the form of a dialogue between mother and child. In **11, 66** the Virgin's voice is heard in the burden, but the stanzas are largely a monologue by Jesus. The tenderness characteristic of the Grimestone lullabies is still present in the later poems, as is the poignant tension between the Virgin's immediate concern for her cold and weeping child and an awareness of the agony of his sufferings to come. This grim prospect draws from the Virgin an exceptionally candid, rueful and

[29] See above, pp. 3–4.

(with its double negative) emphatic comment at the end of the penultimate stanza of **II, 67**:

> 'A! sone, that is a heyvy cas: *sad plight*
>   When Gabrell cnelled before my face,   *knelt before me* (lit. *before my face*)
>   And sayd, "Heylle! Lady, full of grace,"
>   He never told me noothing of this.'

II, 67, 25–8

The Coventry carol, *O sisters too* (**II, 68**), is unique in having as its speakers the mothers of the infant victims of Herod's Slaughter of the Innocents. This lullaby occurs in a mystery play, the Coventry Shearmen and Taylors' Pageant; it is so specific to its dramatic context that it may well have been written for this play.

Middle English religious lyrics served a practical function as aids to devotion. Many were prayers (e.g. **II, 84–87**). Some were used in sermons to lend greater impact to preaching. A rubric in the Harley manuscript of *Wofully araide* (**II, 71**) claims that the recitation of 'this prayer' will bring about one hundred years of pardon.[30] *In a tabernacle of a toure* (**II, 73**) is similarly viewed as a prayer. Below a drawing of the Virgin Mary in one manuscript,[31] a kneeling supplicant says:

> Maria the flowre of virgyns clere
> In al oure nede oure prayer thu here.

This practical devotional function is most evident in Passion lyrics. In *O man unkynde* (**II, 70**), Christ invites man to behold his sufferings and, in particular, his 'pierced heart' (6). As with earlier lyrics like *Whyt is Thi naked brest* (**I, 86**) and *Whan Ich se on rode* (**I, 87**), the aim of this poem was to confront the reader with Christ's sufferings, to stir in him feelings of compassion and so to move him to a response of heartfelt contrition. In later manuscripts such lyrics are sometimes accompanied by illustrations. The text of *O man unkynde* is written down the left side of the manuscript page: to the right there is a drawing of Christ, with blood pouring from the nail-holes in his hands and feet and, especially, from the gash in his side.[32] This is the popular 15th-century *imago pietatis*, the 'image of pity' – not specifically a crucifix (with Christ hanging from the cross), but a timeless image of the wounded Christ as the Man of Sorrows. Echoing the text, Christ in this illustration is offering to man – represented as a figure kneeling in prayer at his feet – his heart. In a scroll above the heart are found the following words which sum up the devotional function of drawing and poem:

> Thies woundës smert,   *these painful wounds*
> Bere in thin hert,   *bear*
> And luf God aye.
>
> If thou do this,
> Thu sal hafe blys   *thou shalt have bliss*
> Withowten delay.

---

[30] See Commentary, **II, 71**.
[31] See Commentary, **II, 73**, 1.
[32] See Gray (1972), illus. 2, opposite p. 23, and Woolf, plate 1, opposite p. 186.

Evidently such drawings, sometimes fairly crude, were thought to enhance the impact of lyric texts.

Complaints of Christ – poems in which Christ addresses man directly – are among the most moving of Middle English Passion lyrics. The early complaints tended to be short, simple poems; longer and more elaborate are the later *Wofully araide* (**II, 71**) and *Brother, abyde, I the desire and pray* (**II, 72**). If these poems were devotional in intention, quite clearly they were also literary in conception. In *Wofully araide* Christ appeals to man in terms of a vivid account of the sufferings he endured on the cross. These agonies, however, are described in the past tense:

Thus wàs I defasëd,	*disfigured*
Thus wàs my flesh rasëd,	*torn*
And I to deth chasëd;	*hounded*
Like a lambe led	
untò sacrefise,	
Slayëne I was	*slain*
in most cruell wise.	

II, 71, 20–24

The speaker is again the timeless figure of the suffering Christ, the *imago pietatis*. Indeed, a small drawing of the *imago pietatis* appears above the first stanza of the poem in the Harley manuscript.

The formal crafting of this lyric is particularly striking. Its nine-line stanzas consist of a quatrain of long lines, a triplet of short lines, and a final couplet of long lines, a structure supported by the rhyme-scheme: a a a a, b b b, c c. The dominant rhythm of half lines and short lines is: × / × × / (×). How far was this metrical norm meant to prevail in the reading (or singing?) of this lyric? And to what effect? For the most part the poem may be read fluently following this rhythm, which easily overrides the occasionally different stress patterns which would result if the lines were read as prose. Deviations from this rhythmic pattern may have been consciously devised for rhetorical effect. The most striking instance comes at the end of the last stanza. Here for the first time the sense of the final line of the triplet (31) runs on into the first line of the final couplet, at the end of which the dactylic rhythm suddenly changes to / × /, lending rhetorical weight to the words *màn, for thè*. John Stevens has observed that in both musical settings of this poem in the Fairfax manuscript, 'the words "O, man, for thy sake" are set in a striking way, apparently emphasizing the central issue of the poem, Christ's Pleading'.[33] It may be that the poet of *Wofully araide* sought to emphasize the same point metrically at the climax of his poem.

In *Brother, abyde, I the desire and pray* (**II, 72**), Christ's appeal is not focused solely on his sufferings at the crucifixion but on a review of his entire life – a life of poverty and sacrifice. The medieval practice of dwelling in the imagination on the events and details of Christ's earthly existence as a form of spiritual exercise promoted the production of such largely fictional accounts of the life of Christ as the *Meditationes Vitae Christi*, a work long attributed to St Bonaventura

---

[33] *M&P*, p. 103.

(*c.* 1217–74).[34] It is from this literary and devotional tradition that the vivid details and human touches in the narrative of this lyric derive: Christ as a youth playing with children in the street dressed in such poor clothes as his mother could make or spin (33–5); Christ like an idealized Franciscan wandering barefoot and capless, suffering so much from hunger, thirst and cold that even his own mother did not know him (43–9); Christ on the cross, his heart like a plummet of ice (164).

However, the impact of this lyric depends crucially on the success with which it creates and sustains an awareness of Christ's speaking voice. Christ had already appealed to man in earlier Middle English devotional lyrics (e.g. **1**, **70**, **72**, **99**, **100**, and **102**); in the unadorned language of these brief, short-lined poems, Christ spoke simply and poignantly. Now, in this later poem, his tone of voice is graver. This results partly from a richer range of diction, but mainly from the weight of the decasyllabic lines here, lines of five stresses sometimes marked by alliteration. This metrical norm is varied in rhythm and stress pattern by the introduction of extra unstressed syllables in some lines, by the positioning of the caesura in others, and also by the use of enjambement (e.g. 19–21). These variations, matching as they do the subtle flexibilities, accents and flow of speech, contribute to the success with which Christ's voice emerges from this poem. Christ's manner of address also varies. At times it is rhetorically articulated: *Harke now therfor, hark now and take goode hede* (57). As narrative turns to drama with Pilate's sudden intervention at line 117 – *'Speke, manne,' quod Pylate, 'how ys thy lyf convayed?'* – Christ is eloquent in his silence: *And I stode styll, seke and sore appalled* (119). The caesura after *styll* and the alliterative linking in *stode styll* seem to accentuate Christ's outward impassivity, while the stress following the caesura and the continuing alliteration lend effective emphasis to the first word, *seke*, in the description of his inner feelings: *seke and sore appalled.* Yet, as in the earlier lyrics, it is a gentle voice which speaks of love in the final stanza of this poem:

> Off tendure love, all this I dyd endure;
> Love dyde me lede, love dyde me thus constrayne;
> And for my dede and grevouse adventure   *death; grievous fate*
> More aske I nott but love for love agayne.   *in return*
>
> **II, 72**, 190–93

The characteristic 15th-century iconographic representation of the Virgin was the pietà, the Virgin depicted as holding the dead Christ on her lap. Representations of the pietà, like those of the *imago pietatis*, must have been common in paintings, carvings and sculpture in late-medieval churches.[35] However effective as an aid to devotion, the pietà may seldom have had as powerful an impact as it had on Margery Kemp, who, on entering a church and seeing an image of our Lady in the form of a pietà, *was compelled to cryen ful lowde and wepen ful sor, as thei* (though) *sche shulde a deyd* (have died).[36] Hardly less arresting, however, is the encounter in *With favoure in her face* (**11, 74**). This carol begins dramatically and enigmatically:

[34] See Commentary, **11, 72**.
[35] See Woolf, p. 391.
[36] Meech and Allen (1997), p. 148.

> *Sodenly afraide,*   suddenly afraid
> *half wakyng, half slepyng,*
> *And gretly dismayde –*
> *a wooman sate weepyng.*

Who is 'suddenly afraid'? Who experiences great dismay, half waking, half sleeping? Is it the weeping woman, or someone else? It turns out to be the poet, the first-person narrator of the poem. The distressed woman he encounters is the Virgin with her dead son on her lap. The pathos of the Virgin's reiterated lament – *'Who cannot wepe, come lerne at me'* – and of the scene as she sobs over her son so *bobbëd, / And of his lif robbëd* (8–9, etc.), moves the 'hard-hearted' (13) poet to answering tears (19). The poem reaches its climax as, looking directly at the poet, the Virgin identifies Christ as his 'brother' and, kissing her dead son with the words, *'Swete, am I not thy modir?'* (34), swoons, yet revives again only to vanish in the midst of her refrain as suddenly as she had appeared. The intense emotionalism here carries conviction partly because in this poem it is supported by an overall sense of formal structure, felt especially in the sustained rhythm of the metre and the refrain-like repetition of the rhymes *sobbëd / bobbëd / robbëd* of the triplet of short lines at the heart of each stanza.[37]

In later Middle English Marian lyrics, the complaint of the Virgin emerges as a genre corresponding to and largely modelled on the complaint of Christ. In earlier lyrics Mary wept at the foot of the cross, lamented her son's sufferings, and entered into anguished dialogue with him.[38] Now, in *In a tabernacle of a toure*:

> A crounëd quene, most of honoure,   *greatest in honour*
> Apered in gostly syght ful sone.   *appeared in a spiritual vision suddenly*
> She made compleynt thus by hyr one,   *on her own*
> For mannës soule was wrapped in wo: *because*
> 'I may nat leve mankynde allone,
>   Quia amore langueo.'   *because I languish for love*
>   **II, 73**, 3–8

Like Christ, Mary here addresses her complaint to man and entreats him to abandon sin for her sake (57). She grieves for man, her 'dear child' (12); she laments the sufferings man has caused Christ, also her 'child' (49ff.). Like Christ, she is patient and long-suffering:

> 'Now wol I syt and sey nomore,
> Leve, and loke with grete longyng;   *leave off, and wait* (lit. *look*)
> Whan man woll calle, I wol restore;   *I will rescue* (him)
> I love to save hym – he ys myne osprynge.' *offspring*
>   **II, 73**, 73–6[39]

Not only as mother, as advocate, and, now, as Queen of Heaven, but again, like

---

[37] See Commentary, **II, 74**.

[38] See especially **I, 90** and **I, 91**.

[39] Cf. *Com when thu wilt, and welcome to me,* Christ's patient invitation to man at the end of *Wofully araide* (**II, 71**).

Christ the lover-knight,[40] as one languishing for love of man (90), she invites man to accept her protection, to 'creep' under her 'wing' (92).

In **II, 75**, with the words *abyde and se* (2) and *beholde wele me* (7) at the beginning of her complaint to 'all women that ever were born', Mary echoes the traditional opening of Christ's complaints derived from the antiphon *O vos omnes …* in the Passiontide liturgy.[41] Poignant contrasts are developed in this complaint between Mary, once again the Virgin of the pietà with her dead son on her lap, and other mothers who dance their children merrily on their knees. Such a mother happily combs her child's hair: Mary picks thorns from her dead son's head; such a mother takes pleasure in making a garland of flowers for her child: Mary's child has a garland of thorns.

O woman, a chaplet chosyn thu has	*garland (of flowers); you have*
Thy childe to were, hit dose the likyng,	*wear; it gives you pleasure*
Thu pynnes hit on, grete joye thou mas;	*you make*
And I sitte with my son sore wepyng,	
His chaplet is thornys sore prickyng,	
His mouth I kys with carfull chere –	*in sorrow*
I sitte wepyng and thu syngyng,	
For now liggus ded my dere son dere.	*lies dead my dear, dear son*

II, 75, 17–24

The details of motherly affection in this complaint recall accounts of Mary and the infant Jesus so lovingly dwelt upon in medieval lives of Christ.[42]

Among surviving Middle English lyrics, those which celebrate Easter are considerably less numerous than those dealing with the Nativity, or the Passion, or the Virgin. One late 15th-century Easter poem in the 'aureate' style – a style clearly felt to be appropriate to the theme of this poem – gives a stirringly triumphant account of the resurrection.

Be glaid, ye angellis and ye archangellis cleir!	
Youre wailyeand prince, victorius in battall,	*valiant prince*
Met with all hevinlie melody and cheir;	
And to youre king ye sing, 'haill, victour, haill!'	
That hes in erd ovrecumyn with gret travell,	*on earth*
And hes of hell the power put to flicht,	*flight*
And thair strang portes privlie done assale,	*strong gates powerfully assailed*
Quhois glaid uprissing blithis every wycht.	*whose; gladdens every man*

Brown XV, no. 112, 9–16

This was the version of Easter which seized the medieval imagination: Christ as mighty victor, descending to hell, bursting open its gates, defeating the Devil, releasing hell's captives – the souls of the righteous who had died before his coming – and leading them in triumph to the bliss of heaven. Known as the Harrowing of Hell, this episode in the Easter narrative between Good Friday and

---

[40] See Woolf, pp. 44–55, and Commentary, **I, 71**.
[41] See Commentary, **II, 72**, 1–3.
[42] See Commentary, **II, 72**.

Easter Sunday derived from the apocryphal, fifth-century Gospel of Nicodemus and was widely represented in medieval visual arts, literature and drama. The finest of Old English religious poems, *The Dream of the Rood*, reaches its climax with Christ as triumphant hero returning to heaven from this final expedition; the Harrowing of Hell also figures prominently in the great 14th-century religious allegory *Piers Plowman*, and in the 15th-century mystery plays.

Nowhere, however, does this legend find more vivid expression than in Dunbar's great resurrection hymn *Done is a battell on the dragon blak* (**II, 77**). The epic protagonists – Christ and Satan – are here depicted in a series of biblically derived images which exploit the symbolic contrast of light and darkness so prominent in the Gospel of Nicodemus.[43] The Devil, once Lucifer (9), the light-bearing archangel (the etymological sense of the name), is now a 'dragon black' (1), vicious and deadly, a cruel serpent (10), a tiger with bared teeth (11) and strong claws (13); Christ, whose light was dimmed (27) as the sacrificial lamb of the crucifixion (18), has now risen again as a lion (19) – the biblical Lion of Judah – and as a giant, and is as radiant as the dawn and as the sun-god Apollo (21–2), the god of the pagan world serving here simply as a poetic comparison. The lamb which 'suffered death' (17) is the 'great victor' (25); the dragon is now 'despoiled of the treasure he had guarded' (39). Hell's darkness has been dispersed (28). Dunbar's poem, like the Nicodemus narrative, is vibrant with noise and drama. The gates of hell are broken 'with a crack' (3); the devils tremble 'with hideous voice' (5); 'the knell of mercy is sounded from the heavens' (29). Yet, only when read aloud can the triumphal impact of the sound of Dunbar's verse be fully appreciated. His decasyllabic lines pound and exult in a dramatic play of alliterative effects and varied stress rhythms: *Dòne is a bàttell on the dràgon blàk* (line 1, four heavy stresses); *The sòne that wòx all pàill now schỳnis brìcht* (line 27, five stresses); *He màid him for to fèlye of that fàng* (line 15, three heavy stresses).

Of the numerous Middle English lyrics on the theme of death, several late lyrics with the refrain *Timor mortis conturbat me* from the Office of the Dead are personal and devotional in character. In *Illa iuventus that is so nyse* (**II, 88**) the voice of the poem is still that of the anonymous, unindividualized speaker characteristic of many Middle English devotional poems, an Everyman persona with whom the medieval reader could readily identify. There are *Timor mortis* poems by three named late-medieval poets – Audelay, Lydgate and Dunbar. The best-known of these is Dunbar's *Lament for the Makaris*.[44] However, Audelay's lyric in carol form, *Dred of deth, sorrow of syn* (**II, 89**), is remarkable for its sustained personal intensity. Exceptionally for a medieval poet, Audelay frequently mentions his own name: in several places he refers to himself as 'the blind Audelay', and at the end of the final poem in the sole manuscript of his works, he states that he *made this bok by Goddës grace, / Deeff, siek, blynd, as he lay*.[45] Old age, the transience of life and fear of death are not merely general themes for him. In particular, blindness is not simply a symptom of age but an autobiographical fact, truly 'a heavy thing' suffered by a poet who knew the grief of being able to 'see' (i.e. 'sense') nothing of

---

[43] See Commentary, **II, 77**.

[44] See Gray (1998), p. 351.

[45] See Whiting (1931), p. 224.

himself *Save filth, unclennes, vile stynkyng* (29). Part of the moving quality of this poem is the way fear is balanced by faith: *Timor mortis* of the burden is answered throughout the poem by *Passio Christi* in the refrain line of each stanza. Again, in the two penultimate stanzas, as the poet records the personal blessing he has derived from Christ's final words to his father – *In manus tuas, Domine* (52) – and speaks of the Virgin as 'mother' and 'merciful maiden' (57), there emerges a sense of assurance that in the face of death his pleas to Mary for help and to Jesus for mercy – reiterated in the burden – will be answered. As Rosemary Woolf observes, in this *Timor mortis* poem 'we see an ancient medieval theme treated with an emphasis which is un-medieval: the "I" is no longer Everyman, but the poet with his individual experience and sensibility'. Indeed, she may be justified in claiming that here 'for perhaps the first time in an English lyric poem, the poet truly speaks in his own voice'.[46]

L ATER MORAL AND PENITENTIAL lyrics continue to dwell upon topics which were already common in earlier Middle English lyrics, such as mankind's wretched lot as the offspring of Adam, the brevity and enigma of life and death summed up in three ominous final questions,[47] the transience of wisdom, beauty and strength in the face of death, 'seven feet wherein to rot' as the sum of man's ultimate gain on earth, and the worthlessness of wealth and wit at the Day of Judgement, themes of successive stanzas of the late 14th-century lyric *When Adam delf* (**II, 90**). Despite the demands of a rather elaborate rhyme-scheme and refrain, the pithy short lines of this lyric flow smoothly – almost ironically so in view of its grim concerns; and well-worn though its themes may be, a chilling end is reached with the image of man as a torch of straw reduced to dust (97–9), in death a 'hideous guest' beyond human embrace (100–102), and with the pun on 'sheet' and 'winding-sheet' in the final line:

With I and E,	
Syker thou be	*be sure*
Thare es nane, I the hete,	*there is none, I promise you*
Of al thi kyth	*of all your acquaintances*
Wald slepe the with,	*would sleep with you*
A nyght under schete.	*one night under (your) sheet*

II, 90, 103–8

As y gan wandre in my walkinge (**II, 94**) and *In a noon-tiid of a somers day* (**II, 95**) continue the tradition of the late 14th-century moralizing refrain poems in the Vernon manuscript,[48] though they lack something of the sustained *gravitas* of the earlier poems. *In a noon-tiid* opens in the manner of a *chanson d'aventure* with the bright sunshine of noon on a summer's day and the poet setting out for some sport with his hawk and his spaniel. The dog raises a hen-pheasant and the hawk takes it; but, as the poet runs forward he encounters not a shepherdess but a briar bush, the leaves of which are inscribed with the word *revertere* (turn back).

[46] Woolf, pp. 335–6.
[47] See Commentary, **II, 90**, 50–4.
[48] See Commentary, **I, 60**.

As he kneels to detach himself from the bush, his attention focuses on this word and his heart, hitherto cheerful, sinks – 'fell down to [his] toe' (19). Abandoning hawk and pheasant, he turns to contemplate the implications of this 'new lesson, *revertere'* (24). He thinks of how his youthful life of pleasure has led him astray into sin. In these thoughts the realistic sunny landscape of the introduction gives way to allegory. The hawk now comes to represent the heart of youth, and the hen-pheasant, the pleasure youth pursues. For salvation it is necessary to 'turn back' (*revertere*) from youth's sinful pleasures.

Some three dozen or so of the 15th-century lyrics dealing with popular topics of religious or moral counsel are carols.[49] These carols, like the four included here (**II, 96–99**), are plain, even homely, in language and direct in manner; they offer shrewd advice which is as relevant now as it was then. Loud talk is dangerous:

> And when thou syttëst at the ale,
> And cryëst lyk an nyghttyngale,   *and sing out* (lit. *cry) like*
> Bewar to whom thou tellest thi tale,
>   But ber a horne and blow it nought.
>
> **II, 98**, 28–31

Don't get above your station:

> Therfor loke that thow be sley: *see that you are discreet*
> For no thyng hew thow tow hey,   *on no account hew too high*
> Last they falle don into thy ey,   *lest they fall down into your eye*
>   The sponës that above the be.   *the chips that are above you*
>
> **II, 97**, 23–6

Other lyrics are couched in 15th-century versions of the 'high' style of Chaucer's moral ballades. Though referred to in one manuscript as a *ballat*, the two rhyme royal stanzas of Halsham's poem *The worlde so wide, the aire so remuàble* (**II, 93**) are not in ballade form; nevertheless, with its decasyllabic lines, its elevated vocabulary, and its play of rhetoric,[50] this poem resembles the Chaucerian ballade in style.

Farewell, this world! I take my leve for evere (**II, 102**) is the finest of several Middle English poems in which a dead man bids farewell to the world. Though its themes and images are largely conventional,[51] this is a distinctive lyric. The intimate tone of voice of the first-person speaker pervades and unifies the poem from the opening address, *Farewell, this world! I take my leve for evere* (with its ring of finality), to the sad and poignant *Farewell, my frendes* of the final stanza. Especially memorable is the beginning of the third stanza (at once pathetic and chilling): *Speke softe, ye folk, for I am leyd aslepe!* The address to 'ye folk' here recalls Christ's words, *O vos omnes* (Oh all ye who pass by …), words also echoed by a voice from the grave in an epitaph poem (**II, 104**). And *softe* here could not be more ironic: not all the shouting in the world could awaken this sleeper in his sleep of death. And yet, even in this sleep, he claims: *I have my dreme* (16). Although somewhat enigmatic, lines 16–18 appear to suggest that this speaker dreams of wishing to leap from Death's

---

[49] See Greene, pp. 197–213.
[50] See Commentary, **II, 93**.
[51] See Commentary, **II, 102**.

clutches, a hope, however, which seems no more than a vain deception: 'in trust is much deception'(16); the very entertaining of such a thought shows the decline of wisdom to feeble speculation (18): idle dreaming, indeed.

However, the apparent finality of this third stanza, ending as it does with a grim reminder of the last trumpet and the Day of Judgement, marks only a stage in the development of this poem as it moves from despair to hope, a hope which depends in some measure on the concept of purgatory, a doctrine which became popular in the later Middle Ages in treatises and homilies on death and the afterlife.[52] The first two stanzas present the sinner in an apparently hopeless plight in the face of sudden death, a situation graphically expressed in an earlier lyric: *Al to latë, al to latë / Whan the bere* [bier] *is at the gatë* (**I, 44**, 13–14). Arrested to appear before God, not even one brief hour is left to him in which to repent. As he bids farewell to this world, belatedly and broken-heartedly regretting his past, he now sees life for what it is. There is no escaping Death's grasp (17); the dream of doing so in stanza 3 was nothing more than a momentary delusion. This world is fickle and false, a truth fully brought home in stanza 4. Yet, in the concluding stanza, as this sinner bids his friends farewell, in his time of parting from life, *this passage*, 'this transition' (31), he recognizes in the words *Requiem aeternam* of the funeral service his 'best song' (31), one which offers hope beyond death, for which he now prays. After all his *adversité* (33) – the punishments of purgatory, presumably – salvation may yet be found in the blood of Christ. In this way, this poem arrives at an appraisal of life and death, not simply in terms of grim details and ominous warnings, but in a broader theological perspective.

This lyric has a poise and restraint which set it apart from earlier death lyrics. The speaker would give the world (3–4) – the very world he is leaving for ever and no longer has to give – for 'one hour's space' (4) to repent his sins; here, however, there follows no recital of these sins, 'in bed or at board' or anywhere else.[53] In death the body is, indeed, food for worms (14), but no grisly details are entered into. Homiletic tones of exhortation and menace are likewise absent. And, in this poem, the simple versification of earlier lyrics has given way to rhyme royal stanzas in decasyllabic lines – a weightier and more sophisticated verse form characteristic of the 'high' style of the ballade, and well matched to the measured, sad and serious tones of this speaker.

Westron wynde when wyll thow blow?
The smalle rayne downe can rayne.   *does rain*
Cryst, yf my love wer in my armes   *if only*
And I yn my bed agayne!

II, 105

I N W H A T S E N S E (or senses) could this or the other poems in the final part of this anthology be called 'popular'? Some may be said to be 'un-courtly'. In *Westron wynde* the dreary, continuous drizzle – not a decent downpour, not even a breath of wind, let alone the promise of a western wind – which exactly expresses

---

[52] See Matsuda (1997).
[53] Contrast **I, 37**, 21 ff.

the poet's amorphous, unrelieved misery, owes nothing to the traditional contrast of the courtly lover's woe with the joy of nature in springtime; and the urgency of *Christ, yf my love wer in my armes* (3), a frank expression of his longing to be in bed with his love 'again' (4), is, refreshingly, a far cry from the love-sick longings of a courtly lover for a distant mistress. The theme (true love), the manner, and the conventions of *The man that I loved altherbest* (II, 106) are essentially those of courtly poetry; in this poem, however, unlike poems in the courtly tradition, the speaker is a woman. In medieval courtly literature ladies of ideal beauty and excellence were traditionally described as being fair, with long golden hair. The speaker of *Summe men sayen that y am blac* (II, 108) – again a woman – offers a spirited challenge to this ubiquitous literary stereotype. Yet, if 'popular' in the sense of 'un-courtly', these poems – and not least *Westron wynde* – are far from unsophisticated; and if, in some ways, they are 'un-courtly', that is not to say that they may not have been current in court circles. *Westron wynde* survives in a manuscript which includes songs of a courtly nature: on this basis it is as courtly by the context of its survival as *A Robyn* (II, 32) in the Henry VIII manuscript. Perhaps the designation 'popular' might be considered more appropriate for poems recounting the exploits of serving girls, for poems of rather crude sexual innuendo, for poems of the tavern or poems akin to folk tradition such as the holly-and-ivy carols. Yet, as Bernard O'Donoghue has aptly observed, however used, 'under scrutiny … the term "popular" proves much more equivocal than might be expected'.[54]

The thematic range of the Middle English carol was wide and unrestricted, as is evident from the fact that carols feature in all four sections of Part II of this anthology. Only towards the end of the 15th century did the specific association of the carol with Christmas begin to emerge. About one-fifth of surviving carols are secular, and many of these are popular in character. Some, like II, 109–112, tell of amorous encounters, typically between serving girls and local priests on occasions of festive merrymaking. Priestly seducers such as Jankin in I, 129 were stock figures in medieval literature, and Midsummer Day, 24 June, the Nativity of St John the Baptist, was a popular occasion for celebration and revelry.

Ladd y the daunce	*led*
a Myssomur Day;	*on Midsummer*
Y made smale trippes,	*I took dainty steps*
soth for to say.	*truth to tell*
Jak, oure haly-watur clerk,	*Jack our holy-water priest*
com be the way,	*came by*
And he lokede me upon;	
he thought that yc was gay –	*that I was attractive*
Thought yc on no gyle.	*on no impropriety (lit. guile)*

II, 110, 6–10

The merry girl of this carol dances so daintily on Midsummer Day that she attracts the attention of 'Jack, our holy-water priest'. He eyes her up: she notices his interest – quite innocently, of course! And as Jack steers her into a corner for a

---

[54] *Companion*, p. 210.

kiss during the dance, tempts her with a gift of white gloves, and invites her home for what becomes an evening of merry and vigorous love-making, this seduction is presented in vivid and dramatic detail, as, indeed, is the outcome – the girl caught sneaking home at daybreak by a furious mistress, and the inevitable pregnancy.

Convivial occasions of one kind or another are subjects of several secular carols. *Jentill butler, bell amy* (**II, 123**) presents a familiar tavern scene – that of a parched customer railing against slow service. In *Is ther any good man here* (**II, 124**), a professional minstrel turns up to challenge members of a household to sing a song. Like many a modern entertainer he deploys the kind of warm-up routine which involves picking on and making fun of individuals in his audience with provocative questions, blunt imperatives and ironic personal remarks. The scene is thus vividly evoked: the thin man, dismissed as a hopeless, miserable creature unaccustomed to 'good sport or play' (38); the fat man, leaden of complexion, scarcely able to hold up his head, whose only 'music' is that of ale and wine and whose daily gluttony is a waste of bread; and, finally, the shy fellow at the back, suddenly pounced upon, jocularly addressed as 'brother', and cruelly mocked as famous for being the worst singer in the country:

Now will ye see wher he stondeth behynde?	
I-wis, brother, ye be unkynd;	*indeed, brother, you are*
Stond forth and wast with me som wynd,	*step forward and spend some breath*
For ye have ben called a synger ay.	*always been called a singer*
Nay, be not ashamed;	
Ye shall not be blamed,	
For ye have ben famed	
The worst in this contrey.	

II, 124, 49–56

Of the Middle English secular lyrics associated with mid-winter festivities, several are holly-and-ivy carols. These are closely related to folk-song. Characteristics of such poems have survived into modern times in popular verse and folk traditions. The well-known Christmas carol *The Holly and the Ivy* continues not only the traditional association of these two evergreens, but also other motifs of the medieval poems: the claim to supremacy for holly is still made – of all trees of the wood it 'bears the crown'; and, like its Middle English ancestors, this poem also speaks of the holly bearing berries. However, unlike the earlier poems, the modern version is overtly religious:

> The holly bears a berry,
> As red as any blood,
> And Mary bore sweet Jesus Christ
> To do poor sinners good.
>
> *The Oxford Book of Carols*, no. 38, stanza 3

Significantly lacking is the battle-of-the-sexes theme so prominent in the medieval poems, where Holly and his merry men are in vigorous contention with Ivy and her gentle women. In some early carols, Holly's claim to supremacy – to have the *maystry* – is vigorously asserted, as in **II, 127** and **128**. The counter claim for Ivy is tellingly strengthened in **II, 129** by her association with the Blessed Virgin. In **II, 130**, the dispute resolves itself in a decorous truce.

The carol, with the potential of its repeated burden for expressing joy and triumph, was particularly well suited to poems of celebration, whether of persons (Christ, Mary, saints) or events (the Nativity, the Christmas season, victories in battle). Among many short historical poems in Middle English – poems dealing with kings, princes, battles and the like – probably the most successful and best known, with its ringing burden *Deo gracias, Anglia, / Redde pro victoria*, is the Agincourt Carol:

> *Deo gracias, Anglia,*   *thanks to God, England,*
>   *Redde pro victoria.*   *render for victory*
> Owre kynge went forth to Normandy
> With grace and myght of chyvalry;   *of mounted knights*
> Ther God for hym wrought mervelusly;
> Wherfore Englonde may calle and cry,
>   'Deo gracias.'   *thanks be to God*
>   *Deo gracias, Anglia*
>   *Redde pro victoria.*
>
>   **II, 132**, 1–9

The same popular note of national triumph is again effectively caught in *Worschip of vertu ys the mede* (**II, 133**), a carol celebrating St George.

Major themes of medieval satire – not least anti-feminism and anti-clericalism – are well represented in Middle English lyrics. A typical account of a termagant wife in *All that I may swynk or swet* (**II, 138**) is matched in the same manuscript with a merry proclamation of the joys of bachelorhood:

> *A, a, a, a,*
>   *Yet I love wherso I go.*
> In all this warld nis a meryar lyfe   *world there is no merrier life*
> Than is a yong man withoutyn a wyfe,   *than a young man*
> For he may lyven withouten stryfe
>   In every place wherso he go.
>   *A, a, a, a, etc.*
>
>   **II, 140**, 1–7

A deal more abusive and venomous in tone is *O wicket wemen, wilfull and variable* (**II, 139**). Despite the import of its refrain – when everything else in the world is topsy-turvy, one may indulge the ultimate absurdity, that of putting trust and confidence in women! – the vitality of *Whan netilles in wynter bere rosis rede* (**II, 136**) depends less on arrant misogyny than on the sense of gusto with which the poet develops his series of impossibilities, the rhetorical figure of adynaton.[55] *Freers, freers, wo ye be!* (**II, 141**) is a blistering attack on friars in general; *Ther was a frier of order gray* (**II, 142**) deals specifically with the friar as seducer, in this case, of a nun – a wholly remarkable lyric in its audacious use of biblical parody and subtle play on the suggestive potential of late medieval musical terminology.[56]

[55] See Commentary, **II, 136**.
[56] See Commentary, **II, 142**.

A mixture of humorous satire and social criticism animates the description of a swaggering, dagger-sporting young braggart who gets his come-uppance from a carter's whip in **II, 143**, and the laments of arse-peppered schoolboys in **II, 144** and **145**. Again, however dramatic the foray of the fox in **II, 147** and plaintive the hare's lament in **II, 148**, these are far from being simple poems of wild life. The seizure of a goose to feed his wife and family may seem the natural action of a fox, but this fox, with his greeting *'Pax vobis'* ('Peace be with you'), a greeting characteristic of friars, is also, here, the type of a predatory friar. Wat, the poor hare of **II, 148**, may seem worthy of sympathy as one of nature's innocent victims. Yet for a hare he is remarkably class-conscious: he is grateful to gentlemen who, with their hounds and hunting etiquette – in contrast to mere peasant women with their dogs and snares – give him a sporting chance; but this almost snobbish preference for gentlemen is ironic, granted the fate that awaits him when caught. For the medieval world, nature was truly a book in which were to be read lessons moral and divine.

Satire is an ingredient of a number of late Middle English lyrics – some witty, some rather crude – dealing with versions of what might (politely) be termed love in a popular vein. The sexual *double entendre* in *At the northe ende of Selver Whyte* (**II, 113**) exploits the vocabulary and imagery of a tournament. The lady (the speaker of the poem) first offers her lover her *ware* (her 'target'), a 'buckler' wide, to 'strike' at – but he misses. He has no better success when her 'target' is offered a 'peck measure' wide, and wider still, a 'bushel measure' wide.[57] The lady is unimpressed with the 'jousting' of a man who cannot hit the 'target'. The general gist of *May no man slepe in youre halle* (**II, 114**), the next poem in the same manuscript, is evident enough though the progression from dogs, to rats, to flies in this lyric may hold greater significance than is immediately apparent. The five late Middle English riddles from another Cambridge manuscript (**II, 115–120**) are, however crude, zestfully merry. Old Hogyn of **II, 121** belongs to the world of the medieval *fabliaux*. His lady's expectation of 'honouring' her family by admitting him (stanza 2), unless wholly ironic, may suggest that Hogyn is to be thought of as wealthy as well as old – i.e. a rich old man (a stock figure in medieval literature), the type Chaucer's Wife of Bath favoured for her first three husbands. In the event, however, this lady is no more impressed with Hogyn's performance as a lover than the lady of *Selver Whyte* with that of her 'jouster'. Here, however, failure is punished: as he departs, the randy but impotent old Hogyn is made the victim of the same crude prank as that suffered by Absolon in Chaucer's *Miller's Tale*. The context of this poem's survival is interesting. It is preserved in Richard Hill's commonplace book.[58] It might surprise a present-day reader to learn that on the very page on which it is copied, it is immediately followed by a hymn to the Virgin. Whatever else, this collocation testifies to the catholicity of late medieval taste.[59]

Finally, among surviving Middle English tomb texts the epitaph of a certain rich Alan is unusually wry and nonchalant:

Here lyeth under this marbyll ston	*here lies under this marble stone*
Riche Alane, the ballid man;	*rich Alan, the bald man*

[57] See Commentary, **II, 113**.
[58] See below, pp. 46–7.
[59] Cf. Commentary, **II, 122**.

> Whether he be safe or noght   *safe* (i.e. *saved*) *or not*
> I recke never – for he ne roght!   *I don't care – for he never did*
>
> II, 150

More common are grimmer texts like **II, 104**, in which a voice from the grave addresses all conditions of men, high and low, with a warning that 'such as I am shall you be' (4). However, rich Alan's epitaph reminds us that even in an age of faith there were some people who apparently lived with a certain wit and insouciance.

Lyric Stanza and Metre

HOW ARE Middle English lyrics to be read? In the Middle Ages they would have been sung or read aloud. To enjoy these poems to the full modern readers must, at the very least, be able to read them with a confident sense of the movement of the verse, and this depends on some understanding of the metre in which they were written.

Old English poetry of all kinds was written in the same verse form, the alliterative line, so called because its two halves were linked by alliteration. Each half had two stressed and a variable number of unstressed syllables. A development of this line continued into Middle English and is used in several of the lyrics in this volume. Rhyme and stanza form, modelled on French and Latin verse, first appeared in English in Middle English poetry. The very structure of the stanza declares its origin in song. Thus, the rhyme scheme a a b; a a b; b a a b of *With longing I am lad* (**1, 1**) marks out a stanza structured as two three-line units followed by a four-line unit, corresponding to the melodic structure A A B – that is, a tune in two parts with the first part sung to the first three lines and repeated for the second three, and the second part sung to the final quatrain of the stanza. However, while originating in song, stanza form continued as a prosodic pattern for so-called 'literary lyrics', that is, lyrics written to be recited rather than sung.

With rhyme schemes as a guide, the stanza forms of the lyrics present few problems. However, the convention of representing units of verse as separate lines is a largely post-medieval practice. The representation of poetic form was often at best a matter of secondary importance for a medieval scribe; his overriding concern was usually with economy, with saving space. Hence, in the manuscripts, these poems were frequently written out as prose or in long lines (i.e. two or more lines written as one) in order to make the maximum use of every page. The way a poem was copied sometimes depended on how the page on which it was begun had been divided for the previous item. Thus, in MS BL Harley 2253, the beginning of *Of rybaudz I ryme* (**1, 115**) is written out in short lines because the page on which it starts had already been divided into two columns; but when the scribe began a fresh page he changed to copying the rest of the poem (from line 24) in long lines. Similarly, John of Grimestone copied the first stanza of **1, 92** as four short lines, and then, to fill space at the bottom of the page, he copied the second stanza as two long lines. Like many others, the scribe of MS London, BL Sloane 2593 sometimes marked the division of his long lines into units by punctuation marks; he also had the habit of saving space by copying the last line of a stanza in the right-hand margin. The line division and stanza form adopted in this volume are, therefore, for the most part editorial, following the modern convention of representing units of verse by separate lines.

If the stanzaic form of Middle English lyrics is generally clear, the same cannot be said of the metre. Even in non-alliterative verse, lines have usually been described in terms of number of stresses. An obvious disadvantage of this is that it is often unclear what is to count as a 'stressed syllable' – a syllable carrying 'natural' stress, or, perhaps, 'metrical', or 'rhetorical' stress? A more serious disadvantage is that unstressed syllables are left out of account. It has commonly been thought that English poets, accustomed to relative freedom with regard to the number of unstressed syllables in traditional native alliterative verse, were happy with some flexibility in the syllable-count when writing non-alliterative verse. This may be true of some verse, but as a generalization it is much too sweeping and may owe more to a quaint form of nationalistic pride than to any systematic analysis. Middle English verse, it has been claimed, by 'the admission of extra unstressed syllables ... refused to surrender ... [to] mere slavish following of French and Latin forms'.[60] Whatever the truth, a crucial question confronts us in assessing the metre of Middle English lyrics: precisely which unstressed syllables in a line *as written* are to be counted? It is difficult to answer this question for two reasons. First, no contemporary account of the metrical principles and practices of Middle English poets survives, if, indeed, any such treatise was ever written. The second is simply this: whereas it is clear to a present-day reader how many syllables are represented in a modern English text, in a Middle English text this, as will be explained, is far from self-evident.

For guidance on this question it is therefore necessary to look, at least in the first instance, to sources of evidence independent of the actual texts. Two such sources immediately suggest themselves: one is the verse tradition from which the lyrics derived, French and Latin songs; the other is the music which survives with some of the Middle English lyrics. A fundamental requirement of a song is that its words should fit the tune, and do so for all stanzas – a requirement which calls for a considerable degree of regularity. Indeed, from a study of troubadour and trouvère songs, John Stevens concluded that in the matching of word and music the 'most important single controlling factor is the number of syllables in any given line or stanza'.[61] It may well be, therefore, that in English stanzaic lyrics within this tradition (whether surviving with music or not) the principal poetic constraint continued to be a matter of a syllabic match, line for line and stanza by stanza. Indeed, of the Middle English songs which survive with music, E. J. Dobson took the view that 'the music ... may require perfect or near-perfect metrical regularity, in syllable-count and in rhythm'.[62] However, while this is, broadly speaking, true, the evidence of the actual surviving musical notation supports greater flexibility than Dobson allowed, especially with regard to two significant matters: first, the variation – common in Middle English verse – of lines beginning with or without an initial unstressed syllable; and second, the extent of freedom acceptable

---

[60] Saintsbury (1907), pp. 376–7.
[61] Stevens (1982), p. 2. See also Stevens (1986), *passim.*
[62] *MES,* p. 32.

in metrical rhythm. A fuller account of the evidence of the music is given in Appendix A.

The syllable count of a line may conveniently be expressed as its number of metrical (i.e. pronounced) syllables, counting from the first stressed syllable to the rhyme syllable (not counting the second syllable of feminine rhymes). Occasionally, as in some lines beginning with the word 'and', metrical or rhetorical stress will determine the first stressed syllable. An initial unstressed syllable may be regarded as an optional extra syllable. As a common variant in lines of this kind, the initial stress pattern × / may be inverted to give / × and so, for instance, an eight-syllable line in the form / × × / × / × /. However, regular alternation of stressed and unstressed syllables often depends on imposing a rhythm of 'metrical' stresses. Thus, though the lines of *With longing I am lad* (**1, 1**) may be described as three-stress lines, such a description only makes sense in terms of 'metrical' stressing, for in natural speech rhythm many of the lines read more convincingly with two stresses (e.g. *With lònging I am làd*, or *For sèlden I am sàd*, or *That sèmly for to sèe*). It makes more sense, then, to view lines of non-alliterative verse not as fixed in number of stresses (some merely 'metrical'), but rather (at least, in careful verse) as basically constant in number of syllables, with flexibility in the number and rhythm of natural stresses. Such a view accords well with John Stevens's claim that the rhythm of Middle English verse is that of 'very speech itself';[63] and although some lyric verse was meant to be sung rather than read aloud,[64] when it is so read a reader may appropriately follow the natural rhythms of speech.

How, then, does this view square with the evidence of the surviving lyric texts? Unfortunately, as already stated, it is not self-evident from a Middle English text *as written* which syllables are to be pronounced. Some may or may not be pronounced depending on the operation of linguistic principles such as elision, hiatus, synizesis, syncope and apocope. These are matters fundamental to any appraisal of metre; however, as they are of a technical nature, they are discussed separately in Appendix B. Even if Middle English lyrics had survived in autograph copies, an understanding of their metrical form would have been possible only in the light of such considerations.

However, none of the surviving lyric texts is demonstrably an author's copy, and most are manifestly the end product of successive scribal transcriptions, and possibly, in some cases, versions made from dictation or from memory. Such copies are notoriously unreliable.[65] Since there was no such thing as a standard form of Middle English – no standard spelling, no standard grammar – scribes wrote in accordance with the pronunciation and usage of their own dialects and the spelling

---

[63] Stevens (1982), p. 7.

[64] This is especially true of *contrafacta*. See Commentary, **1, 109**.

[65] Readers unfamiliar with the extent of textual corruption in Middle English lyrics (words added or omitted, the order of words, lines and even stanzas altered, stanzas added or omitted), not to mention the effects of scribal linguistic revision, need only compare the different versions of **1, 39, 75, 46, 40, 38** and **91** printed by Carleton Brown (Brown XIII, nos. 10, 17, 28, 32, 46 and 49) or the texts of **11, 69** from MS BL Royal 2.F.viii (Brown, XIII, no. 63) and **11, 94** from MS Bodl. Digby 2 (Brown, XIII, no. 64) with the versions of the same lyrics in MS BL Harley 2253 (Brook, nos. 18 and 22).

habits which prevailed in the schools or scriptoria where they had learned to write. Furthermore, Middle English scribes tended to alter the language of the texts they copied to conform with the spellings and forms familiar to them, a widespread practice known as 'linguistic revision'. Metre and rhyme were vulnerable to such changes. Chaucer himself was all too aware of this danger, as his famous plea at the close of *Troilus and Criseyde* makes clear:

> And for ther is so gret diversité   *because; diversity*
> In Englissh and in writyng of oure tonge,
> So prey I God that non myswritë the,   *thee*
> Ne the mysmetre for defaute of tonge.   *lack of skill in language*
>
> *Troilus*, V, 1793–96

Typically, a scribe might copy a word such as *sinne* (sin) as *sunne* or *senne* according to his own dialect, thus spoiling a rhyme. Numerous words in Middle English, including prepositions, adverbs, nouns and especially verbs, had the endings '-en' or '-e' as variant forms. Scribes readily copied '-en' instead of '-e' or *vice versa*. Since final '-e' was often silent or frequently disappeared with elision which was prevented by '-en', it is evident how easily metre could be distorted by such alterations alone.[66] Among other common variants affecting and potentially distorting metre were: *havest / hast*; *haveth / hath*; *haveth / haven / have / han*; *haved / had*; *for to / to*; *upon / on*; *unto / to*; *other / or*; *also / so, as*; *muchel / much*; *loverd / lord*; *lavedy / lady*; *heved / hed*; *ne wot / not*; and single *ne*, *nought* and double *ne … nought* negatives.[67]

Above all, it is in the interpretation of the endings '-e', '-est', '-eth', '-ed' and '-es' that the most obvious difficulty in metrical analysis arises.[68] It is evident, not least from Chaucer's verse, that not infrequently the verb endings '-est' and '-eth', written as full forms, concealed reduced pronunciations; and it is difficult to resist the conclusion that with '-ed', and even '-es', the option of reduced endings was already available to poets even as early as the 13th century. It is also evident that from early Middle English through to the 15th century poets had the metrical option of treating final '-e' as pronounced or silent.

By now it will have become apparent why Middle English lyric scansion is so problematic. Nevertheless, when analysed in the light of the issues outlined above, many of the non-alliterative lyrics in this anthology do reveal a marked consistency in syllable count. When a lyric is characteristically regular in its metre, it is reasonable to assume that an occasional irregularity may well have resulted from the hazards of 'linguistic revision'. Accordingly, in rendering the texts of Part I into London English, where an alternative form (e.g. *drive* instead of *driven*, or *to* instead of *unto*) readily rectifies the metre of a line, such an alternative is silently

---

[66] However, the 'e' of '-en' followed by a vowel could be reduced by syncope; see Appendix B (4). Furthermore, one must be alert to the possibility of reading final '-en' or '-yn' as silent.

[67] Numerous examples of 'mismetering' and spoilt rhymes caused by variants adopted by scribes other than the forms of the original text are readily to be seen by comparing the texts of lyrics printed from more than one manuscript in Brown XIII. See also Commentary, **I, 75**, 14.

[68] See further, p. 45 below.

adopted, as are alternative forms such as those of the third singular present (*haveth* and *hath*), of the present plural (*haveth*, *have(n)* and *han*), and of the past tense (*haved* and *had*) of the verb 'to have'. Likewise, final '-e' is restored, as metrically required. Where such alternative forms are adopted in Part II texts, the manuscript readings are recorded in the Commentary. However, as it would seem that Chaucer's readers must have been used to pronouncing 'never' as 'ner' as metrically required, in other such forms as 'unto', 'other' and 'also' it is frequently left to the reader to adopt the reduced pronunciations 'to', 'or' and 'so' at their discretion. Metrical irregularities occasionally invite emendation, especially where suspect sense or syntax is involved; and even if emendation can never guarantee to restore the original text even with support from another manuscript – for all emendation must always remain to a degree speculative – the restoration of metre is a positive editorial gain. Again, all emendations are recorded with the original readings of the base text in the Commentary.

But not all lyrics are metrically regular. One kind of verse frequently used in lyrics – a long line of seven stresses which usually divides into two lines, one of four and one of three stresses – has lines of three plus three stresses as a common variant. This type of scansion developed from the septenarius, a seven-foot syllabic metre popular in medieval Latin verse; it is the form of verse used in the two dramatic, ballad-like poems about Judas (**1, 112**) and St Stephen (**1, 126**), and was, indeed, the origin of what is now known as ballad metre. Lyrics of a more popular kind, as one might expect, are often freer in their scansion. Occasionally metre defies consistent analysis. *Levedy seynte Marie* (**1, 37**), for instance, seems to fluctuate between lines of four stresses (sometimes marked by alliteration) and syllabic verse. In some of the later lyrics (in striking contrast with Chaucer) lines with extra syllables are common. This is true of the two Vernon lyrics in this anthology (**1, 60** and **61**). The considerable textual discrepancies between the two manuscripts of *In the vaile of restles mind* (**1, 73**) make it impossible to tell how authentic the apparently loose metre of this lyric, written *c.* 1400, really was. Again, textual corruption may account for the metrical irregularities found in some of the lyrics in MS London, BL Sloane 2593.

In alliterative verse and in rhymes it is especially difficult to tell whether unstressed syllables are full or reduced, or, in the case of final '-e', silent. Middle English alliterative verse, unlike its Old English ancestor, appeared to enjoy considerable freedom in the number of weak syllables per line. Guidance on pronunciation in alliterative lyrics is, therefore, largely impressionistic. Again, since it is difficult to tell when final '-e' was sounded in rhymes, it has usually been marked for pronunciation only as required by music. However, the reader is alerted to the strong probability that it may have been pronounced more frequently.

Inevitably, the interpretation of lyric metre depends on hypothesis and personal judgement. Lines will sometimes scan in more ways than one. Thus, lines 86–8 and 90–92 of **1, 3** could be read as given here with *hirë*, or, alternatively, with *hire*, i.e. with a silent final '-e'. In **1, 51**, lines 37 and 49, *hertë ginneth* and *hertë brekëth* could have been *herte ginnëth* and *herte brekëth*, and so on. Especially in earlier lyrics, decisions as to whether final '-e' should be pronounced or silent are inevitably uncertain and tentative. Different readings are sometimes possible.

While it is hoped that the guidance offered here will prove helpful, readers familiar with Middle English may wish, here and there, to opt for alternative interpretations.

Guidance to Metrical Reading

SINCE IN MIDDLE ENGLISH alternative pronunciations arose in some unstressed syllables, internal and final, the vowel 'e' is marked as 'ë' where it was probably pronounced, and left unmarked where it may well have been silent.

(1) It is essential that the reader should be aware that many final '-e's were sounded in Middle English which are silent in modern English; but also, that, as a random or conventional spelling, or because of elision, a final '-e' in Middle English was often silent. Thus, final '-e' is pronounced in *waxë* (**1, 1,** 2), *maidë* (**1, 1,** 3), *rewë* (**1, 1,** 7), *allë* (**1, 1,** 11), etc., but is silent in *molde* (**1, 1,** 2), *grede* (**1, 1,** 4), *grone* (**1, 1,** 4), *routhe* (**1, 1,** 8), etc.

(2) The ending '-eth' of the present tense, third person singular of the verb was sometimes pronounced as a full ending as in *marrëth* (**1, 1,** 3), *revëth* (**1, 1,** 33), *lovëth* (**1, 2,** 11), etc. Frequently, however, the ending was reduced: thus, *bereth* (**1, 1,** 35), *woneth* (**1, 1,** 37), *thinketh* (**1, 2,** 15), etc. were probably pronounced as 'berth', 'wonth', 'thinkth', etc.

(3) Similarly, the ending '-est' of the present tense, second person singular of the verb was sometimes pronounced as a full ending as in *spekëst* (**1, 24,** 66), but was sometimes reduced as in *singestou* (**1, 21,** 18), pronounced with two syllables as 'singstou'.

(4) The endings '-ed' of the past tense and the past participle of the verb, and '-es' of the genitive singular and plural of nouns and of some adverbs, were usually pronounced as full syllables: e.g. *marrëd* (**1, 2,** 38), *sewëd* (**1, 3,** 69), *listenëd* (**1, 3,** 77), etc., and *Godës* (**1, 2,** 17), *whallës* (**1, 2,** 19), *tounës* (**1, 2,** 22), etc. However, these endings were sometimes reduced as in modern English, occasionally so in earlier lyrics – e.g. *y-loved* (**1, 13,** 3), *loved* (**1, 17,** 16), *lovede* (**1, 24,** 51 and 55), *unwarned* (**1, 60,** 170), *deyed* (**1, 65,** 18), etc., and *tales* (**1, 27,** 37), *whiles* (**1, 30,** 7), *tidinges* (**1, 41,** 1), *sawes* (**1, 51,** 10), *sides* (**1, 51,** 78), *mirthes* (**1, 51,** 81), etc. – and increasingly in later lyrics.

(5) Some words could vary in pronunciation. Thus, in words like *comely, dereworthe, dereworthliche, lasteles, levely, leveliche, stedefast*, etc., the unstressed 'e' within the word could be pronounced or not as metrically required. The very common word *hevene* could be pronounced with two syllables as in modern English, or as *hevenë* (with the final '-e' sounded and the middle 'e' lost by syncope – see Appendix B), or with three syllables as *hevënë* (**1, 51,** 107) as required by metre. With syncope, and elision with a following word beginning with a vowel, it could even be reduced to one syllable as in *Hevene I* (**1, 1,** 39) and *heven and* (**1, 2,** 53). Again, see Appendix B.

Manuscript Sources[69]

MEDIEVAL ENGLISH LYRICS are mostly anonymous and have survived only by chance. Some are found haphazardly jotted in margins and on flyleaves, some embedded in sermons, others entered in what had been blank leaves at the end of long (frequently Latin) manuscripts. How many manuscripts with lyrics have perished? Who can tell? Of some, only a single damaged leaf remains. Had MS BL Harley 2253 perished, half of the love lyrics from before Chaucer's time – and those the best – would have been lost. The majority of the early lyrics to survive are found in a few important manuscripts. Of the lyrics in Part I of this volume, eight appear in MS Cambridge, Trinity College B.14.39 (*c.* 1250), six in MS Oxford, Bodl. Digby 86 (*c.* 1275), four in MS London, BL Arundel 248 (*c.* 1280–1300), a manuscript especially important for its music, seven in MS Oxford, Bodl. Rawlinson D.913 (*c.* 1325–50), 29 in MS London, BL Harley 2253 (*c.* 1340), 15 in MS Edinburgh, NLS Advocates 18.7.21 (1372), and five in the Vernon manuscript, MS Oxford, Bodl. eng. poet. a.1 (*c.* 1380–1400). Of these, Rawlinson D.913 is a single leaf of parchment, much faded and partly illegible. The Cambridge and Edinburgh manuscripts are Franciscan compilations of materials for preachers. In the other manuscripts the lyrics are found as part of wide-ranging anthologies of religious and secular texts, in prose and verse, in Latin, French and English.

There are a few manuscripts in which later lyrics and carols figure prominently. Two such are MS London, BL Sloane 2593 (early 15th century) and MS Oxford, Bodl. eng. poet. e.1 (late 15th century), each consisting almost entirely of short poems, mainly carols. Fourteen poems from the former manuscript are to be found in Part I; a further five are included in Part II, as are 12 poems from the latter manuscript, one of which (**II, 47**) is common to both. Both manuscripts are small, approximately 4 × 6 inches in size. It has been claimed that these small, compact volumes of songs and carols may have been carried around by minstrels. However, evidence connecting the Sloane manuscript with the Benedictine monastery of Bury St Edmunds and the Bodley manuscript with Beverley Minster, Yorkshire, suggests that they originated with monks rather than minstrels.

Many late Middle English lyrics and carols survive in commonplace books of the period, the contents of which could range from household accounts, medical remedies, wills and family genealogies to lengthy works, religious and secular, in poetry and prose, sometimes in English, sometimes in Latin and French. Two of the lyrics in this volume appear in a commonplace book written at Glastonbury Abbey *c.* 1450;[70] six are found in a mid-15th-century student's commonplace book;[71] another comes from the commonplace book of Humfrey Newton (1466–1536);[72] and four others occur in the commonplace book of the Findern family.[73] From the point of view of lyrics and carols, Richard Hill's is by far the most

---

[69] An excellent and comprehensive account is given by Julia Boffey in 'Middle English Lyrics and Manuscripts', in *Companion*, pp. 1–18.
[70] Cambridge, Trinity College O.9.38.
[71] Cambridge, Gonville and Caius College 383.
[72] See Commentary, **II, 15**.
[73] See Commentary, **II, 27**.

important manuscript of this kind.[74] Hill, a citizen and grocer in London, compiled his commonplace book over a period of some 30 years up to 1536. Nineteen of the poems included here are found in this manuscript, ten of them uniquely there.

Some manuscripts are poetic miscellanies. MS London, Lambeth Palace Library 835, a small-sized, modest but lengthy manuscript in a fairly formal script dated *c.* 1430, is a fine collection of English poems which includes three of those printed here. Four others are found in a more elaborate 15th-century manuscript of assorted religious pieces, some accompanied by drawings, perhaps compiled at Mount Grace, a Carthusian monastery in Yorkshire.[75] Two manuscripts preserve poems by named poets represented in this anthology: almost all the English poems of Charles d'Orléans survive in MS BL Harley 682 (*c.* 1440), and the poems of John Audelay are found in MS Oxford, Bodl. Douce 302, which may have been copied at his dictation by a monk of Haghmond Abbey early in the second quarter of the 15th century. In some manuscripts lyrics are copied along with musical notation, sometimes roughly written monophonic melodies, sometimes elaborate polyphonic settings. Of the latter sort are seven of the carols in Part II, four of which are from MS Oxford, Bodl. Arch. Selden B.26, and three from MS Cambridge, Trinity College O.3.58. The Trinity manuscript, a most valuable roll of 6 feet 8 inches in length and 8 inches wide, contains some of the finest surviving carols, including *Ther is no rose of swych vertù* (**II, 46**) and the Agincourt Carol (**II, 132**). The lyrics in the early 16th-century Fairfax and Henry VIII manuscripts have polyphonic settings by Tudor composers. Two settings, one by William Cornish Junior and one by Browne, of *Wofully araide* (**II, 71**) are found in the former manuscript. The latter, a handsome, professionally produced volume, offers excellent evidence of the music and poetry enjoyed at the Tudor court in the early 16th century. Five of its poems (**II, 31–35**) are included here. The latest source used for this volume is the Bannatyne manuscript, a large anthology of poetry compiled by George Bannatyne, an Edinburgh merchant, and completed in 1568. Though mainly a collection of Scottish poetry, this manuscript includes English poems by Chaucer, Hoccleve and Lydgate and also a number of anonymous poems.

Language and Texts

A S FOUND IN THE MANUSCRIPT SOURCES, the lyrics in Part I differ widely in dialect and present a great diversity of spellings and grammatical forms. The language of the surviving copies is clearly often the product of scribal transmission and linguistic revision (see pp. 42–3); it is seldom if ever demonstrably the actual language of the original poets. Dialect variants are sometimes of literary significance, as in rhyme or in alliteration. In the main, however, the linguistic diversity of the lyrics, while of interest to philologists, only constitutes a needless barrier between the modern reader and the Middle English poems as poetry.

This barrier is not removed simply by replacing special Middle English characters like 'þ' (thorn) and 'ʒ' (yogh) with their modern equivalents – 'th' for

---

[74] Oxford, Balliol College 354.
[75] London, BL Add. 37049.

'þ', and 'gh' or 'y' for 'ʒ'; for not only is one still left with many different dialect spellings of the same word (e.g. *sunne, senne, zenne, sinne* – some of many spellings of the word 'sin'), but also with such idiosyncratic spellings as *Nv yh she* 'Now I see', the opening words of **1, 69** in MS London, BL Royal 2.F.viii. Worse still, if a manuscript form like *necheð* (**1, 36,** 3) is merely 'normalized' to *necheth*, or if forms like *ho* and *hende* (**1, 47,** 22 and 60) are left unaltered, a non-specialist reader, who does not know that in *necheth* the spelling 'ch' does not represent the initial sound of modern 'cheese', or that in the other forms the *h* is silent, is likely needlessly to be misled.

To avoid such difficulties, the spelling and grammar of the texts of Part I in this volume have been 'revised' in accordance with the language of late 14th-century London English. In effect, this is just the kind of linguistic revision which a London scribe would have made. This process of 'normalization' has two considerable advantages. The first is that the language of the texts remains at all times authentic Middle English and not the medley of half-changed forms produced by other attempts at normalization. The second is that since late 14th-century London English is Chaucer's language, it is the form of Middle English most familiar to modern readers and, moreover, one which most readily allows for the possibility of reading these poems aloud in something approaching a reasonable approximation of one type of Middle English pronunciation – in the case of lyrics, a matter of some consequence. Occasionally, forms from other dialects are retained as required by rhyme or alliteration. The vocabulary of the lyrics is also preserved; words which were regional or archaic, not current in ordinary late 14th-century London, are retained, just as they would have been by a faithful scribe, as an integral part of a poem's texture and diction. An element of dialect mixture of this kind is in no way inauthentic; it was, indeed, typical of many Middle English texts.

The London language itself varied considerably both in spelling and in grammatical forms, as Chaucer manuscripts readily demonstrate. From this diversity the most common forms and the more familiar spellings have generally been adopted. However, the common conventions of Middle English writing have been respected: final '-e', both as a random spelling and as found in such common alternative spellings as *yet / yette, had / hadde, wel / welle*, etc., and in the free variation of the spellings *ou* and *ow* (as in *nou / now* 'now' and *soule / sowle* 'soul'), *o*, *ou* and *ow* (as in *thoght / thought / thowght* 'thought'), and *i* and *y* (as in *him / hym* 'him' or *while / whyle* 'while') have been partly, though not systematically, retained. Such characteristics of authentic written Middle English will scarcely disturb a modern reader. However, the use of the letters 'u' and 'v' has been standardized according to modern usage, and, where appropriate, capital 'F' replaces initial *ff* of the manuscripts.

The language of the later lyrics of Part II poses fewer grammatical problems: for instance, nothing like the diversity of forms of the personal pronouns in earlier Middle English dialects remains to confuse the reader of 15th-century lyrics. Accordingly, the language of the Part II lyrics differs from that of the surviving manuscript copies only where common late Middle English letter forms and spellings replace other variants of the period which would needlessly distract or mislead a modern reader. The alterations made here are as follows:

(1) 'þ' is replaced by 'th'.

(2) 'ʒ' is replaced by 'y', 'gh' or 'w'.

(3) Initial 'ff' (as appropriate) is replaced by capital 'F'.

(4) '&' is replaced by 'and' or (in Latin) 'et'.

(5) Where 'v' and 'u', 'i' and 'j', 'w' and 'v', and also 'w' and 'u' as initial consonants, are equivalent spellings, the alternative familiar from modern usage is adopted.

(6) 'ght' replaces the variant spellings 't', 'tt', 'th', 'ht', 'cht' and 'ʒth'; and 't' replaces the variants 'th' and 'ght'.

(7) 'th' replaces the variants 't', 'tt', and occasional 'ht', 'ʒt', 'ʒth', 'gth' and 'ght'.

(8) 'sh' replaces the variant spellings 'ch' and 'x'.

(9) 'wh' replaces the variant spellings 'qu', 'qw' and 'w'.

(10) Unetymological initial 'h' is omitted.

(11) In final unstressed syllables, 'y', 'i', 'u' or 'a' in the endings '-yst', '-yth', '-ys', '-yn' and '-yd', etc. of verbs, and '-ys', etc. of nouns (genitive and plural) are usually replaced by 'e'.

(12) '-y' is preferred to final '-e' in such variants as *evere / every*, *lade / lady*, etc., except in rhymes with Middle English /e:/.

Examples of such spelling changes are: under (5), *under* replaces *vnder* 'under', *Jesus* replaces *iesus*, and *Judas* replaces *iudas*; under (6), *out* replaces *ought* 'out', and *myght* replaces *myth* 'might'; under (7), *worth* replaces *worʒt* 'worth', and *erth* replaces *ergth* 'earth'; under (7) and (11), *thinketh* replaces *thinkitt* 'thinks'; under (8), *shal* replaces *chal* or *xal* 'shall'; under (9), *whan* replaces *quan, qwan*, or *wan* 'when'. None of these alterations significantly affects pronunciation. Thus, the vowel of the inflexions '-est', '-eth', '-es', '-en' and '-ed' was doubtless the same indeterminate unstressed sound, no matter which of the spelling variants 'e', 'i', 'y', 'u' or 'a' was used. In the Northern and Scottish lyrics in this volume (e.g. those of Dunbar), the alterations detailed in the first five points above are made, but other spellings consistently characteristic of their dialects are left unaltered such as 'cht' for 'ght', and the 'i' or 'y' spellings in endings such as '-it' (for '-ed'), '-is', etc. Changes of idiosyncratic or misleading spellings other than those listed above are recorded in the Commentary along with the spellings of the base manuscripts.

Notwithstanding these alterations, many variants characteristic of late Middle English spelling are preserved unaltered in the texts in this volume; these, however unfamiliar at first sight, should cause little or no difficulty. Many are the kind of alternative spellings still encountered in some 16th- and 17th-century texts, e.g. the common variation of a single final consonant and a double consonant with a final 'e' in spellings such as *ship / shippe, had / hadde*, etc. Other variants like *maydyn* and *maydon* 'maiden' and *wundir, wundor* and *wunder* 'wonder', etc. will be immediately recognizable in context. Occasionally alternative spellings represent different dialect pronunciations, e.g. *vond*, the Southern form with a voiced initial consonant, of *fond* 'found'.

Pronunciation Guide

A<small>N</small> <small>APPROXIMATION</small> to the pronunciation of late 14th-century London English, Chaucer's English, may be achieved if the following significant differences from modern English Received Pronunciation are observed. This pronunciation will also serve well enough for reading the later lyrics even if significant changes in pronunciation (especially with regard to long vowels) were beginning to emerge by the end of the 15th century.

(1) The spellings *a, e (ee), i (y), o (oo), ou (ow),* and *u* for long vowels represent the sounds they have in modern French, Spanish and Italian:

Vowel	as in French	e.g. Middle English
a	*la gare*	*name, tale, maken* 'make'
e (ee)	*le café*	*swete* 'sweet', *meten* 'meet', *see* 'see'
e (ee)	*la mère*	*techen* 'teach', *speken* 'speak', *see* 'sea'
i (y)	*le livre*	*tyme / time* 'time', *while* 'while', *ryden* 'ride'
o (oo)	*le mot*	*gode / good* 'good', *mone* 'moon', *don* 'do'
o (oo)	*l'homme*	*gon* 'go', *hom* 'home', *stone* 'stone'
ou (ow)	*Toulouse*	*house* 'house', *now* 'now'
u	*la lune*	*vertú* 'virtue', *natúre* 'nature'

Modern English spelling and pronunciation can often help in distinguishing the appropriate pronunciation of Middle English *e (ee)* and *o (oo)*, as follows: Middle English *e (ee)* is pronounced as French **é** in words where the modern spelling is *ee*, and as French **è** where the modern spelling is *ea*; Middle English *o (oo)* is pronounced like **o** in French *mot* in words which now have the vowel sound of present-day *moon*, and like **o** in French *homme* in words which now have the vowel sound of present-day *stone*.

(2) Where in modern English the spellings *u* or *o* are pronounced as in *but / hut / love / son* the Middle English pronunciation was as in modern English *put / full* – e.g. ME *but, muchel* 'much', *sunne* 'sun', and *love, comen* 'come', *sone* 'son'.

(3) The diphthong spelt as *ai (ay)* or *ei (ey)* was probably pronounced like modern English *my* – e.g. ME *saide / seyde* as modern English *side*. The diphthong spelt *au (aw)* had the sound of *ow* in modern English *now* – e.g. ME *cause, lawe, drawen* 'draw'.

(4) At the end of a word the letter 'e', when pronounced, had the rather neutral sound of *e* in modern English *enough*, or *a* in modern English *above* – e.g. *swetë, sunnë, lovë*, etc. Where a final '-e' is marked with an acute accent – e.g. ME *beauté* 'beauty', *leauté* 'loyalty', *pité* 'pity' – the pronunciation is as in French *café*. The suffix *-io(u)n*, as in ME *confusioun, nacioun* 'nation', *transmutacioun*, etc., was pronounced '-i-o(u)n', that is, as two syllables.

(5) Consonants.

    (a) The spelling *gh* was pronounced as *ch* in Scottish *loch* after back vowels – e.g. *noght, boughte, foughte, caughte* – and as *ch* in German *ich* after front vowels – e.g. *night, light, fighten* 'fight'.

    (b) Initial *g, k*, and *w* were still sounded in words like *gnawen* 'gnaw', *knowen* 'know' and *writen* 'write', as was *l* before consonants, as in *half* and *folk*. The consonant *r*, often silent in modern English, was always pronounced, and probably trilled, as in present-day Scottish speech.

    (c) The pronunciation of *ng* was as in modern English *hunger*. Thus in Middle English *singer* would rhyme with *finger*.

(6) The accentuation of some words derived from French varied. Thus in *vertù, natùre, miròur, manère, servìce, savòur*, etc. the accent could fall on the second syllable as in French; but sometimes such words occur with initial accentuation as in English – e.g. *mìrror, màner*, etc. Sometimes accentuation could fall on a suffix, as in the rhymes on *-aunce, -esse* and *-nesse* in **I, 30**.

Texts of the Lyrics and Carols

I N PART I the language of the lyrics (except for **1, 95, 102** and **116**) has been normalized in accordance with the spelling and grammar of late 14th-century London English. Occasional non-London forms are retained for the sake of rhyme or alliteration. In the case of common Middle English variants such as *hath / haveth, to / unto, to / for to,* etc. (forms which vary without distinction of meaning from manuscript to manuscript in the course of scribal transmission, see pp. 42–3), a different form from that of the base manuscript has sometimes been silently adopted where metrically preferable.

The spelling of the texts in Part II is that of the base manuscripts except for the modifications detailed on p. 49 and occasional additional changes recorded in the Commentary.

All substantive emendations, with the original readings of the base manuscripts and selected variants from other manuscripts, are recorded in the Commentary. Variants from versions which appear to be reworkings, that is, essentially different poems rather than copies, are ignored unless they offer significant information.

Scribal abbreviations are silently expanded. Strokes above or through final letters which may sometimes be mere scribal flourishes are always regarded as marks of abbreviation where extra syllables are metrically desirable. Capitalization, punctuation, word-division and metrical arrangement are editorial. An 'e' at the end of a word and in the inflections '-est', '-eth' and '-es', in the suffix '-ed', and in unstressed syllables within a word, which may have been silent or sounded, is marked with a diaeresis where it seems to be required by the metre. An acute accent is placed over 'e' where the pronunciation is equivalent to that of English final '-y' or French 'é'; occasionally a grave accent is used to mark a stressed syllable.

PART I

Love Lyrics

I, 1   With longing I am lad

With longing I am lad,	*I go (lit. am led)*
On molde I waxë mad,	*on earth I am going mad*
A maidë marrëth me.	*distresses*
I grede, I grone, unglad,	*cry out; groan; anguished*
5 For selden I am sad	*seldom; tired*
That semly for to see.	*that fair one; of seeing (lit. to see)*
Lady, thou rewë me,	*have pity on me*
To routhe thou hast me rad,	*to grief; brought*
Be bote of that I bad,	*be the remedy for which I have prayed*
10 My lyf is long on thee.	*my life is dependent*
Lady of allë londe,	*all lands*
Les me out of bonde,	*release me; bonds*
Brought Ich am in wo.	*I am*
Have resting on honde,	*bring about respite*
15 And send thou me thy sonde	*response*
Sone, er thou me slo.	*soon, before you slay me*
My reste is with the ro,	*peace of mind; roe*
Though men to me han onde,	*towards me have enmity*
To love nil I nought wonde,	*I will not hesitate*
20 Ne lete for non of tho.	*nor desist for any (lit. none) of them*
Lady, with al my might	
My love is on thee light	*settled (lit. alighted)*
To menskë when I may.	*to honour (you)*
Thou rew and red me ryght,	*pity and guide me aright*
25 To dethe thou hast me dight,	*condemned*
I deye longe er my day.	*before*
Thou leve upon my lay,	*believe in my song*
Trouth Ich have thee plight,	*fidelity; pledged*
To don that Ich have hight	*to do what I have promised*
30 While mi lif lastë may.	
Lylie-whyte she is,	
Hire rode so rose on rys,	*her complexion as; on a stem*
That revëth me my rest.	*who robs me of*
Womman war and wys,	*prudent and wise*
35 Of pride she bereth the pris,	*in excellence she takes the prize*
Byrde one of the best.	*a lady*
This womman woneth by west,	*dwells in the west*
Brightest under bys;	*fairest in fine linen*
Hevene I tolde al his	*I would consider entirely his*
40 That o night were hire gest.	*who for one night might be her guest*

1, 2   A waylë whyte as whallës bon

. . . .
. . . .
. . . .

    Ne half so fre;   *nor half so noble*
5 Whoso wole of love be trewe   *will; true*
    Do listnë me.   *listen to*

    Herknëth me, I you telle,
    In such wondryng for wo I welle,   *perplexity for woe I seethe*
    Nis no fire so hot in helle
10   Al to mon   *as a man*
    That lovëth derne and dar not telle   *in secret; dares*
      What him ys on.   *what is wrong with him*

    Ich unne hire wel, and she me wo,   *I wish her well; she (wishes)*
    Ich am hire frend, and she my fo,   *she (is) my foe*
15 Me thinketh min herte wol breke atwo   *it seems to me; in two*
    For sorwe and syke;   *sighing*
    In Godës greting moote she go,   *in God's grace may she be (lit. go)*
      That waylë whyte.   *beauty; white (i.e. radiant)*

    A waylë whyte as whallës bon,   *a beauty; whale's bone*
20 A greyn in golde that goodly shon,   *a jewel; which shines beautifully*
    A turtel that min herte is on;   *a turtle-dove; is (set) on*
      In tounës trewe   *among men; true*
    Hire gladshipe nis never gon   *her grace will never go (unsung)*
      While I may glewe.   *sing*

25 While I may glewe, when she is glad,   *she is gracious*
    Of al this world namore I bad   *would ask*
    Than be with hire myn one bistad   *alone; settled*
      Withouten strif;   *dispute*
    The care that Ich am in y-brad   *sorrow that I am burnt alive in*
30   I wite a wyf.   *I blame on a woman*

    A wyf nis non so worthly wrought!   *there is no woman as excellently made*
    When she is blythe to bedde y-brought,   *is joyously*
    Wel were him that wiste hire thought,   *who enjoyed her favour*
      That thriven and thro;   *that beautiful and excellent (one)*
35 Wel I wot she nil me nought,   *know she does not want me*
      Myn herte is wo.   *woeful (lit. woe is to my heart)*

    How shal myn herte that lefly syng   *that lovely one; celebrate in song*
    That thus is marrëd in mournyng?   *vexed*
    She me wol to dethë bryng   *will*
40   Longe er my day;   *before my time*

Gret hire wel, that swetë thing	*greet*
With eyen gray.	*eyes*
Hire yen han woundëd me ywisse,	*eyes have; assuredly*
Hire bendë browës bringen blisse,	*arched eyebrows; joy*
45 Hire comely mouth that mightë kisse	*the man who might*
In much mirth were;	*great happiness*
I wolde changë myn for his	*change my (mirth / companion)*
That is hire fere.	*who is her companion*
Wolde hire ferë be so fre,	*companion; noble*
50 And worthës were that so myghte be,	*equivalents (i.e. for exchanging)*
Al for one I wolde yeve three	*give*
Withouten cheep;	*haggling*
From helle to heven and sonne to see	*sun to sea*
Nis none so yeep.	*there is none as prudent*
55 Ich wolde Ich were a thrustelcok,	*song-thrush*
A bountyng other a laverokke;	*bunting; skylark*
Swetë bryd,	*sweet bird*
Bitwen hire kirtel and hire smok	*gown; undergarment*
I wolde ben hid.	

I, 3   Ichot a byrde in bourë bryght

Blow, northerne wind,	
Send thou me my swetyng;	*sweetheart*
Blow, northerne wind,	
Blow, blow, blow.	
5 Ichot a byrde in bourë bryght	*I know a lady; bower*
That selly semly is on syght,	*who wonderfully comely is to see*
Menskful maide of muchel myght,	*a noble; great attraction*
Fair and fre to fonde;	*beautiful and gracious to know*
In al this worthlichë won,	*excellent world*
10 A byrde of blodë and of bon,	*of blood and bone*
Never yet I nistë non,	*knew I any (lit. none)*
Lufsomere in londe.	*lovelier on earth*
Blow, etc.	
With lokkës levëliche and longe,	*tresses lovely and long*
15 With frount and facë fair to fonde,	*forehead; to behold*
With mirthës mony mote she monge,	*with merriment many may she inspire*
That brid so breme in boure;	*maiden so excellent*
With lufsom eyen grete and gode,	*lovely eyes large and good*
With browës blisful under hode,	*eyebrows; under (her) hood*
20 He that reste him on the rode	*may He who rested on the cross*
That leflich lyf honoure.	*that dear creature; honour*
Blow, etc.	

Hirë lerë lemëth light,   *her complexion shines brightly*
Asë a launterne anight,   *as a lantern at night*
25 Hirë ble blikëth so bright,   *her face gleams so radiantly*
   So fair she is and fyn.   *exquisite*
A swetly swire she hath to holde,   *charming neck; to embrace*
With armës, sholdrës, as man wolde,   *shoulders; as one would wish*
And fyngrës fairë for to folde,   *to clasp*
30   God woldë she were myn.   *would God*
    Blow, etc.

Middel she hath menskful smal,   *a waist; gracefully slender*
Hire loveliche cherë as cristal,   *lovely face (is) as crystal*
Thighës, leggës, fet and al
35   Y-wroght was of the beste.   *fashioned*
A lufsom lady lastëles   *faultless*
That sweting is and ever wes,   *was*
A better birdë never nes   *never was (lit. was not)*
   Y-heried with the heste.   *honoured among the best (lit. highest)*
40   *Blow, etc.*

She is derëworthe in day,   *precious*
Graciousë, stout and gay,   *poised*
Gentil, jolif so the jay,   *merry as the jay*
   Worthliche when she waketh;   *splendid; wakens*
45 Maiden, miriest of mouth,
By est, bi west, by north and south
There nis fiëlë ne crouth   *there is neither viol nor fiddle*
   That such mirthës maketh.   *merriment*
    Blow, etc.

50 She is coral of godnesse,
She is rubie of ryghtfulnesse,   *uprightness*
She is cristal of clennesse,   *purity*
   And baner of beuté;   *banner of beauty*
She is lilie of largesse,   *generosity*
55 She is parvenke of prowesse,   *periwinkle of excellence*
She is solsecle of swetnesse,   *marigold*
   And lady of leauté.   *loyalty*
    Blow, etc.

To Love, that leflich is in londe,   *who is dear everywhere*
60 I tolde him, as Ich understonde,   *as I*
How this hende hath hent in honde   *this gracious one has seized*
   An hertë that myn wes;   *a heart that was mine*
And hirë knightës me han soght,   *have sought*
Syking, Sorëwyng and Thoght,   *Sighing, Sorrowing and Perplexity*
65 Tho three me han in balë broght   *those three; grief*
   Ayain the power of Pees.   *against; Peace*
    Blow, etc.

To Love I puttë pleyntës mo,   *I made further complaints*
How Sykyng me hath sewëd so,   *pursued*
70 And ekë Thoght me thret to slo   *also; threatened to slay me*
   With maistrye if he myghte;   *force*
And Sorwë swore in balful bende   *swore; grievous bondage*
That he woldë for this hende   *this gracious one*
Me ledë to my lyvës ende   *lead me*
75   Unlawfulliche in lyghte.   *unlawfully (and) openly*
      Blow, etc.

Love me listenëd ech word
And begh him to me over bord   *leaned to me across the table*
And bad me for to hente that hord   *ordered me to seize that treasure*
80   Of myn hertë hele;   *heart's salvation*
'And biseche that swete and swote,   *that sweet and gentle creature*
Er then thou falle as fen of fote,   *before; as mud from the foot*
That she with thee wol of bote   *will concerning a remedy*
   Derëworthliche dele.   *affectionately negotiate*
85   *Blow, etc.*

For hirë love I carke and care,   *for love of her I grieve and sorrow*
For hirë love I droupne and dare,   *pine and despair*
For hirë love my blisse is bare,
   And al Ich waxë wan;   *grow pale*
90 For hirë love in slep I slake,   *I lose my sleep*
For hirë love al night Ich wake,   *I lie awake*
For hirë love mournyng I make   *I grieve*
   More than any man.
   Blow, etc.

I, 4   Litel wot it any man

Litel wot it any man   *little does anyone know*
   How dernë love may stonde,   *secret love may last (lit. stand)*
But it were a fre womman   *unless; noble woman*
   That muche of love had fonde.   *who; had experienced*
5 The love of hire ne lastëth nowight longe;   *her love lasts not long at all*
She hath me plyght and wytëth me wyth wronge. *promised; blames me wrongly*
   Ever and oo,   *ever and always*
For my lef Ich am in gretë thoghte;   *dear one; perplexity*
I thinke on hire that I ne see noght ofte.   *whom I do not see often*

10 I wolde nempnë hyre to-day   *I would name her*
   And I dorste hire minne;   *if I dared; mention her*
She is that farestë may   *maiden*
   Of ech ende of hire kinne.   *of any member of her sex (lit. kin)*

But she me love of me she havëth sinne.   *unless; she will wrong me*

15   Wo is him   *woe is his (* lit. *to him)*

That loveth the love that he may ner y-winne.   *who loves; whom; never win*

    Ever and oo,

For my lef Ich am in gretë thoghte;

I thinke on hire that I ne see noght ofte.

20 Adoun I fel to hire anon   *down; before her; straightway*

    And crie, 'Lady, thin ore!   *cry; thy mercy*

Lady, ha mercy of thy mon,   *have mercy on your man*

    Leve thou no false lore: *believe; tales*

If thou dost, it wol me rewë sore;   *it will grieve me painfully*

25 Love drecchëth me that I may live namore.'   *afflicts; so that I*

    Ever and oo,

For my lef Ich am in gretë thoghte;

I thinke on hire that I ne see noght ofte.

Mery it is in hyrë tour   *in her (castle) tower*

30   Wyth hathele and wyth hewe;   *with knight and with servant*

So it is in hyrë bour   *in her chamber*

    With gamen and with glewe.   *amorous play; (musical) entertainment*

But she me lovë sore it wol me rewe.

    Wo is him

35 That loveth the love that never nil be trewe.

    Ever and oo,

For my lef Ich am in gretë thoghte;

I thinke on hire that I ne see noght ofte.

Fayrest fodë upon loft,   *fairest creature alive*

40   My gode lef, I thee grete,   *my dear beloved; greet*

As felë sythë and as oft   *as many times*

    As dewës dropës wete,   *of dew; drops; wet*

As sterres in welkne and grassës sour and swete.   *the sky; herbs bitter and sweet*

Whose loveth untrewe his herte is seldë sete.   *whoever loves an unfaithful person;*

45   Ever and oo,   *[seldom at ease*

For my lef Ich am in gretë thoghte;

I thinke on hire that I ne see noght ofte.

1, 5   Ichot a byrde in a bour

Ichot a byrde in a bour	*I know a lady in a bower*
as beryl so bright,	*as bright as beryl*
As saphyr in silver	*as a sapphire (set) in silver*
semly on sight,	*beautiful to behold*
As jaspe the gentil	*as the noble jasper*
that lemëth with light,	*shines*
As gernet in golde	*as garnet and ruby*
and ruby wel right;	*well set in gold*
5 As onycle she is on	*as onyx she is one*
y-holden on hight,	*highly esteemed*
As diamaund the dere	*precious*
in day when she is dight.	*by day; dressed*
She is coral y-kid	*she is coral famous*
with cayser and knight;	*with emperor and knight*
As emeraude amorewen	*as an emerald in the morning*
this may havëth might:	*this maiden has power*
The might of the margarite	*the power of the pearl*
haveth this may mere;	*has this excellent maiden*
10 For charbocle Ich hire ches	*as a carbuncle-stone I esteem her*
by chin and by chere.	*for (her) chin and (her) countenance*
Hire rode is as rose	*her colour is like the rose*
that red is on rys,	*which is red on the spray*
With lilye-white lerës	*lily-white complexion*
lufsom she is;	*lovely*
The primerole she passëth,	*primrose; surpasses*
the pervenke of pris,	*the prized periwinkle*
With alisaundre thereto,	*and alexanders likewise*
ache and anys.	*parsley and anise*
15 Cointe as columbine –	*pretty as columbine*
such hire kinde is –	*such is her nature*
Glad under gore	*delightful in attire*
in grey and in gris;	*in grey furs*
She is blosme upon ble,	*her face is a blossom*
brightest under bis,	*(that) fairest (one) in fine linen*
With celydoyne and sauge	*like celandine and sage*
as thou thyself sis.	*as you yourself see*
That seeth upon that semly	*whoever looks upon that lovely creature*
to blis he is brought;	
20 She is solsecle	*marigold*
to save is forsought.	*(which) for healing is sought out*
She is papejay in pine	*she is a parrot (who) in (my) sorrow*
that betëth me my bale;	*eases for me my distress*
To trewe turtel in a tour	*to (you) true turtle-dove in a tower*
I telle thee my tale;	*I express my opinion*

She is thrustle thriven in thro — *she is a thrush doughty in dispute*
   that singëth in sale, — *sings in the hall*
The wilde laverokke and wolc — *the wild lark and the hawk*
   and the wodëwale; — *and the golden oriole*
25 She is faucon in frith, — *she is a falcon in the forest*
   dernest in dale, — *hidden in the valley*
And with everich a gome — *and to every man*
   gladest in gale. — *most delightful in song*
From Weye she is wisest — *from the Wye*
   into Wyrhale; — *to the Wirral*
Hire name is in a note — *her name is in a note*
   of the nightëgale: —
In annote is hire name – — *in a note is her name*
   nempnëth hit non! — *let no one mention it*
30 Whoso right redëth — *whoever guesses correctly*
   roune to Johòn. — *(let him) whisper to John*

Muge she is and mandrake — *musk; mandrake*
   thurgh might of the mone, — *by the power of the moon*
Trewe triacle y-told, — *as a true remedy esteemed*
   with tongës in trone; — *by reputation enthroned*
Such licoris may leche — *licorice; cure*
   from Lyne to Lone, — *from Lyn to Lune*
Such sucre man sechëth — *sugar is sought after*
   that sanëth men sone; — *which heals men quickly*
35 Blithe y-blessed of Crist — *happily blessed by Christ (she is)*
   that baithëth me my bone — *who grants me my prayer*
When derne dedës in day — *secret deeds by day*
   derne are done. — *are secretly done*
As gromil in greve — *(she is) like gromwell in the grove*
   grene is the grone, — *whose seed is green*
As quibibe and comyn — *(she is) like cubeb and cummin*
   kid is in crone, — *(which is) famed for its crown*
Kid comyn in court, — *esteemed (as) cummin in the court*
   canel in cofre, — *(as) cinnamon in a chest*
40 With gingere and cetewale — *ginger and setwall*
   and the gylofre. — *and the gillyflower*

She is medicine of might, — *a powerful remedy*
   mercie of mede — *gracious in favours*
Rekene as Regnas — *ready as Regnas*
   resoun to rede, — *to give advice*
Trewe as Tegeu in tour, — *true as Tegeu in the tower*
   as Wyrwein in wede, — *as Wyrwein in (her fine) garments*
Bolder than Byrne — *bolder than Byrne*
   that oft the bore bede; — *who often challenged the boar*

45 As Wylcadoun she is wise,   *Wylcadoun*
        doughty of dede,   *doughty in deed*
    Fayrer than Floyres   *Floris*
        folkës to fede,   *to people a pleasure* (lit. *peoples to please*)
    Kid as Cradoc in court   *renouned; Craddock*
        carf the brede,   *who carved the roast*
    Hender than Hilde,   *more gracious than Hilde*
        that haveth me to hede.   *(the one) who has me to care for*
    She haveth me to hede,   *she has me to look after*
        this hendy, anon,   *this fair one, from now on*
50 Gentil as Jonas,   *gracious as Jonas*
        she joyëth with Jon.   *she rejoices with John*

1, 6   Love is soft, love is swet

Love is soft, love is swet,
    love is good sware;   *a kind response*
Love is muche tene,   *great suffering*
    love is muchel care.   *great sorrow*
Love is blissenë mest,   *of joys the most*
    love is bot yare;   *a ready remedy*
Love is wandred and wo,   *misery and woe*
    with for to fare.   *to live* (lit. *travel*) *with*

5 Love is hap who it haveth,   *good luck whoever has it*
    love is god hele;   *good fortune*
Love is lecher and les,   *lewdness and lying*
    and lef for to tele;   *ready to deceive*
Love is doughty in the world,   *honourable*
    with for to dele;   *to deal with*
Love maketh in the land
    many unlele.   *many unfaithful*

Love is stalworthe and strong   *sturdy and strong*
    to striden on stede;   *to mount a horse*
10 Love is loveliche a thing
    to wommanë nede;   *necessary for women*
Love is hardi and hot   *fierce and hot*
    as glowindë glede;   *as glowing coal*
Love maketh mani may   *many a maiden*
    with terës to wede.   *with tears to be distraught*

Love hath his styward   *steward*
    by sti and by strete;   *along paths and highways*
Love maketh mani may   *many a maiden*
    hire wongës to wete;   *her cheeks to wet*

15 Love is hap, who it haveth,	*good luck*
on for to hete;	*one to inflame*
Love is wis, love is war,	*wise; prudent*
and wilful ansète.	*and a strong-willed adversary*
Love is the softeste thing	*gentlest thing*
in hertë may slepe;	*that may sleep*
Love is craft, love is good	*strength*
with carës to kepe;	*for engaging with sorrows*
Love is les, love is lef,	*false; desirable*
love is longinge;	*pining*
20 Love is fol, love is fast,	*foolish; steadfast*
love is frovringe;	*comforting*
Love is sellich an thing,	*a marvellous thing*
whosò shal soth singe.	*tell the truth*
Love is wele, love is wo,	*happiness; woe*
love is gladhede,	*gladness*
Love is lif, love is deth,	*life; death*
love mai us fede.	*feed*
Were love also longdrei	*as long-lasting*
as he is first kene,	*eager*
25 Hit were the wordlokstë thing	*it would be the most precious thing*
in world were, Ich wene.	*in the world that might be, I suppose*
Hit is y-said in an song,	
soth is y-sene,	*the truth is evident*
Love comsëth with care	*begins*
and endëth with tene,	*suffering*
Mid lady, mid wivë,	*with lady, with woman*
mid maidë, mid quene.	*with queen (or, harlot)*

I, 7   Though I can wittës ful-iwis

Though I can wittës ful-iwis,	*I am able in mind most certainly*
Of worldës blissë n'ave Ich non,	*none*
For a lady that is pris	*on account of; the most excellent*
Of allë that in bourë gon.	*bowers; dwell (lit. go)*
5 Sithen first that she was his,	*since*
Y-loken in castel wal of ston,	*locked; wall of stone*
Nas Ich hol ne blithe iwis,	*I was not well nor happy indeed*
Ne thrivinge mon.	*nor a prospering man*
Livëth man non bildëth me	*no man lives who can persuade me*
10 Abide and blithë for to be –	*to be patient and to be happy*
Ned after my deth me longëth.	*of necessity for my death I long*
I may sayen wel by me	*I may say assuredly for my part*
Harde that wo hongëth.	*that grief weighs bitterly*

I, 8   Were ther outher in this toun

Were ther outher in this toun	*were there either*
Ale or wyn,	*wine*
Ich hit woldë bye	*I would buy it*
To lemman myn.	*for my beloved*

5 Welle wo was so hardy   *accursed was (anyone) so rash*
For to make my lef al blody;   *as to harm (i.e. make all bloody) my dear one*
Though he were the kyngës son
Of Normaundy,
Yet Icholde awrekë be   *I would be avenged*
10 For lemman myn.

Welle wo was me tho,   *accursed was I then*
Wo was me tho;   *cursed was I then*
The man that lesëth that he lovëth   *the man who loses the one whom*
Him is also.   *he is likewise cursed*
15 So she me lerdë: *so much she taught me*
Ne more I ne can!   *no more can I do*
But Christ Ich hire bitechë   *to Christ I commend her*
That was my lemman.   *who was my beloved*

I, 9   Of every kinnë tre

Of every kinnë tre,   *every kind of*
Of every kinnë tre,
The hawthorn blowëth swetest,   *blossoms sweetest*
Of every kinnë tre.

5 My lemman she shal be,   *lover*
My lemman she shal be,
The fairest of every kinnë,
My lemman she shal be.

I, 10   Al night by the rosë, rosë

Al night by the rosë, rosë,
Al night bi the rose I lay,
Dorst Ich nought the rosë stele,   *dared; steal*
And yet I bar the flour away.   *bore the flower*

I, 11   Al gold, Janet, is thin her

Al gold, Janet, is thin her,   *hair*
Al gold, Janet, is thin her;
Save thin Jankin, lemman dere,   *sweetheart dear*
Save Jankin, lemman dere,
5 Save thin onlye dere.   *only beloved*

I, 12   Dorë, go thou stillë

Dorë, go thou stillë,	*door; be silent*
Go thou stillë, stillë,	
That Ich havë in the bourë	*until; bower*
Y-don al myn willë, willë.	*accomplished; desire*

I, 13   Ich have y-don al myn youth

Ich have y-don al myn youth,	*I have loved* (lit. *done*)
Oftë, ofte, and ofte;	
Longe y-loved and yerne y-beden –	*eagerly desired*
Ful dere it is y-bought!	*very dearly has it cost me*

I, 14   So longe Ich havë, lady

So longe Ich havë, lady,	
Y-hovëd at thi gate;	*lingered*
That mi fot is frore, faire lady,	*frozen*
For thy love faste to the stake.	*(gate-) post*

I, 15   Bryd onë brerë

Bryd onë brerë, brid, brid onë brerë,	*bird on the briar*
Kynd is comë of Lovë, lovë to cravë;	*Nature; from Love; beg*
Blithful biryd, on me thou rewë,	*joyous bird, have pity on me*
Or greith, lef, greith thou me my gravë.	*or prepare, dear (bird); for me*
5 Ich am so blithe so bright bird onë brerë	*as happy as a*
Whan I see that hendë in hallë;	*that gracious one in the hall*
She is whit of lime, lovely, trewë,	*white in limb*
She is fair and flour of allë.	*flower* (i.e. *best*)
Mightë Ich hirë at willë havë,	
10 Stedfast of lovë, lovëly, trewë,	
Of mi sorwë she may me savë,	
Joy and blissë were me newë.	

I, 16   Foulës in the frith

Foulës in the frith,	*birds; wood*
The fishës in the flod,	*sea*
And I mon waxë wod;	*and I must go mad*
Much sorwe I walkë with	
5 For beste of bon and blod.	*finest (creature) of bone and blood*

Nature.

I, 17　　When the nyghtëgalë singeth

When the nyghtëgalë singeth,
　　the wodës waxen grene;　　　　　*grow green*
Lef and gras and blosmë springe　　*leaf*
　　in Avëryl, I wene;　　　　　　*I know*
5　And love is to myn hertë gon　　*has gone to my heart*
　　with onë spere so kene,　　　　*a spear so sharp*
Night and day my blod hit drynketh;　*blood*
　　myn hertë doth me tene.　　　　*causes me pain*

Ich have lovëd al this yer
10　　that I may love namore;　　　　*no more*
Ich have sikëd moni syk,　　　　　*sighed; sigh*
　　lemman, for thin ore.　　　　　*sweetheart; mercy*
Me nis love never the ner,　　　　*to me is love no nearer*
　　and that me rewëth sore;　　　　*grieves me bitterly*
15　Swetë lemman, think on me,
　　Ich have loved thee yore.　　　　*for a long time*

Swetë lemman, I preyë thee
　　of lovë onë speche,　　　　　　*one word*
Whil I live in world so wyde,
20　　other nil I seche.　　　　　　*another shall I not seek*
With thy love, my swetë leef,　　　*dear*
　　mi blis thou mightëst eche;　　　*happiness; increase*
A swetë cussë of thy mouth　　　　*kiss from your mouth*
　　mightë be my leche.　　　　　　*physician*

25　Swetë lemman, I preyë thee　　　*beg*
　　of a lovë-bene;　　　　　　　*for a love-token*
If thou me lovëst, as men seyth,　　*as it is said (lit. as one says)*
　　lemman, as I wene,　　　　　　*I believe*
And yif hit thy willë be,　　　　　*wish*
30　　thou loke that hit be sene.　　*make sure that it is apparent*
So mochel I thinke upon thee,
　　that al I waxë grene.　　　　　*I become quite green*

Bitwene Lyncolne and Lyndëseye,　*Lindsey*
　　Nòrhamptoun and Lounde,　　　*Lound*
35　Ne wot I non so fair a may　　　*I do not know; maiden*
　　as I go for y-bounde.　　　　　*bound (i.e. in bonds of love)*
Swetë lemman, I preyë thee,
　　thou lovë me a stounde.　　　　*love me soon*
　　Y wol mone my song　　　　　*I will sing (lit. tell)*
40　On whom that hit ys on y-long.　*of the one whom it depends on*

I, 18   Bitwenë March and Avëril

[handwritten: Secular poem]

[handwritten: Courtly love!]

Bitwenë March and Avëril,	*April*
When spray biginneth to springe,	*the twig; sprout* *[handwritten: Spring happening.]*
The litel foul hath hirë wil,	*bird; her desire*
On hyrë lede to synge.	*in her language*
5 Ich live in love-longinge,	*[handwritten: superlative ....]*
For semeliest of allë thynge,	*the fairest; creatures (lit. things)*
She may me blissë bringe,	*joy*
Ich am in hire baundoun.	*power*
An hendy hap Ichave y-hent,	*good fortune I have received*
10 Ichot from hevene it is me sent,	*I know; sent to me*
From allë wommen my love is lent	*has gone*
And light on Alysoun.	*and alighted*
On hew hire her is fair ynogh,	*in colour; hair*
Hire browës broune, hire eyen blake,	*eyebrows brown; eyes black*
15 With lufsom chere she on me logh,	*with a lovely expression; smiled*
With middel smal and wel y-make.	*waist; slender; well made*
But she me wol to hirë take	*unless; will; to herself*
For to ben hire owen make,	*to be; companion*
Longe to live Ichulle forsake	*I will refuse*
20 And feyë falle adoun.	*doomed (to death)*
An hendy hap, etc.	
Nightës when I wende and wake –	*at night; toss and lie awake*
Forthy myn wongës waxen won –	*for which cause my cheeks grow pale*
Lady, al for thinë sake,	
25 Longinge is y-lent me on.	*yearning has come upon me*
In world nis non so wyter mon	*no man so wise*
That al hire bounté tellë con,	*excellence; can give account of*
Hire swyre is whitter then the swon,	*her neck is whiter than the swan*
And fairest may in toune.	*and (she is the); maiden alive*
30 An hendy, etc.	
Ich am for wowyng al forwake,	*loving; worn out (for lack of sleep)*
Wery so water in wore,	*weary; a troubled pool*
Lest any revë me my make	*rob me of my mistress*
Ichave y-yernëd yore.	*yearned for so long*
35 Beter is tholen whilë sore	*suffer for a time grievously*
Then mournen evermore.	*than mourn*
Geynest under gore,	*kindest in the world (lit. in clothing)*
Herknë to my roun.	*song*
An hendy, etc.	

[handwritten: Beautiful under clothing -]

I, 19   In May it mirieth when it dawës

In May it mirieth when it dawës,	*it is pleasant; dawns*
In dounës with thise deerës plawës,	*on hillsides; with these frolicking animals*
And leef is light on lynde;	*leaf; (lime) tree*
Blosmës breden on the bowës,	*flourish; boughs*
5 Al thise wyldë wyghtës wowës,	*these wild creatures make love*
So wel Ich underfynde.	*as I well perceive*
I not non so frely flour	*I do not know any; so excellent; flower*
As ladies that ben bright in bour,	*who are radiant in (their) bower*
With love who mighte hem bynde.	*whoever; them*
10 So worly wommen are by west,	*such splendid women there are in the west*
One of hem Ich herie best,	*I praise above all (lit. best)*
From Irlond into Ynde.	*to India*
Wommen were the bestë thing	
That shoop oure heighë hevenë kyng	*created; king of heaven*
15 If felë falsë nere;	*if many (men) were not false*
They ben too rad upon here red	*they (women) are too hasty in their decision*
To love ther me hem lastës bed	*to love where they are tempted to sin*
When they shulle fongë fere.	*take a companion*
Lite in londë are to leve,	*few (men) anywhere are to be believed*
20 Though me hem trewë trouthë yeve,	*though one give them (women) a true pledge*
For trecherye to yere;	*(men are) too ready to deceive*
When trechour hath his trouthe y-plight,	*when the deceiver has plighted his troth*
Byswike he hath that swetë wyght	*betrayed; that sweet creature*
Though he hire othës swere.	*to her; oaths; should swear*
25 Wommen war thee wyth the swyke	*guard; against the dissembler*
That fair and frely is to fyke,	*pleasant and comely; in flattery (lit. to flatter)*
His fare is o to founde.	*his conduct is always to be tested*
So wide in world is herë won,	*so ubiquitous; their dwelling*
In ech a toune untrewe is on,	*in every town; false; one*
30 From Leycëstrë to Lounde.	*Leicester to Lound*
Of trouthë nis the trechour noght	*fidelity means nothing to the deceiver*
But he have his will y-wroght	*other than having had his way*
At stevenyng embë stounde.	*at a tryst from time to time*
Ah, faire ladies, be on war,	*be on (your) guard*
35 Too latë comëth the yeynchar	*the turning back*
When love you hath y-bounde.	
Wommen ben so fair on hewe	*in appearance*
Ne trowe I none that nerë trewe	*I do not believe any would not have been true*
If trechour hem ne taughte;	*if a dissembler; them; had not taught*
40 Ah, fairë thingës, frely bore,	*fair creatures, nobly born*
When me you woweth, be war bifore	*when you are wooed, be aware beforehand*
Which is worldës aughte.	*what (this) world's danger is like*

Al to late is lend ayein	*all too late it is to turn back*
When the lady lith byleyn	*lies deflowered*
45 And liveth by that she laughte.	*with what she has got*
Ah, woldë lylie-ler in lyn	*would the lily-white one in linen*
Y-herë lefly lorës myn,	*listen willingly to my advice*
With selthe we weren saughte.	*with joy we would be reconciled*

I, 20   Lenten ys come with love to toune

Lenten ys come with love to toune,	*spring has come; to the world*
With blosmës and with briddës roune	*blossoms; birds' song*
That al this blissë bringëth.	
Dayëseyës in this dalës,	*daisies in these dales*
5 Notës swete of nyghtëgalës,	
Ech fowel hire song singëth.	
The threstelcok him thretëth oo,	*the songthrush chides continuously*
Away is herë wynter wo	*gone; their winter sorrow*
When wodërovë springëth.	*the woodruff*
10 This foulës singen ferly fele,	*these birds; wonderfully many*
And wlyten on here wynnë wele,	*warble in their wealth of joys*
That al the wodë ringëth.	
The rosë raylëth hirë rode,	*presents her rosy hue*
The levës on the lightë wode	*leaves in the bright wood*
15 Waxen al with wille.	*grow*
The monë mandëth hirë ble,	*moon sends forth her radiance*
The lilie lufsom is to se,	*lovely*
The fenyl and the fille.	*fennel; chervil*
Wowen thisë wildë drakës,	*make love; these wanton drakes*
20 Milës mirien herë makës	*animals gladden their mates*
As strem ther strikëth stille.	*as the stream; flows softly*
Mody menëth, so don mo,	*the sorrowful man laments; do more*
Ichot Ich am one of tho	*I know; of them*
For love that likëth ille.	*because of love which causes distress*
25 The monë mandëth hirë lyght,	*sends forth*
So doth the semly sonnë bryght	*fair sun*
When briddës singen breme;	*gloriously*
Dewës donken on the dounës,	*the dew (lit. pl.) is moist; downs*
Derës with here dernë rounës	*animals with their secret cries*
30 Domës for to deme;	*(their) wishes to express*
Wormës wowen under cloude,	*worms make love under ground*
Wommen waxen wonder proude,	*amazingly haughty*
So wel it wol hem seme;	*it becomes them*
If me shal wantë wille of on,	*if I must do without the favour of one*
35 This wynnë wele I wil forgon	*wealth of joys; forgo*
And wight in wode be fleme.	*and straightway; be a fugitive*

I, 21   As I me rode this endrë dai

Nou springeth the spray,	*sprouts the twig*
Al for love Ich am so syk	*I am so sick*
That slepen I ne may.	

As I me rode this endrë dai	*went riding the other day*
5 On mi playinge,	*for my pleasure*
Seigh I where a litel may	*saw; maiden*
Bigan to singe:	
'The clot him clinge!	*may the clod (i.e. earth) to him cling*
Wo is him in love-longinge	*woeful is anyone who*
10 Shal liven ay.'	*must live for ever*
Nou springeth etc.	

Sone Ich herde that merye note,	*as soon as*
Thider I drogh;	*thither I drew*
I found hire in an herber swot,	*her; arbour; sweet*
15 Under a bogh,	*bough*
With joie ynogh.	*joyously (lit. with joy enough)*
Sone I asked: 'Thou merye mai,	*straightway I asked*
Why singestou ay?'	*do you sing; always*
Nou springeth, etc.	

20 Than answerde that maiden swote	*sweet*
Mid wordës fewe:	*with*
'Mi lemmàn me hath bihote	*my lover has made me a pledge*
Of lovë trewe:	
He changeth anewe.	*again*
25 If I mai, it shal him rewe,	*he will regret it*
By this day.'	
Nou springeth, etc.	

I, 22   In a fryth as I gan farë fremëde

In a fryth as I	*wood*
gan farë fremëde,	*walked as a stranger*
I founde a wel fair	*very fair*
fenge to fere;	*prize for a companion*
She glystnëde as gold	*shone*
when hit glemëde,	*gleams (lit. gleamed)*
Nas ner gome	*never was anyone*
so gladly on gere.	*so radiant in clothing (i.e. alive)*
5 I wolde wyte in world	*I wished to know*
who hire kenëde,	*had given birth to her*
This byrdë bright,	*maiden*
if hire wil were;	*if she were willing (to tell me)*

She me bad go my gatës — *bade me go away (lit. my ways)*
    lest hire gremëde; — *lest she should get angry*
Ne keptë she — *she did not wish*
    non henyng here. — *any dishonourable proposal; to hear*

'Y-here thou me nou, — *listen to me*
    hendest in helde, — *most comely in grace*
10 N'ave I thee none — *I do not bring (lit. have) any*
    harmës to hethe. — *troubles to mock (you)*
Caste I wol thee — *I will free you*
    from carës and kelde, — *from sorrows and cold*
Comely I wol — *beautifully I will*
    thee nou clethe.' — *clothe*

'Clothës y have
    on for to caste, — *to put on*
Such as I may
    were with wynne; — *wear with pleasure*
15 Better is were — *wear*
    thinne bute laste, — *threadbare (robes) without taint*
Then sydë robës, — *than ample*
    and synke into synne.
Have ye your wyl — *if you have your way*
    ye waxen unwraste, — *you will become fickle*
Afterward
    your thonk be thynne; — *gratitude will be slight*
Better is make
    forewardës faste, — *pledges; firm*
20 Then afterward
    to mene and mynne.' — *moan and regret*

'Of mynning ne minte — *of regretting do not think*
    thou namore; — *any more*
Of menske thou were — *of honour you would be*
    worthe by my myght; — *worth all I could offer*
I take on honde — *I undertake*
    to holde, that I hore, — *to abide, until I grow grey*
Of al that I — *by*
    thee have byhight. — *promised*
25 Why is thee loth — *why are you loath (lit. is it loath to you)*
    to leven on my lore — *to trust in my advice*
Lengere then my love — *(any) longer than*
    were on thee lyght? — *had settled on you*
Another myghte
    yerne thee so yore — *entreat you (ever) so long*
That nolde thee noght — *who would not*
    rede so ryght.' — *advise (you) so well*

'Such reed me myghte   *advice I might*
          spakliche rewe   *soon regret*
30 When al my ro   *peace*
          were me atraght;   *was taken from me*
     Sone thou woldëst
          fecchen anewe   *seek afresh*
     And take another   *another (lover)*
          withinne nyne naght.   *nine nights*
     Thenne might I
          hungren on hewe,   *starve in (my) family*
     In ech an hird   *in every household*
          ben hatëd and forhaght,   *be hated and despised*
35 And ben y-cayrëd   *separated*
          from alle that I knewe,   *had known*
     And bede cleven   *and (be) bidden to cling*
          ther I hade claght.'   *where I had clung (i.e. embraced)*

'. . . . .'   [*Stanza missing*]

'Better is taken
          a comeliche in clothe   *a well-attired person*
     In armës to kepen   *hold*
          to kisse and to clyppe,   *embrace*
     Then a wrecche   *than that a wretch*
          I weddëd so wrothe,   *I should marry; so ill-tempered*
40 Though he me slowe,   *should beat me*
          ne myght I him aslyppe.   *escape*
     The beste red   *advice*
          that I can to us bothe,   *I know for us both*
     That thou me take   *(is) that you should take me*
          and I thee toward hyppe;   *and I should jump at you*
     Though I swore
          by trouthe and othe,   *pledge; oath*
     That God hath shapëd   *what; decreed*
          may non atlyppe.   *may no-one escape*

45 With shaping ne may   *by shape-shifting may not*
          hit me ashunchë;   *it (God's decree) be evaded (* lit. *one evade)*
     Nas I never   *I was never*
          wycche ne wyle;   *a witch nor a sorceress*
     Ich am a maide,
          that me ofthunchëth;   *vexes me*
     Leef me were   *dear to me would be*
          gome but gyle.'   *a man without guile*

I, 23 As I stod on a day

As I stod on a day   *one day*
    me self under a tre: *by myself*

I met in a morweninge   *morning*
    a may in a medë,   *maiden; meadow*
A semlier to min sight   *lovelier*
    saw I ner non;   *never any (lit. none)*
Of a blak burnet   *of dark fine brown cloth*
    al was hir wedë,   *attire*
5 Purfilëd with pellour   *trimmed with fur*
    doun to the ton;   *down; toes*
A red hod on hir heved,   *hood; head*
    shragëd al of shredës,   *edged; with strips (of cloth)*
With a riche riban,   *precious ribbon*
    gold-begon.   *embroidered with gold*
That bird rad on hire boke   *read upon her book*
    evere as she yedë,   *walked*
Was non with hir   *no-one with her*
    but hir selve al on;   *only herself alone*
10   With a cri
    gan she me se;   *see*
She wold awrenchen awey   *would have run away*
    but for I was so ne.   *except that; near*

I sayd to that semly   *fair one*
    that Christ should hir savë
For the fairest may
    that I ever met.
'Sir, God yeve thee grace   *give*
    god happës to havë,   *good fortune*
15 And the lyinges of love,'   *joys*
    thus she me gret.   *greeted*
That I might become hir man   *her*
    I began to cravë;
For nothing in hird   *in public*
    fonden wolde I let.   *to be tried; allow*
She bar me fast on hond   *she speedily accused me*
    that I began to ravë,
And bad me fond ferther   *try elsewhere*
    a fol for to fet;   *fool; find*
20   'Wher gospellëth   *what is the message of*
    al thy speche?   *(pious) talk*
Thou findëst hir noght here   *her not here*
    the sot that thou seche.'   *idiot; seek*

For me thoughtë so fair — *because it seemed to me so attractive*
    hir will wold I tastë, — *her resolve; wished; to test*
And I freynëd hir of love – — *asked her for love*
    therat she lowe. — *laughed*
'A, sire,' she sayd,
    'hurt thou for non hastë; — *tax yourself not out of any haste*
25 If it be your wille, — *by your leave*
    ye an sayd ynowe; — *you have said enough*
It is no mister — *there is no point*
    your word for to wastë. — *in wasting your words*
Ther most a bolder byrd — *finer*
    billen on the bow; — *sing; bough*
I wende be your semblant — *would imagine; demeanour*
    she chese you for chastë. — *she might choose you as chaste*
It is non ned — *there is no need*
    to make it so tow. — *to be so pressing*
30 Why rewen ye — *why do you regret*
    what I redë? — *advise*
Wend fort there ye wenen — *move on to where you may expect*
    better for to spedë.' — *better to succeed*

I, 24   My deth I love, my lyf Ich hate

My deth I love, my lyf Ich hate,
    for a lady shene, — *radiant*
She is bright so dayës light, — *as*
    that is on me wel sene; — *indeed evident*
5 Al I falwe so doth the lef — *I fade as does the leaf*
    in somer when hit is grene,
If my thoght helpëth me noght,
    to whom shal I me mene? — *complain*

Sorwe and syke and drery mod — *sighing; sad mood*
10 bynden me so faste,
That I wene to walkë wod — *expect to go mad*
    if hit me lengere laste; — *longer*
My sorwe, my care, al with a word
    she myghte awey caste;
15 What helpëth thee, my swete lemman, — *what help is it to you*
    my lyf thus for to gaste? — *ruin*

'Do wey, thou clerk, thou art a fol, — *be off; fool*
    with thee bidde I noght chyde; — *wish; argue*
Shalt thou never lyve that day
20 my love that thou shalt byde. — *experience*
If thou in my boure art take, — *caught*
    shame thee may bityde; — *harm; befall*

Thee is better on fotë gon   *on foot to go*
   then wycked hors to ryde.'   *than*

25 'Weylawei, why seist thou so?   *alas, why do you say so*
   thou rewe on me, thy man;   *have pity*
Thou art ever in my thoght
   in londë wher Ich am.   *wherever*
If I deyë for thi love,   *die*
30   hit is thee michel sham;   *to you great dishonour*
Thou lete me lyve and be thy leef,   *let; love (lit. dear one)*
   and thou my swete lemmàn.'   *lover*

'Be stille thou fol, I calle thee right,   *be quiet you fool*
   canst thou never blinne?   *can you never leave off*
35 Thou art waytëd day and nyght   *watched out for*
   with fader and al my kynne.   *by father; relations*
Be thou in mi bour y-take   *if you are; caught*
   lete they for no synne,   *they will (not) refrain for any sin*
Me to holde and thee to slen –   *to kill*
40   the deth so thou might wynne.'   *death; meet*

'Swete lady, thou wend thy mod,   *change your mind*
   sorwe thou wilt me kythe;   *(with) sorrow; you will acquaint me*
Ich am al so sory man   *just as sorrowful a man*
   so Ich was whylom blythe.   *as; once happy*
45 In a window ther we stod   *where we stood*
   we kiste us fyfty sithe;   *fifty times*
Fair biheste maketh mony man   *a gracious promise; many a man*
   al his sorwës mythe.'   *hide*

'Weylawey, why seist thou so?   *alas*
50   my sorwe thou makëst newe.   *anew*
I lovede a clerk al par amour,   *passionately*
   of love he was ful trewe.
He nas noght blythë never a day,   *he was not happy*
   but he me sonë seye;   *unless; soon; saw*
55 I lovede him better then my lyf,
   what bote is hit to leye?'   *what use is it to lie*

'Whil I was a clerk in scole,   *scholar in school*
   wel moche I couthe of lore;   *I knew about learning (i.e. love)*
Ich have tholëd for thy love   *suffered*
60   woundës felë sore,   *many; grievous*
Fer from hom and eke from men,   *far from home; also*
   under the wodë-gore;   *(deep) in the forest*
Swete lady, thou rewe of me,   *have pity on me*
   nou may I no more.'   *now may I (do)*

65 'Thou semëst wel to ben a clerk,   *you appear indeed to be*
     for thou spekëst so stille;   *quietly*
     Shalt thou never for my love
     woundës tholë grylle;   *suffer; terrible*
     Fader, moder and al my kin
70   ne shal me holde so stille,   *keep so subdued*
     That I nam thin and thou art myn,   *that I shall not be yours and you mine*
     to don al thy wille.'   *your pleasure*

I, 25   Moste I ryde by Rybbësdale

Moste I ryde by Rybbësdale   *if I could; through*
Wildë wymmen for to wale,   *vivacious; choose*
     And weldë which Ich wolde;   *could have whichever I desired*
Foundë were the fairest one   *would be*
5 That ever was made of blod and bone,   *blood*
     In bourë best with bolde.   *bower; in noble company*
As sonnëbem hire ble is bright,   *a sunbeam; her face is radiant*
In echë londe she lemëth light,   *in every; shines brightly*
     Thurgh tale as man me tolde.   *by all accounts as I am told*
10 The lylie lufsom is and long,   *lily (i.e. lady); lovely; slender*
     With richë rose and rode among,   *splendid rose and pink intermingled*
     A fyldor fax to folde.   *gold thread; (her) hair; to bind*

Hire hed when Ich biholde upon,   *head; gaze upon (it)*
     The sonnëbem aboutë noon
15   Me thoughtë that I seye;   *it seemed to me that I saw*
Hire yen are grete and gray ynough,   *eyes; large; grey*
That lufsom, when she on me lough,   *that lovely one; smiled*
     Y-bend wax eyther breye.   *arched became either eye-brow*
The mone wyth hirë muchel might,   *moon; its (lit. her) great power*
20 Ne lenëth non such light anight,   *does not send forth any; at night*
     (That is in hevenë heye)   *high*
As hirë forhed doth in day,   *as her forehead does by day*
For whom thus muche I mournë may –   *grieve*
     For dool to deth I dreye.   *for sorrow to the point of death I suffer*

25 She hath browës bend on heigh,   *high-arched*
Whyte bitwene and noght to neigh,   *white between; close*
     Lufsom lyf she ledëth;   *a pleasant life she leads*
Hire nose is set as it wel semëth –   *in seemly fashion*
I deye for deth that she me demëth –   *to which she condemns me*
30   Hire speche as spicës spredëth;   *voice as the (aroma of) spices wafts*
Hire lokkës lefly are and longe,   *beautiful*
For sone she mighte hire mirthës monge   *readily she could; laughter; mingle*
     With blissë when it bredëth;   *with merriment; arises (lit. spreads)*
Hire chin is chosen, and eyther cheke   *excellent*

35 Whit ynough and rode on eke *and pink withall*
    As roser when it redëth. *rose-bush; blossoms (lit. reddens)*

She hath a mery mouth to mele, *for speaking (lit. to speak)*
Wyth lefly redë lippës lele *true*
    Romauncës for to rede;
40 Hire teth are white as bone of whal, *whale-bone*
Even set and atled al, *evenly set; placed; all*
    As hende mowe taken hede; *gentle knights may observe*
Swannës swyre swythe wel y-sette, *a swan's neck very well set*
A spannë lengere than I mette, *a span longer; have met*
45   That frely is to fede; *excellent; and pleasing (lit. to please)*
Me were lever kepe hire come *I would rather await her coming*
Than ben Pope and ryde in Rome, *be Pope*
    Stythest upon stede. *mightiest upon a steed*

When I byholde upon hire hond, *gaze*
50 The lylie-whitë, lef in lond, *lily-white one, dear in the land*
    Best she mightë be;
Eyther arm, an elnë long, *ell*
Balòygnë mengëth al bymong, *whale-bone white mingles overall*
    As baume ys hirë ble; *(fragrant) as balm; skin*
55 Fingrës she hath fair to folde, *clasp*
Mighte Ich hirë have and holde,
    In world wel werë me. *in (this) world well would I be*
Hyre tyttës are anunder bis *breasts; under fine linen*
As apples two of Paradys,
60   Yourself ye mowen se. *may see*

Hire girdel of beten gold is al, *belt of beaten gold*
Umben hirë middel smal, *about her slender waist*
    That trikëth to the to, *hangs down to the toe*
Al with rubies on a rowe, *in a row*
65 Withinnë corven, craft to knowe, *set within, skill to show*
    And emeraudës mo; *and emeralds more*
The bokle is al of whallës bon; *buckle*
There withinnë stont a ston *stands*
    That warnëth men from wo; *protects; woe*
70 The water that it wetëth in, *it is dipped in*
Ywis, hit worthëth al to wyn – *indeed, it turns everything to wine*
    That seyen seyden so. *those who have seen (it) said so*

She hath a metë middel smal, *neat; waist; slender*
Body and brest wel made al,
75   As fenix withoute fere; *the phoenix; without equal*
Eyther sidë soft as sylk,
Whitter than the morwen-milk, *morning milk*
    With lefly lit on lere. *with lovely colour in (her) cheek*

Al that Ich you nempnë noght,   *do not mention*
80 Hit is wonder wel y-wroght,
  And ellës wonder were.   *otherwise strange it would be*
He myghtë seyn that Christ hym seye   *say; had looked after him*
That myghtë nightës neigh hyre leye: *who; by night; near; lie*
  Heven he haddë here.   *heaven he would have here*

I, 26 Alas, hou sholde I singe

Alas, hou sholde I singe;   *should*
Y-loren is my playinge;   *lost; delight*
How sholde I with that oldë man
To live and letë my lemmàn,   *abandon my lover*
5 Swetest of al thing?

I, 27 Weping hath myn wongës wet

Weping hath myn wongës wet   *my cheeks*
For wikked werk and wane of wit;   *wicked deeds; lack of understanding*
Unblithe I be til I ha bet   *unhappy I shall be; have atoned for*
Brechës broken, as bok bit,   *offences committed, as the book requires*
5 Of ladys love, that I ha let,   *concerning the love of ladies; abandoned*
That lemen al with lefly lyt.   *who shine; with beautiful hue*
Oft in song I have hem set   *in verse; them; put*
That is unsemly ther hit syt;   *unseemly where it applies* (lit. *sits*)
  Hit syt and semëth noght   *it applies but* (lit. *and*) *is inappropriate*
10 Ther hit is seid in song;   *where*
  That I have of hem wroght   *what; written* (lit. *wrought*)
  Ywis hit is al wrong.   *indeed*

Al wrong I wroghtë for a wyf   *wrote on account of a woman* (i.e. Eve)
That made us wo in world ful wyde;   *caused*
15 She raftë us allë richesse ryf   *robbed us all (of) wealth abundant*
That durfte us noght in reynës ryde.   *needed us not; reins; ride*
A stythie stinte hire sternë stryf   *an excellent person stopped her fierce discord*
That is in hevenë hert in hyde;   *who is in the heart of heaven in hiding*
In hirë lyght, on ledëth lyf,   *born* (lit. *alighted*); *one* (i.e. Christ) *lives*
20 And shon thurgh hirë semly syde.   *shone*
  Thurgh hirë side he shon
  As sonne doth thurgh the glas;   *glass*
  Womman nas wicked non   *(there) was not; any* (lit. *none*)
  Sithe He y-borë was.   *since; born*

25 Wycked nis non that I wot   *is none; I know*
That durste for werk hire wongës wet;   *who needed for (wicked) deeds wet her cheeks*
Alle they live from last of lot   *(free) from blame as to conduct*
And are al hende as hawk in chete.   *gracious; hall*

Forthy on molde I waxë mot	*therefore on earth I become sorry*
30 That I sawës have seid unsete,	*words; unbecoming*
My fikel flesh, my falsy blod,	*deceitful flesh*
On feld hem fele I falle to fete;	*ground (lit. field); often; at their feet*
To fet I falle hem fele,	*at their feet I fall often*
For falslek fifti-folde,	*for falsehood fifty-fold*
35 Of alle untrewe on tele	*for all (the) false (things) in slander*
With tonge as I er tolde.	*that I hitherto have said*
Though told ben tales untoun in toune –	*evil; among men*
Such tiding may tide, I nil noght teme –	*(that) such a thing may happen; vouch*
Of bridës bryght with browës broune,	*concerning ladies*
40 Your blisse they beye, thise briddës breme.	*joy; purchase; these excellent ladies*
In rudë were roo with hem roune	*in boorish company; peace; to speak*
That hem mighte hente as him were heme.	*who from them might receive what suited him*
Nys kyng, cayser, ne clerk with croune	*there is no king, emperor; tonsure*
Thise semly serve that mene may seme.	*for serving; who; less; would seem*
45 Seme him may on sonde	*it may become him on an errand*
Thise semly serven so,	*these fair ones thus to serve*
Both with fet and honde,	
For on us warp from wo.	*for the sake of one (who); rescued*
Nou wo in world is went away	*has gone*
50 And wele is comen as we wolde,	*joy*
Thurgh a mighty, methful mai	*gentle maiden*
That us hath cast from carës colde.	*freed*
Ever wymmen Ich herie ay	*praise always*
And ever in hyrd with hem Ich holde,	*always in public*
55 And ever at nede I nyckenay	*always when in difficulty I deny*
That I ner nemnëde that they nolde.	*I ever mentioned what they did not wish*
I nolde and nullyt noght	*I would not and do not wish it*
For nothing nou, a nede;	*for anything (lit. nothing); of necessity*
Soth I of hem ha wroght	*truth; have written*
60 As Richard erst gan rede.	*first said*
Richard, rote of resoun right	*source (lit. root) of good sense*
Rekening of rym and ron,	*paragon of verse and poetry*
Of maidnës mekë thou hast might	*over maidens meek; sway*
On molde I holde thee miriest mon.	*on earth I consider you*
65 Kindë comely as a knight	*well-born*
Clerk y-kid that craftës con,	*a scholar; famous; versed in skills*
In ech an hyrd thin athel is hight,	*in every household; excellence; mentioned*
And ech an athel thin hap is on.	*every man; your destiny; is concerned with*
Hap that hathel hath hent	*good fortune that splendid fellow has obtained*
70 With hendelec in halle;	*with courtesy in the hall*
Selthë be him sent,	*happiness*
In londe of ladies alle.	

I, 28   Now welcome, somer, with thy sonnë softe ~ *Geoffrey Chaucer*

Now welcome, somer, with thy sonnë softe, *sun*
That hast thes wintrës wedrës overshake, *these; storms; shaken off*
And driven away the longë nyghtës blake!

Saynt Valentyn, that art ful hy on-lofte, *very highly exalted above*
5 Thus syngen smalë foulës for thy sake:
Now welcome, somer, with thy sonnë softe,
That hast thes wintrës wedrës overshake.

Wel han they causë for to gladen ofte, *greatly have they cause; rejoice*
Sith ech of hem recoverëd hath hys make, *since each; found again; mate*
10 Ful blissful mowe they syngë when they wake: *may*
Now welcome, somer, with thy sonnë softe,
That hast thes wintrës wedrës overshake,
And driven away the longë nyghtës blake!

I, 29   To Rosëmounde ~ *Geoffrey Chaucer*

Madame, ye ben of al beauté shryne *the shrine*
As fer as cerclëd is the mapamounde, *circumscribed; map of the world*
For as the cristal glorious ye shyne,
And lyke ruby ben your chekës rounde.
5 Therwith ye ben so mery and so jocounde, *cheerful*
That at a revel whan I see you daunce, *at a festive occasion*
It is an oynëment unto my wounde, *an ointment for*
Thogh ye to me ne do no daliaunce. *offer no encouragement*

For thogh I wepe of terës ful a tyne, *weep; tears; a barrel*
10 Yet may that wo myn hertë nat confounde; *not overcome*
Your semy voys that ye so smal out twyne *light voice; so ethereally spin out*
Makëth my thoght in joy and blys habounde. *in joy and bliss to abound*
So curtaysly I go wyth lovë bounde *in courtly manner*
That to myself I sey in my penaunce, *say in my suffering*
15 'Suffysëth me to love you, Rosëmounde, *it is sufficient for me*
Thogh ye to me ne do no daliaunce.'

Nas never pyk walwëd in galauntyne, *a pike steeped in galantine* (a sauce)
As I in love am walwëd and y-wounde, *am steeped*
For whych ful ofte I of myself devyne *concerning myself suppose*
20 That I am trewë Tristam the secounde. *Tristan*
My love may not refreydë nor affounde, *grow cold; grow numb*
I brenne ay in an amorous plesaunce. *burn ever; delight*
Do what you lyst, I wyl your thral be founde, *you please; slave*
Thogh ye to me ne do no daliaunce.

I, 30   Womanly Noblesse ~ *Geoffrey Chaucer*

So hath myn hertë caught in remembraunce
Yowre beauté hoole and stidefast governaunce,   *your complete beauty; behaviour*
Yowre vertues al and yowrë hie noblesse,   *exalted honour*
That yow to serve is sette al my plesaunce.   *set; delight*
5   So wel me liketh youre womanly contenaunce,   *pleases me; appearance*
Youre fresshë fetures and youre comlynesse,
That whiles I live myn hert to his maystresse   *while; as its mistress*
Yow hath ful chose in trewe perseveraunce   *utterly chosen; constancy*
Never to chaunge, for no maner distresse.

10   And sith I shal do you this observaunce,   *homage*
Al my life withouten displesaunce,   *displeasure*
Yow for to serve with al my besynesse,   *diligence*
Takëth me, lady, in your obeisaunce,   *under your authority*
And have me somwhat in your souvenaunce.   *remembrance*
15   My woful hertë suffrëth grete duresse,   *great hardship*
And loke how humblëly with al symplesse   *simplicity*
My wil I conforme to youre ordynaunce,   *command*
As yow best list, my peynes for to redresse.   *it best pleases you; to alleviate*

Considryng eke how I hange in balaunce,   *also*
20   In yowre servicë, suche, loo, is my chaunce,   *fortune*
Abidyng grace, whan that yowre gentilnesse   *graciousness*
Of my grete woo list do allegëaunce,   *is pleased to make alleviation*
And with youre pité me som wise avaunce   *in some way to favour*
In ful rebatyng of myn hevynesse;   *abatement; sadness*
25   And thynketh by resoun that wommanly noblesse   *it seems reasonable*
Shuld nat desire for to do the outrance   *cause thee harm*
Ther as she fyndëth non unbuxumnesse.   *no disobedience*

Lenvoye

Auctor of norture, lady of plesaunce,   *originator of good manners; delight*
Soveraigne of beautée, floure of wommanhede,
30   Take ye non hede unto myn ignoraunce,
But this receyvëth of your goodlihede,
Thynkyng that I have caught in remembraunce,
Your beauté hole, your stidefast governaunce.   *your complete beauty*

I, 31   *Canticus Troili* / Troilus's song ~ *Geoffrey Chaucer*

If no love is, O God, what fele I so?	*feel*
And if love is, what thing and which is he?	
If love be good, from whennës cometh my woo?	
If it be wikke, a wonder thinkëth me,	*wicked; it seems to me*
5 When every torment and adversité	
That cometh of hym may to me savory thinke,	*seem pleasant to me*
For ay thurst I, the more that Ich it drynke.	*for always*

And if that at myn owen lust I brenne,	*for my own desire; burn*
From whennës cometh my waillynge and my pleynte?	*lament*
10 If harm agree me, wherto pleyne I thenne?	*is agreeable to me; complain*
I noot, ne whi unwery that I feynte.	*I know not, nor why unweary; faint*
O quikë deth, O swetë harm so queynte,	*O living death; so strange*
How may of the in me swich quantité,	*may (there be) of thee; such a quantity*
But if that I consentë that it be?	*unless I*

15 And if that I consente, I wrongfully	
Compleyne, iwis. Thus possëd to and fro,	*indeed; tossed*
Al sterëlees withinne a boot am I	*rudderless; boat*
Amydde the see, bitwixen wyndës two,	
That in contrarie stonden evere mo.	
20 Allas, what is this wondrë maladie?	*amazing*
For hote of cold, for cold of hote, I dye.	

I, 32   Against Women Unconstant ~ *Geoffrey Chaucer* (?)

Madàme, that throgh your newëfangelnesse	*(you) who; desire for novelty*
Many a servaunt have put out of grace,	*expelled from grace*
I take my leve of your unstedfastnesse,	*inconstancy*
For wel I woot, whyle ye have lyvës space,	*I know, while you live*
5 Ye can not love ful half yere in a place,	*half a year in one place*
To newë thing your lust is ay so kene;	*for new things; desire; keen*
In stede of blew, thus may ye were al grene.	*instead of blue; wear; green*

Right as a mirour nothing may impresse,	*imprint upon*
But, lightly as hit cometh, so mote it pace,	*it comes; must it pass*
10 So fareth your love, your werkës bere witnesse.	
Ther is noo feyth that may your herte enbrace,	*no loyalty; embrace*
But as a wedercok, that turneth his face	*weathercock*
With every wind, ye fare, and that is sene;	*go; evident*
In stede of blew, thus may ye were al grene.	

15 Ye might be shrynëd for your brotelnesse	*enshrined (as a saint); fickleness*
Bet than Dalyda, Creseyde or Candace,	*better; Delilah*
For ever in chaunging stant your sikernesse;	*is your constancy*

That tache may noo wyght from your herte arace.   *that blemish; eradicate*
If ye lese oon, ye can wel tweyn purchace;
20 Alle lyght for somer, ye wote wel what I mene,   *you know well what I mean*
In stede of blew, thus may ye were al grene.

I, 33   Complaynt D'Amours ~ *Geoffrey Chaucer* (?)

I, which that am the sorowfullest man
That in this world was ever yit living,
And leste recoverer of himselven can,   *least; a healer; knows (how to be)*
Beginne right thus my deedly compleyning   *grievous complaint*
5 On hir that may to lyf and dethe me bringe,   *about her; life and death*
Whiche hathe on me no mercy ne no reuthe   *who has; pity*
That love hir beste, but sleethe me for my treuthe.   *who; slays; fidelity*

Can I nought doon ne seye that may yow lyke?   *do; what may please you*
Ne, certës, now; allas, allas the whyle!   *not, indeed, now; the time*
10 Youre plesaunce is to laughen whan I sike,   *pleasure; sigh*
And thus ye me from al my blisse exile.
Ye have me caste in thilkë spitous yle   *that inhospitable island*
Ther never man on lyvë might asterte;   *escape*
This have I, for I love yow beste, swete herte.   *because*

15 Soothe is, that wel I woot, by lyklynesse,   *I know, in all probability*
If it were a thinge possible to doo
For to acounte your beautée and goodnesse,   *to estimate*
I have noo wonder though yee do me woo,   *you cause me grief*
Sithe I, th'unworthiest that may ride or goo,   *since; walk*
20 Durste ever thinken in so hie a place: *dared ever aspire to; high*
What wonder is, though ye do me noo grace?

Allas, thus is my lyf brought to an ende;
My dethe, I see, is my conclusioun.   *my death*
I may wele sing, 'In sorye tyme I spende
25 My lyf.' That song may have confusioun!   *cursed be that song*
For mercy, pitée, and deep affeccioun,
I sey for me, for al my deedly chere,   *for my part; despite; appearance*
Allë this dide, in that, me love yowe dere.   *these made, in this case; dearly*

And in this wyse and in dispayr I lyve   *manner*
30 In love; nay, nay, but in dispayre I dye!
Bùt shal I thus yowe my dethe foryive,   *death forgive*
That causëles dothe me this sorow drye?   *makes me suffer this sorrow*
Yee, certës, I! For she of my folye   *oh yes, indeed; with my folly*
Hath nought to done although she do me sterve;   *nothing; cause me to die*
35 Hit is nought with hir wille that I hir serve.   *it is not with her agreement*

Than sithe I am of my sorowe the cause   *since*
And sithe that I have this withoute hir rede,   *encouragement*
Than may I seyne right shortly in a clause,   *may I say*
It is no blame unto hir womanhede
40 Though suche a wrecche as I be for hir dede.   *such; dead*
Yèt alwey two thingës doone me dye,   *cause me to die*
That is to seyne, hir beauté and myn eye;   *eye*

So, algatës, she is the verray roote   *nevertheless; root (i.e. cause)*
Of my diseese and of my dethe also,   *of my suffering*
45 For with oon worde she mightë be my boote,   *cure*
If that she vouchëd sauf for to do so.   *agreed*
Bùt than is hir gladnesse at my woo?   *is she glad (lit. is her gladness)*
It is hir wonë plesaunce for to take   *her custom pleasure*
To seen hir servaunts dyen for hir sake!

50 But certës, thanne is al my wondering –   *then; my cause for amazement*
Sithen she is the fayrest crëature,
As to my doom, that ever was livinge,   *in my judgement*
The benignest and beste eke that Nature   *kindest and best also*
Hath wrought or shal, whil that the world may dure –   *last*
55 Why that she leftë Pité so behinde?   *why (was it); she (Nature); Pity*
It was, ywis, a greet defaute in Kinde.   *certainly; failing on Nature's part*

Yit is al this noo lak to hir, pardée,   *fault in her, to be sure*
But God or Nature hem soore wolde I blame.   *them bitterly would I*
For though she shewe no pité unto me,
60 Sithen that she dothe othere men the same,
I n'oughtë to despise my ladyes game;   *ought not; conduct*
It is pleye to laughe when that men sykëth,   *amusement; when one sighs*
And I assente al that hir liste and lykëth!   *assent to; delights and pleases her*

Yet wolde I, as I dare, with sorwful herte
65 Biseche unto your mekly womanhede   *gentle*
That I now dorste my sharpë sorwës smerte   *I now dare; painful*
Shewe by word, and ye wolde onës rede   *express; and (that); once read*
The compleynte of me, which I full sore drede   *my complaint; fear*
That I have seid here, through myn unkonnynge,   *lest I have spoken; lack of skill*
70 In any word unto yowre displesinge.   *your displeasure*

Loothest of anything that ever was loth   *most hateful*
Were me, as wisly God my soulë save,   *it would be to me; surely*
To seyne a thing through which ye might be wroth   *say; angry*
And, to that day that I be leyde in grave,   *until; when I am l laid*
75 A trewer servaunt shulle ye never have;
And, though that I have pleyned unto yow here,   *have made my complaint*
Forgyveth it me, myn ownë lady dere.

Ever have I been, and shal, how-so I wende,   *however I fare*
Outher to lyve or dye, youre humble trewe.   *either; true (servant)*
80 Yee ben to me my gynnyng and myn ende,   *you are to me my beginning*
Sonne of the sterre so bright and clere of hewe;   *sun (i.e. source of light); star;*
Alwey in oon to love yow freshly newe,   *continually*   [*in appearance*
By God and by my trouthe, is myn entente;   *intention*
To live or dye, I wolle it never repente!   *I will*

85 This compleynte on Seint Valentinës day,
Whan every foughel cheesen shall his make,   *bird; choose; mate*
To hir, whos I am hole and shall alwey,   *wholly; shall always be*
This woofull songe and this compleynte I make,
That never yit wolde me to mercy take;
90 And yit wolle I evermore her serve   *will I*
And love hir best, although she do me sterve.   *cause me to die*

I, 34   Merciles Beauté ~ *Geoffrey Chaucer* (?)

I

Your yën two wol slee me sodenly;   *eyes; will slay; suddenly*
I may the beautée of hem not sustene,   *bear*
So woundëth hit thourghout my hertë kene.   *keenly*

And but your word wol helen hastily   *unless; heal*
5 My hertës woundë while that hit is grene,   *fresh (lit. green)*
   Your yën two wol slee me sodenly;
   I may the beautée of hem not sustene.

Upon my trouthe I sey you feithfully
That ye ben of my lyf and deeth the quene,   *queen (i.e. ruler)*
10 For with my deeth the trouthë shal be sene.   *evident*
   Your yën two wol slee me sodenly;
   I may the beautée of hem not sustene,
   So woundëth it thourghout my hertë kene.

II

So hath your beautée fro your hertë chaced   *expelled*
15 Pitée, that me n'availëth not to pleyne,   *is of no avail to me to lament*
For Daunger halt your mercy in his cheyne.   *Disdain; holds; chain*

Giltlës my deeth thus han ye me purchased;   *brought about (lit. bought)*
I sey you sooth, me nedëth not to feyne;   *tell you the truth; dissemble*
   So hath your beautée fro your hertë chaced
20   Pitée, that me n'availëth not to pleyne.

Allas, that Nature hath in you compassed   *encompassed*
So greet beautée, that no man may atteyne   *attain*
To mercy though he stervë for the peyne.   *die; anguish*

So hath your beautée fro your hertë chaced
25   Pitée, that me n'availëth not to pleyne,
For Daunger halt your mercy in his cheyne.

III

Sin I fro Love escapëd am so fat,
I never thenk to ben in his prison lene;   *lean*
Sin I am free, I counte him not a bene.   *bean*

30   Hè may answere and seye this and that;
I do no fors, I speke right as I mene.   *I pay no heed; mean*
Sin I fro Love escapëd am so fat,
I never thenk to ben in his prison lene.

Love hath my name y-strike out of his sclat,   *struck; slate*
35   And he is strike out of my bokës clene   *clean*
For evermo; ther is non other mene.   *way* (lit. *means*)
Sin I fro Love escapëd am so fat,
I never thenk to ben in his prison lene;
Sin I am free, I counte him not a bene.

I, 35   A Balade of Complaynte ~ *Geoffrey Chaucer* (?)

Compleyne ne koude ne might myn hertë never   *lament*
My peynës halve, ne what torment I have,   *half (of)*
Thoughe that I shoulde in youre presence ben ever,
Myn hertës lady, as wisly He me save   *as truly may He save me*
5   That Bountée made, and Beautée list to grave   *goodness; was pleased to engrave*
In youre persone, and bade hem bothe in-fere   *together*
Ever t'awayte, and ay be wher ye were.   *remain*

As wisly He gye alle my joyës here   *as truly may He guide*
As I am youres, and to yow sadde and trewe,   *constant and true*
10   And ye my lyf and cause of my gode chere,   *you (are); spirits*
And dethe also, when ye my peynës newe,   *death; pains renew*
My worldës joye, whom I wol serve and sewe,   *follow*
Myn heven hole, and al my suffisaunce,   *complete; fulfilment*
Whom for to serve is sette al my plesaunce.   *set all my delight*

15   Beseching yow in my moste humble wyse   *manner*
T'akcepte in worthe this lytel porë dyte,   *to accept favourably; poor poem*
And for my trouthe my servyce not despyse,   *fidelity*
Myn observaunce eke have not in despyte,   *homage also; scorn*
Ne yit to longe to suffren in this plyte;   *(have me) to suffer; plight*
20   I yow beseche, myn hertës lady, here,   *hear (my complaint)*
Sith I yow serve, and so wil yere by yere.   *since; year by year*

Penitential and Moral Lyrics

I, 36 Miri it is while sumer i-last

Miri it is while sumer i-last   *lasts*
With foulës song;   *birds' song*
Oc now neghëth windës blast   *but; approaches (draws nigh)*
And weder strong.   *weather; rough*
5 Ei, ei, what this night is long,   *how*
And Ich with wel michel wrong   *for very great wrong doing*
Sorwe and murne and fast.   *sorrow; grieve*

I, 37 Lavedy seynte Marie

Lavedy seynte Marie   *Lady saint Mary*
   moder and medë,   *mother and maiden*
Thou wissë me nouthë   *guide me now*
   for Ich am eredë;   *perplexed*
Unnit lif   *a worthless life*
   to longe Ich ledë,   *too long I have led*
Whanne Ich me bethinkë   *take stock of myself*
   well sore Ich me adredë.   *I am afraid*

5 Ich am y-bounde sorë   *grievously*
   mid well felë sennë,   *by very many sins*
Mid smale and mid gretë,   *great*
   mid well felë kennë;   *very many kinds*
Day and night Ich fondë   *I seek*
   to wendendë hennë,   *to go hence*
Weldë God an heven   *let God in heaven decide*
   to whichërë wennë.   *to what bliss*

Slep me hath my lif forstolë   *sleep (i.e. of sin); stolen away*
   right half other morë;   *or more*
10 Away! too late Ich was y-war   *aware*
   now hit me rewëth sorë.   *now I regret it bitterly*
In slepe ne wende Ich endë nought   *I did not intend to end*
   though Ich slepe evermorë;   *shall sleep*
Whoso liveth that wakerer be   *more vigilant*
   think of minë lorë.   *advice*

All too longë slepth the man
   that never nile awakë;
Whose understant well his endeday   *final day*
   well yernë he mot spakë,   *eagerly he must hasten*

15 To dondë sinne away from him   *put*
          and fele almessë makë,   *many acts of charity; perform*
    If him ne shal, whanne he forthwent   *goes hence*
          his breechgirdel quakë!   *let his loins quake with fear*

    Slep me hath my lif forstolë
          er Ich me biseyë,   *myself; paid heed to*
    That Ich well ayittë now   *perceive*
          by sightë of min eyë;
    My brownë heer is whit bicome   *hair; white*
          Ich not for whichë leyë,   *I do not know; hair lotion*
20 And my toughë rode y-turnëd   *my robust complexion*
          all into othrë deyë.   *another hue*

    Biforn Ich have y-sinnëd   *previously*
          mid worke and with wordë,   *deed*
    While in mine bedde   *sometimes*
          and while attë bordë;   *at the table*
    Ofte win y-drunke   *wine*
          and selde of the fordë;   *seldom from the ford (i.e. stream)*
    Muche Ich have y-spendëd
          too lite Ich have on hordë.   *in store*

25 Hord that Ich telle
          is almessë-dedë,   *charitable deeds*
    Yive the hungrie mete   *food*
          and the nakede y-wedë,   *clothing*
    Redë the redlesse   *guide the ignorant person*
          that is withoute redë,   *advice*
    Luve God almighty
          and of Him have dredë.

    Inne mete and inne drinke
          Ich have y-ben overdedë,   *excessive*
30 And inne well-sitting shoon,   *well-becoming shoes*
          in proudere y-wedë;   *more sumptuous clothing*
    Whanne Ich y-herde of Gode spekë
          ne hedd Ich what men sedë;   *I heeded not what was said*
    Whan Ich hereof rekenë shal,   *take account*
          well sorë me may dredë.

    Beforn Ich have y-sinnëd
          mid workës and mid mouthë,   *in deeds*
    And mid alle mine limës   *with all my limbs*
          sith Ich sinnen couthë,   *since I knew how to sin*
35 And well felë sinnes y-don   *very many sins committed*
          that me athinkëth nouthë,   *I repent of now*
    And so me hadde aforn y-don
          if hit me Crist y-youthë.   *had granted*

Moder ful of milce,   *grace*
    I biddë, my mod wendë;   *pray; heart; change*
Lete me stewe my flesh   *curb*
    and mine foo shendë;   *foe (i.e. the Devil); defeat*
Edmodnesse lovë   *humility*
    to mine livës endë;
40 Love to Gode and to man
    Ich biddë that thou me sendë.

Lavedy seynte Marie
    understand now sinnë minë,
Ber min erende well   *bear my petition*
    to derë sonë thinë,   *dear son*
Whos flesh and blod y-halwëd is   *consecrated*
    of bred, of water, of winë,   *from*
That us y-shelde He ever   *may protect*
    fram alle hellë-pinë.   *pains of hell*

1, 38   Worldës blis ne last no throwë

Worldës blis ne last no throwë,   *Worldly bliss; lasts; time*
It went and wit awey anon;   *changes; passes away soon*
The longer that Ich it y-knowë   *I know it*
The lesse Ich findë pris theron,   *less; value in it*
5 For al it is y-meynd mid carë,   *mingled with*
With sorwës and with evel farë,   *misfortune*
And attë lastë poure and barë   *in the end poor and naked*
It lat man whan it ginth agon.   *leaves; when it departs*
Al the blis this her and tharë   *bliss which is*
10 Biloukth at endë wep and mon.   *amounts in the end to weeping and sorrow*

Al the blis of thisë livë   *joy*
Thou shàlt, man, enden innë wep –   *bring to an end in weeping*
Of hous and hom, of child and wivë.   *(the joy) of*
Sely man, nim therof kep!   *wretched man, take heed of this*
15 Thou shalt al bileven herë   *leave*
Th'aghtë wherof lord thou werë;   *the wealth of which*
Whan thou list upon the berë   *you lie; bier*
And slepst that swithë drery slep,   *very dreadful sleep*
Ne shaltou have with thee no ferë   *companion*
20 But thinë werkës on a hep.   *other than your deeds in a heap*

Al shal gon that man here owëth,   *pass away; possesses*
And al it shal bicome to naught;   *come to naught*
The man that here no god ne sowëth,
Whan othrë repe he worth bi-caught.   *others reap he will be ensnared*

25 Think, man, forthy, whilstou hast mightë,	*therefore; while you have the ability*
That thou thy giltë here arightë,	*atone for*
And werchë god by day and nightë,	*do good*
Er than thou be of livë laught.	*before; from life; snatched*
Thòu nost whannë Crist our drightë	*you know not when; lord*
30 Thee askëth that He hath bitaught.	*will ask you; has entrusted*

Man, why setstou thought and hertë	*why do you set*
On worldës blis that nought ne last?	*does not last*
Why tholstou that thee s'ofte y-smertë	*do you allow; should so often anguish*
For thing that is unstedëfast?	*transitory*
35 Thou lickëst hony of thorn iwis,	*you lick honey from a thorn indeed*
That setst thy love o worldës blis	*who set; on*
For ful of bitternes it is.	
Ful sorë thou might ben agast,	*afraid*
That here despendëst aught amis,	*who here spend wealth wrongly*
40 To ben therthurgh into hellë cast.	*to be thereby*

Think, man, wherto Crist thee wroughtë	*to what end; created*
And do way pride and filth and mood.	*put away pride and lust and anger*
Think how derë He thee boughtë	*dearly*
O rodë mid His swetë blood.	*on the cross with*
45 Himself he yaf for thee in pris	*gave; in ransom*
To beyn thee blis yif thou be wis.	*buy; if you are wise*
Bithink thee than and up aris	*then; rise up*
Of sinne, and agin werchen good	*from sin, and begin do good*
Ther whyls timë to werchen is,	*while; to act*
50 For siker ellës thou art wood.	*for certainly, otherwise you are mad*

Al day thou might understondë	*every day*
And thy miròur bifor thee sen,	
What is to don and what to wondë	*to be done and what to be avoided*
And what to holde and what to flen;	*to keep and what to flee*
55 For àl day thou seest with thine eyë	
How thìs world went and how men deyë.	*goes; die*
That witë wel, that thou shalt dreyë	*know this well, that you will suffer*
As othrë dide and eek ded ben;	*as others have done and also die*
Ne helpëth nought ther non to leyë,	*it helps no one then (lit. there) to lie*
60 Ne may no man be deth ayen.	*nor may any man withstand death*

Shal no good ben unforyoldë	*unrequited*
Ne no qued ne worth unbought;	*any evil; be unpaid for*
Whan thou list, man, under moldë	*when you lie; the earth*
Thou shalt have as thou hast wrought.	*earned*
65 Bithink wel forthy, Ich thee redë,	*consider well therefore; advise*
And clensë thee of ech misdedë,	*cleanse; misdeed*

That Crist thee helpe at thinë nedë,   *so that; may help you in your need*
That so derë hath thee bought,
And to hevenë blissë ledë   *lead (you)*
70 That ever last and faillëth nought.   *lasts*

I, 39   Man mai longe him livës wenë

Man mai longe him livës wenë   *for himself; life; expect*
Ac oftë him lyëth the wrench,   *deceives; the trick*
Fair weder ofte him went to renë   *turns to rain*
And ferlichë makëth his blench.   *suddenly plays its trick*
5 Therfore, man, thou thee bi-thench,   *take heed*
Al shal falëwi thy grenë.   *fade; youthful vigour (lit. greenness)*
Weilaway, nis king ne quenë   *alas; nor queen*
That ne shal drinke of Dethës drench.   *of Deaths's draught*
Man, er thou fallë of thy bench,   *off*
10   Thy sinne aquench.   *overcome*

Ne mai strong, ne stark, ne kenë   *may not prevail; nor mighty; bold*
Ayein Dethës wither-clench;   *against Death's hostile grip*
Young and old and bright and shenë,   *beautiful*
Al he rivëth an his strength.   *tears to pieces in his strength*
15 Fox and ferlich is the wrench,   *crafty and sudden is his (lit. the) twist*
Ne may no man thertoyenë,   *no man may prevail thereagainst*
Weylaway, threting ne benë,   *alas, neither threats nor entreaty*
Medë, list, ne lechës drench.   *bribery, cunning, nor a doctor's potion*
Man, let sinne and lustës stench,   *abandon sin and the stench of lust*
20   Wel do, wel thench!   *think*

Do bi Salomonës redë,   *act according to Solomon's advice*
Man, and so thou shalt wel do;
Do als he thee taught, and hedë   *if you do as; and heed*
What thin ending thee bringth to,
25 Nè shaltow never misdo –
Sorë thou might thee adredë!   *sorely you may fear for yourself*
Weylaway, swich wenth wel ledë   *Alas, such a man as fully expects to lead*
Long lyf, and blissë underfo,   *a long life and to enjoy happiness*
There Deth lutëth in his sho   *Death lurks there in his shoe*
30   To him fordo.   *to destroy him*

Màn, why niltow thee bi-knowë?   *will you not acknowledge your nature*
Màn, why niltow thee bi-se?   *consider yourself*
Of foulë filth thou art i-sowë,   *begotten*
Wormës metë thou shalt be.   *food*
35 Her nastou blissë dayës three,   *here you do not have; for three days*
Al thy lif thou drist in wowë;   *you endure in sorrow*
Weylaway, Deth thee shal throwë   *alas*

Doun ther thou wenst hyë ste;   *when (lit. where) you expect; high to rise*
In wo shal thi welë te,   *to misery will your prosperity pass*
40   In wop thy gle.   *to weeping your merriment*

World and welë thee biswikëth,   *prosperity; deceive*
Iwis, they ben thine ifo;   *assuredly; foes*
If thy world mid wele thee slikëth   *with prosperity; flatters you*
That is for to do thee wo.   *cause you harm*
45   Therfore let lust overgo,   *pass*
Man, and eft it wel thee likëth.   *and afterwards it will please you well*
Weylaway, hou sore him wikëth   *how sorely it serves him*
That in one stundë other two   *who in an hour*
Werkth him pinë evermo: *earns himself torment*
50   Ne do, Man, swo!   *Man, do not so*

I, 40   On hire is al mi lif y-long

On hire is al mi lif y-long   *her (Mary); dependent*
    Of whom Ich willë singë,
And herien Him ther-among,   *(will) praise Him (Christ) in the process*
    That gan us botë bringë   *who brought us deliverance*
5   Of hellë-pinë that is strong,   *from the torment of hell; severe*
And brought us blisse that is so long   *enduring*
    Al thourugh hire childingë.   *all through her child-bearing*
Ich biddë hirë in mi song,   *I beseech her*
    He yeve us god endingë,   *that He (Christ) may grant us*
10   Though we do wrong.

Al this world hit shal ago   *pass away*
    With sorwë and with sorë,   *sorrow; grief*
And al this blisse Ich mot forgo,   *I must forgo*
    N'ofthinke it me so sorë.   *though it displease me bitterly*
15 This world nis but ourë fo,   *is nothing but our foe*
Therfor Ich wille hennë go   *hence*
    And lernen Goddës lorë;   *teaching*
This worldës blis nis worth a slo.   *sloe*
    Ich biddë, God, thin orë,   *I pray, God, for Thy mercy*
20   Now and evermo.   *evermore*

To longe Ich havë sot i-be   *too long; a fool; been*
    Ful sore I me adredë;   *right sorely I am afraid*
Y-loved Ich havë gamen and gle   *sport and pleasure*
    And aughte and fayrë wedë.   *and wealth and fair garments*
25 Al that nis nought, ful wel Ich se, *nothing*
Therfore Ich willë sinnës fle
    And letë my sothedë.   *abandon my folly*
Ich biddë hirë me bi-se,   *I beseech her to look upon me*

And helpë me and redë,   *advise*

30   That is so fre.   *who is so gracious*

Thou art hele and lif and light   *salvation and life*
      And helpëst al mankennë;   *mankind*
Thou us hast ful wel i-dight,   *for us; provided*
      Thou yaf us wele and wennë.   *you have given us well-being and joy*

35 Thou broughtëst day, and Evë night,
She brought wo, thou broughtëst right,   *evil*
      Thou àlmesse, and she sennë.   *charity; sin*
Thou do us merci, lady bright,   *have mercy upon us*
      Whan we shullen hennë,   *when we shall go hence*

40   Ful wel thou might.   *can*

Agilt Ich havë, weilawy,   *offended; alas*
      Sinful Ich am and wrechë,   *wretched*
Thou do me merci, lavëdi,   *have mery upon me, lady*
      Er deth me hennë fecchë.   *before death; hence; fetches*

45 Yif me thi love, Ich am redi,   *give me*
Let me live and amendi,   *reform*
      That fendës me ne drecchë.   *so that fiends; may not afflict*
For minë sinne Ich am sori,   *my sins*
      Of thìs lif Ich ne recchë.   *for; I do not care*

50   Lady, merci!

I, 41   Ech day me comëth tydinges thre

Ech day me comëth tydinges thre,
      For wel swithë sore ben he: *very very grievous are they*
      The on is that Ich shal hennë,   *one; I must go hence*
      That other that Ich not whennë,   *I do not know when*

5   The thriddë is my mestë carë,   *greatest grief*
      That Ich not whider Ich shal farë.   *where I must go*

I, 42   Whan I thenkë thingës thre

Whan I thenkë thingës thre,   *ponder*
      Ne may I never blithë be: *happy*
      That on is that I shal away,   *must depart (lit. (go) away)*
      That other is I not which day,   *do not know*

5   The thriddë is my mostë carë,   *my greatest sorrow*
      I ne wot whider I shal farë.   *where I must go*

I, 43   If man him bithoughtë

If man him bithoughtë	*bethought himself*
Inderliche and oftë	*earnestly*
How harde is the forë	*journey*
Fro beddë te florë,	*from bed to floor*
5 How rewful is the flittë	*lamentable is the passing*
Fro florë te pittë,	*to grave*
Fro pittë te pinë	*to torment*
That never shal finë,	*end*
I wenë non sinnë	*think no sins*
10 Should his hertë winnë.	

I, 44   Whan mine eyen mistëth

Whan mine eyen mistëth,	*eyes grow dim*
And mine erës sissëth,	*ears buzz*
And my nosë coldëth,	
And my tongë foldëth,	*speech fails*
5 And my rodë slakëth,	*complexion fades*
And mine lippës blakëth,	*grow pale*
And my mouth grennëth,	*gapes*
And my spotel rennëth,	*spittle runs*
And min her risëth,	*hair stands on end*
10 And min hertë grisëth,	*heart quakes*
And mine hondës biviëth,	*hands tremble*
And mine fet stiviëth –	*feet stiffen*
Al to latë, al to latë,	*all too late*
Whan the bere is at the gatë.	*bier*
15 Than I shal flit	*must pass*
From beddë to florë,	
From florë to herë,	*haircloth shroud*
From herë to berë,	*bier*
From berë to pit,	*grave*
20 And the pit fordit.	*will close*
Than lith myn hous uppë myn nesë:	*my house will lie; upon my nose*
Of al this world ne give Ich a pesë!	*for; I shall not give a pea*

I, 45   Whan the turuf is thy tour

Whan the turuf is thy tour,	*turf; tower*
And thy pit is thy bour,	*grave; bower*
Thy fel and thy whitë throtë	*skin; throat*
Shullen wormës to notë.	*shall (be) good for worms*
5 What helpëth thee thennë	
Al the worildë wennë?	*world's delights*

I, 46   Whan Ich thenche on domës-dai

Whan Ich thenche on domës-dai	*when I think on the Day of Judgement*
ful sore I me adredë;	*I am afraid*
Ther shal after his werek	*according to his deeds* (lit. *work*)
ech man fongen medë.	*receive (his) reward*
5 Ich havë Christ agilt	*sinned against*
with thoughtës and with dedë,	*deeds*
Loverd helend, Goddës sone,	*Lord saviour*
what shal me to redë?	*what shall I do*
That fyr shal comen in this world	*fire; upon this world*
10 on one sonnë-nightë,	*on a Saturday night*
Forbrennen al this middelerd	*to burn up all this earth*
so Crist hit wolë dightë,	*as Christ; will command*
Bothen water and the lond,	
the flourës that ben brightë;	
15 Y-heriëd be oure loverd,	*praised; lord*
muchel is his mightë.	*great*
Four englës in the dai-red	*four angles at dawn*
blowen herë bemë,	*will blow their trumpets*
Thenne comëth Ihesus Crist	*when*
20 His domës for to demë;	*judgements; pronounce*
Ne helpëth hit nought thenne	
to wepen ne to remë	*weep; cry out*
To him that litel hath y-don	*for the person who*
that Cristë was y-quemë.	*which to Christ; pleasing*
25 From that Adam was y-wrought	*from the time that; created*
that comëth domësday,	*until*
Mony of the richë men	
that werden fou and gray,	*who wore lavish furs*
And riden upon stedës	*rode; steeds*
30 and upon palëfray;	*fine mounts*
They shulle attë domë	*at the Judgement*
singen weilaway.	*alas*
Ne shul they ther nought fighten	
with sheldës ne with sperë,	
35 With helmë ne with brinie	*helmet; coat of mail*
ne with non other gerë;	*any other weapons*
Ne shal ther noman other	
with wisë wordës werë;	*attack*
But here almësdedës	*only their charitable deeds*
40 her ernidës shal berë.	*petitions; advance*

They shulle y-sen that maiden
    that Ihesu Crist ofkendë,   *gave birth to*
Bitwenen hirë armës
    Swetëliche him wendë;   *enfold*
45 The whilë that we mighten,   *while we could have*
    to litel we hire sendë,   *too little did we send to her*
That makëdë the worsë,   *that the Devil caused*
    so fule he us ablendë.   *so completely; blinded*

They shulle y-sen the king
50   that al the woriold wroughtë,   *created*
And upon the swetë rodë   *sweet cross*
    with strongë pinës boughtë;   *severe torments; redeemed*
Adam and his ofspring,
    in hellë He hem soughtë –
55 To bidden thennë milcë   *to beg then for mercy*
    to late they ben bithoughtë.   *too late they had considered*

Ther shullen the rightwisë ben   *righteous*
    on Goddës rightë hondë,
And the sinfullë shullen
60   atelichë stondë   *in dread*
With herë sinne y-writen,   *sins recorded*
    that is muchel shondë;   *great shame*
Alle they shullen hem y-sen   *all those they shall see*
    that livëden in londë.   *who lived on earth*

65 To the rightwisë He spekëth   *will speak*
    wordës swithë swetë: *very sweet*
'Comëth her mine frends,
    your sinnës forto letë;   *to abandon*
In mine fader house   *father's*
70   you is y-makëd setë,   *for you is made a lasting home*
Ther you shullen englës
    swetëlichë gretë.'

To the sinfulë He spekëth
    so ye mowe y-herë: *as you may hear*
75 'Goëth ye awariedë,   *damned*
    with fendës y-ferë,   *with devils as companions*
Into brenning fyr;   *burning fire*
    of blissë ye ben skerë   *of bliss you will be bereft*
Forthy that ye your sinnës   *because*
80   out of this world berë.'   *take*

Biddë we our lavëdy,   *let us pray to our lady*
  swetest alrë thingë,   *of all things*
That she bere our erendë   *take our petition*
  to the hevenë kingë,
85 That for his holy name   *that for the sake of*
  and for hir erendingë,   *her advocacy*
That He ourë soulës
  to hevenrichë bringë.   *to the kingdom of heaven; may bring*

I, 47   Where ben they before us weren

Ubi sunt qui ante nos fuerunt

Where ben they beforen us weren,   *where are they who; were*
Houndës ladden and hawkës beren,   *who led hounds; carried hawks*
  And hadden feld and wode;   *possessed*
The richë ladies in here bour   *their bower*
5 That wereden gold in here tressour *wore; head-dress*
  With here brightë rode?   *complexion*

They eten and dronken and maden hem glad,   *made (themselves) merry*
Here life was all with gamen y-lad,   *in pleasure; spent (lit. led)*
  Men kneleden hem biforen;
10 They beren hem wel swithë hye   *bore themselves very proudly*
And in a twinkling of an eye
  Here soulës weren forloren.   *lost*

Where is that laughing and that song,
That trailing and that proudë yong,   *those trailing robes; gait*
15   The hawkës and the houndës;
All that joye is went away,   *has passed away*
That wele is come to weilaway,   *that happiness; lamentation*
  To many hardë stoundës.   *dire times*

Here paradis they nomen here,   *their paradise; took*
20 And now they lye in helle y-fere,   *together*
  The fire hit brennëth ever;   *burns*
Long is 'ay!' and long is 'o!',   *ah! / ever; oh! / always*
Long is 'wy!' and long is 'wo!',   *alas!; woe!*
  Thennës ne come they never.   *thence*

25 Dreye here, man, then if thou wilt *endure*
A litel pine that man thee bit,   *suffering; that is required of you*
  Withdraw thine esës ofte;   *forgo; comforts*
Though thy pinë be unrede,   *pain; should be severe*
And thou thinkë on thy mede   *if you think; reward*
30   It shall thee thinken softe.   *seem mild*

If that fend, that foulë thing,   *fiend*
Thurgh wikkë roun, thurgh fals egging,   *evil counsel; deceitful incitement*
   Nether thee hath y-cast;   *down*
Up and be good champioun,
35 Stond, ne fal namore adoun
   For a litel blast.

Thou take the rodë to thy staf   *cross as*
And think on Him that theron yaf   *gave*
   His lyf that was so leef;   *so dear*
40 He it yaf for thee, thou yelde hit Him,   *He gave it; repay Him for it*
Agains His fo that staf thou nim   *against; take*
   And wreke Him of that theef.   *avenge; on that thief*

Of right bileve thou nim that shell   *take that shield*
The whiles that thou art in that feld,   *while*
45   Thin hand to strengthen fonde;   *try*
And keep thy fo with stavës ord,   *hold; at the point of the staff*
And do that traitour seye that word,   *make*
   Biget that mery londe.   *achieve; happy*

Therin is day withouten night,
50 Withouten endë, strength and might,
   And wreche of everich fo;   *vengeance on*
With God himselven echë lif   *eternal*
And pes and rest withouten strif,   *peace*
   Wele withouten wo.   *bliss*

55 Maiden, moder, hevenë quen,
Thou might, and canst, and owest to ben   *ought*
   Our shell again the fende;   *against the fiend (Devil)*
Help us sinnë for to fleen   *flee*
That we moten Thy son y-seen   *may; see*
60   In joye withouten ende.

I, 48   No more ne will I wiked be

No more ne will I wiked be,   *wicked*
Forsake Ich wille this worldës fe,   *wealth*
This wildës wedes, this folës gle,   *these wantons' clothes; delight of fools*
   Ich wol be mild of chere;   *gentle in manner*
5 Of knottës shal mi girdil be,   *girdle*
   Becomen Ich wil frere.   *a friar*

Frer menour I wil me make,   *minor*
And lecherie I wil asake;   *renounce*
To Ihesu Crist Ich wil me take
10   And serve in holi chirche,
Al in mi hourës for to wake,   *(canonical) hours*
    Goddës wille to wirche.   *do*

Wirche I wil this workës gode,   *do; these good works*
For Him that bought us on the rode; *redeemed us on the cross*
15 From his sidë ran the blode,
    So dere He gan us bye;   *dearly; redeemed us*
For sothe, I tel him mor than wode *truly, I consider him; mad*
    That hauntëth licherie.   *who habitually practises lechery*

I, 49   Lord, thou clepedest me

Lord, thou clepedest me,   *you called me*
An Ich noght n'answerde thee   *and I answered you nothing*
But wordës slow and slepy: *sleepy*
'Thole yet, thole a litel.'   *forbear yet*
5 But 'yet' and 'yet' was endëlis, *endless*
And 'thole a litel' a long wey is.

I, 50   Lullay, lullay, litel child, why wepëstou so sore?

Lullay, lullay, litel child,
    why wepëstou so sore?   *bitterly*
Nedës mostou wepe,   *of necessity must you weep*
    it was i-yarkëd thee of yore   *ordained for you long ago*
5 Ever to live in sorwe,
    and sigh and mournen evermore, *sighing*
As thine eldren did er this,   *forebears*
    whil they alivës wore.   *alive; were*
Lullay, lullay, litel child,
10   child, lullay, lullow,
Into uncouth world   *an alien world*
    y-commen so artou.   *are you*

Bestës and tho foulës,   *beasts and these birds*
    the fishës in the flode,   *sea*
15 And ech shaft alivës,   *creature alive*
    makëd of bone and blode,   *made*
Whan they commen to the world,
    they don hemself some gode,   *some good*

    Allë but the wrecchë brol   *the wretched brat*
20   that is of Adames blode.
    Lullay, lullay, litel child,
        to care artou bemette;   *to sorrow you are destined*
    Thou nost nought this worldës wild   *you know not; power*
        before thee is y-sette.   *(which) is set against you*

25 Child, if it betidëth   *happens*
        that thou shalt thrive and thee,   *prosper*
    Think thou were y-fostrëd   *remember that*
        up thy moder kne;   *upon your mother's knee*
    Ever have mind in thyn hert   *remember*
30   of tho thingës thre,   *those*
    Whan thou commëst, what thou art,   *whence*
        and what shall come of thee.   *become*
    Lullay, lullay, litel child,
        child, lullay, lullay,
35 With sorwe thou com into this world,   *came*
        with sorwe shalt wend away.   *pass away*

    Ne tristou to this world,   *do not trust in*
        it is thy fullë fo;   *declared enemy*
    The rich he makëth pouer,   *he (i.e. the world); poor*
40   the pouer rich also;   *likewise*
    It turnëth wo to wel,   *misery to prosperity*
        and ekë wel to wo;   *also*
    Ne trist no man to this world   *let no one trust in*
        while it turnëth so.   *changes*
45 Lullay, lullay, litel child,
        thy fote is in the whele;   *wheel*
    Thou nost whider it wil turne,   *which way*
        to wo other to wele.   *to misery or to prosperity*

    Child, thou art a pilgrim
50   in wikkednes y-born;
    Thou wandrëst in this falsë world,
        thou lokë thee beforn!   *look ahead*
    Deth shall comen with a blast,
        out of a well dim horn,   *very sombre horn*
55 Adames kin adoun to cast –
        himself hath don beforn.   *(as Adam) himself did previously*
    Lullay, lullay, litel child,
        so wo thee worth Adam,   *Adam caused you woe*
    In the lond of paradis,
60   through wikkednes of Satan.

Child, thou n'art a pilgrim
  but an uncouth gest;   *alien guest*
Thy dawës ben y-told,   *days are numbered*
  thy journeys ben y-cest;   *travels are charted*
65 Whider thou shalt wend,   *wherever; go*
  by north other by est,
Deth thee shall betide   *befall*
  with bitter bale in brest.   *pain*
Lullay, lullay, litel child,
70 this wo Adam thee wrought,   *wrought for you*
Whan he of the appil ete
  and Eve it him betought.   *gave*

I, 51 Hye Loverd, thou here my bone

Hye Loverd, thou here my bone,   *Lord on high; hear my prayer*
That madëst middelerd and mone,   *earth and moon*
  And man of mirthës minne;   *and man to think of pleasures*
Trusty king and trewe in trone,   *on (your) throne*
5 That thou be with me saughtë sone, *reconciled with me soon*
  Assoilë me of sinne.   *absolve*
Fol Ich was in folies fayn,   *a fool I was delighting in folly*
In lithere lastës I am lain,   *in base vices I have lain*
  That maketh myn thriftës thinne; *which makes my lot unhappy*
10 That semly sawes was wont to sain, *one who fair words; wont to utter*
Nou is marrëd al my main,   *destroyed; all my authority*
  Away is al my winne.   *gone; joy*

Unwin haveth myn wongës wet,   *unhappiness; cheeks*
  That maketh me routhës rede.   *(words of) remorse; utter*
15 Ne seme I nought ther I am set,   *I seem not to exist where; put*
Ther me calleth me 'fillë-flet'   *I am called 'floor-filler'*
  And 'waynoun waytëglede'.   *'good-for-nothing fire-gazer'*

While Ich was in willë wolde,   *formerly; in pleasure's mastery*
In ech a bour among the bolde   *in every chamber in noble company*
20 Y-holdë with the heste;   *counted among the best* (lit. *highest*)
Nou I may no finger folde,   *clasp*
Litel loved and less y-tolde,   *less esteemed*
  Y-levëd with the leste.   *abandoned with the least*
A goute me hath y-greythëd so   *gout; afflicted*
25 And other eveles many mo,
  I not what bote is beste;   *I do not know what remedy*
Ther er was wildë as the ro   *where formerly I was wild; roe*
Nou I swyke, I may nought so,   *I give up, I cannot be so*
  Hit sewëth me so faste.   *it (? gout or old age) pursues*

30 Faste I was on horsë heigh   *high*
        And werëde worly wede;   *wore splendid garments*
        Nou is faren al my feigh –   *gone; my wealth*
        With sorwe that Ich hit ever seigh! –   *saw*
        A staf is nou my stede.   *steed*

35 When I se stedës stithe in stalle,   *steeds strong*
        And I go halting in the halle,   *limping*
            Min hertë ginneth to helde.   *sink*
        That er was wildest inwith walle   *one who formerly was; within walls*
        Nou is under fote y-falle
40   And may no finger felde.   *clasp*
        Ther Ich was lef Ich am ful loth,   *where; loved; utterly hated*
        And alle my godës me at-goth,   *desert*
            Myn gamenës waxen gelde;   *pleasures become barren*
        That fairë founde me mete and cloth,   *those who kindly; food and clothes*
45 They wrie away as they were wroth –   *turn; angry*
        Such is evel and elde.   *misfortune and old age*

        Evel and elde and other wo
            Folewen me so faste
        Me thinketh myn hertë breketh atwo;   *will break in two*
50 Swetë God, whi shal hit so,
            How may hit lenger laste?   *longer*

        Whil mi lif was lither and les: *formerly; base and false*
        Glotonie mi gleman wes,   *minstrel*
            With me he wonde a while;   *dwelt*
55 Pridë was my pleïë-fere,   *playfellow*
        Lecherie my lavendere,   *mistress (lit. laundress)*
            With hem is Gabbe and Gile;   *Falsehood and Deceit*
        Coveytise myn keyës bere,   *Covetousness; carried*
        Nithe and Ondë were mi fere,   *Envy and Anger; companions*
60   That ben folkës fyle;   *vile*
        Lyer was mi latymer,   *Liar; interpreter*
        Slouthe and Slep mi beddëfere,   *Sloth and Sleep my bedfellows*
            That wenen me umbe while.   *which attract me at times*

        Umbë while I am to wene,   *at times I am attracted*
65   When I shal mirthës meten;   *merriment; encounter*
        Mannë mest I am to mene,   *most of men; to be pitied*
        Lord, that hast me lif to lene,   *life (i.e. eternal life); to grant*
            Such lotës lef me leten.   *such evils let me abandon*

        Such lif Ich havë lad ful yore,   *led for a long time*
70 Merci, Lord, I nil namore,   *will not (do so) anymore*
            Bowen Ich wille to bete;   *submit; to atone*
        Siker hit sewëth me ful sore,   *truly they (lit. it) pursue me*

Gabbës les and lither lore –   *lies untrue and wicked ideas*
   Sinnës ben unsete;   *sins (which) are evil*
75 Godës heste ne held I nought,   *command; I did not keep*
But ever ayein His wille I wrought –   *against His will I acted*
   Man lerëth me to lete;   *I am urged to desist*
Such sorwë hath myn sides thurghsought   *pierced*
That al I welwe away to nought   *I wither*
80   When I shal mirthës mete.   *merriment; encounter*

To metë mirthes Ich was wel fous   *very eager*
   And comely man to calle;   *and a fine fellow; to be called*
I say by other as by ous: *I speak of others just as of ourselves*
As is hirman halt in hous,   *servant; haughty; house*
85   As heved hount in halle.   *head hound / chief huntsman*

Dredful Deth, why wilt thou dare?   *tarry*
Bring this body that is so bare   *take*
   And in bale y-bounde;   *torment*
Careful man y-cast in care   *a sorrowful man*
90 I falwe as flour y-let forthfare,   *I wither; left to die*
   I have myn dethës wounde;
Mirthës helpen me no more,
Help me, Lord, er than Ich hore,   *before I turn gray*
   And stint my lyf a stounde;   *and end my life soon*
95 That yokkyn hath y-yernëd yore,   *the man who; passion; yearned for*
Nou hit sorwëth him ful sore,   *it pains him most grievously*
   And bringëth him to grounde.

To grounde it havëth him y-brought:
   What is the bestë bote   *remedy*
100 But herie him that hath us bought,   *praise*
Our Lord that al this world hath wrought,
   And fallen him to fote?   *at his feet*

Nou Ich am to dethe y-dight,   *for death; prepared*
   Y-don is al my dede.   *finished*
105 God us lenë of His light   *grant*
That we of seyntës haven sight   *saints*
   And hevënë to mede!   *heaven as (our) reward*

I, 52   Wynter wakenëth al my care

Wynter wakenëth al my care,   *awakens; sorrow*
Nou this levës waxen bare;   *now that these leaves become*
Ofte I sike and mournë sare   *sigh and grieve bitterly*
   When hìt cometh in my thought
5 Of this worldës joie, hou hit goth al to nought.   *how it goes*

Nou hit is and nou hit nys,   *is not*
Also hit ner nere, ywys.   *as if it had never been, indeed*
That many man saith, soth hit is,   *what; true*
  Al gòth but Godës wille,   *passes; except*
10 Allë we shul deyë though us likë ylle.   *shall die; it displeases us*

Al that grein me gravëth grene,   *grain which is planted unripe*
Nou hit falwëth al bydene;   *withers utterly*
Iesu, help that hit be sene,   *this (lit. it) may be made clear*
  And shildë us from helle,   *shield*
15 For I not whider I shal, ne hou longe her dwelle. *know not where I shall (go)*

I, 53   Nou shrinkëth rose and lylie-flour

Nou shrinkëth rose and lylie-flour,   *withers*
That whilom bar that swete savòur   *once bore; scent*
  In somer, that swetë tide;   *time*
Nis no queene so stark ne stour,   *so mighty or strong*
5 Ne no lady so bright in bour   *so radiant in bower*
  That deth ne shal by-glyde.   *whom; steal upon*
Whoso wol flesh-lust forgon   *physical desire; forgo*
  And hevenë blis abyde,   *wait for*
On Iesu be his thought anon   *constantly*
10   That thirlëd was His side.   *whose side was pierced*

From Petrësbourgh in o morning,   *one morning*
As I me wende o my playing,   *took my way for pleasure*
  On my folie I thoughte;   *folly*
Menen I gan my mourning   *I addressed my lament*
15 To hir that bar the hevenë kyng,   *who bore*
  Of merci hire bysoughte.   *for mercy; begged*
Lady, preye thi son for ous   *entreat; us*
  That us derë boughte,   *dearly*
And shild us from the lothë hous   *shield; hateful*
20   That to the fend is wroughte.   *for the Devil; made*

Myn herte of dedës was fordred   *at deeds; terrified*
Of synne that I have my flesh fed   *of sin; fed to*
  And folwëd al my time,
That I not whider I shal be led   *so that I do not know whither; taken*
25 When I ligge on dethës bed,   *lie*
  In joie or into pyne.   *to bliss or to torment*
On o lady myn hope is,   *on one lady*
  Moder and virgyne,
We shulen into hevenë blis   *shall go to*
30   Thurgh hire medicine.

Betere is hire medycyn
Than any mede or any wyn;   *mead; wine*
   Hire herbës smellen swete;
From Catenas to Dyvelyn.   *Caithness to Dublin*
35 Nis ther no lechë so fyn   *physician so excellent*
   Our sorëwës to bete.   *to cure*
Man that felëth any sor   *the person who feels any remorse*
   And his folie wol lete,   *will abandon*
Withouten gold other tresòr   *or treasure*
40 He may be sound and sete.   *healed and at ease*

Of penaunce is hir plaster al,   *remedy*
And ever serven hire I shal
   Nou and al my lyve;
Nou is fre that er was thral   *free who formerly was enslaved*
45 Al thurgh that lady gent and smal,   *graceful and slender*
   Heried be joiës fyve!   *praised be the five joys*
Wherso any man sek is   *wherever anyone; sick*
   Thider hyë blyve;   *thither (to her) let him hasten quickly*
Thurgh hire ben y-brought to blis
50 Bo mayden and wyve.   *both*

For He, that dide his bodi on tre,   *in order that He, who put*
Of ourë sinnës have pitè,   *on our sins may have pity*
   That weldëth hevenë bourës,   *(He) who rules heaven's bowers*
Womman with thi jolitèe,   *gaiety*
55   Thou thench on Godës shourës.   *think; sufferings*
Though thou be whyt and bright on ble,   *fair (lit. white) and radiant of face*
   Falwen shule thy flourës.   *fade*
Iesu, have mercì of me,
   That al this world honourës.   *whom (i.e. Jesus)*
      Amen.

I, 54   Middelerd for man was mad

Middelerd for man was mad,   *earth; made*
Unmighty are his mostë mede;   *puny; its greatest rewards*
This edi hath on hond y-had   *this blessed one; brought it about*
That heven hem is heist to hede.   *for them is most important to heed*
5 Ich herde a blissë bedel us bad   *a herald of joy (who) bid us*
The drery domësday to drede,   *terrible; dread*
Of sinful saughting sone be sad   *of acquiescing in sin; soon to be weary*
That dernë don these dernë dede;   *those who secretly; hidden deeds*
   Though they ben dernë done,   *they are*
10 These wrackful workës under wede,   *wicked deeds under cover (lit. clothes)*
   In soulë sutelen sone.   *(they) become manifest soon*

Sone is sutel as Ich you say,   *is manifest*
This sake, although hit semë swete; *sin; seems sweet*
That I telle a pourë play   *that I count a poor sport*
15 That first is fair and sithe unsete: *afterwards evil*
This wildë willë went away   *passionate desire passes*
With mone and mourning muche unmete; *lamentation; grief; excessive*
That liveth on liking out of lay, *he who lives in unlawful pleasure*
His hap he doth full harde on hete *his fate; violently; call out against*
20 Agains he hovëth henne;   *at the time he goes hence*
Alle his thrivenë thewës threte *virtuous qualities rebuke*
 That thinkëth nought on thenne. *the person who; on that time*

Againës thenne us threten thre. *regarding that time; three (i.e. foes)*
If they ben thriven and thowe in thede, *thriving and prosperous among men*
25 Our soulës bone so broerli be *destroyers as brotherly may be*
As bernë best that bale forbede. *as the best of men who; harm; prevent*
That wil withstonden strength of theo, *the person who; of them*
His rest is revëd with the rede. *peace is robbed like the reed*
Fight of other ne thar he floe *the assault; need he not flee*
30 That fleshës faunyng first foryede, *who; allure; has withstood*
 That falsest is of five;   *most insidious; of the five (i.e. senses)*
If we leven any lede,   *believe any people*
 Werryng is worst of wyve. *the onslaught of women is worst*

Wyvës willë were ded wo   *a woman's will (lust) were deadly peril*
35 If she is wikked for to welde; *hard to control*
That burst shal betë for hem bo, *he who; harm; is to remedy; them both*
Shal him berwen though he hire belde. *must save himself; shelter her*
By body and soule I say also
That some ben founden under felde *on earth*
40 That have to fere his mostë fo; *as a wife his worst enemy*
Of gamenës he may gon al gelde *pleasures; be (lit. go) utterly deprived*
 And sore ben ferde on folde, *and (yet) be sore afraid on earth*
Lest he him to harmës held *himself; submit*
 And happës hente unholde. *suffer (lit. seize) a disastrous outcome*

45 Hom unholdest her is on   *home; the most disastrous; here*
Withouten helle, as Ich hit holde, *outside; maintain*
So fele are founden mannës fon. *so many; foes*
The first of hem biforen I tolde: *I mentioned*
There afterward this worldës won *world's riches*
50 With muche unwynne us woren wolde. *much sorrow; would disturb*
Sonë ben these gamenës gon *pleasures; gone*
That maken us so brag and bolde *so lively*
 And bidden us ben blythe; *merry*
An ende they casten us ful colde *in the end; destine; without compassion*
55 In sinne and sorwë sithe. *to sin and a time of sorrows*

In sinne and sorowe I am seint,   *am sunk*
That sewen me so selly sore;   *which pursue; exceedingly painfully*
My mirth is al with mourning meint,   *with grief; mingled*
Ne may Ich mythen hit namore.   *conceal it*
60 When we ben with this world forwleynt,   *puffed up*
That we ne listnen lyvës lore,   *so that we do not listen to life's teaching*
The fend in fyght us fint so feint   *fiend; finds; so feeble*
We falle so flour when hit is frore,   *as a flower; withered*
    For folkës fader al fleme;   *because of the father of mankind; all fugitives*
65 Wo him was y-warpë yore   *destined long ago*
    That Crist nil nowight queme.   *will in no way please*

To quemë Crist we were y-core   *to please; chosen*
And kend his craftës forto knowe.   *and taught his power to know*
Leve we nought we ben forlore,   *let us not believe; ruined*
70 In lustës though we lyen lowe;   *in pleasures; lie sunk* (lit. *low*)
We shul arise our fader afore,
Though fon us fallen umbë throwe;   *foes defeat us at times*
To borwe us alle He was y-bore.   *to save us; born*
This bannyng when Him bemës blowe,   *summons; for Him; trumpets*
75   He bit us ben of Hyse,   *will command us to be of His company*
And on His right hond hentë rowe   *take (our) position*
    With rightwis men to arise.   *with righteous*

I, 55   Erthe tok of erthe erthe wyth wogh

Erthe tok of erthe   *earth*
    erthe wyth wogh;   *sin*
Erthe other erthe
    to the erthe drogh;   *drew*
Erthe leyde erthe   *laid*
    in erthëne throgh;   *an earthen pit*
Tho hevede erthe of erthe   *had*
    erthe ynogh!   *enough*

I, 56   Wrechë man, why art thou prowde

Wrechë man, why art thou prowde   *wretched man; proud*
    That art of erthë makëd?   *made*
Hider ne broughtëst thou no shroude,   *hither*
    But poure thou come and naked.   *poor you came*
When thy soule is faren out,   *has gone forth*
    Thy body with erthe y-rakëd,   *raked over*
That body that was ranke and loude   *haughty and bold*
    Of allë men is hatëd.

I, 57   Was ther never caren so loth

Was ther never caren so loth	*corpse so hateful*
As man when he to pittë goth	*to the grave goes*
And deth hath layde so lowe.	*laid*
For when deth drawëth man from other,	
5 The sister nil not se the brother,	*see her (lit. the) brother*
Ne fader the sone y-knowe.	*know his (lit. the) son*

I, 58   The Lavëdi Fortunë is bothe frend and fo

The Lavëdi Fortunë	*Lady Fortune*
is bothe frend and fo,	
Of poure she makëth riche	
of richë poure also,	
She turnëth wo al into wele	*misery into prosperity*
and wele al into wo,	
Ne tristë noman to this wele	*let no man trust to this prosperity*
5 the wheel it turnëth so.	*wheel (i.e. of Fortune)*

I, 59   Kynge I syt and loke aboute

[Primus:]

'Kynge I syt and loke aboute,	
Tomorwen I may ben withoute.'	*may be*

Secundus:

'Wo is me, a kynge I was,	
This worlde I loved but that I las.'	*lost*

Tercius:

5 'Nought longe gon I was ful ryche,	
But now is riche and poure ylyche.'	*alike*

Quartus:

'I shal be kyng, that men shul se,	
When the wrechë ded shal be.'	

I, 60   Whan men ben meriest at her mele

Whan men ben meriest at her mele	*at their meal*
With mete and drink to make hem glade,	*food; themselves*
With worship and with worldlich wele	*honour; worldly prosperity*
They ben so set they conne not sade.	*so concerned they cannot have too much*
5 They have no deynté for to dele	*no inclination to have to do*
With thinges that ben devoutli made,	*that are works of devotion*
They weene her honour and here hele	*imagine; their health*
Shal ever last and never diffade.	*fade*

But in her hertes I wolde they hade   *I wish they considered (lit. had)*
10 Whan they gon richest on aray,   *go about in greatest splendour*
Hou sone that God hem may degrade,   *soon; may humble them*
    And sum tyme think on yesterday.   *sometimes*

This day as leef we may be light   *we would as soon be cheerful*
With al the mirthes that men may vise,   *merriment; may devise*
15 To revel with this birdës bright,   *to make merry; these ladies*
Ech man gayest on his gyse.   *most elegant in his own manner*
At the last hit draweth to night
That Slep most maken his maistryse;   *when Sleep must assert his authority*
Whan that he hath y-kid his might,   *he (Sleep) has shown his power*
20 The Morwe he buskëth up to rise,   *the Dawn; prepares*
Then al drawe hem to fantasyse;   *(they) all become an illusion*
Wher they bicome can no man say,   *what became of them*
(And yif they wiste they were ful wise!)   *knew they would be very wise*
    For al is tornd to yesterday.   *changed*

25 Whose wolde thinken upon this   *whoever*
Mighte fynde a good enchesoun why   *good reason*
To preve this world alwey, ywis,   *to prove; always, to be sure*
Hit nis but fantome and fairy;   *is nothing but illusion and fantasy*
This erthly joye, this worldly blis,
30 Is but a fikel fantasy,
For nou hit is and nou hit nis,   *is not*
Ther may no man therin affy;   *trust*
Hit chaungeth so ofte and sodenly,
Today is her, tomorwe away;   *(it) is here, tomorrow gone*
35 A siker ground who wol him gy,   *on sure ground; to make his way*
    I rede he thinke on yesterday.   *I advise (that) he should think*

For ther nis non so strong in stour,   *in battle*
Fro tyme that he ful waxen be,   *from the time; full grown*
From that day forth, everich an hour,   *(who) from; every hour*
40 Of strengthe ne lest a quantité;   *does not lose*
Ne no birde so bright in bour,   *nor any lady*
Of thritty winter, I ensure thee,   *of thirty years (lit. winters); assure*
That she ne shal fade as a flour,
Lite and lite lese hire beauté;   *little by little lose*
45 The soth ye may yourself y-se   *truth; observe*
Be your eldrës, in good fay.   *from your ancestors, truth to tell*
Whan ye ben gretest in your degré,   *reputation*
    I rede ye thinke on yesterday.   *advise*

Nis non so fresh on fote to fare,   *to go*
50 Ne non so fayr on fold to fynde   *on earth; to be found*
Ne shal a bere be brought ful bare –   *who shall not on a bier be borne full naked*
This wrecched world nis but a wynde;   *is nothing but a puff of wind*

Ne non so stif to stynte ne stare,   *so resolute (as) to stand or stare*
Ne non so bold berës to bynde,   *so bold as to chain up bears*
55 That he nath warnynges to be ware,   *who has not; to be wary*
For God is so curtèis and kinde.   *so gracious*
Bihold, the lame, the bedrede, the blynde   *bedridden*
That bid you be war whil that ye may,   *be cautious*
They make a mirour to your mynde   *for your mind*
60   To se the shap of yesterday.   *shape*

The lyf that any man shal lede   *lead*
Ben certein dayës attë last;   *numbered days in the end*
Than moste our termë shortë nede,   *then must our span shorten necessarily*
Be o day come another is past.   *if one day has come*
65 Herof and we wolde take good hede,   *if we would take good heed*
And in our hertes acountës cast,   *tallies; make*
Day bi day, withouten drede,   *without doubt*
Toward our ende we drawe ful fast.
Than shal our bodies in erthe be thrast,   *into the earth be thrust*
70 Our careyns couchëd under clay;   *our corpses lodged*
Herof we oughte ben sore agast   *sorely aghast*
    And we wolde thinke on yesterday.   *if we*

Salamon saide in his poesy
He halt wel beter with an hounde   *(that) he has much greater preference for*
75 That is lyking and joly   *pleasing and frisky*
And of seknesse hol and sounde,   *free and healthy*
Then be a leon though he lye   *than for a lion if*
Cold and ded upon the grounde;
Wherof servëth his victory   *what use is*
80 That was so stif in eche a stounde?   *so valiant on every occasion*
The mostë fool, I herde respounde,   *reply*
Is wiser whil he lyvë may   *is alive*
Than he that hadde a thousand pounde   *he (who)*
    And was buried yesterday.

85 Socrates seith a word ful wys: *speaks*
Hit were wel beter for to se
A man that nou partëth and dys   *departs and dies*
Then a feste of realté.   *a feast of royal splendour*
The feste wol make his flesh to rise
90 And drawe his herte to vanité;
The body that on the berë lys   *bier lies*
Shewëth the same that we shal be.   *what (lit. the same); become (lit. be)*
That ferful fit may no man fle   *fearful seizure*
Ne with no wiles win hit away,   *put it*
95 Therfore among al jolité
    Sum tyme think on yesterday.

But yit me merveilëth over al   *I marvel above all*
That God let many man croke and elde   *allows; to become bent and grow old*
Whan might and strengthe is from hem fal   *(to the point) when*
100   That they may not hemself a-welde,   *so that; control themselves*
And now this beggers most principal   *these beggars; in particular*
That good ne profyt may non yelde.   *yield*
To this purpos answere I shal   *to this point*
Why God sent swich men boote and belde: *sends such men relief and comfort*
105   Crist that made both flour and felde   *flower and field*
Let swich men live, forsothe to say,   *allows*
Whan a yong man on hem bihelde   *(so that) when; looked*
     Sholde se the shap of yesterday.   *(he) should see*

Another skile ther is for whi   *reason*
110   That God let swich men live so longe;
For they ben treacle and remedi   *a salve*
For synful men that han do wronge;
In hem the seven dedes of merci   *works of mercy*
A man may fulfille among;
115   And also this proude men may therbi   *these proud; therein*
A feir mirour underfonge.   *a fair mirror; find*
For ther nis non so stif ne stronge,   *bold; valiant*
Ne no lady stout ne gay –   *stately*
Bihold what over her hed can honge,   *hangs over their heads*
120   And sum tyme think on yesterday.

I have wist sin I cuthe men   *known since I could remember*
That children han bi candel light   *have by*
Her shadewe on the wal i-sen   *their shadow; seen*
And runne therafter al the night.
125   Bisie aboutë they han ben
To cacchen hit with al her might
And whan they cacche hit best wolde wene,   *to catch it; most expect*
Sannest hit shet out of her sight;   *immediately it shoots*
The shadewe cacchen they ne might
130   For no lynës that they couthe lay.   *snares which they could lay*
This shadewe I may likne aright   *liken exactly*
     To this world and yesterday.

Into this world whan we ben brought
We shul be tempt to cuvetise;   *tempted to avarice*
135   And al thi wit shal be thurghsought   *mind; intent*
To more good then thou may suffyse.   *on more possessions; need*
Whan thou thinkest best in thi thought
On richesse for to regne and rise,   *wealth; succeed and rise*
Al thi travaile turnëth to nought,   *effort; nothing*
140   For sodeynly on deth thou dyse,   *you die*

Thi lyf thou hast y-lad with lyes   *spent in lies*
So this world gan thee bitray.   *betrayed you*
Therfore I rede thou this dispyse   *I advise (that) you despise this*
   And sum tyme think on yesterday.

145 Man, yif thi neighbor thee manas   *threatens*
Other to kille other to bete,   *either … or; beat*
I knowe me siker in the cas   *sure in that event*
That thou wolt drede thi neighbores threte,
And never a day thy dore to pas   *leave*
150 Withoute siker defense and grete,   *secure*
And ben purveyed in eche a plas   *arrangements being made; each place*
Of sikernes and help to gete;   *for safety*
Thin enemy woltou not foryete   *forget*
But ay be aferd of his affray.   *(you will) be afraid; assault*
155 Ensaumple herof I wol you trete   *an instance of this; elaborate for you*
   To make you think of yesterday.

Wel thou wost withouten fayle   *know*
That Deth hath manast thee to dye,   *threatened you with death (lit. to die)*
But whan that he wol thee asayle
160 That wost thou not ne never may spye.   *find out*
Yif thou wolt don be my counsayle,   *act on my advice*
With siker defence be ay redye;   *ever ready*
For siker defence in this batayle
Is clenë lyf, parfyt and trye;   *a pure life, perfect and exemplary*
165 Put thi trust in Godes mercye,
Hit is the best at al assay,   *in every trial*
And ever among thou thee envie   *and again and again show hostility*
   Into this world and yesterday.   *towards*

Sum men seyn that Deth is a thef,
170 And al unwarned wol on hem stele,   *without warning will on them steal*
And I sey nay, and make a pref   *say no, and give as proof*
That Deth is stedefast, trewe and lele,   *loyal*
And warnëth ech man of his gref,   *warns; of the (lit. his) suffering*
That he wol o day with him dele.   *he (Death); will one day allot to him*
175 The lyf that is to you so lef,   *so dear*
He wol you reve and eke your hele;   *take from you and also your health*
Thise poyntes may no man him repele,   *these intentions; turn him from*
He cometh so boldely to pyke his pray.   *to select his prey*
Whan men ben meriest at her mele,
180   I rede ye think on yesterday.   *advise you*

I, 61   I wolde wite of sum wys wight

I wolde wite of sum wys wight — *would like to know; wise person*
Witterly what this world were; — *truly what the nature of; might be*
Hit farëth as a foulës flight, — *goes; bird's*
Now is hit henne, now is hit here, — *far off*
5 Ne be we never so muche of might, — *so great in strength*
Now be we on benche, now be we on bere; — *one moment (we are); the next; on a bier*
And be we never so war and wight, — *vigilant and strong*
Now be we sek, now be we fere; — *sick; healthy*
Now is on proud withouten pere, — *one proud; equal*
10 Now is the selve y-set not by; — *the same person thought nothing of*
And whos wol alle thing hertly here, — *whoever; earnestly heed (lit. hear)*
    This world fareth as a fantasy. — *an illusion*

The sonnës cours we may wel kenne, — *perceive*
Arisëth est and goth doun west;
15 The ryvers into the see they renne, — *sea; run*
And hit is never the more almest; — *it (the sea); hardly*
Wyndës roshen her and henne, — *hither and thither*
In snow and rain is non arest; — *ceasing*
Whan this wol stinte, who wot, or whenne, — *stop; or by what cause*
20 But only God, on groundë grest? — *(who is) on earth the greatest*
The erthe in on is ever prest, — *in the same (condition) is always ready*
Now bedroppëd, now al drye; — *bedewed; dry*
But eche gome glit forth as a gest, — *each man glides away like a guest*
    This world fareth as a fantasye.

25 Kinredes come and kinredes gon — *generations*
As joynen generacions; — *join*
But alle they passen everichon — *they all pass away*
For al her preparacions;
Sum are foryetë clene as bon — *forgotten clean as bone*
30 Among alle maner nacions; — *all kinds of peoples*
So shul men thenke us nothing on — *have no thought of us*
That nou han th'ocupacions; — *have the control of affairs*
And alle these disputacions — *disputations*
Ideliche all us occupye, — *in vain*
35 For Crist maketh the creacions, — *makes created things*
    And this world fareth as a fantasye.

Which is man, who wot, and what, — *of what nature is man, who knows*
Whether that he be ought or nought? — *anything or nothing*
Of erthe and eir groweth up a gnat, — *air*
40 And so doth man whan al is sought; — *examined*
Though man be waxen gret and fat, — *should grow*
Man melteth away so doth a mought. — *a moth*
Mannës might nis worth a mat — *is not worth a mat (i.e. is worthless)*

	But noyeth himself and turneth to nought.	*but only vexes him*
45	Who wot, save He that al hath wrought,	*created*
	Wher man bicometh whan he shal dye?	*where man goes to*
	Who knoweth bi deth ought but bi thought?	*about death anything except by speculation*
	For this world fareth as a fantasye.	

	By ensaumple men may se,	*example; see*
50	A gret tre groweth out of the grounde;	
	Nothing abated th'erthe wol be	*reduced*
	Though hit be hugë, gret and rounde.	
	Right ther will rote the selvë tre,	*rot the same tree*
	Whan elde hath made his kinde aswounde;	*age; its natural strength; enfeebled*
55	Though ther were rotë suchë thre,	*to rot three such (trees)*
	The erthe wol not encrece a pounde.	*increase*
	Thus waxe and wane man, hors and hounde,	*wax and wane*
	From nought to nought thus henne we hye;	*hence we hasten*
	And her we stinten but a stounde,	*we remain only for a little while*
60	For this world is but a fantasye.	

	Dyëth man, and bestës dye,	
	And al is on occasioun;	*one occurrence*
	And al o deth bos bothë drye	*and (all) one death must both suffer*
	And han on incarnacioun;	*have one birth*
65	Save that men ben morë slye,	*intelligent*
	Al is o comparisoun.	*all is alike (lit. one comparison)*
	Who wot yif mannës soulë stye,	*ascends*
	And bestës soulës synken doun?	
	Who knoweth bestës entencioun,	*what animals mean*
70	On her creatour how they crie,	*their creator*
	Save only God that knoweth her soun?	*understands their utterance*
	For this world fareth as a fantasye.	

	Ech secte hopëth to be save,	*sect; saved*
	Boldëly bi her bileve;	*confidently according to their belief*
75	And echon upon God they crave –	
	Why sholde God with hem Him greve?	*trouble Himself with them*
	Echon troweth that other rave,	*believes; others are mad*
	But alle they chesen God for cheve,	*choose God as (their) lord (lit. chief)*
	And hope in God echon they have,	
80	And bi her wit her worching preve.	*their (own) practice; justify*
	Thus mony maters men don meve,	*raise (lit. move, i.e. for discussion)*
	Sechen her wittës how and why;	*rack their brains*
	But Godës merci us al biheve,	*let only; be necessary for all*
	For this world fareth as a fantasye.	

85	For thus men stumble and sere her wit	*blight their intelligence*
	And meven maters many and fele;	*and raise; numerous*
	Sum leven on him, sum leven on hit,	*some believe*

As children lernen for to spele.   *learn to speak*
But non seth non that abit,   *anyone who survives*
90 Whan stilly deth wol on him stele.   *silently; steal*
For He that hest in hevenë sit,   *highest; sits*
He is the help and hope of hele;   *of salvation*
For wo is ende of worldës wele –   *woe is the end of the world's bliss*
Eche lif loke wher that I lye –   *let each person judge whether I lie*
95 This world is fals, fikel and frele,   *frail*
    And fareth but as a fantasye.

Wharto wilne we for to knowe   *to what end do we wish*
The poyntes of Godës priveté?   *the particulars; secret purposes*
More than Him list us for to showe   *it pleases Him*
100 We sholde not knowe in no degré;   *no way*
An idel bost is for to blowe   *boast (it) is to brag*
A mayster of divinité.   *(that one is) a Master of Divinity*
Thenk we lyve in erthe her lowe,   *remember that*
And God on hye in magesté;   *on high*
105 Of matryal mortualité   *of material mortal matters*
Melle we, and of no more maistrie.   *let us concern ourselves; knowledge*
The more we trace the Trinité,
    The more we falle in fantasye.

But leve we our disputisoun,   *let us give up our debate*
110 And leve on Him that al hath wrought;   *trust*
We mowe not preve bi no resoun   *may not explain by any argument*
How He was born that al us bought;
But hol in oure entencioun,   *undivided*
Worshipe we Him in herte and thought,   *let us worship*
115 For He may turne kindes upsodoun,   *turn the natural order upside down*
That allë kindës made of nought.   *created things; from nothing*
Whan al our bokës ben forth brought,
And al our craft of cleregie,   *skill in learning*
And al our wittes ben thurghout sought   *thoroughly investigated*
120   Yit we fare as a fantasye.

Of fantasye is al our fare,   *activity*
Olde and yonge and alle y-fere;   *all together*
But make we merye and sle care,   *slay*
And worshipe God whil we ben here;
125 Spende our god and litel spare,   *substance; save*
And ech man cherice otheres chere.   *encourage others' good spirits*
Thinke how we comen hider al bare,   *naked*
Our wey-wendyng is in a were;   *our departure; state of uncertainty*
Prey we the prince that hath no pere,   *equal*
130 Tak us hol to His merci   *in entirety*
And kepe our conciencë clere –
    For this world is but fantasy.

I, 62   Fortune ~ *Geoffrey Chaucer*

Balades de Visage sanz Peinture

I *Le Pleintif countre Fortune*   *The plaintiff against Fortune*

This wrecched worldës transmutacioun,   *mutability*
As wele or wo, now povre and now honour,   *joy or sorrow; poverty*
Withouten ordre or wis discrecioun   *wise judgement*
Governëd is by Fortunës errour.   *fickleness*
5 But natheles, the lakke of hyr favour   *lack; her*
Ne may nat don me syngen, though I dye,   *make me sing*
Jay tout perdu mon temps et mon labour;   *I have lost all my time and effort*
For fynally, Fortune, I thee defye.   *for in the end; defy*

Yit is me left the lyght of my resoun
10 To knowen frend fro foo in thi mirour;   *friend from foe; your mirror*
So muche hath yit thy whirlinge up and doun
Y-taught me for to knowen in an hour.
But trewëly, no force of thi reddour   *it does not matter about your severity*
To hym that over hymself hath the maystrye;   *control*
15 My suffysauncë shal be my socour,   *self-sufficiency; succour*
For fynally, Fortune, I thee defye.

O Socrates, thou stidfast champyoun,
She never myghtë be thi tormentour;
Thou never dreddëst hyr oppressyoun,
20 Ne in hyr cherë founde thou no savour.   *countenance; pleasure*
Thou knewe wel the deceit of hyr colour,   *her pretence*
And that hir mostë worshipe is to lye.   *her greatest reputation*
I knowe hir ek a fals dissimulour,   *her also (as) a false deceiver*
For fynally, Fortune, I thee defye!

II *La respounse de Fortune au Pleintif*   *The reply of Fortune to the plaintiff*

25 No man ys wrecched but hymself yt wene,   *unless; believes it (to be so)*
And he that hath hymself hath suffisaunce.   *sufficiency*
Whi seystow thanne I am to thee so kene,   *why say you then; so cruel*
That hast thyself out of my governaunce?   *(you) who possess; free from*
Sey thus: 'Graunt mercy of thyn haboundaunce   *say; thank you for; abundance*
30 That thou hast lent or this.' Why wolt thou stryve?   *before this; argue*
What woost thow yit how I thee wol avaunce?   *what do you yet know; will advance*
And ek thou hast thy bestë frende alyve.   *moreover*

I have thee taught divisyoun bytwene	*the difference between*
Frend of effect and frend of countenaunce;	*friend in actuality; in appearance*
35 Thee nedëth nat the galle of no hyene,	*bile; hyena*
That curëth eyen derkëd for penaunce;	*dimmed on account of affliction*
Now seestow cleer that were in ignoraunce.	*you see clearly*
Yit halt thyn ancre and yit thou mayst aryve	*hold fast your anchor; arrive*
Ther bounté berth the keye of my substaunce,	*bears the key; wealth*
40 And ek thou hast thy bestë frend alyve.	
How many have I refusëd to sustene	
Sin I thee fostred have in thy plesaunce.	*well-being*
Woltow than make a statute on thy quene	*law applying to; queen*
That I shal been ay at thyn ordinaunce?	*command*
45 Thou born art in my regne of varyaunce,	*realm of mutability*
Aboute the wheel with other most thou dryve.	*around; others; go (lit. drive)*
My loore is bet than wikke is thi grevaunce,	*teaching is better; harmful; affliction*
And ek thou hast thy bestë frende alyve.	

III *La respounse du Pleintif countre Fortune* *The plaintiff's response to Fortune*

Thy loore I dampne, it is adversité.	
50 My frend maystow nat reven, blinde goddesse;	*take away*
That I thy frendës knowe, I thanke it thee –	
Tak hem agayn, lat hem go lye on presse.	*back; in a closet*
The negardye in keping hyr rychesse	*miserliness; their wealth*
Prenostik is thou wolt hir tour assayle;	*is a sign that; their tower*
55 Wikke appetyt comth ay before syknesse.	*excessive appetite*
In general, this reulë may nat fayle.	

La respounse de Fortune countre le Pleintif *The response of Fortune to the Plaintiff*

Thou pynchëst at my mutabylytée	*findest fault with*
For I thee lente a drope of my rychesse,	*because*
And now me lykëth to withdrawë me.	
60 Why sholdëstow my realté opresse?	*sovereign power suppress*
The see may ebbe and flowen more or lesse;	
The welkne hath myght to shynë, reyne, or hayle;	*sky*
Ryght so mot I kythen my brotelnesse.	*manifest my fickleness*
In general this reulë may nat fayle.	
65 Lo, th'execucion of the majestée	*performance; majesty (i.e. God)*
That al purveyëth of his ryghtwysnesse,	*foresees in his righteousness*
That samë thinge 'Fortunë' clepen ye,	
Ye blindë beestës ful of lewëdnesse.	*ignorance*
The hevene hath propreté of sykernesse,	*the characteristic of stability*
70 This world hath ever restëles travayle;	*ceaseless suffering*
Thy lastë day is ende of myn intresse.	*final day; concern*
In general, this reulë may nat fayle.	

Lenvoy de Fortune	*The conclusion of Fortune*
Princes, I prey you of your gentilesse	*nobility*
Lat nat this man on me thus crye and pleyne,	*cry out and complain*
75 And I shal quytë you your bysynesse	*reward you for your effort*
At my requeste, as three of you or tweyne;	*two*
And but you list releve him of hys peyne,	*unless you wish* (lit. *it pleases you*)
Preyëth hys bestë frend of his noblesse	
That to som beter estat he may attayne.	
Explicit	

I, 63   Truth ~ *Geoffrey Chaucer*

Balade de Bon Conseyl	*Ballade of good counsel*
Flee fro the prees and dwelle with sothefastnesse;	*crowd; truth*
Suffyse unto thy thing though it be smal,	*be content with what you have*
For hord hath hate and clymbyng tykelnesse,	*avarice; hatred; ambition; instability*
Prees hathe envye and wele blent overal.	*wealth blinds everywhere*
5 Savour no more thanne thee byhovë shal,	*relish; than is your due*
Reule wel thiself that other folk canst rede,	*control; (you) who; advise*
And trouthe thee shal delyvere it is no drede.	*set free there is no doubt*
Tempest thee nought al croked to redresse	*excite; crooked (things); set right*
In trust of hir that turnëth as a bal;	*in reliance on her; ball*
10 Gret restë stant in litel besynesse.	*peace of mind resides; endeavour*
Be war therfore to spurne ayeyns an al,	*of kicking against an awl*
Stryve not, as doth the crokkë with the wal.	*struggle not; crock*
Daunte thyself, that dauntëst otheres dede,	*subdue; (you) who rule; deeds*
And trouthe thee shal delyvere it is no drede.	
15 That thee is sent, receyve in buxumnesse;	*what; submissively*
The wrastlyng for the worlde axëth a fal.	*wrestling; invites*
Here is non home, here nys but wyldernesse:	*no home; is nothing but*
Forthe, pylgryme, forthe! Forthe, beste, out of thy stal!	*onwards pilgrim; beast*
Knowe thy contré, loke up, thank God of al;	*look up*
20 Holde the heye wey and lat thy gost thee lede,	*keep to the main; let your spirit*
And trouthe thee shal delyvere it is no drede.	
Envoy	
Therfore, thou Vache, leve thine olde wrecchednesse;	*Sir Philip de la Vache*
Unto the world levë now to be thral.	*cease; enslaved*
Crye Hym mercy, that of His hie goodnesse	*exalted goodness*
25 Made thee of nought, and in especial	*above all*
Drawe unto hym, and pray in general	*beg in general terms*
For thee, and eke for other, hevenlich mede;	*yourself; also for others; reward*
And trouthe thee shal delyvere it is no drede.	
Explicit Le bon counseill de G. Chaucer.	

1, 64 Gentilesse ~ *Geoffrey Chaucer*

Moral Balade of Chaucier

The firstë stocke, fader of gentilesse –	*ancestor; nobility*
What man desirëth gentil for to be	*any man who desires; noble*
Must folowe his trace, and alle his wittës dresse	*his (ancestor's) footsteps; direct*
Vertue to love and vicës for to fle.	*flee*
5 For unto vertue longëth dignité	*honour belongs*
And nought the reverse, saufly dar I deme,	*opposite, safely dare I say*
Al were he mytrë, croune, or dyademe.	*although he (a man) should wear*
This firstë stok was fulle of rightwisenesse,	*full of righteousness*
Trewe of his worde, sobrë, pitous, and fre,	*sober, compassionate and generous*
10 Clene of his gost, and lovëd besynesse	*pure in his spirit; activity*
Ayeinst the vyce of slouthe, in honestée;	*against the vice of sloth; honour*
And, but his heir love vertue as did he,	*unless*
He is nought gentil, though he richë seme,	*wealthy; appear*
Al were he mytrë, croune, or dyademe.	
15 Vice may welle be heire to olde richesse,	*well be heir to ancestral wealth*
But there may no man, as men may welle se,	*may well see*
Bequethe his heire his vertuous noblesse	*leave to*
(That is approprid unto no degré	*is the property of no social rank*
But to the firstë fader in magestée,	*but of*
20 That makëth hem his heirës that hym queme),	*who please him*
Alle were he mytrë, croune, or diademe.	

1, 65 Every day thou myghtëst lere

Gay, gay, gay, gay,	*gay / Gay*
Think on dredful domësday.	
Every day thou myghtëst lere	*learn*
To helpe thiself whil thou art here;	
5 Whan thou art ded and leyd on bere,	*bier*
Cryst help thi soule, for thou ne may.	
Thynk, man, on thi wyttës fyve;	*senses*
Do sum good whil thou art on lyve;	*alive*
Go to cherche and do thee shryve,	*make your confession*
10 And bryng thi soule in good aray.	*into a good state*
Thynk, man, on thi synnës seven;	
Think how meri it is in heven;	
Prey to God with myldë steven	*gentle voice*
He be thin help on domësday.	*that He may be*

15 Lokë that thou non thing stere   *see that you offer incense to nothing*
    Ne non fals wytnessë bere;
    Thynk how Cryst was stunge with spere   *pierced*
        Whan he deyed on Good Fryday.

    Lok that thou ne sle non man
20 Ne do non foly with non womman;   *nor commit adultery*
    Thynk, the blod fro Ihesu ran
        Whan he deyed, withouten nay.

I, 66   If thou serve a lord of prys

Bewar, sqwyer, yeman, and page,   *servant*
For servyse is non heritage.   *inheritance*

    If thou serve a lord of prys,   *worth*
    Be not to boystous in thin servys;   *too zealous*
5   Damne not thin sowlë in non wys,   *way*
        For servyse is non heritage.

    Winteres wether and wommanes thought
    And lordës lovë chaungëth oft;
    This is the sothe if it be sought,   *truth*
10   For servyse is non heritage.

    Now thou art gret, tomorwen shal I,   *I shall be*
    As lordës chaungen her baly;   *their bailiff*
    In thin welthe werk sikerly,   *for your (own) prosperity work steadily*
        For servyse is non heritage.

15 Than serve we God in allë wyse,
    He shal us quiten our servyse   *repay*
    And yeve us yiftës most of pryse,   *worth*
        Hevene to be our heritage.

Devotional Lyrics

I, 67   Swetë Jhesu, king of blisse

Swetë Jhesu, king of blisse,
Min hertë love, min hertë lisse,   *heart's love, my heart's joy*
Thou art swetë mid y-wisse,   *sweet indeed*
Wo is him that thee shal misse.   *who will lose you*

5 Swete Jhesù, min hertë light,   *heart's*
Thou art dai withouten night,
Thou yeve me strengthe and ekë might   *give me; and also*
For to loven thee al right.   *aright*

Swete Jhesù, my soulë bote,   *soul's salvation*
10 In min herte thou sette a rote   *may you plant a root*
Of thy love that is so swote,   *so sweet*
And wite hit that hit springë mote.   *guard it so that it may grow*

I, 68   Jhesù, swete is the love of thee

Jhesù, swete is the love of thee,   *sweet is*
Noon other thing so swete may be;
No thing that men may heere and see
Hath no swetnesse ayeyns thee.   *compared with thee*

5 Jhesù, no song may be swettèr,
No thing in hertë blisfullèr,   *in heart more blissful*
Nought may be feelëd lightsomèr,   *be felt more joyous*
Than thou, so swete a lovyèr.   *lover*

Jhesù, thi love was us so fre   *to us so generous*
10 That it fro hevenë broughtë thee;
For love thou derë boughtëst me,   *dearly*
For love thou heng on roodë tre.   *hung on the rood tree (cross)*

Jhesù, for love thou toledëst wrong,   *suffered*
Woundës sore, and peynës strong;   *torments severe*
15 Thine peynës reuthful were and long,   *pitiful*
No man may hem telle, ne song.   *them tell; nor song*

Jhesù, for love thou bood so wo   *experienced such woe*
That blody stremës ronne thee fro;   *ran from you*
Thi whytë sides woxe blew and blo,   *became black and blue*
20 Oure synnes it made so, weylawo!   *alas!*

Jhesù, for love thou stigh on roode,   *ascended upon the cross*
For love thou yaf thin hertë bloode;   *gave your heart's blood*
Love thee made my soulës foode,   *Love made you*
Thi love us boughtë til al goode.   *for all that is good*

25 Jhesù my love, thou were so fre;   *so generous*
    Al that thou didest for love of me;
    What shal I for that yeldë thee?   *render you*
    Thou askëst nought but love of me.   *you ask nothing but love from me*

    Jhesù my God, Jhesù my kyng,
30 Thou askëst me noon other thing,   *ask of me no*
    But trewë love and hert-yernyng,   *heart-felt yearning*
    And lovë-teeres with swete mournyng.   *tears of love; longing*

    Jhesù my love, Jhesù my lyght,
    I wol thee love and that is right;   *I will*
35 Do me love thee with al my myght,   *make me*
    And for thee mourne bothe day and nyght.   *yearn*

    Jhesù, do me so yernë thee   *make me so to desire thee*
    That my thought ever upon thee be;
    With thin eyë loke to me,
40 And myldëly my nedë se.   *gently; need; look upon*

    Jhesù, thi love be al my thought,
    Of other thing ne recche me nought;   *I care nothing*
    Thanne have I thi wille al wrought,
    That havëst me ful derë bought.   *dearly*

I, 69   Now I se blosmë sprynge

    Now I se blosmë sprynge,   *blossom flourish*
    Ich herde a foulës song,   *I heard a bird's song*
    A swetë love-longinge
    Myn hertë thurghout sprong,   *throughout; has sprung up*
5 That is of lovë newe,   *about a new love*
    That is so swete and trewe,   *so sweet and true*
    Hit gladëth al my song;   *it gladdens*
    Ich wot al mid y-wisse   *know with certainty*
    My lyf and eke my blysse   *and also*
10 Is al theron y-long.   *dependent*

    Of Jhesu Crist I synge,
    That is so fayr and fre,   *noble*
    Swetest of allë thynge,
    His owne Ich owe wel be;   *His own I ought indeed to be*

15 Fùl fer He me soughte,   *far*
   Mìd hard He me boughte   *with suffering*
   With woundës two and thre;
   Wel sòre He was y-swonge,   *very painfully; scourged*
   For me mid spere y-stonge,   *with a spear; pierced*
20 Y-nailëd to the tree.

   Whan Ich myselvë stond   *stand*
   And mid herte y-see,   *with (my) heart; see*
   Y-thirlëd fet and honde   *pierced; feet and hands*
   With gretë nailës three –
25 Blody was His heved,   *head*
   Of Him nas nought by-levëd   *was no part left*
   That of pyne was fre –   *from pain was free*
   Wel oughtë myn herte,
   Al for His lovë smerte,   *smart*
30 Syk and sory be.   *sigh and be sorry*

   A way! that I ne can   *alas!*
   To Him turne al my thought,
   And make Him my lemmàn   *lover*
   That thus me hath y-bought   *redeemed*
35 With pine and sorwë longe,   *pain*
   With woundës depe and stronge –
   Of love ne can I nought!   *I am incapable*
   His blod that fel to grounde
   Out of His swetë wound,   *wounds*
40 Of pine us hath y-brought.   *out of torment*

   Jhesu, lemman softe,   *gentle lover*
   Thou yif me strengthe and might,   *give me*
   Longinge sore and ofte   *yearning sore and often*
   To servë thee aright;
45 And leve me pinë drye,   *let me suffer pain*
   For thee, swetë Marie,
   That art so fayr and bryght.
   Mayde and moder milde,
   For love of thinë childe,
50 Ernde us henenë light.   *obtain for us the light of heaven*

   Jhesu, lemman swete,
   I sendë thee this songe,
   And wel ofte I thee grete   *greet*
   And biddë thee among;   *pray to you constantly*
55 Yif me sonë lete,   *grant me soon to forsake*
   And minë sinnës bete,   *atone for*
   That I have do thee wrong.   *whereby; have done*

At mine lyvës ende,   *life's end*
Whan I shal hennë wende,   *hence depart*
60 Jhesù, me underfonge! Amen.   *receive*

I, 70   Love me broughte

Love me broughte,
And love me wroughte,   *created*
   Man, to be thi fere;   *companion*
Love me fedde,
5 And love me ledde,
   And love me letted here.   *kept me here*

Love me slow,   *slew*
And love me drow,   *drew*
   And love me leyde on bere;   *laid on a bier*
10 Love is my pes,   *peace*
For love I ches   *chose*
   Man to byen dere.   *buy (i.e. redeem) at a cost*

Ne dred thee nought,
I have thee sought,
15   Bothen day and night;   *both*
To haven thee,
Wel is me,
   I have thee wonne in fight.   *won*

I, 71   Alas! alas! wel evel I sped!

Alas! alas! wel evel I sped!   *very ill have I fared*
For sinne Jesù fro me ys fled,
   That levely fere.   *dear companion*
At my dore He stant alone   *at my door He stands*
5 And calleth 'Undo!' with rewful mone,   *with pitiful lament*
   On this manere:

'Undo, my leef, my dowvë dere!   *my beloved, my dear dove*
Undo! Why stond I steken out here?   *stand I shut out*
   Ich am thi make!   *your spouse*
10 Lo, mi lokkes and ek myn heved   *my locks and also my head*
Are al wyth blody dropes byweved   *covered*
   For thinë sake.'

1, 72   I am Jhesù, that com to fight

I am Jhesù, that com to fight — *who came*
   Withouten sheld and spere, — *shield and spear*
Ellës were thi deth y-dight, — *otherwise; destined*
   Yif mi fighting ne were. — *if it had not been for*
5 Sithe I am come and have thee brought — *since I have come*
   A blisful bote of bale, — *salvation from torment*
Undo thin herte, tel me thi thought,
   Thi sinnës grete and smale.

1, 73   In the vaile of restles mynd

In the vaile of restles mynd — *vale*
   I sought in mounteyn and in mede, — *meadow*
Trustyng a trewe love for to fynd.
   Upon an hyll than toke I hede, — *took I heed*
5 A voice I herd (and neer I yede) — *nearer I went*
In gret dolour complaynyng tho, — *grief; then*
   'See, dere soule, my sidës blede, — *bleed*
     Quia amore langueo.' — *because I languish for love*

Upon thys mount I found a tree,
10   Under thys tree a man sittyng;
From hede to fote wounded was he,
   Hys hertë-blode I saw bledyng,
   A semely man to be a kyng, — *comely man*
A graciouse face to loke unto. — *look upon*
15   I asked hym how he had paynyng: — *why he suffered*
     He said, *'Quia amore langueo.'*

'I am trew love that fals was never.
   My sister, mannes soule, I loved hir thus;
Bicause I wold on no wyse dissever — *be separated*
20   I left my kyngdome glorious;
   I purveyd hyr a paleis precious; — *provided; palace*
She flytt, I folowed; I loved her so — *fled*
   That I suffred thes paynës piteous, — *pitiable*
     Quia amore langueo.

25 'My faire love, and my spousë bryght,
   I saved hyr fro betyng, and she hath me bet; — *beating; beaten*
I clothed hyr in grace and hevenly lyght,
   This blody surcote she hath on me set. — *surcoat*
   For longyng love I will not let; — *because of love-longing; give up*
30 Swetë strokës be thes, lo!
   I have loved ever as I het, — *promised*
     Quia amore langueo.

'I crouned hyr with blis, and she me with thorne,
   I led hyr to chambre, and she me to dye;
35 I brought hyr to worship, and she me to scorne,   *honour*
   I dyd hyr reverence, and she me vilanye.   *shame*
    To love that loveth is no maystrye,   *to love one who loves; great skill*
    Hyr hate made never my love hyr foo;   *hatred; enemy*
     Ask then no moo questions why,   *no more*
40   *Quia amore langueo.*

'Loke unto myn handës, man!
   Thes gloves were given me whan I hyr sought;
They be nat white, but rede and wan,   *discoloured*
   Embroudred with blode (my spouse them bought!);   *embroidered*
45   They wyll not off – I leve them nought!   *come off; discard them not*
I wowe hyr with them where ever she go.   *woo her; goes*
   Thes handes full frendly for hyr fought,   *so lovingly*
     Quia amore langueo.

'Marvell not, man, though I sitt styll;
50   My love hath shod me wonder strayte.   *shod me wondrously tight*
She bokled my fete, as was hyr wyll,   *buckled*
   With sharpë nailes (well thou mayst waite!).   *may see*
   In my love was never dissaite,   *deceit*
For all my membres I have opend hyr to;   *limbs*
55   My body I made hyr hertës baite,   *bait for her heart*
     Quia amore langueo.

'In my syde I have made hyr nest;
   Loke in, how wide a wound is here!   *inside*
This is hyr chambre, here shall she rest,
60   That she and I may slepe in fere.   *together*
   Here may she wasshe, if any filth were;
Here is socour for all hyr wo;
   Come if she will, she shall have chere,   *be welcome*
     Quia amore langueo.

65 'I will abide till she be redy,
   I will to hir send or she say nay;   *to her send messages until*
If she be recheless, I will be redy,   *heedless; attentive*
   If she be dangerous, I will hyr pray.   *disdainful; beseech*
   If she do wepe, than byd I nay,   *then shall I beg her not to*
70 Myn armes ben spred to clypp hyr to.   *to embrace her*
   Crye ones, 'I come' – now, soule, assay!   *once; try!*
     Quia amore langueo.

'I sitt on an hille for to se fer, *further*
 I loke to the vayle, my spouse I se; *look to the vale*
75 Now renne she away-ward, now come she ner, *should she run; nearer*
 Yet fro myn eye-sight she may nat be.
 Some waite their pray, to make hyr flee; *lie in wait for their prey*
I renne tofore to chastise hyr fo. *ahead; to subdue*
 Recover, my soule, agayne to me, *return*
80 *Quia amore langueo.*

'My swetë spouse, will we go play?
 Apples ben rype in my gardine; *are ripe; garden*
I shall clothe thee in new array,
 Thy mete shall be mylk, honye, and wyne. *your food*
85 Now, dere soule, lat us go dyne; *let us*
Thy sustenaunce is in my scrippë – lo! *bag*
 Tary not now, fayre spousë myne,
  Quia amore langueo.

'If thou be foule, I shall make thee clene,
90 If thou be sike, I shall thee hele, *sick*
If thou ought mourne, I shall thee mene – *for anything; comfort*
 Spouse, why wilt thou nought with me dele? *have anything to do with me*
 Thou foundëst never love so lele; *faithful*
What wilt thou, soule, that I shall do?
95 I may of unkindnes thee appele, *of ingratitude; accuse*
  Quia amore langueo.

'What shall I do now with my spouse?
 Abyde I will hyr gentilnisse. *await; graciousness*
Wold she loke ones out of hyr house *if she would look once*
100 Of fleshly affecciouns and unclennisse, *carnal desires*
 Hyr bed is made, hyr bolster is blysse, *pillow*
Hyr chamber is chosen – such ar no mo! *choice – there are no more such*
 Loke out at the wyndows of kyndnisse, *affection*
  Quia amore langueo.

105 'My spouse is in chamber, hold your pees, *in (her) chamber; peace*
 Make no noyse, but lat hyr slepe. *let*
My babe shall suffrë no disese, *distress*
 I may not here my dere childe wepe,
 For with my pappe I shall hyr kepe. *for close to my breast I shall*
110 No wonder though I tend hyr to – *attend*
 Thys hoole in my side had never ben so depe
  But *quia amore langueo.*

'Long and love thou never so hye,	*though you yearn and love ever so intensely*
Yit is my love more than thyn may be;	
115 Thou gladdest, thou wepest – I sitt thee by;	*you rejoice; weep; I will sit*
Yit myght thou, spouse, loke ones at me!	*yet if you could; once*
Spouse, shold I alway fedë thee	*feed*
With childës mete? Nay, love, nat so –	*food*
I preve thy love with adversité,	*test*
120 *Quia amore langueo*.	

'Wax not wery, myn owne dere wyfe!	*grow*
What mede is aye to live in comfort?	*what reward is there always*
For in tribulacioun I renne more rife,	*I am found more commonly*
Ofter tymes than in disport –	*happiness*
125 In welth, in wo, ever I support.	*prosperity; misery*
Than, dere soule, go never me fro!	*then*
Thy mede is marked, whan thou art mort,	*reward is assigned; dead*
Quia amore langueo. '	

I, 74   Levëdie, Ich thonkë thee

Levëdie, Ich thonkë thee,	*Lady, I thank you*
With hertë swithë milde,	*very humble*
That god that thou hast i-don me	*for that good which*
With thine swetë childe.	
5 Thou art god and swete and bright	
Of alle other y-coren;	*chosen above all others*
Of thee was that swetë wight	*person*
That was Jesùs y-boren.	*born*
Maidë mildë, bidde I thee	*pray*
10 With thinë swetë childe,	
That thou erendië me	*intercede for me*
To haven Godës milde.	*God's mercy*
Moder, lokë thou on me	
With thinë swetë eye;	
15 Reste and blissë yif thou me,	*give*
My lady, then Ich deye.	*when I die*

I, 75   Of on that is so fayr and bright

Of on that is so fayr and bright,	*of one*
Velud maris stella,	*as the star of the sea*
Brighter than the dayës light,	
Parens et puella;	*mother and maiden*

5　Ich crie to thee, thou se to me,	*look upon me*
Lady, preye thi sone for me,	
Tam pia,	*so devoted*
That Ich motë come to thee,	*may*
Maria.	
10　Lady, flour of allë thing,	
Rosa sine spina,	*rose without thorn*
Thou berë Jhesu, hevenë-king,	*bore; king of heaven*
Gratia divina.	*by divine grace*
Of allë thou berëst the pris,	*you bear the prize*
15　Lady, quene of Paradys	*Paradise*
Electa,	*chosen*
Maydë mildë, moder ek	*also*
Effecta.	*proven*
Of carë conseil thou art best,	*in sorrow; counsellor*
20　　*Felix fecundata;*	*happy fruitful one*
Of allë wery thou art rest,	
Mater honorata.	*revered mother*
Bisek thou Him with mildë mod	*beseech; gentle heart*
That for us allë shad His blod	*shed*
25　　*In cruce,*	*on the cross*
That we moten come til Him	*we may come to Him*
In luce.	*in light*
Al this world it was forlore	*lost*
Eva peccatrice,	*through Eve the sinner*
30　Til our Loverd was y-bore	*lord; born*
De te genitrice;	*from you, mother*
With '*Ave*' it went away	*'Hail'; it (dark night)*
Thuster night, and com the day	*dark night; came*
Salutis;	*of salvation*
35　The wellë springëth out of thee	*well*
Virtutis.	*of virtue*
Wel He wot He is thi sone	*knows*
Ventre quem portasti;	*whom you carried in the womb*
He wil nought wernë thee thy bone	*deny you your request*
40　　*Parvum quem lactasti.*	*little one to whom you gave suck*
So hendë and so god He is,	*gracious*
He hath brought us into blis	
Superni,	*of heaven*
That hath y-dit the foulë pit	*who hath shut*
45　　*Inferni.*	*of hell*

I, 76   Edi be thou, hevenë quenë

Edi be thou, hevenë quenë,	*blessed; queen of heaven*
Folkës frovre and englës blis,	*comfort; angels'*
Moder unwemmëd and maiden clenë,	*unspotted; pure*
Swich in world non other nis.	*such; no other is*
5 On thee hit is wel eth-senë	*very evident*
Of allë wommen thou havest the pris.	*you are supreme*
My swetë Levedy, her my benë,	*lady, hear my prayer*
And rew of me yif thi wille is.	*have pity on me if*
Thou asteye so the day-rewë	*arose like the dawn*
10 That delëth from the derkë night;	*which parts; dark night*
Of thee sprang a lemë newë	*from you; light*
That al this world havëth y-light.	*has lit*
Nis non maide of thinë hewë,	*complexion*
So fair, so shene, so rudy, so bright;	*so fair, so beautiful, so rosy*
15 Swetë Lady of me thou rewë	*have pity on me*
And havë merci of thin knight.	
Sprongë blosme of onë rotë,	*blossom sprung from a single root*
The Holy Gost thee reste upon;	*rested*
That was for mankinnës botë	*salvation*
20 And here soule t'alesen for on.	*their souls to free in exchange for one*
Ladi mildë, softe and swotë,	*gentle and sweet*
Ich crie thee merci, Ich am thy mon,	*your servant*
Bothe to hondë and to fotë,	*both hand and foot*
On allë wisë that Ich con.	*in every way that I know*
25 Thou art erthe to godë sedë,	*earth for good seed*
On thee lightë th'evenë-dew;	*alighted the heavenly dew*
Of thee sprang the edi bledë,	*from you; blessed fruit*
The Holy Gost hir on thee sew.	*sowed it in thee*
Thou bring us out of care, of dredë	
30 That Evë bitterliche us brew;	*brewed for us*
Thou shalt us into hevenë ledë –	*lead*
Wel swetë is the ilkë dew.	*that same dew*
Moder ful of thewës hendë,	*gracious virtues*
Maidë dreye and wel y-taught,	*patient*
35 Ich am in thine lovë-bendë,	*love-bonds*
And to thee is al my draught.	*my inclination*
Thou me shild, ye, from the fendë,	*shield me, indeed, from the Devil*
As thou art fre and wilt and maught,	*are generous and willing and can*
Help me to my livës endë,	
40 And make me with thin sone y-saught.	*with your son; reconciled*

I, 77   Gabriel, from hevenë king

Gabriel, from hevenë king	*from the king of heaven*
Sent to the maidë swetë,	
Broughtë hire blisful tiding	*tidings*
And faire he gan hire gretë:	*courteously he greeted her*
5 'Hail be thou, ful of grace aright,	*indeed*
For Goddës sone, this hevenë light,	*light of heaven*
For mannës love	
Wil man bicome,	
And takë	
10 Flesh of thee, maiden bright,	
Mankin fre for to makë	*mankind free*
Of sinne and devlës might.'	
Mildëliche him gan answere	*gently*
The mildë maiden thannë:	*then*
15 'Whichëwisë sholde Ich bere	*in what way; bear*
Child withouten mannë?'	*without a husband*
Th'angel saidë: 'Ne dred thee nought,	
Thurgh th'Holi Gost shal ben y-wrought,	*through; shall be done*
This ilkë thing	*this very thing*
20 Wherof tiding	
Ich bringë;	
Al mankin worth y-bought	*mankind shall be redeemed*
Thurgh thy swetë childingë,	*child-bearing*
And out of pine y-brought.'	*torment*
25 Whan the maiden understod	
And th'angles wordës herdë,	
Mildëliche with mildë mod	*gently with gentle heart*
To th'angel she answerdë:	
'Our lordës thew-maiden i-wis	*handmaiden indeed*
30 Ich am, that her-aboven is.	*who is above*
Anentës me	*concerning me*
Fulforthëd be	*be fulfilled*
Thy sawë;	*your word*
That Ich, sithe His wil is,	*since it is His will*
35 Maiden, withouten lawë,	*against the law of nature*
Of moder have the blis.'	*of a mother; should have*
Th'angel wente away mid than,	*at that*
Al out of hirë sightë;	
Hirë wombe arisë gan	
40 Thurgh th'Holi Gostës mightë.	
In hire was Crist biloke anon,	*enclosed forthwith*
Soth God, soth man in flesh and bon,	*true; bone*

And of hir fles   *flesh*
Y-borë wes   *was born*
45   At timë.   *at the due time*
Wherthrough us cam god won;   *whereby; good hope*
He bought us out of pinë,   *redeemed; torment*
And let Him for us slon.   *allowed himself to be slain for us*

Maiden-moder makëles,   *virgin-mother peerless*
50   Of milcë ful y-boundë,   *with mercy fully endowed*
Bid for us Him that thee ches,   *pray for us to Him who chose you*
At whom thou gracë fundë,   *from whom; found*
That He foryive us sinne and wrake,   *that He may forgive; injury*
And clene of evry gilt us make,   *free from all guilt; make us*
55   And hevnë blis,   *and the bliss of heaven*
Whan our time is   *when it is our time*
  To stervë,   *to die*
Us yive, for thinë sake,   *give us (and grant us)*
Him so her for to servë,   *here*
60   That He us to Him take.   *may take us to Himself*

I, 78   Now this foulës singëth

Now this foulës singëth   *these birds sing*
and makëth herë blis,
Ànd that gres up thringëth   *grass pushes up*
ànd levëth the ris;   *the branch sprouts leaves*
5 Of on Ich willë singen   *one*
that is makëles,   *peerless*
The king of allë kingës
to moder He hire ches.   *as mother; chose*

She is withouten sinne
10   ànd withouten hore,   *stain*
Y-come of kingës kinne   *from a lineage of kings*
ànd of Jessës more;   *stock*
The loverd of mankinne   *lord of mankind*
of hire was y-boren
15 To bringe us out of sinne,
elles we were forloren.   *otherwise we had been lost*

Gabriel hire grette   *greeted*
and saidë hire 'Ave,   *'hail'*
Marie ful of grace,
20   our loverd be with thee,
The fruyt of thinë wombe
y-blessëd mot it be.   *may it be*

Thou shalt go with childe,
    for sothe Ich seye it thee.' *in truth; say*

25 And tharë gretinge, *and about the greeting*
    that angel had y-brought,
She gan to bithenchen *began to think*
    and meindë hirë thought; *and was perplexed*
She saidë to the angel:
30   'How may tiden this? *happen*
Of mannës y-monë *of intercourse with a man*
    not I nought, y-wis.' *I know nothing, for sure*

Maid she was with childe
    and maiden her-biforen, *before that*
35 And maiden er sithen *still after*
    hire child was y-boren;
Maide and moder nas *was not*
    never non but she, *ever any (lit. never none)*
Wel mightë she berigge *the bearer*
40   of Goddës sonë be.

Y-blessëd be that child
    and the moder ek, *also*
And the swetë brestë
    that hire sonë sek; *sucked*
45 Y-herëd be the time *praised be*
    that swich child was y-boren, *such a*
That lesëd al of pinë *delivered everyone from torment*
    that er was forloren. *who previously had been lost*

I, 79   I syng of a mayden

I syng of a mayden
    that is makëles, *peerless*
King of allë kingës
    to here sone she ches. *as her son she chose*

5 He cam also styllë *as silently*
    ther his moder was, *where his mother was*
As dew in Aprylle
    that fallëth on the gras.

He cam also styllë
10   to his moderës bowr, *bower*
As dew in Aprille
    that fallëth on the flour. *flower*

He cam also stillë
    ther his moder lay,   *where*
15 As dew in Aprille
    that fallëth on the spray.   *leafy branch*

Moder and mayden
    was never non but she –   *was never anyone*
    Wel may swych a lady   *such*
20   Godës moder be!

1, 80   I saw a fair maiden

'Lullay, myn lyking,   *beloved*
    my dere sone, myn sweting,   *sweet one*
Lullay, my dere herte,
    myn owyn dere derling.'   *darling*

5 I saw a fair maiden
    sitten and singe,
She lullëd a litel child,
    a swetë lording.   *sweet lord*
    Lullay, etc.

10 That echë Lord is that   *very Lord*
    that made allë thing;   *all things*
Of allë lordës he is Lord,
    of allë kingës King.
    Lullay, etc.

15 Ther was mikel melody   *much*
    at that childës birth;
Allë tho were in hevenë blis,   *those (who); in the bliss of heaven*
    they madë mikel mirth.
    Lullay, etc.

20 Aungelës bright, they sang that night
    and saiden to that child,
'Blissëd be thou, and so be she   *blessed*
    that is both meek and mild.'   *meek and gentle*
    Lullay, etc.

25 Prey we now to that child,
    and to his moder dere,
Graunt hem his blissing   *to grant them; blessing*
    that now maken chere.   *now rejoice (lit. make joy)*
    Lullay, etc.

I, 81   As I lay upon a night

Lullay, lullay, lay lay, lullay:
Mi derë moder, sing lullay.   *dear mother*

As I lay upon a night
   Alone in my longing,   *yearning*
5 Me thoughte I saw a wonder sight,   *it seemed to me; wondrous*
   A maiden child rokking.
      Lullay, lullay, etc.

The maiden wolde withouten song   *wished*
   Hire child o slepë bringe;   *to put her child to sleep*
10 The child thoughtë she dide him wrong,
   And bad his moder singe.
      Lullay, lullay, etc.

'Sing now, moder,' seide that child,
   'What me shal befalle   *what is to happen to me*
15 Here after whan I come to ild,   *come to maturity*
   So don modrës alle.   *as do*
      Lullay, lullay, etc.

'Ech a moder, trewëly,   *every mother, truly*
   That can hire cradel kepe   *who knows how; to watch over*
20 Is wone to lullen lovëly   *is wont to lull lovingly*
   And singe hire child o slepe.   *to sleep*
      Lullay, lullay, etc.

'Swetë moder, fair and fre,   *gracious*
   Sithen that it is so,   *since*
25 I preye thee that thou lullë me   *lull*
   And sing somwhat therto.'   *something as well*
      Lullay, lullay, etc.

'Swetë sonë,' seydë she,
   'Wherof sholde I singe?   *of what*
30 Wist I never yet more of thee   *knew I*
   But Gabrieles gretinge.   *than Gabriel's greeting*
      Lullay, lullay, etc.

'He grette me godli on his kne   *greeted me graciously*
   And seydë, "Hail, Marie
35 Ful of grace, God is with thee;
   Beren thou shalt Messyé."   *bear; the Messiah*
      Lullay, lullay, etc.

'I wondrëd mychel in my thought,   *greatly; mind*
   For man wold I right none.   *a husband; did I wish*
40 "Marie," he seydë, "drede thee nought: *fear not*
   Let God of hevene alone.   *leave it to*
      Lullay, lullay, etc.

'"The Holi Gost shal don al this,"   *will do*
   He seyde withouten wone,   *without delay*
45 That I sholde beren mannës blis,   *man's bliss*
   Thee, my swetë sone.
      Lullay, lullay, etc.

'He seidë, "Thou shalt bere a king   *bear*
   In King Davidës see,"   *kingdom*
50 In al Jacobs wonying,   *the house of Jacob*
   Ther king sholde he be.
      Lullay, lullay, etc.

'He seydë that Elizabeth,
   That baraine was before,   *barren*
55 "A knavë child conceyvëd hath,   *male; conceived*
   To me leve thou the more."   *believe me the more (for that)*
      Lullay, lullay, etc.

'I answërëd blythëly,   *gladly*
   Fòr his word me payde,   *pleased me*
60 "Lo, Godës servant her am I;
   Be it as thou me sayde."
      Lullay, lullay, etc.

'Ther, as he seidë, I thee bare   *bore*
   On midwinter night,
65 On maydenhed, withouten care,   *in virginity, without sorrow*
   Be grace of God almight.   *by the grace; almighty*
      Lullay, lullay, etc.

'The herdes that wakëd in the wolde   *shepherds that kept watch on the hill*
   Herde a wonder mirthe   *wondrous rejoicing*
70 Of aungëlës ther as they tolde,   *angels; sang*
   In timë of thi birthe.   *at the time of*
      Lullay, lullay, etc.

'Swetë sonë, sikerly,   *truly*
   No more can I say;
75 And if I coudë, fayn wold I   *glad would I be*
   To don al at thy pay.'   *all to your liking*
      Lullay, lullay, etc.

. . . .

Certeynly this sight I say,   *saw*
    This song I herdë singe,
80 As I lay this Yolës day   *Christmas Day*
    Alone in my longinge.   *yearning*
        Lullay, lullay, etc.

I, 82   Lullay, lullay, litel child, child rèstë thee a throwe

Lullay, lullay, litel child,
    child rèstë thee a throwe,   *rest you for a while*
Fro heighë hider art thou sent   *from on high hither*
    with us to wonë lowe;   *to dwell below*
5 Poure and litel art thou mad,   *poor; made*
    uncouth and unknowe,   *strange and unknown*
Pine and wo to suffren her   *torment and misery; here*
    for thing that was thin owe.   *for a creature who was your own*
Lullay, lullay, litel child,
10   sorwë might thou make;   *well might you cry*
    Thou art sent into this world,
        as thou were forsake.   *as if you were abandoned*

Lullay, lullay, litel grom,   *lad*
    king of allë thinge,   *things*
15 Whan I thenke of thy mischeef,   *misfortune*
    me list wel litel singe;   *I have very little wish to sing*
But caren I may for sorwë,   *but grieve I may*
    yif love wer in myn herte,
For swichë peynes as thou shalt drye   *such torments; endure*
20   were never non so smerte.   *any so painful*
    Lullay, lullay, litel child
        ful wel might thou crie,
    For than thi body is bleik and blak   *for when; pale and wan*
        sone after shal ben drie.   *soon after it will be shrivelled*

25 Child, it is a weping dale   *vale of tears*
    that thou art comen inne,
Thy pourë cloutes it proven wel,   *poor rags prove it well*
    thy bed mad in the binne;   *made; manger*
Cold and hunger thou must thole   *suffer*
30   as thou were gete in sinne,   *as if you had been begotten*
    And after deyen on the tre   *die*
        for love of al mankinne.   *mankind*
    Lullay, lullay, litel child,
        no wonder though thou care,   *lament*
35 Thou art come amongës hem   *among those*
    that thi deth shullen yare.   *who; will prepare*

Lullay, lullay, litel child,
    for sorwë might thou grete,   *weep*
The anguissh that thou suffren shalt
40   shal don thee blod to swete;   *will make you sweat blood*
Naked, bounden shalt thou ben,
    and sithen sorë bete,   *afterwards sorely beaten*
No thing fre upon thy body   *free*
    of pinë shal be lete.   *of torment; left*
45   Lullay, lullay, litel child,
    it is al for thy fo,   *because of thine enemy (the Devil)*
The hardë bond of love-longing   *the cruel fetter of love-longing*
    that thee hath bounden so.

Lullay, lullay, litel child,
50   litel child thin ore!   *have mercy (lit. thy mercy)*
It is al for our owen gilt
    that thou art peynëd sore;   *punished severely*
But woldë we yet kindë be,   *if we would yet be obedient*
    and live after thy lore,   *according to thy teaching*
55 And leten sinnë for thy love,   *renounce*
    ne keptëst thou no more.   *you would wish for nothing more*
Lullay, lullay, litel child,
    softë slep and faste,   *gently sleep and soundly*
In sorwë endëth every love
60   but thin at the laste.   *except thine*

I, 83   Ler to love as I love thee

'Ler to love as I love thee,   *learn*
On al my limes thou might y-se   *limbs; see*
    How sore they quake for colde;   *painfully they shiver*
For thee I suffrë mychel wo,   *suffer great anguish*
5 Love me, swetë, an no mo,   *sweet one, and no other*
    To thee I take and holde.'

'Jhesu, swetë sonë dere,   *dear*
In porful bed thou list now here,   *on a pitiful bed you lie*
    And that me grevëth sore;   *grieves me bitterly*
10 For thi cradel is as a bere,   *byre*
Ox and assë ben thi fere,   *are your companions*
    Wepe may I therfore.   *weep*

'Jhesu, swetë, be nought wroth,   *angry*
I have nother clout ne cloth   *neither rag nor cloth*
15   Thee inne for to folde;   *wrap*

I n'ave but a clout of lappe,   *I have nothing but a piece of sleeve*
Therefòre lay thi feet to my pappe   *breast*
   And kep thee fro the colde.   *keep yourself from*

'Cold thee taketh, I may wel se –   *cold seizes you*
20 For love of man it motë be,   *must be*
   Thee to suffren wo;
For bet it is thou suffrë this   *for better it is that*
Than man forberë hevenë blis –   *than that man should forgo*
   Thou most him bye therto.   *must; redeem*

25 'Sithe it most nedes that thou be ded   *since it must needs be; dead*
To saven mankin from the qued,   *mankind; Devil*
   Thy swetë wil be do.   *will be done*
But let me nought dwelle her to longe, *too*
After thy deth me underfonge   *take*
30   To ben for evermo.'   *to be (with you) for evermore*

1, 84   Now goth sonnë under wode

Now goth sonnë under wode,   *goes the sun under the wood*
Me reweth, Marie, thi fairë rode.   *I grieve, Mary, for your fair face*
Now goth sonnë under tre,   *the tree*
Me reweth, Marie, thi sone and thee.   *son*

1, 85   Whyt was Hys naked brest

Whyt was Hys naked brest   *white*
   and red of blod Hys syde,   *red with blood*
Bleyk was His fair andlèd,   *pale; fair face*
   His woundës dep and wide,   *deep*
5 And Hys armes y-streight,   *stretched*
   hey upon the rode;   *high upon the cross*
On fif stedes on His body   *five places*
   the stremës ran o blode.   *the streams of blood ran*

1, 86   Whyt is Thi naked brest

Whyt is Thi naked brest
   and blodi is Thi side,
Starkë are Thine armes   *rigid*
   that strecchëde are so wyde.
5 Falwe is Thi fairë ler   *pale; fair cheek*
   and dimmyëth Thi sighte,   *grows dim*
Drie is Thin hendë body   *lifeless; gracious body*
   on rodë so y-tighte.   *stretched*

Thine thighës hongen colde	*hang*
10 al so the marble-ston,	*as marble*
Thinë thirlëde fet	*pierced*
the redë blod by-ron.	*drenched*

I, 87   Whan Ich se on rode

Whan Ich se on rode	*on the cross*
Jhesu mi lemmàn,	*my beloved*
And beside Him stonde	*stand*
Marie an Johàn,	*and*
5 And His rig y-swongen,	*back scourged*
And His side y-stongen,	*pierced*
For the love of man,	
Wel ow Ich to wepen	*ought I to weep*
And sinnës forleten,	*and forsake sins*
10 Yif Ich of lovë can,	*if I am capable of love*
Yif Ich of lovë can,	
Yif Ich of lovë can.	

I, 88   Worldës blissë, have god day!

Worldës blissë, have god day!	*worldly bliss, good day (to you)!*
Now from myn hertë wend away;	*go away*
Him for to loven min hert is went	*heart has turned*
That thurgh His sidë sperë rent.	*through whose side the spear tore*
5 His hertë blod shaddë for me,	*shed*
Naylëd to the hardë tre;	*hard*
That swetë bodi was y-tent,	*stretched*
Prenëd with naylës three.	*pierced*

Ha Jesù! thin holi heved	*holy head*
10 With sharpë thornës was by-wevëd,	*encircled*
Thi fairë neb was al bi-spet,	*fair face; spat upon*
With spot and blod meynd al by-wet;	*spittle; mingled; drenched*
Fro the crounë to the to	*from the crown to the toe*
Thi body was ful of pine and wo,	*pain and woe*
15 And wan and red.	*wan and red*

Ha Jesù! thi smartë ded	*Ah Jesu! your painful death*
Be my sheld, and minë red	*may it be; help*
From develes lorë.	*from the Devil's promptings*
Ha, swète Jesù, thin òrë!	*have mercy*
20 For thinë pinës sorë,	
Tech min herte right lovë thee	*to love you properly*
Whos hertë blod was shad for me.	*heart's blood was shed*

1, 89   The mildë Lamb, y-sprad o rodë

The mildë Lamb, y-sprad o rodë,	gentle; spread on the cross
Heng bi-ronnen al o blodë,	hung drenched all in blood
For oure giltë, for oure godë,	for our guilt, for our benefit
For He ne giltë nevrë nought.	He sinned never at all
5 Fewe of Hise Him were bi-levëd,	His (followers) were left to Him
Dred hem hadde Him al bi-revëd	fear had deprived Him of them all
Whan they sawen herë heved	saw their head (i.e. leader)
To so shanful deth y-brought.	so shameful a death

His moder, ther Him stod bisidë,	
10 Ne let no ter other abidë,	and let no tear await another
Whan she saw hire child bitidë	befall her child
Swich pine and deyen giltëles.	such pain and die guiltless
Saint Johàn, that was Him derë,	who was dear to Him
On other halve Him stod eek ferë,	side; also as His companion
15 And biheld with mournë cherë	with sorrowful countenance
His maister that him loved and ches.	who loved and chose him

Sore and harde He was y-swungen,	beaten
Fet and hondës thurgh y-stungen,	pierced through
Ac most of alle His other wunden	above all his other wounds
20 Him dide His modrës sorwë wo.	His mother's grief caused Him woe
In al His pine, in al His wrakë,	pain; suffering
That He dreigh for mannës sakë,	endured
He saw His moder sorwë makë –	lamenting
Wel rewfuliche He spak hire to.	most compassionately

25 He seydë, 'Woman, lo! me herë,	hear me
Thi child that thou to mannë berë;	whom you in human form bore
Withouten sor and wep thou werë	pain and weeping
Tho Ich was of thee y-born.	when
Ac now thou most thi pinë dreyen,	but now you must; pain endure
30 Whan thou seest me with thin eyen	eyes
Pinë thole o rode and deyen	suffer torment; die
To helen man that was forlorn.'	heal (i.e. redeem); who was lost

Saint Johàn th'evangelistë	
Hir understod thurgh hese of Cristë;	supported her; command
35 Fair he kept hire and biwistë	kept and looked after her
And servëd hire from hond to fot.	
Rewful is the mineyingë	pitiable is the remembrance
Of thìs deth and this dèpartìngë;	parting
Therin is blis meind with wepingë,	joy mingled with weeping
40 For ther-thurgh us cam allë bot.	thereby to us came all salvation

He that starf in ourë kendë,   *died in our natural state*
Leve us so ben ther-of mendë,   *grant us; mindful*
That He yeve us atten endë   *may give us at the end*
    That He hath us to y-bought.   *what He has bought for us*
45 Milsful moder, maiden clenë,   *merciful; pure*
Mak thi milce upon us senë,   *make your mercy evident in us*
And bring us thurgh thi swetë benë   *through thy sweet intercession*
    To the blis that faillëth nought.   *fails not*

1, 90   Jesu Cristës mildë moder

Jesu Cristës mildë moder   *gentle mother*
Stod, biheld hire sone o rodë   *on the cross*
    That he was y-pinëd on;   *tortured*
The sonë heng, the moder stod   *son hung; stood*
5 And biheld hire childës blod,   *blood*
    How it of hise woundës ron.   *from his wounds ran*

Tho He starf that king is of lif,   *when He died who*
Drerier nas never no wif   *sadder was never any woman*
    Than thou werë, lady, tho;   *lady, then*
10 The brightë day went into night   *turned into*
Tho Jesu Christ, thin hertë light,   *when; your heart's light*
    Was y-queynt with pine and wo.   *was quenched with pain*

Thy lif dreigh ful hardë stoundës   *your person suffered very severe pangs*
Tho thou saw hise blodi woundës,   *when*
15   And his bodi o rodë don.   *placed*
Hisë woundës sore and smertë   *sore and painful*
Stongen thurgh and thurgh thi hertë,   *pierced through*
    As thee bihightë Simeon.   *promised*

Now his hed with blod bispronken,   *besprinkled*
20 Now his side with spere y-stongen,   *pierced*
    Thou biheldë, lady fre.   *gracious lady*
Now his hondës sprad o rodë,   *hands spread on the cross*
Now hise fet washen with blodë   *washed*
    And y-naillëd to the tre.

25 Now His bodi with scourgës beten,   *beaten*
And His blod so wide out-leten   *so widely diffused*
    Maden thee thin hertë sor.   *made your heart sore*
Wharso thou castest thin eyen   *wheresoever you cast*
Pinë strong thou saw Him dreyen –   *torment; endure*
30   Ne mightë no man tholë more.   *suffer more*

Now is timë that thou yeldë   *that you should pay*
Kindë that thou him with-heldë   *Nature what you from him*
   Tho thi child was of thee born.   *when*
Now he askëth with goulingë   *with (your) anguished cries*
35 That thou him in thi childingë   *for what you from him; child-bearing*
   Al with-heldë ther biforn.   *completely withheld before*

Now thou fondest, moder mildë,   *you experience*
What woman dreith with hir childë,   *what a woman suffers*
   Though thou clenë maiden be;   *you are a pure virgin*
40 Now thee's yolden hardë and derë   *to you is given hard and dire*
The pinë wherof thou werë   *the pain of which*
   In thy childing quite and fre.   *child-bearing quit and free*

Sone after the night of sorwë,
Sprang the light of edi morwë   *blessed morning*
45   In thin hertë, swetë may;   *maiden*
Thi sorwës wenden al to blissë,   *turned*
Tho thi sone al mid y-wissë   *when; with complete certainty*
   Aros upon the thriddë day.

Weila, what thou werë blithë,   *Lo! how happy you were*
50 Tho H'aros from deth to livë;   *when He rose*
   Thurgh the holë ston He glod   *through the intact stone He glided*
Also He was of thee boren;   *just as; born*
Bothen after and biforen
   Hol bilof thy maidenhod.   *intact remained*

55 Newë blissë He us broughtë
That mankin so derë boughtë   *who mankind so dearly redeemed*
   And for us yaf His derë lif.   *precious life*
Glade and blithë thou us makë   *glad and happy; make us*
For thi swetë sonës sakë,
60   Edi maiden, blisful wif.   *blessed maiden, blissful woman*

Quen of hevenë, for thi blissë,   *for the sake of your bliss*
Lighte al ourë sorinissë,   *lighten all our sorrow*
   And wend our evel al into god.   *and turn*
Bring us, moder, to thi sonë,
65 Mak us ever with Him wonë,   *with Him to dwell*
   That us boughtë with His blod.   *who redeemed us*

I, 91   Stond wel, moder, under rodë

(margin, handwritten) Religion

'Stond wel, moder, under rodë,	*stand well, mother, under the cross*
Bihold thi child wyth gladë modë,	*gladsome heart (mood)*
Blythë moder might thou be.'	*a happy mother you may be*
'Sone, how may I blithë stonden?	*be (lit. stand) happy*
5 I se thin feet, I se thin honden,	*hands*
Naylëd to the hardë tre.'	
'Moder, do wey thi wepingë;	*mother, put away*
I thole this deth for mannës thingë,	*I endure; for man's sake*
For owen giltë thole I non.'	*for my own guilt*
10 'Sone, I fele the dethë-stoundë,	*pangs of death*
The swerd is at min hertë-groundë,	*the bottom of my heart*
That me by-hightë Symeon.)	*which Simeon promised me*
'Moder, rew upon thy beren!	*have pity upon your child*
Thow washe awey tho blodi teren,	*wash away those bloody tears*
15 It don me wersë than mi det.'	*they affect me worse than my death*
'Sone, how might I terës wernen?	*restrain*
I se tho blodi flodës ernen	*those streams of blood run*
Out of thin hertë to min fet.'	
'Moder, now I may thee seyë,	*I may tell you*
20 Better is that Ich onë deyë	*it is better that I alone die*
Than al mankin to hellë go.'	*mankind; should go*
'Sone, I se thi bodi swongen,	*body beaten*
Thi brest, thin hond, thi fot thurgh-stongen,	*pierced through*
No selly nis though me be wo.'	*it is no wonder*
25 'Moder, if I dar thee tellë,	*I dare*
Yif I ne dye thou gost to hellë;	*if I do not die you go to hell*
I thole this deth for thinë sakë.'	*endure*
'Sonë, thou beest me so mindë,	*you are so thoughtful for me*
Ne wit me nought, it is my kindë	*blame me not, it is my nature*
30 That I for thee this sorwë makë.'	
'Moder, merci! let me deyen,	*die*
For Adam owt of hellë beyen,	*in order; to buy (i.e. redeem)*
And al mankin that is forloren.'	*mankind; lost*
'Sonë, what shal me to redë?	*Son, what am I to do?*
35 Thi pinë pinëth me to dedë,	*your agony tortures me to death*
Let me deyen thee biforen.'	*die*
'Moder, now tarst thou might leren	*now for the first time; learn*
What pinë thole that children beren,	*pain (they) suffer who; bear*
What sorwë have that child forgon.'	*(they) have who lose a child*
40 'Sone, I wot, I can thee tellë,	*Son, I know*
Bute it be the pine of hellë	*unless; torment*
Morë sorwë ne wot I non.'	*greater sorrow know I none*

(margin, handwritten beside line 15) More pain than?

'Moder, rew of moder carë!   *have pity on a mother's sorrow*
Now thou wost of moder farë,   *know about a mother's lot*
45   Though thou be clenë mayden-man.'   *a pure virgin*
'Sonë, help at allë nedë   *in every necessity*
Allë tho that to me gredë,   *all those who; cry*
Maiden, wif, and fool womman.'   *foolish*

'Moder, I may no lenger dwellë   *stay*
50   The time is come I fare to hellë,   *to go to hell*
The thriddë day I rise upon.'   *shall rise*
'Sone, I willë with thee founden,   *go with you*
I deye, y-wis, of thinë wounden,   *I die, truly; wounds*
So rewful deth was never non.'   *so pitiable a death*

55   When He ros than fel thi sorwë,   *then your sorrow vanished*
Thy blissë sprong the thriddë morwë,   *on the third morning*
Wel blithë moder wer thou tho.   *a most happy mother; then*
Moder, for that ilkë blissë,   *for that very bliss*
Bisech oure God oure sinnës lissë,   *beseech; to remit*
60   Thou be oure sheld ayayn oure fo.   *be thou our shield against our foe*

Blissed be thou quen of hevenë,
Bring us out of hellë levenë   *hell's flames*
Thurgh thi derë sonës might.
Moder, for that heighë blodë   *noble blood*
65   That He shadde upon the rodë,   *shed*
Led us into hevene light. Amen   *heaven's light*

I, 92   Why have ye no routhe on my child?

Why have ye no routhe on my child?   *no pity*
Have routhe on me ful of mourning;
Tak doun o rode my derworth child,   *from the cross my precious child*
Or prik me o rode with my derling!   *or nail me on the cross; darling*

5   More pine ne may me ben y-don   *more hurt may not be done to me*
Than lete me live in sorwe and shame;   *than to let*
As love me bindëth to my sone,
So let us deyen bothe y-same.   *die both together*

I, 93   Thou sikëst sore

Lovely ter of lovely eye,	*lovely tear*
Why dost thou me so wo?	*do you cause me such grief*
Sorful ter of sorful eye,	*sorrowful*
Thou brekst myn herte a-two.	*you are breaking; in two*

5 Thou sikëst sore,   *you sigh sorely*
    Thi sorwe is more
      Than mannës mouth may telle;
    Thou singest of sorwe,
    Mankin to borwe   *mankind to redeem*
10   Out of the pit of helle.
      Lovely, etc.

    I proud and kene,   *bold*
    Thou meke and clene,   *meek and pure*
      Withouten wo or wile;   *evil or guile*
    Th'art ded for me,   *you are dead*
15 I live thurgh thee,   *through you*
      So blissëd be that while.   *time*
      Lovely, etc.

    Thi moder seeth   *sees*
    How wo thee beeth   *what woe yours is*
      And therfore yerne she yerte; *earnestly she cried out*
20 To hire Thou speke,   *spoke*
    Hire sorwe to sleke –   *alleviate*
      Swet suitë wan thin herte.   *sweet entreaty won*
      Lovely, etc.

    Thin herte is rent,
    Thi body is bent,
25   Upon the rodë tre;
    The weder is went,   *storm is past*
    The devel is shent,   *destroyed*
      Crist, thurgh the might of Thee.
      Lovely, etc.

I, 94   I sike al when I singe

I sike al when I singe,	*I sigh whenever*
For sorwë that I se,	*for the sorrow that I see*
When Ich with wepìnge,	*when I*
Biholde upon the tre.	*look upon the tree (cross)*
5 I se Jhesù mi swete,	
His hertë blode forlete	*shed*
For the love of me.	
His woundës waxen wete –	*grow moist*
Marie, milde and swete,	
10 Thou have mercy of me!	*on me*
Hye upon a doune,	*high upon a hill*
As al folke hit se may,	
A mile withoute the toune,	*outside*
Aboutë the mid-day,	
15 The rode was up arerde;	*rood (cross); raised up*
His frendes were al aferde,	*afraid*
They clungen so the clay.	*shrank like clay*
The rod stondëth in ston.	*stands rooted in stone*
Mari hirselfe alon,	*by herself, alone*
20 Hir songe was 'waylaway'.	*alas, alas!*
Whan Ich Him biholde	
With eye and hertë bo,	*both*
I se his bodi colde,	*grow cold*
His ble waxëth al blo,	*complexion becomes all livid*
25 He hongëth al of blode	*hangs all bleeding*
So hey upon the rode	*high*
Bitwixen thevës two –	
How sholde I singë mor?	
Mari, thou wepë sor,	*wept bitterly*
30 Thou wist of al His wo.	*knew*
Wel oftë when I sike,	*sigh*
I makië mi mon;	*utter my lament*
Evel hit may me like –	*ill; please me*
And wonder nis it non –	*and it is no wonder*
35 Whan I se hongë hey	*hang on high*
And bitter peynës drey	*suffer*
Jhesu, mi lemmòn;	*beloved*
His woundës sorë smerte,	*smart*
The sper is at his herte,	
40 And thurgh His sidë gon.	*has passed*

The nailes ben al to stronge,
The smith is al to sleye,   *skilful*
Thou bledëst al to longe,
The tre is al to heye.   *high*
45 The stonës waxen wete –   *grow moist*
Allas! Jhesù mi swete,
Few frendës haddëst neye,   *had (you) near*
But Seint Jon mourning,
And Mari weping,
50 That al thi sorwë seye.   *who; saw*

Wel oftë whan I slepe
With sorwe Ich am thurgh-sought;   *pierced through*
Whan I wake and wepe,   *weep*
I thenkë in mi thought:
55 Allas that men ben wode!   *mad*
Biholden on the rode   *(they) look upon the cross*
And sellen (Ich ly nought)   *and sell (I lie not)*
Her soulës into sin   *their souls into sin*
For any worldës win,   *for any worldly pleasure*
60 That were so der y-bought.   *(their souls) which were so dearly bought*

I, 95   My trewest tresowre

My trewest tresowre   *truest treasure*
    sa trayturly was taken,   *treacherously*
Sa bytterly bondyn   *bound*
    wyth bytand bandes;   *biting bonds*
How sone of thi servandes   *how soon by your servants*
    was thou forsaken,
And lathly for my lufe   *hatefully for love of me*
    hurld with thair handes.   *buffeted by*

5 My well of my wele   *my fountain of my joy*
    sa wrangwysly wryed,   *so unjustly accused*
Sa pulled owt of preson   *prison*
    to Pilate at prime;   *prime (the first hour)*
Thaire dulles and thaire dyntes   *blows; buffets*
    ful drerely thou dreed   *right sorrowfully you suffered*
Whan thai schot in thi syght   *spat; eyes*
    bath slaver and slyme.   *both spittle and filth*

My hope of my hele   *salvation*
    sa hyed to be hanged,   *thus driven*
10 Sa charged with thi crosce   *so burdened; cross*
    and corond with thorne;   *crowned*

Ful sare to thi hert	*right painfully to your heart*
thi steppes tha stanged,	*your steps then pierced*
Me thynk Thi bak burd breke,	*your back ought to break*
it bendes forborne.	*weighed down*
My salve of my sare	*salve of my pain*
sa saryful in syght,	*so sorrowful to see*
Sa naked and nayled	
Thi ryg on the rode;	*your back on the cross*
15 Ful hydusly hyngand,	*right hideously suspended*
thay heved thee on hyght,	*they raised you on high*
Thai lete thee stab in the stane	*let you be jolted into the rock*
all stekked that thar stode.	*which stood there all fixed in place*
My dere-worthly derlyng,	*my precious darling*
sa dolefully dyght,	*so shamefully treated*
Sa straytly upryght	*tautly*
streyned on the rode;	*stretched*
For Thi mykel mekenes,	*great meekness*
Thi mercy, Thi myght,	
20 Thow bete al my bales	*cured all my ills*
with bote of Thi blode.	*with the remedy*
My fender of my fose,	*my defender from my foes*
sa fonden in the felde,	*so tested in the field (of battle)*
Sa lufly lyghtand	*so graciously descending*
at the evensang tyde;	*evensong time*
Thi moder and hir menyhe	*her companions*
unlaced Thi scheld,	*unfastened your shield*
All weped that thar were,	*all wept who were there*
Thi woundes was sa wyde.	
25 My pereles prynce	*peerless*
als pure I Thee pray,	*so utterly I you beseech*
The mynde of this myrour	*the remembrance of this example*
Thou lat me noght mysse;	*let me not be without*
Bot wynd up my wylle	*increase my desire*
to won wyth thee ay,	*to dwell with you for ever*
That Thou be beryd in my brest	*so that you may be buried*
and bryng me to blysse.	

I, 96   Gold and al this worldës wyn

Gold and al this worldës wyn   *world's joy*
  Is nought but Cristës rode;   *nothing without Christ's cross*
I wolde be clad in Cristës skyn,
  That ran so longe on blode,
5 And gon t'is herte and take myn in   *go to His heart and take my lodging*
  Ther is a fulsum fode;   *where there is abundant food*
Than yeve I litel of kith or kyn,   *then would I give little for*
  For ther is allë gode.   *there (i.e. with Christ)*

I, 97   Crist maketh to man a fair present

Crist maketh to man a fair presènt,
His blody body with lovë brent;   *afire with love*
That blisful body his lyf hath lent,   *has given its life*
For love of man that synne hath blent.   *whom sin has blinded*

5 O lovë, love, what hast thou ment?   *intended*
  Me thinketh that love to wrathe is went.   *has turned to anger*

Thi loveliche hondes love hath to-rent,   *lovely; torn to pieces*
And Thi lithe armes wel streit y-tent;   *gentle arms so tightly stretched*
Thi brest is bare, Thi body is bent,
10 For wrong hath wonne and right is schent. *won; is destroyed*

Thi myldë bones love hath to-drawe,   *gentle bones; pulled apart*
The nayles Thi feet han al to-gnawe;   *have quite gnawed to pieces*
The Lord of love love hath now slawe,   *slain*
Whane love is strong it hath no lawe.   *law (i.e. limit)*

15 His herte is rent,
  His body is bent
    Upon the rodë tre;
  Wrong is went,   *is overthrown*
  The devel is schent,   *is destroyed*
20   Crist, thurgh the might of Thee.   *through*

For thee that herte is leyd to wedde;   *is given as a pledge*
Swych was the love that herte us kedde,   *such; showed*
That hertë barst, that hertë bledde,   *burst*
That hertë blood oure soulës fedde.   *heart's blood; fed*

25 That hertë clefte for treuthe of love,   *broke for constancy of love*
Therfore in him oon is trewe love;   *in it alone*
For love of thee that herte is yove,   *is given*
Kepe thou that herte and thou art above.   *victorious*

Lovë, love, where schalt thou wone?   *dwell*
30 Thi wonyng-stede is thee bi-nome,   *dwelling-place is taken from you*
For Cristës herte, that was thin home –
He is deed, now hast thou none.   *dead*

   Lovë, love, whi doest thou so?
   Love, thou brekest myn herte a-two.   *in two*

35 Love hath schewëd his greet myght,   *great*
For love hath maad of day the nyght;
Love hath slawe the kyng of ryght,   *slain*
And love hath endëd the strong fight.

So inliche love was never noon;   *such deep love*
40 That witen wel Marie and Jon,   *know well*
And also wite thei everychon,   *know they each one*
That love with Him hath maad at oon.   *whom love with Him has made at one*

Love makëth, Crist, Thin hertë myn,
So makëth love myn hertë Thin;
45 Thanne scholdë myn be trewe al tym,   *be true at all times*
And love in love schal make it fyn.   *make it perfect*

1, 98   A sory beverage it is

A sory beverage it is   *sorrowful drink*
   and sore it is abought,   *grievously it is paid for*
Now in this sharpë time   *to this bitter moment*
   this brewing hath me brought.   *has brought me*
5 Fader, if it mowe ben don   *may be done*
   as I have besought   *implored*
Do awey this beverage   *take away*
   that I ne drink it nought.

And if it mowe no better ben,   *if it may no better be*
10   for allë mannës gilt,   *because of all man's guilt*
That it ne mustë nedë   *(than) that it must needs be*
   that my blod be spilt,   *should be*
Swetë Father, I am Thy sone
   Thi wil be fulfilt,   *fulfilled*
15 I am her, thin owen child,   *here*
   I wil don as thou wilt.   *do*

I, 99   Ye that pasen be the wey

Ye that pasen be the wey,
   abide a litel stounde;   *pause a little while*
Beholdëth, al mi felawes,   *my fellows*
   yif ani me lik is founde.   *if anyone like me*
5 To the tre with nalës thre
   wel fast I hangë bounde,   *very fast; hang*
With a spere al thurgh mi side   *through*
   to min herte is made a wounde.   *to my heart*

I, 100   My folk, now answerë me

My folk, now answerë me,
   And sey what is my gilt;   *say; guilt*
What might I mor ha don for thee,   *have done*
   That I ne have fulfilt?   *fulfilled*

5 Out of Egipte I broughë thee,
   Ther thou wer in thi wo;   *where; woe*
And wikkedliche thou nomë me,   *wickedly; took me*
   As I hadde ben thi fo.   *as if; foe*

Over al I leddë thee   *everywhere I led thee*
10   And aforn thee I yede;   *and before you I went*
And no frendschipe fond I in thee   *found I*
   Whan that I haddë nede.   *need*

Fourti winter I sentë thee   *for forty years*
   Angeles mete fro hevene;   *angel's food from heaven*
15 And thou heng me on rodë tre,   *hung me on a cross*
   And greddëst with loud stevene.   *reviled (me) with loud outcry*

Heilsom water I sentë thee   *wholesome*
   Out of the hardë ston;
And eisel and galle thou sentëst me, *vinegar and gall*
20   Other yaf thou me non.   *gave*

The see I parted asonder for thee,   *sea; asunder*
   And ledde thee thurgh wel wide; *through with ample space*
And the hertë blod to sen of me,   *heart's blood to see*
   Thou smottest me thurgh the side. *through*

25 Alle thi fon I slow for thee,   *all your foes I slew*
   And made thee couth of name;   *renowned in name*
And thou heng me on rodë tre,   *hung me*
   And didest me mychel shame.   *great shame*

    A kingës yerde I bitook thee   *king's sceptre I granted you*
30   Til thou wer al beforn;   *until; above all (others)*
    And thou heng me on rodë tre,
      And crounëdest me with thorn.   *crowned*

    I made thin enemies and thee
      For to ben knowen asonder;   *known apart*
35 And on an hey hil thou henge me,   *high hill you hung me*
      Al the world on me to wonder.   *for all; to wonder at me*

I, 101   Jhesus doth him bymene

    Jhesus doth him bymene,   *Jesus complains*
    And speketh to synful mon: *man*
    'Thy garland is of grene,   *green*
    Of flourës many on;   *flowers many a one*
5 Myn of sharpë thornes,
    Myn hewe it makëth won.   *complexion; pale*

    'Thyn hondës streitë glovëd,   *your hands are tightly gloved*
    White and clenë kept;   *clean*
    Myne with nailës thorlëd   *pierced*
10 On rode, and eke my fet.   *on the cross; also*

    'Acros thou berest thyn armes,   *crossed*
    Whan thou dauncëst narwe,   *you dance close together*
    To me hastou non awe   *for me have you no reverence*
    But to worldës glorie;   *but only for worldly glory*
15 Myne for thee on rode,   *my (arms)*
    With the Jewës wode,   *by the mad Jews*
    With gretë ropes to-draw.   *pulled apart*

    'Open thou hast thi syde,
    Spaiers longe and wide,   *(with) slits*
20 For veyn glorie and pride,
    And thi longe knif astrout –   *sticking out*
    Thou art of the gai route;   *company*
    Myn with sperë sherpe   *my (side); a sharp spear*
    Y-stongen to the herte,   *pierced*
25 My body with scourgës smerte   *painful*
    Bi-swongen al aboute.   *beaten all over*

    'Al that I tholede on rode for thee,   *suffered on the cross*
      To me was shame and sorwë;
    Wel litel thou lovëst me,   *very little*
30 And lassë thou thenkëst on me,   *less*
      An evene and eke amorwë.   *night and also morning*

     'Swetë brother, wel might thou se,
     Thes peynës stronge on rodë tre
     Have I tholed for love of thee;   *suffered*
35 They that havë wrought it me   *done it to me*
       Mai syngë weylawo.   *alas*
     Be thou kinde par charité,   *for love's sake*
     Let thy synne and love thou me,   *leave*
     Hevenë blisse I shal yeve thee,   *give*
40   That lastëth ay and oo.'   *for ever and ever*

I, 102   Lo! lemman swete, now may thow se

     Lo! lemman swete, now may thow se   *beloved; may you see*
     That I have lost my lyf for thee –   *my life*
       What myght I do thee mare?   *do for you; more*
     Forthi I pray thee speciali   *therefore; especially*
5 That thow forsake ill company
     That woundës me so sare;   *sorely*

     And take myne armës pryvëly   *my arms (i.e. armour) secretly*
     And do tham in thi tresory,   *and put them in your treasury*
       In what stede sa thow dwellës,   *in whatever place you dwell*
10 And, swete lemmàn, forget thow noght   *not*
     That I thi lufe sa dere have boght,   *your love so dearly have bought*
     And I aske thee noght ellës.   *I shall ask thee nothing else*

I, 103   Stedfast crosse, among alle other

     Stedfast crosse, among alle other   *among all others*
     Thou art a tre michel of pris,   *of great price*
     In braunche and flourë swych another   *branch and blossom such another*
     I ne wot non in wode ne rys.   *I know none in wood nor thicket*
5 Swete the nailes, and swete the tre,   *sweet*
     And swetter the burden that hangeth on thee!   *sweeter*

I, 104   What is he, this lordling ~ *William Herebert*

     'What is he, this lordling   *young lord*
       that comëth from the fight
     With blod-rede wedë   *blood-red garments*
       so grisliche y-dight,   *terribly arrayed*
     So faire y-cointisëd,   *beautifully apparelled*
       so semlich in syght,   *fair to see*
     So stiflichë gangëth,   *who so bravely advances*
       so doughty a knight?'   *valiant*

5 'Ich hit am, Ich hit am,	*it is I*
that ne spekë bute right,	
Champioun to helen	*save*
mankinde in fyght.'	
'Why thenne is thy shroud red,	*thy clothing red*
with blod al y-meind,	*all mingled*
As tredderes in wringe	*like treaders in the wine-press*
with must al bispreynd?'	*with must all spattered*
'The wringe Ich have y-treddëd	*wine-press; trod*
al myself on,	*myself all alone*
10 And of al mankinde	*for all mankind*
ne was non other won.	*no other hope*
Ich hem have y-treddëd	*them*
in wrathe and in grame,	*in wrath and in anger*
And al my wede is bispreynd	*my clothing is spattered*
with here blod y-same,	*with their blood together*
And al my robe y-foulëd	*garment defiled*
to here gretë shame.	*to their great disgrace*
The day of thilke wreche	*of that vengeance*
liveth in my thought,	
15 The yer of medës yelding	*year of reward-giving*
ne foryet Ich nought.	*forget I not*
Ich lokëd al aboute	*looked all about*
som helpynge mon;	*for someone to help (me)*
Ich soughte al the route	*searched all the crowd*
bote help nas ther non.	*was there none*
Hit was myn owne strengthe	
that this bote wroughte,	*salvation wrought*
Myn owne doughtynesse	*own courage*
that help ther me broughte.	
20 Ich have y-treddëd the folk	
in wrathe and in grame,	*in wrath and in anger*
Adreynt al with shennesse,	*drowned; ignominy*
y-drawe doun wyth shame.'	*dragged down*
'On Godës milsfulnesse	*mercifulness*
Ich wole bi-thenche me,	*I will bethink me*
And herien Him in alle thing	*and praise; everything*
that He yeldëth me.'	*grants*

I, 105   As I me rod this ender day

As I me rod this ender day	*as I rode out the other day*
By grenë wode to sechë play,	*by the green wood to seek pleasure*
Mid herte I thoughte al on a may,	*in my heart; entirely on a maiden*
Swetest of allë thinge;	*of all creatures*
5 Lithe, and Ich you tellë may	*listen*
Al of that swetë thinge.	
This maide is swete and fre of blod,	*noble of blood*
Bright and fair, of mildë mod,	*of gentle disposition*
Allë she mai don us god	*do*
10 Thurgh hirë bisechinge;	*her intercession*
Of hirë He tok flesh and blod,	*from her*
Jesus, hevenë kynge.	*king of heaven*
With al my lif I love that may,	*that maiden*
She is my solas night and day,	*comfort*
15 My joie and eke my bestë play,	*and also my greatest pleasure*
And eke my love-longynge;	*and also my love's desire*
Al the bet me is that day	*the better to me*
That Ich of hirë synge.	*of her may sing*
Of allë thinge I love hire mest,	*most*
20 My dayës blis, my nightës rest,	
She counseillëth and helpëth best	
Bothen olde and yinge;	*both old and young*
Now I may, yif that me lest,	*now I may, if I wish*
The fivë joiës mynge.	*call to mind*
25 The firstë joie of that woman	
When Gabriel from hevenë cam	*came*
And seide God sholde bicomen man	*should*
And of hire be bore,	*of her be born*
And bringen up of hellë pyn	*from the torment of hell*
30 Mankyn that was forlore.	*mankind which had been lost*
That other joië of that may	*second joy; maiden*
Was o Cristës-massë day,	*was on*
Whan God was bore on thorogh lay,	*was born in perfect light*
And broughtë us lightnesse;	*and brought us light*
35 The ster was seyn biforë day,	*(that) the star was seen*
This herdës bere wytnesse.	*these shepherds bear witness*

The thriddë joie of that lady,
That men clepe th' Epyphany,   *which men call the Epiphany*
When the kingës come wery   *came weary*
40   To presente hyre sone   *to present her son*
With myrrë, gold, and encens hy,
    That was man bicome.   *who had become man*

The fourthë joie we tellë mawen   *we may tell*
On Ester-morwe when hit gan dawen,   *Easter morning when it dawned*
45 Hyrë sonë, that was slawen,   *who was slain*
    Aros in flesh and bon;   *bone*
Morë joie men have ne mawen,   *may not have*
    Wyf ne mayden non.   *woman nor any maiden*

The fiftë joie of that woman,
50 When hire body to hevene cam,
The soulë to the body nam   *went*
    As hit was wont to bene.   *as (i.e. where) it was wont to be*
Crist leve us alle with that woman   *Christ grant us*
    That joie al for to sene.   *to see*

55 Preye we alle to oure lady,   *pray*
And to the seintes that wone hire by,   *dwell beside her*
That they of us haven merci,   *may have mercy*
    And that we ne misse   *we may not fail*
In this world to ben holy   *be*
60   And wynnë hevenë blysse.   *win the bliss of heaven*

I, 106   Somer is come and winter gon

Somer is come and winter gon,   *has come; gone*
    this day bigineth to longe,   *lengthen*
And this foulës everichon   *these birds every one*
    joyen hem with songe;   *rejoice in singing*
5   So stronge   *such intense*
       care me bint,   *sorrow binds me*
al with joyë that me fint   *despite the joy that is found*
       in londe,   *everywhere*
       Al for a child
10   that is so milde   *gracious*
       of honde.   *in manner (lit. with hand)*

	That child that is so milde and wlanc	*gentle and noble*
	and eke of gretë mounde,	*also of great power*
	Bothe in boskës and in bank	*in woods and on hill-side*
15	y-sought me hath a stounde;	*has sought me for a while*
	Y-founde	*found*
	he havëd me,	*he had (found) me*
	for an appel of a tre,	*on account of an apple from a tree*
	y-bounde;	*bound*
20	He brak the bond,	*broke*
	that was so strong,	
	with wounde.	*through (His) wounds*
	That child that was so wilde and bold	*defiant and daring*
	to me aloutë lowe;	*bowed low*
25	Fram me to Jewës he was sold,	*by me to the Jews*
	ne couthe they Him nought knowe.	*they could not recognize him*
	'Do we',	*'Let us'*
	saiden he,	*said they*
	'naile we Him upon a tre	*'let us nail him*
30	a lowe,	*on a hill*
	Ac erst we shullen	*but first we must*
	shamen Him	*make mock of him*
	a throwe.'	*for a while'*
	Jhesu is the childës name,	
35	king of allë londe;	*lands*
	Of the king they maden game	*made sport*
	and smiten Him with honde;	*smote him*
	To fonde	*to test*
	Him on a tre	
40	they yeve Him woundës two and thre	*gave*
	mid honde;	*by hand*
	Of bitter drink	
	they senden Him	*sent him*
	a sonde.	*a gift*
45	Deth He nam o rodë-tre,	*accepted on the cross*
	that lif is of us alle;	*he who is life of us all*
	Ne mightë hit nought other be	*be otherwise*
	but we sholden falle;	*unless we were to fall*
	And walle	*and to boil*
50	in hellë dep	*deep*
	nerë neverë so swet	*were never*
	with alle;	
	Ne mighte us socour	*nothing could help us*
	castel, tour	*castle, tower*
55	ne halle.	*nor hall*

Mayde and moder ther astod,   *remained there*
   Marie ful of grace,
She let the terës al of blod   *she let her tears, all bloody*
   fallen in the place;   *in that place*
60   The trace   *trail*
   ran of her blode,
changëd herë flesh and rode   *complexion*
   and face;
    He was todrawe,   *rent apart*
65   so deer y-slawe,   *like a deer slain*
      in chace.   *in the chase*

Deth He nam, the swetë man,   *death he accepted*
   wel heigh upon the rode;   *so high upon the cross*
He wessh our sinnës everichan   *washed away; every one*
70   mid His swetë blode.   *with*
     Mid flode   *with a torrent*
   He loute adoun   *he bent down*
and brac the yates of that prisòun   *broke the gates*
   that stode,   *which stood (against him)*
75   And ches here   *and chose from* (lit. out of) *them*
   out that there   *those who there*
    were gode.   *were good*

He ros Him ene the thriddë day   *He rose by His own power*
   and set Him on His trone;   *seated Himself on His throne*
80 He wol come a domës-day   *will come on Doomsday*
   to dem us everich one.   *to judge us every one*
     Grone   *let (the man) groan*
   and wepë ay,   *and ever weep*
the man that deyth withouten lay,   *(who) dies without faith*
85   alone;   *alone*
   Grant us, Christ,
   with thin uprist   *resurrection*
    to gon.   *go*

I, 107   Lullay, lullay, litel child

Lullay, Lullay, litel child,
Why wepëst thou so sore?   *bitterly*

Lullay, lullay, litel child,
Thou that were so sterne and wild,
5 Now art becomë meke and mild
    To save that was forlore.   *what was lost*
        Lullay, etc.

But for my sinne I wot it is   *only; I know*
That Goddës sonë suffrëth this,
10 Merci lord, I have do mis,   *done wrong*
    Y-wis I wile no more.   *certainly*
        Lullay, etc.

Ayeyns my fadrës wille I ches   *against; chose*
An appel with a rewful res,   *on a lamentable impulse*
15 Wherfore myn heritage I les,   *lost*
    And now thou wepest therfore.
        Lullay, etc.

An appel I tok of a tre,   *from a tree*
God it hadde forboden me;   *forbidden*
20 Wherfore I sholde dampnëd be,   *damned*
    Yif thy weping ne wore.   *were*
        Lullay, etc.

Lullay for wo, thou litel thing,
Thou litel barun, thou litel king,   *lord / child*
25 Mankinde is cause of thy mourning,
    That thou hast loved so yore.   *so long since*
        Lullay, etc.

For man that thou hast ay loved so   *always*
Yet shaltou suffren peynës mo,   *more pains*
30 In hed, in feet, in hondës two,
    And yet wepen wel more.   *and still weep much more*
        Lullay, etc.

That peyne us make of sinnë fre,   *may that pain make us free from sin*
That peyne us bringe Jhesù to thee,
35 That peyne us helpë ay to fle
    The wikked fendës lore.   *fiend's promptings.*
        Lullay, etc.

1, 108   Adam lay y-bownden

Adam lay y-bownden,   *bound*
   bownden in a bond,
Fower thousand wynter,   *years*
   thought he not to long.   *too long*

5 And al was for an appil,
   an appil that he took,
As clerkës fynden writen,   *scholars find written*
   writen in here book.   *their*

Ne hadde the appil takë,   *had the apple not taken*
10   the appil takë ben,   *(not) been taken*
Ne haddë never our lady   *our lady would never*
   have ben hevenë quen.   *have been queen of heaven*

Blessëd be the tymë
   that appil takë was,
15 Therfore we mown singen,   *may sing*
   'Deo gratias!'.   *thanks be to God!*

Miscellaneous Lyrics

I, 109   Er ne couthe Ich sorwë non

Er ne couthe Ich sorwë non,	*formerly knew I no sorrow*
Nou Ich mot menen min mon;	*must utter my lament*
Carful, wel sore Ich sichë.	*full of care, most bitterly I sigh*
Giltles Ich tholë muchel shamë;	*guiltless I suffer*
5 Help, God, for thin swetë namë,	
King of hevënë richë.	*King of the kingdom of heaven*
Jesu Crist, soth God, soth man,	*true*
Loverd, thou rew upon me!	*Lord, take pity*
Of prison ther Ich in am	*from the prison which I am in*
10 Bring me out and makë fre.	*make (me) free*
Ich and minë ferës somë	*some of my companions*
(God wot Ich ne lyë nought)	*God knows I do not lie*
For othrë han misnomë,	*because others have done wrong*
Ben in thys prison y-brought.	*are in*
15 Almighty,	
That wel lightly	*who so readily*
Of bale is hele and botë,	*of torment is salvation and remedy*
Hevenë king,	*King of heaven*
Of this woning	*from this misery*
20 Out us bringë motë.	*may you bring us out*
Foryif hem,	*forgive them*
The wykkë men,	*wicked*
God, yif it is thy willë,	
For whos gilt	*whose guilt*
25 We ben y-pilt	*we have been thrust*
In this prison illë.	*into this evil prison*
Ne hopë non to this livë –	*Let no man trust in this life*
Her ne may he bilivë;	*remain*
Heighë though he styë,	*high; ascend*
30 Deth him fellëth to groundë.	*Death fells him*
Nou hath man wele and blissë,	*prosperity and joy*
Rathe he shal ther-of missë;	*soon; lose*
Worldës welë, mid y-wissë,	*worldly prosperity, assuredly*
Ne lastëth bute an stoundë.	*lasts but a moment*
35 Maiden that bare the heven-king,	*bore the King of heaven*
Besech thin sone, that swetë thing,	*beseech*
That he have of us rewsing	*pity*
And bring us of this woning	*from this misery*
For his muchëlë milsë.	*great mercy*

40 He bring us out of this wo
  And us techë werchen so
  In this life, go how s'it go,
  That we moten ay and o
  Haven the echë blissë.

may He bring
so to act
go however it may
that we may for ever and ever
have eternal bliss

I, 110   Somer is y-comen in

Sing cuckòu nou! Sing cuckòu!
Sing cuckòu! Sing cuckòu nou!

  Somer is y-comen in,
    loudë sing, cuckòu!
5 Growëth sed and blowëth med
    and springth the wodë nou.
  Sing cuckòu!

  Ewë bletëth after lamb,
    lowth àfter càlvë còu;
10 Bullok stertëth, bukkë vertëth,
    merye sing, cuckòu!
  Cùckou, cùckou,
  Wèl singèst thou cùckou;
  Ne swik thou never nou!

Sing, cuckoo, now

has come in
sing loudly, cuckoo
seed grows; the meadow blossoms
the wood comes into leaf now

the ewe bleats for
the cow lows for the calf
leaps; the buck cavorts
merrily

do not stop ever

I, 111   Say me, wight in the brom

  'Say me, wight in the brom,   *tell me, creature in the broom*
  Teche me hou I shal don   *what I must do*
  That min housëbondë   *so that my husband*
  Me lovien woldë.'   *should love me*

5 'Hold thine tongë stillë
  And have al thine willë.'– *desire .*

I, 112   Hit was upon a Shere Thorsday

  Hit was upon a Shere Thorsday   *Maundy Thursday*
    that oure Loverd aros,   *our Lord arose*
  Ful mildë were the wordës
    Hè spac to Judàs: *spoke*

5 'Judàs thou most to Jursëlem,   *must (go); Jerusalem*
    oure metë for to bigge;   *our food; to buy*
  Thritty platës of selver   *coins of silver*
    thou bere upon thy rigge;   *you are to carry on your back*

Thou comest fer i the brodë strete,   *you will go far along the highway*
10   fer i the brodë strete;
Some of thinë kinnësmen   *kinsmen*
    ther thou mayst y-mete.'   *may meet*

He mettë with his suster   *he met; sister*
    the swikëlë wommon: *treacherous*
15 'Judas, thou were worthe   *you deserve*
    me stondë thee with ston,   *to be stoned*
Judas, thou were worthe
    me stondë thee with ston,
For the falsë prophete
20   that thou bilevest upon.'

'Be stillë, levë suster,   *be quiet, dear sister*
    thin hertë thee tobreke!   *may your very heart break*
Wiste min Loverd Crist,   *if my Lord Christ knew*
    ful wel He wolde be wreke.'   *right thoroughly; avenged*

25 'Judas, go thou on the rok,   *go on to the cliff*
    heighe upon the ston,   *high upon the crag*
Lay thin heved i my barm,   *head in my lap*
    slep thou thee anon.'   *go straight to sleep*

Sonë so Judàs   *as soon as Judas*
30   of slepë was awake,   *from sleep*
Thritty platës of selver
    from him were y-take.   *had been taken*

He drow hymselvë by the top   *he tore his hair*
    that al it lavede ablode;   *it all streamed with blood*
35 The Jewës out of Jursëlem
    awenden he were wode.   *thought he was mad*

Forth hym com the richë Jew   *forward came*
    that hightë Pilatùs: *who was called*
'Wilt thou sellë thy Loverd   *Lord*
40   that hightë Jesùs?'   *who is called Jesus*

'I nil sellë my Loverd   *I will not*
    for nonës kinnës aughte,   *for money of any kind*
But it be for thritty platës   *unless it is for the thirty coins*
    that He me bitaughte.'   *which he entrusted to me*

45 'Wilt thou selle thy Loverd Crist
    for enës kinnës golde?'   *gold of any kind*
'Nay, but hit be for the platës' –   *no, unless it is*
    that he haven wolde.   *that he wished to have*

In him com our Lord Crist gon | *our Lord Christ came walking in*
50 As his postles satte at mete: | *apostles sat at their meal*
'Hòw sittë ye, postles, | *why are you sitting*
and why nillë ye ete? | *will you not eat*
Hòw sittë ye, postles,
and why nillë ye ete?
55 Ich am abought and y-sold | *I have been bought and sold*
today for ourë mete.' | *food*

Up stod him Judàs, | *Judas stood up*
'Lord am I that frec? | *that man*
I nas never on the stede | *was never in the place*
60 ther me thee evel spec.' | *where evil was spoken of you*

Up him stod Petèr
and spak with al his mighte:
'Though Pilatus him comë | *though Pilate should come*
with ten hundred knighte, | *knights*
65 Though Pilatus him comë,
with ten hundred knighte,
Yet Ich woldë, Loverd, | *would*
for Thy lovë fighte.' | *for the love of you*

'Stillë thou be, Peter, | *be quiet*
70 wel I thee y-cnowe; | *know*
Thou wilt forsake me thryës | *thrice*
er the cok him crowe.' | *before the cock crows*

I, 113   Ich herde men upon mold

Ich herde men upon mold | *I heard men on earth*
makë muche mon, | *utter great lamentation*
Hou he ben y-tened | *how they are harassed*
of herë tilyinge: | *in their farming*
Gode yerës and corn | *good years and corn-crops*
bothe ben a-gon; | *both are gone*
Ne kepen here no sawe | *they care to hear no tales*
ne no song singe. | *nor sing any song*
5 Now we mote werche, | *now we must labour*
nis ther non other won, | *there is no other option*
May Ich no lengere | *I can no longer*
live with my lesinge; | *my losses*
Yet ther is a bitterer | *more bitter*
bit to the bon, | *cut to the bone*
For ever the ferthe peni | *for always every fourth penny*
mot to the kinge. | *must go*

Thus we carpen for the king,	*complain because of the king*
and caren ful colde,	*and are vexed most bitterly*
10 And wenen for to kevere,	*and hope to recover*
and ever ben a-cast;	*and always are cast down*
Whoso hath any god,	*if anyone has anything of value*
hopëth he nought to holde,	*he doesn't expect to keep it*
But ever the levest	*always the dearest possessions*
we lesen a-last.	*we lose in the end*
Lither is to lesen	*wicked it is to lose*
ther as litel is,	*where there is little*
And haven many hynen	*to have many labourers*
that hopen therto;	*who look for their share*
15 The hayward hetëth us harm	*the hayward threatens us trouble*
to haven of his;	*to get his bit*
The bailif becknëth us bale	*the bailiff hints at trouble for us*
and wenëth wel do;	*and expects to do well*
The wodeward waytëth us wo	*the wood-keeper treats us badly*
that loken under rys;	*who forage under trees*
Ne may us rise no rest,	*for us there can be no rest*
richës ne ro.	*prosperity nor peace*
Thus me pilëth the poure	*thus the poor man is robbed*
that is of lite pris:	*who is of little account*
20 Nede in swete and in swink	*inevitably in sweat and in toil*
swindë mot so.	*so must he perish*
Nede he mot swyndë	*he needs must perish*
(though he hade swore)	*though he had vowed (not to)*
That nath nought an hood	*he who has not a hood*
his hed for to hide!	*to cover his head*
Thus Wil walkëth in londe,	*so Will stalks the land*
and lawe is forlore,	*abandoned*
And al is pikëd of the poure	*and stolen from the poor is all*
the prikërës pride.	*the rider's array*
25 Thus me pilëth the poure	*thus the poor are robbed*
and pikëth ful clene,	*and stripped quite clean*
The riche men reimen	*the powerful plunder*
withouten any right;	
Her londes and her ledes	*their lands and their property*
lyen ful lene	*lie completely barren*
Thurgh bidding of bailifs,	*through the demands of bailiffs*
such harm hem han hight.	*have they threatened them*
Men of religioun,	*men in religious orders*
me halt hem ful hene,	*are held in utter contempt*
30 Baroun and bonde,	*by baron and peasant*
the clerk and the knight.	*the cleric and the knight*

Thus Wil walkëth in lond,   *thus Will stalks the land*
    and wandred is wene,   *poverty is expected*
Falsshipe fattëth   *Falsehood grows fat*
    and marrëth with might.   *and brings ruin by his might*

Stont stille in the stede   *he stands there unmoved*
    and halt him ful sturne   *and behaves most sternly*
That makëth beggeres go   *he who causes beggers to go*
    with burdoun and bagges.   *with staff and bags*
35 Thus we ben hunted   *are hunted*
    from halë to hurne;   *from corner to corner*
That er werëde robes,   *we who formerly wore robes*
    nou weren ragges.   *now wear rags*

Yet comen bideles   *furthermore tax-collectors come*
    with ful muchë bost: *with such great arrogance*
'Greythë me silver   *pay me silver*
    to the grene wax;   *for the green wax*
Thou art writen i my writ,   *entered in my schedule*
    that thou well wost!' –   *well know*
40 Mo than ten sithës   *more than ten times*
    told I my tax.   *I have paid my tax*
'Thenne mot Ich have   *then I must have*
    hennës arost,   *roast hens*
Fair on fish-day   *fine; on fish-day*
    laumprey and lax;   *lamprey and salmon*
Forth to the chepinge!' –   *be off to the market*
    gaynëth no chost,   *nothing's to be gained by arguing*
Though I selle my bil   *even though I have to sell my hoe*
    and my borst-ax.   *and my logging axe*

45 Ich mot layë my wed   *I must put down my deposit*
    wel, yif I wille,   *in full, if I am willing*
Other sellë my corn
    on gras that is grene.   *still green on the blade*
Yet I shal be 'foul cherl',   *yet I shall be (called) 'foul peasant'*
    though they han the fille;   *even though they get the full amount*
That Ich allë yer spare,   *what I all the year save*
    thenne I mot spene.   *then I must spend*

Nede I mot spene   *of necessity I have to spend*
    that I sparëd yore;   *what I previously saved*
50 Ayein this cachereles comen   *against the time these catchpolls come*
    thus I mot care;   *thus I have to worry*
Comëth the maister bidel,   *the chief tax-collector*
    brist as a bore,   *bristling like a boar*
Saith he wille my bigging   *my home*
    bringë ful bare.   *strip completely bare*

Mede I mot minten,	*a bribe; I must consider*
a mark other more,	*a mark or more*
Though Ich at the set day	*even though I on the set day*
sellë my mare.	*have to sell my mare*
55 Thus the grene wax	*so taxation*
us grevëth under gore,	*grieves us deeply*
That me us huntëth	*in that we are hunted*
as hound doth the hare.	*as a hound does the hare*
They us hunten as hound	
hare doth on hille;	*on the hill*
Sithe I tok to the lond	*since I took to (tilling) the land*
such tene me was taught.	*such trouble have I been taught*
N'aven ner bideles	*never have tax-collectors*
bodëd her fille,	*declared their full takings*
60 For they may scape	*for they can escape*
and we aren ever caught.	*and we are always caught*
Thus I kippe and cacche	*so I get and come by*
carës ful colde,	*sorrows most bitter*
Sithe I counte and cot	*since I accounts and a smallholding*
hadë to kepe.	*had to keep*
To seche silver to the king	*to find silver for the king*
I my seed solde,	
Forthy my lond leye lith,	*for which reason my land lies fallow*
and lernëth to slepe.	*and learns to sleep*
65 Sithe they my faire fee	*after that; my fine livestock*
fette y my folde.	*took away from my fold*
When I think o my wele,	*of my (former) prosperity*
wel nigh I wepe.	
Thus breden manye	*so are bred many*
beggeres bolde,	*bold beggars*
And oure reye is roted	*and our rye is rotten*
and ruls er we repe	*and useless before we reap it*
Ruls is oure reye	*useless is our rye*
and roted in the stree,	*and rotten on the stalk*
70 For wickëde wederes	*because of severe storms*
by brokes and by brynke.	*by streams and by bank*
Thus wakenëth in the world	*so there awakes in the world*
wandred and wee –	*distress and woe*
As god is swinden anon	*it is as well to perish forthwith*
as so for to swinke!	*as so to toil*

I, 114   Man in the moone stont and strit

Man in the moone
    stont and strit,   *the man in the moon / stands still and strides out*
On his bot-forke   *on his hay-fork*
    his burthen he berëth;   *he carries his bundle*
Hit is muche wonder   *it is a great wonder*
    that he n'adoun slit,   *that he does not fall down*
For doute leste he falle,   *for fear lest he fall*
    he shoddrëth and sherëth.   *he trembles and swerves*
5 When the frost fresëth   *when the frost freezes*
    muche chele he bit;   *great chill he endures*
The thornës beth kene   *the thorns are sharp*
    his hattren to-terëth.   *which tear his clothes to pieces*
Nis no wight in the world   *there is nobody in the world*
    that wot when he sit,   *who knows when he sits down*
Ne, bute hit be the hegge,   *nor, unless it be the hedge*
    what wedës he werëth.   *what garments he wears*

Whider trowëth this man   *where does this man think*
    ha the way take?   *he is going*
10 He hath set his o fot   *he has set one foot*
    his other to-foren.   *in front of the other*
For non highte that he hath   *whatever haste that he may be in*
    ne seeth me him ner shake,   *one never sees him stir*
He is the sloweste man
    that ever was y-boren!
Wher he were o the feld   *wherever he might be in the field*
    pichinge stake,   *planting cuttings*
For hope of his thornës   *hoping with his thorns*
    to ditten his doren,   *to stop up his gaps*
15 He mot mid his twi-bil   *he must with his two-edged axe*
    other trous make   *make another bundle (of thorns)*
Other al his dayës werk   *or else all his day's work*
    ther were y-loren.   *there would be lost*

This ilke man upon heigh   *this same man up there*
    when er he were,   *whatever his origin*
Wher he were i the moone   *whether he was in the moon*
    boren and y-fed,   *born and nurtured*
He lenëth on his forke   *he leans on his fork*
    as a grey frere.   *like a grey friar*
20 This crokede kaynard   *this hunched idler*
    sore he is adred.   *he is sore afraid*
Hit is mony day go   *it is many a day gone*
    that he was here;   *since he was here*
Ichot of his ernde   *I reckon that in his errand*
    he nath nought y-sped: *he has not succeeded*

He hath hewe somwher — *he has cut somewhere*
a burthen of brere, — *a bundle of briars*
Therefore sum hayward — *for this some hedge-keeper*
hath taken his wed. — *has taken his pledge*

25 'If thy wed is y-take, — *if your pledge has been taken*
bring hom the trous, — *bring home the bundle*
Sete forth thyn other fot, — *put forward your other foot*
strid over sty. — *stride along the way*
We shule praye the hayward — *we shall invite the hedge-keeper*
hom to our hous — *home to our house*
And maken him at eise — *and make him at ease*
for the maistry; — *as much as possible*
Drinke to him deerly — *drink to him warmly*
of ful good bous, — *with right good liquor*
30 And our dame douse — *sweet wife*
shal sitten him by.
When that he is drunke
as a dreynt mous, — *as a drowned mouse*
Thenne we shule borwe — *then we shall redeem*
the wed attë baily!' — *the pledge from the bailiff*

This man herëth me nought — *hears me not*
though Ich to him crye; — *shout to him*
Ichot the cherl is def, — *I reckon the churl is deaf*
the del him to-drawe! — *the Devil take him*
35 Though Ich yeiye upon heighe — *I shout at the top of my voice*
nil he nought hye, — *he will not hurry*
The lustlesse ladde — *the lazy fellow*
can nought o lawe. — *cannot get down*
Hippe forth, Hubert, — *leap forth, Hubert*
hosede pye! — *(you) stockinged magpie*
Ichot th'art amarscled — *I reckon you are bewildered*
into the mawe. — *to your very vitals*
Though me tene with him — *though I rage at him*
that my teeth mye, — *till my teeth grind*
40 The cherl nil nought adoun — *the fellow will not come down*
er the day dawe. — *before the day dawns*

I, 115   Of rybaudz I ryme and rede o my rolle

Of rybaudz I ryme	*of menials I rhyme*
and rede o my rolle,	*and tell in my roll*
Of gadelinges, gromës,	*of lackeys, servants,*
of Colyn and of Colle,	
Harlotes, hors-knavës,	*attendants, stable boys*
by pate and by polle,	*one by one*
To devel Ich hem to-livre	*to the Devil I consign them*
and take to tolle!	*and give as payment*
5 The gadelinges were gadered	*the lackeys were gathered*
of Gonnylde gnoste;	*out of Gunnild's spark*
Palfreyours and pagës	*grooms and pages*
and boyës with boste,	*and arrogant boys*
Alle were y-haught	*all were hatched*
of an horsë thost;	*from a horse turd*
The devel hem afrete,	*the Devil devour them*
raw other aroste!	*raw or roasted*
The shapere that hem shoop,	*the creator who made them*
to shame he hem shadde,	*for shame he singled them out*
10 To flees and to flye,	*for fleas and for flies*
to tyke and to tadde;	*for mongrels and for toads*
So saith romaunz,	*as books say*
whoso right radde:	*whoever has read correctly*
Flee com of flour,	*flea came from flower*
and lous com of ladde.	*and louse came from lad*
The harlotes ben horelinges	*the attendants are fornicators*
and haunten the plawe;	*and practise copulation*
The gadelinges ben glotouns	*the lackeys are gluttons*
and drinken er hit dawe;	*and drink before it dawns*
15 Sathanas here syre	*Satan their sire*
saide on his sawe:	*said in his old saying*
Gobelyn made his garner	*Goblin made his granary*
of gromënë mawe.	*of a groom's belly*
The knave crammëth his crop	*the knave crams his crop*
er the cok crawe;	*before the cock crows*
He momelëth and mocchëth	*he mumbles and munches*
and marrëth his mawe;	*and ruins his stomach*
When he is al for-laped	*when he is completely sozzled*
and lad over lawe,	*and filled beyond measure*
20 A dozeyne of doggës	*a dozen dogs*
ne mightë hyre drawe.	*could not drag payment (out of him)*

The rybaud arisëth   *the rascal gets up*
   er the day rewe,   *before the day dawns*
He scrapëth on his scabbës   *he pick at his scabs*
   and drawëth hem to dewe;   *and makes them ooze*
Sene is on his browe   *it is evident from his forehead*
   and on his eye-brewe,   *and from his eyebrow*
That he lousëth a losynger   *that he would free a flatterer*
   and shooëth a shrewe.   *and shoe a shrew*

25 Nou ben capel-claweres   *now are stableboys*
   with shamë to-shride;   *shamefully clothed*
They busken hem with botouns   *they adorn themselves with buttons*
   as hit were a bride,   *like girls*
With lowe-lacëde shoon   *with low-laced shoes*
   of an heifer-hide;   *of heifer's hide*
They piken of here provendre   *they filch from their fodder*
   al herë pride.   *all their finery*

Whoso rekenëth with knavës   *whoever settles with lackeys*
   herë costage –   *their wages*
30 The lithernesse of the ladde,   *the evil of the varlet*
   the pride of the page! –   *the arrogance of the fellow*
Though he yeve hem cattës dryt   *though he gave them cat's shit*
   to here companage,   *for their relish*
Yet hem sholde arewen   *yet they would complain*
   of the arrerage!   *about the balance due*

While God was on erthe
   and wandrede wide,   *and travelled far and wide*
What was the resoun   *reason*
   why He noldë ride?   *did not wish to ride*
35 For He noldë no grom   *because he wanted no groom*
   to go by His side,
Ne grucchyng of no gadeling   *nor the grumbling of any lackey*
   to chaule ne to chide.   *jabbering or quarreling*

Spedëth you to spewen,   *you are as quick to vomit*
   as me doth to spelle;   *as I am to speak*
The fend you afrete   *the fiend devour you*
   with flesh and with felle!   *flesh and skin*
Herknëth hiderward, horsmen,   *listen here, stable men*
   a tidyng Ich you telle,   *a message I have to give you*
40 That ye shulen hangen   *that you will hang*
   and herberewen in helle.   *and lodge in hell*

I, 116   Skottes out of Berwik and of Abirdene ~ *Laurence Minot*

Skottes out of Berwik	*Berwick*
and of Abirdene,	*Aberdeen*
At the Bannok burn	*Bannock burn / stream*
war ye to kene;	*you were too bold*
Thare slogh ye many sakles,	*there you slew many an innocent*
als it was sene,	*as was manifest*
And now has King Edward	
wroken it, I wene.	*avenged it, I reckon*
5 It es wrokin, I wene,	*it is*
wele wurth the while;	*blest be the hour*
War yit with the Skottes,	*beware still of the Scots*
for thai er ful of gile!	*for they are full of guile*
Whare er ye Skottes	*where are you Scots*
of Saint Johnës toune?	*of St. John's town*
The boste of yowre baner	*the pride of your banner*
es betin all doune;	*is beaten*
When ye bosting will bede,	*taunts; offer*
Sir Edward es boune	*ready*
10 For to kindel yow care	*to cause you misery*
and crak yowre crowne.	*crown (i.e. top of head)*
He has crakkëd yowre croune,	
wele worth the while;	
Shame bityde the Skottes,	*befall*
for thai er full of gile!	
Skottes of Striflin	*Stirling*
war steren and stout,	*were fierce and bold*
Of God ne of gude men	*good*
had thai no dout;	*fear*
15 Now have thai, the pelers,	*the raiders*
prikëd obout,	*galloped round about*
Bot at the last Sir Edward	*but in the end*
rifild thaire rout.	*stripped the lot of them*
He has rifild thaire rout,	
wele wurth the while,	
Bot ever er thai under	*but ever are they underneath*
bot gaudes and gile.	*(nothing) but tricks and deceit*
Rugh-fute riveling,	*rough-footed rawhide boot*
now kindels thi care;	*now kindles your woe*
20 Berebag with thy boste,	*bag-carrier with your boasting*
thi biging es bare;	*dwelling*
Fals wretche and forsworn,	*perjured*
whider wiltou fare?	*where will you go*

Busk thee unto Brig	*haste you to Bruges*
and abide thare.	*there*
Thare, wretche, shaltou won	*remain*
and wery the while;	*and curse the time*
Thi dwelling in Donde	*your stay in Dundee*
es done for thi gile.	*is over because of your guile*

25 The Skotte gase in Burghës	*goes to Bruges*
and betes the stretes,	*and pounds the streets*
All thise Inglis men	*(to) all these English*
harmes he hetes;	*he threatens harm*
Fast makes he his mone	*earnestly; complaint*
to men that he metes,	
Bot fone frendes he findes	*but few*
that his bale betës.	*who ease his misery*
Fune betes his bale,	*few*
wele wurth the while,	
30 He uses all threting	*every threat*
with gaudes and gile.	*with tricks and guile*

Bot many man thretes	*makes threats*
and spekes ful ill	
That sum tyme war better	*who sometimes would be better*
to be stane-still.	*to be silent as a stone*
The Skot in his words	
has wind for to spill,	*waste*
For at the last Edward	
sall have al his will.	*shall have*
35 He had his will at Berwik,	
wele wurth the while!	
Skottes broght him the kayes,	*brought him the keys*
but get for thaire gile.	*but look out for their guile*

I, 117   Ich am of Irlande

Ich am of Irlande	*from Ireland*
And of the holy lande	
Of Irlande.	

Gode sire, pray Ich thee,	
5 For of saynte charité	*for holy charity*
Come and daunce with me	
In Irlande.	

I, 118   Maiden in the morë lay

Maiden in the morë lay,   *dwelt in the moor*
  In the morë lay,
Sevenightë fullë –   *for a full seven nights*
Sevenightë fullë –
5 Maiden in the morë lay,
    In the morë lay,
Sevenightë fullë –
Sevenightë fullë –
  Fullë and a day.

10 Well was hirë mete,   *excellent was her food*
    What was hirë mete?
The primerole and the –   *primrose*
The primerole and the –
Well was hirë mete,
15   What was hirë mete?
The primerole and the –
The primerole and the –
  And the violet.

Well was hirë dring,   *drink*
20   What was hirë dring?
The coldë water of the –
The coldë water of the –
Well was hirë dring,
    What was hirë dring?
25 The coldë water of the –
The coldë water of the –
  Of the wellë-spring.   *of the spring*

Well was hirë bour,   *her dwelling*
  What was hirë bour?
30 The redë rose and the –
The redë rose and the –
Well was hirë bour,
    What was hirë bour?
The redë rose and the –
35 The redë rose and the –
  And the lilie flour.

I, 119   D ... dronken

D ... dronken –
dronken, dronken, y-dronken,
... dronken is Tabart attë wyne.   *drunk is Tabart with* (lit. *at the*) *wine*
Hay ... suster, Walter, Peter,   *sister*
5   Ye dronke al depe,   *you all drink deeply*
And Ichulle eke.   *and I shall too*

Stondëth alle stillë -   *stand everyone still*
Stillë, stillë, stillë -
Stondëth allë stillë –
10 Stille as any ston;   *stone*
Trippe a litel with thy fot,
And let thy body gon.   *go*

I, 120   The Complaint of Chaucer to his Purse

To yow, my purse, and to noon other wight   *to no other person*
Complayne I, for ye be my lady dere.   *you are; dear*
I am so sory, now that ye been lyght;   *light (in weight) / fickle*
For certës, but ye make me hevy chere,   *unless you take me seriously*
5   Me were as leef be layd upon my bere;   *I would as readily; bier*
For whiche unto your mercy thus I crye   *for which reason*
Beth hevy ayeyne, or ellës mote I dye.   *be heavy / serious again; or else I must die*

Now vouchëth sauf this day or hyt be nyght   *now grant; before it is night*
That I of yow the blisful soune may here   *sound; hear*
10 Or see your colour lyke the sonnë bryght
That of yelownesse hadde never pere.   *equal*
Ye be my lyfe, ye be myn hertës stere.   *heart's rudder*
Quene of comfort and of good companye
Beth hevy ayeyne, or ellës moote I dye.

15 Now purse that ben to me my lyvës lyght   *(you) who are; light of my life*
And savëour as doune in this worlde here,   *down*
Out of this tounë helpe me thurgh your myght, *town*
Syn that ye wole nat ben my tresorere;   *since; treasurer*
For I am shave as nye as is a frere.   *shaven as close as a friar*
20 But yet I pray unto your curtesye,
Bethe hevy ayen, or ellës moote I dye.

Lenvoy de Chaucer
O conquerour of Brutës Albyon,   *Brutus's Albion*
Which that by lygne and free eleccion   *who by lineage*
Been verray kynge, this song to yow I sende,   *are true king*
25 And ye, that mowen alle oure harmes amende, *who are able; to remedy*
Have mynde upon my supplicacion.

I, 121   Whan I have in myn purs y-now

Syng we alle and say we thus:
'Gramercy, myn owen purs!'   *thank you, my own purse*

    Whan I have in myn purs y-now,   *enough*
    I may have bothe hors and plow,   *plough*
5 And also frendës y-now,   *friends in plenty*
      Through the vertu of myn purs.   *power / excellence*

    Whan my purs gynnëth to slak,
    And ther is nought in my pak,
    They wil sayn: 'Go, farewel, Jak!
10   Thou shalt no more drynke with us.'

    Thus is al myn good y-lorn,   *all my money lost*
    And my purs is al totorn,   *is all torn to pieces*
    I may play me with an horn   *I may amuse myself*
      In the stede al of myn purs.   *instead of*

15 Farewel hors and farewel cow,
    Farewel cart and farewel plow;
    As I played me with a bow,
      I said: 'God, what is al this?'

I, 122   I have a gentil cok

    I have a gentil cok,   *noble cock*
      crowëth me the day;   *who crows for me at day-break*
    He doth me risen erly,   *makes*
      my matins for to say.

5 I have a gentil cok,
      comen he is of gret;   *of great lineage*
    His comb is of red corel,
      his tayil is of jet.

    I have a gentil cok,
10   comen he is of kinde;   *of noble birth*
    His comb is of red corel,
      his tayil is of inde.   *indigo*

    His leggës ben of asur,   *lapis lazuli*
      so gentil and so smale;   *so graceful and so slender*
15 His spurës arn of sylver white   *spurs are of bright silver*
      into the wortëwale.   *down to the root*

His eyen arn of cristal,   *eyes*
    loken al in aumber;   *set; amber*
And every night he perchëth him
20   in myn ladies chaumber.

I, 123   Omnes gentes plaudite!

Omnes gentes plaudite!   *O clap your hands all ye people*
I saw many briddës sitte on a tre,
They token here flight and flowen away   *flew away*
With *Ego dixi* – have good day!   *I said*

5 Many white federes hath the pye –   *magpie*
I may noon more singen, my lippes arn so drye; *no more*
Many white federes hath the swan –
The more that I drinke, the lesse good I can.   *the less sense I have*

Lay stikkes on the fire, wel mot it brenne,   *well may it burn*
10 Yeve us onës drinken er we gon henne.   *give us one more drink; hence*

I, 124   I have a yong suster

I have a yong suster   *sister*
    fer beyond the se,   *far; sea*
Many be the drueries   *are the keepsakes*
    that she sentë me.

5 She sentë me the cherye   *cherry*
    withouten any stone,
And so she did the dove
    withouten any bone.

She sentë me the brere   *briar*
10   withouten any rinde,   *any bark*
She bad me love my lemman   *sweetheart*
    withoutë longìng.

How sholde any cherye
    be withoutë stone?
15 And how sholde any dove
    ben withoutë bone?

How sholde any brere
    ben withoutë rinde?
How sholde I love myn lemman
20   withoutë longìng?

When the cherye was a flour,
    than hadde it non stone;
When the dovë was an ey,   *was an egg*
    than hadde it non bone.

25 When the brerë was onbred   *had not yet sprouted*
    than hadde it non rinde;
When the mayde hath that she loveth   *has what she loves*
    she is without longìng.

I, 125   I have a newe garden

I have a newe garden,
    and newe is begunne;   *and it is newly begun*
Swych another garden   *such*
    know I not under sunne.

5 In the middës of my garden   *in the midst*
    is a perer set,   *pear-tree*
And it wil non pere bern   *and it will bear no pear*
    but a pere-jonet.   *other than an early pear*

The fairest mayde of this toun
10   prayëd me
    For to griffen her a gryf   *to plant her a graft*
    of myn pery-tre.   *from my pear-tree*

When I hadde hem griffëd   *planted*
    alle at herë wille,   *all according to her wishes*
15 The wyn and the alë   *the wine and the ale*
    she dide in fille.   *she poured out*

And I griffëd here
    right up in here home,   *deep inside her*
And be that day twenty wekes   *weeks*
20   it was quik in here womb.

That day twelvë month   *months*
    that mayde I met,
She said it was a pere Robert   *a 'Robert' pear*
    but non pere Jonet.   *but not a 'John' pear*

I, 126   Seynt Stevene was a clerk

Seynt Stevene was a clerk   *attendant*
  in Kyng Heròwdës halle,
And servëd him of bred and cloth,   *with food at table*
  as every kyng befalle.   *as would befit every king*

5 Steven out of kichen cam   *came from the kitchen*
  with borës hed on honde,   *with a boar's head in his hands*
He saw a sterre was fayr and bright   *a star which was*
  over Bedlem stonde.   *Bethlehem*

He cast adoun the borës hed,
10   and went into the halle:
'I forsak thee, Kyng Heròwdës
  and thy werkës alle.

'I forsak thee, Kyng Heròwdës,
  and thy werkës alle,
15 Ther is a chyld in Bedlem born
  is better than we alle.'

'What ailëth thee, Stevene?
  what is thee befalle?   *what has happened to you*
Lakketh thee either mete or drynk   *do you lack either food or drink*
20   in Kyng Heròwdës halle?'

'Lakketh me neither mete ne drynk   *I lack neither*
  in Kyng Heròwdës halle;
Ther is a chyld in Bedlem born
  is beter than we alle.'

25 'What aileth thee, Steven, art thou wod,   *are you mad*
  or thou gynnest to brede?   *or are you beginning to rave*
Lakketh thee either gold or fee   *gold or payment*
  or any rychë wede?'   *fine clothing*

'Lakketh me neither gold ne fee,
30   ne non rychë wede;
Ther is a chyld in Bedlem born,
  shal help us at our nede.'   *in our necessity*

'That is also soth, Stevèn,   *that is just as true*
  also soth y-wis,   *just as true, indeed*
35 As this capoun crowë shal   *capon*
  that lyth here in myn dish.'   *lies*

That word was not so sonë said,   *was no sooner said*
    that word in that halle,
The capoun crew *Christus natus est*   *Christ is born*
40   among the lordës alle.

'Risëth up, myn turmentoures,
    by two and al by on,   *i.e. one and all*
And ledëth Steven out of this town,
    and stonëth him with ston.'

45 Token they Stevènë   *they took*
    and stoned hym in the way;
And therfore is his even   *his eve*
    on Cristës owen day.

I, 127   Yong men, I warne you everychon

How, hey! It is non les: *it is no lie*
I dar not sayn whan she saith 'Pes!'   *I dare not speak; peace / be quiet*

Yong men, I warne you everychon,   *young; every one*
Oldë wivës tak ye non,
5 For I myself at hom have on –
    I dare not sayn whan she saith 'Pes!'

Whan I come fro the plow at non,   *from the plough at noon*
In a riven dish my mete is don,   *in a cracked dish my food is put*
I dar not aske our dame a spon –   *spoon*
10   I dar not sayn whan she saith 'Pes!'

If I aske our damë bred,
She taketh a staf and breketh myn hed,   *head*
And doth me renne under the led –   *an makes me run; cauldron*
    I dar not sayn whan she saith 'Pes!'

15 If I aske our damë flesh,   *meat*
She brekëth myn hed with a dish:
'Boy, thou art not worth a rish!' –   *rush*
    I dar not sayn whan she saith 'Pes!'

If I aske our damë chese,   *cheese*
20 'Boy,' she sayth, al at ese,   *quite unmoved*
'Thou art not worth half a pese!' –   *half a pea*
    I dar not say whan she saith 'Pes!'

I, 128   We bern aboute no cattës skinnes

We ben chapmen light of fote,	*pedlars light of foot*
The foulë weyës for to fle.	*flee*
We bern aboute no cattës skinnes,	*carry about*
Purses, perlës, sylver pynnes,	*pearls*
5 Smale wimpeles for ladies chinnes;	*fine head-dresses*
Damsele, bye sum ware of me.	*buy some wares from me*
I have a poket for the nones,	*for the purpose*
Therin ben tweyne precious stones;	*two*
Damsele, hadde ye assayed hem ones,	*if you once tried them*
10 Ye sholde the rather gon with me.	*you would the sooner go with me*
I have a jelyf of Godes sonde,	*jelly by God's grace*
Withouten feet it can stonde,	*stand*
It can smite and hath non honde;	*no hand*
Red yourself what it may be.	*guess*
15 I have a powder for to selle,	
What it is can I not telle,	
It makëth maydenes wombes to swelle;	
Therof I have a quantité.	

I, 129   As I went on Yol Day

'Kyrië', so 'kyrië',	
Jankin singëth mirië,	*merrily*
With 'alëyson'.	
As I went on Yol Day	*Yule (Christmas) Day*
5 in our prosessyon,	
Knew I jolly Jankin	
by his mery ton.	*tone / voice*
Kyriëlëyson.	
Jankin began the offis	*office (i.e. of the Mass)*
10 on the Yolë Day	
And yet me thinketh it dos me good,	*does*
so merie gan he say	*so merrily did he say*
Kyriëlëyson.	
Jankin red the pistil	*read the Epistle*
15 ful fair and ful wel,	
And yet me thinketh it dos me good,	
as ever have I sel.	*as ever I may have bliss*
Kyriëlëyson.	

Jankin at the *Sanctus*
20   crakëth a merie note,   *divides*
And yet me thinketh it dos me good –
I payëd for his cote.   *coat*
    Kyriëlëyson.

Jankin crakëth notës   *divides his notes*
25   an hundred on a knot,   *a hundred in a phrase*
And yet he hakketh hem smaller   *splits them smaller*
than wortës to the pot.   *than herbs for the pot*
    Kyriëlëyson.

Jankin at the *Angnus*   *Agnus Dei*
30   berëth the pax-brede,   *pax*
He twinkelëd, but said nought,   *winked*
and on myn foot he trede.   *trod*
    Kyriëlëyson.

Benedicamus Domino,   *Let us bless the Lord*
35   Crist fro shame me shilde;   *may Christ shield me from shame*
Deo gratias therto –   *Thanks be to God, as well*
alas, I go with childe!
    Kyriëlëyson.

I, 130   Thou that sellest the worde of God

Thou that sellest the worde of God,
Be thou barfot, be thou shod,   *bare-foot*
    Com thou never here!
In principio erat verbum   *in the beginning was the word*
5   Is the word of God, alle and sum   *all in all*
    That thòu sellest, lewed frere.   *ignorant friar*

Hit is cursëd symonie   *simony*
Eyther to sellen or to bye   *buy*
    Any gostly thinge.   *spiritual*
10 Therfore, frere, go as thou come,   *came*
And hold thee in thy hous at home
    Til we thee almës brynge.

Goddës lawe ye reversèn,   *pervert*
And mennës housës ye persèn   *penetrate*
15   As Paul berëth witnes.
As midday develes goinge aboute   *midday devils*
For money lowëly ye loute,   *low you bow*
    Flatteringe both more and less.   *great and humble*

I, 131   Allas! what shul we frerës do

Allas! what shul we frerës do	*shall we friars*
Now lewed men con holy writ?	*lay men know*
All aboutë where I go	
They aposen me of it.	*they confront me with it*
5 Then wondreth me that it is so	*it amazes me*
How lewed men con allë wite,	*can understand everything*
Certeinly we ben undo	*we shall be ruined*
But if we mo amenden it.	*unless we can rectify it*
I trow the devel brought it about	*I believe*
10 To write the gospel in English,	
For lewed men ben nowe so stout	*are now so defiant*
They yeve us neither flesh ne fish.	*meat nor fish*
When I come into a shoppe	
For to say *'in principio'*,	
15 They bidden me 'Go forth, lewd poppe!	*foolish fop*
And werche', and win my silver so.	*work*
If I say hit longëth not	*it is not fitting*
For prestes to werchen where they go,	*wherever*
They leggen for hem holi writ	*claim in their support*
20 And sayen that Seint Paul did so.	
Than they loke on myn habìte	*habit*
And sayn, 'Forsothe, withouten othes,	*truly, without doubt*
Whether it be russet, black, or white,	*whether; brown*
It is worthe alle our wering-clothes!'	*clothing*
25 I say, 'I biddë not for me,	*I do not beg for myself*
But for them that haven none.'	
They sayn, 'Thou havëst two or three;	
Yeve hem that neden therof one.'	*give them*
Thus our deceitës ben aspide	*deceits are found out*
30 In this maner and many mo;	*more*
Few men bedden us abide	*ask us to tarry*
But hyë fast that we were go.	*but to hurry up and be gone*
If it go forth in this manèr,	*if it goes on*
It wol done us muchë gile;	*harm*
35 Men shul fynde unnethe a frere	*scarcely a friar*
In Englande within a while.	

I, 132   Swarte smekëd smithes smatered with smoke

Swarte smekëd smithes	*black smoke-begrimed smiths*
smatered with smoke	*smutty with smoke*
Drive me to deth	
with din of here dyntes!	*din of their blows*
Swich noys on nyghtes	*such noise at night*
ne herd men never:	
What knavënë cry	*what a shouting of rascals*
and clatering of knockes!	*and clattering of hammer-blows*
5 The cammëde conjouns	*the snub-nosed rogues*
crien after 'col, col!'	*shout for 'coal, coal!'*
And blowen here bellowes	
that al here brain brestes.	*until their very brains burst*
'Huf, puf!' saith that one,	*the one*
'haf, paf!' that other.	*the other*
They spytten and sprawlen	*they spit and stretch*
and spellen many spelles;	*tell many a tale*
They gnawen and gnachen,	*grind and gnash (their teeth)*
they gronen togider,	*they grunt together*
10 And holden hem hote	*and keep themselves hot*
with here hard hamers.	*with their strenuous hammering*
Of a bole-hyde	*of bull-hide*
ben here barm-felles;	*are their leather aprons*
Here shankes ben shakeled	*their legs are protected*
for the fire-flunderes;	*against sparks from the fire*
Hevy hameres they han	*have*
that hard ben handled,	*which are difficult to wield*
Stark strokes they stryken	*stout blows they strike*
on a steled stokke:	*on a steel anvil*
15 Lus, bus! las, das!	
rowten by rowe,	*they strike in turn*
Swich dolful a dreme	*such a dreadful noise*
the devyl it to-dryve!	*the Devil take it*
The mayster longëth a litel	*the master smith lengthens a small piece*
and lashëth a lesse,	*and hammers out a smaller bit*
Twynëth hem twayn	*twists the two together*
and touchëth a treble.	*and strikes a treble note*
Tik, tak! hic, hac!	
tiket, taket! tik, tak!	
20 Lus, bus! lus, das! –	
swych lyf they leden!	*such a life they lead*
Allë clothemeres –	*all blacksmiths*
Crist hem gyve sorwe!	
May no man for bren-wateres	*water-sizzlers*
on night han his rest.	*for a single night have his rest*

PART II

II, 1   Allas, Deth, who made thee so hardy ~ *Charles d'Orléans*

Allas, Deth, who made thee so hardy   *so bold*
To take awey the most nobill princesse
Which comfort was of my liif and body –
Mi wele, my joy, my plesere and ricchesse?   *my well-being; pleasure and wealth*
5 But syn thou hast biraft me my maystres,   *since; my mistress*
Take me, poore wrecche, hir cely serviture,   *her innocent servant*
For levyr had y hastily forto dy   *I would rather; die*
Than langwysshe in this karfull tragedy,   *languish; sorrowful tragedy*
In payne, sorowe and woofull aventure.   *woeful misfortune*

10 Allas, nad she of eche good thing plenté,   *had she not; each; abundance (plenty)*
Flowryng in youthe and in hir lustynes?   *in her vitality*
I biseche God, acursëd mote thou be,   *may*
O falsë Deth, so full of gret rudenes.   *great harshness*
Had thou hir taken in unweldynes,   *in infirmity*
15 As had thou not y-doon so gret rigure;   *then had you not acted so harshly*
But thou, alak, hast take hir hastily,   *taken; with haste (i.e. in her prime)*
And, welaway, this left me pitously   *alas*
In payne, sorow and wooful aventure.

Allas, alone am y out compané!   *without companion*
20 Farewell, my lady, farewell my gladnes!
Now is the love parted twix yow and me.
Yet, what for then, y make yow here promes   *yet, what of that; promise*
That with prayers y shall of gret larges   *plenteous in number*
Here serve yow ded, while my liif may endure,   *dead*
25 Out forgetyng in slouthe or slogardy,   *without; in sloth or sluggishness*
Biwaylyng oft yowre deth with wepyng ey,   *weeping eye*
In payne, sorow and wofull aventure.

O God, that lordëst every creature,   *who rulest over*
Graunt of thi grace thi right forto mesure   *prerogative to exercise moderation*
30 On alle the offens she hath doon wilfully,   *offences; committed*
So that the good sowle of hir now not ly   *should not lie*
In payne, sorow and wofull aventure.

II, 2   For dedy liif, my lyvy deth y wite ~ *Charles d'Orléans*

For dedy liif, my lyvy deth y wite,	*for death-like life, my living death I*
For ese of payne, in payne of ese y dye;	*ease of pain; I die* [*blame*
For lengthe of woo, woo lengtith me so lite	*for prolongation of woe, woe prolongs*
That quyk y dye and yet as ded lyve y.	*living* [*my life so little*
5 Thus nygh afer, y fele the fer is ny	*almost afar, I feel the distance is near*
Of thing certeyne that y, uncerteyn, seche,	*of a certain thing; seek*
Which is the deth, sith Deth hath my lady –	*since Death*
O wofull wrecche, O wrecche, lesse onys thi speche!	*lose once for all thy speech*
O gost formatt, yelde up thi breth attones,	*vanquished spirit, yield up thy breath at*
10 O karkas faynt, take from this liif thi flight,	*feeble body* [*once*
O bollëd hert, forbrest thou with thi grones,	*swollen heart, burst; groans*
O mested eyen, whi fayle ye not yowre sight?	*misted eyes, why do you not lose*
Syn Deth, allas, hath tane my lady bright	*since; taken*
And left this world without on to her leche,	*without anyone like her*
15 To lete me lyve ye do me gret unright –	*let; great injustice*
O wofull wrecche, O wrecche, lesse onys thi speche!	
What is this liif? – a liif or deth y lede?	*lead*
Nay, certës, deth in liif is liklynes;	*indeed; is the likelihood*
For though y fayne me port of lustihede	*I feign a bearing of good cheer*
20 Yet inward, lo! it sleth me, my distres.	*slays me*
For fro me fledde is joy and all gladnes	*for from me fled*
That y may say, in all this world so reche	*(so) that; say (that); so rich*
As y is noon of payne and hevynes –	*as I (there) is no one in pain and woe*
O woofull wrecche, o wrecche, lesse onys thi speche!	
25 Ther nys no thing sauf Deth to do me day,	*save Death to cause me to die*
That may of me the woofull paynës eche;	*(nothing) that can; increase*
But wolde y dey, allas, yet y ne may –	*but though I would wish to die; I cannot*
O wofull wrecche, o wrecche, lesse onys thi speche.	

II, 3   Tofornë Love have y pleyd at the chesse ~ *Charles d'Orléans*

Tofornë Love have y pleyd at the chesse	*before Love*
To passe the tyme with cursëd false Daungere,	*false Disdain*
And kepte eche poynt bi good avysynes	*kept each square by good strategy*
Withouten losse, to that, as wol ye here,	*until, as you will hear*
5 That Fortune came to strengthen his matere.	*strengthen his cause*
O woo worthe she that my game ovyrthrew,	*woe betide her who upset my game*
For tane she hath my lady, welaway.	*for she has taken; alas*
That y am matt, this may y se and say,	*I am checkmated*
Without so be y make a lady newe.	*unless it should be that I regain a lady*

10 In my lady lay all my sikirnes,   *security*
   For ay at nede hir socoure was me nere   *ever in need her succour was near me*
   To helpe me in eche trobill or distres,   *trouble*
   For all my warde, that kepte my lady dere,   *my defence*
   More then knyght, that is of more powere,   *greater strength*
15 Or afyn, pown, or rook, this fynde y trewe;   *or bishop, pawn*
   For all my game y lost hit have, and pley,
   And all my good, God wot, that on hit lay,   *my well-being; that depended on it*
   Without so be y make a lady newe.

   Not kan y skyfte me from the sotilnes   *I cannot escape from the cunning*
20 Of seytfull Fortune with hir dowbil chere,   *deceitful Fortune; ambiguous expression*
   That doth eche game so torne and ovyrdresse   *so turn and overturn*
   That where to drawe not wot y, there or here,   *where to move I know not*
   She cometh on me in a so sodeyn gere,   *in so sudden a way*
   That y may not myn harmës, lo, eschewe,   *eschew / avoid*
25 Mi game is all forcast in suche aray,   *all upset in such a manner*
   That in no wise y hit amenden may,   *in no way can I remedy it*
   Without so be y make a lady newe.

   Farewel, princesse, yowre losse sore doth me rewe *causes me grievous pain*
   And evir shall unto myn endyng-day,
30 For shulde y thenke rekevre me now – nay, nay,   *to recover now*
   Without so be y make a lady newe.

II, 4   In the forest of noyous hevynes ~ *Charles d'Orléans*

   In the forest of noyous hevynes,   *painful grief*
   As y went wandryng in the moneth of May,
   I mette of love the myghti gret goddes,   *great*
   Which axëd me whithir y was away;   *who asked me where I was going*
5 I hir answered, 'As fortune doth convey,   *her; guide*
   As oon exyled from joy, al be me loth,   *as one; hateful though it is to me*
   That passyng well all folke me clepen may   *very fittingly; may call me*
   The man forlost that wot not where he goth.'   *man utterly lost, who knows not*

   Half in a smyle ayen of hir humblesse   *in reply out of her graciousness*
10 She seide, 'My frend, if so y wist, ma fay,   *if I knew, indeed*
   Wherfore that thou art brought in such distresse,
   To shape thyn ese y wolde mysilf assay;   *to contrive relief for you I would; try*
   For heretofore y sett thyn hert in way   *in the way*
   Of gret plesere; y not whoo made thee wroth;   *great happiness; I know not who; sad*
15 Hit grevëth me thee see in suche aray,   *grieves; in such a state*
   The man forlost that wot not where he goth.'

'Allas!' y seide, 'most sovereyne good princesse,
Ye knowe my case, what nedëth to yow say,   *what need is there to tell you*
Hit is thorugh Deth, that sheweth to all rudnesse,   *because Death; harshness*
20 Hath fro me tane that y most lovëd ay,   *has taken from me the one whom; always*
In whom that all myn hope and comfort lay;
So passyng frendship was bitwene us both   *such great*
That y was not, to fals Deth did hir day,   *till false Death caused her to die*
The man forlost that wot not where he goth.

25 'Thus am y blynd, allas and welaway!   *alack and alas*
Al fer myswent, with my staf grapsyng wey,   *gone far astray; groping my way*
That no thyng axe but me a grave to cloth: *who ask nothing but a grave to cover me*
For pity is that y lyue thus a day,   *the pity is that*
The man forlost that wot not where he goth.'

II, 5   O sely ankir, that in thi selle ~ *Charles d'Orléans*

O sely ankir, that in thi selle   *O blessed anchorite; cell*
I-closëd art with stoon and gost not out,   *enclosed; stone*
Thou maist ben gladder so for to dwelle
Then y with wanton wandryng thus abowt,   *unrestricted*
5 That have me pikëd, amongis the rowt,   *who have chosen for myself; crowd*
An endles woo withouten recomfort,   *endless woe without comfort*
That of my poorë liif y stonde in dowt –   *in fear*
Go, dul complaynt, my lady this report.   *sad complaint, to my lady*

The anker hath no more him for to greve   *to trouble him*
10 Then sool, alone, upon the wallës stare.   *than only, alone; to stare*
But, welaway, y stonde in more myscheef,   *but, alas; in greater misfortune*
For he hath helthe and y of helthe am bare.   *salvation; am lacking*
And more and more when y come where ther are
Of fayre folkës to se a goodly sort,   *a goodly company*
15 A thousand fold that doth encrese my care –   *that causes my sorrow to increase*
Go, dull complaynt, my lady this report.

It doth me thynke, 'Yondir is fayre of face!   *causes me to think, 'Yonder one*
But, what! More fayre yet is my ladi dere!
Yond on is small! And yonde streight sidës has!   *slender; has straight sides*
20 Her foot is lite! And she hath eyen clere! –   *dainty; bright eyes*
But all ther stayned my lady were she here!'   *but my lady would eclipse all present*
Thus thynke y, lo, which doth me discomfort,   *causes me*   [*(lit. there)*
Not for the sight, but for y nare hir nere –   *but because I was not near her*
Go, dull complaynt, my lady this report.

25 Wo worthe them which that raft me hir presence! *woe betide them who deprived me of*
Wo worth the tyme to y to hir resort!   *woe betide; until I come to her*
Wo worth is me to be thus in absence!   *woe is me to be thus absent from her*
Go, dull complaynt, my lady this report.

II, 6   Syn that y have a nounparall maystres ~ *Charles d'Orléans*

Syn that y have a nounparall maystres	*since I; an incomparable mistress*
The which hath hool my service and myn hert,	*wholly*
I shall be glad for any greef or smert	*grief or pain*
To serve hir in hir goodly lustynes:	*her; pleasing vivacity*
5 For now y trust to have, dowtles,	*doubtless*
More joy then ther be stiches in my shert –	*than there are stitches in my shirt*
Syn that y have a nounparall maystres	
The whiche hath hool my service and myn hert.	
Though, to envyous, hit be hevynes	*to the envious, it is sadness*
10 And sorow gret, to don hem prike and stert,	*to cause them to prance and rear up*
Yet, bi my trouthe, when that y me advert	*yet, upon my word, when I consider*
Ther displesere, hit is my gret gladnes –	*their*
Syn that y have a nounparall maystres	
The whiche hath hool my service and myn hert.	

II, 7   My gostly fadir y me confesse ~ *Charles d'Orléans*

My gostly fadir y me confesse,	*spiritual father*
First to God and then to yow,	
That at a wyndow – wot ye how?–	*do you know how*
I stale a cosse of gret swetnes,	*I stole a kiss*
5 Which don was out avisynes;	*which was done without thinking*
But hit is doon, not undoon now –	*done*
My gostly fadir y me confesse,	
First to God and then to yow.	
But y restore it shall dowtles	
10 Ageyn, if so be that y mow;	*I can*
And that to God y make avow,	*I vow*
And ellis y axe foryefënes –	*and otherwise I ask forgiveness*
My gostly fadir y me confesse,	
First to God and then to yow.	

II, 8   The smylyng mouth, and laughyng eyen gray ~ *Charles d'Orléans*

The smylyng mouth, and laughyng eyen gray,	*eyes*
The brestës rounde, and long smal armës twayne,	*slender arms*
The hondës smothe, the sidës streight and playne,	*smooth; straight and smooth*
Yowre fetës lite – what shulde y ferther say?	*little feet; further*
5 Hit is my craft when ye are fer away	*my occupation; far*
To muse theron in styntyng of my payne –	*assuaging*
The smylyng mouth, and laughyng eyen gray,	
The brestës rounde, and long smal armës twayne.	

So wolde y pray yow, gef y durste or may,   *would I; if I dared*
10 The sight to se as y have seyne;   *to see as I have seen*
   Forwhi that craft me is most fayne,   *wherefore; to me is most pleasing*
   And wol ben to the howre in which y day –   *and will be; hour; I die*
     The smylyng mouth, and laughyng eyen gray,
     The brestës rounde, and long smal armës twayne.

II, 9   Go forth myn hert wyth my lady ~ *Charles d'Orléans*

    Go forth myn hert wyth my lady,   *my heart*
    Loke that ye spar no besynes   *look that you spare no effort*
    To serve hyr wyth seche lowlynes   *such humility*
    That ye get hyr grace and mercy.   *you may earn*

   5 Pray hyr oftymës pryvely   *beseech her often secretly*
    That sche quippe trewly hyr promes –   *that she keep truly her promise*
     Go forth myn hert wyth my lady,
     Loke that ye spar no besynes.

    I most as a hertles body   *I must; heartless (i.e. without heart)*
10 Abyde alone in hevynes,
    And ye schal dwel wyth your maistres
    In plesans glad and mery –   *in pleasure*
     Go forth myn hert wyth my lady,
     Loke that ye spar no besynes.

II, 10   So fayre, so freshe, so goodely on to se ~ *Charles d'Orléans*

    So fayre, so freshe, so goodely on to se,   *to look upon*
    So welle dymeynet in al your governans   *so well-mannered; conduct*
    That to my hert it is a grete plesans   *heart; great delight*
    Of your godenes when y remembre me.   *when I recall your excellence*

   5 And trusteth fully wher that ever y be   *trust completely that wherever I am*
    I wylle abyde under your obeyssance –   *will remain under your rule*
     So fayre, so freshe, so goodely on to se,
     So welle dymeynet in al your governans.

    For in my thought ther is no mo but ye   *none other but you*
10 Whom y have servëd wythout repentance;
    Wherfore y pray yow sethe to my grevance   *attend (lit. see) to my trouble*
    And put osyde all myn adversité –   *put aside; adversity*
     So fayre, so freshe, so goodely on to se,
     So welle dymeynet in al your governans.

II, 11   Myn hertës joy and all myn hole plesaunce ~ *the Duke of Suffolk*

Myn hertës joy and all myn hole plesaunce   *heart's joy; whole delight*
Whom that I serve and shall do faythfully
Wyth trew entent and humble observaunce,   *loyal diligence; respect*
Yow for to plese in that I can treuly,   *please; truly*
5 Besechyng yow thys lytell byll and I   *little letter*
May hertëly, wyth som symplesse and drede,   *heartily; simplicity and reverence*
Be recomawndëd to your goodlyhede.   *recommended; excellence*

And yf ye lyst have knowlech of my qwert,   *if you wish; my health*
I am in hele (God thankëd mot He be)   *in health; may*
10 As of body, but treuly not in hert,   *heart*
Nor nought shal be to tyme I may you se;   *nor shall be until the time*
But thynke that I as treuly wyll be he
That for your ese shall do my payn and myght,   *your benefit shall exert myself all I can*
As thogh that I were dayly in your syght.   *though*

15 I wryte to yow no more for lak of space,
But I beseche the only trinité   *trinity*
Yow kepe and save be support of hys grace,   *keep and save you by*
And be your sheld from all adversyté.   *shield; adversity*
Go lytill byll, and say thou were wyth me
20 Of verey trouth, as thou canst wele remembre,   *in utter truth; well*
At myn upryst, the fyft day of Decembre.   *uprising*

II, 12   A celuy que pluys eyme en mounde

De Amico ad Amicam   *from a lover to his beloved*
A celuy que pluys eyme en mounde,   *to the one whom most I love in the world*
Of allë tho that I have founde
Carissima,   *dearest*
Saluz od treyé amour,   *greetings with faithful love*
5 With grace and joye and alle honour,
Dulcissima.   *sweetest (lady)*

Sachéz bien, pleysant et beele,   *be well assured, pleasing and beautiful one*
That I am ryght in good heele,   *good health*
Laus Christo!   *praise God (lit. praise be to Christ)*
10 Et moun amour doné vous ay,   *and my love have I given you*
And also thin owene nyght and day   *as your own*
Incisto.   *I persevere*

Ma tresduce et tresamé,   *my most sweet and most beloved*
Nyght and day for love of the   *thee*
15   Suspiro.   *I sigh*

Soyez permenant et leal,	*be constant and faithful*
Love me so that I it fele,	*may feel*
Requiro.	*I ask*
Jeo suy pour toy dolant et tryst,	*I am because of you sorrowful and sad*
20 Thu me peynëst bothe day and nyght	*you cause me pain*
Amore.	*from love*
Mort ha tret tost sun espeye,	*Death has speedily drawn his sword*
Lovë me wel er I deye	*die*
Dolore.	*from grief*
25 Sachés bien, par verité,	*know well, in truth*
Yif I deye I clepë the	*I shall call you*
Causantem;	*the cause*
Et par ceo jeo vous ore ser,	*and so I beg you sweetheart*
Love me well withoute daunger	*without reserve*
30 Amantem.	*(your) lover*
Et de vous enpense tut dyz,	*and of you I think always*
Of al the world thou berest the pris,	*you are the most excellent (lit. take the prize)*
Decora;	*gracious one*
Vous aves moy enpresoné,	*you have imprisoned me*
35 Allas, thin lovë wele me sle	*love of you will slay me*
Cum mora.	*with delay*
Icest est ma volunté,	*this is my wish*
That I mightë be with the	
Ludendo;	*in dalliance*
40 Vostre amour en moun qoer	*your love in my heart*
Brennëth hote as doth the fyr	*burns hot; fire*
Cressendo.	*as it increases (i.e. flares up)*
Douce, bele, plesaunt et chere,	*gentle, fair, pleasing and dear*
In all this lond ne is thin pere	*equal*
45 Inventa;	*found*
Claunchant ou la clere note	*lightly singing with your clear tones*
Thow art in myn hertë rote	*in my heart's core (lit. root)*
Retenta.	*held fast*
Tost serroy joyous et seyn,	*I would immediately be joyful and well*
50 Yif thu woldëst me serteyn	*if you would indeed*
Amare;	*love me*
Et tost serroy joious et lé,	*and immediately I would be joyful and happy*
There nys no thyng that shal me	*there is nothing that would*
Gravare.	*oppress me*

55 Ma tresbele et tresamé,	*my most beautiful and most beloved*
Yif thu wilt I letë be	*if you wish I shall leave off*
Langorem,	*languishing*
De cestis portés entendement	*pay attention to this* (i.e. *this letter*)
And in youre herte takëth entent	*give heed to*
60 Honorem.	*(my) devotion*
A vous jeo suy tut doné,	*to you I am wholly devoted* (lit. *given*)
Myn hertë ful of love to the	*to thee*
Presento;	*I present*
Et pur ceo, jeo vous pry	*and therefore, I beg you*
65 Sweting, for thin curteysy,	*sweet one,*
Memento!	*remember (me)*
Jeo vous pry par charité,	*I beg you for love's sake*
The wordës that here wreten be	*are written*
Tenete;	*hold fast*
70 And turne thyn hertë me toward.	
O, a Dieu, que vous gard!	*may (God) keep you*
Valete.	*farewell*

II, 13   A soun treschere et special

Responcio	*Reply*
A soun treschere et special,	*to her most dear and special one*
Fer and ner and overal	*far and near and everywhere*
In mundo,	*in the world*
Que soy ou salutz et gré,	*that he should be with health and grace*
5 With mouthë, word and hertë free	
Jocundo.	*I rejoice*
Jeo vous pry sanz debat	*I beg you that without demur*
That ye wolde of mynë stat	*you would concerning my situation*
Audire.	*listen*
10 Sertefyés a vous jeo fay,	*assurances to you I give* (lit. *make*)
I wil in tymë, whan I may,	*(that) I will*
Venyre.	*come*
Quaunt a vous venu serray	*when I (shall have) come to you*
(I yow swerë be this day	*I swear to you by this day*
15 Pro certo)	*for certain*
Mes jeo fuyss en maladye,	*even if I should be sick*
Yif ye me lovë sykyrlye	*if you love me truly*
Converto.	*I shall recover*
L'amour de vous moy fayt dolent,	*love of you makes me sad*
20 But ye me lovë I am schent	*unless you love me I shall be destroyed*
Dolendo;	*with grieving*

Sy suyre estoy de vostre amour,	*if I were sure of your love*
I were as lyght as the flour	*I would be light (i.e. joyful) as a flower*
Florendo.	*in blossom (lit. in blossoming)*

25 De moy, jeo pry, aves pyté,	*on me, I beg, have pity*
I falle so doth the lef on tre	*the leaf from the tree*
Tristando;	*with grieving*
Tot le mounde, longe et lé	*all the world, far and wide*
I woldë leve and takë thee	*leave*
30 Zelando.	*with fervour*

Pur vostre amour, allas, allas,	*for love of you*
I am wersë than I was	
Per multa;	*by far*
Jeo suy dolorouse in tut manere,	*I am sad in every way*
35 Wolde God in youre armes I were	
Sepulta.	*buried*

Jeo a vous pleyne grevousement	*I complain to you grievously*
That thyn lovë hath me schent	*that love of you has destroyed me*
Amando;	*with loving*
40 De moy, jeo pry, avez peté,	*on me, I beg, have pity*
Turnëth youre herte and lovëth me	
Letando.	*with gladness (lit. with being glad)*

A cestys ay maundé de vous ore,	*to this (letter) may I have an answer from you now*
What bote ist to strivë more	*what benefit is there in striving more*
45 Amore?	*in love*
Remaundé vostre volunté,	*send (me) back your wishes*
Yif I shal trewely trostë thee	*if I am truly to trust you*
Dulcore.	*with affection (lit. in sweetness)*

Vous estes ma mort et ma vye,	*you are my death and my life*
50 I preye yow, for youre curteysye,	
Amate;	*love (me)*
Cestes maundés, jeo vous pry,	*this letter, I pray you*
In youre hertë stedefastly	*heart*
Notate.	*inscribe*

II, 14   Fresshe lusty beauty, joyned with gentylesse ~ *John Lydgate*

Fresshe lusty beauty, joyned with gentylesse,	*delightful beauty; graciousness*
Demure, appert, glad chere with gouvernaunce,	*reserved, honest, in manner pleasing and*
Yche thing demenëd by avysinesse,	*ruled by discretion [poised*
Prudent of speeche, wisdam of dalyaunce,	*wise in conversation*
5 Gentylesse with wommanly plesaunce,	
Hevenly eyeghen, aungellyk of vysage –	*eyes, angelic*
Al this hathe nature sette in youre ymage.	

Wyfly trouthë with Penelopé,   *wifely fidelity*
And with Gresyldë parfyt pacyence,   *perfect patience*
10 Lyche Polixcenë fayrely on to se,   *like; pleasing to look upon*
Of bounty, beauty, having th'excellence   *of generosity, beauty*
Of qweene Alceste, and al the diligence
Of fayre Dydo, pryncesse of Cartage –
Al this hathe nature sett in your ymage.

15 Of Nyobë the sure perseveraunce,   *endurance*
Of Adryanë the gret stedfastnesse,
Assurëd trouthë, voyde of varyaunce,   *free from fickleness*
With yonge Thesbë, exsaumple of kyndënesse,
Of Cleopatres abydyng stabulnesse,   *stability*
20 Meeknesse of Hester, voyde of al outrage –   *intemperance*
Al this hathe nature sette in your ymage.

Beauty surmounting with feyre Rosamounde,   *outstanding in beauty; fair*
And with Isawdë for to beo secrée,   *in being discreet*
And lych Judith in vertu to abounde,   *abounding in virtue*
25 And seemlynesse with qwenë Bersabée,   *and comeliness*
Innocence, fredame, and hye bountée,   *nobility, and supreme goodness*
Fulfilled of vertu, voyde of al damage –   *all harm*
Al this hathe nature sette in youre ymage.

What shoulde I more reherce of wommanhede?
30 Yee beon the myrrour and verray exemplayre   *you are; and true exemplar*
Of whome that worde and thought acorde in deed,   *of one in whom*
And in my sight fayrest of alle fayre,
Humble and meek, benyngne and debonayre,   *kindly and gracious*
Of other vertues with al the surplusage   *with all the superabundance*
35 Which that nature hathe sette in youre ymage.

I seo no lack but oonly that daunger   *I see no defect except that disdain*
Hathe in you voyded mercy and pytée   *driven out mercy and pity*
That yee list not with youre excellence   *so that you do not care*
Upon youre servantes goodely for to see;   *to regard your servants with favour*
40 Wheron ful soorë I compleynë me,   *whereof right grievously I lament*
That routh is voyde to my disavauntage,   *that pity is absent*
Sithe alle thees vertues be sitte in youre ymage.

L'envoye

Go, lytel balade, and recomaunde me   *little ballade, and recommend me*
Until hir pyty, hir mercy, and hir grace;
45 But first be ware aforne that thou weel see   *wary in advance that you see to it*
Disdayne and daunger be voyde oute of that place;   *and aloofness are driven out from*
For ellys thou mayst have leysier noon, ner space,   *have no opportunity, or scope*
Truwly to hir to done my message,   *truly to present my message to her*
Which hathe alle vertues sette in hir ymage.

II, 15   Go, litull bill, and command me hertëly ~ *Humfrey Newton*

Go, litull bill, and command me hertëly	*little letter; commend; heartily*
Unto her that I call my trulof and lady,	*truelove*
Be this same tru tokynnynge:	*by; true sign*
That sho se me in a kirk on a Friday in a mornyng,	*she saw me in a church*
5 With a sper-hauk on my hand,	*sparrow-hawk*
And my mone did by her stond,	*man (i.e. attendant); stand*
And an old womon sete her by,	*sat beside her*
That litull cold of curtesy;	*who knew little*
And oft on her sho did smile	*she*
10 To loke on me for a wile.	*in order to glance at me for a moment*
And yet be this another token:	*by this*
To the kirke she comme with a gentilwomon;	*came with a lady*
Even byhynd the kirk dore	*right behind the church door*
Thay knelëd bothe on the flore,	*floor*
15 And fast thay did piter-pater –	
I hope thay said matens togeder!	*I expect they said matins*
Yet ones or twyes at the lest,	*once or twice at least*
Sho did on me her ee kest;	*cast her eye*
Then went I forthe prevëly	*I went out unobtrusively*
20 And haylsëd on thaym curtesly.	*and greeted them courteously*
Be alle the tokens, truly,	*by all*
Comand me to her hertëly.	*commend*

II, 16   Have godday, nou, Mergerete

Have godday, nou, Mergerete,	*good day*
With gret lovë y the grete!	*greet*
Y wolde we mighten us ofte mete	*I wish; meet*
In halle, in chaumbre, and in the strete,	
5 Withoutë blame of the contrë –	*of other people* (lit. *the country, neighbourhood*)
God yevë that so mighte hit be!	*God grant*

II, 17   Gracius and gay

Gracius and gay,	*and merry*
On hyr lyyth all my thoght;	*on her rests* (lit. *lies*)*; thought*
Butt sche rew on me today,	*unless she has pity*
To deth sche hath me broght.	*death; brought*
5 Hyr feyngeres long and small,	*long and slender*
Hyr armes byth rown and toght,	*are round and firm*
Hyr mowth as swet as lycory,	*licorice*
On hyr lyyth all my thoght.	

Hyr eyne byth feyr and gray,   *are fair and grey*
10 Hyr brues byth well y-bent,   *eyebrows are well arched*
Hyr rode as rede as roose yn May,   *her complexion as red as a rose*
Hyr medyll small and gent.   *waist slender and elegant*

Sche ys swett under schett,   *attractively dressed*
I lov hyr and no mo.   *love her and no other*
15 Sche hath myne hart to kepe,   *heart to keep*
In londës wher sche go.   *wherever she goes*

Sodenly tell, y pray;   *quickly tell (me your answer)*
To the my lov ys lend;   *on you my love is set*
Kysse me yn my way,   *as I pass (lit. in my way)*
20 Onys ar y wend.   *once before I depart*

II, 18   Myn owne dere ladi fair and fre

Thei y synge and murthës make,   *though I sing and make merry*
It is not y wolde.   *it is not as I would wish*

Myn owne dere ladi fair and fre,   *fair and noble*
Y pray in herte ye ruwe on me,   *that you take pity on me*
5 For al my lykyng is on the   *all my desire is for you*
Whan y on yow beholde.   *when*
Thei y synge, etc.

Were we to togadere beyne,   *two together both*
Thou myght me lyssë of my peyne;   *relieve me of my pain*
10 Y am agast it wol not geyne –   *afraid it will not help*
Myn hertë fallëth colde.
Thei y synge, etc.

Myself y wol myn arende bede;   *I will present my petition*
The betur y hopë for te spede;   *to succeed*
15 Non so wel may do myn nede –   *no one; do what I require*
A womman so me tolde.
Thei y synge, etc.

II, 19   I saw never joy lyk to that sight

My dere an dese that so fayr ys,   *my dear one on the dais*
Of lufe gentyl and fre,   *gentle and noble*
I kan not ly, withowtyn lese   *lie, without falsehood*
My lady lele best lykës me.   *my lady fair best pleases me*

5 I saw never joy lyk to that sight   *like*
     As my fayr lady schen;   *beautiful / radiant*
   Her brows thay er both brant and bright,   *arched and beautiful*
     With two gray lawhyng een.   *laughing eyes*
      My dere an dese, etc.

10 Her syds er lang, shapen of ryght,   *sides are long, well-shaped*
     That semly er to se;   *comely are to see*
   By Crist, and yt wer in my myght,
     Scho suld my treuluf be.   *she would be my true-love*
      My dere an dese, etc.

15 Scho suld be my hertës qwen   *my heart's queen*
     That is so fayr and swete;   *sweet*
   Alas, scho dos me tray and teen: *causes me grief and woe*
     I may noght with her met.   *meet*
      My dere an dese, etc.

II, 20   Thayr ys no myrth under the sky

Thayr ys no myrth under the sky,   *no pleasure*
Harpyng, lutyng, nor mery dance,
That may put owt my swet lady   *may oust*
All fro my daly remembrance.   *entirely from my daily*
5 Yie be the birde of all plesance,   *you are the mistress of all delight*
   My lady gent with love inbraste,   *my gracious lady embraced with love*
   Full comly ys youre countenance –   *comely*
   Be trew, lady, for I you truste.   *be true*

I set not by no gret tresore,   *I place no value on any great treasure*
10 Mony, golde, nor wardly fee,   *money, gold, or worldly wealth*
   So of my lady that I be sure   *as long as I am sure of my lady*
   That she caste not hire love fro me;   *take not her love away from me*
   And yie wolde ay so stabyll be   *if you would ever be so constant*
   Me for to love for any haste,   *as to love me in any circumstances*
15 Thane shuld I leyffe in rialté –   *live in regal state*
   By trew, lady, for I you truste.   *be true*

The doyff whyche wantes discressiòne   *dove which lacks rational understanding*
And hasse no ressone by verray kynde,   *and has no reason by its very nature*
Fro she chesse hir ellecciòn,   *from the time she has made her choice*
20 A love most plesinge to hire mynde,
   She will not stray, os doyth the hynde,   *as does the hind*
   Anoder luffer for to taste;   *another lover to try*
   Take heyd, my swete, for yie ar kynde –   *take heed; you are kind / natural*
   By trew, lady, for I you truste.

25 Seyne bestes that be without rassòn   *since beasts which are without reason*
   Cane love withoutyne varryance,   *without inconstancy*
   Tharfor my hert, for this sessòne,   *season*
   Put not your love to sore grevance,   *your beloved in severe affliction*
   Wherthrugh gret care myght me unhance   *whereby great care might deject me*
30 And mak my hert lyk for to bruste,
   For of all women yie leyd the dance –   *you lead*
   By trew, lady, for I you truste.

   Love ys strange in all degré,   *in every respect*
   Summtyme hoyt and sumtyme colde,   *sometimes hot*
35 Tharfor to dowt, yt caussis me,   *therefore to fear*
   Leyff, that yie shuld fro me foyld;   *beloved, that you should turn from me*
   And fals lovers youe kepe in hold,   *if false lovers should hold you in thrall*
   Than wold my sorow me tobraste.   *my sorrow would shatter me*
   With fals lovers be not to bolde –   *be not too venturous*
40 By trew, lady, for I you truste.

   Yie are the salyfe unto my sore,   *you are the ointment for my wound*
   Medyscyne to myne infirmité;
   My tonge cane not expresse tharfor   *can*
   The secunde parte of youre beauté.   *half (lit. the second part)*
45 Ther yse no surrance may hurte me,   *no affliction*
   Nor no sorow bot I shall cayste,   *which I shall not cast out*
   When I think on your love so fre –   *so noble*
   By trew, lady, for I you truste.

II, 21   Alone walkyng

   Alone walkyng,
   In thought pleynyng,   *complaining*
   And sore syghyng,   *sighing*
   All desolate,
5 Me remembryng
   Of my lyvyng,   *life (lit. living)*
   My deth wyssyng   *wishing*
   Erly and late,

   Infortunate
10 Ys soo my fate,
   That – wote ye whate? –   *do you know what*
   Oute of mesure
   My lyfe I hate;
   Thus desperate,
15 In suche estate   *such a state*
   Do I endure.

Of other cure
Am I nat sure,   *not*
Thus to endure
20 Ys hard, certayn;
Suche ys my ure,   *my custom*
I yow ensure;   *assure you*
What creature
May have more payn?

25 My trouth so pleyn   *my fidelity so apparent*
Ys take in veyn,   *taken*
And gret disdeyn
In remembraunce;
Yet I full feyne   *most readily*
30 Wold me compleyne
Me to absteyne   *to keep myself*
From thys penaunce.   *from this suffering*

But in substaunce,
Noon allegeaunce   *alleviation*
35 Of my grevaunce
Can I nat fynde;
Ryght so my chaunce   *fate*
With displesaunce   *displeasure / sorrow*
Doth me avaunce –   *advance*
40 And thus an ende.

II, 22   Now wolde y fayne sum merthës mak

Now wolde y fayne sum merthës mak,   *would I gladly make merry*
Al only for my ladys sak   *entirely on account of my lady*
　　When y her se;   *see*
But nowe y am so far fro hir   *from her*
5　　It wil not be.

Thow y be far out of her cight,   *though; sight*
I am her man both day and nygth,
　　And so wol be.   *will*
Therfore wolde God as y love her   *would God*
10　　She lovëd me.

Whan she is mery than am y gladde,   *then*
Whan she is sory than am y sadde,   *sad*
　　And cause is whye –   *and this is the reason why*
For he leveth not that lovëd her   *lives not who has loved her*
15　　So wel as y.   *well as I*

She seith that she hath seyn it write   *she says that she has seen it written*
That 'seldyn seyn is sone forgeit'.   *seldom seen is soon forgotten*
    Yt is not so –
For yn good feith, save only her,   *good faith*
20   Y love no moo.   *nobody else* (lit. *no more*)

Wherfor y pray, bothe nygth and day,
That she may cast alle car away   *care*
    And leve in rest,   *live*
And evermor wherever she be
25   To love me best;

And y to her to be so trewe,
And never to chaung hir for no newe,   *new* (i.e. *new love*)
    Unto my ende,
And that y may in her service
30   Ever amend.   *ever improve*

II, 23   Go hert, hurt with adversité

Go hert, hurt with adversité,   *heart*
And let my lady thi wondes see,   *wounds*
And sey hir this, as y say the: *say this to her; to thee*
    'Farwel my joy, and welcom peyne,   *pain*
5   Til y se my lady agayne.'   *until*

II, 24   Thus I complayn my grevous hevynesse

Thus I complayn my grevous hevynesse   *lament*
To you that knoweth the trewth of myn entent.
Alas, why shuld ye be mersyles –   *merciless*
So moch beuty as God hath you sent!   *so much beauty*
5   Ye may my peyn reles.   *pain relieve*
Do as ye list – I hold me content!   *do as you wish*

II, 25   Alas, departyng ys ground of woo

Alas, departyng ys ground of woo –   *parting*
Other songe can y not synge.
But why part y my lady fro,
Syth love was caus of our metyng?   *since*

5 The bitter teres of hir wepyng   *her weeping*
Myn hert hath pershed so mortaly,   *pierced*
That to the deth hit wil me bryng,
But yf y se hir hastily.   *unless I see her soon*

II, 26   My hert ys so plungyt yn greffe

My hert ys so plungyt yn greffe	*plunged in grief*
Ther may no barn my balyes onbynd;	*no-one relieve (lit. unbind) my sorrows*
Tyll y onys may sse my leffe	*once again; dear one*
It wyll not com owt off my mynd.	
5 Alace, Fortune, thou art onkynd!	*unkind*
Why ssuffrys thou my hart to brek yn two?	*why do you suffer / allow*
For y may not my lady ffynd,	*if I cannot*
Y wot y dey ffor greffe and wo.	*I know I shall die for grief and woe*

II, 27   A! mercy, Fortune, have pitye on me

A! mercy, Fortune, have pitye on me,	
And thynke that thu hast done gretely amysse	
To parte asondre them whiche ought to be	
Alwey in on. Why hast thu doo this?	*always united*
5 Have I offended the? I? Nay, y-wysse!	*offended thee; indeed*
Then torne thy whele and be my frende agayn,	*turn thy wheel*
And sende me joy where I am nowe in payn.	
And thynke what sorowe is the departyng	*parting*
Of two trewe hertës lovyng feithfully,	
10 For partyng is the most soroughfull thynge,	*sorrowful*
To myn entent, that ever yet knewe I.	*in my opinion*
Therfore, I pray to the right hertëly	*thee; heartily*
To turne thy whele and be my frende agayn,	
And sende me joy where I am nowe in payn.	
15 For tyll we mete, I dare wel say for trouth	*meet*
That I shall never be in ease of herte.	
Wherfor, I pray you, have of me sume routh,	*some pity*
And release me of all my paynës smerte.	*from all my grievous pains*
Now, sith thu woste hit is nat my deserte,	*since you know it is not what I deserve*
20 Then torne thy whele and be my frynde agayn,	
And sende me joy where I am nowe in payn.	

II, 28   This ys no lyf, alas, that y do lede

This ys no lyf, alas, that y do lede,	*lead*
It is but deth as yn lyves lyckënesse,	*in life's likeness*
Endeles sorow assurëd owte of drede,	*guaranteed without doubt*
Past all despeyre and owte of all gladenesse.	*beyond all despair; devoid of all*
5 Thus well y wote y am remedylesse,	*I know I am without remedy*
For me nothyng may comforte nor amende	
Tyl deith come forthe and make of me an ende.	*death*

II, 29   Sweit rois of vertew and of gentilnes ~ *William Dunbar*

Sweit rois of vertew and of gentilnes,	*sweet rose of virtue and nobility*
Delytsum lyllie of everie lustynes,	*delightful lily of every charm*
Richest in bontie and in bewtie cleir	*in goodness and in beauty fair*
And everie vertew that is held most deir,	*dear*
5 Except onlie that ye ar mercyles.	*only that you are merciless*
Into your garthe this day I did persew;	*garden; did enter*
Thair saw I flowris that fresche wer of hew,	*there; hue*
Baithe quhyte and rid, moist lusty wer to seyne,	*both white and red, most lovely; see*
And halsum herbis upone stalkis grene:	*wholesome herbs*
10 Yit leif nor flour fynd could I nane of rew.	*leaf nor flower; any of rue*
I dout that Merche with his caild blastis keyne	*I fear; March; cold keen blasts*
Hes slane this gentill herbe that I of mene,	*has slain; of which I speak*
Quhois petewous deithe dois to my hart sic pane	*whose piteous death; such pain*
That I wald mak to plant his rute agane,	*I would make to plant its root again*
15 So confortand his levis unto me bene.	*comforting its leaves are to me*

II, 30   O maistres myn, till yow I me commend

O maistres myn, till yow I me commend,	*to you*
Allhaill my hairt sen that ye haif in cure,	*since you have my heart entirely in (your) care*
For, but your grace, my lyfe is neir the end;	*without your grace; near*
Now lat me nocht in danger me endure.	*let me not in disdain*
5 Off lyif, lyk lufe, suppois that I be sure,	*of life, only as of love, suppose*
Quhay wat na God may me sum succur send?	*who knows if God may not send me*
Than for your lufe quhy wald ye I forfure?	*then; why would you wish that I perish*
O maistres myn, till yow I me commend.	
The wynttir nycht ane hour I may nocht sleip,	*the winter night one hour; not sleep*
10 For thocht of yow bot tumland to and fro;	*thought; tossing*
Methink ye ar into my armys, sueit,	*in my arms, sweet*
And quhen I walkyn ye ar so far me fro.	*when I wake you are so far from me*
Allace! allace! than walkynnis my wo,	*then wakens*
Than wary I the tyme that I yow kend;	*then curse I; I came to know you*
15 War nocht gud hoip, my hairt wald birst in two!	*if there were no good hope, my heart; burst*
O maistres myn, til yow I me commend.	
Sen ye ar ane that hes my hairt alhaill,	*since you are the one; completely*
Without fenyeing I may it nocht genstand:	*feigning; resist*
Ye ar the bontie, bliss of all my baill,	*the goodness, joy of all my sorrow*
20 Bayth lyfe and deth standis into your hand.	*both; in your hand*
Sen that I am sair bundin in your band,	*since I am sorely bound; bond*
That nycht or day I wait nocht quhair to wend,	*I do not know where to turn*
Lat me anis say that I your freindschip fand,	*for once let me say; enjoyed*
O maistres myn, till yow I me commend.	

II, 31   Whoso that wyll all feattes optayne ~ *King Henry VIII*

Whoso that wyll all feattes optayne,	*whosoever wishes to accomplish all feats*
In love he must be withowt dysdayne,	*disdain*
For love enforcëth all nobyle kyndes,	*strengthens all noble natures*
And dysdayne dyscorages all gentyl myndes.	*disheartens all gentle spirits*
5 Wherfor to love and be not loved	*why*
Is wors then deth? Let it be proved!	*is it worse than death*
Love encoragëth and makëth on bold;	*makes a man (lit. one) bold*
Dysdayne abattëth and makëth hym colde.	*diminishes (lit. abates)*
Love ys geven to God and man;	*given*
10 To woman also, I thynk, the same.	
But dysdayne ys vice and shuld be refused;	*should be rejected*
Yet never the lesse it ys moch used.	*much*
Grett pyty it ware love for to compell	
With dysdayne bothe falce and subtell.	*with disdain both dissimulated and subtle*

II, 32   A Robyn

A Robyn,	
Gentyl Robyn,	
Tel me how thy lemman doth,	*sweetheart*
And thow shal know of myne.	
5 My lady is unkynde i-wis;	*indeed*
Alac, why is she so?	*alack*
She loveth another better than me	
And yet she will say no.	*she will deny it*
I cannot thynk such doubylnes	*imagine such duplicity*
10 For I fynd women trew;	*true*
In faith my lady loveth me well;	
She will change for no new.	

II, 33   Wherto shuld I expresse ~ *Henry VIII*

Wherto shuld I expresse	*wherefore*
My inward hevynes?	
No myrth can make me fayn	*make me glad*
Tyl that we mete agayne.	*until we meet again*

5 Do way, dere hart, not so.   *stop, dear heart, be not so*
  Let no thought yow dysmaye.   *dismay*
  Thow ye now parte me fro,   *though you now part from me*
  We shall mete when we may.   *meet when we can*

  When I remembyr me   *when I reflect*
10 Of your most gentyll mynde,   *upon your*
  It may no wyse agre   *may in no way allow* (lit. *agree*)
  That I shuld be unkynde.

  The daisy delectable,
  The violett wan and blo;   *pale and blue*
15 Ye ar not varyable;   *inconstant*
  I love you and no mo.   *no other*

  I make you fast and sure;   *I regard you as steadfast and sure*
  It ys to me gret payne
  Thus longe to endure
20 Tyll that we mete agayne.

II, 34   The knyght knokett at the castell gate

Yow and I and Amyas,
*   Amyas and yow and I,*
To the grenewode must we go, alas!   green wood
*   Yow and I, my lyff, and Amyas.*   my dear

5 The knyght knokett at the castell gate;   knocked
  The lady merveled who was therat.   wondered
*   Yow and I and Amyas, etc.*

  To call the porter he wold not blyn;   would not cease
  The lady said he shuld not com in.   should
10 *   Yow and I and Amyas, etc.*

  The portres was a lady bryght;   portress
  Strangënes that lady hyght.   that lady was called
*   Yow and I and Amyas, etc.*

  She askëd hym what was his name;
15 He said, 'Desyre, your man, madame.'
*   Yow and I and Amyas, etc.*

  She said, 'Desyre, what do ye here?'
  He said, 'Madame, as your prisoner.'
*   Yow and I and Amyas, etc.*

No story as such but so catchy!

20 He was cownselled to breffe a byll   *draw up a petition*
    And shew my lady hys oune wyll.
        Yow and I and Amyas, etc.

    Kyndnes said she wold yt bere,   *would it bear*
    And Pyty said she wold be ther.
25   *Yow and I and Amyas, etc.*

    Thus how thay dyd we cannott say –
    We left them ther and went ower way.
        Yow and I and Amyas, etc.

Lyric/song like.

II, 35   Sore this derë stryken ys

Blow thi horne, hunter,
    and blow thi horne on hye!   *on high*
Ther ys a do in yonder wode;   *doe in yonder wood*
    in faith, she woll not dy: *will not die*
5   *Now blow thi horne, hunter,*
    and blow thi horne, joly hunter!

    Sore this derë stryken ys,   *this deer is sorely stricken*
        And yet she bledes no whytt;   *bleeds not at all*
    She lay so fayre, I cowde nott mys;   *could not miss*
10   Lord, I was glad of it!
        Blow thi horne, hunter, etc.

    As I stod under a bank,   *beneath a bank*
        The dere shoffe on the mede;   *deer made her way over the meadow*
    I stroke her so that downe she sanke, *I struck her*
15   But yet she was not dede.   *dead*
        Blow thi horne, hunter, etc.

    There she gothe! Se ye nott
        How she gothe over the playne?   *across the plain*
    And yf ye lust to have a shott,
20   I warrant her barrayne.   *barren (i.e. not pregnant)*
        Blow thi horne, hunter, etc.

    He to go and I to go,   *he advanced and I advanced*
        But he ran fast afore;   *fast ahead*
    I bad hym shott and strik the do,   *shoot and strike*
25   For I myght shott no more.
        Blow thi horne, hunter, etc.

To the covert bothe thay went,	*to the thicket*
For I fownd wher she lay;	
An arrow in her hanch she hent;	*had taken an arrow in her haunch*
30 For faynte she myght nott bray.	*faintness*
Blow thi horne, hunter, etc.	

I was wery of the game;	*weary*
I went to tavern to drynk;	
Now the construccyon of the same –	*meaning*
35 What do yow meane or thynk?	*guess or think*
Blow thi horne, hunter, etc.	

Here I leve and mak an end	*leave off and make an end*
Now of this hunters lore;	
I thynk his bow ys well unbent,	
40 Hys bolt may fle no more.	*fly*
Blow thi horne, hunter, etc.	

II, 36   O mestres, whye

O mestres, whye	*why*
Owtecaste am I	
All utterly	
From your pleasaunce,	*pleasure*
5 Sythe ye and I	*since*
Or thys, truly,	*before this*
Famyliarly	
Have had pastaunce,	*have passed our time*

And lovyngly	
10 Ye wolde aply	*were wont to devote*
Thy company	
To my comforte?	
But now, truly,	
Unlovyngly	
15 Ye do deny	*you refuse*
Me to resorte,	*to visit me*

And me to see	
As strange ye be,	*reluctant you are*
As thowe that ye	*as though*
20 Shuld nowe denoy,	*deny*
Or else possesse	
That nobylnes	
To be Dochess	
Of grete Savoy.	

Men + women
pain

25 But sythe that ye   *since*
   So strange wyl be   *distant*
   As toward me,   *towards me*
      And wyll not melle,   *associate (with me)*
   I truste, percase,   *perhaps*
30 To fynde some grace
   To have <u>free chayse,</u> *free hunting (i.e. in love)* ← *Pursuit.*
      And spede as welle!   *succeed*

II, 37   Love woll I withoute eny variaunce

Love woll I withoute eny variaunce   *will I without any inconstancy*
Trewly to servë with al louelynesse;   *all lowliness*
For yn hit is triste and gentilnesse,   *loyalty and courtesy*
And that may man honour and avaunce.   *may bring a man honour and favour*

II, 38   Luf wil I with variance

Luf wil I with variance,   *inconstancy (i.e. without commitment)*
Because y drede of repentance;   *suffering (i.e. for love)*
For whoso loveth withoutyn governance,   *moderation*
Ofttyme it doth hym grevaunce.   *often it causes him grief*
5 Therfor with avisance   *with prudence*
Love wil I with variaunce.

II, 39   Whatso men seyn

Whatso men seyn,   *whatever men say*
Love is no peyn   *love is no pain*
To them, serteyn,   *certainly*
   Butt varians;   *but (only) inconstancy*
5 For they constreyn   *compel*
   Ther hertes to feyn   *falsely to cause*
   Ther mowthes to pleyn   *utter*
      Ther displesauns.   *their discontent*

Whych is in dede   *in fact*
10 Butt feynëd drede –   *feigned anguish*
   So God me spede –   *so help me God*
      And dowbilnys;   *duplicity*
   Ther othes to bede   *their oaths to promise*
   Ther lyves to lede   *to conduct their lives (properly)*
15 And profer mede –   *and offer reward*
      Newfangellnys.   *(is mere) pursuit of novelty*

For when they pray,	*entreat*
Ye shall have nay	*you will get nothing*
Whatso they sey –	*whatever they say*
20 Beware ffor shame!	
For every daye	
They waite ther pray	*lie in wait for their prey*
Wherso they may,	*wheresoever*
And make butt game.	*and only amuse themselves*

25 Then semëth me	*it seems to me*
Ye may well se	
They be so fre	*are so free*
In every plase,	*place*
Hitt were peté	*it would be a pity*
30 Butt they shold be	*if they were not*
Begeled, pardé,	*beguiled, by God*
Withowtyn grase.	*without mercy*

II, 40   I am sory for her sake

	Care away, away!	*away with care*
	Away murnynge, away!	*away with sorrow*
	Y am forsake,	*I am forsaken*
	Another ys take,	*another is taken*
5	*No more murne yc may.*	*no more can I mourn*

	I am sory for her sake,	
	Yc may wel ete and drynke;	*I can eat and drink well*
	Whanne yc sclepe yc may not wake,	*when I sleep I cannot lie awake*
	So muche on here yc thenke.	*so much on her I think*
10	Care away, etc.	

	I am brought in suche a bale,	*I am brought to such grief*
	And brought in suche a pyne,	*torment*
	Whanne yc ryse up of my bed,	*when I rise*
	Me listë wel to dyne.	*it is my pleasure to dine well*
15	Care away, etc.	

	I am brought in suche a pyne,	
	Y-brought in suche a bale,	
	Whanne yc havë ryghte god wyne,	
	Me listë drynke non ale.	*I have no inclination to drink any ale*
20	Care away, etc.	

II, 41   Of my lady wel me rejoise I may! ~ *Thomas Hoccleve*

La commendacion de ma dame

Of my lady wel me rejoise I may!
Hir golden forheed is ful narw and smal,   *narrow*
Hir browës been lyk to dym reed coral,   *are like lustreless red coral*
And as the jeet hir yën glistren ay.   *jet (i.e. black); eyes glitter*

5   Hir bowgy cheekës been as softe as clay,   *baggy cheeks are*
     With largë jowës and substancial.   *jaws*
        Of my lady wel me rejoise I may!
        Hir golden forheed is ful narw and smal,
        Hir browës been lyk to dym reed coral,
10   And as the jeet hir yën glistren ay.

     Hir nose a pentice is that it ne shal   *an overhanging roof; it cannot*
     Reyne in hir mowth thogh shee uprightës lay.   *rain; lay on her back face up*
        Of my lady wel me rejoise I may!
        Hir golden forheed is ful narw and smal,
15   Hir browës been lyk to dym reed coral,
        And as the jeet hir yën glistren ay.

     Hir mowth is nothyng scant with lippës gray,   *in no way puny*
     Hir chin unnethë may be seen at al,   *scarcely*
     Hir comly body shape as a footbal,   *shaped like*
20 And shee syngeth ful lyk a papëjay.   *parrot*
        Of my lady wel me rejoise I may!
        Hir golden forheed is ful narw and smal,
        Hir browës been lyk to dym reed coral,
        And as the jeet hir yën glistren ay.

Devotional and Doctrinal Lyrics

II, 42   I hafe set my hert so hye

I hafe set my hert so hye,	*have; so high*
Me liketh no love that lowere ys;	*no love pleases me*
And alle the paynes that y may drye,	*pains; suffer*
Me thenk hyt do me good y-wys,	*it seems to me it (suffering) does me good, indeed*
5 Me thenk yt do, i-wys.	

For on that lorde that loved us alle,	
So hertely have I set my thowght,	
Yt ys my joie on hym to calle,	
For love me hath in balës browght,	*has brought me to anguish*
10 Me thenk yt hath, i-wys.	

II, 43   Jhesu, Lorde, that madëst me ~ *Richard de Caistre*

Jhesu, Lorde, that madëst me	
And with thi blyssëd blode hast bowght,	*blessed blood hast bought*
Foryeve that I have grevëd the	*forgive; grieved thee*
In wordë, werkë, will and thowght.	*words, works*

5 Jhesu, for thi woundës smerte	*painful*
Of body, fete and hondës too,	*feet and hands*
Make me meke and lowe in hert,	*meek; lowly*
And the to love as I schulde doo.	*thee*

Jhesu Criste, to the I calle	
10 As thu art Fader, full of myght,	
Kepe me clene, that I ne falle	*that I do not fall*
In fleshely synn, as I have tyght.	*have resolved*

Jhesu, grante me myn askyng,	*my asking (what I ask)*
Pacience in my desesse,	*patience; distress*
15 And never I mot doo that thyng	*may*
That schulde yn ony thyng dysplese.	*in any thing displease*

Jhesu, that art hevene kyng,	*king of heaven*
Sothfast God and man also,	*truly*
Yeve me grace of gode endyng	*give; the grace of a good end*
20 And hem that I am holden to.	*them to whom I am beholden*

Jhesu, for thoo dulful terës	*those sorrowful tears*
That thu gretëst for my gylt,	*you wept; guilt*
Here and spedë my preyèrës,	*hear and answer (lit. prosper) my prayers*
And spare me that I be not spylt.	*damned*

25 Jhesu, for hem I the beseche   *for them I thee beseech*
   That wrathën the in ony wyse;   *who anger you in any way*
   Withhold from hem thi hande of wreche   *them; vengeance*
   And lete hem leven in thi servyse.   *let them live*

   Jhesu, joyfull for to sen   *joyful to behold*
30 Of all thi seyntës everychone,   *for all; every one*
   Comfort hem that carfull ben,   *are full of sorrow*
   And helpe hem that ar woo-begone.

   Jhesu, kepe hem that ben goode,   *protect; who are*
   And mende hem that han grevëd the,   *reform; grieved thee*
35 And sende men frutes of erdely foode,   *earthly*
   As eche man nedeth to hys degré.   *according to his condition*

   Jhesu, that art withowteyn lese   *truly* (lit. *without a lie*)
   Almyghty God in trynyty,
   Cese thise werres and send us pees,   *stop these wars; peace*
40 With lestyng love and cheryty.   *lasting*

   Jhesu, that art the gostly stone   *spiritual*
   Of all Holy Cherche in erde,   *on earth*
   Bryngge thi foldës floke in one   *bring the flock of thy fold into unity*
   And reule hem ryghtly with on herde.   *rule; one shepherd*

45 Jhesu, for thi blyssëd blode,
   Bryng tho soulës into blys   *those souls*
   Of qwom I have had ony goode,   *from whom; any*
   And spare that thei han done amysse.   *forgive what they have done amiss*
       Amen.

II, 44   Fore love is love and ever schal be ~ *John Audelay*

I have a love is Heven Kyng;   *(who) is the king of heaven*
I love his love fore evermor.

Fore love is love and ever schal be,
And love has bene ore we were bore;   *has been before we were born*
5 Fore love he askes non other fe   *fee*
Bot love ayayn – he kepes no more.   *but love in return – he desires*
   I say herefore: *therefore*
     I have a love etc.

Trew love is tresoure, trust is store   *fidelity is a hoard (of riches)*
10 To a love to Godes plesyng,   *love which is to God's liking*
Bot leude love makës men y-lore,   *carnal love causes men to be damned*
To love here lust and here lykyng.   *(causes them) to love their desire; pleasure*
   I say herefore:
     I have a love etc.

15 In good love ther is no syn;
   Without love is hevynes: *there is sadness*
   Herefore to love I nyl not blyn,   *therefore; I will not cease*
   To love my God and his goodnes.
      I say herefore:
20   *I have a love etc.*

   For he me loved or I him knew,   *before*
   Therfore I love him altherbest,   *best of all*
   Ellis my love I myght hit rew;   *otherwise; I might be ashamed of it*
   I love with him to take my rest.
25   I say herefore:
      I have a love etc.

   Of al loveres that ever was borne,
   His love hit passëd everechon;   *his love surpassed every one*
   Nad he us loved we were forelorne;   *if he had not; we would have perished*
30 Without is love trew love is non.   *other than his love there is no true love*
      I say herefore:
      I have a love etc.

II, 45   This flour is fayre and fresche of heue ~ *John Audelay*

There is a floure sprung of a tre,
The rote therof is called Jessé,   *root*
   A floure of pryce;   *a flower of excellence*
Ther is non seche in paradise.   *none such*

5 This flour is fayre and fresche of heue;   *hue*
   Hit fadës never bot ever is new;   *it fades; but*
   The blisful branche this flour on grew
   Was Mary myld, that bare Jhesu,
     A flour of grace;
10 Ayayns al sorow hit is solas.   *against; it is solace*
     There is a floure etc.

   The sede herof was Godës sond,   *seed thereof; God's gift*
   That God himselve sew with his hond,   *sowed; hand*
   In Bedlem, in that holy lond,   *Bethlehem; land*
15 Medis here herbère ther he hir fond;   *in the middle of her garden where he found her*
     This blisful floure
   Sprang never bot in Maris boure.   *but; Mary's bower*
     There is a floure etc.

   When Gabrëël this mayden met,   *Gabriel*
20 With 'Ave Maria' he here gret;   *he greeted her*
   Betwene hem two this flour was set   *by the two of them; planted*
   And kept it was (no mon schul wit)   *no man was to know*

	Hent on a day,	*until*
	In Bedlem hit con spred and spray.	*it began to grow and sprout*
25	*There is a floure etc.*	

	When that floure began to spred	*grow*
	And his blossum for to bede,	*blossom (began) to show*
	Ryche and pore of every lede,	*poor; nation*
	Thai marvelt hou this flour myght sprede,	*how*
30	Til kyngës thre	*three*
	That blesful flourë come to se.	*blissful*
	There is a floure etc.	

	Angeles cam out of here toure	*their tower*
	To loke apon this freschely floure,	*upon this fresh flower*
35	Houe fayre he was in his colòure,	
	And hou sote in his savòur,	*how sweet; fragrance*
	And to behold	
	How soche a flour myght spryng in golde.	*such*
	There is a floure etc.	

40	Of lilly whit, of rose of ryse,	*white; rose upon its stem*
	Of prymrol and of flour-de-lyse,	*primrose; fleur-de-lis*
	Of al the flours, at my devyse,	*in my opinion*
	Yet floure of Jessé bers the prys	*holds the prize*
	As most of hele	*as greatest in healing power*
45	To slake oure sorous everydele.	*relieve every bit of our sorrows*
	There is a floure etc.	

	I pray youe, flours of this cuntré,	*country*
	Whereevere ye go, wereever ye be,	
	Hold up the flour of good Jessé	*exalt*
50	Fore your freschenes and youre beuté,	*above*
	As fayrest of al,	
	And ever was and ever schal.	*shall be*
	There is a floure etc.	

II, 46   Ther is no rose of swych vertù

	Ther is no rose of swych vertù	*such excellence*
	As is the rose that bare Jhesù.	*bore*

	Ther is no rose of swych vertù	
	As is the rose that bar Jhesù;	*bore*
5	Alleluya.	
	Ther is etc.	

For in this rose conteynëd was
Heven and erthe in lytyl space,
    Res miranda.   *a thing to be wondered at*
10   Ther is etc.·

Be that rose we may weel see   *by; well*
That he is God in persones thre,
    Pari forma.   *in one substance*
    Ther is etc.

15 The aungeles sung the sheperdes to: *the angels sang to the shepherds*
    'Gloria in excelcis Deo.'   *'glory to God in the highest'*
    Gaudeamus.   *let us rejoice*
    Ther is etc.

Leve we all this wordly merthe,   *lets us leave; worldly mirth*
20 And folwë we this joyful berthe;   *follow; birth*
    Transeamus.   *let us go*
    Ther is etc.

II, 47   Lyth and lystyn, both old and yyng

Of a rose, a lovely rose,
Of a rose I syng a song.

Lyth and lystyn, both old and yyng,   *attend and listen; young*
How the rose begane to spryng;
5 A fayyrer rose to owr lekyng   *to our liking*
    Sprong ther never in kyngës lond.   *never sprang in (any) kingdom*
    Of a rose, etc.

Five branches of that rose ther ben,   *there are*
The wychë ben both feyer and shene;   *which are both fair and beautiful*
10 Of a maydyn, Mary, hevyn quene,   *queen of heaven*
    Out of hyr bosum the branches sprong.   *her bosom*
    Of a rose, etc.

The first branch was of gret honour:
Ther cam an angell out hevyn toure,   *from heaven's tower*
15 That blyssëd Mary shuld ber the flour,   *should bear the flower*
    To breke the Develes bond.   *break*
    Of a rose, etc.

The secund branch was gret of myght,   *of great might*
That sprong upon Cristmes nyght;
20 The sterrë shone and lemëd bryght,   *star shone and gleamed bright*
    That man schuld se both brod and longe.   *see far and wide*
    Of a rose, etc.

The thridë branch gan spryng and spred;	*began to sprout and spread*
Thre kyngës than the branch gan led	*three kings the branch then led*
25 Tho to owr Lady in hure chyldbed;	*then to our Lady in her*
Into Bethlem that branch ryght sprong.	
Of a rose, etc.	

The fourthë branch, it sprong to hell,	
The Develes power for to fell,	*vanquish*
30 That no soule therin shuld dwell,	*should*
The braunch so blessedfully sprong.	
Of a rose, etc.	

The fifthë branch, it was so swote,	*sweet*
Yt sprong to hevyn, both croppe and rote,	*top and root*
35 In every ball to ben owr bott,	*every tribulation to be our remedy*
So blessedly yt sprong.	
Of a rose, etc.	

II, 48   At a sprynge-wel under a thorn

At a sprynge-wel under a thorn,	*wellspring*
Ther was bote of bale,	*a remedy for sorrow*
A lytel here aforn.	*a little time ago*
Ther bysydë stant a mayde,	*stands*
5 Fulle of love y-bounde;	*completely bound by love*
Hoso wol sechë trwë love,	*whoever wishes to seek true love*
Yn hyr hyt schal be founde.	*in her it*

II, 49   Haill quene of hevin and steren of blis

Haill quene of hevin and steren of blis;	*star*
Sen that thi sone thi fader is,	*since thy son thy father is*
How suld he ony thing the warn,	*how should; thee deny*
And thou his mothir and he thi barn?	*child*

5 Haill fresche fontane that springis new,	*fountain*
The rute and crope of all vertù,	*root and crown; virtue*
Thou polist gem without offence,	*polished; without fault*
Thou bair the lambe of innocence.	*bore*

II, 50   O sterne so brycht

O farest lady, O swetast lady,	*fairest*
O blisful lady, hevynnis quheyne.	*queen of heaven*

O sterne so brycht,	*star so bright*
That gyfys lycht,	*gives light*
5 Til hevyne and Haly Kyrk,	*to heaven and Holy Kirk*

Thi help, thy mycht   *might*
Grant ws ful rycht,   *us completely*
    Raik throw thire clowdis dirk.   *reach through these dark clouds*
Fra hel sa fel convoy ws clene –   *from hell so terrible bring us unharmed*
10 One the, Maré, thus most I meyne.   *upon thee, Mary, thus must I cry*
    O farest lady, etc.

Thow ruby red,
That rasis ded   *who raises the dead*
    And grantis synnarise thare lyf,   *grants sinners their life*
15 For til remeid   *to remedy*
The fendis pleid   *the fiend's dispute*
    Quha can thi help discrif?   *who can thy help describe?*
But the, lady, quha may sustene   *without thee; who may withstand*
Thare warldly lustis bath scharp and kene?   *their worldly desires both*
20   *O farest lady, etc.*

Thow wel of grace,   *well*
Ostend thi face   *reveal*
    Quhen ded sal ws persew.   *when death shall us pursue*
Away thow chase   *chase away*
25 Of fendis the brase;   *the embrace of fiends*
    Ask at thi sone, Jhesu,   *plead with thy son*
One ruyd his blud that bled betwene   *who once shed his blood on the cross*
For oure traspass, before thin eyne.   *eyes*
    O farest lady, etc.

30 Now, lady myne,
Thi ere inclyne   *ear*
    To me thi servitour.   *servant*
Quhen I go hyne,   *when I go hence*
Hef my saul fra pyne;   *raise my soul from torment*
35 Thow keip it in thi cwre,   *keep it in your care*
In place quhare grace ay growis grene,   *in (that) place where grace grows ever green*
Forever in joy thar til contein.   *there to remain*

    O farest lady, O swetast lady,   *fairest*
    O blisful lady, hevynnis quheyne.   *queen of heaven*

II, 51 Goe, lytyll byll, and doe me recommende

Goe, lytyll byll, and doe me recommende   *letter*
Unto my lady with godely countynaunce –
For trusty messanger I the sende.   *as a trusty messenger I thee send*
Pray her that sche make purvyaunce,   *preparation*
5 For my love, thurgh her sufferaunce,   *with her permission*
In her bosome desyreth to reste,
Syth off all women I love here beste.   *since*

She ys lylly off redolence,   *lily; fragrance*
Whych only may doe me plesure;   *which alone may cause me*
10 She is the rose off conffydence,
Most conffortyng to my nature.
Unto that lady I me assure,   *I commit myself*
I wyll hur love and never mo –   *her; no other (lit. never more)*
Goe, lytyll byll, and sey hur so.   *tell her so*

15 She restëth in my remembraunce,   *remains in my thoughts*
Day other nyght wherso I be;   *day or night*
It ys my specyall dalyaunce   *special intimate delight*
For to remembyr hur bewté;   *her beauty*
She is enprented in ych degré   *endowed in every respect*
20 With yftes of nature inexplycable   *gifts; inexpressible*
And eke of grace incomparable.   *and also*

The cause therfor, yf she wyll wytt,   *if she wishes to know*
Why I presume on sych a flowre,
Say, off hyr for yt ys i-wrytt   *(because) it is written of her*
25 She is the feyrest paramour,   *(that) she; fairest beloved*
And to man in ych langour   *every distress*
Most soverayne medyatryce: *intercessor*
Therffor I love that flowre of pryce. *precious flower*

Her bewty holy to dyscryve   *her beauty wholly to describe*
30 Who is he that may ssuffyce?
Forsoth no clerk that is on lyve,   *truly no scholar who is alive*
Syth she is only withowtyn vyce!   *since she alone is*
Her flavour excedeth the fflowr-de-lyce. *fragrance; fleur-de-lis*
Afore all flowres I have hur chose   *before all; chosen her*
35 Enterely in myn herte to close.   *to enclose*

Hyr I beseche – seth I not feyne   *since I do not pretend*
Butt only putt me in hur grace –   *other than to place myself in her*
That off me she not dysdeyne,   *should not be disdainful*
Takyng regarde at old trespace,   *taking into account former sin*
40 Seth myn entent in every place   *since*
Shall be to doe hur obeysaunce   *to be obedient to her*
And hur to love saunce varyaunce.   *to love her without change*

II, 52   O emperesse, the emperoure ~ *James Ryman*

O emperesse, the emperoure
   Quem meruisti portare,   *whom you were worthy to bear*
Of heven and erthe hath made the floure: *hath made thee flower*
   Regina celi, letare!   *queen of heaven, rejoice*

5   O quene of grace, the king of blisse
        Quem meruisti portare,
     Hath made thy sete next unto his: *seat / throne*
        Regina celi, letare!

     O princesse pure, the prince of peas   *peace*
10   Quem meruisti portare,
     Ever thy joye he doth encreas: *increase*
        Regina celi, letare!

     O lady fre, the lorde of alle   *noble lady*
        Quem meruisti portare,
15   Hath made man free, that was moost thralle: *enslaved*
        Regina celi, letare!

     O swete moder, thy sone Jesus   *sweet mother*
        Quem meruisti portare,
     He rose ayene, that died for us: *again*
20   Regina celi, letare!

     O mayden myelde, thy sone so dere   *mild; dear*
        Quem meruisti portare,
     Hath crownëd the in blis so clere: *crowned thee in bliss so pure*
        Regina celi, letare!

25   O spowse of Criest, oure savyoure   *spouse*
        Quem meruisti portare,
     Heven and erthe the doth honoure: *heaven and earth honour thee*
        Regina celi, letare!

     O Marie, of thy sonne aske this
30   Quem meruisti portare,
     That we may dwelle with him and his:
        Regina celi, letare!

II, 53   Com, my swetë, com my flour

     'Com, my swetë, com my flour,
      Com my culver, myn owne boure,   *dove; bower*
      Com my modyr, now wyth me,   *mother*
      For hevyn qwene I makë the!'   *queen of heaven*

5   'My swetë sonne, wyth al my love
      I com wyth the to thyn above;
      Wher thou art now let me be,
      For al my love ys layde on the.'

II, 54   The infinite power essenciall

The infinite power essenciall,   *absolute*
Me thoght I sawë verrement,   *truly*
Procedyng from his trone celestiall   *throne*
To a dere damsell that was gent.   *dear; noble / beautiful*
5 Songes melodious was in their tent,   *were the concern*
Of angells synging with gret solemnyté
Before a quene whiche was present –
    Ecce Virgo, radix Jessé.   *behold the Virgin, the root of Jesse*

Tota pulcra, to the lilly like,   *wholly beautiful*
10 She was set withe saphures celestiall;
The odour of hir mowthe aromatike   *fragrant*
Dyd coumford the world unyversall;   *did comfort*
Moche clerer she was then the cristall,   *clearer; than*
She is the flowre of all formosité,   *beauty*
15 Devoide of actës crymynall –
    Ecce Virgo, radix Jessé.

Oleum effusum, to languentes medsyne –   *oil poured out, medicine to the faint*
O Maria by denominacioun! –   *by name*
Fulgent as the beame celestyne,   *resplendent as the heavenly beam*
20 Called unto hir coronacioun.   [*(i.e. the sun)*
Phebus persplendent made his abdominacioun,   *resplendent; abdication*
Devoidyng all in tenebrosité,   *leaving all in darkness*
For gret love of hir exaltacioun –
    Ecce Virgo, radix Jessé.

25 Ryght diligent were the mynstrells divine,
Trones and Dominaciones, for to expresse,   *Thrones and Dominations*
Angells, Archangells, dubbit in doctryne,   *acclaimed in Church teaching*
To mynystre to that regall arayed in rychesse.   *royal personage*
The prynce perpetuall spake to that pryncesse,
30 Smylyng in his suavyté,   *sweetness*
'Columba mea, the cloystre of clandnesse –   *my dove, the cloister of purity*
    Ecce Virgo, radix Jessé.'

'Surge, true tabernacle of virginité,   *arise*
Bothe mother and maiden inculpable,   *without blame*
35 Cum furthe of thy consanguinité   *from your human family*
Unto glorie incomparable.'
Then kneled this oryent and amyable   *this radiant and lovely one*
Before the pellicane of perpetueté,   *the everlasting pelican*
And he crowned that regyent venerable –   *ruler worthy of reverence*
40   Ecce Virgo, radix Jessé.

By the spectable splendure of hir fulgent face	*visible splendour; radiant face*
My sprete was ravesshed and in my body sprent,	*spirit was ravished; leapt up*
Inflamed was my hert with gret solace	*great joy*
Of the luciant, corruscall, resplendent.	*at the bright, shining, resplendent one*
45 Then this curious cumpany incontynent,	*choice company forthwith*
Withe the seraphynnes in their solemnyté,	
Solemply sang this subsequent –	*solemnly sang as follows*
'Ecce Virgo, radix Jessé.'	
O Deifere delicate and doghter dyvyne,	*Bearer of God*
50 Mother of mercy and meyden melleffluus,	*sweet maiden*
Devoide of dysseyte, dubbet in doctryne,	*deceit*
Trone of the Trinity, treite thow for us.	*throne; intercede for us*
Us defende from the dongeon dolorous,	*grievous dungeon (i.e. hell)*
And bring to abide in blisse withe the,	*with thee*
55 There to love our Godd most glorious –	
Ecce Virgo, radix Jessé.	

II, 55   Hale, sterne superne, hale, in eterne ~ *William Dunbar*

Ane Ballat of Our Lady

Hale, sterne superne, hale, in eterne,	*hail, star on high; in eternity*
In Godis sicht to schyne;	*in God's sight to shine*
Lucerne in derne for to discerne	*lamp in darkness by which to see*
Be glory and grace devyne.	*by; divine*
5 Hodiern, modern, sempitern,	*for this day, this age, for ever*
Angelicall regyne,	*queen of angels*
Our tern inferne for to dispern	*gloom infernal to disperse*
Helpe, rialest rosyne.	*most royal rose*
Ave Maria, gracia plena,	*Hail Mary, full of grace*
10 Haile, fresche floure femynyne,	*fresh flower of femininity*
Yerne us guberne, virgin matern,	*diligently us govern, virgin mother*
Of reuth baith rute and ryne.	*of compassion both root and bark*
Haile, yhyng, benyng, fresche flurising,	*young, gracious, fresh blossom*
Haile, Alphais habitakle;	*Alpha's (i.e. God's) dwelling-place*
15 Thy dyng ofspring maid us to syng	*worthy offspring made us*
Befor his tabernakle.	*tabernacle*
All thing maling we doune thring	*all things evil we thrust down*
Be sicht of his signakle,	*at the sight of his sign (i.e. the Cross)*
Quhilk king us bring unto his ryng	*which; his kingdom*
20 Fro dethis dirk umbrakle.	*from death's dark shadow*
Ave Maria, gracia plena,	
Haile, moder and maide but makle;	*without stain*
Bricht syng, gladyng our languissing	*bright sign, comforting our sorrow*
Be micht of thi mirakle.	*by the power of thy miracle*

25 Haile, bricht be sicht in hevyn on hicht,	*bright to behold in heaven on high*
Haile, day sterne orientale;	*day-star of the east*
Our licht most richt in clud of nycht	*our light most true in cloud of night*
Our dirknes for to scale.	*our darkness to disperse*
Hale, wicht in ficht, puttar to flicht	*valiant in fight, putter to flight*
30 Of fendis in battale;	*foes in battle*
Haile, plicht but sicht, hale, mekle of mycht,	*anchor unseen; great in might*
Haile, glorius virgin, hale.	
Ave Maria, gracia plena,	
Haile, gentill nychttingale,	
35 Way stricht, cler dicht, to wilsome wicht	*straight, clearly marked, for erring creatures*
That irke bene in travale.	*who are weary in journeying*
Hale, qwene serene, hale, most amene,	*queen; most kindly*
Haile, hevinlie hie emprys;	*high empress*
Haile, schene unseyne with carnale eyne,	*beautiful one unseen by mortal eyes*
40 Haile, ros of paradys.	*rose*
Haile, clene bedene ay till conteyne,	*wholly pure ever to remain*
Haile, fair, fresche floure-de-lyce;	*lily*
Haile, grene daseyne, haile fro the splene,	*young (lit. green) daisy; heart (lit. spleen)*
Of Jhesu genitrice.	*mother of Jesus*
45 Ave Maria, gracia plena,	
Thow baire the prince of prys,	*bore the prince of glory*
Our teyne to meyne and ga betweyne	*our sins to mediate and intercede for*
As humile oratrice.	*humble intercessor*
Haile, more decore than of before	*beautiful than ever before*
50 And swetar be sic sevyne,	*seven times sweeter*
Our glore forlore for to restore	*glory lost*
Sen thow art qwene of hevyn.	*since*
Memore of sore, stern in aurore,	*mindful of (our) grief, star at dawn*
Lovit with angellis stevyne,	*praised by angels' voice*
55 Implore, adore, thow indeflore,	*thou undeflowered virgin*
To mak our oddis evyne.	*to make our odds even*
Ave Maria, gracia plena,	
With lovingis lowde ellevyn,	*with praises loud eleven*
Quhill store and hore my youth devore,	*until adversity and old age; devour*
60 Thy name I sall ay nevyne.	*I shall always call upon*
Empryce of prys, imperatrice,	*sovereign of excellence, empress*
Bricht polist precious stane,	*bright polished; stone*
Victrice of vyce, hie genitrice	*conqueror; exalted mother*
Of Jhesu, lord soverayne;	*(our) sovereign lord*
65 Our wys pavys fro enemys,	*wise shield from enemies*
Agane the Feyndis trayne,	*against the Fiend's deception*

Oratrice, mediatrice, salvatrice, *intercessor, mediator, saviour*
 To God gret suffragane. *great assistant*
  Ave Maria, gracia plena,
70 Haile, sterne meridiane, *star of midday*
Spyce, flour-de-lice of paradys *spice, lily*
 That baire the gloryus grayne. *seed (i.e. Jesus)*

Imperiall wall, place palestrall *magnificent palace*
 Of peirles pulcritud, *peerless beauty*
75 Tryumphale hall, hie trone regall *triumphal; high royal throne*
 Of Godis celsitud, *God's sublimity*
Hospitall riall, the lord of all *royal refuge*
 Thy closet did include, *chamber (i.e. womb); enclose*
Bricht ball cristall, ros virginall *bright crystal orb, virginal rose*
80 Fulfillit of angell fude. *filled with angels' food (i.e. Jesus)*
  Ave Maria, gracia plena,
 Thy birth has with his blude *child; blood*
Fra fall mortall originall *from the original death-bringing fall*
 Us raunsound on the rude. *ransomed us; cross*

II, 56 Owt of your slepe aryse and wake

Nowel, nowel, nowel,
Nowel, nowel, nowel!

Owt of your slepe aryse and wake, *sleep*
For God mankynd nowe hath y-take *has now assumed human nature*
5 Al of a maide without eny make; *any mate / peer*
 Of al women she bereth the belle. *takes the prize (lit. bell)*
  Nowel!
   Nowel, nowel, etc.

And thorwe a maidë faire and wys *through; wise*
10 Now man is made of ful grete pris; *very great worth*
Now angeles knelen to mannes servys,
 And at this tyme al this byfel. *befell*
  Nowel!
   Nowel, nowel, etc.

15 Now man is brighter than the sonne; *sun*
Now man in heven an hye shal wone; *on high shall dwell*
Blessed be God this game is begonne, *this process has begun*
 And his moder, Emperesse of Helle.
  Nowel!
20   *Nowel, nowel, etc.*

That ever was thralle, now ys he fre;   *enslaved; free*
That ever was smalle, now grete is she;   *great*
Now shal God deme bothe the and me   *assign*
   Unto his blysse yf we do wel.
25   Nowel!
         Nowel, nowel, etc.

Now man may to heven wende;   *go*
Now heven and erthe to hym they bende;   *they bow*
He that was foo now is oure frende;   *foe; friend*
30   This is no nay that y yowe telle.   *no denying what I tell you*
         Nowel!
         Nowel, nowel, etc.

Now, blessëd brother, graunte us grace
A domësday to se thy face   *on*
35 And in thy courte to have a place,
      That we mow there synge nowel.   *may*
         Nowel!
         Nowel, nowel, etc.

II, 57   The sunne of grace hym schynit in

   Al the meryere is that place   *merrier*
   The sunne of grace hym schynit in.   *the sun of grace shone in*

   The sunne of grace hym schynit in
      In on day whan it was morwë,   *morning (of a new day) /Matins*
5   Whan our Lord God borën was
      Withoutë wem or sorwë.   *stain or sorrow*
         The sunne of grace etc.

   The sunne of grace hym schynit in
      On a day whan it was pryme,   *early morning /Prime*
10   Whan our Lord God borën was,
      So wel he knew his tyme.
         The sunne of grace etc.

   The sunne of grace hym schynit in
      On a day whan it was non,   *noon / None*
15 Whan our Lord God borën was
      And on the rodë don.   *placed on the cross*
         The sunne of grace etc.

   The sunne of grace hym schynit in
      On a day whan it was undyrn,   *afternoon / Sext*
20   Whan our Lord God borën was
      And to the hertë stongen.   *pierced*
         The sunne of grace etc.

II, 58   When Cryst was born of Mary fre

Christo paremus cantica: let us provide songs for Christ
'In excelsis gloria.'   'Glory in the highest'

When Cryst was born of Mary fre   noble
In Bedlem, in that fayre cyté,   city
5 Angelles songen with myrth and gle,   sang with delight and joy
    'In excelsis gloria.'
      Christo paremus etc.

Herdmen beheld thes angelles bryght,   shepherds
To hem apperëd with gret lyght   (who) appeared to them
10 And seyd, 'Goddes sone is born this nyght;
    In excelsis gloria.'
      Christo paremus etc.

A kyng ys comen to save kynde,   mankind
In the scriptur as we fynde;
15 Therfore this song have we in mynde:
    'In excelsis gloria.'
      Christo paremus etc.

Jesu, Lord, for thy gret grace,   great
Graunt us in blys to se thy face,
20 Where we may syng to the solas: for thy pleasure
    'In excelsis gloria.'
      Christo paremus etc.

II, 59   The sheperd upon a hill he satt

Can I not syng but 'hoy',   sing nothing but 'hoy'
Whan the joly sheperd made so mych joy?

The sheperd upon a hill he satt;
He had on hym his tabard and his hat,   cloak
5 Hys tar-box, hys pype, and hys flagat;   flask
Hys name was called Joly, Joly Wat.
    For he was a gud herdes boy,   good shepherd-boy
      With hoy!
    For in hys pype he made so mych joy.   much
10   *Can I not syng etc.*

The sheperd upon a hill was layd;   lay on the hill
Hys doge to hys gyrdyll was tayd;   was tied
He had not slept but a lytill brayd   a little while
But 'Gloria in excelcis' was to hym sayd.   'Glory in the highest'
15   For he was a gud herdes boy,
      With hoy!
    For in his pipe he mad so myche joy.
    Can I not syng etc.

The sheperd on a hill he stode;   *stood*
20 Rownd abowt hym his shepe they yode;   *went*
He put hys hond under hys hode;   *hood*
He saw a star as rede as blod.   *blood*
　　For he was a gud herdes boy,
　　　　With hoy!
25 　For in his pipe he mad so myche joy.
　　　　Can I not syng etc.

'Now farwell Mall, and also Will;
For my love go ye all styll   *quietly*
Unto I cum agayn you till,   *until I come back to you*
30 And evermore, Will, ryng well thy bell.'
　　For he was a gud herdes boy,
　　　　With hoy!
　　For in his pipe he mad so mych joy.
　　　　Can I not syng etc.

35 'Now must I go ther Cryst was borne;   *to where*
Farewell, I cum agayn tomorn;   *I shall come back tomorrow*
Dog, kepe well my shep fro the corn,   *from*
And warn well, Warroke, when I blow my horn.'   *summon*
　　For he was a gud herdes boy,
40 　　With hoy!
　　For in hys pype he made so mych joy.
　　　　Can I not syng etc.

The sheperd sayd anon ryght,   *straightaway*
'I will go se yon farly syght,   *marvellous sight*
45 Wheras the angell syngeth on hight,   *where; sings loudly*
And the star that shyneth so bryght.'
　　For he was a gud herdes boy,
　　　　With hoy!
　　For in his pipe he made so mych joy.
50 　　*Can I not syng etc.*

Whan Wat to Bedlëëm cum was,
He swet – he had gon faster than a pace!   *was sweating; walking-pace*
He fownd Jhesu in a sympyll place
Betwen an ox and an asse.
55 　For he was a gud herdes boy,
　　　　With hoy!
　　For in his pipe he mad so mych joy.
　　　　Can I not syng etc.

'Jhesu, I offer to the here my pype,
60 My skyrte, my tar-box, and my scrype;   *kilt; bag*
    Home to my felowes now will I skype,
    And also loke unto my shepe.'   *see to*
        For he was a gud herdes boy,
            With hoy!
65   For in his pipe he mad so myche joy.
            Can I not syng etc.

    'Now, farewell, myne own herdesman Wat.'   *shepherd Wat*
    'Ye, for God, lady, even so I hat!   *before God; I am called*
    Lull well Jhesu in thy lape
70 And farewell, Joseph, wyth thy rownd cape.'   *round cap*
        For he was a gud herdes boy,
            With hoy!
        For in hys pipe he mad so myche joy.
            Can I not syng etc.

75 'Now may I well both hope and syng,   *hop / dance*
    For I have bene a Crystes beryng.   *at Christ's birth*
    Home to my felowes now wyll I flyng.   *dash*
    Cryst of hevyn to his blis us bryng!'
        For he was a gud herdes boy,
80   With hoy!
        For in his pipe he mad so myche joy.
            Can I not syng etc.

II, 60   Abowt the fyld thei pyped full right

Tyrlé, tyrlo,
So merylye the shepperdes began to blowe.

    Abowt the fyld thei pyped full right,   *piped most excellently*
    Even abowt the middes off the nyght;
5   Adown frome heven thei saw cum a lyght.   *come*
        Tyrlé, tirlo.
            Tyrlé, tyrlo, etc.

    Off angels ther came a company
    With mery songes and melody;
10 The shepperdes annonne gane them aspy.   *immediately caught sight of them*
        Tyrlé, tyrlo.
            Tyrlé, tyrlo, etc.

    'Gloria in excelsis,' the angels song   *'glory in the highest'; sang*
    And said who peace was present among   *how peace was here too*
15 To every man that to the faith wold long.   *for every man; would adhere*
        Tyrlé, tyrlo.
            Tyrlé, tyrlo, etc.

The shepperdes hyed them to Bethleme
To se that blyssëd sonës beme,   *sunbeam*
20 And ther they found that glorious streme.   *glorious ray of light*
    Tyrlé, tyrlo.
        Tyrlé, tyrlo, etc.

Now preye we to that mekë chyld,   *meek*
And to his mothere that is so myld,
25 The which that was never defyld,   *defiled*
    Tyrlé, tyrlo,
        Tyrlé, tyrlo, etc.

That we may cum unto his blysse
Where that joy shall never mysse;   *never come to an end*
30 Than may we syng in paradice,   *then*
    'Tyrlé, tirlo.'
        Tyrlé, tyrlo, etc.

I pray yow allë that be here
Fore to syng and mak good chere
35 In the worschip off God thys yere.   *year*
    Tyrlé, tirlo.
        Tyrlé, tyrlo, etc.

II, 61   A babe is borne of hye natèwre ~ *John Audelay* (?)

'What tythynges bryngst us, messangère,   *tidings*
Of Cristës borth this New Eres Day?'   *birth; New Year's Day*

'A babe is borne of hye natèwre,   *noble lineage*
A Prynce of Pese that ever schal be;
5 Off heven and erthe he hath the cewre;   *charge*
Hys lordship is eterneté.   *his rule is for eternity*
    Seche wonder tythynges ye may here: *such wonderful tidings; hear*
    That God and mon is on in fere,   *God is united as one with man*
    Our syn had mad bot fyndës pray.'   *(whom) our sin; but prey for fiends*
10   'What tythynges etc.'

'A semly selcouth hit is to se: *seemly wonder; see*
The burd that had this barne i-borne   *maiden who had borne this child*
This child conseyved in he degré   *conceived in a noble manner*
And maydyn is as was beforne.   *and is (still) a virgin as she was before*
15   Seche wondur tydynges ye mow here: *may hear*
        That maydon and modur ys won y-fere   *maiden and mother are united as one*
        And lady ys of hye aray.'   *of high rank*
            'What tythynges etc.'

'A wonder thyng is now befall:
20 That Lord that mad both se and sun,   *made; sea*
Heven and erth and angeles al,   *all*
In monkynde ys now becumme.   *has now become man*
    Seche wondur tydynges ye mow here:
    A faunt that is bot of on yere   *infant who is merely in his first year*
25 Ever as ben and schal be ay.'   *ever has been and shall be for ever*
    'What tythynges etc.'

'These lovely lady con grete her chylde: *this lovely lady greeted*
"Hayle, Sun! Haile, Broder! Haile, Fader dere!"   *Hail Son; Brother; Father dear*
"Haile, doghter! Haile, suster! Haile, moder myld!"
30 This haylsyng was on coynt manere.   *this salutation was gracious in manner*
    Seche wonder tythynges ye may here:
    This gretyng wes of so he chere   *was so nobly expressed*
    That mannës pyne hit turned to play.'   *man's pain; joy*
    'What tythynges etc.'

35 'That Lord that al thyng mad of noght   *made of nothing*
Is mon becum fore monnës love;   *has become man for love of man*
For with his blood he schul be boght   *shall be redeemed*
From bale to blys that is above.   *misery*
    Seche wonder tythynges ye may here:
40 That Lord us grawnt now our prayère,   *grant; prayer*
    To dwel in heven that we may.'
    'What tythynges etc.'

II, 62   A ferly thyng it is to mene

Aye! aye! this is the day   *indeed, indeed!*
That we shall worshep ever and aye.   *honour ever and always*

A ferly thyng it is to mene,   *marvellous thing it is to tell*
    That a mayd a chyld have borne   *should have borne*
5 And sythë was a mayden clene,   *afterwards; pure*
    As prophetes sayden herbeforne.   *before now*
I-wys, it was a wonder thyng   *certainly; wondrous*
That thowrow an aungelles gretyng   *through; greeting*
God wold lyght in a mayden yyng,   *would alight; young*
10   With aye!
    Aye! aye! I dar well say,
    Her maydenhed yede no away.   *her virginity went not away*
        Aye! aye! this is the day etc.

Hys moder was a mayden myld,
15   As Holy Kyrke wytnese and we;
    Withouten weme she bar a chyld,   *without blemish she bore*
    And so ded never non but she.   *did*

A farly thyng it schuld befall,
But God hath allë women thrall   *though God; bound*
20 In peynes to ber her chylderne all,   *in pains to bear all their children*
    With aye!
  Aye! aye! I dar wel say,
  She felt non of that aray.   *nothing of that condition*
    Aye! aye! this is the day etc.

25 Hys byrth was know that ylkë nyght   *known that very night*
  In all the lond thorow and thorow;   *through*
Thedyr thei yeden to se that syght,   *thither they went*
  To Bethlem, that fayer borow.   *fair town*
An angel bad that thei shuld go:
30 He seyd that 'Betwenne beestës two
Godes Sonne seker ye fynd so',   *certainly ye shall so find*
    With aye!
  Aye! aye! I dar well say,
  In a crybe thei found hym ther he lay.   *where*
35   *Aye! aye! this is the day etc.*

Thre kyngës out of Yndë lond,   *Asian lands*
  Thei cum to seke that ferly fode   *came to seek that wondrous child*
With rych presantes in ther hond;   *their hands*
  A sterre styffely afor hem yode.   *a star steadily before them went*
40 A ferly thyng it was to se: *marvellous thing*
That sterre was mor than other thre;   *three times bigger than any other*
Yt held the course to that contrée,   *country*
    With aye!
  Aye! aye! I dar wel say,
45   Thei thar not mysse of redy way.   *they had no need to miss the direct way*
    Aye! aye! this is the day etc.

Whan thei with that lady mett,
  Thei fond hyr chyld upon her kne;
Full curttesly thei her grett   *courteously; greeted*
50   And present hym with yaftës thre.   *presented; three gifts*
As kyng thei yeffe hym gold so rede,   *as a king they gave; red*
Myrre and sense to hys manhede,   *myrrh and incense for his manhood*
Of hyr offryng thus we redde,   *concerning their offering thus we read*
    With aye!
55   Aye! aye! I dar well say,
Thei worsheped hyme on the twelfth day.
    Aye! aye! this is the day etc.

Mary moder, maydyn myld,
  To the we cry, to the we call: *thee*
60 Thou be owr socur and owr sheyld;   *our help (succour) and our shield*
  Us thou save fro myscheves all.   *save us from all afflictions*

Thou pray thi Sone, that Prynce of Pees,
Of al owr synnes he us relees   *release*
Out of this warld whane we shal cees,   *beyond this world; cease to be*
65   With aye!
      Aye! aye! so that we may   *may we*
      Wend with hym at domësday.   *go; on the Day of Judgement*
       Aye! aye! this is the day etc.

II, 63   I passëd thoru a garden grene

I passëd thoru a garden grene,   *through; green*
I fond a herbere made full newe,   *found an arbor*
A semelyour syght I haff noght sene,   *seemlier sight I have not seen*
Of ylke treo sange a tyrtull trew.   *from every tree; true turtle-dove*
5 Thereyn a mayden bryght off hew,   *radiant in appearance*
And ever sche sange and never sche sest;   *she sang; she ceased*
Thies were the notes that sche can schew: *these; that she uttered*
     'Verbum caro factum est.'   *the word was made flesh*

I asked that mayden what sche mentt;
10 Sche bad me byde and I schuld here.   *she bade me tarry and I would hear*
What sche sayd I toke gude tent –   *I took good heed of*
Yn hyr songe had sche voice full clere.   *clear / pure*
Sche said, 'A prynce withouten pere   *peer*
Ys borne and layd betwene to best;   *two beasts*
15 Therefore I synge as ye mey here,   *you may hear*
     Verbum caro factum est.'

And thoroght that frythe as I can wend,   *throughout that wood as I wandered*
A blestfull song yit hard I mo;   *blissful; yet heard I another*
And that was of threo scheperdes hend,   *three gracious shepherds*
20 'Gloria in excelsis Deo.'   *glory to God in the highest*
I wold noght they had faren me fro,   *I did not want them to leave me*
And eftyr them full fast I prest;   *I hurried*
Then told thei me that thei sange ssoo   *they sang so*
     For verbum caro factum est.   *because the word was made flesh*

25 They said that songe was this to sey: *amounted to this*
     'To God abovun be joy and blysse!   *God above*
For pece yn erth also we pray   *peace on earth*
Tyll all men that yn goodnesse ys.   *to all men of goodwill*
The may that is withouten mysse   *maiden; fault*
30 Hasse borne a child betwene to best;   *has borne; between two beasts*
Sche is the cause theroff i-wysse   *indeed*
     That verbum caro factum est.'

I farëd me furthe yn that frythe,	*I proceeded onward; wood*
I mett threo commely kynges with crone,	*met three stately kings with crowns*
35 I sped me furth to speke them with,	*I hastened forward*
And on my knees I knelëd done.	*down*
The ryalest of home to me con rone	*the kingliest of them addressed me*
And said, 'We farred wele at the fest;	*we fared well at the feast*
Fro Bethlëëm now ar we bone	*from Bethlehem now are we bound*
40 For verbum caro factum est.	

'For we seo God becomen flech	*we have seen God become flesh*
That bote hasse broght off all oure bale	*who has brought the remedy for all our sorrow*
Awey oure synnës for to wesche.	*to wash*
A mey hym harburd yn hur hall,	*a maiden harboured him in her hall*
45 Sche socourd hym sothly yn hur sale,	*succoured; truly in her chamber*
And held that hend yn hur arest;	*that gracious one in her dwelling*
Foll trewly mey sche tell that tale	*full truly may*
That verbum caro factum est.'	

Untyll that prences wyll we pray	*unto that princess*
50 Als sche is bothe moder and mayd;	*as she*
Sche be oure helpe als sche wele mey	*may she be; well may*
To hyme that yn hur lappe was layd.	*her lap*
To serve hyme we be prest and payd,	*we are eager and willing*
And therto make we oure behest;	*our vow*
55 For I hard when sche sange and said,	*heard*
'Verbum caro factum est.'	

II, 64   I saw a swetë semly syght

'Lullay, lullow, lully, lullay,	
Bewy, bewy, lully,	
Bewy, lully, lullow, lully,	
Lullay, baw, baw, my barne,	*my child*
5 Slepe softly now.'	

I saw a swetë semly syght,	*sweet, pleasing sight*
A blisful birde, a blossum bright,	*lady*
That murnyng made and mirth ofmange;	*who grieved and rejoiced at the same time*
A maydin moder, mek and myld,	*meek*
10 In credil kep a knavë child	*(who) watched over a boy child in a cradle*
That softly slepe; scho sat and sange:	*who slept softly; she sat*

'Lullay, lullow, lully, lullay,	
Bewy, bewy, lully,	
Bewy, lully, lullow, lully,	
15 Lullay, baw, baw, my barne,	
Slepe softly now.'	

II, 65   That lovely lady sat and song

Thys endris nyght	*the other night*
I saw a syght,	
A stare as bryght as day,	*star*
And ever among	*and all the while*
5 *A mayden song,*	*sang*
'Lullay, by-by, lullay.'	

That lovely lady sat and song,	
And to hyr chyld con say,	*her; did say*
'My sone, my broder, my fader der,	*dear*
10 Why lyest thou thus in haye?	
My swetë bryd,	*sweet child (lit. bird)*
Thus it ys betyde,	*thus it has happened*
Thow thou be kyng veray;	*though you are truly a king*
But nevertheles	
15 I wyll not ses	*cease*
To syng "By-by, lullay".'	
Thys endris nyght etc.	

The chyld than spak in hys talkyng,	
And to hys moder sayd:	
20 'I be kydde for Heven-Kyng,	*I am known as King of Heaven*
In crybbe thou I be layd,	*though*
For aungelles bryght	
Done to me lyght –	*descend to me*
Thou knowest it ys no nay;	*there is no denying it*
25 And of that syght	*at that sight*
Thou mayst be lyght	*glad*
To syng "By-by, lullay".'	
Thys endris nyght etc.	

'Now swet son, syn thou art kyng,	*since*
30 Why art thou layd in stall?	
Why nere ordenëde thi beddyng	*why was not your bed placed*
In sum gret kyngës hall?	*great*
Me thynketh it is right	
That kyng or knyght	
35 Shuld ly in good aray;	
And than among	*and then the while*
It were no wrong	*it would not be wrong*
To syng "By-by, lullay".'	
Thys endris nyght etc.	

40 'Mary, moder, I am thi chyld	
Thow I be layd in stall;	*though I am laid in a stall*
Lordes and dukes shal worsshyp me,	

And so shall kyngës all.
  Ye shall well se
45   That kyngës thre
    Shal come the twelfthë day;
For this behest   *promise*
Yefe me thi brest   *give; breast*
    And syng "By-by, lullay".'
50   *Thys endris nyght etc.*

'Now tell me, swet son, I the pray –
  Thou art me leve and dere –   *to me beloved and dear*
How shuld I kepe the to thi pay   *look after you to your liking*
  And mak the glad of chere?   *make you glad in spirit*
55   For all thi wyll
    I wold fullfyll,   *would fulfil*
      Thou wotst full well in fay; *know full well in truth*
    And for all this
    I wyll the kys   *thee kiss*
60   And syng "By-by, lullay".'
       Thys endris nyght etc.

'My der moder, whan tym it be,   *when the time comes*
  Thou take me up on loft,   *pick me up*
And set me ryght upon thi kne,   *knee*
65   And handyll me full soft,   *handle me very gently*
    And in thi arme
    Thou hyl me warme,   *cover me up warm*
      And kepe me nyght and day; *protect me*
    If I wepe   *weep*
70   And may not slepe,   *and cannot sleep*
      Than syng "By-by, lullay".' *then*
       Thys endris nyght etc.

'Now, swet son, syn it is so,   *since*
  That all is at thi wyll,
75 I pray the, grauntë me a bone,   *request*
  Yf it be ryght and skyll,   *reasonable*
    That chyld or man
    That wyl or kan
      Be mery upon my day,
80   To blyse hem bryng,   *them (you will) bring*
    And I shal syng
      "Lullay, by-by, lullay".'
       Thys endris nyght etc.

II, 66   This endrys nyght

'Lullay, my chyld, and wepe no more,   *weep*
  Slepe and be now styll;
The Kyng of Blys thi fader ys,   *father*
  As it was hys wyll.'

5 This endrys nyght   *this other night*
  I saw a syght,
    A mayd a cradyll kepe;   *watched over a cradle*
  And ever she song   *sang*
  And seyd among: *the while*
10   'Lullay, my chyld, and slepe.
    Lullay, my chyld, etc.'

  Me thought I hard   *heard*
  The chyld answard,   *answered*
    And to hys moder he sayd: *mother*
15 'My moder der,   *dear*
  What do I her?   *what am I doing here*
    In crybbe why am I layd?'
    'Lullay, my chyld, etc.'

  'I may not slep,   *I cannot sleep*
20 But I may wepe,   *but I can weep*
    I am so wobegone;
  Slep I wold,   *I would (like to) sleep*
  Butt I am cold,
    And clothës have I none',
25   'Lullay, my chyld, etc.'

  'I was borne
  And layd beforne
    Bestes, both ox and asse;
  Mi moder myld,
30 I am thi chyld,
    But he my fader was.'
    'Lullay, my chyld, etc.'

  'Adams gylt,
  This mane had spylt –   *this had destroyed man*
35   That syn grevyt me sore!   *grieved me bitterly*
  Man, for the   *thee*
  Her shal I be   *here*
    Thyrty wynter and mor.'   *thirty years (lit. winters)*
    'Lullay, my chyld, etc.'

40 'Dole it is to se,   *painful it is to see*
      Her shall I be
          Hang upon the rode,   *hung upon the cross*
      With baleis to-bete,   *with scourges severely beaten*
      My woundes to-wete,   *streaming (lit. wholly wet)*
45   And yeffe my flesche to bote.'   *my body (lit. flesh) given as a ransom*
          'Lullay, my chyld, etc.'

    'Here shal I be
    Hanged on a tre,
        And dye, as it is skyll;   *fitting*
50 That I have bought   *(of) what*
    Lesse wyll I nought: *lose; nothing*
        It is my faders wyll.'
          'Lullay, my chyld, etc.'

    'A spere so scharp   *spear*
55 Shall perse my herte   *pierce my heart*
        For dedes that I have done.   *deeds*
    Fader of Grace,
    Wherto thou hase   *wherefore hast thou*
        Forgeten thi lytyll sonne?'   *forgotten*
60   'Lullay, my chyld, etc.'

    'Without pety   *pity*
    Her shall aby   *here (I) shall endure*
        And mak my fleshe al blo;   *discoloured (i.e. with bruising)*
    Adam, i-wys,   *indeed*
65 That deth it ys
        For the and many mo.'   *for thee and many more*
          'Lullay, my chyld, etc.'

II, 67   A baby ys borne us blys to bryng

A baby ys borne us blys to bryng;
A mayddyn I hard 'Loullay' synge: *heard*
'Dyre son, now leyfe thi wepping,   *dear; leave off; weeping*
    Thy fadyre ys the kyng of blys.'   *father*

5 'Nay, modyre, for yow weppe I noght,   *mother; weep I not*
But for thinges that schall be wroght   *shall be done*
Or that I have mankynd i-boght;   *before I have; bought / redeemed*
    Was never payn lyke yt i-wys.'   *indeed*

'Pes! dyre sone, say me not soo!   *peace, dear son*
10 Thow art my chyld, I have noo moo.   *no more*
Alas! that I schwld see this woo,   *should*
    Hyt were to me gret heyvenys.'   *great sorrow (lit. heaviness)*

'My hondes, modyre, that ye now see,   *hands*
Thay schall be nayllëd one a tre;   *nailed on*
15 My feyt allsoo fastnëd schal be –   *feet*
    Ful monny schall wepe that schall see this.'

'Alas! dyre son, hard ys my happe   *my lot*
To see my chyld that soukes my pappe   *sucks my breast*
So rwthfully taken out of my lape,   *so pitifully*
20   Hyt wer to me gret heyvenys.'   *great sorrow*

'Alsoo, modyre, ther schall a speyre   *also, mother; spear*
My tendure hert all to-teyre;   *tender heart; tear to pieces*
The blud schall kevyre my body ther –   *blood shall cover*
    Gret rwthe yt schall be to see this.'   *great pity*

25 'A! sone, that is a heyvy cas: *sad plight*
When Gabrell cnelled before my face,   *knelt before me (lit. before my face)*
And sayd, "Heylle! Lady, full of grace",
    He never told me noothing of this.'

'Dere modyre, peys! nowe I yow pray,   *peace*
30 And take noo sorrow for that I say,   *feel no sorrow at what I say*
But synnge this song "By-by, lowllay,"   *sing*
    To dryfe away all heyvenys.'   *drive*

II, 68   O sisters too

Lully, lulla, thow littel tiny child,
By-by, lully, lullay, thow littell tyny child,
By-by, lully, lullay!

O sisters too,   *two*
5 How may we do
    For to preserve this day
    This pore yongling   *poor youngling / young child*
    For whom we do singe,
        'By-by, lully, lullay'?
10   *Lully, lulla, etc.*

Herod the king
In his raging,
    Chargëd he hath this day
    His men of might
15 In his owne sight
    All yonge children to slay.
        Lully, lulla, etc.

That wo is me,
Pore child, for thee,   *poor*
20   And ever morne and may   *(I) mourn and can*
For thi parting   *because of*
Nether say nor singe,   *neither*
    'By-by, lully, lullay.'
    Lully, lulla, etc.

II, 69   O man unkynde

O man unkynde,
Have thow yn mynde   *if you bear in mind*
    My passyon smert,   *my painful passion*
Thou shall me fynde
5 To the full kynde –   *to thee*
    Lo, here my hert!   *heart*

II, 70   O man unkynde

Querela divina   *the divine lament*

O man unkynde,
Hafe in mynde   *have in mind*
    My paynës smert;   *my sharp pains*
Beholde and see,
5 That is for the   *thee*
    Percëd my hert.   *pierced*

And yitt I wolde,   *yet I would*
Or than thu schuld   *rather than that you should*
    Thi saule forsake,   *your soul*
10 On cros with payne
Scharp deth agayne   *in return*
    For thi luf take.   *love*

For whilk I aske   *which*
None other taske   *payment*
15   Bot luf agayne;   *love in return*
Me than to luf,   *then*
Al thyng abofe,   *above all things*
    Thow aght be fayne.   *ought to be glad*

Responsio humana   *the human response*

O lord, right dere,   *dear*
20 Thi wordes I here   *hear*
    With hert ful sore;   *most sorrowful*

Therfore fro synne	*from*
I hope to blynne	*desist*
And grefe no more.	*and grieve (thee) no more*

25 Bot in this case	
Now helpe thi grace	*may thy grace now help*
My frelnès;	*frailty*
That I may ever	
Do thi pleser,	*pleasure*
30 With lastyngnès.	

This grace to gytt,	*obtain*
Thi moder eeke	*mother also*
Ever be prone,	*may she ever be ready*
That we may alle	
35 Into thi halle,	
With joy, cum sone. Amen.	*come soon*

II, 71   Wofully araide

Wofully araide,	*woefully arrayed*
My blode, man,	*blood*
For the ran,	*for thee*
Hit may not be naide;	*denied*
5 My body blo and wanne,	*black and blue (lit. blue and dark)*
Wofully araide.	

Beholde me, I pray the,	*thee*
with all thyne hole reson,	*undivided attention*
And be not hard-hertid,	*hard-hearted*
for this encheson	*reason*
That I, for thi saule sake	*thy soul's sake*
was slayne in good seson,	*at the appropriate time*
10 Begiled and betraide	
by Judas fals treson,	*treason*
Unkindly intreted,	*treated*
With sharp corde sore freted,	*bound / bitten into*
The Juës me threted;	*reviled*
They mowëd, they spittëd	*grimaced*
and dispisëd me,	
15 Condemnëd to deth	
as thu maïëste se.	*you may see*

Thus nakid am I nailëd,	*(marked by) nails*
O man, for thi sake.	
I love the, thenne love me –	
why slepest thu? Awake!	

Remember my tender
   hert-rote for the brake,   *heart's core broken for thee*
With paynës my vainës   *veins*
   constraynëd to crake.   *forced to break*
20   Thus wàs I defasëd,   *disfigured*
      Thus wàs my flesh rasëd,   *torn*
      And I to deth chasëd;   *hounded*
      Like a lambe led
         untò sacrefise,
      Slayëne I was   *slain*
         in most cruell wise.

25   Of sharp thòrne, I have worne
         a crowne on my hed,
      So rubbëd, so bobbëd,   *scratched; buffeted*
         so rufulle, so red;
      Sore paynëd, sore straynëd,   *stretched*
         and for thi love ded,
      Unfaynëd, not demëd,   *willingly, not compelled*
         my blod for the shed;   *my blood for thee shed*
      My fete and handes sore,
30   With sturdy nayles bore;   *pierced with cruel nails*
      What myght Ì suffer more
      Thèn I have sufferde,   *than*
         man, for the?   *thee*
      Com when thu wilt,
         and welcome to me.

II, 72   Brother, abyde, I the desire and pray

Brother, abyde, I the desire and pray;   *thee*
Abyde, abyde, and here thy brother speke.   *hear; speak*
Beholde my body in this blody aray,   *bloody state*
Broysed and betene wyth whippes that wold not breke. *bruised and beaten; break*
5 This ferefull force, this wo, this wrongfull wreke, *violence; vengeance*
For the I sufferd; canst thou do lesse agayne   *for thee; less in return*
But stonde a while and harke how I complayne?   *than stand; lament*

Above the sterres, in hevyne emperiall,   *stars; imperial heaven*
Crounëd, I satte, thi lorde and thi soverayne,
10 Servede wyth bodies of nature ymmortall,   *by beings*
In joyes that ever shall endure and remayn.
Hevyn, erth and hell, and all thei contayne,
To me dyde owe dewe obedyence,
As to theyr prynce, most hygh in excellence.

15 I raynyng thus in full felicity,   *reigning*
    Thou lyveddest in erth, subjecte to the fende,   *fiend (i.e. the Devil)*
    Wrapped in wo and grett adversity,
    Voyde of socoure, voyde of comforde fro any ffrende.   *without succoure; comfort from*
    And worst of all, thou knewest no tyme nor ende   [*any friend*
20 Off thy distresse – thou knewest no remedy
    Agaynst thy greffe and mortall mysery.   *for thy grief*

    Pety I hade, beholdyng the this wise   *pity; beholding thee in this way*
    Be thin enmy oppressëde, in distresse;   *by*
    And, of grett love, anoone I dyd devise   *anon I determined*
25 The to delyver out of this wrechidnese.   *thee*
    And by and by, withouten longe procese,   *without delay*
    I lefte my trone and regall magesté,   *throne*
    And hither I came, a maydyns childe to be.   *maiden's*

    Borne in Bedlem, lapped and laide in strawe   *wrapped*
30 Ine a powur howse wher bestës ete ther mete;   *poor; ate their food*
    Brought to the temple after Juës lawe,
    And circumcysed – this ys not to forgette;   *not to be forgotten*
    I lede my youth wyth children in the strette,   *street*
    Poorly arayed in clothës bare and thyne,   *dressed*
35 Suche as my mother for me dyde make and spyne.

    Myn age encresed, and then about I wentt,
    Prechinge scripture; and whersumever I came
    I moved the people for to be penitent,
    And that I saied was in my fathers name.   *and whatever I said*
40 Some praysed my preching, some said I was to blame,
    Some toke my techyng, sum wold nott of my scole,   *accepted; rejected my instruction*
    Sum held me wyse, some said I was a fole.   *fool*

    Thus longe I lyved, passyng frome place to place,
    Barefotyd, caplese, wythout sylver or gold.
45 Payne of my traveylle aperëd in my face,
    Men myght perceyve yf thei listed to behold.   *if they wished*
    Watch and grett labur, sharpe honger, thurst and cold   *wakefulness and great exertion*
    Full ofte me brought so feble and so lowe,
    That myne owne mother sum tyme dyd me not knowe.

50 Thus and mych more for the endurëd I.   *much more for thee*
    Therfor, brother, make thou no hast to starte,   *haste to rush away*
    Nother of my speche be thou no thing wery,   *neither; weary*
    For that yf thou be, to blame thou arte.
    To whom shuld I disclose or brek myne harte,   *or open my heart*
55 To whom shulde I complayne my greffe mortall,   *lament my mortal grief*
    But to the, my brother moost naturall?   *thee*

Harke now therfor, hark now and take goode hede,
And of my troble anoone thou shalt here more.   *anon; hear*
To shewe myself as God and mane in deede,   *man*
60 Lasar I raysed, buried fowre dayes before.   *Lazarus I raised*
The people I cured of every maner sore,   *of every kind of infirmity*
Some deffe, some dome, sum full of dropsy,   *dumb*
And some sore enhawntëd wyth ferefull frensy.   *sorely possessed by*

And some lame, of lidernes that myght not goo nor crepe,   *(who) for infirmity; creep*
65 And sum blynde borne, by ympedyment of natùre,
And some vexed, they cowde nevyr reste ne slepe,   *nor sleep*
And sum that fell dede by sodene adventùre.   *sudden chance*
Bothe powur and ryche I holpe and toke to cure,   *poor; helped; took care of*
Usyng to them noone other medycyne   *for them*
70 But my holy worde, full of vertue divyne.

Then myn enmys begane to rage and rayle,
And said I hade the devyll at my demayne;   *in my control*
Some said I used arte, magike wythout fayle,   *without doubt*
And some said I coude not longe contynew ne rayne.   *continue nor reign*
75 Al this I hard and litle I said agayne;   *heard; little; in return*
All that myne ennymes dyd I sufferd paciently,
And to ther wordes no countraury speche hade I.   *riposte (lit. contrary speech)*

Then they came to me, flamed wyth ire fervent,   *inflamed; vehement rage*
And said the people by me deceyvëd were.   *deceived*
80 Many blynd reasons and miche froward argument   *much hostile*
To me they made, and bade I shuld answere.   *against me*
Answere I dyde, wherto they leyed good ere,   *lent (lit. laid) good ear*
And specyally thei gave sure attendance,   *paid good attention*
To take me wyth some fawlte in utturaunce.   *catch me out in; fault*

85 But to my saying they cowde no thyng replye;   *to what I said*
My resouns wer so playne and apparentte.   *plain and clear*
Neverthelesse, so miche was ther envy,   *so great was their enmity*
That styll they murmorde and wold not be contente.   *be satisfied*
Cownsell they toke and by secrett assentte
90 They were agreed to dethe me for to bete,   *to beat me to death*
Wyth cloddes of erthe and stone hard and grette.   *great*

I me wythdrewe and dyde lette theire fury passe   *let*
And for a seasone fro them I dyd me hyde.
Neverthelese, agayn abrode I wase,   *I was abroad (i.e. out and about)*
95 All there malys redy for to abyde.   *their malice ready*
And by this tyme thei had gotene them a gyde,   *guide*
One that I trustëd, and Judas was his name,   *a man (lit. one)*
Which me betrayed and hynge hymeself for shame.   *who; hanged*

Then to conclude ther cruell appetyt,
100 Thei gatherd them in a great companye,
Wyth bylles and battes, wyth torch and lanterne lyght,   *pikes and clubs*
Me to dystresse; and so takene was I,   *to take me prisoner*
And leede to prysoun wyth clamor and outcry,
Fast bownde in roppes, and left myself alone,
105 For all my frendes were fro me flede and goone.

Petur, my frend, that said wyth wordës bolde   *Peter*
In my quarell he wolde bothe lyve and dye,   *in my cause*
Stode by the fyere to warme hymeself for colde,   *fire*
And for his master thrise he dyde me dinye.   *as his master thrice; deny*
110 Thus was I lefte no frende to stande me by,
Thus was I lefte in fere and grett danger,   *fear*
Amonge myn enymys a wofull prisoner.

Before Pylate erly they dyd me brynge,
He as a juge, to here what shuld be sayde.   *hear what should be said*
115 And too stode forth, agaynst me witnessyng,   *two*
And a fals mattur unto my charge they layde.
'Speke, manne,' quod Pylate, 'how ys thy lyf convayed?'   *said Pilate; conducted*
And wyth that worde, wattur to whasche he callde,   *for water to wash he called*
And I stode styll, seke and sore appalled.   *sick*

120 Then sodenly the folke feelle in roure,   *fell into uproar*
And wyth one voyce they cryed, 'Hang up this theff!'
Pylate stode forth and openly he swoure   *swore*
He cowde lay no thyng to my repreff.   *as accusation against me*
Neverthelesse, fering his propur greeff   *fearing trouble for himself*
125 And wyllyng also noyse to apease and stylle,   *wishing; to allay and calm*
He badde them take and do wyth me ther wyll.   *their*

Then they layde hande and lede me forth that day,
Wyth shotyng and crying, wyth mokry and mych dysdayne;   *shouting; mockery*
Some pulled me forwarde and tare my powur aray,   *tore my poor clothing*
130 And by the here some plukked me bake agayne.   *by the hair; back*
Often I stomelled and felle to the grounde for payne   *stumbled*
And wythout pyty of my grevance or hurte
They spornned me up, all betrodene in durte.   *kicked at me*

And as people most cruell and unkynde,
135 When I for woo blode and water swette,   *(with) blood and sweat was*
Unto a pylar nakyd thei dyde me bynde   *[covered (lit. sweated)*
And wyth sharpe scorgës thei dyde my body bette   *beat*
Unto the bonnes – the synuës dyd freete –   *bones; sinews smarted*
And on my heode sharpe thorns thei dyd dystrayne   *head; they pressed*
140 Thorowgh skyne and skulle, that rane unto my brayne.   *which ran right to*

Thus bete, thus rentte, and all totore,	*beaten; torn to pieces*
Wyth a great crose thei dyd me charge and lade,	*cross; load*
Which on my shuldure up to an hill I bore,	
In steppes of blode as depe as I cowde wade.	*deep*
145 Abowt me rennyng, myche tyrany thei made,	*running; much cruelty*
And as wood men thei dyde me dryve and chace,	*as mad men; hound*
Wyth mowes and knockes and spettyng in my face.	*taunts and blows*
This crosse soo sade apone my shulder ley	*so heavily*
That bake and bone it made to bowe and bende.	*back and bone*
150 Often I stomeled and fell downe by the way	*stumbled*
As I labored the mounteyn to ascende;	
When I came up, my breth was at an ende;	*breath*
I cowde not speke – in me no powur ther was	*speak; strength*
But as in a mane redy for to passe.	*other than in a man ready to die*
155 Then one this crosse thei dyde me strecch and strayn,	*on*
And nayled me faste wyth nayllës gret and longe,	
And hyng me uppe betwene false thevës twayne	*hung*
Most shamefully, wyth moche rebuke and wronge.	*much*
I called for drynke, my thurst was grevous strong;	
160 Thei gave me aysell, tempred wyth bitter galle,	*vinegar*
Which I did taste and dranke therof but smalle.	*only a little*
My visage changed to pale and blew as byse,	*blue as blue-grey pigment*
My fleshe beganne to styff and waxëd drye,	*tauten; became dry*
My hart lokëd lyke a plomett of ise,	*seemed like a plummet of ice*
165 My lyff was spent, myne owre was come to dye;	*hour*
Unto my father I cryed, 'Eli, Eli!'	
And wyth that worde, I layde myne hede asyde,	*head*
And dolfully gave up the spret, and dyed.	*spirit*
Ther honge I dede, a pytyfull fygure,	*hung*
170 And mene in harnesse were sette the place to kepe;	*men in armour; to guard*
And bycawse of me thei wold be sure,	
Wyth a sharpe spere my hart thei lawnsëd depe.	*pierced (lit. lanced)*
My mother stode, but what cowde she doo but weepe?	
And weepe she dyde, terres both whit and rede,	*tears; clear and red*
175 Wrynging her handes, and fill downe by me deede.	*in a swoon (i.e. as if dead)*
Now, gentyll brother, beholde this matur welle,	*matter*
And myndfully marke this rufull reknynge,	*heed this pitiful account*
Loke one this processe, consider it every delle,	*narrative; in every part*
Fro the furst to the laste consider every thynge.	
180 Furst consider I raynëd as a kynge;	*reigned*
Seconde considere, as a frend moost fre,	*most generous*
To make the ryche, I died in poverté.	*thee rich; poverty*

What cowde one brother more for another doo
Then my complaynte presently dothe apere and expresse?   *than; lament now; reveal*
185 What canst thou adde or putte eny thyng thertoo   *any*
That myght be done by brotherly kyndnesse?
Se what I suffred thy grevanse to reddresse!   *see; grievance*
What canst thou aske or more desire of me,
Thy feythfull brother, dyeng in poverté?   *dying*

190 Off tendure love, all this I dyd endure;
Love dyde me lede, love dyde me thus constrayne;
And for my dede and grevouse adventure   *death and grievous fate*
More aske I nott but love for love agayne.   *in return*
Brother, be kynde, and for a good certayne,   *for an absolute certainty*
195 Byside all this, rewardede shalt thou be
In the blysse of hevyne, where ther ys no poverté.

II, 73   In a tabernacle of a toure

In a tabernacle of a toure,   *niche; tower*
As I stode musyng on the mone,   *meditating on the moon*
A crounëd quene, most of honoure,   *greatest in honour*
Apered in gostly syght ful sone.   *appeared in a spiritual vision suddenly*
5 She made compleynt thus by hyr one,   *on her own*
For mannës soule was wrapped in wo: *because*
'I may nat leve mankynde allone,
    Quia amore langueo.   *because I languish for love*

'I longe for love of man my brother,   *pine*
10 I am hys vokete to voyde hys vyce;   *advocate to set aside*
I am hys moder – I can none other –   *mother; I cannot do otherwise*
Why shuld I my dere chylde dispyce?   *despise*
Yef he me wrathe in diverse wyse,   *if he angers me in various ways*
Through flesshes freelty fall me fro,   *(if) through frailty of flesh (he); from*
15 Yet must me rewe hym tyll he ryse,   *I must take pity on him*
    Quia amore langueo.

'I byd, I byde in grete longyng,   *I entreat, I wait*
I love, I loke when man woll crave,   *look for the time; plead*
I pleyne for pyty of his peynyng;   *I lament out of pity for his suffering*
20 Wolde he aske mercy, he shuld hit have.   *if he would ask for*
Say to me, soule, and I shall save,   *speak*
Byd me, my chylde, and I shall go;   *entreat; go (i.e. as advocate)*
Thow prayde me never but my son forgave,
    Quia amore langueo.

25 'O wreche in the worlde, I loke on the,   *thee*
    I se thy trespas day by day,
    With lechery ageyns my chastité,   *against*
    With pryde agene my pore aray;   *against; poor*
    My love abydeth, thyne ys away;
30 My love the calleth, thow stelest me fro;   *thee; steal away from me*
    Sewe to me, synner, I the pray,   *appeal*
        Quia amore langueo.

    'Moder of mercy I was for the made;   *mother; thee*
    Who nedëth hit but thow allone?   *it (i.e. mercy)*
35 To gete the grace I am more glade   *obtain grace for thee*
    Than thow to aske hit; why wylt thou noon?   *none*
    When seyd I nay, tel me, tyll oon?   *to anyone*
    Forsoth never yet, to frende ne foo;
    When thou askest nought, than make I moone,   *then I lament*
40   Quia amore langueo.

    'I seke the in wele and wrechednesse,   *seek; in prosperity*
    I seke the in ryches and poverté;   *in wealth*
    Thow, man, beholde where thy moder ys,
    Why lovest thou me nat syth I love the?   *not since*
45 Synful or sory how evere thow be,
    So welcome to me there ar no mo;   *as welcome; are; more*
    I am thy suster, ryght trust on me,   *sister; trust fully*
        Quia amore langueo.

    'My childe ys outlawed for thy synne,
50 My barne ys bette for thi trespasse;   *my child is beaten*
    It prykketh myne hert that so ny my kynne   *it stabs my heart; so deeply my kin*
    Shuld be dysseased. O Sone, allasse!   *afflicted; O Son, alas!*
    Thow art hys brother, hys moder I was;
    Thow soked my pappe, thow loved man so;   *sucked my breast*
55 Thow dyed for hym, myne hert he has,   *heart*
        Quia amore langueo.

    'Man, leve thy synne than for my sake;   *leave; then*
    Why shulde I gyf the that thou nat walde?   *give thee what you do not wish*
    And yef thow synne, som prayere take,   *if*
60 And trust in me as I have talde.   *as I have bidden*
    Am nat I thy moder called?   *not; mother*
    Why shulde thou flee? I love the – loo,   *thee – see (lit. interj. lo)*
    I am thy frende, I helpe – byhalde,   *friend; behold*
        Quia amore langueo.

65 'Now Sone,' she sayde, 'wylt thou sey nay,   *say no*
      Whan man wolde mende hym of hys mys?   *should want to cure himself of his sin*
      Thow lete me never in veyne yet pray.   *in vain*
      Than, synfull man, see thow to thys,   *then; pay heed to this*
      What day thou comest, welcome thow ys;   *whatever day*
70 Thys hundreth yere yef thow were fro   *even if you were away for a hundred*
      I take the ful fayne, I clyppe, I kysse,   *most gladly; embrace*   [*years*
          Quia amore langueo.

    'Now wol I syt and sey nomore,
      Leve, and loke with grete longyng;   *leave off, and wait (lit. look)*
75 Whan man woll calle, I wol restore;   *I will rescue (him)*
      I love to save hym – he ys myne osprynge;   *offspring*
      No wonder yef myne hert on hym hynge,   *if; hangs on him*
      He was my neyghbore; what may I doo?
      For hym have I thys worshippyng,   *honour*
80   *And therefore amore langueo.*

    'Why was I crouned and made a quene?
      Why was I called of mercy the welle?   *the well of mercy*
      Why shuld an erthly woman bene
      So hygh in heven above aungelle?   *angels*
85 For the, mankynde – the truthe I telle!   *for thee*
      Thou aske me helpe, and I shall do   *ask help from me*
      That I was ordeyned, kepe the fro helle,   *what I was chosen to do, protect you*
          Quia amore langueo.   [*from hell*

    'Nowe man, have mynde on me forever,
90 Loke on thy love thus languysshyng;
      Late us never fro other dissevere,   *let; separate from one another*
      Myne helpe ys thyne oune, crepe under my wynge;
      Thy syster ys a quene, thy brother ys a kynge,
      Thys heritage ys tayled – sone, come therto,   *entailed; son*
95 Take me for thy wyfe and lerne to synge,
          Quia amore langueo.'

II, 74   With favour in her face

      Sodenly afraide,   *suddenly afraid*
        half wakyng, half slepyng,
      And gretly dismayde –
        a wooman sate weepyng.

    With favoure in hir face   *beauty in her face*
        ferr passyng my reason,   *far surpassing my account*
    And of hir sore weepyng,   *her*
        this was the enchesone: *cause*

5 Hir soon in hir lap lay, *son*
  she seid, slayne by treason.
Yif wepyng myght ripe bee, *might be appropriate*
  it seemed than in season. *then*
'Jhesù!' so she sobbëd –
So hir soon was bobbëd, *so buffeted had her son been*
And of his lif robbëd –
10 Saying thies wordes, *these*
  as I say thee: *to thee*
'Who cannot wepe, *whoever*
  come lerne at me.' *learn from me*
   Sodenly afraide, etc.

I said I cowd nòt wepe,
  I was so harde-hartid.
Shee answerd me shortly
  with wordës that smarted: *stung*
15 'Lo, nature shall move the, *nature (i.e. natural instinct); thee*
  thou must be converted;
Thyne owne fader this nyght
  is deed' – thus she thwarted – *dead; countered*
'So my soon is bobbëd,
And of his lif robbëd.'
Forsooth than I sobbëd,
20 Veryfying the wordes,
  she seid to me:
'Who cannot wepe,
  may lern at me.'
   Sodenly afraide, etc.

'Now breke, hert, I the pray! –
  this cors lith so rulye, *this body lies so pitifully*
So beten, so wownded,
  entreted so Jewlye. *treated so Jewishly*
25 What wight may behold *what creature could look on*
  and wepe nat? – noon truly! – *weep not; none*
To see my deed dere soon, *dead dear son*
  lygh bleedyng this newlye.' *lie; thus*
Ever stil she sobbëd – *ever yet*
So hir soon was bobbëd,
And of his lif robbëd –
30 Newyng the wordes, *repeating*
  as I say thee:
'Who cannot wepe,
  com lern at me.'
   Sodenly afraide, etc.

On me she caste hir ey,   *cast her eye*
 said, 'See, man, thy brothir!'
She kissed hym and said, 'Swete,
 am I not thy modir?'   *mother*
35 In sownyng she fill there –   *in a swoon she fell there*
 it wolde be noon othir;   *it could not have been otherwise*
I not which more deedly,   *I do not know which (looked) more deathly*
 the toon or the tothir.   *the one or the other*
Yit she revivëd and sobbëd –
 So hir soon was bobbëd,
And of his lif robbëd –
40 'Who cannot wepe' –
 this was the laye,   *complaint* (lit. *lay*)
 And with that word,
  she vanysht away.
   Sodenly afraide, etc.

II, 75 O alle women that ever were borne

O alle women that ever were borne
That berys childur, abyde and se   *who bear children, abide and see*
How my son liggus me beforne   *lies before me*
Upon my skyrte, takyn fro tre.   *on my lap, taken from the tree (i.e. the*
5 Your childur ye dawnse upon your kne *dance   [cross)*
With laghyng, kyssyng and mery chere; *laughing; merriment*
Beholde my childe, beholde wele me, *well*
 For now liggus ded my dere son dere. *lies dead my dear, dear son*

O woman, woman, wel is the: *you are happy*
10 Thy childis cap thu dose upon,   *you put on*
Thu pykys his here, beholdys his ble – *you comb his hair, look upon his face*
Thu wost not wele when thu hast done. *you are unaware of (your) happiness*
But ever, alas! I make my mone   *lament*
To se my sonnys hed as hit is here; *son's head*
15 I pyke owt thornys be on and on, *I pick out thorns one by one*
 For now liggus ded my dere son dere.

O woman, a chaplet chosyn thu has *garland (of flowers); you have*
Thy childe to were, hit dose the likyng, *wear; it gives you pleasure*
Thu pynnes hit on, grete joye thou mas; *you pin it on; you make*
20 And I sitte with my son sore wepyng,
His chaplet is thornys sore prickyng,
His mouth I kys with carfull chere – *in sorrow*
I sitte wepyng and thu syngyng,
 For now liggus ded my dere son dere.

25 O woman, loke to me agayne,
    That playes and kisses your childur pappys.   *(you) who play; children's breasts*
    To se my son I have gret payne,
    In his brest so gret a gap is   *great*
    And on his body so mony swappys.   *so many blows*
30 With blody lippys I kis hym here,
    Alas! full hard me thynk me happys,   *it seems to me my lot is*
        For now liggus ded my dere son dere.

    O woman, thu takis thi childe be the hand   *you take; by the hand*
    And seis, 'My son gif me a strake!'   *say; give me a caress*
35 My sonnys handis ar sore bledand;   *are; bleeding*
    To loke on hym me list not layke.   *looking at them I have no desire to play*
    His handis he suffyrd for thi sake
    Thus to be boryd with naylës sere;   *several nails*
    When thu makes myrth gret sorow I make,
40   For now liggus ded my dere son dere.

    Beholde women when that ye play
    And hase your childur on knees daunsand;   *have; dancing on your knees*
    Ye fele ther fete, so fete ar thay   *you feel their feet, so neat they are*
    And to your sight ful wel likand.   *so very pleasing*
45 But the most fyngur of my hande   *biggest finger*
    Thorow my sonnys fete I may put here   *through my son's feet*
    And pulle hit out sore bledand,   *bleeding*
        For now liggus ded my dere son dere.

    Therfor, women, be town and strete   *in town and street*
50 Your childur handis when ye beholde,
    Theyr brest, theire body and theire fete,
    Gode were on my son thynk ye wolde,   *it would be good if you would think*
    How care has made my hert full colde
    To se my son, with nayle and speyre,
55 With scourge and thornys manyfolde,
        Woundit and ded, my dere son dere.

    Thu hase thi son full holl and sounde,   *you have; completely whole and sound*
    And myn is ded upon my kne;   *dead*
    Thy childe is lawse and myn is bounde;   *free*
60 Thy childe is an life, and ded is he –   *alive; dead*
    Whi was this oght but for the?   *other than for thee*
    For my childe trespast never here.
    Me thynk ye be holdyne to wepe with me,   *it seems to me that you are bound*
        For now liggus ded my dere son dere.

65 Wepe with me, both man and wyfe,
    My childe is youres and lovys yow wele.   *loves you well*
    If your childe had lost his life
    Ye wolde wepe at every mele;   *continually (lit. on every occasion)*
    But for my son wepe ye never a del.   *never a bit*
70 If ye luf youres, myne has no pere;   *if you love yours, mine has no peer*
    He sendis youris both hap and hele   *good fortune and health / salvation*
        And for yow dyed my dere son dere.

    Now, alle wymmen that has your wytte   *who are of sound mind*
    And sees my childe on my knees ded,   *and (who) see*
75 Wepe not for yours but wepe for hit,   *it (i.e. my child)*
    And ye shall have ful mycull mede.   *a very great reward*
    He wolde agayne for your luf blede   *would; bleed*
    Rather or that ye damnëd were.   *rather than; you should be damned*
    I pray yow alle to hym take hede,   *pay heed to him*
80   For now liggus ded my dere son dere.

    Farewel, woman, I may no more
    For drede of deth reherse his payne.
    Ye may lagh when ye list and I wepe sore,   *laugh when you wish*
    That may ye se and ye loke to me agayne.   *if you look*
85 To luf my son and ye be fayne   *if you are willing*
    I wille luff yours with hert entere,   *with (my) whole heart*
    And he shall brynge your childur and yow sertayne   *certainly*
        To blisse wher is my dere son dere.   *where my dear, dear son is*

II, 76   I have laborede sore and suffered deyth

    I have laborede sore and suffered deyth,
    And now I rest and draw my breyth;   *breath*
    But I shall come and call ryght sone   *soon*
    Hevene and erth and hell to dome;   *to judgement*
  5 And thane schall know both Devyll and mane   *Devil and man*
    What I was and what I ame.

II, 77   Done is a battell on the dragon blak ~ *William Dunbar*

    Done is a battell on the dragon blak;   *ended is a battle against*
    Our campioun Chryst confoundit hes his force;   *champion; has overthrown his power*
    The yettis of hell ar brokin with a crak,   *gates*
    The signe triumphall rasit of the croce.   *victorious symbol of the cross raised*
  5 The divillis trymmillis with hiddous voce;   *devils tremble; hideous voice*
    The saulis ar borrowit and to the bliss can go;   *souls are redeemed*
    Chryst with his blud our ransonis dois indoce: *blood; endorses our ransoms*
        Surrexit Dominus de sepulchro.   *The Lord is risen from the tomb*

Dungin is the deidly dragon Lucifer,   *beaten down; deadly*
10 The crewall serpent with the mortall stang,   *cruel; sting*
The auld kene tegir with his teith on char   *old fierce tiger with his teeth bared*
Quhilk in a wait hes lyne for us so lang   *which in ambush has lain; long*
Thinking to grip us in his clowis strang.   *strong claws*
The mercifull lord wald nocht that it wer so;   *did not wish*
15 He maid him for to felye of that fang: *fail of (i.e. to capture) that prey*
    Surrexit Dominus de sepulchro.

He for our saik that sufferit to be slane   *He who; sake; allowed (himself); slain*
And lyk a lamb in sacrifice wes dicht   *like; was given*
Is lyk a lyone rissin up agane   *like a lion risen up again*
20 And as gyane raxit him on hicht.   *and like a giant stretched himself on high*
Sprungin is Aurora radius and bricht;   *risen; radiant and bright*
On loft is gone the glorius Appollo;   *on high*
The blisfull day depairtit fro the nycht: *separated from the night*
    Surrexit Dominus de sepulchro.

25 The grit victour agane is rissin on hicht   *great; risen on high*
That for our querrell to the deth wes woundit;   *our cause*
The sone that wox all paill now schynis bricht,   *sun which grew all wan now shines*
And dirknes clerit, our fayth is now refoundit;   *darkness cleared; established again*
The knell of mercy fra the hevin is soundit,   *from*
30 The Cristin ar deliverit of thair wo,   *Christians; delivered from their woe*
The Jowis and thair errour ar confoundit: *Jews*
    Surrexit Dominus de sepulchro.

The fo is chasit, the battell is done ceis,   *driven away; made to cease*
The presone brokin, the jevellouris fleit and flemit;   *prison; gaolers scared and put to flight*
35 The weir is gon, confermit is the peis,   *war is over, confirmed; peace*
The fetteris lowsit and the dungeoun temit;   *fetters loosened; dungeon emptied*
The ransoun maid, the presoneris redemit;   *ransom made; prisoners redeemed*
The feild is win, ourcumin is the fo,   *field (i.e. of battle) is won, overcome*
Dispulit of the tresur that he yemit: *despoiled; treasure that he guarded*
40   Surrexit Dominus de sepulchro.

II, 78   Jhesus woundes so wide

Jhesus woundes so wide
Ben welles of lif to the goode,   *are wells of life*
Namely the stronde of hys syde,   *especially the stream from his side*
That ran ful breme on the rode.   *so fiercely; cross*

5 Yif thee liste to drinke,   *if it is your will*
To fle fro the fendes of hell,   *flee; fiends*
Bowe thu doun to the brinke   *bow down*
And mekely taste of the welle.   *meekly*

II, 79   He bare hym up, he bare hym down

Lulley, lulley; lully, lulley;
The fawcon hath born my mak away.   *falcon; mate*

He bare hym up, he bare hym down;
He bare hym into an orchard brown.
5   *Lulley, lulley; etc.*

In that orchard ther was an hall,
That was hanged with purpill and pall.   *with rich purple fabrics*
   Lulley, lulley; etc.

And in that hall ther was a bede;   *bed*
10 Hit was hanged with gold so rede.
   Lulley, lulley; etc.

And yn that bed ther lythe a knyght,   *lies*
His wowndës bledyng day and nyght.
   Lulley, lulley; etc.

15 By that bedes side ther kneleth a may,   *maiden*
And she wepeth both nyght and day.
   Lulley, lulley; etc.

And by that beddes side ther stondeth a ston,
'Corpus Christi' wreten ther-on.   *'the body of Christ' written thereon*
20   *Lulley, lulley; etc.*

II, 80   Byhalde merveyles! A mayde ys moder!

Byhalde merveyles! A mayde ys moder!   *behold marvels; maiden*
Her sone her fader ys and broder!   *her son is her father and brother*
Lyfe faught with dethe and dethe is slayne; *fought with death*
Most high was lowe – he styghe agayne!   *(he who was) most high was (brought)*
                                             low – he rose again

II, 81   A God and yet a man?

A God and yet a man?
   A mayde and yet a mother?
Witt wonders what witt can   *wit (i.e. reason, intellect)*
   Conceave this or the other.

5 A God – and can he die?
   A dead man – can he live?
What witt can well replie?
   What reason reason give?

God, Truth itselfe, doth teach it;
10   Mans witt senckes too farr under   *man's understanding sinks*
By reasons power to reach it.   *reason's*
     Beleeve, and leave to wonder!   *believe, and cease*

II, 82   Whan nothyng was but God alone

Why, why, what is this whi
But virtus verbi Domini?   *the power of the word of God*

Whan nothyng was but God alone,
The Fader, the Holy Gost, with the Son,   *Father*
5 On was three, and three was on.   *one*
     What is this why?
To frayn why I hold but foly;   *to ask; folly*
It is non other sertenly   *certainly*
But virtus verbi Domini.
10   *Why, why, etc.*

'Fiat' was a word ful bold,   *'let there be'*
That mad al thing as He wold,   *wished*
Heveyn and erth and men of mold.   *from earth*
     What is this why?
15 To frayn why I hold but foly;
It is non other sertenly
But virtus verbi Domini.
     Why, why, etc.

The warld gan wax and multiply;   *world began to grow*
20 The planetes mad hem full besy   *made themselves very busy*
To rowll ych thyng by and by.   *to rule each thing one by one*
     What is this why?
To frayne why I hold but foly;
It is non other sertenly
25 But virtus verbi Domini.
     Why, why, etc.

The planetes wark nothyng in veyn,   *do nothing in vain*
But, as thei be ordent, so must thei reygne,   *as they are ordained; reign*
For the word of God wyl not ageyne.   *nothing will prevail against*
30   What is this why?
To frayne why I hold but foly;
It is non other sertenly
But virtus verbi Domini.
     Why, why, etc.

35 Whan Bede had preched the stonës dry, *preached to the dry stones*
 The myght of God mad hem to cry, *made them*
 'Amen!' – certys, this is no ly. *assuredly this is no lie*
  What is this why?
  To frayn why I hold but foly;
40 It is non other sertenly
  But virtus verbi Domini.
   Why, why, etc.

 Herytykes wonder of this thyng most: *heretics*
 How God is put in the Holy Host,
45 Her and at Rome and in every cost. *here; every land (lit. coast)*
  What is this why?
  To frayn why I hold but foly;
  It is non other sertenly
  But virtus verbi Domini.
50 *Why, why, etc.*

II, 83 In the vale of Abraham

 Now bethink the, gentilman, *thee*
 How Adam dalf and Evë span. *delved*

In the vale of Abraham
Cryst hymself he made Adàm,
5 And of his rybbe a fayr wommàn,
 And thus this semly word began. *seemly speech*
  Now bethink the, etc.

'Cum, Adàm, and thou shalt se
The blysse of paradis so fre; *so excellent*
10 Therin stant an appil tre; *stands*
 Lef and frewt growëth theron. *leaf and fruit*
  Now bethink the, etc.

'Adàm, if thou this appil ete,
Alle these joyes thou shalt foryete *lose*
15 And the peynes of hellë gete.' *get*
 Thus God hymself warnëd Adàm.
  Now bethink the, etc.

Whan God was fro Adam gon,
Sone after cam the fend anon; *fiend*
20 A fals tretour he was on! *he was one false traitor!*
 He tok the tre and krep theron. *took hold of the tree and crept on to it*
  Now bethink the, etc.

'What eyleth the, Adam? Art thou wod?   *what ails you; are you mad*
Thi Lord hath tawt the lytil good.   *taught you little of worth*
25 He wolde not thou understod   *he did not want you to understand*
    Of the wyttës that he can.   *the wise things that he knows*
      Now bethink the, etc.

'Tak the appil of the tre   *take*
And ete therof, I biddë the,   *eat; bid thee*
30 And alle hese joyës thou shalt se,   *all his (i.e. God's) joys*
    Fro the He shal heden non.'   *from thee he shall hide none*
      Now bethink the, etc.

Whan Adam hadde that appil ete,   *eaten*
Alle hese joyës wern foryete;   *all his joys were lost*
35 Non word morë myght he speke;
    He stod as nakyd as a ston.
      Now bethink the, etc.

Thann cam an aungil with a swerd   *sword*
And drof Adàm into disert;   *drove; desert*
40 Ther was Adam sore aferd,   *afraid*
    For labour coude he werken non.   *he knew not how to do any work*
      Now bethink the, etc.

II, 84   Almyghty God, fadir of hevene

Almyghty God, fadir of hevene,   *father*
For Cristës love that dyde on rode,   *died on the cross*
I praye the, Lorde, thou here my stevene,   *thee; hear my voice*
And fulfill my will in gode.   *fulfill my wishes in good things*

5 Crist, thi fader for me praye,   *pray to thy father for me*
For hir love thou lighted inne,   *for the love of her; alighted in*
He yeve me myght, or that I dye,   *that he give me strength, before I die*
Me to amende of all my synne.   *myself*

The Holy Gost, thou graunte me grace,
10 With such werkes my lif to lede,   *lead*
That I may se God in his face
On Domësday withouten drede.   *on Doomsday without fear*

Marie, thi sone for me thou praye,   *pray to thy son for me*
He yeve me grace, or that I wende,   *that he may give; before I depart*
15 That I have after I dye   *that I may have*
The blisse of hevene withouten ende.

Fader and Sone and Holy Gost,
All one God and persones thre,
Almyghty God, of myghtës most,   *greatest in power*
20 Lord, thou have mercy on me.

And on alle that mercy nede, for charité.   *need mercy, for love's sake*
   Amen, par amore, Amen.   *for love*

II, 85   Upon my ryght syde y me leye

Upon my ryght syde y me leye,   *I lay myself down*
Blesed Lady, to the y pray;   *thee*
For the terës that ye lete   *that you shed*
Upone yowr swetë sonnës feete,
5 Sende me gracë for to slepe
And good dremës for to mete,   *to dream*
Slepyng, wakyng, til morowe daye bee.   *till tomorrow comes*
   Owre Lorde is the frwte, oure Lady is the tree – *fruit*
   Blessed be the blossome that sprange of the! *from thee*

In nomine patris et filii et spiritus sancti. Amen.   *In the name of the Father, Son,*
                                              and Holy Spirit. Amen

II, 86   O swete angell, to me soo deere

O swete angell, to me soo deere,
That nyght and day standëthe me neere
   Full loveyngly wyth myldë moode;   *gentle disposition*
Thankyng, loveyng, love and praysyng,
5 Offer for me to Jhesu, our kyng,
   For his gyfftës great and goode.

As thow gothe betwix hym and me,
And knowethe my lyffe in every degré,   *life; in every respect*
   Saying it in his presence;
10 Aske me grace to love hym truly,   *for me*
To serve my lorde with hertt duly,
   With my dayly diligence.

Keepe me from vice and all perells,   *perils*
Whiles thowe with me dayly travells   *while thou*
15   In this worlde of wyckednesse;
Sett me my peticions grauntede   *cause my petitions to be granted*
By thy praier dayly haunted,   *daily performed*
   Yff it please thy holynes.

II, 87   God be in my heed

God be in my heed,
And in myn understandynge;
God be in myn eyen,
And in my lokynge;
5   God be in my mouthe,
And in my spekynge;
God be in my herte,
And in my thynkynge;
God be at myn ende,
10 And my departynge.

II, 88   Illa iuventus that is so nyse

Alas, my hart will brek in thre;	*heart will break in three*
Terribilis mors conturbat me.	*dreadful death confounds me*
Illa iuventus that is so nyse	*that time of youth that is so foolish*
Me deduxit into vayn devise;	*led me into idle pleasure*
5 Infirmus sum, I may not rise –	*infirm I am*
Terribilis mors conturbat me.	
Alas, my hart etc.	
Dum iuvenis fui, lytill I dred,	*while I was young little did I fear*
Set semper in sinne I ete my bred;	*but ever*
10 Iam ductus sum into my bed –	*now I am led to*
Terribilis mors conturbat me.	
Alas, my hart etc.	
Corpus migrat and my sowle,	*my body and soul part*
Respicit demon in his rowle,	*the demon looks in his list*
15 Desiderat ipse to have his tolle –	*he wishes to have his toll*
Terribilis mors conturbat me.	
Alas, my hart etc.	
Christus se ipsum, whan he shuld dye,	*Christ himself, when he was to die*
Patri suo his manhode did crye:	*to his father*
20 'Respice me, Pater, that is so hye,	*look upon me, father; so high*
Terribilis mors conturbat me.'	
Alas, my hart etc.	
Queso iam the Trynyté:	*now I entreat*
'Duc me from this vanyté	*lead me*
25 In celum, ther is joy with the' –	*into heaven where there is*
Terribilis mors conturbat me.	
Alas, my hart etc.	

II, 89   Dred of deth, sorrow of syn ~ *John Audelay*

Lady helpe! Jhesu, mercé!	*mercy*
Timor mortis conturbat me.	*the fear of death confounds me*

Dred of deth, sorow of syn	*sorrow for sin*
Trobils my hert ful grevysly,	*troubles; grievously*
5 My soule hit nyth with my lust then –	*is vexed by my evil desires then*
Passio Christi conforta me.	*Passion of Christ strengthen me*
Lady helpe! Jhesu, mercé!	
Timor mortis conturbat me.	

Fore blyndnes is a hevy thyng	*heavy*
10 And to be def therwith only,	*especially*
To lese my lyght and my heryng –	*lose*
Passio Christi conforta me.	
Lady helpe! Jhesu, mercé!	
Timor mortis conturbat me.	

15 And to lese my tast and my smellyng	*lose; taste and sense of smell*
And to be seke in my body:	*sick*
Here have I lost al my lykyng –	*pleasure*
Passio Christi conforta me	
Lady helpe! Jhesu, mercé!	
20 *Timor mortis conturbat me.*	

Thus God He yeves and takes away	*gives*
And as He wil so mot hit be;	*so must it be*
His name be blessed both nyght and daye –	
Passio Christi conforta me.	
25 *Lady helpe! Jhesu, mercé!*	
Timor mortis conturbat me.	

Here is a cause of gret mornyng:	*great mourning*
Of myselfe nothyng I se	
Save filth, unclennes, vile stynkyng –	
30 Passio Christi conforta me.	
Lady helpe! Jhesu, mercé!	
Timor mortis conturbat me.	

Into this word no more I broght,	*this world no more I brought*
No more I gete with me trewly	*shall I take; truly*
35 Save good ded, word, wil and thoght –	*deeds*
Passio Christi conforta me.	
Lady helpe! Jhesu, mercé!	
Timor mortis conturbat me.	

The fivë wondes of Jhesu Crist   *five wounds*
40 My midsyne now mot thai be,   *medicine; must*
The Fyndës pouere downe to cast –   *the Fiend's power*
    Passio Christi conforta me.
        Lady helpe! Jhesu, mercé!
        Timor mortis conturbat me.

45 As I lay seke in my langure,   *sick in my infirmity*
With sorow of hert and teere of ye,   *eye*
This caral I made with gret doloure –   *carol; great sorrow*
    Passio Christi conforta me.
        Lady helpe! Jhesu, mercé!
50   *Timor mortis conturbat me.*

Oft with these prayere I me blest,   *this prayer*
'In manus tuas, Domine: *into your hands, O Lord*
Thou take my soule into thi rest' –   *resting place*
    Passio Christi conforta me.
55   *Lady helpe! Jhesu, mercé!*
        Timor mortis conturbat me.

Mary, moder, mercyful may,   *mother, merciful maiden*
Fore the joys thou hadest, lady,
To thi sun fore me thou pray –   *son*
60 Passio Christi conforta me.
        Lady helpe! Jhesu, mercé!
        Timor mortis conturbat me.

Lerne this lesson of blynd Awdlay:
When bale is hyest then bot may be;   *trouble is at its height; remedy*
65 Yif thou be nyd, nyght or day,   *if you are troubled*
        Say, 'Passio Christi conforta me.'
            Lady helpe! Jhesu, mercé!
            Timor mortis conturbat me.

II, 90   When Adam delf

When Adam delf	*delved*
And Evë span,	*spun*
Spir, if thou wil spede,	*ask, if you wish to succeed*
Whare was than	*where was then*
5 The pride of man	
That now merrës his mede?	*mars his reward*
Of erth and slame	*earth and mud*
Als was Adàm	*as*
Makëd to noyes and nede,	*made for afflictions and distress*
10 Ar we als he	*are we as he*
Makëd to be,	*made to be*
Whil we this lyf sal lede.	*while we this life must lead*
With I and E,	*with oh! and ah! (?)*
Born ar we,	
15 Als Salomon us hyght,	*as Solomon assured us*
To travel here	*to pass here*
Whils we ar fere,	*while we are alive (*lit. *healthy)*
Als fouls unto the flight.	*like birds in flight*
In worlde we ware	*in the world we were*
20 Kast for to kare,	*destined to sorrow*
To we be broght to wende	*till we come to depart*
Til wele or wa,	*to bliss or woe*
An of tha twa,	*one of these two*
To won with-outen ende.	*to dwell without end*
25 Forthi whils thou	*therefore while you*
May helpe the now,	*can help yourself now*
Amend the, and haf mynde,	*reform, and bear in mind (that)*
When thou sal ga,	*when you must go*
He bese thi fa	*he will be your foe*
30 That are was here thi frende.	*who formerly was your friend here*
With E and I,	
I rede forthi	*I advise therefore*
Thou thynk apon thies thre:	*(that) you think about these three (things)*
What we ar,	*what we are*
35 And what we ware,	*were*
And what we sal be.	*we shall be*
War thou als wyse,	*if you were as wise*
Praysëd in pryce,	*(as) acclaimed for excellence*
Als was Salomon,	*as was Solomon*
40 Fayrer fode	*a fairer creature*

Of bone and blode	*of bone and blood*
Then was Absalon,	*than*
Strengthy and strang	*sturdy and strong*
To wreke thi wrang	*to avenge your wrong*
45 As ever was Sampson,	
Thou ne myght a day,	*you could not for one (single) day*
Na mare then thai,	*any more than they*
Dede withstand allon.	*death; alone (i.e. by your own efforts)*
With I and E,	
50 Dede to the	*death to you*
Sal com, als I the kenne;	*shall come, as I tell you*
Thou ne wate	*you do not know*
In what state,	*in what manner*
How, ne whare, ne when.	*how, nor where, nor when*
55 Of erth aght	*of (this) earth anything*
That the was raght	*which was granted to you*
Thou sal not have, I hete,	*you will have nothing, I promise*
Bot seven fote	*but seven foot*
Therin to rote,	*therein to rot*
60 And thi wyndyng-schete.	*and your winding-sheet*
Forthi gyf	*therefore give*
Whils thou may lyf,	*while you are alive*
Or all gase that thou gete:	*before all that you acquire goes*
Thi gast fra God,	*(before) your spirit (goes) from God*
65 Thi godes olod,	*your goods (are) dispersed*
Thi flesch fowled undur fete.	*your flesh trampled under foot*
With I and E,	
Syker thow be	*be sure*
That thi secutowrs	*that your executors*
70 Of the ne wil rek,	*will not care about you*
Bot skelk and skek	*but mock (?) and plunder*
Ful boldly in thi bowrs.	*quite brazenly in your house*
Of welth and witt –	*of the wealth and wisdom*
This sal be hitt –	*– this will come to pass –*
75 In world that thou here wroght	*what you have achieved here in the world*
Rekken thou mon,	*you must render account*
And yelde reson	*and give justification*
Of thyng that thou here thoght.	*for the things which you thought here*
May no fallace	*deception*
80 Help in this case,	
Ne cownsel getes thou noght;	*nor will you get any advocate*
Gyft ne grace,	*bribe nor favour*
Nane thare gase,	*none operates (lit. goes) there*
Bot brok als thou hase boght.	*but (you will) get what you deserved*

85 With I and E,
   The boke biddes the,   *the book (i.e. Bible) bids you*
     Man, be ware of thi werkes;   *be cautious in your doings*
   Terme of the yere   *a day of reckoning*
   Hase thou nan here –   *have you none here*
90   Thi mede bese ther thi merkes.   *your reward there is your goal*

   What may this be
   That I here se?   *see*
     The fayrehede of thi face,   *the beauty of your face*
   Thi ble sa bryght,   *your complexion so bright*
95 Thi mayn, thi myght,   *your strength, your power*
     Thi mowth that miri mas?   *your mouth that makes merry*
   Al mon als was   *all must as a torch of straw*
   To powder passe,   *turn to dust / ashes*
   To dede when that thow gase,   *when you go to death*
100 A grysely geste   *a hideous guest*
   Bese than thi breste,   *shall your body (lit. breast) be then*
     In armës til enbrase.   *in arms to embrace*
   With I and E,
   Syker thou be   *be sure*
105   Thare es nane, I the hete,   *there is none, I promise you*
   Of al thi kyth   *of all your acquaintances*
   Wald slepe the with,   *would sleep with you*
     A nyght under schete.   *one night under (your) sheet*

II, 91   Who hath that conyng, by wysdam or prudènce

Who hath that conyng, by wysdam or prudènce,   *who has the skill; or intelligence*
To know whether his frende be feynt or stable?   *false or trustworthy*
Ther ys no creature, I trow, that hath that sciènce   *I believe, has the knowledge*
To know his ffrende – the world ys so mutàble,   *his friend; changeable*
5 And ffrenship ys double and varry dìsseyvàble;   *deceitful and very treacherous*
The mowthe seythe ane, the hert thinkëth another;   *the mouth says one thing*
Allas to say, hit ys full lèmentàble!   *most lamentable*
Unneth a man now may truste his owne brother.   *hardly can a man now trust*

II, 92   Allas diceyte that in truste ys nowe

Allas diceyte that in truste ys nowe,   *deceit*
Duble as Fortune, turnyng as a balle,   *false (lit. double); ball*
Brotylle at assay lyke the rotyn bowe: *brittle when tested; rotten bough*
Who trusteth to truste ys redy for to falle.   *(he) who trusts in trustworthiness*
5 Suche gyle ys in trust allmost overalle   *such guile (there) is; almost everywhere*
That yn poynte a man no frende fynde shalle.   *that in fact*
Wherfore beware of trust, after my devise;   *by my advice*
Trust to thiselfe and lernë to be wyse.

II, 93   The worlde so wide, the aire so remuàble ~ *Squire Halsham* (?)

The worlde so wide, the aire so remuàble,   *the air so changeable*
The sely man so litel of statùre,   *helpless man so small in stature*
The grove and grounde of clothinge so mutàble,   *and earth so variable in clothing*
The fire so hoote and subtil of natùre,   *hot and ethereal in quality*
5 The water never in oon – what creatùre   *never the same*
That made is of these fourë, thus flyttyng,   *fluctuating*
May stedfast be as here in his lyving?   *as regards his life here*

The more I goo the ferther I am behinde,   *I advance the further*
The ferther behinde the ner my wayës ende,   *the nearer my journey's end*
10 The more I seche the worsë kan I fynde,   *seek the less able am I to find*
The lighter leve the lother for to wende,   *easier to leave; more reluctant to go*
The bet y serve the more al out of mynde.   *the better I serve the more completely forgotten*
Is thys fortùne, not I, or infortùne?   *I know not*
Though I go lowse, tyed am I with a lune.   *free* (lit. *loose*); *with a leash*

II, 94   As y gan wandre in my walkinge

As y gan wandre in my walkinge   *as I wandered on my way*
    Bisidis an holt undir an hille,   *by a wood beneath a hill*
Y say an oolde man sitte wepinge,   *I saw*
    With sighynge sore he seide me tille: *with bitter sighs he said to me*
5 'Sumtime y hadde the world at wille,   *formerly I had the world at will*
    With ricchesse and with rialté,   *riches; kingly rank*
And now it is turned al to ille –   *to tribulation*
    The worlde is but a vanyté.   *is (nothing) but futility*

'My silf I likne unto the morewe,   *I liken myself to the morning* (i.e. *of a new*
10   Whanne y was child, and boren bare;   *born naked*   [*day*)
Mi modir for me suffrede sorewe   *suffered sorrow*
    With gruntynges gril and sighinge sare;   *hideous groaning; grievous sighing*
On me was neither wem ne hore,   *neither blemish nor defilement*
    But sithen in synne y havë be,   *but since then; have been*
15 Now y am oolde, y wepe therfore –
    This world is but a vanyté.

'At mydmore y lerned to go,   *early morning* (lit. *mid-morning*) *I learnt*
    And plaied as children doon in strete;   *do in the street*   [*to walk*
The kinde of childhode y dide also,   *the natural activities of childhood*
20   With my felawes to fighte and threte.   *fellows; fight and quarrel*
Al that y dide, it thoughte me swete,   *it seemed pleasant to me*
    For al this childhode taughtë me;
Now y am oolde, therfore y wepe –   *weep*
    This worlde is but a vanité.

25 'At undren to scole y was sett   *mid-morning; school; put*
    To lernë lore, as othir dooth;   *to learn knowledge, as others do*
  Whanne my maistir wolde me bet,   *beat*
    I wolde him curse, y was ful wrooth.   *I would curse him; very angry*
  To lernë good y was ful looth,   *learn; I was very reluctant*
30   I thoughte on joie and joilité;
  Now certis, for to seie the sooth –   *now indeed, to tell the truth*
    This world is but a vanyté.

  'At mydday y was dubbëd knyght,   *dubbed a knight*
    In route y lernëd for to ryde;   *in an armed band I learned to ride*
35 Was ther noon so hardi a wight   *there was no man so bold*
    That in bataile durste me abide.   *as dared face (lit. abide) me in battle*
  Where is bicome now al my pride,   *what has now become of*
    Mi booldnes, and my fair bewté?   *beauty*
  Now from deeth may y me not hide –   *death*
40   This world is but a vanyté.

  'At high noon y was crownëd king,   *noon (ecclesiastically None, 3 p.m.)*
    This world was oonli at my wille;   *was wholly*
  Evere to lyve was my liking,   *to live for ever*
    And alle my lustës to fulfille.   *all my desires*
45 Now age is cropen on me ful stille,   *has crept up on me very stealthily*
    And maketh me oold and blac of ble,   *and discoloured in complexion*
  And y go downeward with the hille –
    This world is but a vanité.

  'At mydovernoon y droupëd faste,   *at mid-afternoon I declined fast*
50   Mi lust and liking wente away;   *my passion and desire*
  From jolité myn hert is paste   *my heart has passed on*
    From rialté and riche aray.   *from pomp and lavish trappings*
  Mannes liif here is but a day   *man's life*
    Ayens the liif that evere schal be;   *compared with*
55 And oo thing y dare weel say –   *one thing; well*
    This world is but a vanité.

  'At evensong tyme y wax ful coold,   *I became very cold*
    And bigan to go bi stave;   *to walk with a stick*
  Now is deeth on me ful boold,   *death; most pressing*
60   And for his rent he wole me crave.   *he wishes to demand from me his due*
  Whanne y am deed and leid in grave,   *dead and laid   [payment*
    Ther is no thing thanne that savëth me *that will save me*
  But good or yvel that y do have –   *but the good or evil that I have done*
    This world is but a vanité.

65 'Thus is the day come to nyght,
    That me lothëth of my lyvynge,   *that my life is hateful to me*
  And doolful deeth to me is dight,   *and doleful death is ready for me*
    And in coold clay now schal y clinge.' *shall I waste away*
  Thus an oold man y herde mornynge   *I heard mourning*
70   Biside an holte undir a tree.   *by a wood*
  God graunte us His blis everlastinge!
  This world is but a vanité.

II, 95   In a noon-tiid of a somers day

In a noon-tiid of a somers day   *at noon on a summer's day*
  The sunne schoon ful myrie that tide, *shone right merrily that time*
I took myn hauk al for to play,   *hawk*
  Mi spaynel rennyng bi my side.   *my spaniel running by*
5 A feisaunt hen soone gan y se,   *a hen-pheasant I soon saw*
  Myn hound put up ful fair to flight,   *(which) my dog*
I sente my faukun, y leet him flee: *falcon, I let him fly*
  It was to me a deintyuose sight.   *a pretty sight*

My faukun fligh faste to his pray,   *flew fast to its prey*
10   I ran tho with a ful glad chere,   *ran then with most joyful spirit*
I spurnëd ful soone on my way,   *I stumbled immediately*
  Mi leg was hent al with a brere.   *was caught completely on a briar*
This brere forsothë dide me griif,   *caused me pain*
  And soone it made me turne ayé,   *turn again*
15 For he bare written in every leef   *it bore written on every leaf*
  This word in Latyn, *revertere.*   *turn again / turn back*

I kneled and pulled the brere me fro,   *detached myself from the briar*
  And redde this word ful hendëli;   *read; most attentively*
Myn herte fil doun unto my too   *heart fell; toe*
20   That was woont sitten ful likingly.   *was wont to be* (lit. *sit*) *most cheerful*
I leete myn hauke and feysaunt fare,   *I let my hawk and pheasant go*
  Mi spaynel fil doun to my knee;   *lay down at my knee*
Thanne took y me with sighynge sare *I took to myself with grievous sighs*
  This new lessoun, *revertere.*

25 *Revertere* is as myche to say   *is as much as to say*
  In Englisch tunge as 'turne ayen'.   *tongue; 'turn again'*
Turne ayen, man, y thee pray,
  And thinke hertli what thou hast ben; *think earnestly*
Of thi livynge bethinke thee riife   *often*
30   In open and in privité;   *in public and in private*
That thou may come to endles liif,   *to everlasting life*
  Take to thi mynde *revertere.*

This word made me to studie sore,	*ponder deeply*
And binam me al my list;	*took from me all my enjoyment*
35 How y hadde ledde my liif so yore,	*lead my life for so long*
I putt it freischli to my brist.	*breast*
Thanne foond y me ful fer y-flet	*found I myself so far fled*
Al from God in majesté;	
Forsothe there schal no thing me leett	*truly; prevent me*
40 That y ne wole synge *revertere*.	*that I will not sing*
To noon-hete of the someres day,	*to noon-heat; summer's day*
Whanne the sunne moost highest is,	
Yowth may be likened, in good fay,	*youth may be compared; faith*
For Gregorie witnesseth weel this;	*witnesses well to this*
45 For in yonge age men wide doon walke	*men go astray*
To dyvers synnes in fele degré;	*sundry sins in many a way*
Though a yong man make a balke,	*commit a blunder*
Yit take to thi mynde *revertere*.	
For likinge blindëth many oon	*for lust blinds many a man (lit. one)*
50 That he seeth not himself y-wis,	*indeed*
And maketh his herte as hard as stoon:	*stone*
Thanne thenketh he not on heven blis.	*the bliss of heaven*
For Danyel preveth it weel rightfulli,	*demonstrates it absolutely correctly*
As Susannes storie tellëth me:	*the story of Susanna*
55 Two preestes were deemëd worthili;	*priests were rightly condemned*
For likinge thei knew not *revertere*.	*on account of lust*
Youthe bereth the hauke upon his hond	
Whanne joilité foryetëth age:	*revelry forgets age (i.e. maturity)*
This hauke is mannes herte, y undirstonde,	*hawk is man's heart*
60 For it is yong and of high romage.	*young and high-spirited*
He puttëth his hauke fro his fist,	*despatches (lit. puts); from*
He that schulde to God be free;	*who ought to be available to God*
He melteth and wexeth a weel poore gist	*melts (i.e. with contrition) and becomes*
Whanne he cometh to *revertere*.	[*a very poor guest (i.e. of God)*
65 For ful of corage is yougethe in herte,	*full of spirit is youth*
And waitynge evere on his pray,	*ever lying in wait for his prey*
He ne spareth ryver ne thornës smerte	*avoids neither river nor painful thorns*
To gete his myrthe there he beest may.	*to get his pleasure; best*
He that ensercheth the derknes of nyght	*seeks out*
70 And the myst of the morowtide may se;	*the early morning; see (sic. the truth)*
He schal know bi Cristës myght	*by*
If youthe kunne synge *revertere*.	*if youth is able to sing*

This hauk of herte in youthe y-wys, *this hawk, man's heart (lit. of heart)*
 Pursuëth evere this feisaunt hen; *hen-pheasant*
75 This feisaunt hen is likingnes, *is pleasure*
 And evere foleweth hir these yonge men. *young men always follow her*
This is likinge in every synne, *delight in every sin*
 Venial and deedli, whether it be; *venial and deadly, whichever it may be*
With greet likinge he wole bigynne, *he will engage (in sin)*
80 But sorewe bringe forth *revertere*. *unless contrition*

Liking is modir of synnës alle, *desire is mother*
 And norischeth every wickid dede; *nourishes; deed*
In feele myscheves sche maketh to falle, *into many a mischief she causes (a man)*
 Of sorowe sche dooth the dauncë leede. *she leads the dance*
85 This herte of youthe is hie of port, *arrogant (lit. high) in bearing*
 And wildenes maketh him ofte to fle, *fly (i.e. like a hawk)*
And ofte to falle in wickid sort; *into wicked company*
 Thanne is it the beste, *revertere*. *then the best thing is to 'turn again'*

II, 96 A man that shuld of trewthë telle

God be with trewthë wher he be; *wherever he may be*
I wolde he were in this cuntré. *land /country*

A man that shuld of trewthë telle, *who would speak of truth*
With grete lordes he may not dwelle; *great*
5 In trewe story, as klerkës telle, *in true accounts, as the learned tell*
 Trewthe is put in low degré. *placed in low esteem*
  God be with trewthë etc.

In laydyes chaumberes cometh he not;
Ther dar trewthe setten non fot; *dare truth set no foot*
10 Thow he woldë he may not *though he wished to he cannot*
 Comen among the heye mené. *high society*
  God be with trewthë etc.

With men of lawe he hath non spas; *he finds no room (lit. space)*
They loven trewthë in non plas; *place*
15 Me thinketh they han a rewly grace *have pitiful manners*
 That trewthe is put at swych degré. *rated in such a way*
  God be with trewthë etc.

In Holy Cherche he may not sytte; *sit*
Fro man to man they shuln hym flytte; *from; they pass him on*
20 It reweth me sorë in myn wytte; *it grieves me sorely in my mind*
 Of trewthe I havë gret peté. *for truth I have great pity*
  God be with trewthë etc.

Relygius, that shulde be good –	*men of religion, who should*
If trewthe cum ther, I holde hym wood –	*came; I would think him mad*
25 They shulden hym ryndë cote and hood	*they would tear from him coat*
And make hym barë for to flé.	*and make him flee naked*
God be with trewthë etc.	

A man that shulde of trewthe aspye,	*who would search out truth*
He must seken esylye	*seek gently*
30 In the bosum of Marye,	
For there he is forsothe, pardé.	*truly, indeed*
God be with trewthë etc.	

II, 97   If y halde the lowe asyse

Lord, how scholde I roulë me,	*should I conduct myself*
Of al men i-preysed to be?	*praised*

If y halde the lowe asyse	*maintain a lowly demeanour*
And take aray of lytel pryse,	*adopt a life-style of little pretension*
5 Then men wil say, 'He ys nowght wyse;	*not wise*
He ys a fon; let hym be.'	*fool*
Lord, etc.	

And yyf I take the mene astate	*the middle position*
And wyth non man maky debat,	*take issue*
10 Than men wil sey, erly and late,	*then; early and late*
That I am worth no maner fe.	*of no worth (lit. worth no kind of fee)*
Lord, etc.	

And yf y takë gryte aray,	*adopt a grand life-style*
Hors and hondes and clothës gay,	*horse and hounds*
15 Than men wel say every day	*then; will say*
That I passë my degré.	*I have got above my station*
Lord, etc.	

Then take thow hede of the oxe;	*take heed of the ox*
Go nowght to lowë for the foxe,	*for fear of the fox*
20 Nether to hey tyl thow be wox,	*nor (climb) till you have risen too high*
For the kyte that wolde the sle.	*for fear of the kite that would slay you*
Lord, etc.	

Therfor loke that thow be sley:	*see that you are discreet*
For no thyng hew thow tow hey,	*on no account hew too high*
25 Last they falle don into thy ey,	*lest they fall down into your eye*
The sponës that above the be.	*the chips that are above you*
Lord, etc.	

II, 98   Blowyng was mad for gret game

I hold hym wyse and wel i-taught
Can bar an horn and blow it naught.   who knows how to bear (i.e. carry)

Blowyng was mad for gret game;   great entertainment
Of this blowyng cometh mekell grame;   much harm
5 Therfor I hold it for no schame
    To ber a horn and blow it nought.
      I hold hym wyse etc.

Hornes ar mad both loud and shyll;   shrill
Whan tym ys, blow thou thi fyll,   when (the) time is (appropriate)
10 And when ned is, hold the styll,   when it is necessary, keep quiet
    And ber a horne and blow it nought.
      I hold hym wyse etc.

Whatsoever be in thi thought,
Her and se, and sey ryght nought;   hear and see, and say nothing at all
15 Than schall men sey thou art wel tought   taught
    To bere a horne and blow it nought.
      I hold hym wyse etc.

Of al the ryches under the son   sun
Than was ther never betur wonne   a better habit
20 Than is a tawght man for to konne   than for a man to be taught to know how
    To ber a horne and blow it nought.
      I hold hym wyse etc.

Whatsoever be in thi brest,   whatsoever may be; breast
Stop thi mouth with thi fyst,
25 And lok thou thynk well of 'Had I wyst',   known
    And ber a horne and blow it nought.
      I hold hym wyse etc.

And when thou syttëst at the ale,
And cryëst lyk an nyghttyngale,   and sing out (lit. cry) like
30 Bewar to whom thou tellest thi tale,
    But ber a horne and blow it nought.
      I hold hym wyse etc.

II, 99   In what order, or what degré ~ *John Audelay*

Hit is the best, erely and late,	*at all times (lit. early and late)*
Uche mon kepe his ounë state.	*each man should keep to his own position*

In what order, or what degré	*in whatever rank, or whatever station*
Holy Cherche hath bownd the to,	*has bound thee to*
5 Kepe hit wele, I cownsel the;	*keep to it well, I counsel thee*
Dissire thou never to go therfro.	*never desire; therefrom*
I say allgate:	*I say at all events*
Hit is the best, etc.	

A hye worship hit is to the	*high honour; thee*
10 To kepe thi state and thi good name,	*to hold to your position*
Leud or lered, where-ere hit be,	*unlettered or educated, wherever*
Ellis God and mon thay wol the blame.	*and man they will thee blame*
I say algate:	
Hit is the best, etc.	

15 Fore four obisions now schul ye here	*four abuses; you shall hear*
That God hates ilë in his syght:	*hates bitterly*
A hardë prest, a proud frere,	*priest; friar*
An old man lechoure, a couard knyght.	*lecherous*
I say algate:	
20 *Hit is the best, etc.*	

A prest schuld scheu uche mon mekenes	*show each man meekness*
And leve in love and charité;	*live; charity*
Throgh his grace and his goodnes	*through*
Set al other in unité.	*others in unity*
25 I say algate:	
Hit is the best, etc.	

A frere schuld love all holynes,	*friar*
Prayers, penans and poverté;	*penance and poverty*
Relegious men, Crist hem ches	*chose them*
30 To foresake pride and vayn glory.	
I say algate:	
Hit is the best, etc.	

An old mon schuld kepe him chast	*keep himself chaste*
And leve the synne of lechoré;	*leave; lechery*
35 Al weded men schuld be stedfast	*wedded*
And foresake the syn of avowtré.	*adultery*
I sai algate:	
Hit is the best, etc.	

A knyght schuld feght ayayns falsnes,   *fight against falsehood*
40   And schew his monhod and his myght,   *show his manhood*
And mayntene trouth and ryghtwysnes,   *maintain truth and righteousness*
And Holy Cherche and wedowes ryght.   *widows' rights*
        I say algate:
            Hit is the best, etc.

45 Here be al the foure astates   *four estates*
In Holy Cherche God hath ordent;   *which God has ordained*
He bedes you kepe hem wel algates;   *bids; well in any circumstances*
Whosever hem shomes, he wyl be schent.   *whoever dishonours them, he will be destroyed*
        I say algate:
50   *Hit is the best, etc.*

II, 100   Maist thou now glade, with all thi fresshe aray

Cest le myrroure pur lez jofenes   *this is the mirror for the*
dames a regardir aud maytyne   *young ladies to look into in the morning*
pur lour testes bealment adressere.   *in order to beautify themselves (lit. their heads / [faces)*

Maist thou now glade, with all thi fresshe aray,   *you can be happy now; fresh appearance*
One me to loke that wyll dystene thi face.   *look; stain your face*
Rew one thyself and all thi synne uprace;   *take pity on yourself; uproot*
Sone shalte thu flytte and seche another place;   *soon; depart and seek*
5 Shorte is thy sesoun here, thogh thou go gay.   *though you live (lit. go) joyously*

O maset wriche, I marke the with my mace.   *crazy wretch; mace / club*
Lyfte up thy ieye, beholde now and assay.   *eye; and learn*
Uche loke one me aught put the in affray;   *each look; ought to alarm thee*
I wyll not spare the, for thou arte my pray.   *thee; prey*
10 Take hede, and turne fro synne while thu hast space.   *time (lit. space)*

O th'oughte wel the hede this, thaught ye say nay. *oughtest to heed this well, though*
My tyme muste nedis comme as I manace;   *must of necessity come as I warn*
No lengthe one lyfe may lepe oute of my lace.   *in life; leap; my snare*
I smyte, I sle, I woll graunte no mane grace.   *slay; no man*
15 Aryse! awake! amend here while thou may.

II, 101   I weende to dede, a kynge i-wisse

'I weende to dede, a kynge i-wisse;   *I go to death; truly*
What helpes honòr or werldës blysse?   *what good is honour or worldly joy*
Dede is to mane the kyndë wai –   *death is to man the natural way*
I wendë to be clade in clay.'   *clad (i.e. clothed)*

5 'I wende to dede, knight stithe in stoure,   *a knight valiant in battle*
Thurghe fyght in felde I wane the flour;   *through fighting; I won the flower*
Na fightes me taght the dede to quell –   *no battles taught me to slay death*
I weend to dede, soth I yow tell.'   *truth*

'I wende to dede, clerk ful of skill,   *a scholar full of wisdom*
10 That couth with worde men mare and dill.   *knew; to confound and stupefy (?)*
Sone has me made the dede ane ende –   *death has soon put an end to me*
Beese ware with me, to dede I wende.'   *take heed from me*

II, 102   Farewell, this world! I take my leve for evere

Farewell, this world! I take my leve for evere;   *leave*
I am arested to apere at Goddës face.   *before God (lit. God's face)*
O myghtyfull God, thu knowest that I had levere   *I had rather*
Than all this world, to have oone hourë space   *the space of one hour*
5 To make asythe for all my grete trespace.   *reparation*
My hert, alas, is brokene for that sorowe:
Sum are today that shall not be tomorowe.   *some are (alive) this day*

This lyfe, I see, is but a cheyry feyre;   *cherry fair*
All thynges passene, and so most I algate.   *so must I in any case*
10 Today I sat full ryall in a cheyere,   *right royally; chair / throne*
Tyll sotell Deth knokëd at my gate,   *subtle*
And onavysed he seyd to me, 'Chek-mate!'   *and without warning*
Lo, how sodeyn he makëth a devors!   *suddenly; a separation*
And wormes to fede he hath here leyd my cors.   *feed; laid my body*

15 Speke softe, ye folk, for I am leyd aslepe!   *softly; laid asleep*
I have my dreme – in trust is mochë treson –   *dream; much deception*
Fram Dethës hold feyne wold I make a lepe,   *fain / gladly would I; leap*
But my wysdom is turned to feble resoun.   *has turned into feeble speculation*
I see this worldes joye lasteth but a season –
20 Wold God, I had remembyrd me beforne!   *I had taken heed before*
I sey no more, but be ware of ane horne!   *beware of a horn*

This fekyll world, so fals and so unstable,	*fickle*
Promoteth his lovers for a lytell while,	*advances*
But at the last he yevëth hem a bable	*he gives them a bauble*
25 Whene his peyntëd trowth is torned to gile.	*his feigned good faith; deceit*
Experyence cawseth me the trowth to compile,	*to put the truth together*
Thynkyng this – to late, alas, that I began!	
For foly and hope disseyvëth many a man.	*deceive*
Farewell, my frendes! the tide abideth no man:	*time waits for*
30 I moste departe hens, and so shall ye;	
But in this passage, the beste song that I can	*this transition; that I know*
Is *Requiem Eternam* – I pray God grant it me!	*rest eternal; God may grant*
Whan I have ended all myn adversité,	
Graunte me in paradise to have a mancyon,	*may he grant; mansion*
35 That shede his blode for my redempcion.	*(he) who; blood*
Beati mortui qui in Domino moriuntur.	*Blessed are the dead who die*
Humiliatus sum vermis.	*in the Lord. / I am brought low as the worms.*

II, 103   This warldly joy is onely fantasy

This warldly joy is onely fantasy,	*worldly; mere delusion*
Of quhich none erdly wicht can be content;	*with which no earthly being*
Quho most has wit, leste suld in it affy,	*who; understanding, least should in it*
Quho taistis it most, most sall him repent.	*who tastes; shall repent* [*trust*
5 Quhat valis all this richess and this rent,	*what value has; wealth; income*
Sin no man wate quho sall his tresour have?	*since no man knows who shall*
Presume nocht gevin that God has done bot lent –	*not given what God has only lent*
Within schort tyme the quhiche He thinkis to crave.	*which he is minded to ask for*

II, 104   All ye that passe be thys holy place

All ye that passe be thys holy place,	*pass by*
Both spirituall and temporall of every degré,	*spiritual and temporal; status*
Remembyr yourselfe well duryng tyme and space:	
I was as ye are nowe, and as I ye shal be.	
5 Wherfor I beseche you of your benygnité,	
For the love of Jhesu and hys mothyr Maré,	
For my sowle to say a Pater Noster and an Avé.	

II, 105 Westron wynde when wyll thow blow?

Westron wynde when wyll thow blow?
The smalle rayne downe can rayne.   *does rain*
Cryst, yf my love wer in my armes   *if only*
And I yn my bed agayne!

II, 106 The man that I loved altherbest

Woldë God that hyt were so   *would God*
As I cowde wysshe bytuyxt us too!   *between us two*

The man that I loved altherbest   *best of all*
In al thys contry, est other west,   *east or west*
5 To me he ys a strangë gest;   *distant stranger*
  What wonder es't thow I be woo?   *is it if I am woeful*
    Woldë God etc.

When me were levest that he schold duelle,   *when I most wished; stay*
He wold noght sey onys farewelle;   *he would not once say farewell*
10 He wold noght sey onës farewell
   When tyme was come that he most go.   *he had to go*
     Woldë God etc.

In places ofte when I hym mete,
  (I dar noght speke, but forth I go);   *I dare not speak, but on I go*
15 With herte and eyës I hym grete;   *greeted him*
   So trywe of love I know no mo.   *true; know no-one else*
     Woldë God etc.

As he ys myn hertë love,   *my heart's love*
  My dyrward dyre, i-blessed he be;   *precious darling, blest may he be*
20 I swere by God that ys above,   *swear*
   Non hath my love but only he.   *none has my love but he alone*
     Woldë God etc.

I am i-comforted in every syde;   *comforted on every side*
  The colures wexe both fres and newe;   *colours grow both fresh*
25 When he ys come and wyl abyde –   *he has come*
   I wott ful wel that he ys trywe.   *I know*
     Woldë God etc.

I love hym trywely and no mo;   *truly and no other*
  Woldë God that he hyt knywe!   *would God that he knew it*
30 And ever I hope hyt schal be so;   *I trust*
   Then schal I chaungë for no new.   *no new (love)*
     Woldë God etc.

II, 107   Y lovede a child of this cuntré

Were it undo that is y-do,	*were it undone that has been done*
I wold be war.	*would be cautious*
Y lovede a child of this cuntré,	*loved a young man of this district*
And so y wende he had do me;	*so I thought that he did me*
5 Now myself the sothe y see,	*the truth*
That he is far.	*distant*
Were it undo etc.	
He seyde to me he wolde be trewe	*true*
And chaunge me for none othur newe;	*no other new love*
10 Now y sykke and am pale of hewe,	*I sigh; pale of hue*
For he is far.	
Were it undo etc.	
He seide his sawes he wolde fulfille,	*his promises*
Therfore y lat him have al his wille;	
15 Now y sykke and mournë stille,	*mourn secretly*
For he is far.	
Were it undo etc.	

II, 108   Summe men sayen that y am blac

Summe men sayen that y am blac;	*I am dark*
Yt ys a colour for my prow.	*to my advantage*
Ther y love ther ys no lac,	*where I love there is no lack / fault*
Y may not be so whyte as thou.	*(though) I may not be as fair as thou*
5 Blac ys a colur that ys god –	*good*
So say y and many mo;	*and many more*
Blac ys my hat, blac ys my hod,	*hood*
Blac ys al that longeth therto.	*everything that belongs thereto*
Blac wol do as god a nede	*will do as well when required*
10 As the whyte at bord and bedde;	*at table and in bed*
And therto also treu in dede –	*also just as true*
Therto y ley my lyf to wedde.	*on that I stake (lit. lay as a pledge) my life*
Wynd and watur may steyne the whyte,	*stain*
Y-wys the blac yt may not so;	*indeed*
15 Ther yse the blac ys al my delyte,	*where dark is*
Y am y-holde be schyle therto.	*I am with reason devoted to it*
Peper wythoute yt ys wel blac,	*pepper outside*
Y-wys wythinne yt ys not so;	*certainly*
Lat go the colur and tak the smac,	*ignore the colour and take the taste*
20 Thys y sey by me and mo.	*this I say for myself and others*

God save ale hem that buth broune,   *all them who are dark*
   For they buth trew as any stel;   *they are true as any steel*
God kepe hem bothe in feld and toune,   *everywhere (lit. in field and town)*
   And thanne schal y be kept ful wel.

II, 109   Al this day ic han sought

Rybbe ne rele ne spynne yc may   *I cannot scrape flax, nor reel thread, nor spin*
For joy that it ys holyday.

Al this day ic han sought;   *I have looked*
   Spyndul ne werve ne vond y nought;   *spindle nor whorl found I not*
5   To mychë blisse ic am brought   *great joy (lit. much bliss)*
     Ayen this hyghë holyday.   *at the approach of (lit. against) this high*
     Rybbe ne rele etc.

Al unswope ys owrë vlet,   *unswept is our floor*
   And owrë fyre ys unbet;   *our fire is not made up*
10 Oure ruschen ben unrepë yet   *our rushes are still uncut*
     Ayen this hyë halyday.
     Rybbe ne rele etc.

Yc mostë feschen worten in;   *I must fetch herbs in*
   Predele my kerchef undur my chyn;   *fasten (?)*
15 Levë Jakke, lend me a pyn   *dear Jack*
     To predele me this holiday.
     Rybbe ne rele etc.

Now yt drawëth to the none,   *draws towards noon*
   And al my cherrës ben undone;   *chores are (still) not done*
20 Y moste a lyte solas mye schone   *I must ease my shoes a little*
     To make hem dowze this holiday.   *to make them comfortable*
     Rybbe ne rele etc.

Y mostë mylken in this payl;
   Ought me bred al this schayl;   *I have to spread out all this bowl (of dough)*
25 Yut is the dow undur my nayl   *still there is dough*
     As ic knad this holyday.   *as I kneaded*
     Rybbe ne rele etc.

Jakke wol brynge me in my wey,   *will accompany me*
   Wyth me desyrë for te pleye;   *(will) wish to have fun with me*
30 Of my dame stant me non eye   *I stand in no awe of my mistress*
     An never a god haliday.   *on any good holiday*
     Rybbe ne rele etc.

Jacke wol pay for my scot	*my share*
A Sonday atte the alë-scot;	*on Sunday at the scotale*
35 Jacke wol sowsë wel my throt	*drench (lit. souse) my throat well*
Every god haliday.	
Rybbe ne rele etc.	
Sone he wolle take me be the hond,	*soon he will; hand*
And he wolle legge me on the lond,	*will lay me on the ground*
40 That al my buttockes ben of sond,	*are covered with sand*
Opon this hyë holyday.	*high*
Rybbe ne rele etc.	
In he pult, and out he drow,	*in he thrust, and out he drew*
And ever yc lay on hym y-low:	*I lay beneath him*
45 'By Godës deth, thou dest me wow	*you do me wrong*
Upon this heyë holyday!'	
Rybbe ne rele etc.	
Sone my wombe began te swelle	*to swell*
Also gret as a belle;	*as large (lit. great)*
50 Durst y nat my damë telle	*dared I not*
What me betydde this holyday.	*what befell me*
Rybbe ne rele etc.	

II, 110   Ladd y the daunce a Myssomur Day

Alas, ales, the whyle!	*time*
Thought y on no gyle,	*no impropriety (lit. guile)*
So have y god chaunce.	*as I may have good luck*
Alas, ales, the whyle	
5 *That ever y cowde daunce!*	*could dance*
Ladd y the daunce	*led*
a Myssomur Day;	*on Midsummer*
Y made smale trippes,	*I took dainty steps*
soth for to say.	*truth to tell*
Jak, oure haly-watur clerk,	*Jack our holy-water priest*
com be the way,	*came by*
And he lokede me upon;	
he thought that yc was gay –	*that I was attractive*
10 Thought yc on no gyle.	
Alas, ales, etc.	
Jak, oure haly-watur clerk,	
the yonge strippelyng,	
For the chesoun of me	*because of me*
he come to the ryng,	*he came to the ring-dance*
And he trippede on my to	*he stepped lightly on my toe*
and made a twynkelyng;	*and gave a wink*

15 Ever he cam ner;   *ever nearer he came*
          he sparet for no thynge –   *he held back for nothing*
     Thought y on no gyle.
          Alas, ales, etc.

     Jak, ic wot, preyede   *Jack, I know, gazed*
          in my fayre face;   *into my fair face*
     He thought me ful werly,   *very attractive*
          so have y god grace;   *as I may have good grace*
20 As we turnden owre daunce
          in a narw place,   *into a narrow*
     Jak bed me the mouth;   *offered me his mouth*
          a cussynge ther was –   *kissing*
     Thought y on no gyle.
          Alas, ales, etc.

     Jak tho began   *then began*
          to rowne in myn ere: *to whisper in my ear*
25 'Loke that thou be privey,   *see that you are circumspect*
          and graunte that thou the bere;   *and promise to behave discreetly*
     A peyre whyt gloves   *a pair of white gloves*
          ic ha to thyn were.'   *I have for you to wear*
     'Gramercy, Jacke!'   *thanks very much, Jack*
          that was myn answere –
     Thoughte yc on no gyle.
          Alas, ales, etc.

30 Sone aftur evensong   *soon*
          Jak me mette: *Jack met me*
     'Com hom aftur thy gloves   *come home for your gloves*
          that yc the byhette.'   *which I promised you*
     Whan ic to his chambre com,   *when I; came*
          doun he me sette;   *down he sat me*
     From hym myghtte y nat go   *not*
          whan we were mette –
     Thought y on no gyle.
35   *Alas, ales, etc.*

     Schetes and chalones,   *sheets and blankets*
          ic wot, were y-spredde;   *I know*
     Forsothe tho Jak and yc   *indeed then*
          wenten to bedde;
     He prikede and he pransede;
          nolde he never lynne;   *he would not leave off*
     Yt was the muryust nyght   *merriest*
          that ever y cam ynne –
40   Thought y on no gyle.
          Alas, ales, etc.

Whan Jak had don,   *done*
    tho he rong the bell;   *then he rang*
Al nyght ther
    he made me to dwelle;
Of y-trewe we hadden y-served   *assuredly*
    the reaggeth devel of helle;   *shaggy devil*
45 Of othur smale burdes   *small trifles (?)*
    kep y nought to telle –   *care I not to tell*
Thought y on no gyle.
    Alas, ales, etc.

The other day at prime   *the next day at Prime (i.e. at sunrise)*
    Y com hom, as ic wene;   *I came home, as I suppose*
Met y my dame,   *I met my mistress*
    coppud and kene: *ill-tempered and fierce*
50 'Sey, thou stronge strumpet,   *say, you bold strumpet*
    whare hastu bene?   *where have you been*
Thy trippyng and thy dauncyng,
    wel it wol be sene' –   *well it will be seen (i.e. for the wickedness it is)*
Thought y on no gyle.
    Alas, ales, etc.

Ever bi on and by on   *over and over again*
    my damme reched me clot;   *gave me a clout*
55 Ever y ber it privey   *still I kept it secret*
    whyle that y mought,   *while I could*
Tyl my gurdul aros,   *until my girdle / waistband rose*
    my wombe wax out;   *my belly grew out*
Evel y-spunne yern,   *ill-spun yarn*
    ever it wole out –   *will always ravel*
Thought y on no gyle.
    Alas, ales, etc.

II, 111   The last tyme I the well-ey woke

I have forsworne hit whil I life   *live*
    To wake the well-ey.   *to spend the night at the well*

The last tyme I the well-ey woke,   *spent the night at the well*
Ser John caght me with a croke;   *crook*
5 He made me to swere be bel and boke   *swear by bell and book*
    I shuld not tell-ey.
    I have forsworne etc.

Yet he did me a wel wors turne:
He leyde my hed agayn the burne,   *well*
10 He gafe my maydenhed a spurne   *gave my maidenhead a thrust*
    And rofe my bell-ey.   *and tore my pretty (thing)*
    I have forsworne etc.

Sir John came to oure hows to play   *house*
Fro evensong tyme til light of the day;   *from evensong time (i.e. evening)*
15 We made as mery as flowres in May –
I was begyled-ay.   *seduced* (lit. *beguiled*)
    I have forsworne etc.

Sir John he came to our hows,
He made hit wondur copious,   *he was wonderfully plentiful (with gifts)*
20 He seyd that I was gracious   *fortunate*
    To beyre a childe-ey.   *to bear*
    I have forsworne etc.

I go with childe, wel I wot;   *well I know*
I schrew the fadur that hit gate   *I curse the father who begot it*
25 Withouten he fynde hit mylke and pap   *unless he find it milk and food*
    A long while-ey.   *for a long while*
    I have forsworne etc.

II, 112 O Lord, so swett Ser John dothe kys

Hey, noyney!
I wyll love our Ser John
And I love eny.   *if I love any*

O Lord, so swett Ser John dothe kys   *so sweetly*
5 At every tyme when he wolde pley;   *would play*
Off hymselfe so plesant he ys,
    I have no powre to say hym nay.   *power*
    Hey, noyney! etc.

Ser John loves me and I love hym;
10 The more I love hym the more I maye;
He says, 'Swett hart, cum kys me trym';   *sweet heart, come kiss me nicely*
    I have no powre to say hym nay.
    Hey, noyney! etc.

Ser John to me is proferyng   *offering*
15 For hys plesure ryght well to pay,
And in my box he puttes hys offryng;
    I have no powre to say hym nay.
    Hey, noyney! etc.

Ser John ys taken in my mouse-trappe;
20 Fayne wold I have hem bothe nyght and day;   *have him*
He gropeth so nyslye about my lape,   *gropes so lasciviously about my lap*
    I have no powre to say hym nay.
    Hey, noyney! etc.

Ser John geveth me relyus rynges   *glittering rings*
25 With praty plesure for to assay,   *with sweet pleasure to try out*
   Furres off the fynest with othyr thynges –
     I have no powre to say hym nay.
       Hey, noyney! etc.

II, 113   At the northe ende of Selver Whyte

   At the northe ende of Selver Whyte   *Silver White*
     My lef me bat –   *my beloved begged me*
   At the northe ende of Selver Whyte
     My lef me bat I scholde abyde.   *begged me that I should tarry*
5 I leyde my ware a bogeler brode,   *I laid my target a buckler wide*
     And ever he smote –   *struck*
   I leyde my ware a bogeler brode,
     And ever he smote by syde.   *struck to the side (i.e. missed)*
   Shalle ther never man justy therat,   *joust at it*
10   But yyf he can –   *unless he can*
   Shalle ther never man justy therat
     But yf he can hyt smyte.   *hit it*

   At the suthe ende of Selver Whyte   *south*
     My lef me bat –
15 At the suthe ende of Selver Whyte
     My lef me bat I scholde abyde.
   Leyde I my ware a peckel wyde,   *a peck measure wide*
     And ever he smote –
   Leyde I my ware a peckel wyde,
20   And ever he smote by syde.
   Shalle ther never man justy therat,
     But yyf he can –
   Shalle ther never man justy therat,
     But yf he can hyt smyte.

25 At the weste ende of Selver Whyte
     My lef me bade –
   At the weste ende of Selver Whyte
     My lef me bade I scholde abyde.
   Layde I my ware a bosshelle brode,   *a bushel measure wide*
30   And ever he smote –
   Leyde I my ware a bosshelle brode,
     And ever he smote by syde.
   Shalle ther never man justy therat,
     But yyf he can –
35 Shalle ther never man justy therat,
     But yf he can hyt smyte.

II, 114   May no man slepe in youre halle

May no man slepe in youre halle   *sleep*
For dogges, madame, for dogges, madame,
But yyf he have a tent of fifteen ynche   *unless he have a probe of 15 inches*
   With twey clogges,   *with two blocks (i.e. testicles)*
5 To dryve awey the dogges, madame.
    I-blessed be such clogges
     That yyvëth such bogges   *give such thrusts (?)*
    Bytwyne my lady legges   *lady's legs*
To dryve awey the dogges, madame.

10 May no man slepe in youre halle,
For rattes, madame, for rattes, madame,
But yyf he have a tent of fifteen enche
   Wyth letheryn knappes,   *leather knobs*
To dryve awey the rattes, madame.
15   I-blessd be suche knappes,
    That yyvëth such swappes,   *give such blows*
    Under my lady lappes,   *lady's skirts*
To dryve awey the rattes, madame.

May no man slepe in youre halle
20 For flyes, madame, for flyes, madame,   *flies*
But yyf he have a tent of fifteen enche
   Wyth twey byes   *with two rings*
To dryve awey the flyes, madame.
   I-blessed be such byes
25   That makëth such suyes   *such movements*
    Bytuynne my lady thyes   *between my lady's thighs*
To dryve awey the flyes, madame.

II, 115   Ther was a ladie leaned her backe to a wall

     A shoon   *shoe*
Ther was a ladie leaned her backe to a wall;
He tokke uppe peticote, smocke and all;
He laid her legges uppon his knee;
It was as white as white might bee.
5 He took a thing that stiffe did stand,
  And hunched her and punched her and made great game.
'O Godes bodie,' says she, 'fie, for shame!'
Yet he would not leave her so
But he did ease her and please her befor he would goo.

II, 116   Two stones hathe yt or els yt is wrong

A clocke

Two stones hathe yt or els yt is wrong,
With a bald hed and a tag somwhat long;
And in the night when wymen lie awake,
With ther conscience they doe yt take.   *their*

II, 117   I have a hole above my knee

Sheath   *sheath (i.e. for a knife or sword)*

I have a hole above my knee,
And pricked yt was and pricked shal be,
And yet it is not sore,
And yet yt shal be prickëd more.

II, 118   I have a thing and roughe yt is

A glove

I have a thing and roughe yt is,
And in the middest a hole ther is;
Ther cam a yong man with his gin   *young man with his instrument*
And thrust yt even a handfull in.

II, 119   Backe bent, smocke rent

A test (?)

Backe bent, smocke rent,   *smock*
Slipperie yt was and in yt went;
Thrust in stiffe standing,
But comes out lither dropping;   *limply drooping*
5 Stiff standing, roughe handling,
Between a womans legges in a morning.

II, 120   Ther ys a thyng, as I suppose

A placht (?)   *placket (?)*

Ther ys a thyng, as I suppose,
Which hath a face but never a nose,
Hath a mouthe but no toth therin,   *tooth*
Hath a bearde but never a chin.

II, 121   Hogyn cam to bowers dore

Hogyn cam to bowers dore,   *came to the chamber door*
Hogyn cam to bowers dore;
   He tryld upon the pyn for love,   *he rattled at the door-latch*
      Hum, ha, trill go bell –   *let the bell ring*
5   He tryld upon the pyn for love,
      Hum, ha, trill go bell.

Up she rose and lett hym yn,
Up she rose and let hym yn;
   She had a-went she had worshipped all her kyn,   *she thought; honoured; family*
10   Hum, ha, trill go bell –
   She had a-went she had worshipped all her kyn,
      Hum, ha, trill go bell.

When thei were to beddë browght,
Whan thei were to beddë browght,
15   The oldë chorle he cowld do nowght,   *the old chap could do nothing*
      Hum, ha, trill go bell –
   The oldë chorle he cowld do nowght,
      Hum, ha, trill go bell.

Go ye furth to yonder wyndow,
20 Go ye furth to yonder wyndow,
   And I will cum to you within a throw,   *in a little while*
      Hum, ha, trill go bell –
   And I will cum to you withyn a throw,
      Hum, ha, trill go bell.

25 Whan she hym at the wyndow wyst,   *knew*
Whan she hym at the wyndow wyst,
   She torned owt her ars and that he kyst,   *put out her bottom*
      Hum, ha, trill go bell –
   She torned owt her ars and that he kyst,
30   Hum, ha, trill go bell.

Y-wys, leman, ye do me wrong,   *indeed, (my) love, you*
Y-wis, leman, ye do me wrong,
   Or elles your breth ys wonder strong,   *breath is remarkably strong*
      Hum, ha, trill go bell –
35   Or elles your breth ys wonder strong,
      Hum, ha, trill go bell.

II, 122   It was a mayde of brenten ars

Synge dyllum, dyllum, dyllum, dyll!
I can tell you, and I wyll,
Of my ladyes water-myll.

It was a mayde of brenten ars;   *there was a girl; hot*
5 She rode to myll upon a horse;
  Yet was she mayden never the worse.   *none the worse*
    Synge dyllum, etc.

Layde she was upon a sacke;
'Stryke softe,' she sayd, 'hurt not my backe,
10 And spare not – let the myll clacke!'   *let the mill clatter*
    Synge dyllum, etc.

I-wys, the myller was full nyce;   *indeed; was very fastidious / lascivious*
His mylstones hanged bothe by a vyce   *millstones hung both by a screw*
And wolde be walkynge at a tryce.   *would be active in a trice*
15   *Synge dyllum, etc.*

This mayd to myll ofte dyd resorte
And of her game made no reporte,
But to her it was full great conforte.
    Synge dyllum, etc.

II, 123   Jentill butler, bell amy

How, butler, how! Bevis a towt!   *Hoy, butler, hoy! drink to all!*
Fill the boll, jentill butler, and let the cup rowt.   *bowl; cup go round*

Jentill butler, bell amy,   *gentle / noble butler, fine friend*
Fyll the boll by the eye,   *to the brim*
5 That we may drynk by and by.   *one and all*
    With how, butler, how! Bevis a towt!
    Fill the boll, butler, and let the cup rowt.

Here is mete for us all,   *here is food*
Both for gret and for small;   *great*
10 I trow we must the butlar call.   *I believe*
    With how, butler, how! Bevis a towt!
    Fill the boll, butler, and lett the cupe rowt.

I am so dry I cannot spek;   *speak*
I am nygh chokëd with my mete;   *my food*
15 I trow the butler be aslepe.   *is asleep*
    With how, butler, how! Bevis a towt!
    Fill the boll, butler, and let the cup rowt.

Butler, butler, fill the boll,
Or ellës I beshrewe thy noll;   *a curse upon* (lit. *I curse*) *your head*
20 I trow we must the bell toll.   *ring the bell*
     With how, butler, how! Bevis a towt!
     Fill the boll, butler, and let the cup rowt.

Iff the butlers name be Water,
I wold he were a galow-claper   *I would he were a gallows-bird*
25 But if he bryng us drynk the rather.   *unless he bring us drink quicker*
     With how, butler, how! Bevis a towt!
     Fill the boll, butler, and let the cup rowt.

II, 124   Is ther any good man here

Bon jowre, bon jowre a vous!   *good day, good day to you*
I am cum unto this hows   *house*
     With par la pompe, I say.   *with ceremony (?)*

Is ther any good man here
5 That will make me any chere?   *who will offer me any entertainment*
And if ther were, I wold cum nere   *come near*
     To wit what he wold say.   *to know what he would say*
          A! will ye be wild?   *will you shy away*
          By Mary myld
10   And her swete child,
     I trow ye will synge gay.   *I reckon you will sing merrily*
          Bon jowre, etc.

Be gladly, master, everychon;   *be merry, sirs, every one of you*
I am cum myself alone   *I have come all by myself*
15 To appose you on by on;   *to test you one by one*
     Let se who dare say nay.   *let (us) see*
          Sir, what say ye?
          Syng on; lett us see.
          Now will it be
20   Thys or another day?
          Bon jowre, etc.

Loo, this is he that will do the dede!   *do the deed*
He tempereth his mowth; therfore take hede.   *he tunes his voice* (lit. *mouth*); *heed*
Syng softe, I say, lest yowr nose blede,   *bleed*
25 For hurt yowrself ye may.
          But, by God that me bowght,   *bought* (i.e. *redeemed*)
          Your brest is so towght,   *your chest is so congested*
          Tyll ye have well cowght   *until you have coughed thoroughly*
     Ye may not therwith away.   *you cannot get rid of it*
30   *Bon jowre, etc.*

Sir, what say ye with your face so lene?   *lean*
Ye syng nother good tenowre, treble, ne mene;   *neither a good tenor, treble, nor mean*
Utter not your voice withowt your brest be clene,   *unless your chest is clear*
   Hartely I you pray.   *heartily*
35   I hold you excused;
      Ye shall be refused,
      For ye have not be used   *been used*
   To no good sport nor play.   *to any good entertainment or amusement*
    Bon jowre, etc.

40 Sir, what say ye with your fat face?
Me thynketh ye shuld bere a very good bace   *should sustain a very good bass*
To a pot of good ale or ipocras,   *ale or spiced wine*
   Truly as I you say.
     Hold up your hede;   *head*
45   Ye loke lyke lede;   *look like lead*
      Ye wast myche bred   *you waste much bread*
   Evermore from day to day.
    Bon jowre, etc.

Now will ye see wher he stondeth behynde?
50 I-wis, brother, ye be unkynd;   *indeed, brother, you are*
Stond forth and wast with me som wynd,   *step forward and spend some breath*
   For ye have ben called a synger ay.   *always been called a singer*
     Nay, be not ashamed;
     Ye shall not be blamed,
55   For ye have ben famed
   The worst in this contrey.
    Bon jowre, etc.

II, 125   Now ys Yole comen with gentyll chere

   Hay, ay, hay, ay,
   Make we mery as we may.

   Now ys Yole comen with gentyll chere;   *Yule has come with kindly cheer*
   Of merthe and gomyn he has no pere;   *for mirth and merriment; peer*
5   In every londe where he comes nere   *near*
     Is merthe and gomyn, I dar wele say.   *dare well*
    Hay, ay, etc.

   Now ys comen a messyngere
   Of yore lorde, Ser Nu Yere,   *from your lord, Sir New Year*
10 Byddes us all be mery here
     And make as mery as we may.
    Hay, ay, etc.

Therefore every mon that ys here	
Synge a caroll on hys manere;	*(let) every man*
15 Yf he con non we schall hym lere,	*in his own manner*
So that we be mery allway.	*knows none we shall teach him*
Hay, ay, etc.	*we may be merry*

Whosoever makes hevy chere,	*is in a gloomy mood*
Were he never to me dere;	*he would never be dear to me*
20 In a dyche I wolde he were,	*in a ditch I would he were*
To dry hys clothes tyll hyt were day.	
Hay, ay, etc.	

Mende the fyre and make gud chere!	*good cheer*
Fyll the cuppe, Ser Botëlere!	*Sir Butler*
25 Let every mon drynke to hys fere!	*to his companion*
Thys endes my caroll with care away.	*away with care*
Hay, ay, etc.	

II, 126   Lett no man cum into this hall

Make we mery, bothe more and lasse,	*both high and low (in rank)*
For now ys the tyme of Crystymas.	

Lett no man cum into this hall,	*come*
Grome, page, nor yet marshall,	*man-servant, page, nor even steward*
5 But that sum sport he bryng withall,	*some entertainment*
For now ys the tyme of Crystmas.	
Make we mery etc.	

Yff that he say he can not syng,	
Sum oder sport then lett hym bryng,	*some other entertainment*
10 That yt may please at thys festyng,	*this feasting*
For now ys the tyme of Crystmas.	
Make we mery etc.	

Yff he say he can nowght do,	*can do nothing*
Then for my love aske hym no mo,	*for my sake; no more*
15 But to the stokkes then lett hym go,	*stocks*
For now ys the tyme of Crystmas.	
Make we mery etc.	

II, 127   Holy stond in the hall

Nay! Ivy, nay!
    hyt shal not be, i-wys;   *indeed*
Let Holy hafe the maystry,   *let Holly have the upper hand*
    as the maner ys.   *as is customary*

5 Holy stond in the hall,   *holly stands*
     fayre to behold;   *fair*
   Ivy stond without the dore –   *outside the door*
     she ys ful sore a-cold.   *bitterly cold*
       Nay! Ivy, nay! etc.

10 Holy and hys mery men,
     they dawnsen and they syng;
   Ivy and hur maydenes,   *her*
     they wepen and they wryng.   *wring (their hands)*
       Nay! Ivy, nay! etc.

15 Ivy hath a kybe,   *chilblain*
     she kaght yt with the colde;   *caught*
   So mot they all haf ay   *so may they all have always*
     that with Ivy hold.   *who*
       Nay! Ivy, nay! etc.

20 Holy hath berys   *berries*
     as rede as any rose;
   The foster, the hunters   *forester*
     kepe hem fro the doos.   *keep (i.e. protect) them from the does*
       Nay! Ivy, nay! etc.

25 Ivy hath berys
     as blake as any slo;   *black as any sloe*
   Ther com the oule   *there came the owl*
     and ete hym as she goo.   *and ate them in passing (lit. as she goes)*
       Nay! Ivy, nay! etc.

30 Holy hath byrdes,   *birds*
     a ful fayre flok,   *flock*
   The nyghtyngale, the poppynguy,   *parrot*
     the gayntyl lavyrok.   *gentle / noble lark*
       Nay! Ivy, nay! etc.

35 Gode Ivy,   *good*
     what byrdes ast thou?   *have you*
   Non but the howlat,   *none but the young owl*
     that kreye 'How, how!'   *which cries*
       Nay! Ivy, nay! etc.

II, 128   Holy berëth beris

Nay! nay! Ivy,	
it may not be, i-wis,	*indeed*
For Holy must have the mastry,	*Holly; the upper hand*
as the maner is.	*as is customary*
5 Holy berëth beris,	*bears berries*
beris rede ynowgh;	*red enough (i.e. really red)*
The thristilcok, the popyngay,	*the cock thrush, the parrot*
daunce in every bow.	
Welaway, sory Ivy,	*alas, poor Ivy*
10 what fowlës hast thow	*what birds have you*
But the sory howlet,	*other than the miserable owlet*
that syngëth 'How, how'?	
Nay! nay! Ivy, etc.	
Ivy berëth beris	
15 as black as any slo;	*sloe*
Ther commëth the woode-colver	*wood-pigeon*
and fedëth her of tho.	*and feeds herself on them*
She liftëth up her tayll	
and she cakkës or she go;	*and she craps before she goes*
20 She wold not for a hundred	*would not*
poundes serve Holy soo.	
Nay! nay! Ivy, etc.	
Holy with his mery men,	
they can daunce in hall;	
25 Ivy and her jentyl women	*gentle / noble*
can not daunce at all,	
But lyke a meyny of bullokkes	*except like a herd*
in a waterfall,	
Or on a hot somers day,	
30 whan they be mad all.	
Nay! nay! Ivy, etc.	
Holy and his mery men	
sytt in cheyres of gold;	*chairs*
Ivy and her jentyll women	
35 sytt withowt in fold,	*sit outside on the ground*
With a payre of kybid	*pair of chilblained*
helës cawght with cold;	*heels*
So wold I that every man had	*would I*
that with Yvy will hold.	
40 *Nay! nay! Ivy, etc.*	

II, 129   The most worthye she is in towne

Ivy, chefe off trees it is;   chief of trees
Veni, coronaberis.   come, you shall be crowned

The most worthye she is in towne –   in the world
 He that seyth other doth amysse –   says otherwise does amiss
5 And worthy to bere the crowne: bear
 Veni, coronaberis.
  Ivy, chefe etc.

Ivy is soft and mek off spech,   meek of speech
 Ageynst all bale she is blysse,   as opposed to all misery she is joy
10 Well is he that may hyre rech: attain her
 Veni, coronaberis.
  Ivy, chefe etc.

Ivy is green with coloure bright;
 Of all treis best she is;
15 And that I preve well now be right: and that I now most justly prove
 Veni, coronaberis.
  Ivy, chefe etc.

Ivy berëth berys black –
 God graunt us all his blysse!
20 Fore there shall we nothyng lack: for there (i.e. in heaven)
 Veni, coronaberis.
  Ivy, chefe etc.

II, 130   Holvyr and Ivy mad a gret party

Holvyr and Ivy mad a gret party,   Holly and Ivy made a great dispute
 Who shuld have the maystry,   should have the upper hand
  In londës wher thei goo.   wherever they are together (lit. in places
             [where they go)

Than spake Holvyr: 'I am frece and joly;   fresh and jolly
5 I wol have the maystry   I will
  In londës wher we goo.'

Than spake Ivy: 'I am lowd and prowd,
 And I wyl have the maystry
  In londës wher we goo.'

10 Than spak Holvyr, and set hym downe on his kne:
 'I prey the, jentyl Ivy,
 Sey me no veleny   say nothing unkind of me
  In londës wher we goo.'

II, 131   The boris hed in hondes I brynge

Caput apri refero,   *the boar's head I bring*
Resonens laudes Domino.   *sounding praises to the Lord*

The boris hed in hondes I brynge,
With garlondes gay and byrdes syngynge;
5 I pray you all, helpe me to synge,
    Qui estis in convivio.   *who are at this feast*
      Caput apri etc.

The boris hede, I understond,
Ys cheff servyce in all this londe;   *is the best dish*
10 Whersoever it may be fonde,   *found*
    Servitur cum sinapio.   *it is served with mustard*
      Caput apri etc.

The boris hede, I dare well say,
Anon, after the Twelfth Day
15 He taketh his leve and goth away: *goes away*
    Exivit tunc de patria   *he has then left the country*
      Caput apri etc.

II, 132   Owre kynge went forth to Normandy

Deo gracias, Anglia,   *thanks to God, England,*
Redde pro victoria.   *render for victory*

Owre kynge went forth to Normandy
With grace and myght of chyvalry;   *of mounted knights*
5 Ther God for hym wrought mervelusly;
Wherfore Englonde may calle and cry,
    'Deo gracias.'   *thanks be to God*
      Deo gracias, Anglia
      Redde pro victoria.

10 He sette a sege, sothe for to say,   *laid seige, truth to tell*
To Harflu toune with ryal aray;   *Harfleur; royal array*
That toune he wan and made afray   *won and made an assault*
That Fraunce shal rywe tyl domësday;   *that France will regret until*
    Deo gracias.
15   Deo gracias, Anglia
      Redde pro victoria.

Than went oure kynge with alle his oste   *host*
Thorwe Fraunce, for alle the Frenshë boste; *through; in spite of all; boasting*
He spared no drede of lest ne moste   *spared nor feared the least nor the greatest*
20 Tyl he come to Agincourt coste;   *until; district of Agincourt*

Deo gracias.
Deo gracias, Anglia
Redde pro victoria.

Than, forsoth, that knyght comely,   *then, truly, that comely knight*
25 In Agincourt feld he faught manly;   *field he fought manfully*
Thorw grace of God most mervelowsly   *through*
He had bothe felde and victory;
Deo gracias.
Deo gracias, Anglia
30   *Redde pro victoria.*

There dukes and erles, lorde and barone
Were take and slayne, and that wel sone,   *and that right soon*
And summe were ladde into Lundone   *to London*
With joye and merthe and grete renone;   *and great acclaim*
35   Deo gracias.
Deo gracias, Anglia
Redde pro victoria.

Now gracious God He save oure kynge,   *may he save*
His peple, and alle his wel-wyllynge;   *well-wishers*
40 Yef hym gode lyfe and gode endynge,   *give him*
That we with merth mowe savely synge,   *may confidently (lit. safely) sing*
'Deo gracias.'
Deo gracias, Anglia
Redde pro victoria.

II, 133   Worschip of vertu ys the mede

Enfors we us with all our myght   *let us exert ourselves*
To love Seynt Georg, owr Lady knyght.   *our Lady's knight*

Worschip of vertu ys the mede   *honour is the reward of virtue*
And seweth hym ay of ryght;   *and follows it always appropriately*
5 To worschip George than have we ned,   *to honour George; need*
Whych is our sovereyn Ladys knyght.   *Lady's knight*
Enfors we us etc.

He keped the mad from dragons dred   *saved the maid; the dragon's terror*
And fraid al France and put to flight.   *made afraid*
10 At Agyncourt – the crownecle ye red –   *if you read the chronicle*
The French hym se formest in fyght.   *him saw foremost*
Enfors we us etc.

In hys vertu he wol us led   *virtue / strength he will lead us*
Agaynes the fend, the fulë wyght,   *against the fiend, the foul creature*

15 And with hys banner us oversprede   *protect us*
    Yf we hym love with all our myght.
      Enfors we us etc.

II, 134   And by a chapell as y came

Mery hyt ys in May mornyng,
Mery wayës for to gone.   *to go*

And by a chapell as y came,
Mett y wythe Jhesu to chyrcheward gone,   *going to church*
5 Petur and Pawle, Thomas and Jhon,
  And hys desyples everychone.   *every one*
    Mery hyt ys etc.

Sente Thomas the belles gane ryng,   *did ring*
And Sent Collas the mas gane syng;   *Saint Nicholas the Mass did sing*
10 Sente Jhon toke that swete offeryng –
   And by a chapell as y came.
     Mery hyt ys etc.

Owre Lorde offered whate He wollde,   *what he wished*
A challes alle off ryche rede gollde;   *chalice*
15 Owre Lady the crowne off hyr mowlde –   *(offered) the crown from her head*
   The son owte off hyr bosom schone.   *the sun / Son out of*
     Mery hyt ys etc.

Sent Jorge, that ys owre Lady knyghte,   *our Lady's knight*
He tende the tapyres fayre and bryghte,   *lit the tapers*
20 To myn yye a semley syghte –   *to my eyes*
   And by a chapell as y came.
     Mery hyt ys etc.

II, 135   The merthe of alle this londe

The merthe of alle this londe   *the happiness of all this land*
Makëth the gode husbonde   *the good farmer creates*
  With erynge of his plowe.   *with the ploughing of his plough*
I-blessed be Cristës sonde,   *blest be Christ's grace*
5 That hath us sent in honde   *which has placed in our hands*
  Merthe and joye y-nowe.   *happiness and joy in plenty*

The plowe goth mony a gate,   *many a way*
Bothe erly and eke late,   *and also late*
  In wynter in the clay,   *in the earth*
10 Aboute barly and whete –   *to produce (lit. about) barley and wheat*
   That maketh men to swete! –   *sweat*
     God spede the plowe al day!   *God speed the plough every day*

Browne, Morel and Gore,
Drawen the plowe ful sore,   *draw the plough with great effort*
15 Al in the morwënynge;   *all the morning*
Rewarde hem therfòre   *them*
With a shefe or more,   *sheaf*
    Alle in the evënynge.

Whan men bygynne to sowe,
20 Ful wel here corne they knowe   *their corn they anticipate*
    In the mounthe of May.
Howe-ever Janyver blowe,   *January may blow*
Whether hye or lowe,   *high or low*
    God spede the plowe allway!

25 Whan men bygynne to wede   *weed*
The thystle fro the sede,   *from the seed*
    In somer whan they may,
God lete hem wel to spede,   *God grant them to prosper well*
And longe gode lyfe to lede,   *and a good long life to lead*
30   All that for plowemen pray.   *all who pray for ploughmen*

II, 136   Whan netilles in wynter bere rosis rede

Whan netilles in wynter   *nettles*
        bere rosis rede,   *bear*
And thornes bere figges
        naturally,
And bromes bere appylles   *broom bushes*
        in every mede,   *meadow*
And lorelles bere cheris   *laurels bear cherries*
        in the croppes so hie,   *in their lofty branches*
5 And okes bere dates   *oaks*
        so plentuosly,
And lekes geve hony   *leeks give honey*
        in ther superfluens –   *in (their) superabundance*
Than put in a woman
        your trust and confidens.   *confidence*

Whan whityng walk in forestes   *whiting (fish)*
        hartes for to chase,
And herynges in parkes   *herrings*
        hornes boldly blowe,
10 And flownders more-hennes   *flounders moor-hens*
        in fennes enbrace,   *capture (lit. embrace) in the fens*
And gornardes shote grengese   *gurnards shoot goslings*
        owt of a crosse bowe,
And rolyons ride huntyng   *fish*
        the wolf to overthrowe,

And sperlynges rone with speres	*smelts run with spears*
in harnes to defence –	*in armour for protection*
Than put in a woman	
your trust and confidence.	
15 Whan sparowes bild chirches	*sparrows build churches*
and stepulles hie,	*and high steeples*
And wrennes cary sakkes	*wrens carry sacks*
to the mylle,	
And curlews cary clothes	*cloths*
horses for to drye,	*to wipe horses dry*
And se-mewes bryng butter	*sea-mews*
to the market to sell,	
And wod-dowes were wod-knyffes	*wood-pigeons wear hunting knives*
theves to kyll,	*thieves*
20 And griffons to goslynges	*vultures /griffins*
don obedyence –	*are obedient*
Than put in a woman	
your trust and confidence.	
Whan crabbes tak wodcokes	*crabs take woodcocks*
in forestes and parkes,	
And hares ben taken	*are taken*
with swetnes of snayles,	*with (the) sweetness of snails*
And camelles with ther here	*camels with their hair*
tak swalowes and perches,	*take swallows and perch*
25 And myse mowe corn	*and mice mow corn*
with wafeyyng of ther tayles,	*with waving of their tails*
Whan dukkes of the dunghill	*ducks from*
sek the blod of Hayles,	*seek the blood of Hales*
Whan shrewd wyffes to ther husbondes	*when shrewish wives*
do non offens –	*cause no offence*
Than put in a woman	
your trust and confidence.	

II, 137   Tutivillus, the devyl of hell

Tutivillus, the devyl of hell,	
He wrytëth har names, sothe to tel,	*their names, truth to tell*
Ad missam garulantes.	*(of those) chattering at mass*
Bett wer be attome for ay,	*it were better to be at home for ever*
5 Than her to serve the devil to pay,	*here (in church); to the devil's liking*
Sic vana famulantes.	*thus serving vainly*
Thes women that sittëth the church about,	
Thai beth al of the develes rowte,	*they are all of the devil's company*
Divina impedientes.	*hindering devotions*

10 But thai be stil, he wil ham quell,   *unless they are quiet, he will destroy them*
   With kene crokes draw hem to hell,   *with sharp hooks draw them*
      Ad puteum, multum flentes.   *to the pit, greatly wailing*

   For his love that you der boght,   *for the love of him who dearly bought you*
   Hold you stil and jangel noght,   *keep silent and chatter not*
15   *Sed prece deponentes.*   *but (remain) bowed in prayer*

   The blis of heven than may ye wyn;   *then may you win*
   God bryng us al to his in,   *to his lodging*
      Amen! amen! dicentes.   *saying, Amen! Amen!*

II, 138   All that I may swynk or swet

    Care away, away, away,   *away with care*
    Care away for evermore.

   All that I may swynk or swet,   *all that I may may toil or sweat for*
   My wyfe it wyll both drynk and ete;   *eat*
5 And I sey ought, she wyl me bete: *if I say anything; beat*
      Carfull ys my hart therfor.   *sorrowful; heart*
        Care away, etc.

   If I sey ought of hyr but good,   *say anything*
   She loke on me as she war wod   *she looks at me as if she were mad*
10 And wyll me clout about the hod: *hood (i.e. head)*
      Carfull ys my hart therfor.
        Care away, etc.

   If she wyll to the gud ale ryd,   *to the good (i.e. strong) ale ride*
   Me must trot all be hyr syd,   *I must; at her side*
15 And whan she drynk I must abyd: *is drinking I must wait*
      Carfull ys my hart therfor.
        Care away, etc.

   If I say 'It shal be thus,'
   She sey, 'Thou lyëst, charll, i-wous!   *she says, 'you lie, churl, indeed'*
20 Wenest thou to overcome me thus?'   *do you expect*
      Carfull ys my hart therfor.
        Care away, etc.

   Yf ony man have such a wyfe to lede,   *a wife to manage*
   He shal know how 'judicare' cam in the Cred;   *how 'to judge' came into the creed*
25 Of hys penans God do hym med!   *for his penance may God reward him*
      Carfull ys my hart therfor.
        Care away, etc.

II, 139   O wicket wemen, wilfull and variable

O wicket wemen, wilfull and variable, — *wicked; changeable*
Richt fals, feckle, fell and frivolus, — *false, fickle, fierce*
Dowgit, dispytfull, dour and dissavable, — *obstinate, malicious, sullen and deceitful*
Unkynd, crewall, curst and covettus, — *cruel, evil and avaricious*
5 Ouirlicht of laitis, unleill and licherus, — *shallow in behaviour, disloyal and lecherous*
Turnit fra trewth and taiclit with treichery, — *entangled in trechery*
Unferme of faith, fulfillit of fellony! — *faltering in; filled with treachery*

O stowt, stif, standfra and unstable, — *obstinate, obdurate, aloof*
Unmeik but mesur and malitius, — *arrogant beyond measure and malicious*
10 Angry, awstern and till all evillis able, — *harsh and capable of all evils*
Skornand, skaithful, skald and most sklandrus, — *scornful, harmful, shrewish; slanderous*
Gredy not gude, grym, gray and ungratius
Noyus but neid and full of iniquitie, — *vexatious without need*
Ungentill, jugeit and full of jolesie! — *condemned and full of jealousy*

15 Als terne as tygir, of tung untollerable, — *as fierce as a tiger; tongue*
O thow violent virago vennemouss!
Blasterand, bald, brym and abhominable, — *blustering, brazen, fierce*
Ourperte, reprevivable, peirles and perrellous, — *over-pert, reprehensible, unequalled*
Evill Cristiane, unknawin, crafty and cawtelus, — *uncouth, crafty and wily*
20 Unchest, evill chosin and all but cheretie, — *impure; entirely without charity*
Mellit with misdeid and all mensworne ar ye! — *mixed with misconduct; perjured*

    Finis, quod Chauceir. — *the end, said Chaucer*

II, 140   In all this warld nis a meryar lyfe

A, a, a, a,
Yet I love wherso I go.

In all this warld nis a meryar lyfe — *world there is no merrier life*
Than is a yong man withoutyn a wyfe, — *than a young man*
5 For he may lyven withouten stryfe
    In every place wherso he go.
        A, a, a, a, etc.

In every place he is loved over all — *above all*
Among maydyns gret and small,
10 In daunsyng, in pypynge, and rennyng at the ball, — *running*
    In every place wherso he go.
        A, a, a, a, etc.

Thei lat lyght be husbondmen — *they think little of married men*
Whan thei at the ballë rene; — *run*
15 Thei cast hyr love to yongë men — *they direct their love*
    In every place wherso thei go.
        A, a, a, a, etc.

Than sey maydens, 'Farwell, Jacke,   *say*
Thi love is pressed al in thi pake;   *pack (knapsack)*
20 Thou berest thi love behynd thi back,   *you carry your love*
   In every place wherso thou go'.
   A, a, a, a, etc.

II, 141   Freers, freers, wo ye be!

Freers, freers, wo ye be!   *friars; cursed be ye*
   ministri malorum,   *ministers of evils*
For many a mannës soule brynge ye
   ad penas infernorum.   *to the punishments of hell*
5 Whan seyntës fellë fryst from heven,   *angels first fell from heaven*
   quo prius habitabant,   *where they formerly dwelt*
In erthë leyftt the synnës seven   *they left the seven sins*
   et fratres communicabant.   *and friars passed (them) on*
Folines was the fryst floure   *folly was the first flower*
10   quem fratres pertulerunt,   *which the friars brought*
For folines and fals derei   *because of folly and treacherous violence*
   multi perierunt.   *many have perished*
Freers, ye that can weyl lye   *you who well know how to lie*
   ad falandum gentem,   *to deceive people*
15 And weyl can blere a mannës ye   *and can easily hoodwink a man*
   pecunias habentem.   *who has money*
Yf thei may no morë geytte,   *if they (i.e. friars) can get no more*
   fruges petunt isti,   *they seek out the thrifty*
For folines walde thei not lette,   *out of folly they would not spare*
20   qui sunt de grege Cristi.   *(those) who are of Christ's flock*
Lat a freer of sum ordur   *let a friar of some order*
   tecum pernoctare,   *pass the night with you*
Odur thi wyf or thi dougtour   *either your wife or your daughter*
   hic vult violare;   *this (friar) will seek to violate*
25 Or thi sun he weyl prefur,   *or your son he will prefer*
   sicut furcam fortis –   *as (he prefers) the crotch of a (strong) man*
God gyffe syche a freer peyn   *God give such a friar pain*
   in inferni portis!   *in the gates of hell*
Thei weyl assaylle boyth Jacke and Gylle   *they will assail both Jack and Jill*
30   licet sint predones;   *even if they are thieves*
And parte of pennans take hem tylle,   *part of the penance take upon themselves*
   quia sunt latrones.   *because they (too) are robbers*
Ther may no lorde of this cuntré   *country*
   sic edificare,   *build in such a way*
35 As may thes freers, where thei be,   *wherever they are*
   qui vadunt mendicare.   *who go about begging*
Mony-makers I trow thei be,   *counterfeiters I reckon they are*
   regis proditores,   *traitors to the king*

Therfore yll mowëth thei thee,	*ill may they prosper*
40 falsi deceptores.	*false deceivers*
Fader fyrst in trinité,	
Filius atque flamen,	*Son and spirit*
All one God and persones thre,	
Omnes dicant 'Amen'.	*let all say 'Amen'*

II, 142   Ther was a frier of order gray

Inducas, inducas,	*lead (us), lead (us)*
In temptacionibus.	*in temptations*
Ther was a frier of order gray,	*friar of the grey order*
Inducas,	
5 Which loved a nunne full meny a day	*who; many*
In temptacionibus.	
Inducas, etc.	
This fryer was lusty, proper and yong,	*handsome and young*
Inducas,	
10 He offerd the nunne to lerne her syng	*to teach her to sing*
In temptacionibus.	
Inducas, etc.	
Othe, re, me, fa, the frier her tawght,	*ut, re, mi, fa*
Inducas,	
15 *Sol, la,* this nunne he kyst full oft	*so, la*
In temptacionibus.	
Inducas, etc.	
By proper chaunt and Bequory,	*proper chant and B natural*
Inducas,	
20 This nunne he groped with flattery	*he groped and flattered*
In temptacionibus.	
Inducas, etc.	
The fryers first lesson was *'Veni ad me'*,	*'Come to me'*
Inducas,	
25 *'Et ponam tollum meum ad te'*	*'and I shall put my peg to you'*
In temptacionibus.	
Inducas, etc.	
The frier sang all by Bemoll,	*B flat*
Inducas,	
30 Of the nunne he begate a cristenyd sowle	*by the nun he begot a Christian soul*
In temptacionibus.	
Inducas, etc.	

The nunne was taught to syng *'Sepe',*   *'Often'*
Inducas,
35 *'Lapides expungnaverunt me'*   *'the stones have overcome me'*
In temptacionibus.
      Inducas, etc.

Thus the fryer lyke a prety man,   *the friar like a fine fellow*
Inducas,
40 Ofte rokked the nunnës quoniam   *nun's thingy*
In temptacionibus
      Inducas, etc.

II, 143   Lesteneth, lordynges, I you beseke

Prenëgard, prenëgard!   *take care! take care!*
Thus bere I myn basëlard.   *thus I sport my dagger*

Lesteneth, lordynges, I you beseke: *listen; beseech*
Ther is non man worth a leke,   *leek*
5 Be he sturdy, be he meke,   *meek*
      But he bere a basëlard.   *unless he sport a dagger*
      Prenëgard, etc.

Myn baselard hath a schede of red   *sheath*
And a clene loket of led;   *neat band of lead*
10 Me thinketh I may bere up myn hed,   *hold up my head*
      For I bere myn basëlard.   *because I*
      Prenëgard, etc.

Myn baselard hath a wrethin hafte;   *damascened (lit. twisted) hilt*
Whan I am ful of alë cawghte,   *when I am full of ale*
15 It is gret dred of mannësslawghte,   *there is great danger of manslaughter*
      For then I bere myn basëlard.
      Prenëgard, etc.

My baselard hath a sylver schape;   *silver plate (on its scabbard)*
Therfore I may bothe gaspe and gape;   *both yah and boo*
20 Me thinketh I go lyk non knape,   *no ordinary fellow*
      For I bere a basëlard.
      Prenëgard, etc.

My baselard hath a trencher kene,   *has a keen blade*
Fayr as rasour, scharp and schene;   *good as a razor, sharp and bright*
25 Evere me thinketh I may be kene,   *be bold*
      For I bere myn basëlard.
      Prenëgard, etc.

As I yede up in the strete,   *went up the street*
With a cartere I gan mete;   *with a carter I did meet*
30 'Felawe,' he seyde, 'so mot I the,   *fellow; so may I prosper*
    Thou shalt forgo thi basëlard.'
        Prenëgard, etc.

The cartere his whyppe began to take,
And al myn fleysh began to qwake,   *flesh began to quake*
35 And I was lef for to ascape,   *I was glad to escape*
    And there I left myn basëlard.
        Prenëgard, etc.

Whan I cam forth onto myn damme,
Myn hed was broken to the panne;   *to the skull*
40 She seyde I was a praty manne,   *I was a fine fellow* (lit. *pretty man*)
    And wel cowde bere myn basëlard.   *well could sport*
        Prenëgard, etc.

II, 144   I wold fayn be a clarke

Hay, hay, by this day,
What avayleth it me thowgh I say nay?   *what good would it do me*

I wold fayn be a clarke,   *I would gladly be a scholar*
But yet hit is a strange werke;   *a hard undertaking*
5 The byrchyn twyggës be so sharpe –   *birch twigs are*
Hit makëth me have a faynt harte.   *causes me to have*
    What avayleth it me thowgh I say nay?
        Hay, hay, etc.

On Monday in the mornyng whan I shall rise,   *I must rise*
10 At six of the clok, hyt is the gise,   *clock; it is the custom*
To go to skole withowt avise –   *school without arguing*
I had lever go twenti myle twyse.   *rather go twenty miles twice*
    What avayleth it me thowgh I say nay?
        Hay, hay, etc.

15 My master loketh as he were madde:
'Wher hast thou be, thow sory ladde?'   *where have you been*
'Milkë dukkes, my moder badde' –   *my mother bade (me) milk ducks*
Hit was no mervayle thow I were sadde.   *no wonder if* (lit. *though*)
    What vayleth it me thowgh I say nay?
20   Hay, hay, etc.

My master pepered my ars with well good spede;   *peppered; very successfully*
Hit was worse than fynkyll sede;   *fennel seed*
He wold not leve till it did blede –   *would not leave off; bleed*
Myche sorow have he for his dede!   *much sorrow may he have; deed*

25   What vayleth it me thowgh I say nay?
      Hay, hay, etc.

I wold my master were a watt,   *I wish; a hare*
And my boke a wyld catt,   *my book a wild cat*
And a brase of grehowndes in his toppe –   *brace; after him* (lit. *in his hair*)
30 I wold be glade for to se that!   *I would; see*
      What vayleth it me thowgh I say nay?
      Hay, hay, etc.

I wold my master were an hare,   *I wish*
And all his bokës howndës were,
35 And I myself a joly hontère: *hunter*
To blow my horn I wold not spare,
For if he were dede I wold not care.
      What vaylith me thowgh I say nay?
      Hay, hay, etc.

II, 145   Wenest thu, usch, with thi coyntyse

Wenest thu, usch, with thi coyntyse,   *Think you, teacher; cunning*
Iche day beten us on this wyse,   *each day to beat us in this way*
    As thu wer lord of toun?   *as if you were*
We had levur scole forsake,   *had rather leave school*
5 And ilche anothur craftë take,   *and each; occupation*
    Then long in thi bandoun.   *than remain under your control*

But woldë God that we myght ones   *we might for once*
Cache the at the mulnë-stones,   *catch you; mill stones*
    Or at the crabbë-tre!
10 We schuld leve in the such probeyt   *leave in you such testimony*
For that thu hast us don and seyt,   *for what you have done to us and said*
    That alle thi kyn suld rwe the.   *would pity you*

And thow Sire Robert, with his cloke,   *though; gown*
Wold the helpe and be thi Poke,   *your Puck*
15 The werrë thu schust fare;   *worse you would fare*
And for his prayer the rathur we wold   *despite his entreaty*
Yyven hym stripës al uncolde,   *give him stinging blows*
    Not for hym the spare.   *not on his account spare you*

For oftë sorë we abye   *we pay for*
20 The twynkëlingës of his ye,   *the winks of his (the master's) eye*
    The maystur, us to bete;   *to have us beaten*
For he and thu are at asent,   *in collusion*
Al day yyven agagëment   *always pledged*
    To yyven us strokës grete.   *to give us severe beatings*

II, 146   At a place wher he me sett

As I walked by a forest side,
I met with a foster; he bad me abide.   *a hunter*

At a place wher he me sett   *where he positioned me*
He bad me, what tyme an hart I met,   *when I encountered a hart*
5 That I shuld lett slyppe and say 'Go bett!'   *should release (my hounds); 'go*
   With 'Hay, go bet! Hay, go bett! Hay, go bett! How!'   *quickly' ('lit. 'go better')*
   We shall have game and sport ynow.   *in plenty (lit. enough)*
      As I walked etc.

I had not stond ther but a while,   *I had stood there but a (little) while*
10 Ye, not the mountenaunce of a myle,   *indeed, not as long as it would take*
   But a gret hart cam rennyng, withowt any gile.   *running, truth to tell* [*to go a mile*
   With 'Ther he goth! Ther he goth! Ther he gothe! How!'
   We shall have game and sport ynow.
      As I walked etc.

15 I had no sonner my howndes lat goo   *sooner let my hounds go*
   But the hart was overthrowe;   *than the hart*
   Than every man began to blowe,
   With 'Tro-ro-ro! Tro-ro-ro! Tro-ro-ro! Trow!'
   We shall have game and sport ynow.
20   *As I walked etc.*

II, 147   It fell ageyns the nextë nyght

   'Pax vobis,' quod the ffox,   *'Peace be with you', said the fox*
   'For I am come to toowne.'   *have come*

   It fell ageyns the nextë nyght   *it happened on the next evening*
   The fox yede to with all hys myghte,   *fox went to (work)*
5 Withoouten cole or candelight,   *without light of coal or candle*
      Whan that he cam unto the toowne.   *when he came to*
         'Pax vobis,' etc.

   Whan he cam all in the yerde,   *right into the yard*
   Soore the geys wer ill aferde: *the geese were all badly frightened*
10 'I shall macke some of yow lerde   *teach some of you something*
      Or that I goo from the toowne.'   *before I go*
         'Pax vobis,' etc.

   Whan he cam all in the croofte,   *right into the enclosure*
   There he stalkëd wundirfull soofte: *quietly*
15 'For here have I be frayed full ofte   *been attacked very often*
      Whan that I haue come to toowne.'
         'Pax vobis,' etc.

He hente a goose all be the heye;   seized; right by the fence
Faste the goos began to creye;   immediately; cry out
20 Oowte yede men as they myght heye   out rushed the men as fast as they could
   And sayde, 'Fals fox, ley it doowne!'
   '*Pax vobis,*' etc.

'Nay,' he saide, 'soo mot I the,   as I may thrive
Sche shall goo unto the wode with me,
25 Sche and I under a tre,
   Emonge the beryes browne.   among the berries
   '*Pax vobis,*' etc.

'I have a wyf, and sche lyeth seke;   lies sick
Many smale whelppes sche have to-eke;   she has besides
30 Many bonës they muste pike   pick clean
   Whill they ley adowne!'   while they lie down (i.e. as they lie there)
   '*Pax vobis,*' etc.

II, 148   Bi a forrest as I gan fare

Bi a forrest as I gan fare,   as I went
   Walkyng al myselven alone,
I hard a mornyng of an haare,   I heard a lament of a hare
   Rouffully sche mad here mone.   piteously (lit. ruefully) she made her
                                                [complaint
5 'Dereworth God, how schal I leve   most worthy God; live
   Er thus, and leyd my lyve in lond?   ever thus, and lead my life in (this) land
Fro dale to doune I am i-drevfe;   from dale to hill I am driven
   I not where I may syte or stond!   I do not know where

'I may nother rest nor slepe   neither
10   By no vallay that is so derne,   in any valley however secluded
Nor no covert may me kepe,   nor may any thicket protect me
   But ever I rene fro herne to herne.   run from hiding-place to hiding-place

'Hontteres wyll not heyre ther mase   hunters will not hear their mass
   In hope of hunttyng for to wend;   in the expectation of going hunting
15 They cowpulleth ther howndes, more and lase, couple their hounds, great and small
   And bryngeth theme to the feldës ende.

'Rochës rennen on every syde   hounds run
   In forrows that hoppë me to fynd;   hope
Honteres takethe ther horse and ryde,   hunters take their horses
20   And cast the conttray to the wynd.   and scour the country down wind

'Anone as they commeth me behynde,   as soon as
   I loke and syt ful style and lowe;   I watch and sit very still and low down
The furstë mane that me doth fynde   first man who finds me
   Anon he cryeth: "So howe! so hoowe!"   immediately he cries

25 '"Lo", he sayth, "where sytteth an haare!
       Aryse upe, Watte, and go forth blyve!"   *quickly*
    With sorroe and with mychë care   *sorrow and with great anxiety*
       I scape away with my lyve.   *escape*

    'Att wyntter in the depë snowe   *in winter*
30   Men wyl me sechë for to trace –   *men will seek to track me*
    And by my steyppes I ame i-knowe –   *by my tracks (lit. steps) I am recognized*
       And followeth me fro place to place.

    'And yf I to the tounë torne,   *turn to the farm*
       Be hit in worttës or in leyke,   *for cabbages or for leeks*
35 Then wyl the wyffës also yeorne   *immediately*
       Fleche me with here dogës eyke.   *drive me out with their dogs also*

    'And yf I syt and crope the koule,   *eat the kale*
       And the wyfe be in the waye,   *should be around*
    Anone sche wyll swere, "By Cokkes soule!   *straightaway; swear, "By God's soul!"*
40   There is an haare in my haye!"   *within my fence*

    'Anone sche wyle clepe forth hure knave   *then she will call out her boy*
       And loke ryght weel wher I syte;   *look directly (lit. right well) where*
    Byhynd sche wyl with a stave
       Ful wel porpos me to hitte.   *intend to hit me*

45 '"Go forthe, Wate, wit Crystës curse,   *get out, Wat, with*
       And yf I leve, thou schalt be take;   *live; caught (lit. taken)*
    I have an hare-pype in my purse,   *hare-trap in my bag*
       Hit schal be set al for thi sake."

    'Then hath this wyffe two doggës grete,
50   On me sche byddëth heme goe,   *she orders them to set upon me*
    And as a schrowe sche wyll me thret,   *like a shrew; threaten*
       And ever sche cryëth, "Go, dooge, gooe!"

    'But all way this most I goo,   *thus must*
       By no banke I may abyde;
55 Lord God, that me is woo!
       Many a hape hath me bytyde.   *many a mishap has befallen me*

    'There is no best in the word, I wene,   *no creature in the world, I think*
       Hert, hynd, buke ne doe,   *hart, hind, buck nor doe*
    That suffures halfe so mychë tene   *misery*
60   As sylly Wat – go where he go.   *as harmless Wat*

    Yeyfe a genttylmane wyl have any game,
       And fynd me in forme where I syte,   *in (my) form*
    For dred of lossynge of his name   *for fear of losing his reputation*
       I wot wele he wyle not me hyte.   *I know well*

65 'For an acures bred he wyll me leve,   *acre's breadth he will allow me*
    Or he wyll let his hondës rene;   *before; dogs run*
    Of all the men that beth alyve   *are alive*
        I am most behold to genttylmen!   *most beholden*

    'As sone as I can ren to the laye,   *soon; run to open ground*
70   Anon the grey-hondes wyl me have;   *immediately*
    My bowels beth i-throwe awaye,   *are thrown away*
        And I ame bore home on a stavfe.   *borne home on a staff*

    'Als son as I am come home,
        I ame i-honge hye upon a pyne,   *hung up high on a peg*
75 With leke-worttes I am eette anone,   *with leeks; eaten*
        And whelpës play with my skyne.'   *puppies (whelps)*

II, 149   Spende, and God schal sende

    Spende, and God schal sende;
    Spare, and ermor care;   *hoard, and evermore worry*
        Non peni, non ware,   *no penny, no wares (i.e. material goods)*
        Non catel, non care –   *no wares, no worries*
5   Go! peni, go!

II, 150   Here lyeth under this marbyll ston

    Here lyeth under this marbyll ston   *here lies under this marble stone*
    Riche Alane, the ballid man;   *rich Alan, the bald man*
    Whether he be safe or noght   *safe (i.e. saved) or not*
    I recke never – for he ne roght!   *I don't care – for he never did*

Commentary

THE READINGS of the base manuscript along with selected variants are given where substantive emendations have been made. In the case of shared readings the spelling of the first cited MS is quoted. Scribal abbreviations are silently expanded. Erasures, scribal alterations, transposition indications and minor palaeographical peculiarities are not recorded; nor are varying indications for the repetition of carol burdens or sporadic spelling confusions in MSS of Part I texts (e.g. of þ and h, þ and y, þ and ȝ, w (as wynn) and þ or ȝ, w and wh, th and ht, etc.).

PART I

I, 1 With longing I am lad [*NIMEV* 4194]

MS: London, BL Harley 2253.

17 The roe deer, ME *ro* from OE *rā*, is commonly associated with restlessness, as in the alliterative phrase *rooles ase þe ro* in which the adjective *rooles*, 'restless', is formed from ME *ro*, 'peace, rest', derived from OE *rōw*. See *MED*, **roles** adj. and **ro** n. (1) (c).

18 *onde*: Perhaps the enmity of malicious gossips (cf. **I, 4**, 23, and Commentary) is meant.

36 It is tempting to think that the *of* in this line may have been introduced by scribal error, for *one the best*, meaning 'the very best' (in such phrases in ME *one* has an intensifying function) would seem more appropriate than 'one of the best' for a lady of such excellence as the poet's beloved. However, the shift of focus from submissive adoration of the lady herself to a more detached stance, that of regarding her as one among others, is in keeping with the change in tone at the end of this and other Harley lyrics where the poet indulges in surprisingly frank sexual comment or speculation concerning his lady. Cf. **I, 2**, 55–9, and **I, 25**, 82–4.

38 *under bys*: lit. 'in fine linen'. This is one of several conventional tags used for convenience of alliteration in describing a lady. Cf. *under bis* (**I, 5**, 17), *under gore* (**I, 5**, 16), *in lyn* (**I, 19**, 46), *on gere* (**I, 22**, 4, and Commentary), etc.

I, 2 A waylë whyte as whallës bon [*NIMEV* 105]

MS: London, BL Harley 2253.

Text: 25 While I may glewe] *added*; 37 myn herte] *added*; 44 bringen] þat bringeþ MS; 46 were] he were MS.

The title is the well-known first line of this poem as it is found in the MS, line 19 of the present text. For the ordering of the stanzas and the emendations adopted here, see Duncan (1992), pp. 111–20.

20 *shon*: past tense form for sake of rhyme.

22 The word *toune* appears in the Harley lyrics in the general sense of 'where men live' in such phrases as *in tounës,* here, and *to toune* in **1, 20**, 1, which may be translated as 'among men', 'in the world', or the like. The adjective *trewe* is commonly associated with the turtle-dove.

30 The verb *wite* ('to lay blame for') has the person blamed in the dative; see *OED* **Wite**, v^1, 1. The sense is therefore: 'I blame on a woman.' Beneath the immediate reference here to the poet's beloved there may also lurk an implicit reference to that archetypal cause of woe, Eve, referred to in **1, 27**, 13–16, another Harley love lyric.

47 The object of *changë* may be understood (ironically) from *mirth* in the previous line or as 'companion' from *fere* in line 48.

57 *Swetë bryd*: The poet wittily exploits the ambiguity of *Swetë bryd* here. Following on lines 55–6, it would first seem that the skylark is meant, and Brook punctuates accordingly. However, with lines 58–9 *Swetë bryd* may more appropriately be taken as referring to the lady than to any one of the three birds previously mentioned, with *bryd* as 'bird', a term of endearment (see *MED* **brid** n. **3b.** (a)), or as 'lady' (by association with *bride* from OE *brȳd*; see *EMEVP*, Glossary, under **burde** n.). Cf. *brid* (**1, 3**, 17) and *briddës* (**1, 27**, 40).

I, 3   Ichot a byrde in bourë bryght [*NIMEV* 1395]

MS: London, BL Harley 2253.

Text: 7 muchel] *added*; 18 eyen] eye MS; 63 soght] so soht MS; 77 Love] hire loue MS; 79 for to] *added*; 81 biseche] bisecheþ MS. The burden is indicated in the MS only after stanzas 1 and 2; *Blow, etc.* is added after the other stanzas in the text here.

This lyric is 'among the earliest preserved secular carols' (Greene, p. 483).

   5 *bourë*: 'bower'. In ME lyrics this word usually means a lady's chamber and not a flowery arbour, the sense more familiar to present-day readers.

   7 *muchel myght*: The MS reading of this line is two syllables short. For the addition of *muchel* here, cf. *muchel might*, **1, 25**, 19.

10 *of blodë and of bon*: 'of blood and bone', a common tag, equivalent to modern English 'of flesh and blood'. Cf. **1, 16**, 5, and **1, 25**, 5.

12 *in londe*: another common tag with the general sense of 'anywhere', 'everywhere', 'on earth'. Cf. line 59 and **1, 19**, 19.

16 For the sense of this line see *EMEVP*, p. 328, note to VIII K, line 15.

43 *jolif so the jay*: a common comparison aided by the alliteration. For this, and the association of *jolif* with other birds, see *MED* **joli** adj. 1. (a).

47 Both *fiëlë* and *crouth* were kinds of medieval stringed instruments. See Panum (1941), pp. 239–45. The word *fiele* may be taken as a form of OF *viele*. However, the viol as such makes its appearance much later; see *OED* **Viol** sb.^{1}

72 *swore*: For MS *sore* as a form of *swore* (with loss of *w* before a lip-rounded vowel), see *EMEVP*, p. 329, note to VIII K, line 65.

75 *in lyghte*: lit. 'in the light'.

77 For the removal of MS *hire*, see Brook, p. 82, note to no. 14, line 71. Brandl and Zippel (1917), p. 128, removed *hire* in their text and also altered MS *bisecheþ* to *biseche* in line 81.

I, 4   Litel wot it any man [*NIMEV* 1921]

MS: London, BL Harley 2253.

Text: 16 may] ne may MS; 25 may] ne may MS; 30 hathele] haþeles MS; hewe] heowes MS; 32 gamen] gomenes MS; glewe] gleowes MS; 41 as(2)] *added*; 42 wete] beþ weete MS; 43 in] beþ in MS. Lines 17–19, 26–8, 36–8 and 45–7 are abbreviated in the MS to *Euer ant oo etc.*

This poem is preceded in the MS by a religious lyric opening with the same words and in the same form as stanzas 1, 3 and 5 of this poem. Carleton Brown took the religious poem to be an adaptation of the secular (Brown XIII, pp. 235–6).

3   *fre*: If the *fre womman* is the same as *hire* in line 5, the sense 'noble' for *fre* is ironic since the poet's lady (it is implied) has more experience of love than is compatible with the aristocratic ideal of true love (*dernë love*), and apparently feels *fre* (in the sense of 'free to do as she pleases') to ignore her pledge of love, possibly influenced by malicious gossip, as suggested in line 23.

9   Lit. 'whom I do not often see'. This is an instance of litotes, the rhetorical use of understatement for ironic emphasis: the meaning is, in effect, 'whom I never see'. See also line 44, where 'seldom at ease' really means 'never at ease'.

11 By the conventions of *dernë love*, the poet dared not mention his beloved's name.

21 *crie*: the historical present, i.e. the use of the present tense to lend immediacy to an action or emotional situation which actually occurred in the past.

23 In medieval love poetry the courtly lover frequently laments the harm caused by malicious gossips.

30 Since *hewe* (30) and *glewe* (32) rhyme with *rewe* (33) and *trewe* (35), the plurals in the MS readings in lines 30 and 32 (and presumably those within the line as well as those in the rhymes) are probably to be viewed as scribal corruptions.

39 *upon loft*: lit. 'in the air', but one of several conventional phrases simply meaning 'alive'.

44 For the pronunciation of *whose* as a monosyllable, cf. Commentary, **I, 61**, 11.

I, 5   Ichot a byrde in a bour [*NIMEV* 1394]

MS: London, BL Harley 2253.

Text: 31 thurgh] þouh MS; 35 baithëth] bayeþ MS; 36 dedës in day] dede is in dayne MS; 41 medicine] medierne MS; 44 oft] of MS.

It was not unusual in medieval literature to sing the praises of a lady by evoking lists of comparisons (precious stones, flowers, birds, etc.; cf. **I, 3**, 50–57), but seldom in a manner as sustained as in this lyric. A rather loose form of the alliterative line is used: most half lines have two stresses, but some lines (e.g. 23 and 43) seem to have three in the first half. The only other Harley love lyric in alliterative form is **I, 22.**

9 *haveth*: perhaps to be read as *hath* here and in lines 48 and 49.

10 In conventional medieval descriptions of a beautiful lady, the parts of the body which are itemized as features of particular excellence include chin and face. Cf. **1, 25**, 34–6.

16 The alliterating pair *grei and gris* (both words mean 'grey', the former of English, the latter of French derivation) was commonly used in ME of fine garments of grey fur.

28–30 Courtly convention prevented a poet from naming his beloved; cf. **1, 4**, 10–11. Here, however, this poet (presumably John of line 30) plays with the convention by introducing the lady's name by means of a pun on *a note* (meaning 'a note' but implying the name Annot) in line 28 and again as *annote* in line 29, with the spelling *nn* confirming the pun.

34 *man secheth*: lit. 'one seeks'.

37–40 The comparisons must still be with the lady, but the mode of expression in these lines is highly elliptical.

38 *crone*: 'crown, head', here of a plant. 'The cummin is an umbelliferous plant and so has a conspicuous flower' (Brook, p. 76, note to line 38).

41 *of might*: a descriptive genitive; see Mustanoja, pp. 80–81. For *mercie* as an adjective, see *MED* **merci** n. (1), **11**.

42ff. The proper names in this stanza (some of them heroes and heroines of romance) have been traced in Germanic, Celtic and Romance sources. See Brown XIII, pp. 226–8. Doubtless the poet expected his audience to be familiar with those named and with their deeds and reputations. Thus *Cradoc* (47) was famous because he, alone among King Arthur's knights, succeeded in carving a boar's head, thereby proving the fidelity of his wife.

1, 6 Love is soft, love is swet [*NIMEV* 2009]

MS: Oxford, Bodl. Digby 86.

Text: 13 hath] had MS; 16 ansète] an wede MS; 22 gladhede] geddede MS.

24 *longdrei*: cf. *MED* **dri(e** adj. (2) 1. (b): 'lasting'.

1, 7 Though I can wittës ful-iwis [*NIMEV* 3512]

MS: London, BL Royal 8.D.xiii.

This poem is found jotted in pencil as prose in the margin at the top of fol. 25r. The text here is based on the transcription by Carleton Brown, who observes that 'in places the text is so nearly illegible that it can be deciphered only with difficulty, and the reading of a few letters is not certain' (Brown XIII, p. xii). I cannot make out anything before *I can* in line 1, and cannot be sure of many other readings, especially from line 8 on, as the MS copy is now so faint.

Text: 1 though] [þe]h þet (Brown XIII, p. xii); 2 non] nout MS; 5 that] þe MS; 8 thrivinge] þriminde (Brown XIII, p. xii).

I, 8   Were ther outher in this toun [*NIMEV* 3898]

MS: Oxford, Bodl. Rawlinson D.913.

Text: 15–16 *are based on the text as read by* Dronke (1961), p. 245.

For the text and interpretation of this lyric, see *Companion*, p. xvii and fn. 4.

I, 9   Of every kinnë tre [*NIMEV* 2622]

MS: Oxford, Bodl. Rawlinson D.913.

Text: 3 swetest] suotes MS; 7 every kinnë] euer[y k]inne MS, *so* Dronke (1961), p. 245.

I, 10   Al night by the rosë, rosë [*NIMEV* 194]

MS: Oxford, Bodl. Rawlinson D.913.

Text: 3 Dorst] darst MS, *so* Dronke (1961), p. 246.

The *rose* here is presumably a girl, the *flour* (4), her maidenhood.

I, 11   Al gold, Janet, is thin her [*NIMEV* 179]

MS: Oxford, Bodl. Rawlinson D.913.

I, 12   Dorë, go thou stillë [*NIMEV* 2288]

MS: Worcester, Cathedral Library Q.50.

Text: 3 That] þat *or* yat MS – *the initial letter may be* þ *or* y.

The *NIMEV* reference is to ten lines of verse (written as prose by a certain *Robertus seynte Mary Clericus*) which are now taken to be 'three unrelated scraps of song' (Sisam (1965), p. 245). The first 'scrap' consists of the intriguing words:

> Ne shaltou never, levedi,
>> Twynklen wyth thin eyen.
>>> Wilson (1970), p. 167

Dorë, go thou stillë is the third, and **I, 13** (below) the second 'scrap'.

3 Different interpretations of this poem arise from the alternative readings of the first word in line 3. Either, with the reading *That* 'until', the poet, on entering the chamber, bids the door be silent until his love-encounter is completed, or, with the reading *Yat* 'gate', he addresses first the chamber door and then the outside gate as he leaves after a fulfilling tryst.

I, 13   Ich have y-don al myn youth [*NIMEV* 2288]

MS: Worcester, Cathedral Library Q.50.

I, 14   So longe Ich havë, lady [*NIMEV* 3167.3]

MS: Berlin-Dahlem, Stiftung Preußischer Kulturbesitz, Staatsbibliothek theol. lat. fol. 249, fol. 131.

From the Latin words *Deum ad cor intrare volentem excludunt* (God wishing to enter the heart they exclude) which precede this little poem in the MS, it would seem that it was a devotional lyric on the theme of Christ the lover-knight seeking entry to man's soul (see I, 71 and Commentary); but it may originally have been a secular love lyric adapted to this devotional purpose. See Gray, *Selection*, p. 124.

I, 15   Bryd onë brerë [*NIMEV* 521]

MS: Cambridge, King's College Muniment Roll 2 W.32, with music. A facsimile is given in Saltmarsh (1935), opposite p. 3.

Text: 12 were] were were MS.

This song is irregular. Words, music or both may have been incorrectly copied. A second part in the music may be missing, to judge from a blank second stave above the first line of words; and it seems likely that in the second stave with music the scribe has written his clef sign on the wrong line. See F. McD. C. Turner, 'The Music of *Bryd One Brere*', in Saltmarsh (1935), pp. 19–20. However, attempts to regularize this lyric by the Sisams (*MEV*, p. 163) and especially by Dobson (*MES*, p. 183) are speculative and unconvincing. The MS text is followed here except in line 12 where the repetition of *were* has been omitted as it is by Robbins (*Sec.*, p. 147). Final '-e' is marked for pronunciation in the first stanza as required by the musical notation; and with final '-e' as marked in stanzas 2 and 3, the words can easily be fitted to the tune if one assumes, here and there, a slight alteration of the grouping of notes to syllables in these stanzas. Since this presents a modern performer with no difficulty, it is hard to believe that a medieval singer would have been any less capable of such modest flexibility.

1 Another instance of a poet addressing a *bryd one brere* is found in a scrap of ME verse:

> Bryd on brere y tell yt to
> none othur y ne dar.
>
> Greene, p. 491

2 The poet, responding to *Kind*, the law of nature within him, seeks love from Love, personified as is often the case in medieval literature. Perhaps the bird, possibly by association with the nightingale (a frequent representative of love in ME poetry as elsewhere) is here thought of as Love's representative and a confidant of lovers. Thus, in the rest of the stanza, the poet appeals to the bird for compassion.

3 *Blithful biryd*: Taken by some to be the poet's lady; but so abrupt a switch in address from the bird in line 1 is unconvincing, and the ambiguous spelling *biryd* of the MS cannot be taken to confirm the sense 'lady' (ME *birde*) rather than 'bird' (ME *brid*). Whatever the underlying senses that may be felt in this suggestive lyric, the immediate and overt sense here is that the poet continues his address to the *bryd onë brerë*.

I, 16   Foulës in the frith [*NIMEV* 864]

MS: Oxford, Bodl. Douce 139, with music. A facsimile is found in Wooldridge (1897), plate 7.

1 *Foulës*: The MS spelling is *foweles*. Since, however, the music for this word has two ligatured groups of notes in each part in this two-part song, the pronunciation *foulës*, with two syllables, is evidently required.

3 The sense (with *mon* as 'man') may also be: 'And I, a man, go mad', making the usual contrast in medieval lyrics between the springtime happiness of animals in matters of love and the miseries suffered by men. Cf. **I, 20, 32**, and Commentary.

I, 17   When the nyghtëgalë singeth [*NIMEV* 4037]

MS: London, BL Harley 2253.

24 *leche*: 'physician'. It is a common convention of medieval love literature that only the lady can heal the wounds of love, wounds so graphically described here in lines 5–8.

32 *waxë grene*: lit. 'grow green', i.e. become ill, in contrast with the flourishing woods of line 2.

33–4 Lincoln, Lindsey, Northampton and Lound are all located in the East Midlands.

38 *a stounde*: 'soon'. For *a stounde* with this sense, see *MED* **stound(e** n. 1b. (a), where **I, 51** (another Harley lyric), 94 is quoted.

39–40 In the MS this lyric is written in long lines. In this line, the division into two parts is indicated not only by rhyme (*song* and *y-long*) but also by a large *punctus elevatus* after *song*. This final stanza is thereby marked, not only by a departure from the rhyme scheme of the other stanzas but also by a change in rhythm. All the other long lines (as written in the MS) divide into two short lines of four stresses followed by three; here the rhythmic order is reversed to three stresses followed by four, thus emphasizing the finality of the concluding cadence.

I, 18   Bitwenë March and Avëril [*NIMEV* 515]

MS: London, BL Harley 2253.

The stanza form varies in this lyric: stanzas 2 and 3 are alike; stanzas 1 and 4 are similar, but differ in their fifth and sixth lines.

29 *in toune*: a conventional tag meaning 'anywhere' or, simply, 'alive'. Cf. **I, 2, 22**, and Commentary, **I, 3, 12**, and Commentary, and **I, 4, 39**, and Commentary.

35–6 The sense is that it is better to suffer the pangs of love for a time in the hope of ultimate success than never to endure the trials of love and, therefore, never to have any hope of attaining that one state, love, which, in troubadour thinking, made life worthwhile.

I, 19   In May it mirieth when it dawës [*NIMEV* 1504]

MS: London, BL Harley 2253.

Text: 43 lend] send MS.

1 & 5 The Northern or North-Midland endings '-es' of the 3 sg. present in *dawës* and 3 pl. present in *wowës* are kept for the rhymes with the plural nouns *plawës* and *bowës*.

2 *thise deerës plawës*: lit. 'the frolickings of these animals'.

15 *if felë falsë nere*: Not, as at first sight, 'if many women were not false', but, 'if many men were not false', as the following lines show. Throughout this stanza a certain initial ambiguity confronts the reader as to the identity of the subject. This was presumably the poet's intention; he may have been seeking to play upon the reactions of his audience, and perhaps especially of the ladies present. The basic argument, that women are less than perfect because men are false – ironically reversing the usual notion of women (through Eve) as the source of deception – is ostensibly the poet's way of excusing his beloved for whatever the problem may be (her susceptibility to the charms of other men?) which has come between them and which requires reconciliation (48). In terms of this argument the conclusion of the poem is itself ironic with the poet advising his beloved to trust him, a man!

17 Lit. 'where one (*me*) has tempted (*bed*) them to sinful conduct (*lastës*)'. The dialect form *bed* (equivalent to London English *bad*), past tense of *bidden*, 'to bid, request', meaning here 'to tempt, entice', is preserved for the rhyme.

19 *in londe*: cf. **I, 3**, 12, and Commentary.

20 Lit. 'though one (*me*) should give them (*hem*, i.e. women) a true pledge'; cf. line 22.

31 Lit. 'concerning fidelity it is nothing to the deceiver'.

43 *lend*: This emendation is suggested under *MED* **lenden** v. 2. (b), though the sense is rather that of 2. (a), 'go back'. Alliteration and excellent sense support *lend*; the common confusion of the letters 'l' and long 's' would readily explain *send* as a scribal error.

45 'And live with what she has got', i.e. either, in a general sense, the situation she has got herself into or, perhaps, the child she has got from an illicit union. Cf. **I, 22**, 33–6, and Commentary.

I, 20   Lenten ys come with love to toune [*NIMEV* 1861]

MS: London, BL Harley 2253.

Text: 6 hire] *added*; 11 wynne] wynter MS; 17 lufsom is] is lossom MS; 21 ther] þat MS; 22 don] doh MS; 28 on] *added*.

1 *to toune*: cf. **I, 2**, 22, and Commentary.

11 *wynnë*: 'of joys'. Here and in line 35 this is a genitive pl. form with the ending '-e' from the OE genitive pl. ending '-a'.

17 For the emended word-order, cf. *lufsom is*, **I, 25**, 10.

20 *Milës* (? from Welsh *mil* 'animal') occurs only here in ME. However, as Brook

notes, *wolc* and *crouþ* are other possible examples of Welsh loan-words in the lyrics of MS Harley 2253. See Brook, p. 80, note to no. 11, line 20.

21 The emendation *ther* assumes scribal corruption of *þer* to *þat*, possibly through the misinterpretation of a 'þ', with or without an abbreviation mark. Cf. **1, 25,** 17, where *þ* in the MS stands for *þat*. 'Animals gladden their mates as the stream flows softly there' is preferable to 'Animals gladden their mates as a stream that flows softly', a comparison which makes little if any sense.

29 *dernë rounës*: 'secret cries'. Along with the usual association of *derne* 'secret' with love, there is also here the notion of animal language as 'secret' in the sense of unintelligible to man. Cf. **1, 61,** 69–71.

32 Love, so easy and natural for animals (even worms!) in springtime, is, by bitter contrast, difficult and painful for man precisely because women become *wonder proude*! This conventional view of the disparity between the happy lot of animals and the misery endured by man is briefly and poignantly expressed in **1, 16.**

33 'So well it becomes them': a bitterly ironic comment on the haughtiness of women.

34 Lit: 'If the favour of one will be lacking to me'; *wantë* is an impersonal verb.

1, 21   As I me rode this endrë dai [*NIMEV* 360]

MS: London, Lincoln's Inn, Hale 135.

Text: 4 As I me rode this endrë dai] þis endre dai als i me rode MS; 8 clinge] clingges MS; 27 springeth etc.] sprink MS. This poem is written as prose on fol. 137v, the left-hand top corner of which is badly faded. The readings for *Nou springeth* (1), *playinge* (5) and *in* (14) are illegible, and for *Seigh* (6), *him* (9), *longinge* (9), and *singestou* (18), partly illegible.

'This graceful *chanson d'aventure* is one of the very earliest preserved in the carol-form.' (Greene, p. 487)

  1 'Now the twig is sprouting', i.e. now spring is here.
  8 'May the clod (earth, i.e. of the grave!) cling to him.'
  9 *Wo is him*: lit. 'woe is to him (who)'.
  25 *it shal him rewe*: an impersonal construction.

1, 22   In a fryth as I gan farë fremëde [*NIMEV* 1449]

MS: London, BL Harley 2253.

Text: 31 thou] þo MS; 33 hungren] hengren MS; 38 to kepen] *added*; 47 ofthunchëth] ofþunche MS.

  3 *glemëde*: The past tense form for the sake of rhyme, but the sense is simply 'gleams'.
  4 'Never was a living person so radiant'. Here, as with various other alliterating tags found in the Harley lyrics, *on gere*, literally 'in clothing', simply means 'alive'.

7 *hire gremëde*: an impersonal verb.

22 *by my myght*: lit: 'according to my power'.

33–6 The heartbreak, the social ostracism and the predicament of bearing a fatherless child are, as Woolf points out, 'strikingly reminiscent of the lyric genre of the complaint of the betrayed maiden' (Woolf (1969), p. 56).

37 The fact that the girl now speaks in two successive stanzas and that verbal linking of stanzas, found elsewhere in this poem, is lacking between lines 36 and 37, suggests the loss, at this point, of a stanza in which the male speaker may have warned against the miserable lot of the *mal mariée* (cf. **1, 26**), the girl married to a bad husband, the *wrecche ... so wroth* referred to in line 39. See Anderson (1980), p. 258.

39 'Than that I should marry so ill-tempered a wretch'. See *EMEVP*, p. 325, note to VIII F, line 39.

45 Since, as the girl regretfully observes, she is neither a witch nor a sorceress, she cannot escape her fate by shape-shifting, a reference, according to Woolf, to the *chanson des transformations*, a genre 'in which the maiden posits various shapes that she will assume in order to elude her suitor, and the suitor outwits her by inventing shapes for himself that will capture hers'. In illustration, Woolf (1969), p. 58, quotes the ballad of 'The Twa Magicians':

> Then she became a turtle dow,
> > To fly up in the air,
> And he became another dow,
> > And they flew pair by pair.

> She turned hersell into an eel,
> > To swim into yon burn,
> And he became a speckled trout,
> > To gie the eel a turn.

45/47 *ashunchë / ofthunchëth*: For rhymes involving words with unidentical unstressed endings such as '-e' with '-eth', '-es', etc., see *EMEVP*, p. 279, note to lines 83–4.

48 This line may be subtly ambiguous. The surface meaning is: 'Welcome (*leef* 'dear') to me would be a man without guile', a rueful comment on the artful suitor of this poem. However, following upon the girl's regrets at being a girl (47), the underlying sense of 'Gladly would I be a man, without question' (with the verb 'to be' understood) may be hinted at.

1, 23   As I stod on a day [*NIMEV* 371]

MS: London, College of Arms, Arundel 27.

Text: 2 medë] medwe MS; 8 rad] bad MS; 10 se] sey MS; 19 fet] feche MS; 28 she] a MS; 30 Why rewen] Wri wet MS.

1 The first line neither forms part of the first stanza nor does it alliterate. It may have been a later addition prompted by the popular 'As I etc.' opening of the *chanson d'aventure* tradition.

2 The alternative ME forms *mede* and *medwe* (derived from the oblique stem

mǣdw- of OE *mǣd*) are synonyms. Clearly *medë* is required by the rhyme rather than MS *medwe*.

6 *shredës*: For the rhymes here involving the unstressed endings '-es' and '-e', cf. **I, 22**, 45/47, and Commentary.

8 *rad on*: At best, any conceivable sense which might be made of the MS reading, such as 'she prayed on her book', would not only be strained but unparalleled; MED records no such use of *bidden* with the preposition *on*. Alliteration in this line could easily have prompted a scribe to write *bad* instead of *rad*, obviously the correct reading.

10–11 The sense is clearly: 'with a cry she spotted me; she would have run off if I had not been so near', and not, as with the MS reading *sey* 'say': 'with a cry she said to me (that) she would have run off, etc.' The girl does not speak at this point; the poet simply observes her startled reaction on seeing him. If *gan* (10) is rejected as a scribal addition, the rhymes may have been *sei(gh)*, past singular, 'saw', and *nei(gh)*; a short half-line *she me seigh* for 10b would parallel *al my speche* and *what I redë* in stanzas 2 and 3. Alternatively, since OE *nē(a)h(e)* gives rise to a variety of forms in ME, the rhyme here may have been of *se* 'see' and *ne* 'near', as adopted in the text.

15 *lyinges*: see MED **liinge** ger. (1) 1. (d) 'act of sexual intercourse'. Is there meant to be a saucy subtext in the girl's greeting?

17 The poet, assuming an air of gallantry and the manner of a courtly lover, proposes, as *hir man* (16), that version of refined love (*fin amor*) which is characteristically *derne*, that is, 'secret'.

19 *fet*: as the rhyme requires. The corrupt MS reading *feche* has arisen from association with the rhyme which follows.

20 *gospellëth*: This word is not recorded as a verb in MED.

27 *billen*: 'sing'? 'Peck' and 'blow' (a horn) are the senses given for this late ME verb under MED **bilen** v. (1). OED quotes 'bill' as in 'bill and coo' first from Shakespeare.

28 'She might choose you as chaste' – a wry joke! The MS form *a* is taken here as a weakened form of the feminine personal pronoun.

I, 24   My deth I love, my lyf Ich hate [*NIMEV* 2236]

MS: London, BL Harley 2253.

Text: 61 hom] *added*.

17 *clerk*: This word had a wide range of meanings in ME: an ecclesiastic, a parish priest, an ecclesiastic lower in rank than a priest, a person in minor orders, a scholar, a student, etc. The 'hende Nicholas' and 'Absolon, that jolif was and gay' of *The Miller's Tale* (CT, I, 3199 and 3339), not to mention 'jolly Jankin' (**I, 129**, 6), were all 'clerks' and ardent lovers.

38 *for no synne*: 'for any sin', i.e. no matter how wicked it would be.

47–8 The sense is not immediately clear. Perhaps the *fair biheste* refers to an exchange of vows on a previous occasion, the time when the *clerk* was happy (44), when the lovers kissed fifty times (46). The poet observes that such a *fair biheste*, a gracious promise, makes many a man hide his sorrow, i.e. his initial pangs of love-longing before the lady commits herself. But, alternatively, this may simply be a hint to the lady that a *fair biheste* from her now would 'hide', that is, dispel his present sorrows. Whether moved by such a hint, or rather, as the next stanza suggests, by the memory of their previous love, the girl, now, suddenly and dramatically, changes her attitude from scorn to affection.

I, 25   Moste I ryde by Rybbësdale [*NIMEV* 2207]

MS: London, BL Harley 2253.

Text: 29 she] *added.*

7ff. From this point there follows a detailed description of the lady from head to toe exactly in the manner advocated by medieval writers on the art of poetry in their accounts of how the description of a beautiful woman should be handled. An excellent example of this descriptive convention is found in the *Poetria Nova,* a treatise on poetics written in the early 13th century by the Englishman Geoffrey of Vinsauf. His model description begins with the head and, in order, details the following features: hair (golden), forehead (lily-white), eyebrows (dark and snow-white between), nose, eyes (shining), face (bright and rosy), mouth (gleaming), lips (red and warm), teeth (even), breath (fragrance like scent), chin (polished), neck (a milk-white column), throat (radiant as crystal), shoulders (even), arms (long and slender), fingers (long, straight, white), breasts (jewels side by side), waist (slender), leg (long and slender), foot (small and dainty). Following the account of the waist Geoffrey remarks: *Taceo de partibus infra: / Aptius hic loquitur animus quam lingua* (I am silent concerning the parts below; more aptly does the imagination speak at this point than the tongue). See Faral (1962), pp. 214–15, lines 562–99, translated in Murphy (1971), pp. 54–5. See also Brewer (1955). This lyric follows and exploits this medieval literary convention brilliantly; without the slightest sense of stiffness or cataloguing the sustained description flows easily within the verse form.

11 This line refers to the lady's complexion.

29 The addition of *she* (linking with *hire* in the previous and following lines) improves metre and sense. By common convention in medieval love poetry, it is the lady who condemns the poet to death, not Death (personified); cf. **I, 1,** 25, and **I, 2,** 39.

49–51 'When I gaze upon her hand, the lily-white one, dear in the land, the best (sc. of ladies) she might be'. The very perfection of her hands evokes the poet's ecstatic response to his lady, 'the lily-white one'.

75 The immediate sense is: 'like the Phoenix she is without equal'. Perhaps there is also the suggestion here that like the Phoenix, she is 'without a companion'.

79–80 See Geoffrey of Vinsauf, *Taceo de partibus infra,* etc., in the note to line 7ff. above.

I, 26   Alas, hou sholde I sing [*NIMEV* 1265]

MS: Kilkenny, Bishop's Palace, Red Book of Ossory.

I, 27   Weping hath myn wongës wet [*nimev* 3874]

MS: London, BL Harley 2253.

Text: 16 durfte] durþe MS; 48 on] on þat MS; 59 Soth] soþ is þat MS.

4 *bok*: the Bible?

7 *in song ... hem set*: i.e. written about them in poems.

16 'who had no need to ride us on reins (to show her mastery over us)', so Brook, p. 77, note to no. 6, line 16. This is an allusion to a legend, popular in the Middle Ages, in which Aristotle was humiliated by being bridled, saddled, and ridden like a horse by an Indian girl with whom he had fallen in love.

17–18 The *stythie* is the Virgin, often referred to as Queen of Heaven.

21–2 An image commonly found in medieval literature to express the great mystery of Christ being born of a Virgin: she remained as untouched by the natural concomitants of conception and childbirth as glass by the sun's rays. Thus the lines:

> As sunne shineth thurgh the glas,
> So Iesu in his moder was.

28 *chete*: 'hall'. Some editors adopt this gloss as what is required by the context: *Pearl*, line 184, *I stod as hende as hawk in hall*, is quoted in support of this view. However, *chete* is an uncommon word in ME, and elsewhere means 'cabin, cottage'; see *MED* **chete** n. (1). For a wholly different interpretation of *hende as hawk in chete* as 'courteous as a hawk in a hutch', see Ransom (1985), pp. 15–16, who takes this as one of many instances in this poem of ironic undercutting of the status of women.

32 *hem ... to fete*: 'at their feet', lit. 'to them ... at the feet'; *hem* is a dative of possession.

41 Brook (p. 78, note to no. 6, line 41) renders this line: 'Among the violent it would be peace to speak with them'.

43–4 'There is no king, emperor, or tonsured clerk who would seem to be humiliated by serving these seemly ones (i.e. women)', so Brook, p. 78, note to no. 6, line 43f.

58–60 As they stand in the MS, and as punctuated by Brook, these lines may be construed as: 'For nothing now, of necessity, is true which I have written of them'. But this reading contradicts the preceding lines, lines 55–7, in which the poet strongly denies (albeit 'when in difficulty'!) that he has ever maligned women, and adds: 'I would not and will not do so', line 57. It is noteworthy, however, that as it is found in the MS, line 59 is metrically suspect, having eight instead of six syllables. In a poem as deliberately and skilfully crafted as this, a metrical inconsistency of this order is questionable. I assume that in the MS reading of line 59, *is þat* after *soþ* has been added in error. If the line is read as: *Soth I of hem ha wroght*, the sudden, emphatic and rather surprising denial of lines 55–8, with lines 57–8 as 'I would not and will not do so for anything' (albeit again undercut by the ambiguous *nou, a nede*, 'now, of necessity'), reaches its logical climax in the claim, 'I have written the truth about them' (59). But why the qualification 'now, of necessity'? Is it because (however ironically) now (under pressure?) the poet dare not say anything against women, or because women are now self-evidently beyond reproach after the advent of the Blessed Virgin? Again, it is noteworthy that the claim, 'I have written the truth about them' (59), is corroborated by none other than Richard, the paragon of the final stanza. This Richard, however, is perhaps a dubious witness, as one whose success with ladies owes no little to charm (69–70). This blatant and ironic volte-face in the last two stanzas constitutes the brilliant final twist of a highly oblique and ironic poem.

66   *that craftës con*: lit. 'who has mastery of skills'.

I, 28   Now welcome, somer, with thy sonnë softe

MSS: Cambridge, University Library Gg.4.27 (C); Oxford, Bodl. Digby 181 (D); Oxford, St John's College LVII (J). For further details, see Benson, p. 1150, note on lines 680–92. Text based on C.

Text: 1 thy] *om.* C; 3 longe] large C; 10 synge] D, ben C.

This roundel is sung by the birds at the end of Chaucer's *Parlement of Foules* (680–92) as they depart with their mates.

I, 29   To Rosëmounde

MS: Oxford, Bodl. Rawlinson poet. 163. Facsimile in Skeat (1892), plate XII.

Text: 6 whan] whan that MS; 11 small] synall MS.

2   Sense: 'throughout the whole world'. The medieval *mappa mundi* presented the world as roughly circular in shape, surrounded at its circumference by ocean.
20   Tristan was the idealized lover of Isolde in medieval romance.

I, 30   Womanly Noblesse

MS: London, BL Add. 34360.

Text: 10 you] *added by* Skeat; 13 *as conjectured by* Furnivall *to supply the line missing at this point in the MS*; 16 loke how humblëly] how humbly MS, loke how humblely *as emended by* Skeat.

5   *womanly*: For the two syllables required by the metre, Skeat suggested emending to *wyfly*. Perhaps, however, the first two syllables *womanly* may, in a slurred pronunciation, be reduced to one to accommodate the metre here and at line 25, and similarly in *wommen my* in I, 18, 11.

I, 31   Canticus Troili

For MS and printed authorities, see Benson, pp. 1161–2. Text follows Benson, pp. 478–9.

These lines (*Troilus and Criseyde*, Book I, 400–420), which Troilus sings after falling in love with Criseyde, are a fairly close adaptation of Petrarch's 'S'amor non è', Sonnet 88 (in Vita), no. 132 in the Canzoniere. The 14 lines of the Italian sonnet are rendered in three seven-line rhyme royal stanzas to accord with the scansion of Chaucer's poem. However, the form of the sonnet is respected in that Chaucer gives two stanzas to the octave, and one stanza to the sestet of Petrarch's poem. With Chaucer, the Petrarchan sonnet is first found in English literature; it was not to appear in English again until the 16th century. See Gray (1983), p. 97.

I, 32   Against Women Unconstant

MSS: Oxford, Bodl. Fairfax 16 (F); London, BL Cotton Cleopatra D.vii (C); London, BL Harley 7578 (H); and Stowe's edition, 1561 (St). Text is based on F.

Text: 2 grace] your grace FCHSt; 7 & 14 thus may ye] thus may ye CHSt, *and line 21 in* F, ye may wel F; 8 as] CHSt, as in F; 12 his] CHSt, ay his F; 16 Bet] Better FCHSt; 17 stant] stondeth FCHSt.

7 Blue is the colour of fidelity, and green, that of infidelity.
11 The subject in this line may either be *feyth* or *herte*.
16 Delilah, who betrayed Samson; Criseyde, Troilus' unfaithful lover; Candace, a queen of India who tricked Alexander to get him into her power.
17 There is an implied comparison here with Lady Fortune, whose one constant attribute is her changeability.
20 *Alle lyght for somer*: The sense of this phrase may be that the lady is as changeable as the seasons, *light* ('bright', 'friendly', even 'wanton'?) in summer, but, by implication, also 'dark, hostile, cold' in winter, though the rest of the line hints at some further, more personal significance.

I, 33   Complaynt D'Amours

MSS: London, BL Harley 7333 (H); Oxford, Bodl. Fairfax 16 (F); Oxford, Bodl. Bodley 638 (B). Text is based on H.

Text: 8 doon] *om.* H; 12 thilkë] that H; 16 a] *om.* H; 24 sing] FB, say H; 29 in] *om.* H; 48 plesaunce] to plesaunce H; 54 that] *om.* H; 55 leftë] lefe H; 66 sorwës] FB, shoures H; 68 which] þe which H; 69 unkonnynge] FB, unknowynge H; 70 unto] to HFB; 75 shulle] ne shulle H; 77 lady dere] hert dere FB, lady so dere H; 82 Alwey in oon] FB, And I ay oon H.

12 *thilkë spitous yle*: perhaps Naxos, where Ariadne was deserted by Theseus.
26 *pitée and*: pronounced as two syllables: 'pi-tyand'.
70 *unto*: for metre.
76 The H reading could be kept either with the change of *unto* to *to* (cf. line 70) or by assuming a reduced pronunciation for the '-ed' of *pleyned*.
81 The star, so clear and bright in appearance, is Venus, the star of lovers.

I, 34   Merciles Beauté

MS: Cambridge, Magdalene College Pepys 2006.

Text: 1 Your yën two] Yowre two yen MS, *but* Youre yen etc., *when repeated in lines 6 and* 11; 36 ther] this MS. All repeated lines (i.e. lines 6–7, 11–13, 19–20, 24–6, 32–3 and 37–9) are abbreviated in the MS.

16 *Daunger*: an allegorical figure in the *Romance of the Rose* representing an attitude of disdainful rejection on the part of a lady towards her lover.

I, 35   A Balade of Complaynte

MS: London, BL Add. 16165.

I, 36   Miri it is while sumer i-last [*NIMEV* 2163]

MS: Oxford, Bodl. Rawlinson G.22, with music.

Text: 1 Miri] M *not completed* MS; 4 weder] e (1) *lost* MS; 5 is] *lost* MS; 7 fast *supplied*, MS *damaged*.

On music and versification, see Duncan (1994).

 1 *foulës*: MS *fugheles*. For the disyllabic form here, see Duncan (1994).
 6 This line might alternatively be taken to mean: 'and I with very great injustice'.

I, 37   Lavedy seynte Marie [*NIMEV* 1839]

MS: London, BL Add. 27909.

Text: 23 selde] selð *corrected from* sele MS.

At some point in the transmission of this poem stanza 8 (29–32) was accidentally omitted and then copied at the end of the poem, where it appears in the surviving copy. It is here restored to its correct place in the text. See Duncan (1992). This poem frequently echoes the *Poema Morale*, a poem which perhaps best characterizes the themes of the penitential tradition in early ME literature. Specific parallels are found in lines 3–4, 9, 10, 17, 18, 21, 24 and 25. See Patterson (1911), pp. 165–6.

As it survives this lyric is metrically irregular. It seems to begin as alliterative verse (*Làvedy seynte Màrie / mòder and mèdë*), but alliteration is not consistently maintained. At stanza 3 the metre seems to change to lines of 4 + 3 stresses (*Slèp me hàth my lȳf forstòlë / rìght half òther mòrë*), but nor is this structure sustained; some later stanzas vary considerably. Suggestions offered for the pronunciation of unstressed syllables are at best tentative: some final '-e's marked for pronunciation may have been silent or so treated by some readers.

 7–8 The poet seeks to escape from his many sins by 'going hence' from this life to 'whatever joy', the joy of heaven or (ironically) of purgatory or hell, God should decide.
 8 *whichërë*: The MS form is *hwuechere* (with 'w' written as wynn). Here '-ere' may be a survival of the OE dative sg. feminine inflexion. If taken as a reduced form of 'ever', this would be an exceptionally early occurence of 'whichever' which is first reorded in *MED* from Wyclif (a1382); see *MED* **which-ever** pron.
 9 *Slep*: The equating of sleep and the state of sin is a commonplace in penitential writings.
 11 The sense is that the poet intended to repent before it was too late, before, that is, the eternal sleep of death (cf. **1, 38**, 18), an idea continued in the next stanza.
 16 'If he does not do so, when he goes hence let his loins quake with fear', i.e. at

the prospect of eternal punishment. A vivid, if unpleasant, interpretation of the image here may well be appropriate; see *MED* **quaken** v. 1b. (c) 'of one's bowels or loins: to be stirred by fear, etc.'

36 *if hit me Crist y-youthë*: 'if Christ had granted it to me (to do so)'.

I, 38   Worldës blis ne last no throwë [*NIMEV* 4223]

MSS: London, BL Arundel 248 (A), with music; Oxford, Bodl. Rawlinson G.18 (R), with music; Oxford, Bodl. Digby 86 (D). Text based on A; lines 51–60 from R. Variant readings for English songs from before 1400 surviving in more than one MS are listed (with some inaccuracies) in *MES*.

Text: 23 The man] þe mon RD, þe A; 28 Er] ar RD, þar A; 37 *from* RD, *om. in* A; 51–60 *om. in* A, *text from* R; 53 and what] an R, wat is D; 54 and what (2)] and R, and wat D; 58 As … ben] ase þe dede and eke ded ben D, det al so an oþer det R; 65 Ich thee] I þe D, us ics A, hic R; 66 thee] þe RD, *om.* A.

This poem also echoes the 12th-century *Poema Morale*. See Brown, XIII, p. 201.

  5 *mid*: The form *mid* is kept here and elsewhere although by the late 14th century it had largely been displaced by *with*. This displacement is already found in D and R which have *wiþ* instead of *mid*. Likewise, in line 14, instead of *nim* D and R read *tak*, the Scandinavian borrowing which came in ME to replace the native verb.

  9 *this*: The spelling *þis* (for *þe is*) in A and R represents the elision required by the metre. D has *þat is*.

  33 *s'ofte*: Again, in A, the spelling *softe* represents the required elision. R has *so ofte*.

  35 A proverbial saying, cf. *Dere is boht þe hony þat is licked of þe þorne*, in the *Proverbs of Hendyng*.

  40 *into hellë*: The second syllable of *into* is lost by elision; this is more obvious in the MS spelling *into elle*.

  42 *pride and filth and mood*: 'pride', 'lust' and 'anger', three of the Seven Deadly Sins.

  52 Cf. **I, 60**, 116, and Commentary.

  58 For this line as emended, see *MES*, pp. 141–2.

I, 39   Man mai longe him livës wenë [*NIMEV* 2070]

MSS: Maidstone Museum A.13 (M), with music; Oxford, Bodl. Laud misc. 471 (L); London, BL Cotton Caligula A.ix (C); Oxford, Jesus College 29 (J). Text based on M. Quotations from this song appear in other works; see *MES*, p. 123. Variants for lines 43–50 have been accidentally omitted in *MES* (see p. 125). A transcription of the music by M. Bukofzer is given in Reese (1941), p. 243.

Text: 12 Ayein] þat may agein L, þat may ago CJ, a ȝlye *altered from* a slye M; 13 and shenë] and schene CJ, an siene M, ne sene L; 17 threting] þreting CJ, *originally* ne þratȝing M, weping L; 23 hedë] sede ML, seide CJ; 29 sho] scho CJ, soo L, swo M; 31 bi-knowë] bicnowe CJ, bicnowen L, biþenchen M; 33 foulë filth] fole fulþe CJ, felþe ML; 37–8 throwë / Doun] þrowen dun M, dun þr … L, adun þrowe CJ; 39 te] enden M, endi CJ, *lacuna in* L; 41 biswikëth] biswikeþ JCL, bipecheth M; 46

eft it wel] eft it sal M, eft hit JL, eft-zones hit C; 48 that] þat CJ, þanne L, þar M; 49 werkth] wurh M, wurcheþ CJ, a winnet L.

1 *livës wenë*: Here, as in OE, the verb *wene* takes the genitive: 'a man may often expect a long life for himself'. Lines 1–2 echo *The Proverbs of Alfred*, lines 108–9:

> Monymon weneþ þat he wene ne þarf,
> longes lyues, ac him lyeþ þe wrench.

2 'But the trick often deceives him'. The subject, *wrench*, comes at the end of the line.

15 *fox*: 'crafty', see *MED* **fox** n. **3.** As with *wither-clench* (12), the metaphor here probably derives from wrestling.

23 *do*: 'if you do', the conditional imperative; see Mustanoja, p. 477. For the emendation *hede*, see *MES*, p. 128.

35 The reduced forms *nastou* here and *wenst* in line 38 are adopted for the metre; the MSS have the full forms.

39 *te*: Dobson's emendation; see *MES*, p. 129.

46 *wel*: For this emendation, see *MES*, pp. 129–30. Dobson also notes that lines 45–6 are a quotation of a popular ME proverb found in the *Poema Morale*, *The Proverbs of Hendyng* and *The Ancrene Riwle*.

47 *wikëth*: 'serves'. The sense is: 'what a grievous service he does himself'; see *MES*, p. 130.

I, 40   On hire is al mi lif y-long [*NIMEV* 2687]

MSS: Cambridge, Trinity College B.14.39 (T); London, BL Cotton Caligula A.ix (C); Oxford, Jesus College 29 (J); London, BL Royal 2.F.viii (R). Text based mainly on T.

Text: 8 Ich biddë] CJR, we biddit T; mi] CJR, ure T; 20 evermo] euer mo J, eueremo C, heuer more T, hevre more R; 24 And aughte and] heyte and R, and heuir T, and prude and C, *lacking in* J; 26 Ich willë] yg wlle R, ich þenche C, we sulin T, *lacking in* J; sinnës] sunne C, ur sunnis T, henne R, *lacking in* J; 27 letë] R, alle C, *om.* T, *lacking in* J; my] R, mine C, ure T, *lacking in* J; 28 Ich biddë] CR, we biddit T, *lacking in* J; me bi-se] to me biseo C, us to seo T, þet ys so free R, *lacking in* J; 29 And helpë me] C, helpen hus R, þad con wissin T, *lacking in* J; 31 Thou art] þu art CJR, heo is T; 32 helpëst] CJ, helpe R, helpit T; 33 Thou] þu CJR, ho T; hast] hauest CJR, hauet T; 34 Thou] þu CJR, ho T; 35 broughtëst] brohtest CJR, brutis us T; 42 and] R, an C, a T, *lacking in* J; 43 lavëdi] leuedi C, suete leuedy R, lauedi brit T, *lacking in* J; 44 fecchë] C, vezge (*or* vezge) R, wecche T, *lacking in* J; 47 drecchë] CR, letten T, *lacking in* J; 48 For] CR, of T, *lacking in* J; 49 this lif] þis world C, my lif T, lyues R, *lacking in* J.

3 *Him*: The T reading *him* (CJR *hire*), not listed in *MES* (see p. 132), may be right. The poet 'sings' of Mary but celebrates *ther-amonge* Jesus who saved us from hell. Accordingly, in line 9, the reading *he* of T is 'He' and not 'she' as required if *hire* of the other MSS at line 3 is accepted. Thus, it is Christ (not Mary) who gives a good ending; Mary's role is to intercede for such. Cf. **I, 37,**

42–4 and **1, 46**, 81–8. Although such a theologically correct interpretation may be appropriate in what is essentially a penitential lyric, this poem opens as if it were a Marian devotional lyric, and it is easy to see how a change of *him* to *hire* in line 3, making Mary the focus of the whole stanza, could have taken place; it would not, perhaps, have seemed out of place to beseech her, the Queen of Heaven, to grant us a good ending.

8 It seems preferable to continue here in the first person singular as in CJR.

18 *nis worth a slo*: This is a ME equivalent to the modern English idiom 'not worth a bean'.

20 *evermo*: The rhyme requires '-mo' as the final syllable. Perhaps the reduced form *ermo* (cf. *ermor* in Robbins, *Sec.,* no. 60, line 2) is to be understood, as four syllables are required in this line.

23 This line should perhaps be read with the '-ed' of *y-loved Ich* and the '-en' of *gamen and* reduced by syncope.

26–8 Again, the first person singular forms of the other MSS are adopted.

35 *Thou*: In T, *Thou* comes as an abrupt change after the third person singular forms of lines 31–4. In the other MSS (followed here) the Virgin is addressed from the beginning of the stanza.

48 *sinne*: pl. 'sins'. The variant ME plural endings '-e', '-es' and '-en' are all represented in the MSS: *svnne* R, *sunnes* C and *sunnin* T. The final '-e' of R allows for the desired elision here and is therefore adopted in the text. Cf. **1, 46**, 61, and Commentary.

1, 41   Ech day me cometh tydinges thre [NIMEV 695]

MS: Oxford, Jesus College 29. There are many other versions.

Brown gives an account of various other versions of this text (one of which is given here as **1, 42**) and quotes the following Latin version from MS Oxford, Bodl. Ashmole 1393:

> Sunt tria que vere faciunt me sepe dolere.
> Est primum durum quia scio me moriturum:
> Secundum timeo, quia tempus nescio quando;
> Unde magis flebo, quia nescio quo remanebo.

He considers the Latin 'to be a translation of the corresponding English verses, rather than their source' (Brown, XIII, pp. 171–3).

2 *he*: This non-London form of the plural pronoun 'they' is retained here for the rhyme.

1, 42   Whan I thenkë thingës thre [NIMEV 3969]

MS: London, BL Arundel 292. There are many other versions.

6 *ne wot*: Metrically the line may read as / × × / × / × /, or, with syncope of *whider I,* as / × / × / × /. However, it may well be that *ne wot* should be *not*; cf. *not* in line 4.

I, 43   If man him bithoughtë [*NIMEV* 1422]

MS: London, BL Arundel 292. There are many other versions and variants.

According to Carleton Brown, this poem 'seems to be the original from which a variety of others developed' (Brown, XIII, p. 173). A closely related version is used as the concluding lines of the following poem (**1, 44**) on the signs of death. Like **1, 44** and **45**, this is one of several short poems the scansion of which is described by Woolf as 'quick-moving, metrically free, two-stressed couplets' (Woolf, p. 78).

> 3–4 A reference to the custom of removing the body at death from the bed to lie on the floor before burial.

I, 44   Whan mine eyen mistëth [*NIMEV* 3998]

MS: Cambridge, Trinity College B.1.45. There are other versions.

Metrical lists of the signs of death are found in Latin as well as in ME. The English tradition may well derive from the OE period; such a list is found in the 'Address of the Soul to the Body' (?11th century) recorded in the 12th-century *Worcester Fragments*.

> 5–6 The rhyme with the third singular *slakëth* shows that the MS form *blaken* (6) is a corruption of the alternative plural form *blakëth*. The Southern '-eth' plural ending, a minority late 14th-century London form, has been restored in lines 1, 2, 6, 11 and 12; the sustained '-ëth' endings of the rhyme words lend added force and cohesion to this rhetorical catalogue of the signs of death.
> 16 See Commentary, **1, 43**, 3–4.

I, 45   Whan the turuf is thy tour [*NIMEV* 4044]

MS: Cambridge, Trinity College B.14.39.

This brief lyric is preceded in the MS by the Latin text of which it is a translation.

I, 46   Whan Ich thenche on domës-day [*NIMEV* 3967]

MSS: Cambridge, Trinity College B.14.39 (T); London, BL Cotton Caligula A.ix (C); Oxford, Jesus College 29 (J); Oxford, Bodl. Digby 86 (D). Text based mainly on T.

Text: 6 thoughtës] þoȝtes CJ, þonc T, worde D; 13 the] þe DJ, þat C, þed T; 21 nought] noht CDJ, noþinc T; 29 And riden] JC, riden DT; 36 non other] non oþer CJ, none DT; 37 ther] þer CJ, *om.* DT; 40 her] heore CDJ, þat hore T; 41–56 *Stanza order as in* CJ; *in* DT *stanzas 6 and 7 are in reverse order*; 42 ofkendë] CJ, kende D, inne kennede T; 44 him] hine T, he CDJ; 61 sinne] sunnen CDJ, sunnes T; 71 Ther you] þer ow CDJ, þer inne T.

> 8 *what shal me to redë*: lit: 'what shall (be) for me an advisable course of action?', i.e. what shall I do?
> 18 *bemë*: The ME plural form with final '-e' (*beme* CJ, *bemen* T) is kept as required for the rhyme.

28 *fou and gray*: a kind of particoloured fur associated with lavish display; see *MED* **fou** adj. 2.

30 *palëfray*: a fine riding horse as opposed to a war horse; see *MED* **palefrei** n. (a).

39–40 The sense is: 'only their good deeds will act as advocates for them'; see *MED* **beren** v. (1) **1.** (e).

46 *to litel we hire sendë*: The sense is: 'too little did we send (petitions, prayers) to her (for help)'.

56 With *heo* (the form of the plural pronoun in T) the final '-e' of *late* (here) and of *Alle* (in line 63) would, of course, have elided.

57ff. The Judgement scene as described in this and the following stanzas would have been familiar to the medieval reader from the vivid depictions to be found in stained glass, in paintings, and especially in the tympanum over the west door of many a cathedral or church.

61 *sinne*: Again a plural form with '-e', which elides with the following *y-writen*, is preferable to the endings of *sunnes* (T) and *sunnen* (CJ). Cf. Commentary, I, **40**, 48.

67 *frends*: The T reading *frents* suggests that a reduction of the ending '-es' following a monosyllabic stem was already possible in the 13th century. C, D and J have the endingless plural form *freond*.

75 *Goëth*: probably pronounced as two syllables; cf. *gooid* T.

82 *alrë*: The early ME ending '-re' derives from the OE '-ra' inflexion of the genitive plural of the adjective. In J *alre* has become *alle*. In later ME, forms of *alre* only survived in compounds, as in Chaucer's *alderbeste* 'best of all'.

I, 47   Where ben they before us weren [*NIMEV* 3310]

MSS: Oxford, Bodl. Digby 86 (D); Oxford, Bodl. eng. poet. a.1 [Vernon MS] (V); London, BL Harley 2253 (H); Oxford, Bodl. Laud misc. 108 (L); Edinburgh, NLS Advocates 19.2.1 [Auchinleck MS] (A). Text based on D.

Text: 7 They] þei VA, huy L, hue H, *om.* D; 33 Nether thee hath] þere neþere þe haueþ D, adoun þe haþ A, adoun haþ þe H, haueȝ þe ene L, V lacks.

Originally part of a longer poem known as the 'Sayings of St Bernard', these verses appear in the Digby and Auchinleck MSS as an independent lyric. In Digby, *Vbi sount qui ante nos fuerount* (Where are those who were before us) appears as a title to this poem.

14 *That trailing*: i.e. trailing of long splendid robes.

22–3 The words *ay* and *o* are both adverbs meaning 'ever, always', commonly combined in the ME phrase *ai and o*; they are also exclamations of grief. The word *wy* is both a form of the interrogative 'why' and an exclamation meaning 'alas'; see *OED* **Wi**, *int. Obs.* Line 23, reduplicating the punning *ay* and *o* of line 22, is unique to MS Digby 86. Such exclamations vividly recall the anguished faces and cries of woe of medieval depictions of the tormented in hell.

25 *then*: This marks the turning-point in the poem from the *Ubi sunt* motif to the preaching based on it.

26 *that man thee bit*: lit. 'that one requires of you'.

37 By the staff is meant the cross, used as a weapon in this holy war against the devil. This and the following stanza echo Paul's account of the 'whole armour of God'; see Eph. 6:11ff.

40 *He it*: These words may be elided and pronounced as 'hyit'.

43 Cf. Eph. 6:16: 'Above all, taking the shield of faith, wherewith ye shall be able to quench all the fiery darts of the wicked'.

47 *that word*: i.e. a word meaning 'surrender', whatever the actual word may have been that the poet had in mind.

I, 48   No more ne will I wiked be [*NIMEV* 2293]

MS: Oxford, Bodl. Digby 2.

3 *folës*: a plural form as indicated by the MS plural ending '-en'.

7 *Frer menour*: a friar of the Franciscan order.

I, 49   Lord, thou clepedest me [*NIMEV* 1978]

MS: Oxford, New College 88.

On scansion, see Duncan (1994).

In the MS this lyric is preceded by the following passage from St Augustine's *Confessions* (VIII, v, 12) of which it is a close translation: *Non erat quid responderem tibi …, nisi uerba lenta & sompnolenta: 'modo, ecce modo, sine paululum.' Sed 'modo & modo' non habebant modum & 'sine paululum' in longum ibat.*

1 *clepedest*: This is the MS spelling; perhaps a reduced pronunciation such as 'cleptest' was to be understood in reading the line.

5–6 For emendation of the rhyme words to *endëles* and *wes* thus restoring in this ME translation the past tense of the Latin *ibat*, see Duncan (1996), pp. 231–3.

I, 50   Lullay, lullay, litel child, why wepëstou so sore? [*NIMEV* 2025]

MS: London, BL Harley 913.

Text: 4 of yore] ʒore MS; 6 evermore] euer MS; 8 wore] were MS; 25 it betidëth] betidiþ MS; 31 what thou] whan þou MS; 46 thy] þe MS; 47 it wil turne] turne MS; 48 to wele] wele MS; 54 horn] horre MS; 55 adoun] dun MS; 66 by north other by est] norþ oþer est MS. In lines 1, 21, 33, 45, 57 and 69 the second *lullay* is abbreviated to '.l.', and in line 9, is omitted.

This is the first English lullaby. It is different from other ME lullabies in that the baby addressed here is a human child, not the Christ-child. Woolf quotes lines 13–16 of I, 81 in support of the view that traditionally 'the subject-matter of a lullaby was often a prophecy of the baby's future (presumably a romantic promise of great and happy achievements)' (Woolf, p. 151). In this melancholy poem, however, the mother offers only grimly moralizing predictions for her child in the light of such common themes as the three last things (cf. I, 41 and 42), the legacy of Adam, and the malign operations of Fortune, all familiar to ME moral lyrics. The scribe copied this poem in long lines and marked the division of each line with a point or a *punctus elevatus*. The line division is adopted in the text. Exceptionally, in the case of lines 3–4 and 5–6, the scribe, following the sense, divides his long line to give a shorter first part. In line 31, an extra point is inserted after *comest* – again following the sense. Though not marked, the final '-e's at the end of some lines may have been sounded.

20 The final '-es' of *Adames* may have been reduced here and in line 55.

37–40 Here 'this world' is responsible for the changes attributed to Lady Fortune in the closely parallel lines of **I, 58**.

39 *he*: Despite *it* in the previous and following lines, the world seems suddenly to be personified here.

47 *it wil turne*: The MS reading *þou nost whoder turne* of this line means 'Thou knowest not which way to turn'; only by an implausibly oblique ellipsis could it be taken to mean 'Thou knowest not which way it will turn', the required sense, since the reference is to Fortune's wheel. As emended, lines 47–8 conform to the pattern of 4 + 3 stresses of the majority of lines.

54 *horn*: For this emendation and the alteration of the forms of the rhyme words in lines 50, 52 and 56 from the MS readings *ibor*, *bifor* and *befor*, see *MEV*, p. 578. For the notion of Death summoning man with a trumpet blast, see Woolf, p. 354 and fn. 3.

58 Lit: 'So woe to thee became Adam'.

65–6 With only nine syllables, the MS reading of these lines (one long line in the MS) is metrically anomalous. Support, albeit slight, for the speculative emendation adopted here *metri causa* may be claimed from the common currency in ME of such phrases as 'by north and by south'. See *MED* **north** n. **1.** (b). Also cf. **I, 3, 46**.

I, 51   Hye Loverd, thou here my bone [*NIMEV* 1216]

MS: London, BL Harley 2253.

The stanzaic structure of this poem is varied with its alternation of twelve- and five-line stanzas ending with two five-line stanzas.

10 *wont*: MS *woned*. Reduced forms were current in the 14th century. See *OED* **Wont**, *pa. pple.*

15 The old man is a mere nobody; erstwhile accustomed to move in high places, he is now reduced to enduring insults as, stuck by the fire, he seems useless, a creature who simply takes up space.

27 For the roe in ME as a symbol of wildness, see *MED* **ro** n. (1) (c). Also, cf. Commentary, **I, 1, 17**.

38 *inwith walle*: castle walls are meant. The sense is: 'one who formerly was most lively in the courtly company of the castle'. Now (39–40) he has 'fallen under foot' and may no longer 'clasp any finger', that is, enjoy dalliance with courtly ladies.

54 *wonde*: MS *wonede*. The reduced form may have been understood as metrically preferable. Cf. line 10, and comment above.

63 *wenen*: The change to the present tense is continued in the next stanza; temptations are not yet entirely a thing of the past. Here, however, the present tense may also signal an ironic comment by the old man for whom, doubtless, sloth and sleep are indeed now all too frequent companions.

64 *to wene*: '(to be) attracted'. For the passive use of the infinitive in ME, see Mustanoja, pp. 519–21, and cf. *to mene* (66) and *to calle* (82).

66 *Mannë*: the historical form of the genitive plural from OE *manna*.

85 *heved hount*: 'head hound' or 'chief huntsman'; see Brook, p. 81, note to no. 13, line 85.

95 'One who long has yearned for passion.' The sense of the rare word *yokkyn* (MS *ȝokkyn*) is uncertain. Brook, in his glossary, gives its meaning as 'desire, craving'.

I, 52 Wynter wakenëth al my care [*NIMEV* 4177]

MS: London, BL Harley 2253.

4 *cometh*: A reduced pronunciation 'comth' is essential for the metre; the fourth line of each stanza is of six syllables in this poem.

I, 53 Nou shrinkëth rose and lylie-flour [*NIMEV* 2359]

MS: London, BL Harley 2253.

Text: 1 shrinkëth] skrnkeþ MS; 39 other] oþer eny MS; 41 hir] his MS; 46 be] be hir MS; 47 any man] eny MS; 58 me] vs MS.

13 *folie*: In ME this word could mean 'lechery, fornication, adultery'; see *MED* **folie** n. **2.** (b).

41 *plaster*: In the medical sense a 'compress made from herbs, meal, or other substance, often applied on a cloth to the affected area'; see *MED* **plastre** n. **1.** (a). Here it is used figuratively as 'remedy'.

46 The five joys of the Virgin.

47 *any man*: 'any one'; cf. *any man,* **I, 4** (another Harley lyric), 1.

51–9 There may be a line missing in this stanza; it has only nine lines whereas the other stanzas have ten. However, several Harley lyrics have final stanzas which differ from their other stanzas. Cf. **I, 2** and **17**.

55 The point of thinking of Christ's torment on the cross for mankind's salvation is, of course, that such meditation should evoke an appropriate response of penitential gratitude.

I, 54 Middelerd for man was mad [*NIMEV* 2166]

MS: London, BL Harley 2253.

Text: 29 thar] darþ MS; 37 shal] he shal MS; 43 him] *added*; 58 meint] meind MS; 71 afore] byfore MS.

Final '-e' is frequently pronounced within the line and may well have been sounded in rhyme words in this poem. If so, in the rhyme scheme masculine a-rhymes would contrast with feminine b-rhymes in every stanza until the last where all the rhymes would be feminine.

3 *This edi*: Probably Christ, who earned heaven for us, is meant.

5 *blissë bedel*: perhaps John the Baptist with his call to repentance or, more generally, any preacher proclaiming the joy of salvation and the terror of Doomsday – a fitting introduction to a poem which is, in effect, a sermon in verse on the theme of temptation, sin and final judgement.

20 *hovëth*: 'proceed, go'; see *MED* **hoven** v. (1). 3.

23 The traditional three foes of man are the World, the Flesh and the Devil. Lust (the Flesh) is the poet's main concern. Only at line 49 does he turn to *this worldës won* (the World), and at line 62 to *the fend* (the Devil).

23ff. The a-rhymes here depend on the vowel sound required for *theo* (MS *þeo*), a Western variant of the pronoun *þo* 'those', a sound similar to that of the vowel 'ö' in German 'schön'. This was a Western dialect pronunciation not found in 14th-century London English nor, indeed, in present-day English. The vowel spellings of all four rhyme words have been left as they appear in the MS; the 'eo' and 'oe' of *theo* and *floe* will alert the reader to the unfamiliar requirements of these rhymes.

25 *broerli*: a reduced form of *brotherli*; see *MED* **brotherli** adj. and compare the more recent reduction of 'brother' to 'brer' in Brer Rabbit. Brook's emendation to *broþerli*, with its extra syllable, is metrically suspect.

28 The association of restlessness with the reed is conventional.

29 'The assault of other (senses) need he not flee.' The MS form *darþ* (in form derived from OE *dear* with the addition of an analogical 3 sg. '-þ') clearly means 'need' and reflects the ME confusion in meaning and form of the reflexes of the OE verbs *þearf* 'need' and *durran* 'dare'. The equivalent in Chaucer's English is *thar*.

54 *casten ... colde*: see *MED* **colde** adv. (b) 'unfeelingly' and **casten** v. 24. (a) 'destine'.

64 *folkës fader*: i.e. Adam.

74 'When trumpets blow this summons for him', i.e. on the Day of Judgement.

I, 55   Erthe tok of erthe erthe wyth wogh [*NIMEV* 3939]

MS: London, BL Harley 2253. Some 40 other MSS contain versions (some considerably expanded) of these popular verses.

This ironic, epigrammatic, riddle-like poem is a punning elaboration of the Biblical text, *Memento homo quod cinis es et in cinerem reverteris* (Remember man that thou art dust and to dust thou shalt return), used in the Ash Wednesday liturgy. It offers a satirically brief, reductive view of man's existence, of his birth (in sin), marriage (or accumulation of wealth) and death.

I, 56   Wrechë man, why art thou prowde [*NIMEV* 4239]

MS: Oxford, Bodl. Rawlinson C.670; also in other (mostly *Fasc. Mor.*) MSS.

I, 57   Was ther never caren so loth

MS: Oxford, Bodl. Rawlinson C.670; also in other *Fasc. Mor.* MSS.

These verses are preceded in the *Fasciculus Morum* by a Latin quatrain beginning *Vilior est humana caro quam pellis ovina* (Man's flesh is viler than the skin of sheep), along with a comment from St Bernard which (in translation) runs: 'When a man dies, his nose grows cold, his face turns pale, his nerves and veins break, his heart splits in two. Nothing is more abhorrent than his corpse: it is not left in the house lest his family die; it is not thrown into the water lest it become polluted; it is not hung in the air lest it become tainted; but it is thrown in a ditch like deadly poison so that it may not be seen any further, it is surrounded with earth so that its stench may not rise, it is firmly trodden down so that it may not rise again but stay, earth in earth, and the eyes of man shall not behold it any further.' (*Fasc. Mor.*, p. 99) The mention of sister and brother, father and son is reminiscent of the *Poema Morale*.

I, 58   The Lavëdi Fortunë is bothe frend and fo [*NIMEV* 3408]

MS: Cambridge, University Library Oo.7.32; also in other (mostly *Fasc. Mor.*) MSS.

These verses also appear in a French translation. Their traditional, proverbial character is confirmed by the words *Unde de illa Fortuna est antiquum proverbium sic canens* (Whence there is an old proverb about Lady Fortune, which goes thus) which introduce the version found in the *Fasciculus Morum*. See *Fasc. Mor.*, pp. 330, 331. Also, cf. **I, 50**, 37–44.

I, 59   Kynge I syt and loke aboute [*NIMEV* 1822]

MS: Oxford, Bodl. Rawlinson C.670; also in other (mostly *Fasc. Mor.*) MSS.

In the *Fasciculus Morum* these verses follow a version of *The Lavëdi Fortunë* (**I, 58**). The Latin text they render is an expansion of inscriptions often found on representations of Fortune's wheel, and, along with some words of introduction, is translated by Siegfried Wenzel as follows:

> Therefore we must not grieve about the loss of temporal goods of fortune, which now are here, now are gone, now abound, now fail, just as various people are depicted as rising and falling on that wheel turned by Lady Fortune. The first of them, sitting on top, says:
>
>> As king I rule; perhaps I lose my realm tomorrow.
>
> The second:
>
>> Alas, I was a king. What use is what I loved?
>
> The third:
>
>> Shortly ago I was rich; now hardly I cover my limbs.
>
> And the fourth:
>
>> I shall be king when you, o wretch, will go to death.
>
> *Fasc. Mor.*, p. 333

8 'When the wretch is dead'. The 'wretch' is the present king (still at the top of

Fortune's wheel) whose death will make way for the speaker's succession (a further turn of the wheel). Instead of the definite article some MSS have the second singular pronoun: 'When thou, wretch, dead shall be'.

1, 60   Whan men ben meriest at her mele [*NIMEV* 3996]

MSS: Oxford, Bodl. eng. poet. a.1 [Vernon MS] (V); London, BL Add. 22283 (A). Text based on V.

Text: 10 on] men on V, men A; 22 they] he is VA; 33 sodenly] so sodeynly VA; 40 strengthe] his strengþe VA; ne] he VA; 51 Ne] Þat þei ne VA; 56 kinde] so kynde VA; 70 couchëd] chouched V, chaunged A; 95 among] among A, a mon V; 146 other (2)] oþur A, or V.

This and **1, 61** which follows are two of a collection of moralizing refrain poems known as the Vernon lyrics.

Here, as in other Vernon poems, although the scansion is fairly regular, there is a small but significant minority of lines with extra weak syllables. Other lines could be read with or without such an extra syllable depending on the interpretation of forms such as *thinges* (6), *hertes* (9), *mirthes* (14), *warnynges* (55), *hertes* (66), *wiles* (94), *purveyed* (151), *Godes* (165), *unwarned* (170), and *poyntes* (177); and reduced spellings, e.g. *tornd* (*turned* A) and *tempt* (*tempted* A) in lines 24 and 134, occur sufficiently frequently here and in other texts as to suggest that many such words may have been read with reduced endings.

10   The A reading could reflect an original *richest men a rai* with *a rai* representing *of rai*, 'in clothing'; see *MED* **rai(e** n. (1) (c). However, the text adopted here assumes an original *richest of array* with *men* of the MSS viewed as a superfluous addition.

12   One should not be thoughtlessly absorbed in the present but should rather reflect on the past and draw appropriate conclusions. The import is similar to that of the *ubi sunt* topos.

20   *Morwe*: the dawn personified; cf. *Slep* (18) and *Deth* in the final two stanzas. The pronoun *he* is used pleonastically; see Mustanoja, pp. 137–8.

21   'They all become a figment of the imagination', i.e. as if they had never been. For the reflexive *drawe hem*, see *MED* **drawen** v. 3b. **refl.**

21   *fantasyse*: Brown supplies the ending '-yse' (V '-ye', A '-ie') for the sake of rhyme. *MED*, however, records no such form.

22   In the light of the plural *al drawe hem* in line 21, the reading *he is* (both MSS) must be erroneous.

24   'For all is changed to yesterday', i.e. as if it had never been.

25   *whose*: perhaps monosyllabic; cf. Commentary, **1, 61**, 11.

52   *wynde*: 'puff of wind', perhaps an ironic reference to the fleeting breath of the man now dead on the bier.

53   Such common alliterative phrases tend to be semantically vague. The sense here may well be: 'nor anyone so resolute as to stand his ground or stare unflinchingly', i.e. to look the world in the face; see *MED* **stinten** v. 3. (a) and **staren** v. 1. (a).

74 *halt*: MSS *holdeth.*

77 *though*: For the sense 'if' as required here, see *OED* **Though** adv. and conj. 4.c.

116 Medieval books of moral instruction were often called 'mirrors'. The understanding was that just as a man may order his appearance in a mirror, so too he can correct his morals in the mirror of a book of instruction or from the mirror of life. Cf. Commentary, **II, 100**. Here the latter reflects the example of the good deeds (acts of mercy) of others. Cf. **I, 38**, 51–4.

I, 61   I wolde wite of sum wys wight [*NIMEV* 1402]

MSS: Oxford, Bodl. eng. poet. a.1 [Vernon MS] (V); London, BL Add. 22283 (A). Text based on V.

Text: 57 wane] wanteþ VA; 63 bos] hos VA; 85 wit] witte A, wittes V; 99 list us] lust us A, lustnes V.

For the restoration of the fifth stanza (49–60), which comes at the end of the poem in both MSS, to its proper place, see Burrow (1977), p. 250. A similar error of scribal transmission occurred in **I, 37**. Again in this Vernon lyric (as in **I, 60**, above), the scansion is fairly regular, but some lines have extra syllables, e.g. line 6, which, as it stands in both MSS, has at least ten syllables.

In developing the theme of the vanity of human life, this poem draws considerably on Ecclesiastes and other Biblical sources.

6 The metre could be improved here by reading *Now be we on benche, now on bere* assuming that *be we* had mistakenly been repeated after *now* in the second half of this line.

11 *whos*: 'whoso'. This, the spelling in V (A has *whose*), suggests a monosyllabic pronunciation.

12 The refrain line varies. It is usually of nine or ten syllables, but sometimes it is shorter, the same length as the other lines.

13–17 Cf. Eccles. 1:5–7: 'The sun also ariseth, and the sun goeth down, and hasteth to his place where he arose. The wind goeth toward the south, and turneth about unto the north; it whirleth about continually, and the wind returneth again according to his circuits. All the rivers run into the sea; yet the sea is not full; unto the place from whence the rivers come, thither they return again.'

21 Cf. Eccles. 1:4, quoted below.

25–6 Cf. Eccles. 1:4: 'One generation passeth away, and another generation cometh: but the world abideth for ever.'

29 Cf. Eccles. 1:11; 2:16; 9:5–6.

43 Mats, commonly made of rushes, straw, or the like, were readily disposable and relatively worthless.

61–8 Cf. Eccles. 3:19–21: 'For that which befalleth the sons of men befalleth beasts; even one thing befalleth them: as the one dieth, so dieth the other; yea, they have all one breath; so that a man hath no preeminence above a beast: for all is vanity. All go unto one place; all are of dust, and all turn to dust again. Who knoweth the spirit of man that goeth upward, and the spirit of the beast that goeth downward to the earth?'

63   'And both must endure the same death.' The form *bos* (MSS *hos*) is a Northern and North Midland 3 sg. present of the verb *bihoven*, 'to be obliged (to do something)'; see *MED* **bihoven** v. 1c. (b). It may well have been unfamiliar to the scribes.

I, 62   Fortune

See Benson, p. 1188 for the textual authorities, 10 MSS and the editions of Caxton (1477–8) and of Thynne (1532). The text is based on MS Cambridge, University Library Ii.3.21.

Text: 51 it thee] to thee MS; 65 th'execution] excussyon MS; 77 And] That MS, And *most other copies*. After line 64 the MS reads *Le pleintif*; a similar error is found in all copies.

See Benson, p. 1084 for variant readings and different interpretations of the French subtitle. The ideas of this poem are largely derived from Book 2, proses 1–4 and 8 of *The Consolation of Philosophy* by Boethius. For detailed references to *Boece* (Chaucer's translation), and to *The Romance of the Rose* (also partly translated by Chaucer), see Robinson (1957), p. 860.

7   This line is quoted as a *newe Frenshe song* in the *The Parson's Tale*, X, 248.
10   That poverty, the result of adverse fortune, shows a man who his true friends are, is a Boethian theme widely echoed in medieval literature.
11   The reference is to Fortune's wheel.
32   *bestë frend*: Possibly a reference to a passage in the famous 13th-century French allegorical poem, *The Romance of the Rose*, where Friend explains to the Lover that when Poverty had banished his friends,

> … Fortune straightway in their stead bestowed
> The open-faced, true love of one real friend.
>
> Robbins (1962), p. 163, 64–5

Alternatively, the reference may be to King Richard II, as is probably the case in line 78.
43   *quene*: In ME this word means both 'queen' and 'harlot', both applicable to Lady Fortune.
47   'My teaching benefits you more than your affliction injures you' (Robinson (1957), p. 860).
52   *go lye on presse*: 'keep to themselves, stay away (as in a closet)', so Benson, p. 652.
71   With a man's death Fortune has no more control over, and, therefore, interest in him. Cf. *Boece*, Book 2, prose 3, 87ff.
73   *Princes*: usually taken to be the Dukes of Lancaster, York, and Gloucester.
76   Probably a reference to the ordinance of the Privy Council of 1390 which required that no royal gift or grant should be authorized without the consent of at least two of the three dukes.
77–9   A final irony! To attain to *som beter estat* (79) would increase rather than relieve pain since material advancement would leave its recipient even more at Fortune's mercy.

I, 63   Truth

See Benson, p. 1189 for the textual authorities, 21 MSS, two with two copies of the poem, a transcript of a Cotton MS, and the editions of Caxton (1477–8) and of Thynne (1532). The text is based on MS London, BL Add. 10340, which alone gives the envoy.

Text: 2 unto thy thing] *some* MSS, þin owen þing MS; 7, 14, 21 *and* 28 thee] *some* MSS, *om.* MS; 10 Gret restë] *some* MSS, Muche wele MS. The heading and the *Explicit* do not appear in the base MS.

Kean has pointed out that Chaucer, not least in his shorter moral poems, frequently dwelt on 'the Stoic ideal of the philosophical good man who triumphs, by his inner victory over himself, over fortune and mutability', themes common to Boethius and Seneca. However, she noted in such poems the 'use of a style which is unlike the rather discursive one of Boethius, but which is very reminiscent of the short, pithy, familiarly turned, and at times epigrammatic, sentences of Seneca' (Kean (1972), I, pp. 38–9).

1 *prees*: This probably refers specifically to the ambitious and often envious company which thronged the royal court.
2 This line renders the Latin: *Si res tue tibi non sufficiant, fac ut rebus tuis sufficias* (If your goods don't accommodate you, accommodate yourself to your goods), a sentence thought by Gower (and possibly by Chaucer) to be from Seneca though in fact from the *de Nugis Philosophorum* of Caecilius Balbus. See Kean (1972), I, p. 41.
3 *hord hath hate*: cf. *Boece*, Book 2, prose 5, 15–16: *For avaryce maketh alwey mokereres* [hoarders] *to ben hated.*
9 Fortune's symbol was sometimes a wheel, sometimes a revolving sphere.
11 The awl was a sharp tool used by shoemakers for piercing leather. Cf. the Biblical 'kick against the pricks' (Acts 9:5).
12 A proverbial expression to the effect that an earthenware pot should not (for obvious reasons) strike a wall.
17 This wilderness, the world, is man's place of exile, not his true home. Cf. *Boece*, Book 1, prose 5.
22 *thou Vache*: Sir Philip de Vache (1346–1408) was a country gentleman who, like Chaucer, was out of favour at court during the years 1386–9.

I, 64   Gentilesse

See Benson, p. 1189 for the textual authorities, 10 MSS and the editions of Caxton (1477–8) and of Thynne (1532). The text is based on MS London, BL Cotton Cleopatra D.vii.

Text: 1 gentilesse] *two* MSS, gentilnes(se) MS *and others*; 7 mytrë, croune] coroune miter MS, *but* mytre croune *in lines 14 and 21*; 15 Vice] Vicesse MS; 20 hem his heirës] his heires hem MS, *other* MSS vary. The heading is not in the base MS.

1 *firstë stocke*: taken as 'Christ' or 'God' by Henry Scogan (1361?–1407), who, in his *Moral Balade*, quotes the entire text of Chaucer's poem. Compare the words of the old hag in *The Wife of Bath's Tale*:

> Christ wole we clayme of hym oure gentilesse,
> Nat of oure eldres for hire old richesse.
>
> *CT*, III, 1117–18

The concept of *gentilesse* in this poem derives mainly from Boethius.

5–6 The sense is that virtue possesses honour but that honour (derived from social status) does not necessarily possess virtue.

I, 65   Every day thou myghtëst lere [*NIMEV* 739]

MS: London, BL Sloane 2593.

1–2 In the MS the beginning of each stanza is marked in the left-hand margin. The burden is copied at the beginning of the poem only but was doubtless to be repeated after each stanza, though no further indication of this is given.

1 *Gay*: At first sight it seems that the repeated word *gay* is to be taken as an adjective used here as a noun in addressing the frivolous, light-hearted, carefree fellow who is to be warned to think of Doomsday. This would also seem to be the immediate sense of the first two lines of another carol in Sloane 2593:

> Yyng men that bern hem so gay,
> They think not on domysday.
>
> Greene, p. 217

However, Siegfried Wenzel has shown that the medieval reader would have recognized a further sense in the repetitions of *gay* here 'related to a Latin *exemplum* about a false judge or chamberlain named Gayus who, on his deathbed, sees devils dancing around him and singing a carol-like song which includes his name' (Wenzel (1976), p. 85). In MS Cambridge, Jesus College 13, the devils sing:

> Gay, Gay, tu morieris.
> Gay, Gay, tu ponderaberis.
> Gay, Gay, tu morieris.
> Gay, Gay, tu iudicaberis.
> Gay, Gay, tu morieris.
> Gay, Gay, tu dampnaberis.

A version of the Latin verses is followed in MS Worcester, Cathedral Library F.126 by a translation into ME which begins:

> Gay, Gay, þou ert yhent,
> Gay, þou schalt deyn.
> Gay, Gay, þou ert iblent,
> Gay, þou etc.
>
> Wenzel (1976), p. 89

15 *stere*: 'to burn or offer incense'; see *MED* **steren** v. (2) (a). The reference is to the Commandment, 'Thou shalt not make unto thee any graven image, etc.' (Exodus 20:4). Similarly, lines 16, 19 and 20 allude to the Commandments, 'Thou shalt not bear false witness against thy neighbour', 'Thou shalt not kill', and 'Thou shalt not commit adultery' (Exodus 20:16, 13, 14).

I, 66   If thou serve a lord of prys [NIMEV 1433]

MS: London, BL Sloane 2593.

Text: 10 *abbreviated as* for seruyse etc. MS; 14 *abbreviated as* for etc. MS.

 1–2 Cf. Commentary, **I, 65**, 1–2.
 2 This line 'is one of the commonest and longest-lived of medieval proverbs' (Greene, p. 445). It is quoted in *All's Well That Ends Well*, Act 1, scene 3.

I, 67   Swetë Jhesu, king of blisse [NIMEV 3236]

MSS: Oxford, Bodl. Digby 86; London, BL Harley 2253 (a longer version of 15 stanzas); Oxford, Bodl. eng. poet. a.1 [Vernon MS] (as stanzas 2–4 of a longer poem, 'Swete Ihesu, now wol I synge', which also echoes **I, 68**). Text based on MS Digby 86.

 5 & 9 *Swete Jhesù*: The accent here may fall on the second syllable of *Jhesù*, as in **I, 68**. *Swete Jhesù* may be read either in the rhythm / × /, with apocope of the final '-e' of *Swete*, or as *Swetë Jhesù* in the rhythm / × × /.

I, 68   Jhesù, swete is the love of thee [NIMEV 1747]

MSS: Glasgow, Glasgow University Library, Hunter 512; London, BL Harley 2253 (H); Oxford, Bodl. eng. poet. a.1 [Vernon MS] (V), an expanded version of the poem; Chicago, Newberry Library, Ry 8 (N). Text based on G.

Text: 7 lightsomèr] lightsomere V, lykerusere H, delitfullere G, swettur N; 8 lovyèr] louyere V, alumere H, louere G, staluyere N; 15 reuthful were and] reuþful weore and V, rykene hit were H, weren ful G, N *differs*.

The first two stanzas loosely render those of the popular and much-copied poem *Jesu dulcis memoria*, an expression of piety inspired by devotion to the Holy Name of Jesus (see Woolf, pp. 172–9), formerly attributed to St Bernard but probably written by an English Cistercian from Yorkshire at the end of the 12th century. This poem is still familiar today in J. M. Neale's translation:

> Jesu! the very thought is sweet;
> In that dear Name all heart-joys meet:
> But oh, than honey sweeter far
> The glimpses of His presence are.

Devotion to the Holy Name of Jesus flourished in England from the 12th century onwards and featured prominently as a theme in the poetry and prose of Richard Rolle and the writings of other 14th-century mystics.

 7 *lightsomèr*: The range in sense from 'delightful' to something verging on 'wanton' of the V and H readings is more suggestive in this context, i.e. that of a love song addressed to Christ. These readings are also the *difficiliores lectiones* beside the weaker *delitfullere* of G and *swettur* of N. The V reading is rhythmically preferable.
 8 *lovyèr*: Metrically preferable; with the G reading the seemingly obvious elision in *swete a* would have to be ignored.

24 *us boughtë til al goode*: 'bought us for all good', i.e. to enjoy all that is good, salvation. Cf. **1, 96**, 8. The MS readings *bouʒte* G, *brouhte* V, and *brohte* H (the word has been omitted in N) show the common confusion of 'bought' and 'brought' in this context; cf. **1, 69**, 40.

26 *didest*: The reduced pronunciation 'did'st' is clearly required.

1, 69   Now I se blosmë sprynge [*NIMEV* 3963]

MSS: London, BL Royal 2.F.viii (R); London, BL Harley 2253 (H). Text based on R. H omits one stanza and orders the others 1, 3, 5, 4, and 6 (by R's numbering).

Text: 3 love-longinge] loue-longynge H, longinge R; 7 song] H, þong R; 8 al] H, *om.* R; 19 For] and for R, *stanza om. in* H; 21 myselvë] miselue H, myself R; 27 of pyne was] wes of peynes H, of pine were R; 38 that fel to] þat feol to H, fel to þe R; 40 of] of H, þat of R; hath y-brought] haþ yboht H, hauet hy-brovt R; 41 softe] H, suete R; 45 And leve me pinë drye] a[..] leue (*or* lene) pine drye R, pyne to þolie and dreʒe H; 46 For] for H, al for R; 48–50 *not in* R, *supplied from* H.

  3 The R reading manifestly lacks a syllable.

17 *woundës two and thre*: the five wounds of Christ. Cf. **1, 106**, 40.

40 The R reading *þat of pyne hvs hauet hy-brovt* makes the line too long. Again the H reading is metrically correct. The error in R may have arisen from the omission of *þat* in line 38 and its subsequent restoration, mistakenly in line 40, to complete the syntax. Cf. **1, 68**, 24 for confusion of *brought* and *bought* in the MS readings.

45 *And leve me*: as emended by the Sisams (*MEV*, p. 45).

50 *ernde*: 'obtain by intercession'.

1, 70   Love me broughte [*NIMEV* 2012]

MS: Edinburgh, NLS Advocates 18.7.21.

In this lyric Christ himself expresses the paradox of the crucifixion, namely, that when through love He became man's *fere* 'companion' (3) to redeem mankind, He was cruelly slain by that very love. Cf. **1, 97**, on the same theme.

1, 71   Alas! alas! wel evel I sped! [*NIMEV* 143, cf. *NIMEV* 3825]

MSS: London, Lambeth Palace Library 557 (L); Edinburgh, NLS Advocates 18.7.21 (A). In A the stanza order is reversed and further lines are added. Text from L.

Text: 8 I] i A, *om.* L; 10 mi lokkes and ek myn heved] mi lokkes & ek myn heued A, my heued and myne lockys L; 11 Are al wyth blody dropes bywevëd] & al my bodi with blod be-weued A, ar al bywevyd wyth blody dropys L.

This poem reflects the medieval allegory in which Christ as a lover-knight dies for his lady (man's soul) to win her love, and, in particular, the version of the allegory in which the knight comes to the lady's door which she has hard-heartedly barred against him. As the poem opens, Christ, having fled (i.e. repulsed by sin), now returns to make his entreaty, echoing two poignant Biblical texts: Rev. 3:20: *Ecce sto ad ostium et pulso* (Behold, I stand at the door and knock), and S. of S. 5:2: *Aperi mihi, soror mea, amica mea* (Open to me, my sister, my love). The drops of blood on Christ's head, lines 10–11, further echo the dew on the lover's head in S. of S. 5:2: *caput meum plenum est rore, et cincinni mei guttis noctium* (my head is filled with dew, and my locks with the drops of the night). See Woolf, pp. 51–2.

  3 *lively*: As Gray notes (*Selection*, p. 125), the MS form *lyvely* 'probably represents *lefly / levely*'; thus the sense is 'dear' rather than 'lively, life-giving'.

10–11 The A rhyme *heued / beweued* is better than *lockys / dropys* in L. The emendations adopted in these lines were proposed by Woolf (p. 51, fn. 2).

I, 72   I am Jhesù, that com to fight [*NIMEV* 1274]

MS: Edinburgh, NLS Advocates 18.7.21.

  2 Christ, the champion of man's soul against the Devil, fights not with 'shield and spear', but rather, as in *Piers Plowman*, wearing Piers's armour, human nature:

> This Jesus of his gentries wol juste in Piers armes   *for his nobility*
> In his helm and in his haubergeon – *humana natura*.
>   *Piers Plowman*, B, xviii, 22–3

I, 73   In the vaile of restles mynd [*NIMEV* 1463]

MSS: Cambridge, University Library Hh.4.12 (C); London, Lambeth Palace Library 853 (L). Text based on C.

Text: 21 a paleis] L, a place full C; 31 ever] euere L, ouer C; 40 *Quia*] L, but *Quia* C; 58 in] L, in me C; 75 come] L, cummyth C; 89 make thee] þee make L, make C; 91 thee mene] þee meene L, be-mene C; 92 wilt] wolt L, will C; 101 is (2)] L, is in C; 105–120: *these two stanzas ordered as in L, order reversed in C*; 119 I preve thy] I wole preue þi L, I pray the C; 128 *Quia*] L, in blysse *Quia* C.

The wooer of this lyric is the crucified Christ presented as king, knight, lover, mother and husband; a considerable play of wit is evident in the handling of the metaphors employed. The phrase *Quia amore langueo* derives from S. of S. 2:5; 5:8. It recurs in ME devotional literature and again as a refrain in another lyric, II, 73. Evocative echoes of the Song of Solomon, as in lines 81–4, give rise to 'an unusual sensuousness of descriptive detail in this poem' (Woolf, p. 188). The metre is loose; extra weak syllables are common and in many cases (especially with final '-es' and '-ed') it is difficult to tell if the syllable is to be pronounced in full or reduced. However, the many divergent readings of the two surviving MSS show that the text is often unreliable.

  3 *trewe love*: In the pastoral setting of the opening lines – characteristic of the *Chanson d'aventure* – *trewe love* is ambiguous: the poet could be seeking the flower 'true love' or, as it turns out, a true lover, Christ (17).

9–12 The quasi-pastoral description of a wounded man sitting under a tree on a hill-top evokes the image of the medieval 'iconographic theme of "Christ in distress" (*Christus im Elend*), in which the wounded Christ is seated beneath the Cross' (Woolf, p. 188).

18 & 25 Cf. S. of S. 4:9: *Vulnerasti cor meum, soror mea sponsa* (Thou hast ravished my heart, my sister, my spouse); and also S. of S. 4:10.

25ff. The series of bitter contrasts in these lines alluding to the events of the passion (the scourging of Christ, the crown of thorns, etc.) echo the Reproaches, sung on Good Friday, in which Christ addresses mankind with the words *Popule meus, quid feci tibi?* (O my people, what have I done to thee?). He reproaches His people for their ingratitude, and contrasts occasions of His compassion (as God) to Israel in the OT with the outrages now inflicted on Him. Thus, an early 14th-century rendering of the Reproaches in ME verse by Friar William Herebert opens with

> For from Egypte Ich ladde thee,
> Thou me ledest to rode tre.
> My folk, what have I do the?

See also the rendering in John of Grimestone's Commonplace Book, **1, 100,** below.

28 *surcote*: an outer garment worn over armour, here 'bloody', representing Christ's scourged back and wounded side.

45 *I leve them nought*: lit. 'I leave them not', i.e. (ironically), the lover never discards the blood-embroidered gloves (his hands) bought for him by his spouse.

57 The wound in Christ's side is commonly referred to as a nest or place of refuge in medieval devotional writings.

66 The notion here is that of the exchange of messages between lovers. Cf. **1, 1,** 14–16.

68 Both *dangerous* here and *gentilnisse* at line 98 are words of special resonance in the courtly tradition of medieval love literature; they signify the opposite extremes of 'disdainful rejection' and 'gracious acceptance' in a lady's attitude to her lover.

75–6 The sense is: 'Whether she runs away or comes closer, yet …'

77–8 The word *pray* may mean 'a catch, quarry' as in hunting or 'a victim, a captive' as in warfare (or, indeed, in the 'warfare' of love); see *MED* **prei(e** n. (2), **2.** & **3.** The basic contrast is between those enemies who lie in wait for their victim and then give chase to 'her' (in this case, man's soul), presumably to slay her, and the speaker (Christ) who in some sense runs on ahead to protect her by subduing her enemy.

81–4 Cf. S. of S. 5:1 (AV, S. of S. 4:16; 5:1): *Veniat dilectus meus in hortum suum, et comedat fructum pomorum suorum. Veni in hortum meum, soror mea sponsa; messui myrrham meam cum aromatibus meis, comedi favum cum melle meo, bibi vinum meum cum lacte meo* (Let my beloved come into his garden, and eat his pleasant fruits. I am come into my garden, my sister, my spouse: I have gathered my myrrh with my spice; I have eaten my honey-comb with my honey; I have drunk my wine with my milk). Also Rev. 19:8: *et datum est illi ut cooperiat se byssino splendenti et candido* (And to her was granted that she should be arrayed in fine linen, clean and white).

99–104 In medieval allegory the body could be represented as a house containing vices and virtues, in this case carnal vices from which the soul could turn by looking out from the windows of *kyndenisse,* 'natural affection'. The 'choice chamber' of line 102, like the *paleis precious* of line 21, is heaven. Line 103 may echo S. of S. 2:9, where the beloved stands *respiciens per fenestras, prospiciens per cancellos* (looking forth at the windows, showing himself through the lattice).

107–9 Christ as husband changes abruptly to Christ as mother. Devotion to 'Jesus our mother' was a late medieval form of piety, and the image itself was elaborated by Julian of Norwich. See Woolf, pp. 189–90.

I, 74   Levëdie, Ich thonkë thee [NIMEV 1836]

MS: Cambridge, Trinity College B.14.39.

Text: 11 erendië] herdie MS; 12 milde] milce MS; 13 thou] *added*; 15 yif] ges MS.

11 *erendië*: commonly emended to *erndie,* but the metre requires the full form with four syllables.

12 For *milde* as a noun (as required by rhyme), see *MED* **milde** n. 'Pity, compassion'.

I, 75   Of on that is so fayr and bright [NIMEV 2645]

MSS: London, BL Egerton 613 (E); Cambridge, Trinity College B.14.39 (T). Text based on E, in which the stanza order is 1, 3, 4, 2, 5, but with correction, indicated by the letters 'a' and 'b' beside stanzas 2 and 4, to the order as printed here and as found in T.

Text: 17 ek] ec T, es E; 23 thou] T, *om.* E; 28 it] T, *om.* E; 33 com] T, com3 E.

1ff. Anacoluthon. The poem begins 'Of one …' as if it were to continue with a verb like '… I sing'. T reads *For ou.* Gray suggests that an earlier version may have begun *O þou* (*Selection,* p. 102).

2 *maris stella*: Beside such obvious references to the Virgin as *Parens et puella* (4), this poem uses images traditional in Christian literature such as Mary as 'star of the sea' here (cf. the ninth-century hymn *Ave Maris Stella*) and *Rosa sine spina* ('rose without thorn') in line 11.

14 The readings *berëst* (here), *thou* (23), *it* (28) and *into* (42) are from T; E has *berst* and *to,* and omits *thou* and *it,* all clear illustrations of 'mismetering' due to scribal error or linguistic revision.

32 *Ave*: 'hail'. In the Latin form of Gabriel's greeting was commonly seen the Latin name *Eva* ('Eve') in reverse. This accidental link appealed to the medieval habit of making associations between elements in the OT and NT. Thus, as Christ was seen as the 'second Adam', so the Virgin was the 'second Eve' who undid the harm caused by the first Eve. Cf. *Ave maris stella*:

Sumens illud Ave	Receiving that '*Ave*'
Gabrielis ore	from Gabriel's lips
Funda nos in pace	establish us in peace
Mutans Evae nomen	changing Eve's name.

I, 76   Edi be thou, hevenë quenë [*NIMEV* 708]

MS: Oxford, Corpus Christi College 59, with music.

Text: 6 the] þet MS.

Of the eight stanzas of this poem, only the first five are given in the text. The fifth stanza makes a natural conclusion to a self-contained poem; the final three stanzas may be a later addition. For the evidence of the music with regard to the metre in this lyric, see Appendix A.

6–7 *havest / Levedy*: These forms (MS *hauest / leuedi*) may represent *hast* and *levdi / lady* here. Cf. Commentary, I, 75, 14, and see Appendix A.

7–8 Here, as frequently in medieval devotional poetry, the conventions and language of secular love literature are used. The poet addresses the Virgin as a knight would his lady. He begs her for her pity and mercy as her 'knight' (15–16) and as her 'man' in the bondage of love (21–4 and 35).

17 The reference is to Isaiah 11:1: 'And there shall come forth a rod out of the stem of Jesse, and a Branch shall grow out of his roots'. The descent of Jesus from King David was often represented (e.g. in stained-glass 'Jesse' windows) as a tree springing from Jesse, the father of David, with his descendants represented by its branches and ending with Jesus or with the Virgin and Holy Child. Mary was thus a 'blossom sprung from a single root'.

25–8 Cf. Commentary, I, 79, 7.

28 *hir*: The use of the feminine pronoun to refer back to *bledë* in the previous line is an instance of the sporadic survival of grammatical gender in earlier ME.

I, 77   Gabriel, from hevenë king [*NIMEV* 888]

MS: London, BL Arundel 248, with music.

Text: 3 hire] þire MS; *the scribe frequently confuses* 'þ' *and* 'h'.

43 *fles*: a ME variant of *flesh* with a final 's' sound to rhyme with *wes*, itself a dialect variant of *was*.

54–5 The syncopated pronunciation required for *evry* (54) and *hevnë* (55) is here represented in the MS spellings *euri* and *heune*.

58 *yive*: The syntax here is elliptical. Following *bid* 'pray' of line 51, *yive* has two objects, *hevnë blis* (55) and the noun clause of lines 59–60; 'that He give us' must therefore be understood again before that final clause.

I, 78   Now this foulës singëth [*NIMEV* 2366]

MS: Cambridge, Trinity College B.14.39.

Text: 7 king] kind MS; 12 and] *om.* MS; 38 non] non wimon MS; 41 child] suete chid MS.

1 The '-eth' plural of *singëth* is retained for the sake of the rhyme with *thringëth* of line 3. Though not sustained beyond the second stanza, these rhymes seem to be a characteristic of the opening of this poem. In line 7 *kingës* may originally have been *kingen* (with an 'en' plural) to rhyme with *singen* of line 5.

25 *tharë*: This early ME inflected form (feminine, genitive) of the article is retained
    for its disyllabic form here. Other archaic forms, *thire* (21) and *þen* (29), have
    been replaced by the later 14th-century London forms *thine* and *the*.
28 *meindë hirë thought*: lit. 'mingled, mixed her thought'.

I, 79   I syng of a mayden [*NIMEV* 1367]

MS: London, BL Sloane 2593.

Text: 1 I syng of] I syng A of MS.

From a surprising opening, with a matchless maiden choosing the king of kings,
through the simple language and incantational repetitions of the middle three
stanzas, with the gentle but sensuous suggestivity of the imagery (that of dew
falling on grass, flower and leaf, and the stealthy coming of a king to his mother's
bower), to the joyous exclamation of the final lines, this brief lyric gives an
immediate and unique expression of the mystery of Christ's incarnation. However,
beyond the simplicity and immediacy lie deeper and more subtle resonances to be
understood in the light of the responses of a reader familiar with the Bible and the
liturgy, and with medieval love poetry in which the spring season and the courtly
conventions of *fin amor* lent rich overtones to the month of April and the setting of
the bower. See Gray (1972), pp. 101–6. For evidence that this poem was originally a
song, see Fletcher, *Companion*, pp. 208–9.

7 *dew*: The Biblical story of the dew which fell on Gideon's fleece (see Judges 6)
    was allegorically interpreted as representing the descent of the Holy Ghost
    upon Mary at the Incarnation. Cf. Luke 1:35: 'The Holy Ghost shall come
    upon her'. Gideon's fleece ('uellus gedionus') is accordingly represented in the
    Annunciation scene by Martin Schongauer reproduced on the front cover of
    this volume.
10 *bowr*: one of many terms also used in ME to refer to the Virgin's womb.
    Cf. **II, 53**, 1–2, where Christ, addressing his mother, refers to her womb as 'my
    own bower'.
12 *flour*: The Virgin was commonly represented as a flower.
16 *spray*: Mary's bearing of Jesus was represented by the image of a branch bearing
    a flower, and specifically as a branch of the tree of Jesse; see Commentary,
    I, 76, 17.

I, 80   I saw a fair maiden [*NIMEV* 1351]

MS: London, BL Sloane 2593.

The repetition of the burden is twice indicated, at line 9 by *lull myn*, and at line 14
by *lullay*.

Greene describes this as the 'masterpiece of lullaby carols'. He likens its metre
to that of *I syng of a mayden* (**I, 79**), claiming that both poems make 'the same
effective use of the "rest"' (i.e. the mid-point division of the long line) (Greene,
p. 385). However, unlike **I, 79**, this lyric is markedly irregular in its metre.

I, 81   As I lay upon a night [*NIMEV* 352]

MSS: Edinburgh, NLS Advocates 18.7.21 (A); Cambridge, University Library Add. 5943, with music (C); Cambridge, St John's College S.54 (J); London, BL Harley 2330 (H). Text based on A. C has stanza 1, H has stanzas 1–5, J stanzas 1–9, and A has 37 stanzas. Stanzas 1–15 and 37 from A are printed here.

Text: 1 lay lay] la A; 2 sing lullay] lullay A; 49 King] kinges A; 55 knavë child] child A; 68 herdes] sepperdis A; 70 ther] t A; 76 al at] at al A.

Dobson also omits stanzas 16–36 of A, though his reasons for doing so (see *MES*, p. 201) depend partly on unacceptably rigid metrical assumptions. For the repetition of the burden after each stanza (it is indicated, by *Lullay*, only after the final stanza in the MS), see Greene, pp. 94, 95, 387.

> 1–2   For this expansion of the A version of the burden in the light of the readings of J and H and of the musical notation of C, see *MES*, p. 202.
>
> 55   *knavë child*: Dobson's emendation (*MES*, p. 204, note to line 45).

I, 82   Lullay, lullay, litel child, child rëstë thee a throwe
[*NIMEV* 2023]

MS: Edinburgh, NLS Advocates 18.7.21.

Text: 22 ful wel] wel MS. In lines 9, 13, 21, 33, 37, 45, 49 and 57, the second *lullay* is abbreviated as 'l'.

In this adaptation of an earlier secular lullaby (**1, 50**, above), the speaker is the Virgin who reflects on the Christ child's heavenly origin, on His present miseries as a cold, hungry, crying baby, and on the anguish of the crucifixion which it will be this child's lot to endure. Unlike the earlier poem which, as written in the MS, has long lines of six stresses (3 + 3) as well as lines of seven (4 + 3), this lyric has seven-stress lines throughout (again, as copied in the MS).

> 8   *thing that was thin owe*: i.e. man, created by God.
>
> 16   *list*: The common ME reduced form is metrically preferable to MS *listet*.
>
> 22   The MS reading of this line is a syllable short. An original *ful* may have been lost by haplography since confusable and even identical forms of 'full' and 'well' occurred in ME MSS.
>
> 24   *drie*: lit. 'dry', here 'shrivelled', i.e. 'dead'.
>
> 40   Cf. Luke 22:44: 'And being in an agony [in the Garden of Gethsemane] he [Jesus] prayed more earnestly: and his sweat was as it were great drops of blood falling down to the ground.'
>
> 47–8   An expansion and explanation of *it* (46), i.e. the cruel duty of love that Christ had to undergo for man. The vocabulary and associations of the secular poetry of *fin amor* are found in *bond of love-longing* here and in *thin ore* in line 50.

I, 83   Ler to love as I love thee [*NIMEV* 1847]

MSS: Edinburgh, NLS Advocates 18.7.21 (A); London, BL Harley 7322 (H), stanzas 1–3 only. Text based on A.

Text: 16 lappe] a lappe A, H *differs and has an extra line*; 26 mankin] man A.

A rubric in H suggests that the initial stanza is to be taken as addressed by Christ to the Virgin. Woolf (pp. 156–7) argues that stanza 1 is a separate poem, 'an appeal from the Christ-Child to man'. Gray (*Selection*, p. 106) views stanzas 2–3 as 'a self-contained and impressive lullaby'.

I, 84   Now goth sonnë under wode [NIMEV 2320]

MS: Oxford, Bodl. Arch. Selden, supra 74. Versions in other MSS.

These lines are found in the *Merure de Seinte Eglise* by St Edmund of Canterbury (d. 1240), a popular work surviving in over 60 MSS in French, Latin and English. In one ME translation (in MS Cambridge, University Library Ii.6.40) the quatrain is introduced as follows:

> Also bihold his moder, what sorow sche had whan sche saw here swete son suffer al þat peyne; & for þis sorow & wo sche becam blake & blo as sche seiþ of hersilf, 'Ne clepe ȝe me no more faire, lesse ne more, but clepiþ me fro hens forþ ward "woman ful of sorow & wo & colure boþ blake & blo."' As Seynt Barnard seiþ in a songe of love 'Ne merveile ȝe þat þouȝe I be broune & pale, for þe sunne haþ mis coloured me.' And þerfore men sey in Englische in þis maner ...
>
> Robbins (1925), pp. 249–50

Here are found both the traditional notion that the Virgin's 'fair countenance' (i.e. the *faire rode* of line 2) was darkened by grief at the sight of Christ's suffering and the association of this with the effect of the sun in the reference to S. of S. 1:5 (the *songe of love* above): *Nolite me considerare quod fusca sim, quia decoloravit me sol* (AV, S. of S. 1:6: Look not upon me, because I am black, because the sun hath looked upon me), ideas fused in this poem.

1   *wode*: 'wood', here both 'wood' and a single 'tree', i.e. the cross, as in *tre* (3). The setting sun was a common image for Christ's dying. Cf.

> ... the sonne to reste goinge
> Was the deth of Hevene kinge.
>
> BL Add. 22283, fol. 1a

The setting of the sun and imminent darkness also evoke Luke 23:44–6: 'And it was about the sixth hour, and there was a darkness over all the earth until the ninth hour. And the sun was darkened, and the veil of the temple was rent in the midst. And when Jesus had cried with a loud voice, he said, Father, into thy hands I commend my spirit; and having said thus, he gave up the ghost.'

I, 85   Whyt was Hys naked brest [NIMEV 4088]

MS: Durham Cathedral A.III.12. Versions in other MSS, see Woolf, p. 28, fn. 4.

This lyric, dated *c.* 1240 on palaeographical grounds (see Thomson (1935), pp. 101–5), is the earliest of various renderings into ME verse of the following passage from the *Liber Meditationum* of John of Fécamp:

Candet nudatum pectus. Rubet cruentum latus. Tensa arent viscera. Decora languent lumina. Regia pallent ora. Procera rigent brachia. Crura dependent marmorea. Et rigat terebratos pedes beati sanguinis unda.

Woolf (pp. 28–30) gives a full account of all versions, including this poem and **1, 86**.

I, 86   Whyt is Thi naked brest [*NIMEV* 4087]

MS: Oxford, Bodl. Digby 55.

Text: 3–4 are ... are] weren ... weren MS; 6 dimmyeth] dummes MS.

3–4 For the emendation, see Woolf, p. 29, fn. 3: 'In the copying of Middle English lyrics tenses were often confused: *weren* in line 2 [3–4 here] should surely be emended to *aren*'.

6 An original *dimmieþ* (OE *dimmian*) may have been rendered as *dummes* by a Northerly scribe unfamiliar with the '-i-' element of weak verbs of Class II which gives the extra syllable needed here.

I, 87   Whan Ich se on rode [*NIMEV* 3964]

MS: London, BL Royal 12.E.i. Similar versions in various MSS.

Woolf (pp. 33–4) gives an illuminating account of this poem and suggests that the source of the 'outline description of the Crucifixion ... could well be one of the paintings of the Passion, which by the second half of the 13th century were becoming quite common in churches'. Lines 5–6, 'by contrast, have the precision of the *Respice* imitations', i.e. lyrics listing details of the crucifixion based on the commonplace Latin text beginning *Respice in faciem Christi tui.*

I, 88   Worldës blissë, have god day! [*NIMEV* 4221]

MSS: Cambridge, Corpus Christi College 8, with music (C); Edinburgh, NLS Advocates 18.7.21, lines 9–16 only (A). Text based on C.

Text: 5 shadde] ssade C.

The music of this poem is 'through composed', i.e. each stanza has its own music. It constitutes the first English motet; see Bukofzer (1936), pp. 225–33.

1 *have*: In the music two notes appear above *have*; they could be sung to one syllable or (with *have* as *havë*) to two.

3 *loven*: The MS form *louen* has a treble 'f' repeated above 'en'. This repeated note may be merely scribal; the original form may have been *loue* with a single long note in keeping with the prevailing rhythm of the tune.

8 The stanzas of this lyric vary in their number of lines and their rhyme schemes. In this first stanza, the rhyme scheme may be a a b b c c b c (with *y-tent* for MS *y-tend* in line 7). Dobson's emendation (see *MES*, p. 195) for the sake of rhythm as well as rhyme is unnecessary.

17 The form *minë* (instead of MS *my*) requires the breaking of a ligature in the music. However, at this point in the MS the verbal underlay appears to be haphazard and the metre requires an extra syllable.

I, 89   The mildë Lamb, y-sprad o rodë [*NIMEV* 3432]

MS: London, BL Arundel 248, with music.

Text: 9 His] þis MS – *the Arundel scribe frequently writes þ for* h; 10 abide] vnbiden MS.

19 *wunden*: The MS form *wunden* (*woundes* in late 14th-century London English) is retained here for the rhyme. The usual short vowels of *y-swungen* and *y-stungen* must be assumed to have been long or, the less likely alternative, the vowel of *wunden* short. For rhymes of the consonants 'nd' with 'ng', see Commentary, **I, 106**, 8ff.

40 *allë*: The pl. form with '-e' was commonly found in later ME before a sg. noun.

43 *atten*: from OE *æt þæm* 'at the'.

I, 90   Jesu Cristës mildë moder [*NIMEV* 1697]

MS: London, BL Arundel 248, with music.

Text: 29 saw] soie MS.

This is a version of the Latin Sequence *Stabat iuxta Christi crucem*.

1–2 The rhyme *moder / rodë* is not exact.

18 See Commentary, **I, 91**, 11–12.

29 *saw*: The MS form *soie* is an error for *seie,* a variant form of the past tense of this verb.

34 *goulinge*: 'anguished cries'; see *MED* **gouling(e** ger. (a) Howling, lamenting, etc. However, Dobson takes this word to mean 'usury, interest' (*MES*, p. 164, note to line 34, and p. 162) which would echo *cum usura* of the Latin Sequence: *Nunc extorquet cum usura.* The sense is that the Virgin at the crucifixion endured the pain which she had, against the law of nature, been spared at Christ's birth.

40 *thee's*: MS *þes* represents the elision of *thee is.*

50 *H'aros*: MS *þaros.* The MS spelling (with 'þ' for 'h', a confusion common in this MS) represents the elision of *he aros.*

51–4 Cf. Commentary, **I, 27**, 21–2.

54 *bilof*: an early ME past tense form of the verb *biliven.*

I, 91   Stond wel, moder, under rodë [*NIMEV* 3211]

MSS: London, BL Royal 12.E.i, complete text with music for stanzas 1–6 (R); London, BL Harley 2253, complete text without music (H); Oxford, Bodl. Digby 86, lacks last two stanzas, without music (D); Cambridge, St John's College 111, text of *Stabat juxta Christi crucem* with music for Latin text, English words added beneath not properly aligned, both texts to line 27 only (J); Dublin, Trinity College 301, complete text without music (T); London, BL Royal 8.F.ii, first stanza, without music (F). Variants listed in full in *MES*, pp. 155–6. Text from R with *lacunae* (because of a torn page) supplied from H.

Text: 4 I] T, y H, hi F, ich D, *om*. RJ; 24 No selly nis] no selli RJ, no sellik T, no wonder H, hit is no wonder D; 29 Ne wit me nought] ne wyt me naht H, with me nout R, wite ye me noth T, Icomen hit is D; 30 this sorwë] þis sorewe H, sorghe T, serewe D, sorye R; 37 now tarst] nutarst R, nou H, *readings differ in T and D*; 46 at allë] H, at alne T, alle at R, alle D; 56 Thy] thi T, þe R, hire H; 57 Wel] wen R, *om*. HT; 58 Moder] [M]oder T, mod .. R, leuedy H.

According to Carleton Brown, 'The ultimate source of this dialogue between the Blessed Virgin and her Son is without doubt a Latin prose narrative of the Passion represented as spoken by the Virgin to St Anselm … or to St Bernard' (Brown XIII, p. 204).

11–12 These lines refer to Simeon's words to Mary, Luke 2:35: *et tuam ipsius animam pertransivit gladius* (Yea, a sword shall pierce through thy own soul also). Cf. the popular Franciscan poem *Stabat mater dolorosa*:

> *Cujus animam gementem*   Through her lamenting soul,
> *Contristantem et dolentem*   anguished and sorrowful,
> *Pertransivit gladius*   penetrated the sword.

24 *nis*: See *MES*, p. 158, note to line 24.

37 *now tarst*: 'now for the first time'. For the rare word *tarst*, see *MES*, pp. 158–9, note to line 37.

I, 92   Why have ye no routhe on my child? [*NIMEV* 4159]

MS: Edinburgh, NLS Advocates 18.7.21.

Text: 3 o] on MS.

3 The metre is easily restored by adopting the alternative forms *tak* (the endingless imperative plural) and *derworth* instead of the MS forms *taket* and *derworþi*. The prepositions *on* and *of* both have the weakly stressed form *o*; it seems likely that *o rode* (for *of rode*, 'from the cross') has been miscopied as *on rode*.

I, 93   Thou sikëst sore [*NIMEV* 3691]

MS: Edinburgh, NLS Advocates 18.7.21.

Text: 15 I] & i MS; 19 yerte] ȝepte MS.

This lyric is in the form of a carol. The burden is addressed to a tear in Christ's eye; the stanzas are addressed to Christ. The poem may well have been inspired by meditation before a crucifix or a painting of Christ on the cross. An altered version of the final stanza has been incorporated as lines 15–20 of I, 97.

8 *singest*: The metre requires the reduced form *singst* here; cf. *brekst* (the MS spelling), line 4.

13 *wo*: 'evil', from OE *wōh*, as distinct from *wo*, 'woe', from OE *wā*.

14 *Th'art*: The elision of MS *þu art* is metrically preferable.

I, 94   I sike al when I singe [*NIMEV* 1365]

MSS: Oxford, Bodl. Digby 2 (D); London, BL Harley 2253 (H). Text based on D.

Text: 9 swete] sute D, *line differs in* H; 18 stondëth] stonit D, stond H; 20 waylaway] wayla …, *final letters illegible* D, weylaway H; 22 bo] H, boþe D; 25 He hongëth] he honge D, þou hengest H; 32 makië] H, make D; 41 stronge] H, longe D; 52 thurgh-sought] þourhsoht H, þoit soit D; 53 wepe] wende D, wyke (*rhyming with* syke) H; 60 were] was D, H *differs*.

In this lyric, in which the poet sighs for sorrow as he sings of Jesus his *lemmòn* (37), the language and conventions of the courtly love lyric are 'deftly blended with the tone of elegiac love-longing that colours the whole' (Woolf, pp. 65–6).

17–18 A telling contrast of images – of clay shrivelling and crumbling (as it dries out) for the shrinking, dispirited friends of Jesus, and of the impassive, unyielding solidity of the rock in which the cross was implanted. See *MED* for **clingen** in this sense of 'shrivel'.

60 The MS form *was* is best viewed as a dialect variant of the past plural equivalent to *were* or *weren* in Chaucer's language.

I, 95   My trewest tresowre sa trayturly was taken [*NIMEV* 2273]

MS: Cambridge, University Library Dd.5.64 (3).

Text: 26 The] þi MS.

This MS contains works by the 14th-century English mystic Richard Rolle and also a number of lyrics possibly to be ascribed to him.

The language of this lyric as found in the MS, fairly consistently that of a North-East Midland dialect, is preserved in the text, except for the changes of the letters 'þ' to 'th', 'u' (consonant) to 'v', 'v' (vowel) to 'u', 'ʒ' to 'y', and of þe ('thee') to *thee*. A reduced spelling *hurld* occurs in line 4, but, though not specifically marked for pronunciation, '-es' and '-ed' were probably for the most part full endings.

14–16 Christ was nailed to the cross as it lay on the ground. It was then raised to the upright position and, with an agonizing jolt, the base dropped into a hole in the rock whereby the cross was held upright. The process is vividly described in the ME translation of the *Merure de Seinte Eglise* (see Commentary, **I, 84**) as follows:

> … & whanne þe false Iewis hadyn þus fastyned Cristis body on þe crosse as men doun cloþe on a tenconier, þan þei lift up þe crosse for malice of hemsilfe as hiʒe as þei miʒten & lete it squat sodenly into a morteis; & wiþ þat squatynge al þe synows, veyns, & ioyntes of his blissid body to-brosten.
>
> Robbins (1925), p. 250

22–3 Christ the Champion descends from the cross having done battle; his mother and her companions unfasten his shield. A comparable heroic presentation is found in the description of Christ mounting the cross as a young warrior and thereafter being taken down in the OE poem *The Dream of the Rood*.

I, 96   Gold and al this worldës wyn [*NIMEV* 1002]

MS: Edinburgh, NLS Advocates 18.7.21.

  5 For the notion of the wound in Christ's side as a place of refuge, cf. Commentary, **I, 73**, 57.

I, 97   Crist maketh to man a fair present [*NIMEV* 611]

MSS: Glasgow, Glasgow University Library, Hunter 512 (G); Cambridge, Trinity College B.15.17 (T); San Marino, California, Huntington Library HM 127 [Powis MS] (P). Text based on G.

Text: 42 hath maad] haþ made P, is maad GT.

For the literary and devotional background to this moving expression of the paradox of love, both compassionate and harsh, in the doctrine of the Atonement, see Woolf, pp. 166–8.

15–20 These lines, dramatically used here, are a version of the final stanza of **I, 93**.
28 *thou art*: possibly to be elided as *th'art* here. Cf. **I, 93**, 14.
33–4 Clearly *doest* and *brekest* represent the reduced forms *dost* and *brekst* here.

I, 98   A sory beverage it is [*NIMEV* 94]

MS: Edinburgh, NLS Advocates 18.7.21.

This lyric is a moving expression of Christ's anguished prayer in the Garden of Gethsemane. Cf. Mark 14:36: 'And he said, Abba, Father, all things are possible unto thee; take away this cup from me: nevertheless not what I will, but what thou wilt', and also Matt. 26:42.

I, 99   Ye that pasen be the wey [*NIMEV* 4263]

MSS: Edinburgh, NLS Advocates 18.7.21 (A); Cambridge, University Library Ii.3.8 (C). Text based on A. C offers no help with the metrical irregularities in A because the two versions differ so greatly.

This is one of several ME paraphrases of the text from Lam. 1:12: *O vos omnes qui transitis per viam, attendite et videte si est dolor sicut meus* ([O] all ye that pass by, behold, and see if there be any sorrow like unto my sorrow). These words were originally a lament for the city of Jerusalem; in Good Friday services, they were transferred to Christ on the cross. See Woolf, pp. 42–4.

I, 100   My folk, now answerë me [*NIMEV* 2240]

MSS: Edinburgh, NLS Advocates 18.7.21 (A); Cambridge, Jesus College 13 (C). Text based on A. C adds stanzas, but lacks the two final stanzas of A.

Text: 9 al] C, al aboute A; 29 bitook thee] þe be-tok, þe *marked for transposition* A; 32 thorn] a þorn A.

This complaint of Christ, prefaced and concluded in the MS with the words *Popule meus* etc., is a paraphrase of the Reproaches sung as part of the Good Friday services. See Commentary, **1, 73**, 25ff. The OT events referred to here took place in the desert as the Israelites journeyed from captivity in Egypt to the Promised Land. See Exodus, chapters 12–17. For an earlier 14th-century versification of the Reproaches by the Franciscan William Herebert, see Brown XIV, no. 15.

14 *Angeles mete*: i.e. manna, see Exodus 16:15.

23 *the herte*: perhaps to be elided as *th'erte*.

36 The line is a syllable too long. Perhaps *Al* at the beginning has been added.

1, 101 Jhesus doth him bymene [*NIMEV* 1699]

MS: Oxford, Bodl. Bodley 416.

'This poem, which ironically relates the appearance of Christ in the Passion to the fashionable dress and habits of a dandy, shows a quite striking ability to control paradoxical antitheses' (Woolf, p. 41). For further discussion, see Woolf, pp. 41–2. The series of contrasts are in the form of Christ's Reproaches; see **1, 100**, above. The source of this lyric is a popular passage attributed to St Bernard, quoted by Gray from the version in Caxton's translation of the *Golden Legend* (in Ellis (1900), I, pp. 72–3) as follows:

> … whereof saith S. Bernard: *Tu es homo*, etc. – He saith thus: Thou art a man and hast a chaplet of flowers, and I am God and have a chaplet of thorns. Thou hast gloves on thine hands, and I have nails fixed in my hands. Thou dancest in white vestures, and I God am mocked and vilipended, and in the house of Herod had received a white vesture. Thou dancest and playest with thy feet, and I with my feet have laboured in great pain. Thou liftest up thine arms in joy, and I have stretched them in great reproof. Thou stretchest out thine arms across in caroling and gladness, and I stretch mine in the cross in great opprobrium and villainy. Thou hast thy side and thy breast open in sign of vain glory, and I have mine opened with a spear …
>
> Gray, *Selection,* p. 116

As it survives in MS Bodley 416, this lyric is quite irregular in stanza form, rhyme scheme and metre.

11 *acros … armes*: arms crossed in dancing in contrast with Christ's arms outstretched on the cross, as in the above quotation.

18–19 Man's side is 'open' because fashionable garments had long, wide slits (*spaiers*). Christ's side is 'open' from the spear wound (23).

1, 102 Lo! lemman swete, now may thou se [*NIMEV* 1930]

MS: Cambridge, University Library Dd.5.64 (3).

As with **1, 95**, from the same MS, the largely consistent Northerly forms of this poem are retained; they are not difficult to understand and include *mare, woundes, sare, dwelles* (rhyming with *elles*), *sa*, and *lufe*, for which Chaucer's forms would have been *more, woundeth, sore, dwellest, so* and *love*.

7 A reference to the armour of Christ the lover-knight. For the theme of Christ as
   lover-knight, see Woolf, pp. 44–56. See also Commentary, **I, 71**.

I, 103   Stedfast crosse, among alle other [*NIMEV* 3212]

MS: Oxford, Merton College 248.

Text: 5 swete (2x)] swete be (2x) MS; 6 swetter] sweter be MS.

These verses are a translation of the following stanza from the famous hymn *Pange lingua gloriosi* by Venantius Fortunatus (*c.* 530–*c.* 600):

> Crux fidelis, inter omnes arbor una nobilis,
> Nulla silva talem profert fronde, flore, germine
> Dulce lignum, dulces clavos, dulce pondus sustinet.

This hymn was sung at the Adoration of the Cross during Good Friday services. This particular stanza was sometimes sung on its own and sometimes repeated between other stanzas.

5–6 The metre of lines 1–4 is smooth. In view of this, the MS text of the final
     couplet (as marked by the rhymes *tre* / *thee*) is suspiciously loose. For the
     emendations adopted here, see Duncan (1996 [b]).

I, 104   What is he, this lordling [*NIMEV* 3906]

MS: London, BL Add. 46919 (formerly Phillipps 8336).

This lyric by the 14th-century friar William Herebert is a paraphrase of Isaiah 63:1–7. The heroic Messianic champion returning in triumph from Edom where he had subdued the enemies of the Hebrews, was understood as an OT prefiguring of, and in this poem becomes, Christ the vanquisher of Death. As adapted to the Passion, certain irrelevant details of the OT passage are here omitted, e.g. the names of Bosra and Edom. In this new context, other details acquire fuller, and sometimes ironic, significance. Thus, the clothing of the Messianic hero *tinctis vestibus ... formosus in stola* 'with dyed garments ... beautiful in his robe', becomes *With blod-rede wede ... So faire y-cointised* (2–3), still, indeed, the battle dress of Christ the conquerer but also, now, the blood-stained garments of Christ crucified. Moreover, as in **I, 103** above, the beauty of the hero Christ thus clothed is also the ironic beauty of the nails and the cross as instruments of salvation.

8 The OT image of the wine-press for crushing defeat (Isaiah 63:3: 'I have trodden
   the wine-press alone; ... for I will tread them in mine anger, and trample them
   in my fury') acquires here the additional sense of the agony of the cross where
   Christ trod and also was trodden.

15 Here *The yer of medës yelding* is more than the *Dies ... ultionis ... annus
    redemptionis meae* ('day of vengeance, year of my redemption') of the OT
    passage; it is also the Day of Judgement.

16–17 Here the words of Isaiah 63:5: 'And I looked, and there was none to help;
       and I wondered that there was none to uphold' become not just the statement
       of an indignant, single-handed hero, but also the pathos of the solitary and
       rejected Christ. The tone is that of Psalm 69:20: 'I looked for some to take pity,

but there was none; and for comforters, but I found none', a passage associated with the loneliness of Christ on the cross.

20–23   These lines appear in the MS in the order 22–3, 20–21. The order in the text, adopted by some editors, follows that of Isaiah 63:7. Thus, the poem opens with the speaker's question 'Who is he, this young lord?' and ends with his affirmation of faith following upon the dramatic revelation of the identity of the blood-stained champion.

I, 105   As I me rod this ender day [*NIMEV* 359]

MS: London, BL Harley 2253.

Text: 17 bet] betere MS; 23 that me lest] y wole MS; 41 encens hy] encenʒ MS; 47 men have ne mawen] ne mai me hauen MS.

A song of the five joys of the Blessed Virgin.

23   In the MS reading this line is short and lacks a rhyme. Both difficulties are overcome by reading *me lest* on the assumption that a scribe has replaced an impersonal construction with the equivalent personal one, *y wole*.

41   The MS reading for this line is short and lacks a rhyme. For *hy* (adopted here as a conjecture to restore metre and rhyme) as 'holy', or possibly 'strong', see *MED*.

47   The MS reading of this line lacks a rhyme. The emendation assumes error arising from scribal transposition of *have* and *mawen,* the latter subsequently altered to *mai*. Cf. lines 4 and 6 for identical rhyme words.

51–2   For the reuniting of Mary's soul with her body cf. Commentary, **II, 53**.

52   *wont*: a one-syllable variant of MS *woned* is required. Cf. Commentary, **I, 51**, 10.

I, 106   Somer is come and winter gon [*NIMEV* 3221]

MS: London, BL Egerton 613.

Text: 7 me fint] is funde MS; 23 bold] wlong MS; 32 shamen him] scumi him, *with* scumi *added at end of line for insertion, as marked, before* him MS; 46 that lif is] þe lif MS; 47 Ne mightë hit] *erasure, part of second word illegible,* ne mytte hit *in margin in 14th-century hand*; 48 falle] walle MS; 53 socour] saui MS; 58 She let the terës al of blod] MS *illegible except for final* d, Hii let þe teres al of blod *in margin in 14th-century hand*; 62 changëd herë] changedere MS; rode] blod MS; 82 Grone] grone he may MS; 88 gon] gene MS.

For an excellent analysis of this lyric, see Dronke (1974), from whom the stanza form adopted in the text and the emendation at line 53 are derived. In the MS the poem is written out in four long lines per stanza.

7   *me fint*: as emended by the Sisams (*MEV*, p. 17).

8ff.   For rhymes involving words ending with the consonants 'ng' and 'nd' as *longe, songe, stronge, londe* and *honde* in this stanza, and *bond* and *strong* at lines 20 and 21, compare the opening rhymes *bond* and *long* in **I, 108**.

9   *child*: In the context of the nature opening here and the theme of love-longing characteristic of the love lyric, the word *child* evokes not only the notion of

the Christ child but also that of Christ the lover knight. The word *child* was 'a favourite word in ballads and romances for a knight' (Woolf, p. 65).

28 *he*: an earlier ME form of the plural pronoun 'they' kept here for the sake of the rhyme.

31–2 Here, and at 42–3, the rhyme fails. The text may be corrupt, but no convincing emendations suggest themselves.

40 *woundës two and three*: the five wounds of Christ.

48 *falle*: as emended by the Sisams (*MEV*, p. 18).

62 *rode*: The repetition of *blod* in the MS makes poor sense and gives a third rhyme on the same word. The emendation *rode* makes good sense in conjunction with *face* of the following line.

65 *deer*: Dronke notes that the image of Christ as *cervus* ('deer') is as old as Christian symbolism, but can offer no parallel 'for the concreteness and succinct savageness of its use here (a use that clearly has no literal counterpart in the passion)' (Dronke (1974), p. 402).

71 *Mid flode*: Dronke suggests that the poet was developing Fortunatus' notion of the 'cosmic dimension' of the power of Christ's blood, *terra pontus astra mundus quo lavantur flumine* (a stream in which earth, sea, stars, universe are washed). Here it forms a torrent which swept open the gates of hell (Dronke (1974), p. 403).

82 Emendation is required here since the line as found in the MS is too long.

1, 107   Lullay, lullay, litel child [*NIMEV* 2024]

MSS: Edinburgh, NLS Advocates 18.7.21 (A); London, BL Harley 7358 (H).

Text based on A.

In this carol the Christ child is addressed not by the Virgin but by the poet who imaginatively becomes Eve and then a spokesman for mankind. As such, it is 'unique among lullabies ... addressed to the infant Christ' (Greene, p. 390).

1–2 This burden is a quotation from the opening of an earlier lullaby (**1, 50**). Its repetition is twice indicated in H.

24 *barun*: The reading *barun* (in both MSS) gives this line an extra syllable. However, this poem is careful in its versification; all other lines are regular, and concern with form is seen in the repetition of the same rhyme sound at the end of each stanza. The original reading may have been *bern* or *barn*. The sense of *bern* could be 'lord' or 'infant'. For the former, see *MED* **bern** n. (1) **2.** (b) 'a nobleman, a lord; ... often equated with **baroun** baron'. For the latter, see *MED* **barn** n., where *bern* is quoted as an alternative form along with *baren* and *barun*. A pun, with both senses present, may have been intended; but certainly the sense 'child' is appropriate and, in association with *king* in the same line, evokes the common contrastive topos of *humilitas* versus *sublimitas*.

1, 108   Adam lay y-bownden [*NIMEV* 117]

MS: London, BL Sloane 2593.

Text: 8 writen] *om.* MS; 9 takë] take ben MS.

For these emendations, see Duncan (1987).

9–16 Adam's lapse was known paradoxically as the *felix culpa*, the 'happy fault', since it precipitated all the joy of Christ's redemption of mankind and the necessity, here, of having Mary as Queen of Heaven. The words *felix culpa* occur in the *Exultet* sung in the liturgy for the Eve of Easter:

> O certe necessarium Adæ peccatum:
>> quod Christi morte deletum est!
> O felix culpa:
>> quae talem ac tantum meruit habere redemptorem!

O necessary sin of Adam, which was expurged by Christ's death!
O happy fault, which merited such and so great a redeemer!

I, 109 Er ne couthe Ich sorwë non [*NIMEV* 322]

MS: London, Guildhall, Records Office, *Liber de antiquis Legibus*, with music.

Text: 4 tholë] sholye MS; 27 this] his MS.

Although penitential in character, this is more specifically an occasional poem, 'A prisoner's prayer', as it is sometimes entitled.

In the MS a French text, and, below it, an English text, accompany the musical notation. The French poem was probably written first (see *MES*, p. 111). If so, the English poem is a *contrafactum* of the French, that is, a version in a different language reproducing, line by line, the syllable-count of the first poem so as to be singable to the tune of that poem.

The structure of this lyric reflects that of the early sequence. This was a type of medieval church music which differed from the hymn in having stanzas varying in metrical pattern and melody, each of which, however, consisted of two halves corresponding exactly in number and length of lines. The French and English poems follow these metrical principles closely but not always exactly.

15–26 The MS text of this stanza is retained here: its strained syntax may have arisen from the difficulty of matching the French in line length and rhyme scheme.

19 *woning*: Comparison with the *peine* and *dolur e peine* of the French text shows that here and at line 38 the sense is 'misery' (from OE *wānung*) and not 'dwelling' (from OE *wunung*).

27 *this live*: The emendation of MS *his* to *this* here is supported by *ceste morteu uie* of the French text.

I, 110 Somer is y-comen in [*NIMEV* 3223]

MS: London, BL Harley 978, with music.

The words of this famous song are to be sung in canon. According to the instructions given in the MS, this canon may be sung by four, three, or even two companions. The second singer starts when the first has sung the first line, then the third when the second has sung the first line, and so on. There is also a bass part marked *pes* (i.e. 'foot') for two additional voices; both sing together, the one singing *Sing cuckòu nou! Sing cuckòu*, and the other *Sing cuckòu! Sing cuckòu nou!* Although in the MS these lines are copied at the end, after the other words and music, they are in fact meant to be sung accompanying the upper voices from the start and to be repeated as two-bar phrases throughout the song as long as it lasts. For this reason they are given in the text here at the beginning of the song.

As a type of part-song, the rhythm of the music here is, of necessity, strict and measured, unlike the freer rhythms of plainsong-like tunes. In the text some of the syllables have been marked as accented; this is in accordance with the requirements of the *ictus* (the accented beat) of the music. Thus, in lines 4, 7, and 11, and in the lines of the *pes*, the word *cuckòu* has final stress as in French *coucòu*, but in lines 12 and 13 the stress is on the initial syllable as in English. Again, lines 9 and 13, are sung as *Lowth àfter càlve còu* and *Wèl singèst thou cùckou;* they need not, of course, be spoken in this way. These instances clearly illustrate the fact that even in measured, accentual music a singer readily altered the natural stress and rhythm of speech to conform with the accentual requirements of music.

10 *verteth*: Most editors have taken MS *uerteþ* here as a form of *ferteth*, politely glossed as 'breaks wind'. Silverstein questions whether bucks farting is a very apt expression of summer joy; and who would hear it anyway? He suggests instead that this may be an early instance of the verb *vert* (see *OED* **vert**, *v.* 1) from the Latin *vertere*, and here glosses 'cavorts' (Silverstein (1971), p. 37). While this verb is only recorded in *OED* from the late 16th century, it is to be noted that the verb *ferten* (other than this doubtful instance here) is not attested before the end of the 14th century (see *MED* **ferten** v.).

I, 111   Say me, wight in the brom [*NIMEV* 3078]

MS: Cambridge, Trinity College B.14.39.

Another version of this piece of popular traditional wisdom is found in a narrative setting in a Latin exemplum in MS London, BL Add. 11579, where a woman is told by a fortune-teller to go to a wood and repeat her complaint about her husband. There follows this version of the dialogue:

> 'Say, wight y the brom,
> What is me for to don?
> Ich have the worstë bonde
> That is in any londe.'

> *Responsio sortilege anglice:*
> 'Yif thy bonde is ille
> Hold thy tongë stille.'

I, 112   Hit was upon a Shere Thorsday [*NIMEV* 1649]

MS: Cambridge, Trinity College B.14.39.

Text: 13 He mettë] I mette MS; 49 Lord Crist] crist *erased after* lord MS; 58 frec] *added*; 64 & 66 knighte] cnistes MS. In the right-hand margin the sign '.ii.' indicates the repeat of 15–16, 51–2 and 63–4 (written as single long lines in the MS).

No source has been discovered for this story of Judas and his sister. It may have derived from accounts of Judas in which he is exploited by his wife. See Brown XIII, p. 183.

16 *me stonde thee*: lit. 'that one should stone thee'. Here *me* is a weakened form of the indefinite pronoun *man*, 'one'. Cf. line 60.

48 This line has elsewhere been taken as part of Judas's reply, with *he* referring to Christ. However, it is Judas who wished to have the stolen 30 coins of silver back, not Christ, who had given them to Judas to buy food with. Thus, line 47 is Judas's direct speech; line 48 is a comment thereon, and *he* refers to Judas.

64 & 66 *knighte*: MS *cnistes*. The rhyme requires the plural form with the ending '-e' (whether sounded here or not) derived historically from the OE genitive plural *cnihta*.

I, 113   Ich herde men upon mold [*NIMEV* 1320.5]

MS: London, BL Harley 2253.

Text: 7 bit] bid MS; 26 men] me MS; 28 bidding] bddyng MS; 29 Men] meni MS; 43 no] ne MS; 59 her fille] ar fulle MS.

2 *he*: 'they'. This earlier dialect form of the plural pronoun is retained here for the alliteration with *herë* ('their') in the second half of the line.

7 *bit*: See *MED* **bite** n. **3.** (a) where *bid* (the MS form) in this line is quoted with the sense 'bite', though *bid* is not listed initially among the variant forms.

15 The hayward's duties included responsibility for maintaining the fences which separated the common land from enclosed lands.

16 The bailiff was in charge of administering the lord's land and upholding his rights in law.

17 The peasant would forage for firewood or perhaps, like the man in the moon in **I, 114** (below), who is also caught in the act, for briar cuttings for mending fences. The woodward was the official in charge of forests and forest timber.

19 Lit. 'thus one robs the poor': *me* is a form of the ME indefinite pronoun 'one'.

23 Here and in lines 31 and 32 the forces of corruption, unbridled power (*Will*) and dishonesty (*Falsshipe*), are personified.

24 *pikërës*: 'horseman's, rider's'. A contrast is commonly made in ME verse between the rich and powerful mounted on horseback with all their finery and the poor and destitute often walking barefoot and ragged.

33 *in the stede*: lit. 'in the place'.

34 The beggars here are those who have been cheated and driven out of land and property and forced to take to the road like pilgrims, i.e. with staff and bag.

37 The beadle was an official working under the authority of the bailiff, here acting as a tax-collector.

38 *grene wax*: A seal of green wax was affixed to Exchequer documents containing the names of those to be taxed. Thus 'silver for the green wax' meant money for the payment of taxes. See *OED* **Green wax**.

42 *fish-day*: a religious fast day on which fish was eaten.

43 Though the spelling *chost* is questioned under *MED* **chest** n., it is clearly required for the rhyme scheme here.

55 *under gore*: lit. 'under clothes'.

70 Flooding caused by the overflowing of streams and the breaching of banks.

I, 114   Man in the moone stont and strit [*NIMEV* 2066]

MS: London, BL Harley 2253.

Text: 9 trowëth] trowe MS; 35 nil he] nulle MS; 40 cherl] cherld MS.

The man in the moon was popularly supposed to have been a peasant who was banished to the moon for stealing thorns which he still carries in a bundle on his fork.

6 *hattren*: Plurals ending in '-en', as here and in *doren* (needed for the rhyme) in line 14, were occasionally used in late 14th-century London English; so also were the '(e)th' plural forms of the verb, as in *beth* and *to-terëth* (again required for the rhyme).

8 The apparent personification of the hedge here may simply be taken as a touch of wry humour – i.e. so elusive is the man in the moon that only the hedge he works on knows anything about him – what he wears, for example.

9 Lit. 'Where does this man believe (himself) to have taken (his) way?'

13–16 What is described here is the contemporary method of mending hedges, which involved two stages. First, cuttings (commonly of whitethorn) were planted in the hope that they would grow to fill the gaps. Secondly, to prevent the new shoots from being eaten or trampled by animals, these cuttings were protected by a further layer of branches, again preferably of thorns. Thus, if the man in the moon did not cut a second bundle (the *other trous*, line 15), of thorns for this purpose, his cuttings would be left unprotected and his day's work thereby wasted. See Menner (1949), pp. 6–11.

17 *when er he were*: lit. 'whenever he may have been (sc. born)'.

22–32 The man in the moon is imagined as having been off on an errand, namely that of cutting briars; he has not succeeded simply because he has been caught by the hayward. The hayward had the duty of protecting his lord's property from thieves; he has therefore exacted from the man in the moon a promise of payment in the form of a *wed*, that is, a pledge, which could have been any item such as a hat, a pair of gloves, or the like (see *Piers Plowman* C XIV, 44–5, and Skeat (1886), II, p. 174) which could later be redeemed by the payment of money.

32 *baily*: 'bailiff, steward'. In the general sense of 'an agent of a Lord, responsible … for the management of a manor' (*MED* **baillif** n. **3.**) this term may overlap with *hayward*, an official whose duties included, but were by no means confined to, maintaining hedges (see *MED* **hei-ward** n.). Thus the *baily* here – the word perhaps chosen because it alliterates with *borwe* in the first half of the line – may be the same person as the *hayward* of line 24. This would make for the simplest and most satisfactory reading of the situation here. The trick proposed (doubtless one common enough in the poet's day) was to fill the hayward / bailiff full of liquor and, presumably, to steal the pledge back from him when he

was too drunk to notice. Alternatively, if the *hayward* and the *baily* here are to be taken as referring to different officials, one has to suppose with Menner that when the *hayward* is drunk they will steal some money from him with which they will then redeem the pledge from the bailiff (Menner (1949), p. 12).

36 *can nought o lawe*: For *o lawe* with a verb of motion (understood here with *can*) meaning 'get down', cf. *MED* **loue** n. (3) (b).

37 The man in the moon may be called a magpie here because of his activities in stealing thorn cuttings. The magpie is described as *hosede* because its black legs beneath its white belly look as if they were clad in leggings or stockings. See Menner (1949), p. 13.

38 *amarscled*: 'bewildered', i.e. by 'the sinister power of the moon which has made the man a prisoner' (*EMEVP*, p. 332, n. 36, and see also n. 38).

38 *mawe*: 'stomach'. For *into the mawe* as 'to your very vitals', see *EMEVP*, glossary, under **mawe** n.

I, 115 Of rybaudz I ryme and rede o my rolle [NIMEV 2649]

MS: London, BL Harley 2253.

Text: 21 rybaud] rybaudz MS.

3 *by pate and by polle*: lit. 'head by head'.

4 For *take* as 'give' and *tolle* as 'payment' see *MED* **taken** v. **31a.** and *OED* **Toll** sb. 1.

5 *Gonnylde gnoste*: According to *OED* (under **Gun**, *sb.*) *Gonnylde* here (ultimately derived from ON *Gunnhild-r*) was a name used for a cannon.

16 *Gobelyn*: 'a mischievous and ugly demon'. In the 12th century Odericus Vitalis mentions *Gobelinus* as the popular name of a spirit. *Gobelyn* here is the first occurrence of the word in English. See *OED* **Goblin**.

16 *groměně*: The ending '-ene' was originally genitive plural (from OE '-ena') but came also to have adjectival force in ME.

22 *dewe*: 'dew' or simply 'moisture'; see *MED* **deu** n. 1. The choice of word here is dictated by the alliteration.

24 *shooëth a shrewe*: possibly a proverbial saying; see Robbins, *Hist.*, p. 260, n. 24. The sense is that this is the kind of rascal from whose very looks it is obvious that he is given to every kind of mischief and futile activity.

26 *as hit were a bride*: lit. 'as if it were a girl'. In ME *bride* had the general sense of 'young woman, maiden' as well as the modern sense 'bride'. See *MED* **brid(e** n. (1) **2.**

27 *lowe-lacěde shoon*: i.e. fashionable, effeminate footwear, rather than boots or leggings laced up the leg.

28 This line is quoted in *MED* under **piken** v. (1) **8.** (a), under **provendre** n. (a), and under **pride** n. 2 **1b.** (d) with meanings given respectively as 'steal, rob, plunder', 'food for domesticated animals, fodder', and 'worldly wealth or possessions; extravagant finery'. However, it is not altogether clear how 'they steal from their fodder all their finery' makes sense unless 'fodder' is taken to refer not only to food but (derisively) to any sustenance *knavës* can come by from their superiors including items of clothing. This would then amount to

a final dismissive comment to the effect that all their vaunted finery is merely scavenged from anything such lackeys can get.

31–2 *companage*: items of food other than the basics, bread or meat; see *MED* **companage** n. (1). Robbins translates 'relish' (*Hist.,* p. 260, n. 31). The coarsely ironic sense of these lines is: no matter what he gave them ('even if he gave them cats' shit'!) yet they would complain about the balance due to them. The translation of line 32 as 'yet he shall grieve about the expense' given by Robbins (*Hist.,* p. 260, n. 32) ignores the fact that *arrerage* essentially involves the sense of what is owing. See *MED* **arrerage** n.

I, 116   Skottes out of Berwik and of Abirdene [*NIMEV* 3080]

MS: London, BL Cotton Galba E.ix.

Text: 25 Skotte] skottes MS.

The 11 political / historical poems of Laurence Minot (probably a Yorkshireman writing between 1333 and 1352, the period of the events he deals with) appear in the early 15th-century MS BL Cotton Galba E.ix, along with a miscellany of romances and religious and didactic poems. This poem celebrates the victory of the English over the Scots at Halidon Hill in 1333 as revenge for the earlier Scottish victory at Bannockburn. Minot's chauvinistic, anti-Scottish rhetoric is characteristically personal in tone and gains force from his use of alliterative formulae and colloquial vocabulary. On Minot, see Turville-Petre in *Companion*, 181–6.

The Northern dialect of this poem has not been normalized to that of late 14th-century London. As is evident from the *Reeve's Tale*, Chaucer was not unfamiliar with this form of English. Nor does it present much difficulty to the modern reader since some of its characteristics were to establish themselves in Standard English in the course of the ensuing two centuries, e.g. the pronoun 'their' (here *thaire*) and the '-es' ending of the third person singular present indicative of the verb. The MS forms are altered here only in the substitution of the letters 'th', 'y', 'J', 'u' (for the vowel) and 'ee' (in *thee*) for 'þ', 'ȝ', 'I', 'v' and 'e'. Unstressed 'e' may have been sounded more frequently here than indicated in the text.

1 *Skottes out of Berwick and of Abirdene*: i.e. Scots from all parts, South and North.
2 The battle in 1314 at Bannockburn outside Stirling, in which the Scots defeated the English, ushered in a period of success for the Scots in their struggles against the English.
4 The revenge was the English victory in 1333, at Halidon Hill near Berwick.
7 *Saint Johnës toune*: a name for Perth, then capital of Scotland, taken from the medieval town church of St John the Baptist.
9 *bosting*: possibly a reference to songs sung by the Scots abusing the English, some to the effect that the Scots would drag the English to the gallows by their tails.
15 *the pelers*: Border raids by the Scots were used by Edward III as a pretext for his renewal of war against the Scots which led to the battle of Halidon Hill.
16 *rifild thaire rout*: lit. 'stripped their band', i.e. the band of raiders.
19 *riveling*: 'rawhide boot', 'a derogatory nickname for a Scot' (*MED,* **riveling** n. (b)).

20 *Berebag*: The Scots were noted for the fact that when on campaign, instead of hampering their progress by having a baggage-train with provisions, each man simply carried a bag of oatmeal for food.

22 *Brig*: 'Bruges'. The Scots had close trading links with Flanders.

36 After the battle of Halidon Hill, Berwick, which had been besieged by Edward III, surrendered to the English.

I, 117   Ich am of Irlande [*NIMEV* 1008]

MS: Oxford, Bodl. Rawlinson D.913.

1–3 This lyric may have been a dance song in the form of a carol. As such, these lines would be the burden (sung by all the dancers), and lines 4–7 a stanza to be sung by a soloist.

5 Old French *par seinte charite* was rendered as *for seint charite* and as *of seint charite* in ME. Both prepositions have been combined here in *For of*.

I, 118   Maiden in the morë lay [*NIMEV* 2037.5]

MS: Oxford, Bodl. Rawlinson D.913.

Text: 10 was] wat MS; 21, 22, 25 *and* 26 the] *supplied, MS has a four-letter space at the beginning of which the blurred form of the letter* 'þ' *is perhaps to be made out.*

This dance song is recorded in a highly abbreviated form in the Rawlinson MS. For the MS forms *mor* (1, 2, 5 and 6), *seuenyst* (3), *seuenist* (4) and *seuenistes* (7 and 8) as scribal revisions of *more* and *seueniste*, and the rationale of the expansion given here of the Rawlinson text, see Duncan (1996 [a]).

3 *Sevenightë fullë*: After numerals some nouns in ME (of which 'night' was one) had plural forms with final '-e' or without an ending (cf. Chaucer's *she was seven nyght old*, CT, VIII, 2873) as well as forms with the '-es' plural ending. See Mustanoja (1960), pp. 57–8.

27 *wellë-spring*: the source of a stream where the water rises (i.e. 'wells up') to the surface.

28 *bour*: ME *bour* had both the general sense of 'dwelling' and the more specific sense of 'lady's chamber'.

I, 119   D ... dronken [*NIMEV* 694.11]

MS: Oxford, Bodl. Rawlinson D.913.

In the MS this lyric is so faded and illegible in many places that the readings and the arrangement of the text arrived at by various editors differ widely. What is given here is substantially the version printed by Robbins (*Sec.*, p. 106) who interpreted this piece as the work of a poet 'trying to represent the emotions of a drunken man, who wants everything to stand still; then when he trips, is able to relax his body' (Robbins, *Sec.*, p. 265). However, to judge from other Rawlinson poems (e.g. **I, 117** and **118**), this may, as John Burrow has persuasively argued, be a dance song rather than simply a drinking song (Burrow (1984), pp. 1–12). The following is Burrow's version of the text with two additions: (1) *Robin*, as suggested by the Sisams (*MEV*,

p. 169), for the space in the MS between *Hay* and *Malkin* which may well have contained a name; and (2) the repetition of line 8 as line 9, a repetition which could easily have been omitted in error or as an abbreviation of the text (cf. **I, 118**). These alterations give three stanzas of five lines with 3, 2, 3, 3 and 3 strong accents, a rhythmic regularity required of a dance song. The six lines Burrow left 'formally unaccounted for' (Burrow (1984), p. 11) thus form another complete stanza and a final couplet. However, this reconstruction is admittedly speculative.

> Tàbart ìs y-drònken,
>   Drònken, drònken,
> Y-drònken ìs Tabàrt,
> Y-drònken ìs Tabàrt,
> 5 Y-drònken àttë wìnë.
>
> Hay Ròbin, Màlkin, sùster,
>   Wàlter, Pèter!
> Ye drònken àllë dèpë,
> Ye drònken àllë dèpë,
> 10 Ànd Ichùllë èkë.
>
> Stòndëth àllë stìllë,
>   Stìllë, stìllë,
> Stìllë stòndëth àllë,
> Stìllë stòndëth àllë,
> 15 Stìlle as àny stòn.
>
> Trìppe a littel wìth thy fòt
> And lèt thy bòdy gòn.

I, 120   The Complaint of Chaucer to his Purse

See Benson (1988), p. 1191 for the textual authorities, 11 MSS, a transcript of a Cotton MS, and the editions of Caxton (1477–8) and of Thynne (1532). Text based on MS Oxford, Bodl. Fairfax 16.

Text: 4 but] *some* MSS, but yf MS; 25 oure harmes] *some* MSS, myn harme MS.

The envoy appears in only five of the eleven MSS; it differs in form, tone and diction from the preceding stanzas and may have been a later addition. With the envoy, the poem is specifically a begging poem; poems of this kind were written by Chaucer's contemporaries Deschamps and Machaut. Without the envoy, it stands in a tradition of popular poems about money which is well represented by **I, 121**, below. However, 'Chaucer's poem is unique in its humorous application of the language of a lover's appeal to his mistress to this well-worn theme' (Benson, p. 1088).

  4 *make me hevy chere*: 'look gravely / seriously upon me'. Again, as with *lyght* in line 3, pun is involved with *hevy chere* as 'serious in manner' but also with *hevy* as 'heavy in weight'. Lady Purse should be both!
13 *Quene of comfort*: a phrase used referring to the Blessed Virgin in Chaucer's poem 'An ABC', line 77. Cf. his reference to his purse here as 'saviour', in line 16.

15 *that ben*: '(you) who are'; cf. *Been* in line 24. Throughout this poem the plural of polite address is used.

17 *Out of this tounë*: Various interpretations have been offered. Skeat took this to be an expression of Chaucer's wish to quit the expense of London for some cheaper place.

19 *shave as nye as is a frere*: i.e. 'stripped clean of money'. Chaucer playfully combines the sense of the friar's tonsure and the notion of the friar's vow of poverty.

22 A common tradition in medieval literature deriving from the pseudo-historical early 12th-century *Historia Regum Britanniae* of Geoffrey of Monmouth had it that Albion, another name for Britain, had been founded by a certain Brutus, a descendant of Aeneas. The 'conqueror' here is Henry IV, who came to the throne by deposing Richard II.

I, 121   Whan I have in myn purs y-now [*NIMEV* 3959]

MS: London, BL Sloane 2593.

Text: 12 is] *added*.

1–2 Cf. Commentary, **I, 65**, 1–2.

9 Jak was a name commonly used for an ordinary fellow of low social status. See Greene, p. 448.

13 Greene takes the references to *horn* here and *bow* in line 17 as indicating rather 'that Jack has taken to hunting the deer than that he has become a "vagabond musician", as suggested in the note in the first edition of this work' (Greene, p. 448).

I, 122   I have a gentil cok [*NIMEV* 1299]

MS: London, BL Sloane 2593.

Text: 2 the day] day MS; 11 corel] scorel MS.

Compare Chaucer's description of Chauntecleer in *The Nun's Priest's Tale*:

> His coomb was redder than the fyn coral,
> And batailled as it were a castel wal;
> His byle was black, and as the jeet it shoon;
> Lyk asure were his leggës and his toon;
> His naylës whitter than the lylye flour,
> And lyk the burnëd gold was his colour.

CT, VII. 2859–64

8 The MS spelling *tayil* might be taken to indicate a disyllabic pronunciation as required here and in line 12. However, *yi* simply represents 'i' in MS *matyins* (4).

15 & 19 In the Sloane lyrics the variation of three- and four-stress lines is not uncommon.

19–20 For the sexual innuendo here, compare the nursery rhyme:

> Goosey, goosey, gancer,
> Whither shall I wander?

Upstairs and downstairs
And in my lady's chamber.

I, 123   Omnes gentes plaudite! [*NIMEV* 2675]

MS: London, BL Sloane 2593.

Text: 9 it] is MS.

This lyric reads convincingly with four stresses per line.

1 With these words from the beginning of Psalm 47 (AV: 'O clap your hands all ye people'), the singer of this nonsense-cum-drinking song may wryly have been inviting the encouragement of a bit of applause.

4 If the words *Ego dixi* are meant to echo the beginning of the canticle of Hezekiah (Isaiah, 38:10–22), this reference (with the following *have good day*) is blatantly ironic since King Hezekiah's observations are far from cheerful, as, for instance, in verse 14, where there is mention of birds: 'Like a crane or a swallow, so did I chatter: I did mourn as a dove: mine eyes fail with looking upward: O Lord, I am oppressed; undertake for me'.

10 *Yeve us onës drinken*: lit. 'Give us once more [something] to drink'.

I, 124   I have a yong suster [*NIMEV* 1303]

MS: London, BL Sloane 2593.

Text: 2 beyond the] beʒondyn þe MS; 7 the] *added*; 19 I] ony MS, *with* ony *struck through, a deletion then revised, with only the letters* on *subpuncted for deletion.*

12 *longing*: The rhyme with *rinde* here and in lines 20 and 28 is on the second syllable. For 'nd' rhyming with 'ng', cf. *bond* and *long* in **I, 108**, 2 and 4.

21–8 The change in the last two stanzas from the riddle-like questions previously asked to the answers now given is marked by a change in metre; the first and third lines of the last two stanzas now have seven or eight syllables and four stresses instead of the five or six syllables and three stresses of equivalent lines in earlier stanzas.

I, 125   I have a newe garden [*NIMEV* 1302]

MS: London, BL Sloane 2593.

Text: 18 right] *two small letters* – ag (?) – *added above*; home] honde MS; 24 Jonet] jon- *(ending obscured by mending tape)* MS.

1–8 In this, another Sloane lyric of sexual innuendo (cf. **I, 122** and **128**), the poet's unique new garden and its pear-tree are suggestive of various signs of puberty.

8 *pere-jonet*: an early-ripening pear, ripe by St John's Day, 24 June. The association of this fruit with the name 'John', presumably the speaker's name here, is wittily exploited in lines 23–4, where the fair maiden claims that the child is a *pere Robert*, 'a Robert pear', rather than a *pere Jonet*, 'a John pear', i.e. a 'pear' from 'grafting' with one Robert rather than with John.

16 *in fille*: 'pour out'. For this sense with wine etc., see *MED* **fillen** v. 1. (b).

18   *home*: Robbins's emendation of MS *honde* to supply a rhyme with *womb* (20).

I, 126   Seynt Stevene was a clerk [*NIMEV* 3058]

MS: London, BL Sloane 2593.

The variation of three- and four-stress lines is not uncommon in Sloane lyrics. However, in three of the four possible three-stress variants here the name *Stevene* appears. Perhaps the pronunciation varied between *Stevènë* (cf. Latin 'Stephànus') and *Stèven* (cf. *Heròwdës* and *Hèrod*). Line 33 seems to require stress on the second syllable, i.e. *Stevèn*, and *Stevènë* would allow (if the text is sound) for three stresses in line 45. In line 17, *Stevene* could be read as *Stèven* or *Stevènë*. Likewise, line 1 could be read as *Sèynt Stevènë wàs a clèrk.*

   1 *clerk*: Among other senses, this word could mean a household official of various kinds, and here, an attendant at table.
   3 *of bred and cloth*: This could mean 'with food and clothes', but it seems better here to take the sense as (literally) 'with regard to food and table-cloth' – see *MED* **cloth** n. **1b.** (a) – and so as 'with food at table'.
  26 *brede*: 'rave'; see *MED* **breiden** v. (1) **11.** (a).
  43 *Steven out*: pronounced as two syllables here ('Stev'n out') with the medial syllable lost by syncopation.
  47 The Feast of St Stephen is on 26 December; Christmas Day is, therefore, the eve of the feast.

I, 127   Yong men, I warne you everychon [*NIMEV* 4279]

MS: London, BL Sloane 2593.

Text: 5 at hom have on] haue on at hom MS. The repeated final line of each stanza is abbreviated as *I dar not etc* for stanzas 2 and 3, and *I dar etc.* in stanza 4.

Early widowhood and the importance of marriage in respect of property rights in the Middle Ages commonly gave rise to the marriage of young men to older women. For other carols on the perils of marriage, see Greene, nos. 403–11.

  1–2 Cf. Commentary, **I, 65**, 1–2.
  17   *rish*: 'rush', a thing of little value; cf. *pese* (21), and Whiting, *Proverbs*, R 250.

I, 128   We bern aboute no cattës skinnes [*NIMEV* 3864]

MS: London, BL Sloane 2593.

  1–2 Cf. Commentary, **I, 65**, 1–2.
   2 *foulë weyës*: Medieval roads were not only frequently 'foul' in their physical condition but also dangerous on account of robbers. It was therefore especially advantageous to travel light. However, the 'foul ways' the rogue of this poem had to flee doubtless included predicaments over and above the perils of travelling.
  3–5 The wares of ordinary pedlars or friars are listed by Wycliffe as including *knyues, pursis, pynnys and girdlis and spices and sylk and precious pellure and*

forrouris for wymmen (Matthew (1880), p. 12). This 'pedlar' offers something quite different!

5 A wimple was a head-dress covering chin and neck.

11 *jelyf*: 'jelly', slang for penis.

I, 129   As I went on Yol Day [*NIMEV* 377]

MS: London, BL Sloane 2593.

Text: 37 childe] schylde MS. The repetition of the burden is indicated by *Kyrieleyson* in the right-hand margin opposite stanza 2, and by *K* opposite stanzas 5 and 7.

In a witty and irreverent manner, the course of Jankin's seduction of Alison is paralleled in this poem with the structure of the mass, beginnning with the procession, and then the divisions of the Office – the Kyrie, the Epistle, the Sanctus, the Agnus Dei, the words 'Benedicamus Domino' with which the mass ends at solemn feasts such as Christmas, and the people's response 'Deo gratias'. The lines repeated after each stanza in this poem as the burden are a parody of the words 'Kyrie eleison' (Lord have mercy) which are six times repeated early in the mass. The metre again varies with lines of three and of four stresses in the first and third lines of the stanzas.

3 *aleyson*: This spelling, instead of *eleyson,* suggests a pun on the girl's name, Alison.

11 *dos*: The Northern ending '-(e)s' of the third person singular present of the verb was already to be found in the language of London by the late 14th century and is used occasionally by Chaucer, mostly in rhymes.

20 *crakëth a merie note*: This refers to the elaborate style of singing in which long notes were divided into numerous short ('small') notes for ornamentation. Thus, the shepherds in 'The First Shepherds' Play', admire the *small noytys* of the angels which produce *foure & twenty to a long.* See Greene, p. 494.

22 *cote*: The type of coat in question would have been a close-fitting tunic or a surcoat. See *MED* **cote** n. (2) 1. (a).

30 *pax-brede*: a 'disc of silver or gilt with a handle and a sacred symbol used in giving the "kiss of peace" to the congregation' (Greene, p. 494).

I, 130   Thou that sellest the worde of God [*NIMEV* 3697]

MS: Cambridge, St John's College 195.

Text: 3 Com thou] cum MS.

2 Some held that the friars, like their founder, St Francis, should go barefoot; others allowed that in view of the difference in the climate of England from that of Italy, the wearing of sandals was permissible.

4 *In principio erat verbum* (John 1:1) was the conventional greeting of the friars.

7 *symonie*: 'simony', trading in sacred things.

14–15 See 2 Tim. 3:6: *Ex his enim sunt qui penetrant domos, et captivas ducunt mulierculas oneratas peccatis, quae ducuntur variis desideriis* (For of this sort are they which creep into houses, and lead captive silly women laden with sins, led away with divers lusts).

16 *midday develes*: This echoes *daemonio meridiano* of Psalm 90:6, translated as 'noon-day devil' in the Douay version.

I, 131   Allas! what shul we frerës do [NIMEV 161]

MS: Cambridge, St John's College 195.

Text: 12 They] þat þei MS; 25 biddë] *added*.

  6 *allë*: plural, lit. 'all [sc. things]', here, everything to do with scripture.
 14 Cf. **I, 130**, Commantary, 4.
 15 *poppe*: 'fop'; see *MED* **poppe** n. (2).
 21 *myn habite*: to be pronounced 'my nabìbe' cf. MS *my nabete*.
 34 *gile*: As Robbins notes (*Hist.*, p. 339), the sense 'harm' required here is not otherwise recorded for this word.

I, 132   Swarte smekëd smithes smatered with smoke [NIMEV 3227]

MS: London, BL Arundel 292.

  4 *knavënë cry*: The ending '-ene' of *knavënë* derives historically from the OE ending '-ena' of the genitive plural.
  8 *spellen many spelles*: lit. 'tell many tales'. Above these words in the MS, *ech of hem at othyr* ('each of them against the other') has been added in fainter ink.
 21 *clothemeres*: lit. 'those who clothe mares'; see *MED* **clothe-mere** n.

PART II

II, 1   Allas, Deth, who made thee so hardy [NIMEV 144]

MS: London, BL Harley 682.

Steele (1941), Ballade no. 57; French equivalent in Champion, p. 81.

Text: 14 Had] Haddist MS, dist *erased*; taken] taken yet MS, yet *erased*; 16 take] taken MS, n *erased*; 17 this] *written over* has *erased*; 19 out] without MS, wit *erased*; 25 Out] Without MS, wit *erased*; in] *inserted above the line before* slouthe; 30 offens] offensis MS, is *erased*.

That the textual alterations in the MS were made (largely under authorial direction; see Steele (1941), p. xxvii, and Arn (1994), pp. 109–13) to restore, rather than to improve, the metre of this lyric is evident from the reinstatement in line 19, and again in line 25, of *out* (meaning 'without'), a characteristic feature of Charles d'Orléans's vocabulary. Obviously a copyist, without regard to metre, had replaced Charles's *out* with the more familiar *without*. The word *in* added in line 25 restores sense as well as metre.

The poems in MS Harley 682 are in English. Some have counterparts in the French poems of Charles d'Orléans. Charles's authorship of the English poems has been disputed. However, not only does the poet of Harley 682 name himself as *Yowre servaunt Charlis duk of Orlyaunce* – see Steele (1941), p. 92, line 2720, and elsewhere – but a convincing analysis of evidence bearing on the question of authorship led the editor of the EETS edition of the Harley poems to the conclusion that Charles first composed these poems in English and subsequently rewrote them in French. In her edition of 1994, Mary-Jo Arn accepts the premise of Charles's authorship. The French versions have all the appearance of 'polished' revisions (Steele (1941), p. xxvi), while the English poems exhibit the vividness and vigour of original composition (see, e.g., Commentary, **II, 6**, 6 and 10). Though largely Chaucerian, the vocabulary of these poems contains many un-Chaucerian words: some are English malformations; others, mainly used in rhyme, are of French derivation (see Steele (1941), pp. xlii–xliii). Further telling evidence supporting French authorship of the English poems is to be found in occasional lines which can be read fluently only on the assumption that they were written by a poet whose patterns of stress and intonation were French rather than English (see Commentary, **II, 5**, 1 & 3).

The poems of MS Harley 682 are in three parts. The first – mainly a sequence of ballades – is an account of the poet's courtship of a certain Lady Beauty, of the development of their love, of her death, of the poet's grief, and, finally, of his renunciation of Love's service. The second part is called a Jubilee – a banquet of song and dance marking the poet's retirement from love. It consists mainly of a series of roundels (originally 100 in all). This second part concludes with the mention of the poet's 'new fortune', a love affair with a new lady which is recounted in the third part, once again in a sequence of ballades.

    1 Charles d'Orléans occasionally, as here, omits a syllable before the second stress in lines which begin with an exclamation or a question; see Steele and Day (1946), p. 47. Thus, the pattern of stresses in this line is: × / / × / × / × / with stress (albeit without exaggeration) falling on the second syllable of *hardy* as the rhyme-scheme here requires. Similarly, stress must fall on the second syllable of *body* in line 3. Cf. Commentary, **II, 5**, 1 & 3.

    7 *hastily*: pronounced here as two syllables, with the medial vowel elided.

  15 *As … rigure*: lit. 'then had you not committed (an act of) such great severity'.

  28 *creature*: pronounced with three syllables as 'cre-a-ture'.

II, 2   For dedy liif, my lyvy deth y wite [*NIMEV* 816]

MSS: London, BL Harley 682; Cambridge, University Library Add. 2585. The Cambridge MS lacks the envoy (25–8). Text from the Harley MS.

Text: 28 *supplied*.

Steele (1941), Ballade no. 60; no French equivalent.

This ballade skilfully exploits rhetorical devices widely favoured by medieval poets writing in the 'high' style, devices exhaustively described in medieval Latin treatises on rhetoric, or the art of poetry. Oxymoron, the juxtaposition of self-contradictory words (e.g. Chaucer's definition of love as *dredful joye* (*The Parliament of Fowls*, 3) and phrases like 'pleasing pains' and 'loving hate' in Elizabethan love poetry), aptly introduces the paradoxes of this lyric with *dedy liif* and *lyvy deth* in the opening line. Chiasmus, the pattern *a b: b a* formed by reversing in a second clause or phrase the order of words in the first (e.g. **ese** *of* **payne**: **payne** *of* **ese** in line 2), recurs throughout the first stanza. Conduplicatio, the repetition of the same words in successive phrases to accentuate emotion, is used in *O wofull wrecche, O wrecche* of the refrain lines. Exclamatio, where not only persons but also inanimate objects are directly addressed, serves to accentuate the expression of grief in lines 9–12. Anaphora, the repetition of the same word at the beginning of successive lines, is found in lines 1–3 and 9–12. Interrogatio, rhetorical question, is twice repeated at the opening of stanza 3, and followed there by expolitio, the repetition of the same idea in various ways. Such a rhetorical *tour de force* as this is not to be dismissed as mere ingenuity; Charles d'Orléans, in common with Chaucer and other medieval writers, considered the 'high' style to be the mode of writing most appropriate to the expression of deeply felt emotion.

8 *onys*: 'once', pronounced here, as in modern English, as one syllable.

9 *formatt*: 'vanquished', lit. 'checkmated'. Since Death 'has his lady' (7) the poet is vanquished or, metaphorically, in the language of chess, 'checkmated'. Cf. **11, 3** for the same use of the chess metaphor.

12 *eyen*: sometimes spelt *eyn* and here pronounced as a monosyllable.

11, 3 Toforn Love have y pleyd at the chesse [*NIMEV* 3795]

MS: London, BL Harley 682.

Steele (1941), Ballade 61; French equivalent in Champion, p. 82.

In writing this ballade Charles d'Orléans may well have had in mind the passage in Chaucer's *Book of the Duchess* in which the Black Knight speaks of playing a disastrous game of chess with Fortune and, on the loss of his queen, of being checkmated (*Book of the Duchess*, 652–61).

2 *Daungere*: 'Disdain'. In the first part of *The Romance of the Rose* (see Introduction, p. 15–16), a love affair is described in an allegorical dream-vision. The Lover encounters a Rose-bud (his beloved) in a walled garden and is first encouraged in his suit by Fair Welcome, a figure representing the receptive side of the Lady's response. However, Fair Welcome is then driven away by another figure, Danger, who represents the opposite disposition, the Lady's disdain and standoffishness.

3 *kepte eche poynt*: Steele and Day (1946), p. 16, state that 'the squares of the chess-board were called points'. Arn claims that 'the sense is that he kept each *piece* without losing any of them, at first', unless there is 'scribal error' here (Arn (1994), p. 466).

9 This line is equivalent to the French: *Se je ne fais une Dame nouvelle* (Champion, p. 83). The interpretation offered in the Introduction (see p. 16) depends on the assumption that a pawn could be queened. However, the state of the rules of chess in this regard in the late medieval period is a matter of dispute; see Arn (1994), pp. 57–9, and p. 466, note on line 2116. If the rules prevailing at the time Charles was writing did not allow for renewing a queen, the ironic contrast here would then be between an impossibility in chess and a possibility – finding a new lady – in actual life, however unthinkable that possibility to this poet in his grief-stricken circumstances.

20 *dowbil chere*: lit. 'double face', as in 'two-faced', 'deceitful'. In Charles's description of Fortune in the third part of the three-part sequence of the Harley poems her face is described as sometimes frowning, sometimes glad; see Steele (1941), lines 5037–39. Cf. Commentary, **II, 92**, 2.

30 *rekevre me*: 'recover', the verb is reflexive. The next ballade in the sequence (Steele (1941), no. 62, p. 73, lines 1–2) rejects the notion of recovery by finding a new lady just as decisively:

> Shulde y me make a lady newe, Fy, Fy!
> Nay rathir dey than doon so fowl a dede   *I would rather die than commit*
> *so foul a deed*

II, 4   In the forest of noyous hevynes [*NIMEV* 1549]

MS: London, BL Harley 682.

Steele (1941), Ballade no. 70; French equivalent in Champion, p. 88.

1–4 Charles d'Orléans draws on the conventions of the *chanson d'aventure* (see Introduction, p. 3) for the opening of this ballade.

2 *moneth*: 'month', here a monosyllable, as in modern pronunciation.

5 *answered*: pronounced here as two syllables with a reduced ending, as in modern English.

7 *passyng well*: 'very fittingly'; cf. *passyng frendship* (22). However unlikely, an alternative reading (with a comma after *passyng*) suggesting an audacious parallel between the poet as a figure of *noyous hevynes* (1) and the suffering Christ observed by *omnes qui transitis*, 'all who pass by' (see Commentary, **I, 99**, and Commentary, **II, 72**, 1–3) may be felt to lurk here.

17 *sovereyne*: 'sovereign', here pronounced as two syllables with syncope of the middle vowel.

19 *thorugh*: to be pronouced here as a monosyllable like modern English 'through'; *sheweth* should also be pronounced as one syllable, i.e. with a reduced ending.

27 *me a grave to cloth*: 'a grave to cover me'. Although the vocabulary of Charles's English poems is largely Chaucerian, there are several un-Chaucerian expressions, of which one is the word *cloth* in the sense of 'cover' with reference to a grave, here and elsewhere. See Steele (1941), p. xlii.

II, 5   O sely ankir, that in thi selle [*NIMEV* 2550]

MS: London, BL Harley 682.

Steele (1941), Ballade no. 97; no French equivalent.

1 & 3 According to Davies (1963), p. 342, both lines 'stumble', i.e. are, at first sight, awkward to read within the decasyllabic, five-stress norm of this poem. Arn (1994), p. 530, note to lines 5784–86, remarks, without explanation, that 'Charles has omitted a stressed syllable after *Ankir*, as well as after *gladder* in 5786'. However, it may not be fanciful to imagine that for someone used, as a native speaker, to French rather than to English accentuation, the first three words of line 1 could be read in a manner approaching the pattern / × / × / with

light stress on the second syllables of *sely* and *ankir* in the manner of French. Likewise, if one imagines *gladder* (3) pronounced in a French manner – again, that is, with slight accentuation on the second rather than the first syllable – the reading of line 3 becomes more fluent. So read, stress falls on the initial *Thou*, appropriately accentuating the contrast between *Thou* (the anchorite) here and *y* (Charles) in the next line. Other lines of Charles's verse are easier to read if account is taken of the influence of his mother tongue in his versification, e.g. **II, 1**, 1, and **II, 9**, 9 and 12. This is an interpretation which Arn might well have arrived at granted her observation that 'Charles allows some stress patterns that are not always comfortable for English readers', and that these point to verse which is 'the work of a Frenchman' (Arn (1994), p. 85).

8 *complaynt*: 'complaint', here as a literary form, i.e. a poem of complaint (see *MED* **compleint(e** n. **3.**). It is such a poem that the poet sends to 'report' to his lady. Like the present poem, 'complaints' were frequently written in ballade form.

19 *streight sidës*: 'Straight' or 'long' sides (like the other physical attributes mentioned in this stanza) were frequently listed among the features characteristic of conventional medieval beauty. See Commentary, **I, 25**, 7ff., and compare the features mentioned in **II, 8** (especially the *sidës streight* in line 3) and in **II, 19** (particularly in line 10).

25–7 The repetition of *Wo worthe* at the beginning of these successive lines is an instance of the rhetorical device of anaphora; see Commentary, **II, 2**.

II, 6   Syn that y have a nounparall maystres [*NIMEV* 3142]

MSS: London, BL Harley 682; Cambridge, University Library Add. 2585. Text from the Harley MS.

Steele (1941), Roundel no. 5; French equivalent in Champion, p. 206.

Text: 7, 13 Syn … maystres] Syn that MS; 8, 14 The … hert] The whiche MS.

This lyric is a roundel, a form, French in origin, the most characteristic feature of which is the repetition of the opening lines (the refrain), in whole or in part, after further groups of lines, and again, complete, at the end of the poem. Roundels varied in length. Though in Steele's EETS edition the majority (58) of Charles d'Orléans's English roundels are 14-line, decasyllabic poems like this, 12 (e.g. **II, 7** and **9**) are octosyllabic, and two vary decasyllabic and octosyllabic lines (see Commentary, **II, 8**, 10–11). There are also eight 19-line roundels, and one of 21 lines. Arn adopts a 16-line arrangement of the 14-line roundels included here; see her discussion in Arn (1994), pp. 79–81.

5 Charles occasionally introduces octosyllabic lines into decasyllabic verse; see Commentary, **II, 8**, 10–11. This may be such a line. However, assuming a trisyllabic pronunciation of *dowtles* as *dowtëles*, it can easily be read decasyllabically, i.e. *For now y trust to havë, dowtëles*.

6 The striking and homely image of the stitches in his shirt as a measure of the poet's joy here is not found in the French counterpart which simply reads: *D'avoir de tous biens largement* (Champion, p. 206, no. 5, line 6). Charles makes

several such references to his shirt (see Steele (1941), p. xliii), a peculiarity, it would seem, of his poetry.

10 The vivid image of the envious as horses prancing and rearing in rage is, again, not found in the equivalent French poem, which merely states that the envious suffer pain or sadness *sans allegement* ('without alleviation') (Champion, p. 207, no. 5, line 10) at the poet's happiness in his *nompareille maistresse*.

II, 7 My gostly fadir y me confesse [*NIMEV* 2243]

MS: London, BL Harley 682.

Steele (1941), Roundel no. 57; no French equivalent.

Text: 7, 13 My ... confesse] My gostly MS; 8, 14 First ... yow] First to MS; 11 to] *supplied*; 12 foryefënes] foryefnes MS.

12 The required syllabic count of this line could be met by taking *ellis* or *axe* as disyllabic. However, Steele and Day (1946), p. 47, note that 'ellis' in Charles d'Orléans's poems 'is regularly monosyllabic (except 3933)'. A more natural reading of the line is achieved by following the Sisams (see *MEV*, p. 424) in altering MS *foryefnes* here to the four-syllable form *foryefënes*.

II, 8 The smylyng mouth, and laughyng eyen gray [*NIMEV* 3465]

MS: London, BL Harley 682.

Steele (1941), Roundel no. 69; no French equivalent.

Text: 7, 13: The ... gray] The smyling MS; 8, 14 The ... twayne] The brestis MS.

10 I.e. 'To have (lit. to see) sight of you as I have seen (you) before'.

10–11 While describing Charles d'Orléans as a 'careful metrist', Steele and Day note his 'tendency to drop into octosyllables'. These octosyllabic lines here in an otherwise decasyllabic poem are two instances of 'about 150 in all'; Steele and Day (1946), p. 47.

II, 9 Go forth myn hert wyth my lady [*NIMEV* 922]

MSS: Paris, Bibl. Nat. fonds français 25458; London, BL Royal 16.F.ii. Text from the Paris MS.

Steele (1941), Appendix, no. 2; no French equivalent.

Text: 7–8, 13–14 Go ... besynes] Go forth etc. MS.

A copy of this poem (and of **II, 10**, below) is found in the Grenoble MS, a MS of Charles d'Orléans's poems derived from a copy of MS Paris, Bibl. Nat. fonds français 25458, Charles's personal MS, largely written in his own hand, the source of the texts as printed here.

6 *quippe*: 'keep', the spelling of a Frenchman writing English phonetically. See Steele (1941), p. xxv.

12 This line is to be read with accents on initial *In* and (as the rhyme requires) on the final syllable.

II, 10   So fayre, so freshe, so goodely on to se [*NIMEV* 3162]

MS: Paris, Bibl. Nat. fonds français 25458.

Steele (1941), Appendix, no. 6; no French equivalent.

Text: 7–8, 13–14 So … governans] So fayre etc. MS.

  2 *dymeynet*: may be pronounced (with reduced ending) as two syllables.

  5 *ever y*: may be pronounced (with syncope) as 'e-vri'.

II, 11   Myn hertës joy and all myn hole plesaunce [*NIMEV* 2182]

MSS: Oxford, Bodl. Fairfax 16 (B); London, Lambeth Palace Library 306 (L). Lines have been added in L to convert the poem into three eight-line stanzas with a concluding quatrain in short, eight-syllable lines. Text from B.

Text: 6 hertëly, with som] L, hertly with B.

The convention of the verse epistle – a poem written as a letter – was especially popular in 15th-century love poetry. Directions such as *Go lytill byll* (19) were typical of such poems. Here, however, Suffolk exploits the convention to the full by quaintly incorporating the date of his letter as part of the final line. Lyrics **II, 12–15** are also love epistles.

William de la Pole, Duke of Suffolk, a member of the inner council of nobles who governed England during the childhood of Henry VI, was a close personal friend of Charles d'Orléans, with whom he shared an enthusiasm for composing courtly verse. For four years (1432–6) during Charles's long captivity in England from 1415 until 1440, Suffolk acted as Charles's guardian; in this period they spent much time together living at Wallingford Castle and elsewhere.

II, 12   A celuy que pluys eyme en mounde [*NIMEV* 16]

MSS: Cambridge, University Library Gg.4.27, Part I a (C); London, BL Harley 3362 (H); Manchester, Chetham's Library Mun. E.6.10 (4) (A). Text from C.

Text: 2 founde] founde A, fonde H, found C; 12 Incisto] Incisto H, In cisto C, Consisto A; 22 ha tret] hatt3 CH; 26 clepë] clepe to CH; 28 ore ser] oreser H, creser C; 29 withoute] withoutyn CH; 37 Icest] Cest CH; 46 clere] H, cler C; 62 hertë] herte is CH.

This and the following poem form a pair of love epistles, the first from a lover to his beloved, and the second, her reply. The three languages – French, English and Latin – of these macaronic stanzas are skilfully interwoven.

It is assumed that the French lines in this poem are to be read metrically in the same manner as the English and that final 'e's of words in the French (as in the English) should be sounded as required by the metre.

A close textual analysis led Leo Spitzer (1952), fn. 1, pp. 151–2, to the interesting conclusion that 'our macaronic poems have been conceived, consciously and with some sophistication, on three separate linguistic levels every one of which has its specific climate: the English – that of genuine feeling, the French – of conventional courtesy, the Latin – of epigrammatic terseness. The order in which the three climates appear is not arbitrary; the courtly French must needs "open the conversation", to be followed by the mother tongue with its note of corroborative sincerity, the "period" ending with the pointed Latin.'

For textual evidence from a partial copy of **II, 12** in a recently discovered third MS (A), and for the defense and interpretation of the MS readings *od treyé* (4), *ore ser* (28) and *Incisto* (12), see Putter (2009), where further excellent analysis of the literary and socio-linguistic contexts of this lyric and of **II, 13** is also given.

   1 *celuy*: This masculine form of the tonic demonstrative instead of the feminine *celi* is an instance of the levelling of genders in Anglo-Norman.

 22 In the reading *hattʒ* of C and H the final *tʒ* is assumed to be an abbreviation.

 26 The accusative, *Causantem*, in the following line suggests that MS *clepe to* here should be emended to *clepë*. This gives excellent sense ('If I die I shall call you the cause') and good grammar, with *the Causantem* (26–7) matching *me ... Amantem* of lines 29–30.

 31 *de vous enpense*: 'I think of you'. See *AND* **empenser** for this verb in this sense.

 36 *Cum mora*: 'with delay', i.e. the intolerable delay he suffers waiting to be united with his beloved again.

 37 *Icest*: This alternative form to MS *cest* is required for the metre.

 44 *ne is*: perhaps to be elided; cf. H *nys*.

 46 Singing was a frequently mentioned accomplishment of courtly ladies in medieval literature. The manner of singing here, 'lightly singing with clear tones', is reminiscent of Chaucer's praise of Rosemounde: *Your semy voys that ye so smal out twyne* (Your light voice which you so ethereally spin out); see **I, 29**, 11.

 62 The omission of MS *is* here makes for good grammar and sense with *hertë* as the object of *Presento* (63). A scribe with little understanding of the Latin and assuming a verb to be missing in the English could easily have added *is*.

 64 The omission of a syllable after the caesura is assumed in this line and in line 71.

II, 13   A soun treschere et special [*NIMEV* 19]

MSS: Cambridge, University Library Gg.4.27 (C); London, BL Harley 3362 (H). The H text breaks off at line 15 at the bottom of fol. 91. Text from C.

Text: 4 salutz] saltz CH; 5 mouthë] mouth MS; 7 pry] *supplied, om.* CH; 8 mynë] myn MS; 10 fay] say CH; 26 tre] the tre MS; 44 strivë] strue MS.

 10 *Sertefyés*: 'assurances'. This interpretation assumes the use of the p.p. *sertefyés* in the sense '(things) certified' as equivalent to a noun, 'assurances'.

 43–6 The interpretation of the French here follows Spitzer (1952), p. 155.

II, 14   Fresshe lusty beauty, joyned with gentylesse [*NIMEV* 869]

MSS: Cambridge, Trinity College R.3.20 (T); London, BL Add. 29729 (B). Text from the Trinity MS.

Text: 7 ymage] visage TB.

In the Trinity MS this poem is preceded by a rubric by John Shirley (see Commentary, **II, 93**) which reads: 'Loo, here begynnethe a balade which that Lydegate wrote at the request of a squyer that served in loves court'. This rubric, repeated in the Additional MS which was copied from the Trinity MS, suggests that Lydgate, as a professional poet, supplied love lyrics on commission.

Although Lydgate's versification is notoriously awkward, this lyric reads quite smoothly on the whole, notwithstanding a few lines (e.g. 30, 42, 44, 46) with an extra syllable. Lydgate still (like Chaucer) made use of pronounced final '-e'. It may be assumed that despite the spelling, probably Shirley's spelling (which was eccentric) rather than Lydgate's, *eyeghen* (6) was pronounced as a monosyllable; cf. Commentary, **II, 2**, 12.

1 *gentylesse*: 'graciousness'. 'Nobility' or 'elegance' are also possible meanings of *gentylesse* here.

7 *ymage*: As all other refrain lines end with *ymage*, the emendation assumes that the reading *visage* here (albeit in both MSS) is erroneously repeated from the previous line.

8 *Penelopé*: Penelope, wife of Odysseus, was the model of wifely fidelity in classical and medieval literature. Though beset by various suitors during her husband's 20-year absence – his ten years at Troy and ten further years of adventures during his return home – she remained steadfastly loyal.

9 *Gresyldë*: Griselda, the heroine of *The Clerk's Tale* in Chaucer's *Canterbury Tales,* was resolutely patient in all adversity.

10 *Polixcenë*: Polixena, daughter of King Priam of Troy, loved by Achilles, was renowned for her beauty.

12 *Alceste*: Alcestis showed such devotion that she died as a sacrifice in place of her husband. However, in Euripides' play *Alcestis* Hercules brought her back from Hades.

13 *Dydo*: Dido, founder and Queen of Carthage, fell in love with Aeneas and, when he left her, killed herself on her funeral pyre with his sword. Boccaccio praises her for being clever and considerate, and presents her as a chaste queen who chose to mount her funeral pyre rather than remarry on the advice of her counsellors.

15 *Nyobë*: Niobe challenged the goddess Leto; her 14 children were killed as a punishment. She endured her suffering weeping, but proudly silent.

16 *Adryanë*: Ariadne, daughter of Minos, King of Crete. The virtues Lydgate attributes to her may reflect her steadfast love and loyalty to Theseus whom she helped by giving him a thread by means of which he was able to mark his route and so to escape from the Labyrinth after killing the Minotaur. She is mentioned for her discretion in Lydgate's *Floure of Curtesy.*

18 *Thesbë*: The tale of the young lovers, Pyramus and Thisbe, is familiar from the play on the subject performed by Bottom and his friends in Shakespeare's *A Midsummer Night's Dream.* Thinking Thisbe had been killed by a lion, Pyramus stabbed himself with his sword. When Thisbe discovered the dying Pyramus, she took her own life with the same sword.

19 *Cleopatres*: Cleopatra, Queen of Egypt (68–30 BC), was usually noted for her ruthless ambition and many lovers (who included Julius Caesar and

Marc Antony). However, Lydgate's notion of her *stabulnesse* here may reflect Chaucer's wholly unhistorical version of Cleopatra as a worthy and devoted wife to Antony.

20 *Hester*: Esther, heroine of the Book of Esther in the OT, was in medieval literature known for her beauty, her heroism, and, as here, her meekness.

22 *Rosamounde*: A lady of great beauty famously addressed in a ballade by Chaucer. See **I, 29**. Her identity is uncertain.

23 *Isawdë*: Yseult (or Ysolde), an Irish princess, who, as result of a love potion, fell in love with her escort Tristan while on a voyage to Cornwall to become the bride of Tristan's uncle, Mark, King of Cornwall. After the marriage, the secret love of Tristan and Yseult was discovered.

24 *Judith*: Judith, the heroine of the apocryphal Book of Judith, resisted the advances of Holofernes and, while he lay drunk, cut off his head.

25 *Bersabée*: Bathsheba, the beautiful wife of Uriah the Hittite, seduced by King David who, having arranged the death of her husband, took her as his wife and queen. See 2 Sam. 11.

39 *servantes*: i.e. servants in love.

II, 15   Go, litull bill, and command me hertëly [*NIMEV* 926]

MS: Oxford, Bodl. Lat. misc. c.66.

Text: 9 her] her her MS.

This MS, written *c.* 1500, was the commonplace book of Humfrey Newton, esquire (1466–1536), a gentleman of the county of Cheshire, who was related by family and by marriage to most of the leading families of that county. Newton was at best a modest, minor poet; his work is perhaps typical of the achievement of many a versifying 'country squire or town gentleman … in every century' (Robbins (1950), p. 279). However accidentally, his rough versification here seems to mirror the jauntily humorous and teasingly ironic tone of this short verse epistle.

5 & 6 *hand / stond*: The rhyme could be *hand / stand* or *hond / stond*.

II, 16   Have godday, nou, Mergerete [*NIMEV* 1121]

MS: Cambridge, Gonville and Caius College 54.

This brief poem is found in a French love letter at the end of a Latin MS.

II, 17   Gracius and gay [*NIMEV* 1010]

MS: Ireland, Kilkenny Castle, Ormond MS.

Text: 5 long] bytt long MS; 8 On] Vn MS; thoght] toth MS; 11 Hyr] Ass MS; 12 small] ys small MS; 14 and] *supplied*; 18 the] *supplied*; 20 wend] d *supplied*.

At first sight this lyric appears to offer a typical account of feminine beauty according to medieval convention (see Commentary, **II, 19**). However, usually descriptions proceed from head to toe, and this begins with fingers and arms before reaching mouth, eyes, and eyebrows. Even more unusual is the fact that this lady's arms are said to be 'round and firm' (6) rather than long and slender. The two stanza-structures used here are of the simplest kind. An introductory stanza followed by two of physical description are in the form: 5(6), 6, 7(8), 6 syllables per line; the two final stanzas change to 6, 6, 5(6), 5(6). It seems probable that an insensitive scribe with a preference for complete sentences has added the verbs in lines 5 and 12 on the model of lines 6, 9 and 10, thus destroying the ellipsis required (as in lines 7 and 11) by the metre.

1   *Gracius*: three syllables, with the ending '-ius' pronounced '-i-us', that is, as two syllables.
2   *lyyth*: The spelling 'yy' may represent the long vowel /i:/ here; the metre requires a monosyllable and not 'li-eth'.
5 & 7   The rhyme fails here; in 13 and 15 it is only approximate.
13   *under schett*: 'in clothing', lit. 'under sheet'. This is reminiscent of such conventional tags as *under bys* ('in fine linen') and *under gore* ('in a gown') used for the convenience of alliteration in describing ladies in the earlier ME Harley lyrics. See Commentary, **I, 1**, 38.
16   *In londës*: 'anywhere, everywhere', another tag reminiscent of the Harley lyrics. Cf. Commentary, **I, 3**, 12.

II, 18   Myn owne dere ladi fair and fre [*NIMEV* 2185]

MS: Cambridge, Gonville and Caius College 383, with music (for burden only).

Text: 4 pray] pray ow MS; ruwe] ruwen MS; 13 arende] arnde MS.

10   The *it* which 'will not help' here is the lover's languishing, his *peyne* (9). Recognizing this, he resorts, on a woman's advice (16), to the more positive approach of petitioning his lady in person.

II, 19   I saw never joy lyk to that sight [*NIMEV* 2232]

MS: Oxford, Lincoln College Lat. 100.

Text: 4 *lykës*] lyks MS; 6 As] os MS; 8 two] ii MS; 15 qwen] sqwen MS; 16 swete] sqwete MS.

The physical features of the lady in this poem – her arched eyebrows, her grey eyes, her long, shapely sides – are all conventional characteristics of feminine beauty in medieval literature. Cf. **I, 25**, 25, 16, and 76, and **I, 2**, 44 and 42. For a fuller account of the ideal medieval beauty, see Commentary, **I, 25**, 7ff.

4   *lele*: 'fair' or 'noble', a word chosen here partly, no doubt, for alliteration. The burden focuses on the lady's beauty and nobility and the poet's pleasure in her. However, the striking contrast between the buoyant tone of this burden and the sad truth of the current state of affairs admitted in the last two lines of stanza 3, accentuates the gap between the lady on the dais (1) – perhaps unaware of the poet, let alone (as yet) his 'true love' (13) – and this grief-stricken lover at a distance in the hall, unable to meet with her (17–18).

II, 20   Thayr ys no myrth under the sky [*NIMEV* 3534]

MS: Oxford, Bodl. Arch. Selden supra 52.

Text: 2 nor] nor no MS; 19 Fro] Fro that MS; chesse] chesse ons MS; 20 to] vnto MS; 27 for] now for MS; 28 to] vnto MS; 29 unhance] inhance MS; 35 yt] lady yt MS; 38 me tobraste] *supplied*; 39 be] yie be MS; 42 Medyscyne] And medyscyne MS; 45 may] that may MS; 47 on] apon MS.

Sadly, no other copy of this lyric survives to offer some measure of support for the emendations (none in any way altering the sense) made here *metri causa*. A sceptical reader may readily reinstate the MS readings from the textual apparatus above.

17 *doyff*: 'dove'. The dove, in particular the turtle-dove, frequently appears in medieval love literature as the representative of loyalty and true devotion.

17 & 19 The rhyme words are pronounced with four syllables with accents on the second and final syllables.

21 *hynde*: 'hind', the female of the deer. The deer was associated with wildness, restlessness, and, therefore, inconstancy. Cf. Commentary, **I, 1**, 17, and Commentary, **I, 51**, 27.

23 *kynde*: 'kind / natural'. If the sense 'kind' (i.e. 'kind-hearted') is politely present here, *yie ar kynde* also means 'you are natural', i.e. 'you are part of the natural order' (see *MED* **kind(e** adj. **1.**), the same natural order that includes the hind's inconstancy as well as the dove's constancy. It is for this reason that the poet urges his beloved to 'take heed'.

27 *for this sessòne*: 'for this season'. The mention of 'this season' here may reflect the seasonal aspect of some of the activities of the late medieval courtly game of love. Thus, as part of love ceremonies in May, knights and ladies might choose for that season to give their allegiance to the party of the Flower or of the Leaf, two amorous orders into which courtly society sometimes divided itself. On St Valentine's Day (14 February) lovers chose their partners for the coming year. See Stevens, *M&P*, pp. 181–5.

38 Other words ending in '-aste' rhyming with *truste* of the refrain line in this poem lend support to the conjecture adopted to complete this line, which, in the MS, ends at *sorrow*.

41 *salyfe*: 'ointment', commonly spelt *salve* in ME and perhaps to be pronounced as a monosyllable here. Alternatively, *unto* in this line may be a scribal alteration from *to*.

42 *Medyscyne*: by syncope, pronounced as two syllables. The reduced spelling 'medcin(e' occurs in ME; cf. *midsyne* (**II, 89**, 40), and see *MED* **medicin(e** n.

II, 21   Alone walkyng [*NIMEV* 267]

MS: Cambridge, Trinity College R.3.19.

Text: 8 Erly] Bothe erly MS; 15 estate] pore estate MS.

Of the three main French-derived lyric forms (ballade, roundel, and virelai) the virelai was by far the least common in French poetry and rare in ME. It was a flexible form, 'extremely flexible, if not chaotic, in the structure of its text' (Wilkins

(1968), p. 74). One form consisted of stanzas of short lines which employed two rhymes, the second of which, as tail-rhyme of one stanza, became the first and chief rhyme of the following stanza. This is a form of the virelai in eight-line stanzas. Cf. **II, 36** and **39** which have the same stanza form but do not carry on the tail-rhyme from one stanza to the next.

The MS readings of lines 8 and 15 (with five syllables) spoil the rhythm of this lyric and are clearly corrupt; all the other lines have four syllables. *Bothe* in line 8, and *pore* (or perhaps *suche*) in line 15 may well have been added by a careless and insensitive copyist, possibly writing from memory. In line 15, alternatively, the MS reading *pore estate* may originally have been *pore state*.

23 *creature*: pronounced 'cre-a-ture', with three syllables.

II, 22   Now wolde y fayne sum merthës mak [*NIMEV* 2381]

MSS: Oxford, Bodl. Ashmole 191, with music (B); Cambridge, University Library Ff.1.6 (C). Text from B.

Text: 6 far] for B, long C; 8 And] C, A B; 9 wolde God] wold god C, wolde B; 12 sadde] sad C, shadde B; 14 her] C, *om.* B; 16 it] hit C, hith it B; 20 no] C, & no B; 27 hir] C, *om.* B; 30 amend] C, to amend B.

16–17 *write / forgeit*: The rhyme words here (despite the MS spellings) should probably be pronounced as 'writ / forgit'.

II, 23   Go hert, hurt with adversité [*NIMEV* 925]

MS: Oxford, Bodl. Ashmole 191, with music.

For the conceit of the poet sending his heart to plead on his behalf to his lady, cf. **II, 9**.

II, 24   Thus I complayn my grevous hevynesse [*NIMEV* 3722]

MS: Oxford, Bodl. Ashmole 191, with music.

Text: 3 mersyles] mersles MS.

II, 25   Alas, departyng ys ground of woo [*NIMEV* 146]

MS: Oxford, Bodl. Ashmole 191, with music.

1 *ground*: 'basis'. Parting is the basis of the poet's woe: he can sing no other tune (2). Although 'ground' as a musical term in the sense of a 'plain-song or melody on which a descant is raised' is first recorded by *OED* for 1592 – see *OED* **Ground**, *sb.* **II. 6. c.** – it is tempting to suspect that this may be an early, pre-technical use of *ground* in the sense of 'basic tune'; the poet cannot rise above this *ground* (i.e. create any other tune, descant or whatever), for no other melody can he sing. This line is echoed in line 5 of a lyric in the Mellon Chansonnier: *The ground oof Wo Is al de-partyng* (Robbins, *Sec.*, no. 157, line 5),

and a similar line – *Departyng ys the grownde of dysplesaunce* – appears in one of the Findern lyrics (Robbins (1954), p. 639).

II, 26   My hert ys so plungyt yn greffe [*NIMEV* 2245]

MS: Dublin, Trinity College 158, with music.

Text: 2 barn my balyes onbynd] bran my balyes no byne MS.

  2 Emendation as in Robbins, *Sec.*, no. 158, p. 151.
  6 Although this line is exceptionally long, its syllables are all accommodated by the music in this MS.

II, 27   A! mercy, Fortune, have pitye on me [*NIMEV* 12]

MS: Cambridge, University Library Ff.1.6.

Text: 4 this] thus MS; 9 two] ij. MS; 17 have] to haue MS.

This, the Findern MS, was the anthology of the Finderns, a leading Derbyshire family. Its contents (in some 30 hands writing between 1450 and 1550) range from poems by Chaucer, Gower, Hoccleve and Lydgate to sundry household accounts. The 24 lyrics found here make this one of the main lyric anthologies of the late ME period. The names of five women and of various scribes recorded in this MS suggest that it was written partly by local ladies and partly by itinerant scribes. It offers important testimony to the taste for love poetry in the courtly manner in a well-to-do provincial household of this period. For a facsimile of the MS, see Beadle and Owen (1977). See also Robbins (1954) and Harris (1983).

This is a form of ballade in rhyme royal. However, unlike the 'classical' ballade (such as Chaucer's *To Rosëmounde* (**I, 29**)) and Charles d'Orléans's ballades in nine- and eight-line stanzas (**II, 1, 3,** and **4**), the rhyming sounds of stanza 1 of this poem are not repeated in stanzas 2 and 3; and the refrain here is a couplet rather than a single line.

  1 *pitye*: 'pity', with accentuation here on the second syllable as in French.
  4 *this*: As the rhyme shows, the scribe was mistaken in copying *thus* here.

II, 28   This ys no lyf, alas, that y do lede [*NIMEV* 3613]

MS: Cambridge, University Library Ff.1.6.

II, 29   Sweit rois of vertew and of gentilnes [*NIMEV* 3243.3]

MS: Cambridge, Magdalene College, Pepys 2553 [Maitland Folio MS].

Text: 4 held most] *not in MS; supplied as by most editors.*

The flower imagery here belongs to the tradition of love poetry stemming from the 13th-century French allegory of courtly love, *The Romance of the Rose*; see Commentary, **II, 3,** 2.

  10 *nane of rew*: 'any (lit. none) of rue'. The primary reference here is to the plant,

common rue (*Ruta graveolens*) (*MED* **rue** n., from OF **rue**), the bitter leaves of which were used as a herb in cooking and in medicine from the 14th century. The import of this lyric turns elegantly here on a pun. *Rew* also has the sense 'pity' (*MED* **reu(e** n. (1), from OE **hreow**). The virtue of 'pity' which could bring comfort to the poet (15) is as lacking in this 'merciless' (5) rose as the medicinal plant is absent from her garden.

II, 30   O maistres myn, till yow I me commend [*NIMEV* 2517]

MS: Edinburgh, NLS Advocates 1.1.6 [Bannatyne MS].

Text: 5 that] *supplied*; 21 bundin] bunding MS.

This ballade in eight-line stanzas from the Bannatyne MS shows how both the forms and the conventions of Chaucerian courtly love poetry were still flourishing a century and a half later in Scotland.

4 *danger*: For the kind of 'danger' lovers endured, cf. Commentary, **II**, 3, 2.

II, 31   Whoso that wyll all feattes optayne [*NIMEV* 4143.3]

MS: London, BL Add. 31922 [Henry VIII's MS], with music.

Why is it worse than death to love and be not loved? The answer appears to be that in such circumstances the gentle lover is subject to disdain; this, unlike God-given love, is a wasting vice which 'makes a man cold' (8) and therefore incapable of worthy attainments (1–2).

II, 32   A Robyn [*NIMEV* 13.8]

MS: London, BL Add. 31922 [Henry VIII's MS], with music by William Cornish.

The musical setting, perhaps based on a popular song, is for three voices in canon. Stevens (*M&P*, p. 405) is of the opinion that Sir Thomas Wyatt's longer poem (Muir and Thomson (1969), no. 55) is 'a later handling of the song, using this courtly version as a start'.

The first stanza, like the other stanzas, fits the four-phrase structure of the music and is therefore set out in four lines here. Each phrase is equivalent in length to four crotchets of a modern transcription. In stanza 1 the match of syllables and music is as follows (with crotchets divided into quavers to accommodate the syllables of longer lines):

A Robyn,	3 crotchets + rest
Gentyl Robyn,	crotchet + 2 quavers + crotchet + rest
Tel me how thy lemman doth	equivalent of 8 quavers*
And* / thow shal know of myne	4 quavers + crotchet + rest

* 'And', as the up-beat of line 4, is accommodated in the music by the final quaver of line 3. See Stevens (1962), no. 49, pp. 38–9.

An appropriate reading of this stanza – if this lyric is read rather than sung – would, arguably, match the rhythm and pace of the music. In Cornish's canonic setting this stanza acts as a kind of refrain or burden. It is sung throughout by the upper two voices. The third voice (which enters last in the canonic sequence) sings as follows: stanza 1, stanza 2, stanza 1, stanza 3, stanza 1.

II, 33   Wherto shuld I expresse [*NIMEV* 4070.5]

MS: London, BL Add. 31922 [Henry VIII's MS], with music.

Text: 11 no wyse] in no wyse MS; 13 delectable] delectale MS.

This poem appears to be a dialogue. A lover expresses sorrow at parting from his lady (stanza 1). She then replies, bidding the lover take comfort from the prospect of their next meeting and from their steadfast love.

13–16   The sense (here elliptically expressed) is: 'As the daisy is delectable, as the violet is pale and blue, so you are constant, and I love you only'. In the colour code of courtly love literature, blue was the colour of constancy, as green was the colour of inconstancy, cf. **I, 32**, 7, and Commentary.

17   *make*: 'regard as'; see *MED* **maken** v. (1) **17**. (a).

II, 34   The knyght knokett at the castell gate [*NIMEV* 3405.5]

MS: London, BL Add. 31922 [Henry VIII's MS], with music for three voices (burden only) by William Cornish.

This carol, which begins ostensibly as a narrative, almost like a ballad – a knight knocks at a castle gate, the lady of the castle wonders who is there, the knight summons the porter, the lady denies the knight access – rapidly becomes an allegory of courtship. The two opposing aspects of a lady's initial response in courtship, familiar from *The Romance of the Rose* (see Commentary, **II, 3**, 2), may possibly be understood as allegorized in the portress, a *lady bright*, perhaps representing Fair Welcome of the *Romance*, and in the lady herself, here called *Strangënes*, equivalent to Danger, an attitude of disdain. The knight as lover is appropriately named Desire, and is helped in his suit by *Kyndnes* and *Pyty*. Following the conventions of courtly love, he seeks to be the lady's prisoner.

Chambers and Sidgwick (1926), pp. 337–8, cite evidence concerning the name Amyas showing that it 'is not uncommon in Tudor records, and, as it happens, occurs more than once in connection with woodcraft'. However, any reference or topical issue which may have linked a specific Amyas and the 'greenwood' of the burden of this carol with the love allegory of the stanzas is now lost. It has been suggested that the story of this carol may have been enacted in the court as part of a disguising at festive revelries. See Stevens, *M&P*, chapter 11: 'Music in Ceremonies, Entertainments and Plays'.

11–12   At first sight it might appear that only one lady is mentioned here, a portress called *Strangënes*. However, *Strangënes* is not the portress but rather the lady of the castle; it is the lady who continues as the speaker in the following stanza, and the knight's words, *Desire, your man, madame*, and his wish to be her 'prisoner' (18) would be oddly addressed to a portress.

II, 35   Sore this derë stryken ys [*NIMEV* 3199.8]

MS: London, BL Add. 31922 [Henry VIII's MS], with music for three voices (burden only) by William Cornish.

Text: 25 more] mere MS.

Hunting and its rituals and conventions frequently carried a sexual *double entendre* in medieval literature. In particular, from Ovid onwards, the goddess of love, Venus, was thought of as a huntress, and her service a form of hunting. These ideas are made explicit in the following lines from Lydgate's translation of Deguileville's *Pilgrimage of the Life of Man*:

> For ther ys huntë nor foster   *hunter nor huntsman*
> That chacëth ay the wyldë deer,
> Nor other bestes that byth savage,
> That may be lykned to the rage
> Off Dame Venus; wherfor tak hede
> How gretly she ys to drede.
> And yiff thow kanst the trouthe espye,
> Venus ys sayd off venerye.
>
> Furnivall (1899), lines 8143–50

To emphasize the point, 'Venus dicitur a venandi' is written beside the final line of this quotation in the Stowe MS of this text.

In ME the word *foster* means 'forester' or 'huntsman'. There are other 'foster' songs in the Henry VIII MS. In one, an old man speaks with regret:

> Hang I wyl my nobyl bow
>   Upon the grenewod bough,
> For I cannott shote in playne
>   Nor yett in rough;
> Yet have I bene a foster.
>
> *M&P*, H62, pp. 408–9, stanza 2

Venus has commanded him out of her court (stanza 4)! In another, a 'jolly' foster revels in the fact that he can still 'shoot well' and sees no reason to 'hang up his bow' (*M&P*, H65, pp. 410–11). Stevens observes that such songs 'are courtly versions of popular "outdoor" songs … [which] may have been sung on the "pageant" during a disguising'. He instances an occasion when 'there were six foresters "sitting and going" on the "pageant" as it was drawn in front of the Queen' (Stevens (1962), pp. xviii–xix).

20 *barrayne*: 'barren'. The deer here, because she is barren – i.e. without fawn – is fair game for the hunters.

34 *construccyon*: 'meaning', i.e. the meaning of the poem at the level of *double entendre*.

II, 36   O mestres, whye [*NIMEV* 2518]

MS: London, BL Harley 2252.

Text: 11 Thy] my MS; 20 denoy] deny MS; 21 possesse] possede MS; 28 melle] medyll MS.

The stanza form of this poem – eight short lines of four syllables and two stresses arranged in two triplets each followed by a single line with the rhyme-scheme a a a b a a a b – was common in late ME and Tudor lyrics. It is a form which resembles the French virelai (see Commentary, **II, 21**), and similar stanza structures are found in medieval Latin poetry.

17ff. It is not evident why the 'Duchess of great Savoy' should be mentioned in this stanza (unless, perhaps, simply for the rhyme?) or why she in particular should be instanced as the epitome of *nobylnes*. However, the *nobylnes* associated with her appears to be of a rather ambiguous nature. The lady's reluctance now to see the poet is construed either as a denial of that *nobylnes* ('graciousness'?) or as a possession of it ('hauteur'?).

20 *denoy*: the form of this verb required here by the rhyme with *Savoy* (24). See *MED* **denien** v. for the alternative form **denoien**.

28 The rhyme with *welle* (32) requires *melle* rather than the alternative form *medyll* of the MS reading. Along with the sense 'associate with', another sense of this verb, 'to have sexual intercourse with' (see *MED* **medlen** v. **4**), was doubtless understood here.

II, 37   Love woll I withoute eny variaunce [*NIMEV* 2017]

MS: Oxford, Bodl. Ashmole 1393, with music.

Text: 3 gentilnesse] g *supplied.*

3 *hit*: 'it', i.e. service without inconstancy.

II, 38   Luf wil I with variance [*NIMEV* 2016]

MS: Oxford, Bodl. Ashmole 191, with music.

Text: 1 *and* 6 I] *supplied.*

This and another four (**II, 22–25**) of the six songs in this MS are given in this volume. The remaining song may be found in Robbins *Sec.*, p. 149, no. 153.

II, 39   Whatso men seyn [*NIMEV* 3917]

MS: Cambridge, University Library Ff.1.6.

Text: 15 profer] proferith MS.

This lyric, also from the Findern anthology (see Commentary, **II, 27**), is in the same verse form as **II, 36** above.

27 *fre*: 'free'. The range of meaning of ME *fre* would allow here for the senses 'generous (with their favours)', 'promiscuous', 'irresponsible', or, ironically, 'noble'.

II, 40   I am sory for her sake [*NIMEV* 1280]

MS: Cambridge, Gonville and Caius College 383.

This poem is written out as prose in the MS. The arrangement of the burden in lines is an editorial decision; the form adopted here differs slightly from that found in either Robbins or Greene.

14 *Me listë.* This 1 sg. form of the verb (instead of the 3 sg. form *listeth)* reflects the ME development whereby a dative or accusative pronoun in an impersonal construction (*Me* here) 'comes to be taken as the subject of the verb and consequently understood as a nominative' (Mustanoja, p. 435).

II, 41   Of my lady wel me rejoise I may! [*NIMEV* 2640]

MS: San Marino, California, Huntington Library HM 744.

Text: 7–10 wel … ay] *supplied*; 13–16, 21–4 my … ay] *supplied.*

This poem in roundel form begins as a humorous and ironic caricature of the conventional medieval description of a beautiful courtly lady (for which see Commentary, **I, 25**, 7ff.). 'Golden' was indeed the colour of beautiful hair, but certainly not of the forehead, which, ideally, was white, and which was also wide, not 'narrow and thin'; eyebrows were arched and beautiful (cf. **II, 19**, 7), not 'lustreless' and 'coral red'; and eyes were grey and shining (again, cf. **II, 19**, 8), not 'black' and 'glittering'. However, parody is virtually left behind as Hoccleve continues with a merciless itemization of this lady's baggy cheeks, large jaws, bizarrely described hooked nose, her large mouth and all but invisible chin, her football-like figure and parrot-like voice. This would seem a truly savage attack if one did not know that the lady the poet had in mind was none other than Lady Money. This roundel is the third in a series of three: in the first Hoccleve appeals to Lady Money for help, and in the second Lady Money rejects his plea; this, the third, is Hoccleve's humorous response.

II, 42   I hafe set my hert so hye [*NIMEV* 1311]

MS: Oxford, Bodl. Douce 381, with music.

Text: 3 drye] dryue MS.

As Dobson points out (*MES*, p. 210) the musical setting of this lyric shows that its stanza-form consists of a quatrain followed by a one-line refrain. In the MS the refrain line is only copied once, in the form required for the first stanza. (This was common practice with such lines: the repetition of the refrain line in other stanzas was left as understood in performance). As the verb *do* of the refrain line in this stanza echoes the *do* of the previous line, so in the second stanza the verb required for the refrain line is *hath*, again repeated from the preceding line and giving appropriate sense. Such variable refrains were common in later ME lyrics; cf. Commentary, **II, 140**, 16.

9 The anguish of love-longing of this devout poet for Christ, 'that Lord who loved us all' (6), is here expressed in terms of the *balës* ('anguish') conventionally

suffered by poets yearning for their mistresses in secular love lyrics. And just as such poets viewed suffering as beneficial, being a necessary prelude to the ultimate reward of their mistresses' 'mercy', so it is implicit here that the 'good' to be achieved by the love pains (pains of contrition, perhaps?) suffered by this poet (3–4) is none other than Christ's mercy and forgiveness. This, the goal of all true lovers of Christ, is made explicit in the opening stanza of another 15th-century lyric:

> O Jhesu, to all thy true lovers
> Graunt peace of hert and stedffast mynde;
> To theym that thi love dothe seke
> Thou graunt theym thy grace and solas eke   *solace also*
>
>   Brown XV, no. 66

II, 43 Jhesu, Lorde, that madëst me [*NIMEV* 1727]

MSS: London, BL Harley Charter 58. C.14 (H); Oxford, Bodl. Rawlinson liturgical e.3 (R); Oxford, Merton College 204 (M); London, Lambeth Palace Library 853 (L); Cambridge, Trinity College B.14.19 (T); etc. Other MSS are listed in the *NIMEV*. Parallel texts of the versions in ten MSS (including those listed above) are given in 'Richard of Caister, and his Metrical Prayer' by the Rev. Dundas Harford, *Norfolk and Norwich Archaeological Society*, XVII, 221–44. Text based on H.

Text: 4 will] *supplied*; 6 Of … too] R, On fote and handys too H; 9 Criste] *supplied*; 10 Fader] *some MSS*, God H; 14 Pacience] *some MSS*, Perfyte pacyonis H *and most* MSS; 18 Sothfast] th *(for* þ*) supplied*; God] *most MSS*, bothe God H; 19 gode] *supplied*; 20 holden to] *most MSS*, beholdyn to H; 23 preyèrës] preyorys MS; 24 me] *supplied*; 25 I the] *most MSS*, þat I H; 29 for] *supplied*; 31 Comfort] Chomfort MS; 40 lestyng] g *supplied*; 41 gostly] t *supplied*; 42 in] *most MSS*, and H; 46 Bryng … blys] M *and other* MSS, om. H. *The supplied words omitted in H are found in most other* MSS.

The Harley text, written on the back of a charter, is very badly rubbed and faded. I have relied on Carleton Brown's text (Brown, XV, no. 64) at points where I could not make out readings in the MS.

The many surviving MSS testify to the popularity of this poem which is a 15th-century expansion of an earlier 14th-century lyric of eight stanzas (Brown XIV, no. 94). In several MSS it is attributed to Richard de Caistre, vicar of St Stephen's, Norwich, who died in 1420. Richard de Caistre, a priest known for his strict, humble and devout life, befriended Margery Kemp, acted as her confessor when she visited Norwich, and defended her against her detractors.

12 *tyght*: 'resolved'; see *MED* **tighten** v. (2).

14 *Pacience*: pronounced as three syllables.

39 *werres*: 'wars', in this context, spiritual wars.

41–2 Cf. Matt. 21:42: 'Jesus saith unto them, Did ye never read in the scriptures, The stone which the builders rejected, the same is become the head of the corner.' Also 1 Peter 2:6: 'Wherefore also it is contained in the scripture, Behold, I lay in Sion a chief corner stone, elect, precious: and he that believeth on him shall not be confounded.' Also Isaiah 28:16.

43–4 Cf. John 10:16: 'And other sheep I have, which are not of this fold: them also I must bring, and they shall hear my voice; and there shall be one fold, and one shepherd.'

II, 44   Fore love is love and ever schal be [*NIMEV* 831]

MS: Oxford, Bodl. Douce 302.

Text: 11 y-lore] e lore MS; 16 Without] u *supplied*; 17 blyn] n *supplied*; 29 loved] d *supplied*; 30 Without] out *supplied*.

In the MS this poem has the heading: *De amore Dei etc.*

The way in which Audelay works the word 'love' (as noun, agent noun, or verb) into every line except the refrain lines makes this carol something of a *tour de force*. For Audelay, see Commentary, **II, 89**.

The majority of 15th-century carols are religious, though, like this poem, they are by no means all Christmas songs. The carol is defined by its form: it is a poem with a 'burden', that is, a line or group of lines which precedes the first stanza and which is then repeated after the first stanza and after all other stanzas. Although the commonest carol stanza form consists of four lines rhyming a a a b, carol stanzas show considerable variation from a simple two-line structure to much fuller and more complex forms. Another common feature of carols is the refrain, that is, a line or lines which recur (sometimes with slight variation) usually at the end of each stanza. The refrain is to be distinguished from the burden; the refrain is part of the stanza structure whereas the burden is a separate entity. Before 1400 the word 'carol' in ME meant a dance, probably a form of ring dance. The burden-and-stanza form doubtless originated in popular songs sung with such dances, the stanzas sung by the leader of the dance and the burden sung in chorus by the other dancers. However, the earliest ME carols (e.g. **I, 3** and **21**) are not like simple dance songs, and it is unlikely that they developed directly from such songs; as with other ME stanzaic lyrics, it seems more probable that as a literary form the carol was borrowed into English from Latin and Old French carols. Over 80 carols are found with elaborate polyphonic settings in four choir MSS dating from the second quarter of the 15th century. The claim, based mainly on this evidence, that the earliest ME carols were composed by clerics for singing in church processions on the model of Latin processional hymns, has been effectively dismissed by Greene (pp. cvi–cix).

II, 45   This flour is fayre and fresche of heue [*NIMEV* 3603]

MSS: Oxford, Bodl. Douce 302 (D); Oxford, Balliol College 354 (B). Text based on D.

Text: 1 sprung] u *supplied*; 19 mayden] maydyn B, mayd D; 22 it was] yt ys B, was D; 27 his] his his MS; for to] B, to D; 30 kyngës thre] kyngnys iii MS; 33 cam] B, þer cam D; 40 lilly whit, of] lilly whit and B, lille of D; 43 bers] beryth B, ȝet bers D.

For Audelay, see Commentary, **II, 89**.

1–3 The lineage of Mary and Jesus was commonly represented in medieval art and literature as a tree springing from Jesse, father of King David, as its root. See Commentary, **I, 76,** 17.

7–8 Mary sometimes appeared as a branch at the top of the Jesse tree; Jesus was represented as a flower on that branch.

15 *Medis*: assume the pronunciation of the reduced form, ME *midst*.

15 *Medis here herbère*: Representations of the Annunciation in medieval art often depict the angel Gabriel as appearing to the Virgin in an enclosed garden (suggested by the 'hortus conclusus' (garden enclosed) of S. of S. 4:12).

17 For Mary's 'bower' as her 'womb', cf. Commentary, **I, 79,** 10, and Commentary, **II, 53,** 2.

27 *bede*: 'show'; see *MED* **beden** v. 3. (b).

33 Angels are sometimes shown as looking down from the towers of heaven in medieval MS illuminations, stained-glass windows and sculpture.

35 The flower is, of course, 'he', i.e. Jesus.

II, 46   Ther is no rose of swych vertù [*NIMEV* 3536]

MS: Cambridge, Trinity College O.3.58, with music.

Text: 1 Ther] T *supplied*; no] n *supplied*; 3 rose of] se of *supplied*; 15 sung] sungyn MS; 19 Leve] L *supplied. The supplied letters are illegible because the MS, a roll, is worn and damaged.*

1 Already a symbol of the perfection of feminine beauty in classical literature, the rose was particularly associated in medieval literature with the ideal of courtly love. In *The Romance of the Rose* the poet's idealized beloved is represented as a rose. For medieval readers, the association of the rose and the Virgin also recalled a rich array of traditional biblical, patristic and liturgical references: e.g. Mary as the 'exalted … rose plant in Jericho' (Ecclus 24:18), Mary as a rose on the tree of Jesse, Mary as the *rosa sine spina* ('the rose without thorn'), suggesting the Virgin's beauty, excellence, humility and purity. The word *virtù* here means not only 'moral excellence' but also 'strength' (its etymological sense) and, in this context, as an essential characteristic of a rose, 'fragrance'.

5 To a medieval listener, *Alleluya* (5), *Res miranda* (9) and *Pari forma* (13) would all have been familiar from the liturgy, as lines from the *Laetabundus*, a popular sequence attributed to St Bernard of Clairvaux. (A 'sequence' was a non-scriptural text in verse or rhythmic prose sung during the mass after the Alleluia or Tract. For its structure, see Commentary, **I, 109.**)

7–8 Mary's womb was the 'little space' in which heaven and earth (God and man) became one.

12 The word *persones* here, and *aungeles* and *shepherdes* in line 15, may all be pronounced with two syllables (as in modern pronunciation) and are so printed by Stevens (see *MC*, p. 11). So wholly (and effectively) regular is the metre of this carol that it is probable that *sung*, rather than the MS form *sungyn*, may have been the original form of the verb in line 15.

21 *Transeamus*: 'let us go', from Luke 2:15: *Transeamus usque Bethlehem* (Let us now go even unto Bethlehem).

II, 47   Lyth and lystyn, both old and yyng [*NIMEV* 1893]

MSS: Oxford, Bodl. eng. poet. e.1 (A); Oxford, Balliol College 354 (B); London, BL Sloane 2593 (C). Text based on A.

Text: 8 Five] v MS; 11 bosum] s *supplied*; branches] braich A, blossum BC; 13 first] *supplied*; 14 *and* 15, MS *order reversed*; 20 lemëd] leme3d MS; 21 both brod and longe] BC, it both day and þ ny3t A; 23 thridë] iij MS; 24 Thre] iiij MS; the] to MS; 25 chyldbed] chyld hed MS; 26 ryght sprong] sprong ry3t MS; 28 fourthë] iiij MS; 29 power] powr MS; 33 fifthë] v MS.

This carol is structured on the five joys of the Virgin (the Annunciation, the Nativity, the Epiphany, the Resurrection and the Ascension), here represented in terms of five branches of a rose-tree springing from the Virgin's bosom. It may have been based on an emblematic representation (in painting, stained glass, or MS drawing) of a rose tree with five branches, each representing one of the respective scenes.

14–15   The reversal of the order of these lines in the MS gives correct sense; Jesus (the flower of Mary), not the angel, breaks the Devil's bond. This emendation is supported by the order of the rhymes *towr* and *flowr* in the equivalent stanzas in B and C. For angels shown as emerging from heaven's towers, cf. **II, 45**, 33, and Commentary.

21   The sudden alteration of the rhyme scheme from a a a b (the scheme of the other stanzas and other versions) to a a a a in this stanza is suspect. The reading *day and nyght* in A has all the appearance of a cliché prompted by the preceding three rhymes, *myght, nyght* and *bryght*. The scribe may have been influenced by the tradition (not found in the Gospel story) of the star shining both night and day as expressed in the burden of another carol:

> The sterre hym schon bothe nyght and day
> To lede thre kynges ther our lord lay.
>
> Greene, no. 124 A

26   The sounds '-ong' and '-ond' of the b-rhymes of the quatrains of this poem commonly rhymed in ME. Cf. *Adam lay y-bownden* (**I, 108**, 2 and 4). The emendation here restores *sprong* to its correct place as the final word of stanza 5, matching in sound of the final words of the other stanzas.

II, 48   At a sprynge-wel under a thorn [*NIMEV* 420]

MS: Oxford, Magdalen College 60.

This brief lyric, quoted in a Latin homily, survives in a 15th-century MS. It has, however, all the feel of earlier ME verse. Its language and imagery are immediately suggestive of popular and romantic secular love. In medieval lyrics, dance-songs and romances, girls sometimes met their lovers or dreamt about them at wells. From the earliest ME love lyrics, poet-lovers referred to their ladies as their *bote of bale*, the 'remedy for [their] suffering'. Again, the love-bound maiden standing by a well as presented here, could indeed suggest 'a scene from romance, such as a meeting with an Otherworld *fée*' (Gray, *Selection*, p. 131).

However, the evocative power of these lines goes much further. As Dronke notes, 'It was at a fountain, beside a thornbush that, according to some of the early Christian apocryphal writings, the angel's annunciation to Mary took place' (Dronke (1968), p. 70). Thus, as an awareness of a possible religious significance engages the reader, the *bote of bale*, the 'deliverance from torment', located in past time (albeit understated in line 3 as merely 'a little time ago'), becomes the salvation brought about by Christ the Redeemer; and the maiden becomes none other than the Virgin Mary in whom alone true love in perfect form (and not merely the *fin amor* of secular love) is to be found. The religious interpretation was, naturally, uppermost in the mind of the homilist who identified the *springe-wel* as the wound in Christ's side (frequently referred to as a well; cf. **11, 78**, 2, and Commentary) and the maiden as the Virgin. The 'thorn' is also suggestive of Christ's crown of thorns.

The earlier the origin supposed for this brief lyric, the more plausible the pronounced final 'e's in the metrical reading proposed in the text. Of course, it is perfectly possible to read the penultimate line with six syllables – *Hoso wol seche trwe love* – with *trwe* as an unstressed syllable. However, with eight syllables in the line, *trwë* gains appropriate weight and emphasis, and the final quatrain acquires metrical symmetry.

11, 49   Haill quene of hevin and steren of blis [*NIMEV* 1077]

MS: London, BL Arundel 285.

> 2 This play on literal and figurative senses of 'son' and 'father' – Jesus is literally (in a human sense) Mary's son while he is figuratively, as God, Mary's heavenly father – is found in other lyrics on the paradox of the Trinity. Cf. **11, 80** and Commentary.

11, 50   O sterne so brycht [*NIMEV* 2557]

MS: Edinburgh, University Library Laing 149.

Text: 3 sterne] strene MS.

For this as a poem in carol form, see A. A. MacDonald in *Companion*, 251.

> 3 Star (especially in the salutation *Ave stella maris* 'Hail star of the sea') and Well (as here, line 21, *wel of grace*) are two of the many titles given to the Virgin in medieval literature. Cf. **11, 49**, where Mary is addressed as the 'star of bliss' (1) and as a 'fresh fountain' (5).
>
> 28 *before thin eyne*: The reference is to Mary at the foot of the cross witnessing Christ's sacrifice.

11, 51   Goe, lytyll byll, and doe me recommende [*NIMEV* 927]

MS: Oxford, Bodl. Douce 326.

Text: *In* Syth 7, She 8, Say 24, Syth 32, *and* Shall 41 MS *initial* ss *has been altered to* S; 15 restëth] restyd MS; 23 Why] Wyll MS; 30 he] she MS.

The opening stanzas of this poem, beginning with the notion of the poet sending a letter to his lady, are couched in the language and conventions of medieval secular love poems addressed to a courtly mistress. However, as *feyrest paramour* (25) of the S. of S. and *Most soverayne medyatryce* (27), the lady here turns out to be none other than the Virgin, whose beauty is beyond description (29–31), who is without vice (32), who is the flower above all other flowers (34), and who may accept the poet's love and obedience despite *old trespace* ('original sin'?, 39).

1–2 The long lines of the epistolary formula with which this poem opens contrast with the shorter lines of the rest of the poem. The same formula begins the final stanza of another poem addressed to the Virgin:

> Go lytill balett, and doe me recommende
> Unto my lady with godely countynaunce.
>
> Brown XV, p. 308

8 & 10 Description of the beloved in terms of flowers, especially the lily and rose, is common in medieval courtly love poetry. These flowers are also often associated with the Virgin Mary, who is to emerge as the addressee of this poem.

23 For the emendation adopted here, see Brown XV, p. 75.

24–5 The poet justifies his presumption by appealing to Scripture. The reference (quoted in the margin in the MS) is to *pulcherrima mulierum* (fairest among women) of S. of S. 5:9, 17 (Vulgate).

II, 52   O emperesse, the emperoure [*NIMEV* 2415]

MS: Cambridge, University Library Ee.1.12.

This MS contains English carols, songs and translations of Latin hymns attributed in a colophon on fol. 80, dated 1492, to the Franciscan, James Ryman. The Latin refrains of this lyric are taken from the antiphon, *Regina caeli laetare.*

II, 53   Com, my swetë, com my flour

MS: Oxford, Bodl. Gough Eccl. Top. 4.

This lyric appears written out continuously as prose, and in no way distinguished from the surrounding text, in Mirk's sermon for the Feast of the Assumption. Mirk tells how at the Virgin's death Christ took her soul in his arms and bore it up to heaven. Three days later Christ returns with a host of angels and St Michael who now carries the soul of the Virgin. Christ tells St Michael to replace Mary's soul in her body, and addresses the first stanza of this lyric to Mary. Mary then sits up, bows to Christ, and replies to him in the words of the second stanza. Thereafter, with great *myrthe and melody thay beren our lady ynto hevyn, bothe body and soule, and soo Crist set hur ther by hym yn his trone, and crowned hur qwene of heven, and emperice of hell, and lady of al the worlde* (Erbe (1905), p. 224).

1–2 'My sweet' and 'my dove' echo the endearments used in the Song of Solomon.

2 *myn owne boure*: Christ's 'bower' was Mary's womb.

II, 54   The infinite power essenciall [*NIMEV* 3391]

MS: London, BL Add. 20059.

Text: 21 abdominacioun] abhominacioun MS; 41 spectable] spectacle MS.

A feeling for the metre of this poem is best arrived at by first reading the heavily alliterative last stanza from which the pattern of four stresses per line emerges clearly. Throughout the rest of the poem there are lines in which, by virtue of extra unstressed syllables, the stress pattern is not obvious to the modern reader (and, indeed, may not have been immediately clear to every medieval reader either); but difficulty usually evaporates when it is recognized that the final three syllables of Latinate rhyme words carry two stresses in the pattern / × / – as is readily apparent in, for instance, *essènciàll* and *celèstiàll* (1 and 3) – and that this pattern governs the reading of the rest of the line within the metrical norm of four stresses per line. Thus, in line 6, the rhythm × / × / of the final word *solemnyté* ends a line which (granted the norm of four stresses and the validity of the MS reading) has four consecutive unstressed syllables giving × / × / × × × × / × / as the rhythmic pattern of the complete line (though readers may initially be tempted to read the line with five stresses, with stress on *gret*).

> 1–4 The 'infinite power' the poet sees 'proceeding from his celestial throne to a dear damsel' is Christ coming to the Virgin at her coronation. For Mirk's account of the occasion, see Commentary, **II, 53**.
>
> 5 For *was* as a past pl. form, see *OED* **Be** *v.* **A.** III. 6. The syntax here is elliptical: 'Melodious songs were their concern, [the concern] of angels singing with great solemnity.'
>
> 8 *radix Jessé*: The Virgin is 'the root of Jesse' in that she is part of the lineage springing from Jesse and ending in Christ. See Commentary, **I, 76**, 17, and Commentary, **II, 45**, 1–3.
>
> 9 *Tota pulcra*: cf. S. of S. 4:7: *Tota pulchra es, amica mea, et macula non est in te* (Thou art all fair, my love; there is no spot in thee).
>
> 15 *Devoide of actës crymynall*: Mary was immaculate, spotless. Cf. S. of S. 4:7, above.
>
> 18 Davies (1963), p. 199, alters *O Maria* to *A 'Maria'*. But there is no need to emend here. This line is a parenthetic exclamation of joy at the scene and at the very name, Mary – 'O Maria by name!' – by the onlooking poet.
>
> 21–3 Cf. Milton's *On the Morning of Christ's Nativity*, 77–84, where the sun 'hid his head for shame' at the birth of Christ.
>
> 26 Thrones and Dominations were the third and fourth of the nine orders of angels as described in a work entitled the *Celestial Hierarchy* by the mystical theologian Dionysius the Pseudo-Areopagite (*c.* 500).
>
> 27 *dubbit in doctrine*: lit. 'knighted in doctrine'. If the quest for alliteration prompted the pairing of *dubbit* and *doctrine* here, the image is not without appeal as a metaphorical expression of the status, the honour accorded to angels and archangels in Church teaching.
>
> 29 *The prynce perpetuall*: i.e. Christ.
>
> 31 *Columba mea*: 'my dove'. Cf. S. of S. 2:13–14: *Surge, amica mea, speciosa mea; et veni, columba mea, in foraminibus petrae, in caverna maceriae* (Douay: Arise,

my love, my beautiful one, and come: My dove in the clifts of the rock, in the hollow places of the wall).

33 *Surge*: 'arise'. The word occurs several times in the Song of Solomon, as in S. of S. 2:13, above.

38 The pelican as a symbol of Christ arose from the tradition that pelicans fed their young with their own blood.

II, 55   Hale, sterne superne, hale, in eterne [*NIMEV* 1082.5]

MS: Edinburgh, NLS 16500 [Asloan MS].

Ave Maria, gracia plena, the internal refrain repeated as the ninth line of each stanza, derives from Gabriel's greeting to Mary, *Ave, gratia plena* (Luke 1:28). Dunbar combines, seemingly effortlessly in a natural flow of verse, lines of simple vernacular language (*In Godis sicht to schyne* (2), *Be glory and grace devyne* (4), etc.) with lines richly studded with aureate vocabulary linked both by triple internal rhyme and lavish alliteration, and all within a 12-line stanza-form of 11 English lines (employing only two rhymes) and the Latin refrain line. Aureate diction and internal rhyming were characteristic of late medieval hymns to the Virgin, but Dunbar's performance here is an unsurpassed technical *tour de force*. With the urgent and repeated 'hail's addressed to the Virgin, this poem is developed as an exuberant parade of her traditional titles. Some of these simply describe her special roles and status – as virgin mother of Christ, as intercessor for sinners, as heavenly queen. She is *virgin matern* (11), *maide but makle* (22), *humile oratrice* (48) and *Oratrice, mediatrice, salvatrice* (67). Many other titles reflect the addiction of the medieval imagination to finding references in the OT which could be interpreted as prefiguring, or pointing forward to the Virgin. Such references thereby generated further symbols or titles of the Virgin. Thus, because as Christ's mother *the lord of all* [*her*] *closet did include* (77–8), she was the 'temple of God', here *Alphais habitakle* (14) and *his tabernakle* (16), titles echoing Psalm 19:4: 'In them hath he set a tabernacle for the sun', and Psalm 46:4: 'the holy place of the tabernacles of the most High'. Solomon's enthronement of his mother in 1 Kings 2:19 was seen as prefiguring Christ's coronation of the Virgin. She was, therefore, the throne of Solomon, the *hie trone regall* (75), and also *hevinlie hie emprys* (38), *qwene of hevyn* (52) and *Empryce of prys, imperatrice* (61). This interpretation was associated with 1 Kings 10:18: 'Moreover the king made a great throne of ivory, and overlaid it with the best gold': the ivory was taken to symbolize the Virgin's chastity, the gold, her charity. The richest source of these symbols was the sensuous language of the Song of Solomon. Thus Mary is *floure-de-lyce* (42 and 71) and *Spyce* (71), echoing S. of S. 2:2: *Sicut lilium inter spinas, sic amica mea inter filias* (As the lily among thorns, so is my love among the daughters) and S. of S. 4:16: *perfla hortum meum, et fluant aromata illius* (blow upon my garden, that the spices thereof may flow out). Mary is a wall or tower because of her strength and inviolable chastity: here *Imperiall wall* (73) derives from the *Turris David*, the Tower of David, in the S. of S. Long lists of such titles, references and interpretations were given by patristic commentators such as Honorius of Autun, St Bernard of Clairvaux and Richard of St Victor. See Raby (1953), p. 368. Thus, Richard of St Victor in his sermon on the

Nativity or Assumption of the Virgin speaks of her as *Castrum securitate, murus vel turris fortitudine*, 'castle in her security, wall or tower in her fortitude' (*Pat. Lat.* 177, col. 980). However, many of the references to Mary – Mary as star, lamp, rose, fresh flower, nightingale, daisy, precious stone, etc. – evoked just as much the beauty of the natural world and the associations of romance as the learned interpretations of patristic tradition.

11 *virgin matern*: 'virgin mother'. Mary as mother and yet a virgin, the paradox of the Incarnation.

12 *Of reuth baith rute and ryne*: 'of compassion both root and bark', i.e. the all-encompassing source of compassion.

14 *Alphais habitakle*: 'Alpha's (i.e. God's) dwelling-place'. In Rev. 1:8 God is called Alpha and Omega (the first and last letters of the Greek alphabet, and, therefore, beginning and end).

29–30 The notion of the Virgin doing battle against the Devil and putting him to flight derived from the interpretation with reference to Mary and the Devil of God's words to the serpent concerning Eve in Gen. 3:15: 'And I will put enmity between thee and the woman, and between thy seed and her seed; it shall bruise thy head, and thou shalt bruise his heel.' Accordingly, Mary is sometimes represented in Christian art as treading on a devil or dragon.

31 *plicht*: 'main anchor'. For the anchor as a symbol of Christian hope, cf. Heb. 6:19: 'Which hope we have as an anchor of the soul, both sure and stedfast'. 'Anchor' was one of Mary's many titles; Lydgate, for instance, addresses her as 'Of hope our Anker' in *To Mary the Queen of Heaven*, stanza 7.

40 *ros of paradys*: 'rose of paradise', i.e. the rose without thorn (*rosa sina spina*) as in paradise; the thorns developed after the Fall. Cf. Milton's description of paradise which included 'Flours of all hue, and without Thorn the Rose', *Paradise Lost*, Book IV, 256.

42 *floure-de-lyce*: A variety of lily associated with the Virgin as a symbol of purity in Christian art.

51 *Our glore forlore*: 'our lost glory', i.e. the glory of man's unfallen state in paradise. The restoration of this lost glory was achieved through Mary, the second Eve (cf. Milton, *Paradise Lost*, Book V, 387: 'blest *Marie, second Eve*') as mother of Christ, the second Adam.

56 *mak our oddis evyne*: The precise reference of this phrase is unknown but the sense here seems to be something like 'redress the balance (of our sins)'. Kinsley suggests that the reference may be to the Last Judgement 'in representations of which the Virgin intercedes and sometimes tips the scales in the weighing of souls' (Kinsley (1979), p. 228).

58 *ellevyn*: Why 'eleven'? There seems little point to this particular number here unless it is used solely for the sake of rhyme, which seems unlikely for a poet of Dunbar's skill. Bawcutt and Riddy (1992), p. 228, suggest that 'it may perhaps be a variant of *all evin*, an intensive phrase – "all equally, without exception" – sometimes used rather vaguely, as a line-filler'. Gray suspects a scribal error for *ilk evyn*, 'every evening'. This would give excellent sense as the occasion for the *lovingis lowde*, namely, 'the evening recitation of the "Ave Maria", a medieval antecedent of the Angelus' (Gray (1998), p. 383).

73 *place palestrall*: Kinsley glosses as 'palace', suggesting that Dunbar here misused *palestrall* (which should mean 'to do with wrestling') for *palatial* perhaps because he 'may have misread or faultily recalled Troilus' "feste and pleyes palestral" (athletic games) (Chaucer, *Troilus and Criseyde*, v. 304)'; Kinsley (1979), p. 229. A suggestion by Gray that *palestrall* is 'a scribal misreading of an otherwise unattested aureate word *prelustral* invented by Dunbar (Latin *praelustris*, 'magnificent'), especially if, as was often the case, *pre-* was represented in abbreviated form' (Gray (1998), p. 383) would give excellent sense here.

80 *angell fude*: *panis angelorum* of the Vulgate text of Psalm 77:25 – *panem angelorum manducavit homo, cibaria misit eis in abundantia* (Douay: Man ate the bread of angels: he sent them provisions in abundance) – interpreted in patristic tradition as referring to Christ as the Communion bread.

II, 56   Owt of your slepe aryse and wake [*NIMEV* 2733]

MSS: Oxford, Bodl. Arch. Selden B.26 (B), with music; Cambridge, University Library Ll.1.11 (C), with music, a version of stanzas 1, 2 and 4 of B in the order 1, 4, 2. Text from B.

Text: 13, 19 Nowel] *supplied*.

3 This is here not only a joyous reveille – 'wake up to the occasion, it's Christmas!' – but also an exhortation to arise and awake out of the sleep of sin. Cf. Rom. 13:11–12: 'And that, knowing the time, that now it is high time to awake out of sleep: for now is our salvation nearer than when we believed. The night is far spent, the day is at hand: let us therefore cast off the works of darkness, and let us put on the armour of light.'

6 *she bereth the belle*: The allusion may be to the bell as a prize awarded at country races or the bell carried by the bell-wether leading the flock.

17 The metre suggests that *game is* should be elided as 'game's' and, possibly, *Blessed* read as 'blest' in this line.

18 For Empress of Hell as one of the Virgin's titles, see the passage quoted from Mirk's sermon on the Assumption in Commentary, **II, 53**.

21–2 Although the musical notation poses no problem in accommodating the two syllables of *ever*, the metrically preferable monosyllabic pronunciation is supported by the C reading *ere* in both lines.

29 Usually mankind's foe is the Devil. Here however, the foe who has become a friend is God, for now the enmity between God and man brought about by Adam's sin (as a result of which God became, in a sense, man's foe) is to be ended by the reconciliation achieved by the sacrifice made by the second Adam, Christ.

33 Man's *blessëd brother* here is Christ incarnate, often referred to as the brother of mankind, and, in the affective language of St Francis, as 'the little brother of mankind'.

II, 57   The sunne of grace hym schynit in [*NIMEV* 3472]

MS: London, BL Sloane 2593.

Text: 4 morwë] wë *supplied*; 5, 10, 15, 20 borën] born MS; 19 undyrn] rn *supplied*.

Repetition of lines and phrases, a popular characteristic that many carols have in common with folk-songs, is a striking feature of this carol. Its structure is simple: the stanzas are ordered in terms of a progression of times of day: *morwë*, the beginning of a new day; *pryme*, early morning; *non*, noon; and *undyrn*, afternoon. These were also terms for the monastic 'hours' or times of prayer: *morwë* (Matins, the midnight office); *pryme* (Prime, the first hour of the day, observed at about 6 a.m.); *non* (None, the ninth hour, about 3 p.m.); and *undyrn* (Sext, the sixth hour, about midday). Cf. Commentary, **II, 94**. However, the order of *non* (the ninth hour) and *undyrn* of stanzas 3 and 4 does not fit in with the sequence of the monastic hours, since in ME *undern* was usually equivalent to the earlier hours of Sext (the sixth hour) or, in OE and some ME contexts, Tierce (the third hour); see *OED* **Undern** *sb.* **2.** and **1.** respectively. The sense 'afternoon' or 'evening' – as required for *undern* following *non* here – is first recorded in *OED* from the late 15th century; see *OED* **Undern** *sb.* **3.** Moreover, Greene notes that times and events in this poem do not match traditional correspondences between the canonical hours and the events of the Passion, instancing 'Sext as the hour for the fixing to the cross and None as the time of piercing' in the Sarum *De Horis Canonicis Hymnus* (Greene, p. 349).

2   *hym schynit*: 'shone'. The pronoun *hym* here is reflexive.
5   *borën*: Here, and in the repeats of this line, the MS spelling masks the disyllabic pronunciation required by the metre.

II, 58   When Cryst was born of Mary fre [*NIMEV* 3932]

MS: London, BL Harley 5396.

Text: 9 To] T *supplied*; 10 And] A *supplied*; 13 A kyng] A ky *supplied*; 14 In the] *supplied*; 15 Therfore] Therfor *supplied*; 18 Jesu, Lord] Jesu L *supplied*; 19 Graunt] Grau *supplied*; 20 Where] Wh *supplied*. *Manuscript damage has resulted in a loss of letters at the margin.*

For a version of this carol which survived among gipsies in southern England into the last century, see Gillington (1910), no. 10, p. 15. Greene prints Gillington's text (Greene, pp. 360–61).

18   *Jesu*: Greene follows Chambers and Sidgwick in supplying 'Then' as the first word of this line, while observing that 'there is no more reason for restoring this word as "Then" than as "Jhesu" or something else' (Greene, p. 361). However, it is obvious from the metre that the lost word was of two syllables.

II, 59   The sheperd upon a hill he satt [*NIMEV* 3460]

MS: Oxford, Balliol College 354.

Text: 13 brayd] broyd MS; 49 his] *supplied*; 51 Bedlëëm] Bedlem MS; 60 skyrte *and* scrype *transposed in* MS.

As found in the MS, the first stanza of this poem is one line longer than the other stanzas. Greene's suggestion (p. 359) that this extra line, *For he was a gud herdes boy*, was meant to be repeated as the first line of the refrain in the subsequent stanzas has been followed in the text given here. If sung, all the stanzas would have to have been structured alike. With the repetition of this line, all the stanzas end with a three-line refrain. In this form the refrain not only makes good and complete sense in itself, but also adds emphasis to the poignant contrast sustained throughout the poem, that of the simple, spontaneous joy at Christ's birth of Wat, *a gud herdes boy*, and the sense of a sadly limited and inadequate response on the part of the speaker, the 'I' of the burden, who can merely echo the *hoy* of the *mych joy* of Wat's piping: 'Can I do no more than sing "hoy" when the jolly shepherd made such joy?'.

1   *hoy*: a syllable used in singing equivalent to 'hey' in 'hey-nonny-nonny' or 'tra' in modern 'tra-la-la'. Compare the shirkers in Langland's *Piers Plowman*:

> Thenne seten some and songen atten ale,   *some sat and sang over drink*
> And holpen to erie this half-acre with 'hoy! troly! lolly!'   *helped plough*
> *Piers Plowman*, C IX, 122–3

4   *tabard*: See *MED* **tabard(e** n. (1) (a) 'An overgarment, usu[ally] sleeveless, worn primarily by members of the lower classes or by monks'.

5   *tar-box*: See *MED* **ter** n. (2) (c) 'a small container used primarily by shepherds to store tar used as a salve for sheep'.

27   *Mall ... Will*: These seem to be names of Wat's sheep, Mall, perhaps his favourite ewe, and Will (see line 30), the bell-wether of the flock.

38   *Warroke*: A word of obscure origin, probably the name of Wat's dog.

51   *Bedlëëm*: This form with three syllables is metrically preferable to the disyllabic form of the MS.

70   *rownd cape*: Gray compares 'the Adoration of the Shepherds in the east window of St Peter Mancroft, Norwich, where Joseph, sitting warming himself at a brazier, wears a round fur cap' (*Selection*, p. 105).

II, 60   Abowt the fyld thei pyped full right [*NIMEV* 112]

MSS: Oxford, Bodl. eng. poet. e.1 (A); Oxford, Balliol College 354 (B), burden and stanzas 1–5. Another MS, destroyed by fire in 1879, contained versions, with music, of two stanzas of this carol used as two separate songs in the Pageant of the Coventry Shearmen and Taylors. Text from A.

Text: 19 sonës] sons A, son B; 23 mekë] meke B, mek A; 25 which that] wich AB; defyld] defylyd AB; 29 that] *supplied*; 33 allë] all MS.

19   *sonës beme*: There is present here the traditional play on the words 'sun' and 'son'. The sunbeam the shepherds go to Bethlehem to see is Christ, *that glorious streme* (that glorious ray of light), line 20, the Son of Man.

25 *defyld*: This spelling is adopted to indicate the disyllabic pronunciation required by the rhymes in this stanza.

II, 61   A babe is borne of hye natèwre [*NIMEV* 21]

MSS: Oxford, Bodl. Douce 302 (D); Cambridge, Trinity College O.3.58 (burden and stanzas 1, 3, 2, 4), with music (T); Oxford, Bodl. Arch. Selden B.26 (burden and stanzas 1, 2, 4, 3), with music (B). Text based on D.

Text: 1 *What*] H what MS; *after* 7 What tyþyngis bryngis þe messangere *in MS, om. in text*; 23 Seche … here] Swich wunder etc. T, Suche etc. B, What tydyngus bryngu vt supra D, *written in the margin to the right of the stanza in a second hand*; 27 These] iese D, This B, That T; 31 wonder] n *supplied*; ye may here] vt supra MS; 33 mannës] mannys BT, mans D; 36 monnës] mons MS; 39 ye may here] vt supra MS; 40 prayère] prayoure MS; 41 dwel] twel MS; 42 *What tythynges etc.*] Seche wonder tyþyngis vt supra MS.

 7 Following Greene's assumption that originally, 'in regular carol-fashion' (p. 372), the stanzas of this carol were intended to be sung wholly by a soloist representing the messenger with the chorus only singing the burden, the incipit of the burden copied after the fifth line of this stanza has been omitted from the text. However, it may well be that this line should not only be retained here but included as the sixth line in the other stanzas. This is the form of the poem as found in B where, after the fifth line of the first stanza, the first three notes of the music of the burden appear with the words *What tydynges vt supra* and the direction that they are to be sung by the chorus. See *MC*, p. 20, and notes to no. 11 (p. 117) and no. 27 (p. 118).

23 The first line of the refrain has been omitted in D and the beginning of the burden copied in its place by a second hand in the margin. This lends support to the possibility that the first line of the burden (sung by the chorus) was intended to be included after the fifth line as part of each stanza.

42 The beginning of the refrain, instead of the beginning of the burden, has mistakenly been copied after the last stanza.

II, 62   A ferly thyng it is to mene [*NIMEV* 34]

MS: Oxford, Bodl. eng. poet. e.1.

Text: 5 sythë] syth MS; 19 allë] all MS; 25 ylkë] ylk MS; 45 thar] *erased, with* dede *written over in later hand*; 56 Thei] i *supplied*; twelfth] xij MS; 61 fro] for fro MS.

 1 *Aye! aye!*: interjections expressing joy.
51–2 The gifts the three kings presented to Christ were traditionally understood as follows: gold betokened his kingship, incense his godhead, and myrrh his manhood. Here myrrh and incense are both associated with Christ's manhood.

II, 63   I passèd thoru a garden grene [*NIMEV* 378]

MSS: Edinburgh, NLS Advocates 19.3.1 (A); London, BL Sloane 2593 (S). Text from A.

Text: 6 sest] sesest A, lest S; 18 song] *supplied from* S; 41 becomen flech] becomyn is fleych S, becomun yn mannus flech A.

The conventional *chanson d'aventure* opening in this poem is more immediately evident from the first line in the Sloane version: *As I went throw a gardyn grene.*

1   *thoru*: 'through', pronounced here (as the metre shows) as a monosyllable; cf. Sloane spelling *throw.* Likewise *asked* (9) is to be pronounced as one syllable.

4   *tyrtull trew*: The turtle-dove, a 'common European species … noted for its graceful form, harmonious colouring, and affection for its mate' (*OED* **Turtle- dove** 1), figured frequently in medieval love poetry (usually with the alliterating adjective 'true') as a symbol of constancy and affection in love.

6   *sest*: The Sloane reading *lest* is in a different version of this line.

8   *Verbum caro factum est*: from John 1:14: *Et Verbum caro factum est* (And the Word was made flesh).

21   Lit: 'I wished not (that) they should have gone from me'.

38   *fest*: 'feast', i.e. the Feast of the Epiphany. Here the three kings, on their way home from the Bethlehem nativity scene, are imagined anachronistically, in true medieval fashion, as referring to what they had just witnessed as a 'feast', a word belonging to the terminology of the later Christian liturgy.

44–6   *hall, sale, arest*: three of a range of images used in ME poetry to describe the Virgin's womb in which Jesus 'dwelt'. Cf. Commentary, **II, 53**, 2.

51   *oure helpe*: i.e. Mary our help as intercessor.

II, 64   I saw a swetë semly syght [*NIMEV* 1352]

MS: London, BL Add. 5666, with music.

II, 65   That lovely lady sat and song [*NIMEV* 3627]

MSS: Edinburgh, NLS Advocates 19.3.1 (A); Oxford, Bodl. eng. poet. e.1 (B); Oxford, Balliol College 354 (C); London, BL Royal Appendix 58, with music (D). Text from B.

Text: 8 con say] A, gan say D, gan she say C, sayd B; 11 bryd] A, byrd B, CD *differ*; 20 kydde for Heven-Kyng] kidde for (*altered to* kyndde ame *by later hand)* kyng B, kend for Heuun Kyng A, knowen as hevyn kyng C, a kyng above all thyng D; 31 nere] MS, *altered by later hand to* ne þou; ordenëde] ordende MS; 46 twelfthë] xij MS; 57 wotst] wotyste MS; 64 ryght] A, *om.* B, CD *differ*; 66 in] i *supplied*; 68 And kepe me] D, And kepe B, Both be A, C *differs*; 74 all is] all ys D, it be C, all thyng is AB; 76 ryght] AD, both ryght B, C *differs*.

12   *it ys*: The monosyllabic pronunciation 'tis' is required here, in 33, and perhaps in 24.

23   *Done to me lyght*: The meaning could be 'make light for me', as glossed in *MEV*, p. 467. However, the readings *Shall to me lyght* of A and *To me shall light* of C suggest that it is preferable to take *done* here the adverb 'down' (cf. *done*: 'down', **II, 63**, 36) and the meaning as '[angels] descend to me' reflecting the traditional

presence of adoring angels at the Nativity and, in this context, confirming Christ's kingship.

79 *upon my day*: This is not a reference to 'Lady Day', 25 March, the Feast of the Annunciation; as confirmed by the readings *on this gud day* of A and *on this day* of C and D, in this context Mary's day is the day of the Nativity, one of her five joys.

II, 66   This endrys nyght [*NIMEV* 3596]

MSS: Oxford, Bodl. eng. poet. e.1 (B); London, BL Add. 5666, stanzas 1–3, 5–6, and 8 of B, with music (L); Cambridge, University Library Add. 5943, stanzas 1, 2, and 5 of B (C). Text from B.

Text: 12–17 *and* 19–24] MS *order reversed*; 22 wold] w *supplied*; 58 Wherto] Wartu L, Wher B; 61 Without] Withoutyn MS.

12ff. Stanzas 2 and 3 are in the wrong order in both MSS (B and L) in which they survive, for the words *Me thought I hard / The chyld answard* (12–13) must introduce the child's response to his mother. The mistake may have arisen from a scribe assuming that the stanza beginning *I may not slep* (19) had to follow immediately on the Virgin's words at the end of the first stanza, *Lullay, my chyld, and slepe.*

31 *he*: God. Despite his lowly place of birth (a stall, with ox and ass) and the humility of his mild mother, this child's father is no less than God.

50–51 What Christ has 'bought' (i.e. saved) through his sacrifice, and of which he will lose nothing, is mankind. Cf. John 17:12: 'While I was with them in the world, I kept them in thy name; those that thou gavest me I have kept, and none of them is lost'.

II, 67   A baby ys borne us blys to bryng [*NIMEV* 22]

MSS: Oxford, Balliol College 354, with burden and 11 stanzas (A); Oxford, Bodl. Laud misc. 683, with burden and stanzas 1–6 of A (B); Aberystwyth, NLW, Porkington 10, stanzas 1, 3–8, and 11 of A, with no burden (C). Text from C.

Text: 3 wepping] i *supplied*; 5 modyre] moder B, dere moder AC; 8 never] AB, þer neuer C; 9 say] tell AB, say þou C; 16 schall see this] shall se this A, seeth this B, hit schall see C; 17 hard] AB, sowerov now C; 24 this] *supplied, line in* A *and* B *differs but ends with* this; 25 sone] dere sone ABC, *but line differs in* A *and* B.

In C the English verses alternate with stanzas of the Latin hymn *Christe qui lux es et dies*. However, no indication is given as to how this exceptional arrangement of Latin and English stanzas might have been sung or recited together.

16 The emendations to C here and in 24 restore the a a a b rhyme scheme.

II, 68   O sisters too [*NIMEV* 2551.8]

The MS was destroyed by fire in 1879, but the text was preserved in Sharp's edition of 1825. See Craig (1957). Text from Craig.

Text: 20 may] say *Sharp transcript.*

12 *In his raging*: Traditionally the part of Herod in mystery plays called for ranting
and raging; hence Hamlet's comment, 'it out-herods Herod', on the noisy
performance of the kind of actor who aimed 'to split the ears of the groundlings'
(*Hamlet*, Act 3, scene 2).

II, 69   O man unkynde [*NIMEV* 2507]

MSS: Cambridge, Trinity College O.2.53; London, BL Add. 37049; Oxford, Bodl.
Tanner 407. Text from the Trinity MS. This text is also found in two early printed
books.

6 *hert*: In the Tanner MS this word is replaced by the drawing of a heart.

II, 70   O man unkynde [*NIMEV* 2504]

MSS: London, BL Add. 37049 (A); London, BL Add. 36505 (B). Text from A. B
is a variant text of A, a transcription of verses, dated 1522, found on the walls of
Almondbury Church, Yorkshire.

This poem may have been developed out of the single stanza of **II, 69**, above.

In the drawing accompanying this poem (see Introduction, p. 27), Christ is offering
man his heart, a heart in which his wounds are represented, those of hands and feet
by bleeding holes, and that made by the spear by a large lozenge-shaped gash the
width of the heart, surrounded by the words *This is the mesure of the wounde that
our Jesus Crist sufferd for oure redempcion*, the so-called *mensura vulneris*. See Gray
(1972), p. 34. The emphasis on Christ's heart reflects the devotion inspired by the
late medieval cult of the Sacred Heart. Christ's wounded heart was a place of refuge
offered to the sinner. It was also sometimes seen as a token of love paralleling the
broken heart of the secular love poet; and Christ, offering his heart to man, his
beloved, may also have evoked the notion of the exchange of hearts of romantic
lovers.

II, 71   Wofully araide [*NIMEV* 497]

MSS: London, BL Harley 4012 (H); London, BL Add. 5465 ['Fairfax' MS],
two copies, fols. 63v–67 and fols. 73v–77, with music (F). Text from H. For a
15th-century copy of the burden and stanza 2 only, and the 'Heber' copy, see Brown
XV, p. 326.

Text: 14 They] F, The H; 15 maiëste] maiste HF; 20 Thus] This MS; 21 Thus] This
MS; 24 Slayëne] Slayne MS.

The Harley MS gives a fourth stanza, as follows:

> Dere brother, non other thing I desire,
> But geve me thi hert fre, to rewarde myne hire.
> I am he that made the erth, water and fire.
> Sathanas, that slouen and right lothely sire,   *that knave*

> Hym have I over-caste,
> In hell presoune bounde faste,
> Wher ay his woo shall laste.
> I have purvaide a place full clere
> For mankynde, whom I have bought dere.
>
> Brown XV, pp. 157–8

The three stanzas of the Fairfax copies may well represent the original form of this lyric. The extra stanza in the Harley MS, with its generalities and clichés, differs in tone from, and is markedly inferior to the other stanzas, which focus on man's response to beholding the details of Christ's sufferings. Moreover, the poem comes to a wholly convincing conclusion without the fourth stanza. In the Harley MS the text is preceded by

> *Hosumever saith this praier in the worship of the passion shall have .c. yere of pardon*

and followed by

> *Who-sumever saith this devotely hathe grauntid be divers Bisshopis saing at the laste ende five pater nosters and five Aues .cccccc. dayes of pardon.*

Clearly the writer of these rubrics viewed this poem as a devotional prayer the recitation of which could earn a sinner a significant measure of pardon. Perhaps the fourth stanza was added to make more obvious this didactic and penitential conception of the poem.

The similarity of its initial burden-like lines and stanza form to *Sodenly afraide* (**11, 74**), on which it appears to have been modelled (see Rigg (1968), pp. 86–7), suggests that this poem may originally have been a carol despite the lack of any indication for the repetition of the introductory lines as a burden in the Harley MS. (The later through-composed musical settings by William Cornish, junior, and by Browne in the Fairfax MS do not allow for a burden: however, later musical settings need not necessarily represent the original form of a poem.)

Wofully araide is attributed to Skelton on the flyleaf of Richard Heber's 16th-century copy of the pseudo-Boethian *De Discip. schol. cum notabili commento* (see Brown XV, p. 326). Again, a poem *Wofully arayd, and shamefully betrayd* is listed among Skelton's poems in the *Garlande of Laurell* (Dyce (1843), i, p. 417, line 1418). But the words *and shamefully betrayed* are not found in this lyric; the reference may have been to the burden of another lyric. Rigg notes Skelton's 'jocular use' of lines from *Sodenly afraide* in the *Garlande of Laurell* (Dyce (1843), i, p. 403, lines 1038–40) and suggests that if Skelton knew *Sodenly afraide* well enough to quote from it, 'he might well have actually adapted it as "Wofully araid"' (Rigg (1968), pp. 86–7). However, as Gray points out, Skelton was given to using 'snatches of popular songs' (*LMVP*, p. 382). In the rubrics accompanying the text in the Harley MS (see above) no author is named.

1 *Wofully araide*: 'woefully arrayed', i.e. 'clad' in blood and bruises. The sense could also be 'woefully treated'; see *MED* **arraien** v. 1. (d).

12 *freted*: For various possible senses here see *MED* **freten** v. (3) (a) 'To bind or fasten etc.', **freten** v. (1) 1a. (c) '... to chew or gnaw', and 2. (b) 'to rub or chafe etc.'

15 *maiëste*: The full rather than the reduced form of the verb is required. Notwithstanding the MS spelling, a medieval reader would doubtless have adopted the disyllabic pronunciation to fit the dactylic metre here. Cf. line 4.

16 *nakid*: This disyllabic form would have been resolved (i.e. read as a single accent) as the first stress in the rhythm of this line.

17 *slepest*: pronounced here as 'slepst'.

24 *Slayëne*: Cf. line 15.

11, 72   Brother, abyde, I the desire and pray [*NIMEV* 550]

MS: Japan, Tokyo, Takamiya 6 (formerly Helmingham Hall MS LJ. i. 10, now MS 6 in the library of Professor Toshiyuki Takamiya).

Text: 6 canst thou do] what canst thou do then MS; 18 fro] for MS; 26 withouten] without MS; 53 that yf] yf MS; 113 me] be MS; 117 quod] qd MS; 134 And as] As as MS; 139 dystrayne] dystayne MS; 147 mowes] mobbes MS; 177 marke] make MS.

A few lines of this poem read awkwardly and may be open to question: e.g. do the 12 syllables of line 18 arise from a mistaken repetition of the words *voyde of*? Yet, while in so long a poem some lines may well be corrupt, in view of the flexibility of its versification emendation for the sake of metre has only been ventured in lines 6, 26, and 53.

The details of the description of Christ's life in this poem derive from late medieval lives of Christ, the most influential of which was the *Meditationes Vitae Christi*, a work long attributed to St Bonaventura (*c.* 1217–74) but now thought to have been written by a contemporary Franciscan monk living in Tuscany. The style of this narrative is simple; the emphasis throughout is on the Franciscan values of humility and poverty. Particular attention is paid to the infancy of Jesus (the Virgin's gentle, motherly care of her child is lovingly described), to Christ's boyhood, and to the events of the Passion. Details and episodes unrecorded in the Gospels or in such traditional sources as the writings of the Church fathers, the *Glossa ordinaria* and the *Legenda aurea*, are vividly and sympathetically supplied by the author 'as they might have occurred according to the devout belief of the imagination and the varying interpretation of the mind' (*Meditations*, p. xxviii). Several English translations of parts of this text were made in the 14th century, and the complete 15th-century translation by Nicholas Love, *The Mirror of the Blessed Life of Jesu Christ*, became one of the most popular books of the 15th and 16th centuries.

1–3 The words *abyde* (1 and 2) and *Behold* (3) echo *attendite* and *videte* from Lam. 1:12: *O vos omnes qui transitis per viam, attendite et videte, si est dolor sicut dolor meus* (Douay: O all ye that pass by the way attend, and see if there be any sorrow like to my sorrow), OT words used as an antiphon at Lauds on Holy Saturday with reference to Christ's suffering, and reiterated in lyrics such as this in which Christ addresses his complaint to man. Cf. **i, 99**.

6 The MS version of this line is so awkwardly long – egregiously at variance with the regularity of the other lines in this first stanza – that emendation, however speculative, to restore the metre seems desirable. Perhaps *what* and *then* were added by a scribe more concerned with emphasis than with metre.

33–5 A detailed account of the Virgin spinning and sewing in order to clothe herself and her child, and of the child Jesus acting as her messenger as the Virgin sewed for others to earn a living, is given in the *Meditations*, pp. 69–71.

44 On his journey from Nazareth to his baptism in the river Jordan, Christ is described in the *Meditations* as travelling barefoot (see *Meditations*, pp. 104–5) and as 'asking for alms along the way for love of poverty, since He did not carry money' (*Meditations*, p. 106).

46 *listed*: perhaps to be pronounced here as 'list'; *list* was an alternative past tense form of this verb.

47 *Watch*: 'wakefulness', a vigil as a devotional exercise. Christ spent his forty days and forty nights in the desert 'fasting, praying, watching, lying and sleeping on the bare earth', living a life 'everywhere difficult and physically painful' (*Meditations*, p. 117).

55 *greffe mortall*: the 'mortal grief', including death, suffered by Christ as man.

56 *brother moost naturall*: Christ became man's brother 'most natural' by virtue of his human birth.

101 As well as the weapons mentioned in the accounts of Christ's arrest in the Garden of Gethsemane in Matt. 26:47 and Mark 14:43, lanterns and torches are mentioned in John 18:3: 'Judas then, having received a band of men and officers from the chief priests and Pharisees, cometh thither with lanterns and torches and weapons.'

147 *mowes*: 'taunts'; see *MED* **moue** n. (2) **1**. (a). The MS reading is *mobbes*, but no such word is recorded in *MED*. The noun 'mob' meaning 'rabble' first appears in the 17th century, and the related verb meaning 'to attack in a mob or disorderly crowd' in the 18th century. See *OED* **Mob** *sb*. 1 and **Mob** *v*. 2. The emendation to *mowes* is convincing: in some late medieval hands 'bb' and 'w' are easily confusable and this word (as a verb) is used in the same context in **II, 71**, 14: *They mowëd, they spittëd and dispisëd me*.

166 The fourth of the seven last words Christ uttered from the cross: 'E-li, E-li, la-ma sa-bach-tha-ni? that is to say, My God, my God, why hast thou forsaken me?' (Matt. 27:46).

II, 73   In a tabernacle of a toure [*NIMEV* 1460]

MSS: Oxford, Bodl. Douce 322 (D); London, BL Add. 37049 (A); and seven other MSS, one a fragment of one stanza; see *NIMEV*. Text from D, with emendations from A. Of the surviving copies, the Northerly A version is closest to the dialect of the original; it is printed in Alexander and Riddy (1989), pp. 422–5.

Text: 14 Through] Þorow A, Though D; 15 me rewe] A, we rewe D; 19 his] A, *om.* D; 31 Sewe] Shewe D, Turne A; 50 My barne] A, Mankynde D; thi] þi A, hys D; 51 It] A, Yet D; 58 walde] A, wolde D; 59 yef] if A, yet yef D; 60 And] A, Or D; talde] A, tolde D; 62 thou flee] þu flee A, I flee the D; 63 byhalde] A, beholde D; 79 have I] I hafe A, had I D.

The language of love-longing of the Virgin's lament in this moonlight vision echoes that of lovers yearning for their mistresses in secular love lyrics. The refrain *Quia amore langueo* here, as in **I, 73**, derives from S. of S. 2:5; 5:8. Likewise the address of the beloved as 'my spouse' of the Song of Solomon is movingly adopted here in the final stanza as the Virgin implores man to take her, 'thy love thus languishing' (90), as his spouse, 'as [his] wife' (95). Granted the erotic intensity of the Virgin's appeal to man, her beloved – 'very gladly would I take you, embrace and kiss you' (71) – it may, at first sight, seem odd to a modern reader that she also speaks of man as 'my brother' (9), 'my dear child' (12), 'my offspring' (76), and 'son' (94), and refers to herself as man's 'mother' (11) and 'sister' (47, 93). However, as seen in **II, 49** and **80**, the late medieval Christian imagination was given to dwelling upon and even revelling in the emotive, theological, and mystic implications of the ways in which the relationships of man, the Virgin and Christ could be thought of in both human and divine terms; the Virgin is thus at once man's 'sister' and a 'queen', Christ, man's 'brother' and a 'king' (93); as Queen of Heaven, this Virgin may fittingly invite man, her 'son' (94), to take her as his 'wife' (95).

1   *tabernacle*: here, a canopied niche in a statue. In a drawing in MS A, a crowned Virgin stands in just such a niche in a tower holding the infant Jesus.

22   *I shall go*: The sense is that the Virgin will go to act as man's advocate (cf. line 10) before God.

52–6   *O Sone, allasse!* ... These lines are addressed by the Virgin to Christ.

58–64   The Northern forms *walde* (58), *talde* (60) and *byhalde* (63) are adopted from A. They are required to rhyme with *called* (61) and thus indicate that this poem was originally written in a Northerly dialect.

65–7   Again, in these lines the Virgin turns to address Christ.

79   'On account of him (i.e. man) I have this honour'. As stated in the following stanza, it was because of man that Mary had the honour of being crowned Queen of Heaven, of being called the source of mercy, and of being placed above the angels. Man was the cause of this honour in that it was man's original sin which made salvation by Christ necessary and thus, within the scheme of salvation, necessitated Mary's role as Mother of God and her subsequent coronation as Queen of Heaven. For this reason, man's fall in the Garden of Eden was, paradoxically, seen as a 'happy fault', a *felix culpa*. See Commentary, **I, 108**, 9–16.

94   *Thys heritage ys tayled*: An inheritance was 'entailed' when it was vested in the eldest son. In this context, man is 'son' (94) and heir in the lineage of Mary, his sister (also his 'mother'), Queen of Heaven, and of Christ, his brother (also, as God, his 'father'), King of Heaven; man's inheritance is an eternal life of singing in heaven with Mary, now not only his 'mother' and 'sister' but also his 'wife' (95).

II, 74   With favoure in her face [*NIMEV* 4189]

MSS: Manchester, John Rylands Library Lat. 395 (R); Cambridge, Trinity College O.9.38 (T). Text from R.

Text: 14 shortly with wordës] schortly with wordys T, with wordys shortly R; 16 thus] thys T, lo thus R; 21 me] T, þe R; 25 behold] T, me behold R; 26 this] lo this RT; 27 Ever] Euer T, Evuer R.

Like **11, 71**, this poem has the metrical pattern (×) / × × / (×) as the norm of its short lines and the half lines of its long lines and may be read fluently following this rhythm. In some lines it may be that this rhythmic norm was used to rhetorical effect: e.g. 13 *I sàid I cowd nòt wepe* (with emphasis on 'not'), or 33 *On mè she caste hìr ey* (suggesting the tension of the challenging eye-contact between the poet ('me') and the Virgin ('her'). An especially intriguing case is line 16. Could it be that the rhythmic norm of the poem is to be taken as imparting rhetorical stress to 'owne' and 'this'? If so read – i.e. as *Thyne òwne fader thìs nyght* – the sequence of stresses, including the next stress, which falls on *deed* – i.e. thine **own** father, **this** night, is **dead** – might be felt as emphatically underlining the enormity of the situation, the impact of which must enable 'nature' to 'convert' the hitherto unresponsive poet. However, occasional variation in the number of initial weak syllables occurs; line 37 must be read with three such syllables – i.e. as: *Yit she revivëd and sòbbëd* – and line 20 with two initial weak syllables as: *Veryfỳing the wòrdes*. Accordingly, line 16 may easily be read with two initial weak syllables as: *Thyne owne fàder this nỳght*. The sense of the metrical norm is also important in determining cases where two syllables are to be resolved as a single stress; thus, the two syllables of *Ever* (27) resolve readily as a single stress to maintain the rhythmic norm.

16 Whatever view is taken of the metrical interpretation of this line, it is evident that the T version (without the extra word *lo* found in R) correctly accords with the 12-syllable norm for the *a*-rhyme lines.

25 The T reading without the pronoun *me* is metrically preferable. It also makes better sense since the focus of attention at this point is not the Virgin but the pitiful *cors* (23) of Jesus, *So beten, so wownded* (24).

26 Both MSS read *lo this*. However, as in line 16, *lo* here may well be an addition by a scribe seeking to add emphasis without regard to metre.

11, 75   O alle women that ever were borne [*NIMEV* 2619]

MSS: Cambridge, University Library Ff.5.48 (C); Cambridge, University Library Ff.2.38 (U); Manchester, Chetham's Library 8009 (M); Oxford, Bodl. Rawlinson C.86 (R); Oxford, Bodl. Ashmole 61 (A). R and A lack stanzas 5 and 7. Text from C. M, with variants from U, C and R, is printed by Förster (1918), pp. 167–72, R and A, by Sandison (1913), pp. 104–9.

Text: 1 O alle women] Off alle women CUM, All women A, All mankynde R; 4 skyrte] UMA, kne C, lappe R; 7 beholde wele] UM, beholde now C, and beholde RA; 18 likyng] lykyng UMA, gret likyng C, plesyng R; 19 grete joye thou mas] UMA, gret joye makest R, with gret solas C; 22 with carfull] RA, with a carfull CUM; 28 so gret a gap is] so grete a gappe ys U, so gret gap is C, to se so gret gappys R, to se gret gappys A, so meny gappis M; 34 strake] M, stoke CU; 38 naylës sere] U, nayles sore M, nayle and speyre C; 43 Ye … thay] UM, He fele þerfor fittys or day C, Thow handilist his fete, fetys arn þey R, Thou beholdes hys fase and hys aray A; 45 my] MURA, any C; 49 town] towm MS; 52 Gode were] U, Good it were M, Then gode hit were C; 59 bounde] bonde MS; 60 and ded is he] RA, and myn is dede M, and myn ded is he CU; 78 damned] dāmed MS.

The version of this poem in R and A begins in the form of a *chanson d'aventure*:

> In a chirche as I gan knele
> This enders daye to here a masse,
> I sawe a sight me liked wele;
> I shall yow tell what it was.
> I saw a pite in a place,
> Owre lady and her sonne in feere;
> Ofte she wepte and sayde, 'Alas!
> Now lith here dede my dere sonne dere.'
>
> R, 1–8

The 'pite' the poet sees here is a pietà, a sculpture of the Virgin holding the dead Christ on her lap. After a second stanza addressed to 'all women' and a third addressed to 'all mankynde', come stanzas 1, 2, 3, 6, 4, 8, 9, 10 and 11 of the poem as found in the other MSS.

1 *O alle women*: For the emendation of *Off* to *O*, see Gray, *Selection*, p. 22.

12 Although there is no ostensible reason for questioning the text of this line – all MSS give the same reading – the meaning is not immediately obvious. The literal sense is either 'You know not well (i.e. are not well aware) when you have finished' or 'You know not (are not aware of) happiness when you have finished'. The latter interpretation is more probable in that *wele* in this line seems to echo *wel* of line 9. Perhaps the sense is that the mother's joy in caring for her child is so natural, so unselfconscious, so taken for granted, that she is blissfully unaware of it as she finishes with putting on the child's cap and combing its hair, and looks upon its face with motherly love. By contrast, the Virgin, picking thorns out of her son's bleeding head, is acutely aware of her grief as *ever, alas! I make my mone* (13). Alternatively, Gray tentatively suggests the sense to be: 'when you have finished (fondling your child), you feel sorrow (whereas I continually lament)' (Gray, *Selection*, p. 169, Glossary, under **wel(e)**).

19 The C reading, *with gret solas*, may have arisen from a scribe's wish to avoid the Northern form *mas*, which, as a rhyme word, he could not alter to *makest*.

31 *me happys*: an impersonal construction, '(it) happens to me'.

36 *hym*: 'them'. The sense of *hym* here is probably 'them' rather than 'him'; hands (those of the child and those of the crucified Christ) are the focus of attention. U reads *them*. The form *hym* for the plural pronoun 'them', which derived from the OE form *him*, was still current in the 15th century though, by this time, largely ousted by the form *them* borrowed into ME from ON.

43 The sense is probably: 'You feel their feet, so neat are they'. However, the R reading *fetys arn þey* (M reads *fetes*, the same analogical plural form for *fete*, 'feet', in the first half of this line) suggests that the sense might alternatively be taken as: 'You feel their feet, they are like feet [as feet are they]', in contrast, that is, to Christ's wounded feet, unrecognizable as such.

73 *that has your wytte*: lit. 'who have your understanding'.

II, 76   I have laborede sore and suffered deyth [*NIMEV* 1308]

MS: Edinburgh, NLS Advocates 19.1.11.

II, 77   Done is a battell on the dragon blak [*NIMEV* 688.3]

MS: NLS Advocates 1.1.6 [Bannatyne MS].

Text: 4 rasit] rasit is MS; 13 clowis] clowss MS; 16, 24, 32 *abbreviated in* MS.

The battle with the Dragon in this poem is the Harrowing of Hell, a legend which derived from the apocryphal Gospel of Nicodemus (see Introduction, p. 32). The impact of the Nicodemus narrative owed not a little to noise and drama, as the following brief extract illustrates.

> Again was heard the voice like that of thunder, saying 'Lift up your gates, O ye princes, and be ye lifted up, O eternal gates, and the King of Glory shall enter in.' And the Lord of Glory appeared in the form of a man, and he lighted the eternal gloom, and he broke the bonds, and his invincible virtue visited us who were sunk in the depths of the darkness of sin, and in the shadow of the death of sinners. The prince of Tartarus, Death and all the infernal legions seized with fear cried, 'Who art thou? Whence comest thou?' But he did not deign to answer them. Then the King of Glory, in his majesty treading Death under foot, and laying hold on Satan, deprived hell of its power, and led Adam to the light of the sun. And the Lord said, 'Come to me, all my saints, who have borne my image and likeness'.
>
> Quoted from Male (1961), p. 225

1   *the dragon*: For the Devil as a dragon, cf. Rev. 12, and in particular verse 9: 'And the great dragon was cast out, that old serpent, called the Devil'.

5   *divillis trymmillis*: The ending '-is' is sometimes reduced (as in *divillis*) and sometimes pronounced as a full syllable (as in *trymmillis,* trisyllabic here).

8   The refrain *Surrexit Dominus de sepulchro* (The Lord has risen from the tomb) is a versicle from the Mass for Easter Sunday.

18   *lyk a lamb in sacrifice*: Christ the 'Lamb of God' (John 1:29) was, like the lamb eaten at the Jewish Passover, 'our Passover … sacrificed for us' (1 Cor. 5:7).

19   *lyk a lyone*: Dunbar may well have had in mind the celebrated reference to Christ as Judah's Lion (cf. Gen. 49:9) in a stanza of the famous early 11th-century Easter hymn attributed to Fulbert of Chartres:

> How Judah's Lion burst his chains,
> And crushed the serpent's head;
> And brought with him, from death's domains,
> The long-imprisoned dead.
>
> Translation from *The English Hymnal*, no. 139

20   *as gyane*: The mighty Samson bearing off the gates of Gaza (see Judges 16:3) was seen as prefiguring Christ's breaking of the gates of hell.

21–2   *Aurora … Appollo*: Both were Classical deities, here associated with Christ. Aurora, goddess of the dawn, 'risen radiant and bright', echoes Mal. 4:2: 'But unto you that fear my name shall the Sun of righteousness arise with healing in his wings'. Apollo, god of the sun, likewise represents Christ, 'the Sun of righteousness'.

27   The setting of the sun was commonly associated with the darkness from the sixth to the ninth hour on Good Friday (see Luke 23:44–5) and the approach of

Christ's death on the cross (cf. Commentary, **I, 84**, 1); the rising sun offered an obvious image of Christ's resurrection.

II, 78   Jhesus woundes so wide [*NIMEV* 1787]

MS: London, BL Arundel 286.

2 Jesus' wounds are commonly referred to as wells of life. Cf. **II, 48** and Commentary, and see Brown XV, note on no. 100, p. 324.

II, 79   He bare hym up, he bare hym down [*NIMEV* 1132]

MS: Oxford, Balliol College 354.

For later, albeit considerably altered versions (two English and one Scottish from the 19th century, and one 20th-century American version, all without burdens) which testify to the continuing popularity of this carol in oral tradition, see Greene, pp. 196–7.

The allure of this carol – ostensibly a lullaby – is partly that of mystery and puzzlement. Who or what is the falcon (2)? Who is 'my mate' (2)? Why has this falcon borne my mate away to an orchard (4)? What hall (6) is this hung with rich fabrics (7) in the orchard? The mystery deepens from couplet to couplet. Indeed, it would almost seem that to read backwards from the end offers the most promising entry into some of the potential layers of meaning in this poem. The words 'Corpus Christi' inscribed on the stone (18–19) immediately suggest the Christian feast of that name and the words of the Eucharist: 'Hoc est corpus meum'. From this point of departure, the poem begins to unravel with the weeping maid (15–16) as the Virgin Mary, the wounded knight (12–13) as Christ. But what of the hall, the orchard and the falcon? Could the falcon symbolize Death? Is 'my mate' (2) Christ himself? Could the dark orchard be the Garden of Gethsemene? Could the hall be the tomb of Christ, appropriately draped with fabrics of royal and funereal purple, which then becomes a chapel in which, day and night, from the altar (Christ's bed) the sacrament (Christ's blood) is continuously available? In another reading, the wounded knight has been taken to be the keeper of the Holy Grail, and the hall as his castle. Greene interprets the poem as a political allegory: the falcon is Anne Boleyn (whose heraldic badge was a white falcon) who took King Henry VIII away from his first wife, Catherine of Aragon (Greene, pp. 423–7). This interpretation has not found general acceptance. It is difficult to see why Anne (the falcon) should take Henry away only to bring him to the very place where his former wife Catherine, here the maiden of lines 15–16, kneels weeping. Indeed, 'the dominant central image of the wounded knight does not seem to have much to do with the royal separation' (Gray (1972), p. 166). Exposed to the reductive process of interpretation, this poem seems singularly vulnerable; great critical tact is essential if one is to avoid brutally violating its subtlety and evocative appeal. Its language and symbolism seem so richly suggestive that an insistence on any one 'reading' is likely to strain credulity and to leave much unsaid and unaccounted for. It seems more attractive to allow for various layers of meaning – including that of the central concept of the Eucharist with, perhaps, additional overtones of the potent myth of the Holy Grail. See further, the excellent discussion in Gray (1972), pp. 164–7.

1 Although this opening line of the burden immediately suggests a lullaby, Greene points out that the words 'lullay' and 'by by' were words which in the 16th century were 'in well-established use as slang or colloquial language for the lamenting song of a rejected lover' (Greene, p. 426).

3–4 *He bare hym*: In support of his political interpretation of this carol, Greene claims (p. 427) that *hym* in lines 3 and 4 is not an object pronoun referring to *my mak* of line 2 but simply a reflexive pronoun as part of a reflexive construction, *bare hym*, meaning 'went'. This, however, is most improbable in view of the fact that *my mak* (2) is the object of the same verb. In any case, it would still seem odd that the falcon (Anne Boleyn), even if not bearing her stolen mate, should herself fly to the scene of the weeping maiden (Catherine of Aragon).

18 The *And* at the beginning of this line is questionable. If the line began with *By* (as does the first line of the previous couplet – cf. couplets 3 and 4 which both begin with *And*) and the monosyllabic form *stant* were adopted instead of, or assumed to be understood as the pronunciation of *stondeth*, this line would be in better metrical accord with the first lines of the other couplets.

19 The Feast of Corpus Christi, commemorating the institution of the Eucharist and celebrated on the Thursday after Trinity Sunday, was established in 1264 by Pope Urban IV.

II, 80   Byhalde merveyles! A mayde ys moder! [NIMEV 496]

MS: Oxford, Bodl. Laud misc. 108.

There are other late ME verses of this kind (like II, 81, below) in which paradoxes of the Christian faith – Christ as God and man, Mary as virgin and mother, the Host as bread and flesh – are handled in terms of a witty play on words.

II, 81   A God and yet a man? [NIMEV 37]

MS: Oxford, Bodl. Rawlinson B.332.

II, 82   Whan nothyng was but God alone [NIMEV 4000]

MS: Oxford, Bodl. eng. poet. e.1.

Text: 5 three (2x)] iij MS; 13 Heveyn] n *supplied*; 14, 22, 30, 38, 46 this] *supplied*; 16–17, 24–5, 32–3 It … Domini] etc. MS; 21 ych] ychy MS; 23 *and* 31 hold] hold it MS; 39–41, 47–9 To … Domini] To frayn why etc. MS.

The first two lines of the refrain as found in stanza 1 (6–7) are altered in subsequent stanzas. The omission of *this* in lines 14, 22, 30, 38 and 46 gives less convincing sense; the additional *it* in lines 23 and 31 spoils the metre.

This carol offers a robust affirmation of unqualified faith as against intellectual speculation about the ways of God. It is as if the propositions offered in each stanza are being questioned: when, in the beginning, there was nothing but God, how was he then three persons ? (stanza 1); how did God create the world? (stanza 2); why did the world evolve as it did, and what is the role of the planets? (stanzas 3 and 4); why do miracles occur? (stanzas 5 and 6). To ask such things is folly: there is no answer other than the power of the word of God.

6 *What is this why?*: i.e. what is this question 'why'?

7 I.e. it is nothing short of folly to question mysteries of the faith.

11 *Fiat*: 'let there be', God's word of command in Gen. 1:3: *Dixitque Deus: Fiat lux. Et facta est lux* (And God said, Let there be light: and there was light), repeated in Gen. 1:6, and in the plural form *Fiant* in Gen. 1:14.

20–21 The influence of the planets on this world and on the characters and destinies of men and women was a topic which occurred frequently in medieval literature. The orthodox view – i.e. that this influence was part of God's providence – is emphasized in 27–8.

35–7 In the *Venerabilis Bedae Vita Anonymo Auctore* (*Pat. Lat.* 40, cols. 53–4), an account of the character and last days of the Venerable Bede (673–735), this miracle is described. Now blind in old age, Bede, led by a disciple, arrived at a pile of stones. The disciple persuaded him that a great crowd of people was there waiting to hear him preach. This Bede did in a fervent manner, and when he uttered the concluding words *Per omnia saecula saeculorum* (throughout all ages), the stones miraculously gave voice and answered *Amen, Venerabilis Presbyter* (Amen, Venerable Priest).

44–5 I.e. how does the Host, the consecrated bread in the Eucharist, become the body of Christ and do so everywhere at the same time? The mention of heretics who question this miracle (43) may be a reference to Wycliff and the Lollards who rejected the orthodox doctrine of Transubstantiation, the doctrine that in the Eucharist the substance of the bread and wine were wholly converted into the substance of the Body and Blood of Christ.

II, 83   In the vale of Abraham [*NIMEV* 1568]

MS: London, BL Sloane 2593.

Text: 1, 7, 12, 17, 22, 27, 32, 37, 42 *bethink*] beþing MS; 2 span] an *supplied*; 9 so] that is so MS; 33 appil] appil t MS.

1–2 This burden echoes a popular proverb, a version of which is already found as the opening lines of the earlier, late 14th-century lyric *When Adam delf and Evë span* (II, 90). The Tudor historian Holinshed describes how John Ball, a leading figure in the Peasants' Revolt of 1381, preached to an assembly at Blackheath using as his text another version – *Whan Adam dalfe and Eve span, who was than a Gentleman?* – to prove 'that from the beginning all men by nature were created alike, and that bondage or servitude came in by unjust oppression of naughtie men' (quoted from Wright (1856), p. 103). Such sentiments, however, do not emerge in this carol, which is concerned with Adam's fall rather than the equality of men.

1 *bethink*: In the MS spelling *beþing*, the final 'ng' may have represented a variant pronunciation with a voiced final consonant or may derive from the equivalence of 'nk' and 'ng' in ME dialects where final 'ng' was unvoiced to 'nk'.

3 *vale of Abraham*: the valley of Hebron, chosen by Abraham as his home when he arrived in Palestine (see Gen. 13:18), and therefore referred to as the vale of Abraham here. In medieval tradition the valley of Hebron was also held to be place where God created Adam. Thus in the 14th century Sir John Mandeville states in his *Travels* that Abraham had his house in the valley of Hebron and that *righte fast by that place is a cave in the roche where Adam and Eve duelleden, whan thei weren putt out of Paradyse, and there goten thei here children. And in that same place was Adam formed and made, aftre that that sum men seyn* (quoted from Wright (1856), p. 104).

6 *semly word*: 'seemly speech', i.e. the speech beginning at line 8. The speaker, 'Christ himself' in stanza 1, becomes 'God himself' by line 16.

10 *appil tre*: The tree of knowledge – 'the tree of the knowledge of good and evil' (Gen. 2:17) – came, in popular medieval tradition, to be thought of specifically as an apple-tree.

36 An immediate consequence of eating the forbidden fruit was that Adam and Eve were suddenly (and ashamedly) aware of their nakedness; see Gen. 3:7: 'And the eyes of them both were opened, and they knew that they were naked; and they sewed fig leaves together, and made themselves aprons.'

II, 84   Almyghty God, fadir of hevene [*NIMEV* 241]

MSS: London, BL Harley 2406; Cambridge, University Library Ii.6.43, two copies (on fols. 20 and 99v); Cambridge, University Library Dd.8.2; Oxford, Bodl. Bodley 789. Text from the Harley MS.

Text: 18 thre] .iij. MS.

This is a prayer to the Trinity – Father, Son and Holy Ghost – and, additionally, in three copies, to the Virgin as well, almost as if she were of equivalent status to the other three persons.

II, 85   Upon my ryght syde y me leye [*NIMEV* 3844]

MS: London, BL Harley 541.

Text: 9 sprange] sprange lady MS.

In language and manner this ME bed-time prayer to the Virgin has an appealing simplicity akin to that of the modern prayer, 'This night as I lie down to sleep'.

8–9 The final line in the MS is awkwardly long, possibly as a result of *Lady* having been incorrectly repeated from line 8. Granted that ME spelling often masks metre, it may well be that the final couplet was meant to be read as:

> Our Lord's the fruit, our Lady's the tree,
> Blest be the blossom that sprang of thee.

For Mary as part of the tree of Jesse, and Jesus as a blossom thereon, cf. Commentary, **I, 76**, 17, and Commentary, **II, 45**, 1–3 and 7–8.

II, 86   O swete angell, to me soo deere [NIMEV 2560]

MS: San Marino, California, Huntington Library EL 34.B.7.

The practical, devotional purpose of this poem is made absolutely clear in the MS, where it has the heading: 'A praier to the goode Angell'. The third stanza is followed first by:

> The versicull:
>
> O swete angell, that keepith me,
> Bryng me to blysse, I pray the

and then by a collect beginning:

> O my lorde, Jhesu Crist, as it hathe pleasede the to assigne an angell to wayte on me dayly and nyghtly.

II, 87   God be in my heed [NIMEV 940]

Source: Pynson's *Hore Beate Marie Virginis* (1514).

'The first occurrence of the English text seems to be in a Rouen book of hours from 1506, but a French version is attested earlier' (Gray, *Selection*, p. 144). There is an excellent and well-known musical setting of this prayer by Henry Walford Davies (1869–1941).

II, 88   Illa iuventus that is so nyse [NIMEV 1444]

MS: Oxford, Balliol College 354.

Text: 3 iuventus] juventis MS; 8 iuvenis] juvinus MS; 9 sinne] sinni MS; 11, 16, 21 conturbat me] *supplied*; 13 and] in MS.

2   This Latin line, used here as the second line of the burden and also as the refrain line of each stanza, is a version of *Timor mortis conturbat me*, words derived from one of the responses in the Office of the Dead and used in three other late ME carols on the theme of death (Audelay's carol, **II, 89**, below, and Greene, nos. 370 and 371, in the latter translated into English) and as a refrain line in poems by Lydgate, Ryman and Dunbar.

13 Davies (1963), p. 279, prints *Corpus migrat in my soule* (following the MS reading of this line) with the gloss: 'My body parts from my soul.' But the preposition *in* cannot mean 'from', and it is perhaps a little odd to speak of the body parting from the soul rather than of the more usual parting of the soul from the body. Greene offers no comment but clearly understands the text differently as he punctuates:

> Corpus migrat; in my sowle
> Respicit demon, in his rowle.

The word *in* (abbreviated in the MS) may easily have arisen from a misreading of an ampersand. The emendation gives the required sense – 'My body and soul part' (lit. 'My body parts and my soul') – and a reading which is closer to the parallel line quoted by Patterson: *Whan my sowle & my body departyd shall be* (Patterson (1911), p. 182).

14–15 For the popular notion of the Devil (or, as here, a demon) having a 'roll', a document in which he records the names of sinners from whom, after death, he will exact his payment, or 'toll', cf. Tutivillus, the Devil of hell, in **II, 137**, who writes down the names of those who chatter during the mass, and the mention of the Devil's 'toll' in **I, 115**, 4.

20–21 Cf. Greene, no. 370, stanza 4:

> Jhesu Cryst, whane he schuld dey,
> To hys Fader he gan sey;
> 'Fader,' he seyd, 'in Trinyte,
> Timor mortis conturbat me.'

As Greene notes (p. 443), 'These words are not recorded in the canonical Scriptures as said by Jesus'.

II, 89   Dred of deth, sorrow of syn [NIMEV 693]

MS: Oxford, Bodl. Douce 302.

Text: 39 fivë] v MS.

Timor mortis conturbat me appears as the heading of this poem in the MS.

In poem 55 in the unique MS of his work John Audelay states that he was a chantry priest to Richard le Strange of Knockin Castle near Oswestry in Shropshire. It is further recorded in a Latin colophon dated 1426 found at the end of the 18th poem that he was a chaplain, that he was blind and deaf, and that his poems were written as an example for others (i.e. other religious) in Haghmond Abbey, a house of Augustinian Canons near Shrewsbury, where he may well have spent his final days. See further, Fein (2003).

  2 These words are from the Response to the seventh Lectio in the third Nocturn of Matins in the Office of the Dead.

  6 This refrain line comes from the 14th-century eucharistic prayer *Anima Christi sanctifica me*, which Audelay quotes in his didactic poem *De psalterio passionis* (Whiting (1931), no. 6).

  52 The final words of Jesus from the cross; see Luke 23:46: *Et clamans voce magna Iesus ait: Pater, in manus tuas commendo spiritum meum. Et haec dicens expiravit.* (And when Jesus had cried with a loud voice, he said, Father, into thy hands I commend my spirit: and having said thus, he gave up the ghost.)

  64 'When trouble is at its height then a remedy may be at hand' – a proverb common in ME, versions of which were already found in OE.

II, 90   When Adam delf [NIMEV 3921]

MSS: Cambridge, University Library Dd.5.64 (3) (C); Lincoln, Cathedral Library 91 [Thornton MS], held in Nottingham University Library (L). L has two stanzas not found in C. Text from C.

Text: 18 unto] vnto L, to C; 79 fallace] L, fals C; 99 when that] when þat L, when C.

Forms characteristic of the North-East Midland dialect of this poem retained here – e.g. *merrës* (6), *sal* (12) and *ga* (28), Northern counterparts of Southern *merreth, shall* and *go* – should cause the reader little difficulty.

1–6 Cf. **II, 83**, 1–2, and Commentary.

3 *spede*: 'succeed'. Success lies in recognizing the answer to the question posed here, namely, that pride is a sin and was, therefore, unknown in Paradise before the Fall which, unlike this miserable word beset with pride, was a place of bliss and innocence.

6 *merrës his mede*: 'mars his reward'. Perhaps: 'stands in the way of his (heavenly) reward' – so Davies (1963), p. 143. John Ball (see Commentary, **II, 83**, 1–2) would probably have taken the sense as being that while, originally, Adam and Eve enjoyed the fruits of delving and spinning in innocence, now the rewards of labour are marred by inequalities caused by a social hierarchy stemming from the sin of pride. However, with the reference to Solomon later in the stanza, the sense here may simply be that on account of sin – pride in particular – man's rewards in this life are nullified. See note to lines 14–18, below.

13 The *I* and *E* of the *With I and E* refrain (versions of which are found in other lyrics) would seem to be cries or exclamations of sorrow, regret, lamentation, and the like. Cf. *ay* and *o* of Commentary, **I, 47**, 22–3.

14–18 See Wisdom 5:11: 'Or as when a bird flieth through the air, of the passage of which no mark can be found, but only the sound of the wings beating the light air, and parting it by the force of her flight; she moved her wings, and hath flown through, and there is no mark found afterwards of her way.' The apocryphal Book of Wisdom is written in the person of Solomon. In this chapter he asks (verse 8): 'What hath pride profited us? or what advantage hath the boasting of riches brought us?' The answer is: absolutely nothing. As a ship passes through the sea, or a bird or an arrow through air, and leaves no trace, 'so we also being born, forthwith ceased to be: and have been able to shew no mark of virtue: but are consumed in our wickedness' (Wisdom 5:13).

21 Lit. 'Till we are brought [to the time] to depart'.

29–30 The 'friend' in this life who, after death, will become a foe, is the Devil. For the notion of the three traditional foes of man – the world, the flesh and the Devil – masquerading as friends in this life, cf. **I, 54**, 25–6:

> Our soulës bone so broerli be   *our souls' destroyers are as brotherly*
> As bernë best that bale forbede   *as the best of men who prevent harm*

33–6 Cf. lines 50–54 and comments, below.

40–42 Cf. 2 Sam. 14:25: 'But in all Israel there was none to be so much praised as Absalom for his beauty: from the sole of his foot even to the crown of his head there was no blemish in him.' Just as Solomon (39) was renowned for wisdom and Samson (45) was the archetypal man of strength, Absalom (42) was frequently mentioned in medieval literature as the epitome of masculine beauty.

50–54 The inevitability of death, and man's ignorance concerning the time of his death and his destination thereafter, were recurrent themes in medieval moral verse. Cf. **I, 41**, **I, 42**, and **I, 52**, 15. Another related set of three questions asked where we came from, who we are, and where we are going – cf. **I, 50**, 31–2.

64 *fra God*: 'from God', i.e. to Hell.

66 *undur fete*: lit. 'under feet', i.e. in the grave.

70 *ne wil*: to be read here as the reduced, monosyllabic form *nil*.

74 *hitt*: See *MED* **hitten** v. **3.** (c) **ben hit**, 'be fulfilled'.

84 *brok als thou hase boght*: lit. 'enjoy as you have bought' – a pithy and potentially ironic way of expressing the sense 'get what you have deserved'.

88 *Terme*: The sense here is as in ME *terme day*, 'a day appointed for … payment of money that is owed' (*MED* **Terme** n. **4.** (a)).

97 *was*: 'a torch of straw'; see *OED* **Wase 1.**

101 *breste*: 'breast', i.e. 'body'. Synechdoche, a figure of speech whereby the part is used to express the whole, is adopted here, with 'breast' for 'body' for the sake of rhyme.

II, 91   Who hath that conyng, by wysdam or prudènce
[*NIMEV* 4092]

MS: Oxford, Bodl. Rawlinson D.82.

Lines 1, 3 and 5 are metrically awkward. The removal of *that* (1), *that*, or even *I trow that*, granted a trisyllabic pronunciation of *creature* as 'cre-a-ture' (3), and *ys* (5) – all plausibly suspect scribal additions – would restore the decasyllabic metre of this poem.

II, 92   Allas diceyte that in truste ys nowe [*NIMEV* 145]

MS: Oxford, Bodl. Laud misc. 108.

Text: *The edge of the MS has been cut away; the initial letter of each line is supplied.*

1 That trust – i.e. the trustworthiness, the good faith one relies upon in others – is now contaminated with deceit is the theme of this short lyric. No one is to be trusted. Cf. **II, 102**, 16.

2 Lady Fortune, traditionally false and two-faced, is graphically depicted by Chaucer:

> She ys fals, and ever laughynge
> With oon eye, and that other wepynge.
> *The Book of the Duchess*, 633–4

The turning ball or sphere represented the ever-changing nature of Fortune, as did the more familiar symbol of her ever-turning wheel.

II, 93   The worlde so wide, the aire so remuàble [*NIMEV* 3504, 3436]

MSS: Oxford, Bodl. Fairfax 16 (F); London, BL Harley 7333 (H); San Marino, California, Huntington Library HM 144 (P). For further MSS and information, see *NIMEV*. Text from F.

Text: 1 the aire] þe ayer HP *and other* MSS, thaire F; 3 of] HP *and other* MSS, and F.

The attribution of these verses to Halsham is found only in MSS connected with the 15th-century scribe and literary entrepreneur John Shirley, either in his autograph

MSS (BL Add. 16165 and the single quire at the beginning of Ellesmere 26. A. 13), or in MSS derived from Shirley exemplars (BL Harley 7333 and Add. 34360, which latter contains only the first stanza). This 'Halsham' was identified by South (1935) as John Halsham of West Grinstead in Sussex, who was dead by 1415. Authorship was claimed by Bühler (1940) for Lydgate on the basis that he used these verses. More recently, Doyle (1961) suggested that the reference may rather have been to either Richard or Hugh Halsham, sons of John Halsham and his first wife Philippa. According to Margaret Connolly, 'Shirley would have known Richard from his service in France in 1415 when both men served in Warwick's military retinue at Calais'; and it may also be that the term 'squyer' was used by Shirley 'to draw a distinction between Richard and his brother Hugh who was a knight' (Connolly (1998), p. 39).

These seven-line stanzas are in rhyme royal except that the rhyme scheme of stanza 2 ends with a c c instead of b c c. They are composed in a rhetorical manner exploiting devices drawn from medieval Latin handbooks of rhetoric much favoured by medieval poets writing in the 'high' style. Thus, the repetition of a single word for emphasis (the device of traductio) is found in the repetition of 'so' five times in the first four lines. The second stanza is largely a series of balanced opposites (the device of contentio). The crossing *a b b a* sequence of lines 8 and 9 (*more I go – ferther … behind / ferther behind – the ner*) represents a instance of the device of chiasmus. Cf. Chaucer, *The Parliament of Fowls*, 1–3, where all three devices are used:

> The lyf so short, the craft so long to lerne,
> Th'assay so hard, so sharp the conquerynge,
> The dredful joye alwey that slit so yerne.

Cf. Commentary, **II, 2**.

 6 *these fourë*: i.e. the four elements just mentioned – air (1), earth (*grounde*) (3), fire (4) and water (5) – the simple substances from which, according to ancient and medieval philosophers, all things were composed, including *sely man* (2).

II, 94   As y gan wandre in my walkinge [*NIMEV* 349]

MSS: London, Lambeth Palace Library 853 (L); Aberystwyth, NLW, Porkington 10 (P); Oxford, Bodl. Lat. misc. e.85 (B). Stanza 2 of P and B is lacking in L. Text from L.

Text: 10 boren] born MS; 56 This] PB, That this L.

In this poem the different stages of man's life are expressed in terms of different times in the course of a day. These times can clearly be distinguished only when the vernacular terms in this poem (which were often variable or, at the very least, vague in their time reference) are understood in terms of the sequence of the canonical hours (the times of monastic services) with which they were, albeit loosely and sometimes inconsistently, associated. Thus *morewe* (9), lit. 'morning', is equivalent to Matins (the midnight service), and here, therefore, means 'morning' in the sense of 'the beginning of the new day'; *mydmore* (17), lit. 'midmorning', is equivalent to Prime (the 6 a.m. service), and here, therefore, means 'early morning'; *undren* (25), equivalent to Tierce (the 9 a.m. service), here means 'midmorning'; *mydday* (33), lit. 'mid-day', is equivalent to Sext (the midday service); *noon* (41), lit. 'noon' in its vernacular sense, in ecclesiastical usage means None (the 3 p.m. service); *mydovernoon* (49), lit. 'mid-afternoon', is equivalent to Vespers (the late-afternoon service); *evensong* (57), lit. 'evensong', is equivalent in the canonical sequence to Compline, the last of the canonical day-hours. Cf. Commentary, II, 57.

For another moralizing poem in the form of an old man's lament, cf. an earlier lyric from MS Harley 2253 (I, 51). With their refrains, this and the following poem (II, 95) follow in the tradition of the late 14th-century moralizing refrain poems in the Vernon MS. See Commentary, I, 60.

  8 This refrain derives from Eccles. 1:2: 'Vanity of vanities, saith the Preacher, vanity of vanities; all is vanity', words repeated in Eccles. 12:8.

15 *therfore*: either 'on that account' (i.e. old age) or 'for them' (i.e. his sins, mentioned in the previous line).

17 *mydmore*: This word was used for both the canonical hours Prime (6 a.m.) and Tierce (9 a.m.); see *MED* **mid-morwe** n. and *OED* **Undern** *sb*. 1. As this poem is structured in terms of progressive stages of the day, equivalent to different stages of life, it is appropriate to translate *mydmore* (lit. 'mid-morning') as 'early morning' here since, clearly, an earlier time is meant than *undren* 'mid-morning' at line 25.

25 *undren*: The time reference of this term varied considerably; see *OED* **Undern** *sb*.

41 *high noon*: In terms of the structure of this poem based on advancing stages of the day, this time must be understood as later than *mydday* of line 33.

69–72 The ending in P differs. With its echo of the beginning of the poem, it seems better, and may have been the original version:

> As I went on my playing,
> Undure an holt by a tre,
> This hard I an old man mak mournyng –
> This world ys but a vannyté.

II, 95 In a noon-tiid of a somers day [*NIMEV* 1454]

MSS: Cambridge, Trinity College O.9.38 (T); London, Lambeth Palace Library 853 (L); Oxford, Balliol College 354 (B). Text from L, stanzas 1–11. L has 15 stanzas, T has stanzas 1–11, and B has stanzas 1–3 and 11.

Text: 14 turne] to turne LTB; 28 hertli] hertly T, hertili L; 31 endles] T, everlastinge L; 36 to] T, into L; 41 To] T, This L; 43 Yowth] T, It L; 84 Of] T, Of al L.

15 Drawings of trees with words in leaves or branches used for the schematic representation of vices and virtues, etc., were common in late medieval MSS.

16 The refrain lines of this lyric vary. Each follows on in sense and syntax from the preceding line, but always ends with the word *revertere* which probably derives from Isaiah 44:22: *revertere ad me, quoniam redemi te* (return unto me; for I have redeemed thee), where God states that he has blotted out the transgressions of Israel.

40 *ne wole*: may be read as the reduced form *nil*.

44 *Gregorie*: St Gregory (*c.* 540–604), Gregory the Great, the last of the four early Doctors of the Church (the others being Ambrose, Augustine and Jerome).

53ff. The story of Susanna, the beautiful wife of Joakim, is found in one of the shorter apocryphal texts associated with the Book of Daniel. Two elders, consumed with lust for Susanna as they secretly watched her bathing privately in her garden, emerge from their concealment and threaten to accuse her of adultery if she does not yield to their desires. Susanna refuses and, when falsely accused by the two elders before the people, is condemned to death. However, the perfidy of the elders is exposed by Daniel, and they are put to death.

60 *of high romage*: 'high-spirited'; cf. *MED* **ramage** n. and adj.

61–2 I.e. a young man, who should set his heart on God, instead sends his hawk (his heart) off in pursuit of pleasure.

69ff. Only the young man who prays in the darkness of the night and in the mist of the morning is, through the strength of Christ, able to sing 'turn back', i.e. is able to repent.

86 *fle*: 'fly'. In ME the verbs 'flee' (OE flēon) and 'fly' (OE flēogan) were often confused. See *MED* **flen** v. (1). The heart of youth (like a hawk), arrogant and wild, flies in pursuit of pleasure (the hen-pheasant).

87 *wickid sort*: 'wicked company'; see *MED* **sort(e** n. The sense may, alternatively, be 'evil circumstances', see *MED* **sort** n. (1).

II, 96   A man that shuld of trewthë telle [*NIMEV* 72]

MS: London, BL Sloane 2593.

Text: 5 In] n *supplied*; 16 *and* 21 trewthe] w *supplied*; 23 Relygius] Relygiuus MS; 31 pardé] *supplied*.

 8 *cometh*: pronounced as a monosyllable, i.e. 'comth'; so, also, 15 *thinketh* (as 'thinkth').

31 For the addition *pardé* to complete the line and the rhyme scheme, cf. *MEV*, p. 431, no. 186, line 26.

II, 97   If y halde the lowe asyse [*NIMEV* 1415]

MS: Cambridge, University Library Add. 5943.

Text: 6 fon] fow MS; 21 the (2)] they MS; 23 sley] scley MS.

The theme of this poem – whatever life-style one adopts it will attract adverse comment – is the same as Dunbar's poem *How sould I rewill me or in quhat wys* (Kinsley (1979), no. 82). Perhaps, as Greene suggests (pp. 436–7), Dunbar knew this carol (or a common source).

 6 *fon*: 'fool' is a fairly common word in ME; see *OED* **Fon**, *sb.* and *a.* If retained, the MS form *fow* would have to be taken as a rare instance of a borrowing from OF *fou*, not recorded in *MED*.

18 The ox, a symbol of endurance and strength, represented those who bear their yoke with forbearance and labour silently for the common good. Also, as a

sacrificial animal of the Jews, the ox was viewed by some early Christian fathers as a symbol of Christ, the true sacrifice.

19 The fox, the traditional representative of guile and cunning, was frequently found in medieval carving and sculpture, sometimes, indeed, symbolizing the Devil. The sense here is: if one is too 'low', too humble and trusting, one will lay oneself open to trickery and exploitation.

21 *kyte*: The most celebrated instance in medieval literature of the kite – a bird of prey also formerly called, among other names, a 'glede' (see *OED* **Kite** *sb.*) – as an agent of death is found in Henryson's Fable, *The Paddock and the Mouse*, in which both *paddock* (frog) and mouse are seized and slain by a *gredie gled* (greedy glede).

II, 98   Blowyng was mad for gret game [*NIMEV* 543]

MS: Oxford, Bodl. eng. poet. e.1.

Text: 6 nought] ght *supplied*; 16, 21, 26, 31 a horne and blow it nought] etc. MS; 24 Stop] and stop MS.

II, 99   In what order, or what degré [*NIMEV* 1588]

MS: Oxford, Bodl. Douce 302.

Text: 15 four] iiii MS; 28 poverté] é *supplied*; 47 algates] s *supplied*.

In the hard priest, proud friar, lecherous old man and cowardly knight of stanza 3, Audelay may have had in mind lists of abuses found in other medieval verse as, for instance, the 'three points of mischief' – a poor man proud, a rich man a thief, an old man a lecher – in the 15th-century lyric, *Ther ben iij poyntis of myscheff* (Brown XV, no. 177). Exceptionally, priest, friar, old man and knight of stanzas 4–7 are called the four estates ordained by God in the final stanza. The usual division of medieval society was into three estates: priests, knights and labourers.

For John Audelay, see Commentary, **II, 89**.

II, 100   Maist thou now glade, with all thi fresshe aray [*NIMEV* 2136]

MS: London, BL Harley 116.

Text: 1 glade] be glade MS; 8 Uche] Yche MS; put] to put MS; 11 wel the hede] welthe heele to MS; 13 No] Be MS.

For the emendations of *Yche* to *Uche* (8) and *Be* to *No* (13) which restore the acrostic MORS SOLUIT OMNIA (Death dissolves all things) formed from the initial letters of the lines of this poem, see Cutler (1955). Acrostics are used in a few (fewer than 20) ME poems, religious and secular, dating from before 1500: e.g. four hymns to the Virgin with acrostics on MARIA or AVE MARIA, two poems with acrostics on the name St Katherine, two on death or MORS, several on the name of a poet's beloved (e.g. those in Humfrey Newton's commonplace book, see Commentary, **II, 15**). These acrostics are largely contrived, mechanical and non-structural – i.e. they do not determine the structure of poems of any length.

In this lyric, however, the acrostic is not only structural, dictating the first letter of each of the 15 lines, but so cleverly contrived that prior to Cutler (1955) it had passed unnoticed by modern editors. The rhyme-scheme is also remarkable: a b b b a; b a a a b; a b b b a. As in the classical ballade, the same rhyming sounds are used in each of the stanzas.

 1 A scribe having failed to read *glade* as a verb ('rejoice', 'be happy') may have altered the text here to *be glade* (with *glade* as an adjective), thus spoiling the metre.
 2 *dystene*: 'stain'. Beside 'to colo[u]r or stain', other senses of this verb include 'to deprive of colo[u]r, brightness, or beauty' and 'defile'; see *MED* **disteinen** v. **1.** (a), **2.** (a), and **3.** (b).
 6 The image of Death 'marking with his mace' is an ironic parody of marking with the sign of the cross in a Christian blessing. See *MED* **marken** v. (1) **7.** Death's mace is to be seen both as his symbol of office (equivalent to the Christian cross) and as his menacing club, just as Christ's cross was sometimes viewed as a weapon against the Devil. The 13th-century author of a guide to anchoresses, the *Ancrene Wisse,* urges an anchoress to deal with the 'dog of hell' (i.e. the Devil) as follows: 'But seize the crucifix at once, and with the words of the sign of the Cross on your lips, the cross itself in your hand, with the thought of it in your mind, order him out sternly, foul cur that he is, and fall upon him fiercely, with heavy blows on his back from the holy crucifix' (Salu (1955), p. 129). Also cf. **1, 47,** 37 and 46.

The reading of this poem depends significantly on how the French rubric is viewed. Emphasis on the autonomy of poetry is characteristically modern rather than medieval. Late medieval practice frequently associated texts and images. Wall paintings often had explanatory *tituli* (texts, sometimes in verse), and poems were sometimes accompanied by illustrations. It is not, therefore, implausible to suppose that the rubric here was written by the poet to specify the subject-matter of his poem.

If rubric and poem are integrally related, the images of the mirror and Death may be seen as subtly fused in this lyric. Clearly it is the mirror (the *me* of line 2) which first addresses the beautiful young woman who is happy to look therein admiring her appearance. By the end of the poem the mirror has become the reflection of Death, who proclaims 'I smite, I slay' (14). This development is the outcome of the staining process of physical decay announced in line 2. Rapidly the beauty of youth acquires the stain of decay: the mirror reveals this as the young girl's fair countenance changes to reveal (in Donne's words) 'the scull beneath the skin', and to become the image of Death itself.

Ironically, the dressing mirror, initially a source of joy reflecting physical beauty in youth, becomes a moral mirror, reflecting corruption in body and soul. The mirror was commonly understood in this way in medieval homiletic literature. The title, *Mirror,* of a 14th-century cycle of ME sermons translated from Robert de Gretham's 13th-century Anglo-Norman *Miroir,* is explained as follows:

> In the mirur a man seth his body, and bi this writ [writing], body and soule …
> the mirur maketh thes wimmen fair to be sen in the world that hij [they] ben

the more covaited when hij ben fair atired, and this scheweth the fairnes that Jhesus loveth in truthe and maketh the soules to dresse hem that God will covait hem.

Quoted from Duncan and Connolly (2003), pp. 5–7

However, there is no guarantee that the French rubric was necessarily written by the poet to accompany his poem. If one analyses the poem on its own, it will be seen that it contains no specific mention of mirrors, let alone of women. It may be felt that if the poet had really been concerned with these ideas he would have incorporated them expressly within the poem itself. It is therefore possible (perhaps preferable?) to read this lyric without involving what might be regarded as a confusing shift of speaker (i.e. from Mirror to Death). The speaker may be taken as Death throughout. The addressee, with all the *fresshe aray* (1) of youth, may as readily be thought of as a young man as a young woman. Youth may for 'now' (1), while fresh and merry, be happy to look on Death without concern (1–2). Death, however, in the face of such insouciance, urges the addressee to 'take pity' (3) on himself (or herself) and repent. It may be that the French heading was added by some moralistic, anti-feminist scribe who, with a certain grim irony, saw this poem – a poem on death reflecting a 'Memento mori' message – as an appropriate mirror for young ladies to look into to make themselves beautiful (i.e. morally beautiful). However, even ignoring the rubric, it would still be possible to take 'me' of the second line – the thing that fresh youth may rejoice to look upon (1–2) – as referring to a mirror rather than to death.

Whatever view is taken of the French rubric, the fundamental message of this poem is clear whether it is read horizontally across the page or detected vertically in the acrostic: MORS SOLUIT OMNIA.

II, 101   I weende to dede, a kynge i-wisse [*NIMEV* 1387]

MSS: London, BL Cotton Faustina B.vii, Part II (C); London, BL Add. 37049 (B); London, BL Stowe 39 (S). Text from C.

Text: 1 to dede] BS, *om.* C.

This poem is based on a sequence of medieval Latin verse couplets beginning and ending with the words *vado mori*, in which a series of figures – kings, popes, knights, bishops, scholars, etc., usually in approximately hierarchical order – lamented the inevitability of death. The King spoke thus:

> Vado mori, rex sum, quid honor, quid gloria mundi?
> Est via mors hominis regia: vado mori.

I go to die, a king I am, what value honour, what value worldly glory? Death is man's royal road: I go to die.

In MS Stowe 39 Death speaks in an additional final stanza:

> Be ye wele now warre with me!
> My namë then is Ded;
> May ther nonë fro me fle,
> That any lyfe gun led.

> Kynge, kasere, theyn, no knyght,
> Ne clerke that cane on bokë rede,
> Beest, ne foghel, ne other wyght,
> Bot I sal make tham dedde!

All three MSS are illustrated. In Cotton Faustina B.vii each victim is presented holding a scroll containing the stanza he speaks; see Gray (1972), plate 11, opposite p. 214. In Stowe 39 Death is depicted as a skeleton menacing his victims with a spear. Add. 37049 has three skeletons with spears. See Gray (1972), plate 10, opposite p. 183, and also pp. 209–11.

6 *I wane the flour*: 'I won the flower', i.e. 'I was pre-eminent'.

II, 102   Farewell, this world! I take my leve for evere [*NIMEV* 769]

MSS: Cambridge, Trinity College O.2.53 (T); Oxford, Balliol College 354 (B); London, BL Lansdowne 762, final stanza only. The T text ends at *peyntëd* (25); the second half of this line is erased except for a single letter 'e' which survives before the erasure. The text here is from T with the final stanza and a half and the Latin rubric supplied from B.

Text: 7 that] B, *om.* T; 13 sodeyn] sodeynly B, sotell T; 18 to] into TB; 19 I … season] B, *om.* T; 20 Wold God] B, Wold to God T; 22 fekyll] B, febyll T; 25–35] trowth … redempcion] *lacking in* T, *supplied from* B; 25 to] into B, T *lacks.*

In T, *sotell* (13) and *febyll* (22) look like misreadings by a scribe influenced by words he had already copied – *sotell* (11) and *feble* (18). The readings *sodeyn* (13) and *fekyll* (22) adopted here, derived from the B text, are manifestly superior. The metre of this poem is fairly regular. Granted the discrepant readings in T and B it is not unreasonable to suspect that irregularities may be due to scribal corruption. The B reading *Wold God* (20) has been adopted as metrically preferable. Further tentative suggestions, offered below, are excluded from the text as purely speculative.

The final stanza, which appears by itself with the heading *Epitaphium* along with a number of Latin epitaphs in the Lansdowne MS, frequently served as an epitaph in the late 15th century. For seven known instances, see Gray (1961).

The themes and images of this poem are those commonly found in other ME mortality lyrics. Death is the grim Leveller, no respecter of rank (10–11); he comes unannounced, subtle and sudden (11–13); in the chess-game of life he is the victor (12); his grasp is inescapable (17) – cf. *Dethës wither-clench*, 'Death's hostile grip' (**1, 39**, 12); this life is transient, like a cherry fair (8), fickle, false and unstable (22); man may revel in momentary pride (10) only to become food for worms (14); folly and hope deceive (28); time awaits no man (29); *in trust is mochë treson* (16) – cf. **II, 92**; repent while you can; beware of the last trumpet – and so on.

2 *I am arested to apere*: Since *arest* is an alternative form of the past participle of the verb *aresten* (see *MED* **aresten** v.), and the adjacent vowels in *to apere* invite elision, it is quite possible that this line was originally read as: 'I am arest t'apere at Goddës face', i.e. as metrically regular. The image of Death as a sergeant

making his arrest, familiar from Hamlet's words, 'this fell sergeant Death / Is strict in in his arrest' (*Hamlet*, Act 5, scene 2, lines 328–9), had been common since the late 14th century.

3 *myghtyfull*: It would be metrically preferable to assume the disyllabic pronunciation here of the alternative ME form *myghtfull*; see *MED* **mightful** adj.

8 *cheyry feyre*: 'cherry fair', 'a fair or festival held at the time when cherries are harvested' (*MED* **cheri** n. **2**). These fairs, often occasions of merry-making and licence, were held in cherry-orchards where the fruit was sold. Significantly, the cherry season was short and the cherry fair became a 'frequent symbol of the shortness of life and the fleeting nature of its pleasures' (*OED* **Cherry-fair**).

11 Woolf (p. 323) suggests that the image of Death knocking at the door may be a 'bitter parody' of Rev. 3:20: *Ecce sto ad ostium et pulso* (Behold, I stand at the door and knock), words associated with Christ seeking entry to the sinner's soul. Cf. **I, 71** and Commentary.

12 For this use of the chess image, cf. Brown XV, no. 151, 33: *Yit in a whyle thu schall be cheke-mate*. For chess matches with Death (or, in Chaucer's *Book of the Duchess*, with Fortune), see **II, 3** and Commentary.

21 *horne*: Either the trumpet with which, in late medieval literature and art, Death is frequently depicted, or a reference to the last trumpet of 1 Cor. 15:51–2: 'Behold, I shew you a mystery; We shall not all sleep, but we shall all be changed, In a moment, in the twinkling of an eye, at the last trump: for the trumpet shall sound, and the dead shall be raised incorruptible, and we shall be changed.'

22 *world*: The world is personified in this stanza.

26–7 The omission of *to* (26) and *this* (27) would restore the metre without altering the sense.

29 The still familiar proverb, 'Time and tide wait for no man', was already current in late ME. See Whiting, *Proverbs*, T 318. If the verb *abideth* is read as *abit* (the alternative, reduced 3 sg. pres. form) the final stress falls more naturally on the rhyme word *man*.

31 The metre is improved if *But* in this line is omitted as in one, but only one (the Royston, Hertfordshire brass inscription) of the nine surviving versions of this stanza. See Gray (1961), p. 134.

II, 103   This warldly joy is onely fantasy [*NIMEV* 3660]

MSS: Oxford, Bodl. Arch. Selden B.24; Cambridge, Magdalene College Pepys 2553; Cambridge, University Library Ll.5.10; Edinburgh, NLS Advocates 1.1.6 [Bannatyne MS]. Text from the Bodleian MS.

II, 104   All ye that passe be thys holy place [*NIMEV* 237]

MS: Cambridge, Trinity College B.15.31.

Text: 4 as I] j as MS.

2 *spirituall and temporall*: 'spiritual and temporal', i.e. clergy and laity.

II, 105   Westron wynde when wyll thow blow? [*NIMEV* 3899.3]

MS: London, BL Royal Appendix 58, with music.

The tune of this popular song was used as the *cantus firmus* for settings of the mass by three early Tudor composers – Taverner, Tye and Shepherd. See *M&P*, pp. 130, 236–7, and 458.

  2 *smalle rayne*: 'fine rain, drizzle'. For *smalle* as 'consisting of minute particles, … fine', see *MED* **smal** adj. 4. (a). The sense of the line is: 'The drizzling rain keeps on falling'.

II, 106   The man that I loved altherbest [*NIMEV* 3418]

MS: Cambridge, University Library Add. 5943.

Text: 18 hertë] hert MS; 24 wexe] wexeth MS.

The speaker here is a woman, but the theme (true love), manner, and conventions of this poem are so essentially those of courtly poetry, that a later hand has seen fit to alter *The man* in line 3 to *sche* and thereafter to change all masculine pronouns throughout the poem to their equivalent feminine forms.

  9 This line has been regarded as a miscopying from the following line. Robbins (*Sec.*, p. 16), following a suggestion by Greene, supplies the supposedly missing line as: *he maketh haste fro me to go*. However, with the repeated line of the MS reading, the rhyme-scheme of the second stanza, albeit different from that of the following stanzas, matches that of the first, and the sense could be taken, somewhat poignantly, as: 'When first we met, when I wanted him to stay he would not go (i.e. say "farewell"); and when he had to go, still he would not say "farewell" (i.e. he was so reluctant to go)'.
 19 *i-blessed*: may be pronounced as 'i-blest'.
 23 *i-comforted*: may be pronounced as 'i-comfort' or 'i-comford', alternative reduced past participle forms.
 24 I.e. she takes comfort from the hope engendered by spring, the time when flowers bloom afresh, the traditional season of love.
 25 In line 14 she says she dare not speak of the circumstances of their love, and yet her words run on. Now her anticipation of the joy of her beloved's returning and remaining, seems to climax in an assertion of her belief that he is true, and that despite his distant attitude mentioned in the first stanza.
 29 *he hyt knywe*: Above these words *sche were trewe* has been written as part of the alterations made to change the speaker of this poem from a woman to a man.

II, 107   Y lovede a child of this cuntré [*NIMEV* 1330]

MS: Cambridge, Gonville and Caius College 383.

Text: 13 fulfille] fulfulle MS.

The words *bryd on brere y tell yt to none othur y ne dar* written in the MS before the burden of this carol may indicate the tune to which it was to be sung, i.e. that of another carol beginning with these words. This tune cannot, however, be that of

Bryd onë brerë (**1, 15**) since that lyric is not in carol form. Alternatively, since *brid on the brere etc.* – with additional *the* by mistake? – was again written (and then deleted) after the first stanza, it is possible that this was intended to indicate an original four-line burden for this carol, i.e.

> Bryd on brere y tell yt to,
> None othur y ne dar;
> Were it undo that is y-do,
> I wold be war.

This seems all the more likely in view of the fact that the rhymes of the first two lines match those of the two-line burden as otherwise indicated.

II, 108   Summe men sayen that y am blac [*NIMEV* 3174]

MS: Cambridge, Gonville and Caius College 383.

Text: 2 prow] þrow MS; 12 Therto] & þerto MS; 14 Y-wys] Wyn wys MS.

  3 *lac*: 'lack', 'fault'. Both meanings are relevant here.
10 *at bord and bedde*: 'at table and in bed', i.e. 'in all conjugal duties and relationships' (*MED* **bed** n. (1) **2b.** (b)).
23 *in feld and toune*: lit. 'in field and town', a tag meaning 'everywhere'. Cf. Commentary, **II, 129**, 3.

II, 109   Al this day ic han sought [*NIMEV* 225]

MS: Cambridge, Gonville and Caius College 383.

Text: 1 *may*] ne may MS; 2 *joy*] joyȝe MS; 3 *sought*] ght *supplied*; 6 holyday] ho *and* y *supplied*; 11 hyë] hy MS; 14 chyn] khyn MS; 21 dowze] dowge MS; 24 Ought] outh MS; 28 in] onward in MS; 29 pleye] pleyȝe MS; 30 eye] eyȝe MS; 34 alë-scot] ale-schoth MS; 35 throt] wroth MS; 36 haliday] y *supplied*; 39 me] men MS; 40 sond] d *supplied*; 46 heyë] hey MS; 49 Also] lso *supplied*; 50 Durst] drurst MS.

  6 Since repeats of this line may be supposed to have followed the same metrical pattern, final *ë* has been added to the MS spellings *hy* (11) and *hey* (46).
21 *dowze*: The MS reading *dowge* may conceivably represent a rare instance of a borrowing from OF *dougié*, 'soft'. Alternatively, MS *dowge* may be a spelling for *dowze* (i.e. with 'g' written for 'ȝ', representing 'z') from OF *douz*, 'sweet', pleasant'.
24 The meaning of this line is far from clear. In the gloss adopted here, the first word of the text (MS *outh*) is taken as *ought,* i.e. with *th* as a spelling for *ght*. For a wholly different interpretation, see Greene, p. 488.
34 *alë-scot*: 'scotale', 'an "ale" or festival at which ale was drunk at the invitation of the lord of the manor or of a forester or other bailiff, for which ale a forced contribution was levied' (*OED* **Scotale**).

II, 110   Ladd y the daunce a Myssomur Day [*NIMEV* 1849]

MS: Cambridge, Gonville and Caius College 383.

Text: 4 Alas] s *supplied*; 8 clerk] r *supplied*; 10 no] ne MS; 16 no gyle] *supplied*; 20 daunce] e *supplied*; 22 gyle] yle *supplied*; 28, 34, 40, 46, 52 on no gyle] *supplied*; 33 we] *supplied*; 36 were] a were MS; 39 muryust] murgust MS.

The five lines of the burden of this carol are found after stanza 1; only the last two lines are written before the first stanza.

  3 *So have y god chaunce*: 'as I may have good luck', i.e. 'as I hope for a good end', an oath by which the girl merrily seeks to assert her innocence.
  8 *haly-watur clerk*: the cleric who carried the vessel containing the holy water.
  9 *gay*: 'attractive'. Jak may, indeed, have thought her more than simply attractive: the range of senses of ME *gay* includes 'wanton' and 'lascivious'; see *MED* **gai** adj. 1.
 38 *prikede*: The ME verb *priken*, which had, among other meanings, the senses 'to prick' and 'to ride a horse', was rich in sexual innuendo. See *MED* **priken** v.
 42 *he rong the bell*: 'he rang the bell'. Greene (p. 490) claims that this phrase here 'must mean "achieve orgasm", as in sexual slang still current, which also has "ring my chimes"'. However, this ringing occurs after Jak 'had done', and the text here speaks of ringing 'the' bell, not 'my' bell. Could it be that Jak rang a bell literally – perhaps an angelus or curfew as part of his duties (and after which his partner had to stay the night!); or, out of high spirits, did he mimic in blasphemous parody the ringing of the bell during the mass at the elevation of the Host?
 44 *the reaggeth devel*: In medieval literature, art and drama the Devil was often represented as ragged or shaggy. See *MED* **ragged(e** adj. **2.** (a).
 57 A proverb. See Greene, p. 490, where other ME instances are quoted.

II, 111   The last tyme I the well-ey woke [*NIMEV* 3409]

MS: Cambridge, University Library Ff.5.48.

Text: 3 well-ey] wel MS; 6 tell-ey] tell MS; 11 bell-ey] bell MS.

  2 *wake*: See *MED* **waken** v. (1), **1.** (c) 'to spend all or part of the night engaged in frivolous or nefarious pursuits'. Wells were sometimes locations for nocturnal revelry.
  3 *well-ey*: Clearly the rhyme-scheme of this poem requires that ending '-ey' has to be added to the MS readings *tell* (6) and *bell* (11). Likewise, the metre of this line requires *well-ey* (as in line 2) rather than the monosyllabic *wel* of the MS here.
  4 *Ser John*: probably the local priest. In ME the title 'Sir' was commonly used of priests and other clergy; and amorous, not to say lecherous priests were stock figures of later medieval literature. Cf. **II, 112,** and Jolly Jankin of **I, 129.**
  4 *croke*: 'crook', as in shepherd's or bishop's crook, a staff with a curved top; also 'hockey stick' and, allusively, 'penis'. See *MED* **crok** n. **2.**
  5 *swere be bel and boke*: 'swear by bell and book'. A form of solemn oath, common

in the Middle Ages; the bell and book referred to are those used in the service of the mass. See *OED* **Bell** sb.¹ **8.**

11 *bell-ey*: probably short for *bele chose*, 'female sex organ' (see *MED* **bell** n.), a euphemism used by Chaucer's Wife of Bath:

> For if I wolde selle my belë chose,
> I koude walke as fressh as is a rose.
>
> CT, III, 447–8

20 *gracious*: 'fortunate'; see *MED* **gracious** adj. **2.**

II, 112   O Lord, so swett Ser John dothe kys [*NIMEV* 2494]

MS: San Marino, California, Huntington Library EL 1160.

Text: 9 loves] loue MS; 14 is] In MS; 17 *and* 27 I … nay] *supplied*; 20 and] a *supplied*; 22 powre] w *supplied*; -y hym nay] *supplied*.

2 *Ser John*: see Commentary, **II, 111,** 4.

16 *box*: ostensibly a 'money box', but obviously with an additional sexual suggestion here, as, again, with *mouse-trappe* in line 19.

21 *lape*: 'lap', but also, 'sexual organ'. See *MED* **lap(pe** n. **6a.** (b).

II, 113   At the northe ende of Selver Whyte [*NIMEV* 438]

MS: Cambridge, University Library Add. 5943.

Text: 8 he smote] he suy smote MS; 33 man] *supplied*. *Supplied by expansion*: 3–4 (of … bat), 14–16, 19–24, 27–8, 31–2 (I … syde), 34–36.

In the MS the text of this poem (written out as prose) is considerably abbreviated. Where expansion is required to reconstruct the full text, this is indicated by *etc.* or *etc. vt supra.* These expansions are fairly obvious, consisting of the repetition of lines or half lines in stanzas 2 and 3 on the model of stanza 1, which is given in its complete form except for line 3 where *etc.* after *ende* indicates the required repetition of omitted text, i.e. *of Selver Whyte / My lef me bat* from lines 1 and 2. Poems involving considerable repetition – like this and **II, 114,** the next poem in this MS – were frequently copied in abbreviated form by ME scribes. In many cases these poems were songs, and the music would have served as a prompt in reconstructing the full text. The text of *Maiden in the morë lay* (**I, 118**) in MS Oxford, Bodl. Rawlinson D.913 is an extreme example of such scribal abbreviation. See Duncan (1996a).

This, the unique text of this poem, seems incomplete, since a stanza for the east end of Silver White is lacking. There is evidence of carelessness in copying in that the letter 'w' was first written and then deleted before *suthe* in line 13; clearly the scribe was about to write *weste* – i.e. to go on to stanza 3, omitting stanza 2 – but, luckily, noticed and corrected his error.

The sequence 'buckler', 'peck' and 'bushel' seems to indicate an ever-widening of the offered target; a bushel measure is four times larger than a peck measure, and, in size, a buckler was specifically a small shield. 'Buckler', as the first of the three terms, may have been chosen on account of the suggestivity of its shape – 'round, oval, or half-moon' (*MED* **bokeler** n. (1) **1.** (a)). These terms may also suggest further sexual innuendo by association with 'the hidden verbs in bogeler (buck), peckel, and bosshelle (buss)' (Robbins, *Sec.*, p. 236). Thus, the 'target' is offered wide enough for 'bucking', 'pecking' and 'bussing'. Cf. *MED* **bukking** ger. ('rutting' as of deer), and the potentially suggestive actions of *MED* **pekken** v. and **busshen** v. (2).

1 *Selver Whyte*: evidently a place where the lovers met.

17 *peckel*: a nonce word here formed on the model of ME *busshel*; see *MED* **peckel** n. The usual term, ME *pek(ke,* was a vessel used to measure a 'peck' of grain. See *MED* **pek)ke** n. **1.** (a).

29 *bosshelle*: a vessel used for measuring grain, salt, or the like. A bushel measure was some four times larger than a peck measure. See *MED* **busshel** n. (1) **1.** (a).

II, 114   May no man slepe in youre halle [*NIMEV* 2135]

MS: Cambridge, University Library Add. 5943.

Text: 3 *and* 12 tent] ten tent MS; fifteen] xv MS; 5 To … dogges] *supplied*; 7 yyvëth] 3yuef MS; 8 Bytwyne] my twyne MS; lady] la *supplied*; 9 To … madame] *supplied*; 19 May] y *supplied*; halle] *supplied*; 20 for … madame] *supplied*; 21–23 But … madame] *supplied*.

The fact that the stanza which is copied in full – thus serving as the model for expanding the abbreviated texts of the other stanzas – is stanza 2 suggests that it may originally have been the first stanza of this poem.

3 *tent*: lit. 'surgical probe', here for 'penis'. See *MED* **tent(e** n. (3) (b).

17 *lappes*: 'skirts'. There may also be involved a reference to the female genitalia. See *MED* **lap(pe** n. **6a.** (b), where *lappes* here is glossed as '? the lips of the pudendum'.

22 *Wyth twey byes*: Unlike the fourth lines of stanzas 1 and 2, this line in stanza 3 is lacking, whether by abbreviation or accidental omission. It is reconstructed with initial *Wyth* of the corresponding lines in the other stanzas, with *twey* (by conjecture, on the analogy of stanza 1, line 4), and with *byes* supplied from line 24, again on the model of the other stanzas.

II, 115   Ther was a ladie leaned her backe to a wall

MS: Cambridge, University Library Dd.5.75. The page on the verso of which this and the following five poems are written was formerly the flyleaf opposite fol. 1 of Dd.5.76; now, subsequent to rebinding in 1956, it is the final folio of Dd.5.75.

Text: 4 as (1)] a MS.

Riddles are typically short poems on a wide range of subjects (often drawn from the natural world and ordinary life) in which the reader is invited to identify unnamed objects from ingenious and often witty descriptions 'which are intended to be at once accurate and misleading; the more misleadingly accurate and accurately misleading, the better' (Wyatt (1912), p. xxviii). Latin riddles were already popular as literary exercises in the early Middle Ages, and especially so in England of the seventh and eighth centuries as the collections by Aldhelm, Bishop of Sherborne (640?–709), Tatwine, Archbishop of Canterbury (d. 734), Eusebius (Hwætberht), Abbot of Wearmouth (*c.* 680–*c.* 747), Alcuin, Archbishop of York (735–804) and others bear witness. Most remarkable, however, are the 95 or so OE riddles of the Exeter Book, which testify to the mastery in this genre of poets writing in the English vernacular. These riddles range from the literary to the popular, from the sophisticated to the downright crude. Representatives of the latter kind 'consist of the joke of describing some apparently obscene object which in fact turns out to represent something else' (Hamer (1972), p. 95). The late ME riddles included here (**II, 115–120**) are also of this sort. They are self-evidently instances of riddles in which 'the formally stated solution is so overshadowed by the obscene subject … that little attention is paid to the aptness of this' (Tupper (1910), p. xxv). Yet, however crude, there is a merry zestfulness in these short pieces.

II, 116   Two stones hathe yt or els yt is wrong

MS: Cambridge, University Library Dd.5.75.

4 *With ther conscience*: lit. 'with their conscience'. The word *conscience* in ME had the moral sense of modern English 'conscience'; it also had the emotional senses of 'desire' or 'conviction'. See *MED* **conscience** n. The phrase here seems ambiguous, suggesting (ironically) 'with moral concern' and also 'with desire', 'enthusiastically'.

II, 117   I have a hole above my knee

MS: Cambridge, University Library Dd.5.75.

II, 118   I have a thing and roughe yt is

MS: Cambridge, University Library Dd.5.75.
Text: 2 the] th MS.

II, 119   Backe bent, smocke rent

MS: Cambridge, University Library Dd.5.75
Text: 5 standing] standinging MS.
Some kind of surgical probe may be meant if the answer to this riddle is to be read as *A test*. Cf. Commentary, **II, 114**, 3.

II, 120   Ther ys a thyng, as I suppose

MS: Cambridge, University Library Dd.5.75.
This quatrain is enclosed in an oblong box drawn in light brown ink unlike the dark ink of the text. The answer, in the same light brown ink and perhaps to be

read as *Placht*, is in a different hand. It may, as Person (1953) p. 84, suggests, be an early form of *OED* **Placket**², a petticoat. Cloth has a face side, and a petticoat has a mouth (i.e. an opening at the top) and (granted some lace hem or the like) a beard.

II, 121   Hogyn cam to bowers dore [*NIMEV* 1222]

MS: Oxford, Balliol College 354.

Text: 11 her] he MS; 13 *and* 14 beddë] bed MS; 15 *and* 17 oldë] old MS.

1 *bowers dore*: lit. 'chamber's door', as in lady's chamber or bedroom.

3 *He tryld upon the pyn* For this phrase in the sense 'rattled at the door-latch', see *OED* **Tirl**, *v.*³ **II. 3. a.** There may also be a sexual *double entendre* here; for *pyn* as 'penis', see *MED* **pin** n. **5.** (e).

4 *trill go bell*: 'let the bell ring'. The first *OED* quotation for the verb 'trill' in the sense of making a musical trilling sound by voice or instrument is from the 17th century; see *OED* **Trill**, *v.*³ However, in the 15th century the phrase *Trylle upon my harpe* is found as the name of a church window; see *MED* **trillen** v. (2) (c).

II, 122   It was a mayde of brenten ars [*NIMEV* 1641.5]

Source: San Marino, California, Huntington Library, *Christmas carolles newely Inprynted*, a collection of one complete and five incomplete pamphlets, the first certainly, the others possibly, printed by Richard Kele.

Text: 1 *dyll*] dyllum *in source.*

For reasons evident in this poem and obvious enough not to require comment, mills and millers readily lent themselves to exploitation in verse of obscene *double entendre*.

A modern reader may be surprised to learn that this carol occurs in a mid-16th-century collection of Christmas carols; and another carol, equally crude (Greene, no. 460. 1, *NIMEV* 1344.5), is likewise found along with religious Christmas carols in a late 15th-century MS (Add. 7350, Box 2) in Cambridge University Library. In medieval times the Christmas period still reverberated with the revelries, songs and dances associated with older mid-winter pagan festivities. In an Advent sermon in MS Lincoln, Cathedral Library A.6.2, fol. 23b, one ME preacher – typical of many – warns his congregation to *be well ware that ye syng not the songs of fowle rebawdry and of unclennes; for then ye do disworship to the tyme of Cristes burthe.* Christmas carols – as distinct from the wide range of other kinds of medieval carols represented in this volume – came to be increasingly numerous partly because of the activities of the church in promoting religious songs for Christmastide to combat and discourage such 'songs of foul ribaldry'. See further, Greene, pp. clvii–clviii.

1 *dyll*: In view of the rhymes *wyll* and *water-myll* of lines 2 and 3, the source reading *dyllum* here is probably a mistake for *dyll*, which is adopted in the text.

4 *brenten*: lit. 'burnt'. The gloss 'hot' (i.e. 'lascivious') perhaps catches the crudely vulgar import of *brenten* here.

10 *let the myll clacke!*: The verb *clacke* derives 'from the "clacker" or beater of a mill,

the agitator which strikes the hopper and dislodges the corn to the ground'
(Greene, p. 496).

12 *nyce*: 'fastidious', 'lascivious'. For these and other senses of this word in ME,
see *MED* **nice** adj.

II, 123   Jentill butler, bell amy [*NIMEV* 903]

MS: Oxford, Balliol College 354.

Text: 2 *butler*] butlet MS; 2, 7, 12 *rowt*] rowght MS; 16, 21, 26 *towt*] towght MS; 17
Fill … rowt] Fill … butler etc. MS; 22 *Fill … rowt*] Fill … boll etc. MS; 27 *Fill …
rowt*] Fill etc. MS.

1 *How!*: a call to attract attention. See *MED* **hou** interj. (2) (b).
1 *Bevis a towt*: equivalent to modern French *buvez à tous*, 'drink to all'.
23 *Water*: a pun. 'Walter' (the butler's name) could be pronounced in exactly the
same way as the despised drink 'water'!

II, 124   Is ther any good man here [*NIMEV* 1609]

MS: Oxford, Balliol College 354.

Text: 10 And … child] *supplied in MEV, p. 540, for line missing in MS.*

10 Where the sense is not affected in any crucial way and the rhythm and flow of
the stanza can be saved it is surely much better to supply a line (albeit by pure
conjecture) as the Sisams do here than to leave a blank in the text.
32 *mene*: 'mean', in musical terminology, a middle part, especially tenor or alto,
and also a person performing that part.
41 *ye shuld bere a very good bace*: The bass part that this fellow, the glutton with the
fat face, is likely to sustain is not a musical part, as with the tenor, treble and
mean parts mentioned above, but, ironically, a different kind of bass part in a
harmony and counterpoint not of music but of food and drink.

II, 125   Now ys Yole comen with gentyll chere [*NIMEV* 2343]

MS: London, BL Add. 14997.

Text: 3 gentyll chere] gentyll g chere MS.

A Latin rubric in a different hand at the end of this carol states that it was first
written on 4 October 1500.

Again in this carol, as in **II, 126**, the obligation of being merry at Christmas and of
contributing to the seasonal entertainment – in this instance by singing a carol – is
stressed. The use of the same rhyming sounds throughout the stanzas of this carol
is unusual.

20–21 An ironic comment: a miserable fellow would deserve to 'dry his clothes in
a ditch' (i.e. remain wet and cold outside) rather than be allowed to be part of
the merry company indoors at the fire.
26 *care away*: 'away with care'. These words are frequently found in the refrains
and burdens of popular songs, cf. **II, 138**. See Greene, p. 345.

II, 126   Lett no man cum into this hall [*NIMEV* 1866]

MS: Oxford, Balliol College 354.

The obligation common to all, 'both high and low', to contribute to Christmas entertainment in the hall is here proclaimed by a master of ceremonies or 'Lord of Misrule' who evidently had the power to commit to the stocks such persons as fail to meet his requirement.

2 *Crystymas*: This three-syllable form of Christmas (see *MED* **Criste-mas(se** n.) should perhaps – if felt to be rhythically preferable – be repeated in lines 6, 11 and 16 instead of the two-syllable form *Crystmas*.

4 *marshall*: 'steward', a senior household official 'in charge of ceremonies, protocol, seating, service, etc.' (*MED* **marshal** n. 2).

15 *stokkes*: For evidence of the use of actual stocks by a Lord of Misrule at Christmas, see Schoeck (1953), p. 356.

II, 127   Holy stond in the hall [*NIMEV* 1226]

MS: London, BL Harley 5396.

Text: 17 ay] ae MS; 23 doos] doo MS.

The traditional strife between the sexes found in ME holly-and-ivy poems, but absent from the modern carol, *The Holly and the Ivy*, continued in folk tradition. 'A writer in *The Gentleman's Magazine* (1779), p. 137, describes a Shrovetide custom in East Kent, in which the girls of a village burnt a 'Holly Boy' stolen from the boys, and the boys burnt an Ivy-Girl stolen from the girls' (Chambers and Sidgwick (1926), p. 374). Greene associates the motif of excluding women from the hall at Christmas (here and in **II, 128**) with the tradition of 'first-footing'. In this custom, until recently common at New Year in Scotland, good luck is considered to be brought into a house by a man being the first person (the 'first foot') to enter at the beginning of the year. See Greene, pp. cxxv–cxxvi.

5–8 Greene (p. cxxiv) suggests that this carol may have been sung during some kind of dramatic game 'in which the feminine party of Ivy would be excluded from a company representing those in the "hall" and would be grouped by itself "without the door"'.

25–8 For the traditional association of the owl with ivy here and in the final stanza, compare the excellent ME poem *The Owl and the Nightingale* in which the owl's dwelling-place is an ivy-covered tree-stump.

II, 128   Holy berëth beris [*NIMEV* 1226]

MS: Oxford, Balliol College 354.

Text: 15 slo] sho MS; 20–21 a hundred / poundes] C libra MS; 29 hot] whot MS.

9–12 Cf. **II, 127**, 25–8.

II, 129   The most worthye she is in towne [*NIMEV* 3438]

MS: Oxford, Bodl. eng. poet. e.1.

Text: 4 doth] do MS.

> 1–2   Ivy's alleged supremacy as chief of trees here echoes the Virgin's supreme status as blessed among women (see Luke 1:28, 42) and leads naturally to the quotation from S. of S. 4:8: *Veni, coronaberis* (Douay: Come: thou shalt be crowned), OT words associated with the coronation of the Virgin. This association of Ivy with the Virgin is continued in the language of lines 5 and 8, which contain phrases elsewhere used in Marian lyrics. The words *Veni, coronaberis* are also used in the burden and in the refrain of a carol to the Virgin by James Ryman, *Come, my dere spowse and lady free* (Greene, no. 262). In another carol in praise of Ivy (Greene, no. 139) it is explained that Ivy is to be loved because the significance of the letters of her name, in ME spelling, *Ive*: 'I' stands for 'Ihesus' (Jesus, in medieval spelling), 'V' for the Virgin, and 'E' for Emmanuel.
>
> 3   *in towne*: This tag, the literal sense of which is 'in a settlement or place where people live', was especially common in earlier ME lyrics in the general sense of 'in the world', 'anywhere', or simply, 'alive'; see Commentary, **I**, 18, 29. For the similar use of *in londe*, see Commentary, **I**, 3, 12.

II, 130   Holvyr and Ivy mad a gret party [*NIMEV* 1225]

MS: Oxford, Bodl. eng. poet. e.1.

Text: 1, 7, 11 Ivy] heyvy MS; 4 joly] ly *supplied*; 6, 9 we] þei MS.

> 1   *Holvyr*: This late ME term for holly probably derives from Old Icelandic *hulfr*, 'dogwood'. See *MED* **hulver** n. The word 'holly' (ME *holin, holi*, and other spellings) comes from OE *hole(g)n*. See *MED* **holin** n.

II, 131   The boris hed in hondes I brynge [*NIMEV* 3313]

MS: Oxford, Balliol College 354.

Text: 14 Twelfth] xii^th MS.

This carol exists in various forms. For a version of the text sung every Christmas at Queen's College, Oxford, see *The Oxford Book of Carols*, no. 19.

II, 132   Owre kynge went forth to Normandy [*NIMEV* 2716]

MSS: Oxford, Bodl. Arch. Selden B.26, with music (B); Cambridge, Trinity College O.3.58, stanzas 1, 2, 4, 5 and 6, with music (T). Text from B.

Text: 10 sothe for] for sothe T, þe sothe for B; 26 mervelowsly] T, my3ty B; 27 felde and victory] feld and vyctory T, the felde and the victory B.

This, the well-known Agincourt Carol, celebrates Henry V's famous victory over the French at the Battle of Agincourt in 1415 and is, as Greene (p. 474) notes, 'perhaps the best-known carol in English not concerned with the Nativity'.

1–2 'England, render thanks to God for the victory.' Henry V claimed no credit for his part in the battle, insisting that the victory at Agincourt was the work of God. Robbins (*Hist.*, p. 297) quotes as follows from the *First English Life of Henry V*, p. 65:

> But that victorious and goodly Kinge suffered not those honnours to be referred unto him, but to the laude and honnour of God.

40 Robbins (*Hist.*, p. 297) compares the account in the chronicle of Jehan de Waurin of the enthusiastic response of Henry V's troops to his address on the field of battle: 'Sire! Dieu vous doinst bonne vye et victore de vos annemis!' (Sire, God give you good life and victory over your enemies).

II, 133   Worschip of vertu ys the mede [*NIMEV* 4229.5]

MS: London, BL Egerton 3307, with music.

Text: 9 flight] t *supplied*; 14 fulë] ful MS.

2 *owr Lady knyght*: 'our Lady's knight'. St George is commonly so called; cf. **II, 134**, 18.

10 By common report, an apparition of St George appeared above the field of battle at Agincourt. The fact that a chronicle is referred to as the source of this information here suggests that this poem is to be dated some time after the famous victory of the English over the French in 1415. See **II, 132.**

14 In fitting this line to the music Stevens reads: *againës the fiend, the foul wight* (*MC*, p. 49). However, the version of this line as adopted here reads better and could probably be fitted to the music equally well.

II, 134   And by a chapell as y came [*NIMEV* 298]

MS: Aberystwyth, NLW, Porkington 10.

3 The *chanson d'aventure* opening here introduces a remarkable vision in which, after encountering Jesus and the disciples on their way to church, the poet witnessed a mass at which St Thomas rang the bells, St Nicholas sang, St John took the offering, the Virgin offered her crown, St George lit the tapers, and Christ himself celebrated.

13–14 The depiction of Christ officiating as priest at the mass is unusual. The notion may derive from Paul's statement that Christ was 'made an high priest for ever after the order of Melchisedec' (Heb. 6:20). See also Heb. 5:6, 10. See Gray (1963), p. 431.

16 *son*: 'sun' and 'Son' (Christ). The radiance of both are fused in the image here.

18 Cf. **II, 133**, 2, and Commentary.

II, 135   The merthe of alle this londe [*NIMEV* 3434]

MS: Oxford, Bodl. Arch. Selden B.26, with music.

Text: 25 bygynne] bygynneth MS.

The rhyme-scheme a a b a a b suggests a six-line stanza form for this poem.

However, it may be a carol in three-line stanzas with the opening three lines as the burden. Stevens favours this interpretation; he notes that each three-line group 'is marked in the MS with the symbol conventionally reserved to show the start of each verse' and therefore considers it 'a reasonable deduction that, despite the rhyme-scheme, [lines 1–3 are] in fact a burden' (*MC*, p. 124). Greene prints this poem as a carol (no. 418.2) having previously omitted it in his first edition. Under *NIMEV* 1405.5 it is listed as a carol.

This idyllic picture, with the happiness in all this land dependent on the worthy ploughman, and with the ringingly confident repetition of 'God speed the plough' (12 and 24), presents a version of Merry England which is in striking contrast to the vivid account of rural hardship and exploitation found in the 14th-century lyric *Ich herde men upon mold* from MS Harley 2253 (**1, 113**).

4   *i-blessed*: may be pronounced 'i-blest'.

12   *spede*: 'speed', i.e. 'prosper'. Another ME lyric (*NIMEV* 363) has the refrain: *I praye to God, spede wele the plough,* and 'God speed the plough' occurs as the title of a play and of a book in the 16th century. See Robbins, *Hist.*, no. 37, p. 301.

13   *Browne, Morel and Gore*: These appear to be the names of the oxen (or horses?) in the team which draws the plough.

II, 136   Whan netilles in wynter bere rosis rede [*NIMEV* 3999]

MSS: Oxford, Balliol College 354 (A); Oxford, Bodl. eng. poet. e.1 (B); London, BL Printed Book IB. 55242 (C). The Bodleian MS gives a longer version of seven stanzas, reformed, by the addition of a burden, into a carol. The Balliol MS has stanzas 1, 3, 5 and 6 of the Bodleian version; the BL version gives a partly defective text of stanzas 1, 3, 5, 6 and 7. Text from A.

Text: 11 grengese] rolyons A, rullions C, rokes B; 12 rolyons] grengese A, goslynges BC.

This seven-line stanza with the rhyme scheme a b a b b c c is a form of rhyme royal, but instead of the decasyllabic lines of Chaucer's verse the metrical norm here seems to be that of a four-stress line. The lines have therefore been set out in half lines on the analogy of the presentation of traditional alliterative four-stress verse in this volume. Like Machaut and Deschamps before him, Chaucer used rhyme royal in some of his ballades (see p. 5). This poem resembles a ballade in that the final line of each stanza recurs as a refrain. However, the classical ballade had three stanzas (not four, as here), and continued the same rhyming sounds from stanza to stanza.

The rhetorical figure of adynaton is employed here. This device, involving the stringing together of a series of impossibilities, originated in classical literature. It is a characteristic means of expressing the common medieval poetic motif (or 'topos') of the 'world upside-down' – i.e. the depiction of a crazy world in which absurdities prevail and, typically, roles are reversed: the ass plays the lute, the ox dances, the hare is bold, the lion timorous, etc. See Curtius (1953), pp. 94–8. The adynata ('impossibilities') here represent the same imaginative mode as the grotesques and fancies of medieval misericords, of marginal drawings in MSS, and of sculpture in churches and cathedrals: foxes preaching, hares hunting men, bizarre creatures sporting in gargoyles and capitals, and so on.

4   *in the croppes so hie*: lit. 'in the tree-tops so high'.

11 *gornardes*: 'gurnards'. The gurnard is a sea fish 'characterized by a large spiny head with mailed cheeks and three free pectoral rays' (*OED* **Gurnard 1**).

12 The thematic absurdity of this stanza (i.e. that of fish as hunters) breaks down in this line if the readings of A (or of the other sources) are retained. This defect is easily made good if it is assumed that a scribe has mistakenly transposed *grengese* and *rolyons* in lines 11 and 12. The resultant alliteration of *gornardes* and *grengese* (11) and *rolyons* and *ride* (12) supports this emendation. It would appear from the B reading – *rokes* (for *rolyons*) in line 11 – that at least one medieval scribe spotted the inconsistency of fish hunting fish in this stanza.

12 *rolyons*: This (as the spelling *rullions* of C makes clear) is a ME adoption from OF *rouillon*, defined vaguely as a kind of fish by Godefroy. See Godefroy, **rouillon**.

13 *sperlynges*: 'smelts'. The smelt is 'a small fish, *Osmerus eperlanus,* allied to the salmon, and emitting a peculiar odour' (*OED* **Smelt**, sb.^{1} 1).

20 *griffons*: 'vultures'; see *MED* **griffoun** n. (2) (c). However, since the sense here involves the notion of noble creatures giving obedience to lesser creatures, *griffons* here may mean 'griffins', the fabulous animals with the head and wings of an eagle and the body and hind quarters of a lion, frequently found in heraldic devices.

24 The notion of camels catching birds (swallows) and fish (perch) in nets (?) or with lines (?) made of camel hair is certainly bizarre. (For cloth made of camel's hair, see *MED* **camel** n. (b).) In B and C this line appears as: *And cammels in the ayer tak swalows and larkes.* This reading, with the humorous absurdity of flying camels catching birds, may seem preferable in so far as *larkes* (unlike *perches*) gives a satisfactory rhyme.

26 *the blod of Hayles*: The reference is to Hailes Abbey in Gloucestershire, to which what was claimed to be the blood of Christ was given in 1270 by Richard, Earl of Cornwall, and preserved there as a relic.

II, 137   Tutivillus, the devyl of hell [*NIMEV* 3812]

MS: Oxford, Bodl. Douce 104.

Text: 7 Thes] s *supplied*; 12 *multum*] *as read by the Sisams* (*MEV*, p. 598). The MS is badly faded; some of the Latin is almost illegible.

Tutivillus (or Titivillus), a name for a devil which appears in various medieval Latin writings from the 13th century, is first mentioned in English in the late 15th-century mystery plays; and in the late ME *Myroure of Oure Ladye* he says:

> I am a poure dyvel, and my name ys Tytyvyllus … I muste eche day … brynge my master a thousande pokes full of faylynges, and of neglygences in syllables and wordes.

See *OED* **Titivil.**

Chattering in church was a charge frequently levelled at women by medieval anti-feminist writers. Various stories were directed against this vice. In one such, found in *The Book of the Knight of La Tour-Landry*, a hermit who was saying mass observed knights, ladies and gentlewomen in his congregation whispering, laughing and jesting with each other. And as he watched, he became aware

> that there was atte everiche of her eeres [their ears] an orrible fende [fiend], that wrote all that thei saide, and lough hem [laughed them] to scorne; and the blak orible fendes yede lepinge [went leaping] on her [their] hedys, hornes [i.e. of ladies' head-dresses], and riche atyre, as dothe the briddes that sittethe on trees and lepethe from braunche to braunche.
>
> Wright (1906), p. 40

6 *vana*: an accusative (sometimes designated an 'inner accusative') used adverbially.

II, 138   All that I may swynk or swet [*NIMEV* 210]

MS: Oxford, Bodl. eng. poet. e.1.

Text: 11, 16, 21, 26 Carfull ... therfor] carfull etc. MS.

24 *judicare*: 'to judge', as found in the words of the Creed: *Et iterum venturus est cum gloria judicare vivos et mortuos* (And he shall come again with glory to judge both the living and the dead). In dealing with a termagant of a wife this hen-pecked husband indeed knows what it is to be judged – and to suffer accordingly. For him, 'every day [is] a time of Judgement' (Utley (1946), p. 309).

II, 139   O wicket wemen, wilfull and variable [*NIMEV* 2580]

MS: Edinburgh, NLS Advocates 1.1.6 [Bannatyne MS].

In the MS, 'ffinis quod Chauceir' is written after the final line of this poem. Silverstein (1971), p. 154, remarks: 'The attribution to Chaucer looks to us like a Scots scribe's joke, but medieval readers had, on the whole, remarkably little sense of an author's canon.'

This poem is something of a technical *tour de force* reminiscent of Dunbar. The verse form – seven lines rhyming a b a b b c c – is that of Chaucer's rhyme royal stanza. Like the classical ballade, the same rhyming sounds are sustained throughout the three stanzas. However, the vigour of the poem depends essentially on a rugged roughness of metre and the forceful impact of sustained alliteration.

II, 140   In all this warld nis a meryar lyfe [*NIMEV* 1468]

MS: Oxford, Bodl. eng. poet. e.1.

Text: 3 nis] is MS; 11, 16, 21 In ... go] In euery etc. MS; 14 ballë] ball MS; 15 yongë] yong MS.

10 *rennyng at the ball*: obviously some kind of ball game. Greene (p. 461) refers to

F. W. Hackwood, *Old English Sports* (London, 1907), p. 141, and suggests that 'stool-ball' (a game resembling cricket) may have been meant 'as that was the principal ball-game in which maidens joined with men and which involved running'.

16 *thei*: The refrain line varies here and in line 21 as the appropriate pronoun is adopted from the preceding line. Cf Commentary, **II, 42**.

18–20. This young bachelor, as these maidens recognize, is not for settling down with a wife; he loves his roving life (symbolized by his knapsack), possibly as a chapman or pedlar. Compare the 'chapmen light of foot' of **I, 128**, 1.

II, 141   Freers, freers, wo ye be! [*NIMEV* 871]

MS: Cambridge, Trinity College O.2.40.

Text: 2 ministri] minstri MS; 7 seven] vij MS; 9, 11 *and* 19 folines] folnes MS; 13 that] *supplied*; 20 sunt] non sunt MS; 26 furcam] ffurtam MS; 32 quia] qui MS; 43 All … thre] *supplied from* **II, 84**, 18.

In the text here the scribe's frequent idiosyncratic 'ff' spellings have been replaced by 'f'.

The metrical norm of this poem – a line of 13 syllables with a caesura after the seventh – was characteristic of Goliardic verse and is familiar to the modern student from the famous poem *Gaudeamus igitur, iuvenes dum sumus*. In such an accomplished macaronic satire, occasional metrically defective lines are hardly be viewed as other than products of scribal corruption. It therefore seems appropriate to restore the metre by adopting *folines* (the usual ME form of this word) in lines 9, 11 and 19, and by making small emendations (however speculative) in lines 13, 20 and 32.

1 *Freers*: pronounced as two syllables (i.e. 'fre-ers') throughout the poem except for *freer* in line 21.

5 *seyntës*: 'angels'; see *MED* **seint(e** n. **1.** (d). The reference is, of course, to Satan and his followers, who, having rebelled against God, fell from heaven.

7 *the synnës seven*: the seven deadly sins – Pride, Covetousness, Lust, Envy, Gluttony, Anger, and Sloth.

9 *folines*: MS *folnes* here, and in lines 11 and 19, is not recorded in *MED*; see *MED* **foliness(e** n.).

14 *falandum*: i.e. classical Latin *fallendam*.

15 *blere a mannës ye*: lit. 'make bleary a man's eye', a common ME expression meaning 'deceive' or 'hoodwink'; see *MED* **bleren** v. (1) 2. bleren eie(s.

18 *fruges*: Normally the plural of Latin *frux*: 'fruit, success', *fruges* here may (with the plural in '-es' by analogy) represent classical Latin *frugi*, an indeclinable adjective (see *OLD* **frugi** *indecl. adj.*) equivalent to *frugales*, meaning 'thrifty, frugal, honest, virtuous, etc.'

20 As it stands in the MS this line is too long. The metre may be restored by omitting *non*, and good sense is achieved with 'those who are of Christ's flock' (20) as the object of *lette* (19). The friars dupe not only the rich but, in their folly, they will not even spare the thrifty, the virtuous folk of Christ's flock.

The word *non* here may have been added by a scribe who took line 20 to refer to the friars.

21 From the 13th century there were various orders of friars in England; see Commentary, **II, 142**, 3.

26 *furcam*: It is difficult to make sense of the MS reading *ffurtam* in this line even if it is taken to be equivalent to classical Latin *furtum*: 'something stolen, deceit, love intrigue, etc.' – see Niermeyer (1976), under **furtus**. Granted the common confusion of 't' and 'c', it is perhaps better to view *ffurtam* as an error for *ffurcam* (Latin *furca*: 'fork') and assume the sense 'crotch', which would fit the context here.

29 *boyth Jacke and Gylle*: lit. 'both Jack and Jill', meaning, here, 'anyone at all'.

32 The emendation of MS *qui* to *quia* restores the metre and gives more plausible sense. The error could easily have arisen from a misreading of *quia* in abbreviated form.

34 This ironic comment reflects the criticism increasingly levelled against the friars (especially the Franciscans) from the later 14th century that they were too concerned with amassing wealth and with building themselves grand churches and large houses.

44 As written in the MS, *Omnes dicant 'Amen'* is clearly the last line of the poem and not an appendage, as printed by Robbins (*Hist.*, p. 165). It is obvious that the penultimate line (43) has been accidentally omitted. This missing line must have rhymed with *trinité* of line 41 and, as part of this Trinitarian conclusion, must have been something like 'Three in one and one in three'. The required rhyme and sense are met by the line *All one God and persones thre* supplied here from **II, 84**, 18.

II, 142   Ther was a frier of order gray [*NIMEV* 3543.55]

MS: Cambridge, University Library Add. 7350, Box 2. The text here follows Croft (1981), pp. 15–6.

Text: 33 taught] tauȝght MS.

An appreciation of the wit and audacity of this carol depends partly on a reader's awareness of the irreverent biblical parody in the series of slightly altered quotations or echoes from the Vulgate used here. Furthermore, some knowledge of the nature and operation of hexachords in late medieval music is needed if the subtleties of the musical references deployed in this account of the nun's singing lessons and seduction are fully to be understood. See Pike (1998), pp. 13–16. For a later instance of a music lesson as a cover for courtship involving the six notes of the gamut, or hexachord, see *The Taming of the Shrew*, Act 3, scene 1.

1–2 This burden echoes the words of the Lord's Prayer from Luke 11:4: *Et ne nos inducas in tentationem* (And lead us not into temptation), but omits the crucial negative and flippantly alters the accusative singular *tentationem* of the Vulgate to the ablative plural *temptacionibus*. Thus, 'Lead us not into temptation' blasphemously becomes 'Lead us in the midst of temptations.'

3 *frier of order gray*: Readers of Chaucer are familiar with the friar as a butt of anti-clerical satire. Of the religious orders of friars founded from the 13th century

onwards the chief were the four mendicant orders, partly distinguished by the colours of their mantles: these were the Franciscans ('Grey Friars'), the Augustines, the Dominicans ('Black Friars'), and Carmelites ('White Friars'). Croft suggests that this carol is to be seen in relation to the two carols which precede it in the MS. These are by a 'friar of order grey', the Franciscan James Ryman. They are pious carols with burdens drawn from the Latin liturgy. This bawdy carol, also with its Latin burden, about a very different 'friar of order grey', may have been written as a parody of Ryman's carols, and as 'a sophisticated human reaction to the unremitting piety of Ryman and his kind' (Croft (1981), p. 2).

8 *lusty*: The ME adjective had a range of meanings from 'pleasant, handsome', through 'spirited, merry', to 'amorous, lustful'.

13 *Othe*: a spelling for *Ut*, the first syllable of the hexachord, the medieval six-note scale the friar teaches the nun here.

18 *proper chaunt*: 'proper chant', the six-note scale (or hexachord) beginning on C, one of the scheme of hexachords attributed to Guido of Arezzo (11th century) in which all recognized notes were accommodated. There were three fundamental hexachords: the *Naturale* ('natural') which began on C; the *Durum* ('hard') which began on G; and the *Molle* ('soft' or 'sweet') which began on F.

18 *Bequory*: 'B natural'. The old name for the note B natural, ME *bequarre*, from OF *béquarré*, equivalent to Lat. *B quadratum* – i.e. 'B squared' – arose from the fact the sign used to denote it was a squared-off version of the letter b. See *OED* **Bequarre** and Croft (1981), p. 3. B natural occurs in the *Durum*, the 'hard' hexachord. It is crucial to note that this nun's singing lesson begins with the 'natural' hexachord – *proper chaunt* (18) – and then the 'hard' hexachord.

23 *Veni ad me*: 'Come to me', a profane echo of the opening words of Matt. 11:28: *Venite ad me, omnes qui laboratis et onerati estis, et ego reficiam vos* (Come unto me, all ye that labour and are heavy laden, and I will give you rest).

25 *Et ponam tollum meum ad te*: a daringly obscene echo of Matt. 12:18 – *ponam spiritum meum super eum* (I will put my spirit upon him). The friar is far from having anything spiritual in mind. Greene (p. 497) takes the meaning here as: 'And I shall put my weapon to you', with *tollum* as a form of Latin *telum*, 'weapon'. Alternatively, Croft (1981), p. 5, suggests that *tollum* is a Latinization of ME *thole*, 'a peg' (*MED* **thole** n. (1)). The sense, equally indecent, would then be something like: 'I shall put my peg to you.'

28 *Bemoll*: 'B flat'. The word *bemoll* derives, *via* French, from Latin 'B mollis', i.e. 'B soft'. See *MED* **be-mol** n. The six notes of a hexachord gave five intervals: i.e. tone – tone – semitone – tone – tone. Each hexachord was determined by the semitone which was its central interval. The mention of B flat indicates that the friar is now singing in the *Molle*, or 'sweet' hexachord since it was in the semitone at the centre of this hexachord, beginning on F, that the note B flat occurred. The transition from 'hard' to 'soft', from the 'hard' hexachord in which part of the singing lesson was previously conducted (see the comment on line 8, above) to the 'soft' (or 'sweet') hexachord here, wittily parallels the progress of this seduction from its early stages to its emotional and sexual climax.

33 & 35 *Sepe … Lapides expungnaverunt me*: 'often the stones have overcome me', words which echo *Saepe expugnaverunt me* (Many a time have they afflicted me) from Psalm 129:1–2 (one of the psalms recited at Compline in the Office of the Blessed Virgin) used here with obvious sexual innuendo.

40 *quoniam*: 'thingy', i.e. 'pudendum'. A well-known instance of *quoniam* used in this sense is found in Chaucer, in the *Wife of Bath's Prologue*, line 608, where the more common ME word *queynte* occurs as a variant in some MSS:

> And trewely, as myne housbondes toldë me,
> I hadde the bestë *quoniam* myghte be.

CT, III, 807–8

Latin *quoniam* means 'whereas'. *MED* suggests that the crude sense represents a 'humorous use of L. **quoniam,** perh[aps] punning on OF **conin** a rabbit' (*MED* **quoniam** n.). However, OF **con** (from Latin *cunnus*, 'vulva') would seem much more plausible as the implied taboo word for which *quoniam* is substituted – an ostensibly polite word of some (albeit slight) similarity.

II, 143   Lesteneth, lordynges, I you beseke [*NIMEV* 1896]

MS: London, BL Sloane 2593.

Text: 10 hed] d *supplied*; 15 mannësslawghte] manslawtte MS; 16 *and* 26 myn basëlard] *supplied*; 41 basëlard] rd *supplied*.

1 *Prenëgard*: 'take care', from OF *prenez garde*.
4 *worth a leke*: an expression of contempt. Cf. Chaucer:

> I holde a mousës herte nat worth a leek   *mouse's heart not worth a leek*
> That hath but oon hole for to stertë to,   *to rush to*
> And if that faillë, thanne is al y-do   *then all is up*

CT, III, 572–4

19 *both gaspe and gape*: The basic meaning of both verbs of this alliterative phrase is 'to open the mouth wide'; see *MED* **gapen** v. **1.** (a) and **gaspen** v. Greene (p. 462) glosses this phrase as 'yawn as a sign of nonchalance', and *MED* records the senses 'yawn' and 'exhale' for the verbs in this quotation. However, the suggestion that this phrase may mean 'brag' (made in *MEV*, p. 443) – perhaps with 'open-mouthed' taken as equivalent to 'loud-mouthed'? – seems attractive in this context, and 'yah and boo' may serve as an approximate gloss.

II, 144   I wold fayn be a clarke [*NIMEV* 1399]

MSS: Oxford, Balliol College 354; Oxford, Bodl. Laud misc. 601 (fragment).

Text: 10 six] vi MS; 12 twenti] xx^{ti} MS; 17 Milkë] Milked MS.

The metre is irregular.

2 'What good would it do me though I were to say no?' – i.e. refused to go to school.
5–6 As is evident from stanza 4, medieval school discipline was harsh, with beatings carried to the point of drawing blood. On such beatings with birch twigs, cf. John Hall, *The Court of Virtue* (1565) (quoted in Greene, p. 460):

> As fyrst the smalle twygges do serue a good shyft,   *serve*
> The buttockes of boyes to hoyse vp or lyft   *raise up*
> From which it is sometymes nedefull to draw,
> Abundance of bloud to kepe them in awe.

17 'My mother told me to milk ducks', a reply which is as disrespectful as it is ludicrous.

22 *worse than fynkyll sede*: Greene (p. 460) notes: 'the beating was sharper than fennel sauce'. However, since the seeds in a head of fennel are densely packed, the sense may rather be that, in like manner, this scholar's bottom is just as closely spattered with marks from the 'peppering' administered by the master.

II, 145   Wenest thu, usch, with thi coyntyse [*NIMEV* 3895]

MS: Lincoln, Cathedral Library 132, now in Nottingham University Library.

Text: 5 ilche] ilche of us MS; 6 long] long to be MS; 10 the] *supplied*; probeyt] a probeyt MS; 11 seyt] seyd MS; 14 Poke] ppoke MS; 22 thu are] tire af ? MS.

This poem, as Robbins observes (*Sec.*, p. 265), 'gives a vigorous picture of schoolboy venom'.

1 *usch*: 'assistant schoolmaster'; see *MED* **usher** n. 3. Editors may be correct in emending MS *husch* (a spelling with intrusive 'h') to *huscher*. However, the MS form (which is metrically preferable) may perhaps represent a schoolboy's colloquial and contemptuous abbreviation in keeping with the disrespectfully familiar second singular form of address used here.

5 In MS *ilche of us*, the words *of us* (which spoil the metre) may have arisen from careless scribal expansion.

6 As found in the MS, this line is too long compared with the final lines of the other stanzas. Again, it may be that a scribe has added *to be* having misunderstood *long* as an adverb, 'long', rather than as a verb with the sense 'belong' or 'remain'.

13 *Sire Robert, with his cloke*: i.e. Sir Robert (the schoolmaster) with his gown. The title 'Sir' was commonly accorded to priests and other clergy in ME; see *MED* **sir(e** n. 1. (b). A medieval schoolmaster would have been in holy orders.

14 *Poke*: 'Puck'. For ME *pouke* as an evil spirit or as a name for such, see *MED* **pouk(e** n. Sir Robert here is represented as an evil genius aiding and abetting his vindictive assistant.

II, 146   At a place wher he me sett [*NIMEV* 418]

MS: Oxford, Balliol College 354.

2 *foster*: 'forest officer' or 'hunter'; see *MED* **foster** n. (2).

6 *With 'Hay, go bet! etc.'* For similar cries of encouragement to dogs in hunting, cf. Chaucer, *Legend of Good Women*, 1212–13:

> The herde of hertës founden is anon,
> With 'Hay! go bet! ppryke thow! lat gon, lat gon!'

For the use of *how(e* as a hunting cry, see Commentary, **II, 148**, 24.

10 *mountenaunce of a myle*: lit. 'the extent of a mile'.
11 *withowt any gile*: lit. 'without (any) deceit'.

II, 147   It fell ageyns the nextë nyght [*NIMEV* 1622]

MS: London, BL Royal 19.B.iv.

Text: 2 *come*] comyn MS; 3 nextë] next MS; 8 yerde] yarde MS; 10 yow] yowre MS; 25 under] wnther MS.

The popular character of this carol is borne out by the survival of similar accounts of predatory visits of the fox to a farmyard in modern folk-song. See Perkins (1961 and 1964).

18 *heye*: 'hedge' or 'fence'. The sense is that the fox cornered and seized a goose up against a hedge or fence. Robbins (*Sec.,* no. 48, p. 242) takes MS *heye* as 'eye' and glosses *all be the heye* as 'in a twinkling' citing *by the eye* of II, 123, 4 in support. However, it is more likely that the latter phrase means 'to the brim'; cf. *MED* **eie** n. (1) **7c.** (a).

II, 148   Bi a forrest as I gan fare [*NIMEV* 559]

MSS: Aberystwyth, NLW, Porkington 10, 19 stanzas (P); Cambridge, University Library Ff.5.48 (C), a variant text of 15 stanzas, stanzas 1, 2, 4–11, 13 and 12 of P, and three other stanzas, one between stanzas 7 and 8, and two after 12. Text from P.

Text: 4 sche] she C, schew P; mad here] made hir C, mad he here P; 6 Er thus] C, *om.* P; 7 Fro] ffro C, ffrov P; 22 I loke … lowe] I loke alowe and syt ful style and love P, j loke asyde j lurke full lowe C; 23 furstë] furst PC; 27 mychë] mych P, C *differs*; 28 scape] C, schape P; 30 sechë] sche P, C *differs*; 33 torne] come or torne P, drawe C; 35 yeorne] ȝe wyne P, C *differs*; 36 Fleche] flece P, dere C; 39 sche] she C, schowe P; soule] sov MS *cut*; 44 hitte] hitt C, hette P; 48 sake] sake C, sauke P; 49 Then] Then C, Ten P; wyffe] wyffes P, thei C; two] ij MS; 51 schrowe] scrowe P, swyne C; 58 doe] dowe MS; 60 As] As doth þe MS; 61 game] gam MS, *stanza not in C*; 65 leve] le MS.

1–4 A conventional *chanson d'aventure* opening (see Introduction, p. 3); but here the poet wandering alone in a forest overhears the lament not of a shepherdess but of a hare.

24 *So howe! so hoowe!*: A hunting cry: *howe* is from OF *hou*; see *MED* **hou** interj. (1), **1.** (a). Compare the description of fox-hunting in *The Craft of Venery* (quoted from Tolkien and Gordon, rev. Davis (1967), p. 119):

> 'Syre hunter, hou schalt thou seche the fox?' 'Y schall blow at the furst iij motez [notes on a hunting-horn], and afturward y schall let myn houndez out of coupull, and y schall sey "so howȝe" iij tymes al in hyȝe [loudly].'

26 *Watte*: 'Wat' was a name used for the hare; see *OED* **Wat**[2].
34 *in*: 'for'; see *MED* **in** prep. **22.**

36 *fleche*: 'drive out'. MS *flece* is presumably a mistake (or a spelling variant) for *fleche*. The verb 'to fleece' is first recorded in the 16th century (see *OED* **Fleece** v.) and would not, in any case, be appropriate here.

44 *hitte*: The alternative spelling *hitte* (MS *hette*) is adopted here to make the rhyme clear. So also, *sake* (MS *sauke*) 48, and *doe* (MS *dowe*) 58.

49 *wyffe*: The singular is required in view of the singular *sche* in the other lines of this stanza despite the fact that the corresponding stanza in C has plural pronouns throughout.

61–4 I.e. a gentleman would no more attack a sitting hare than shoot a sitting bird.

II, 149   Spende, and God schal sende [*NIMEV* 3209]

MS: Cambridge, Gonville and Caius College 261.

The penny is personified in several medieval vernacular and Latin texts. The power of 'Sir Penny' is celebrated in the 15th-century lyric, *In erth it es a litill thing* (Robbins, *Sec.*, no. 58). MS Sloane 2593 in the British Library contains a carol, *Peny is an hardy knyght* (Greene, no. 392), with the burden:

> Go bet, Peny, go bet, go,
> For thou mat maken bothe frynd and fo,

and also a carol addressing *myn owen purs* (**I, 121**). The burden of another carol (Greene, no. 393) begins: *Money, money, now hay goode day!* The most famous ME address to a purse is, of course, Chaucer's ballade of complaint beginning:

> To yow, my purse, and to noon other wight   *to no other person*
> Complayne I, for ye be my lady dere.
>
> **I, 120**

II, 150   Here lyeth under this marbyll ston [*NIMEV* 1207]

MS: London, BL Harley 665.

The following Latin verses precede the English translation in the MS:

> Alanus calvus   *Alan the bald*
> Iacet hic sub marmore duro;   *lies here under hard marble*
> Utrum sit salvus,   *whether he be saved*
> Non curavit, necque curo   *he cared not, nor do I*

On epitaph verses, see Gray (1972), pp. 200ff.

Music and Metre

T HE EVIDENCE OF THE MUSICAL NOTATION which survives with Middle English lyrics supports a measure of flexibility in the scansion of these lyrics. In Middle English verse, lines beginning with an unstressed syllable frequently varied with lines beginning with a stressed syllable. Because in regular stanzaic lyrics music is given with the first stanza only, it is normally impossible to appeal to music for evidence as to whether or not lines could vary in this regard from stanza to stanza. However, the music of the carol *As I lay upon a night* (**1, 81**) shows exactly how this variation was accommodated. The first line of the first stanza begins with a stressed syllable. However, the first line of the burden begins with a weak syllable. The music for the first full bar of the burden is identical with that of the music for the first line of the stanza except that an extra note has been supplied before that bar as a leading-in note to allow for the extra syllable. In *Man may longe him livës wenë* (**1, 39**) lines 3 and 4 are sung to the tune of the first two lines. The music is not given twice, but one note (a repeat of the final note of the phrase) is added, being the extra leading-in note needed for the initial weak syllable of line 3. Thus, extra syllables were accommodated by adding a note at the beginning or by splitting a note at the end of the musical phrase. It is obvious that without this kind of flexibility it would not have been possible to allow for the variation of masculine with feminine rhymes.

Another important issue concerns the extent to which musical rhythm and word accent should coincide. The question of rhythm in medieval music is notoriously problematic. With unmeasured music (that is, music of a plainsong kind) the flow of the melody appears to have a flexibility which is very little if at all constrained by verbal accent. Measured music, on the other hand, familiar in the 3/4 and 6/8 rhythms of modern performances of medieval songs, clearly has a regular beat. But even here, the implications of the musical rhythm for the stress-patterns of a verbal text are not self-evident; one must be wary, as Harrison warns, of 'presuppositions about stress connected with present-day use of bar-lines'.[1] The fact that strict coincidence of musical beat and word accent was not required may readily be demonstrated from *Somer is y-cumen in* (**1, 110**). The rhythm of this part song is of necessity strict and measured, and requires that line 9 should be sung in the rhythm *Lowth àfter càlvë còu* rather than (with natural word stress) *Lòwth after càlvë còu*. Likewise, a reader would naturally render line 13 as *Wel sìngest thòu cuckòu*, matching the rhythm of line 14; the rhythm of the music, however, requires *Wèl singèst thou cùckou*. Again, in *Stond wel, moder, under rodë* (**1, 91**) the natural accentual pattern of the first four syllables of line 39 – *What sòrwë hàve* – is the opposite of that of the first four syllables of line 42 – *Mòrë sòrwë*. Both lines, nevertheless, as corresponding lines within the matching halves of a stanza in

[1] *MES*, p. 69.

sequence form, are sung to the same musical phrase. It therefore appears that this difference in the pattern of word accent in the two lines does not matter from the point of view of singing; what counts is that the lines are identical in their syllable count. These instances clearly illustrate what, indeed, any musician knows, namely, that even in measured, accentual music, a singer can readily alter the natural stress and rhythm of speech to conform with the accentual requirements of music.

The evidence of the musical notation is not, however, unequivocal. Musical notes are frequently found above syllables which should be subject to elision or syncope. For instance, in *Man may longe him livës wenë* (**1, 39**), the note G above the first written syllable of *longe* and *ofte* (lines 1 and 3) is repeated over the second syllable of both words, although in each case the final '-e' would be expected to elide with the following word *him*. The words of a song were usually written first under blank staves and the music added thereafter. It seems that in adding musical notes above the words, scribes tended, without regard to the metre of a song, to write a note above every written syllable, repeating notes as necessary. An extreme instance of this habit is found in the lyric *Miri it is while sumer i-last* (**1, 36**). The first line, *as written* in the manuscript, has 11 syllables: *Mirie it is while sumer ilast*. In adding the music, the scribe simply placed a note above every written syllable by repeating notes – giving, by repetition, four notes over *Mirie it*, and two over *while* and over *sumer*. At first sight the music thus appears to confirm an egregiously long 11-syllable line; fortunately, the repeat of the musical phrase (now without the repeated notes) in line 3 confirms a count of seven syllables for the first line.[2] In the face of this scribal habit of repeating notes over syllables *as written* without regard to metrical requirements, it is sometimes difficult to know how far to trust the evidence of the musical notation in the question of the metrical acceptability of an occasional extra unstressed syllable. Thus, in the first stanza of *Edi be thou, hevenë quenë* (**1, 76**), the words *hevene* (line 1), *havest the* (line 6) and *Levedy* (line 7) are all accompanied by three musical notes; but metrically all could be taken as syncopated or reduced forms of two syllables. However, only in *heuene* is a repeated note involved; all three notes in *havest þe* and in *Levedi* are different, and so, arguably, integral to the melody.[3] Moreover, in measured music in triple time, the singing of three quavers instead of a crotchet and quaver presents no problem as the parallel melody of this two-part song demonstrates. It is therefore difficult to resist the view that at least in music of this kind an extra weak syllable within the line was an acceptable if occasional metrical variation.

[2] See Duncan (1994), pp. 59–62.
[3] Again, whereas the repeated note over *-er* of *Moder* (line 3) may be discounted by assuming reduction by syncope before the initial vowel of the following word *unwemmed*, the extra syllable represented by *and* in the same line, in this case accompanied by a note which is not merely a repetition, can only be set aside, as in Dobson's text (*MES*, p. 166), by emendation.

The Syllabic Analysis of Middle English Verse

A NY APPRAISAL OF METRE must take account of several important factors affecting the pronunciation of unstressed syllables in Middle English.

By the early 15th century, 'e' at the end of words had ceased to be pronounced. It has commonly been held that this was the result of a gradual and steady loss of sounded final '-e', a process which began in more Northerly dialects in the 13th century and advanced through Midland and then Southern dialects in the course of the 14th century. However, the linguistic processes which led to the loss of final '-e' were complex. Probably from early Middle English the possibility of elision within the spoken chain of language would have given rise to the existence of forms of the same word with and without sounded final '-e' in any dialect. Furthermore, the process of the loss or reduction of unstressed syllables in Middle English doubtless first took place at a colloquial level of speech, from which endingless or reduced forms would begin to appear, however gradually, in more formal registers. In effect, in Midland and Southern dialects until the end of the 14th century, historical final '-e' (that is, the grammatically or etymologically authentic inflexion as distinct from mere random spellings) would have remained available as a sounded syllable for the more conservative register of poetry, while poets would also have at their disposal optional forms of words without final '-e'. [1]

Reduced forms of '-est' and '-eth' of the second and third person singular present indicative of verbs had been current in Southern dialects since the Old English period. They may have been available to poets in other dialects either from their awareness of the Southern forms, or from the operation of syncope (see below), or by analogy with such contracted forms as *saist* and *saith* beside *sayëst* and *sayëth*. As the evidence of Chaucer's metre conclusively demonstrates, even when the endings '-est' and '-eth' were spelt as full forms they would sometimes be pronounced as reduced forms. The evidence of metre would suggest that this was also true for many of the lyrics in this volume. Where lyrics survive in more than one manuscript, variation from copy to copy between full and reduced spellings of the same words is not uncommon.

Again, it has usually been supposed that after monosyllabic stems the verbal suffix '-ed' and '-es' endings in nouns, verbs and adverbs retained their full forms until the 15th century. However, as with the loss of final '-e', it is likely that reduced forms first arose in colloquial usage before establishing themselves in more formal speech. The reduction of these endings has been attributed to the effect of syncope (see below),[2] a process which was not new in Middle English and which

---

[1] See Smithers (1983) for a detailed discussion of this issue in the light of the evidence of *Havelok the Dane*.

[2] See Luick (1964), §456.2.

was operative long before the 15th century. Even in lyrics from the mid-13th and early 14th centuries, it seems metrically plausible to view '-ed' and '-es' in sequences like *Y-lòved Ich hàve* (**1, 40**, 23) and *tàles untòun* (**1, 27**, 37) as early instances of reduction by syncope. Occasional 13th-century reduced spellings also occur as, for instance, *frents* 'friends'[3] and *þar wils* 'there whiles'.[4] It is true that such spelling evidence is scarce, but if the loss of sounded final '-e' is more often signalled by a tendency on the part of scribes to add '-e' to words at random rather than to omit silent '-e' from spelling, there is no reason why the conventional spellings '-es' and '-ed' should not sometimes mask reduced forms. Indeed, even in the late 14th century, when spellings like *tornd* 'turned' and *tempt* 'tempted' are found in the Vernon MS,[5] such evidence of reduction disappears under the cloak of spelling convention in the spellings *turned* and *tempted* of the companion manuscript, BL Add. 22283.

Other linguistic operations vital for the appreciation of metre, but again obscured by Middle English spelling, must also be taken into account. These include the following phonetic processes operative in ordinary speech and in verse as it was read aloud, as it commonly would have been in the Middle Ages.

(1) *Elision*   By this process, a vowel at the end of a word was absorbed by an initial vowel (or 'h' plus vowel) of a following word. This affects the many words ending in '-e' in Middle English. Thus the final '-e's of *grede* and *grone* are elided in *I grede, I grone, unglad* (**1, 1**, 4). The words *the* and *ne* are often subject to elision – e.g. *Th'aghtë* (**1, 38**, 16),[6] *n'answerde* (**1, 49**, 2), and, frequently, *nis* for *ne is*. Among many other common words ending in a vowel which may be reduced by this phonetic process are *he, me, thee, to, into* and *so*, and the reductions are sometimes represented in the manuscript spellings – e.g. *H'aros* 'He arose', **1, 90**, 50 (MS *þaros* for *haros*), *thee's* 'thee is', **1, 90**, 40 (MS *þes*), *s'ofte* 'so oft', **1, 38**, 33 (MS *softe*), *s'it* 'so it', **1, 109**, 42 (MS *sit*).

(2) *Hiatus*   Hiatus is the opposite of elision: it is the term for cases where, for the sake of metre, a vowel at the end of a word is retained and not elided with the initial vowel (or 'h' plus vowel) of a following word: e.g. *cherë as* (**1, 3**, 33), *cussë of* (**1, 17**, 23), *yowrë hie* (**1, 30**, 3), *derë He* (**1, 38**, 43), *wildë as* (**1, 51**, 27), etc.

(3) *Synizesis*   This is a form of elision in which the vowel 'i' (spelt 'i' or 'y'), immediately followed by another vowel either within a word on in the following word, becomes the corresponding semi-vowel /j/ (the sound of 'y' in 'yet') and so the first element of a diphthong with the following vowel, and, thereby, a single syllable. Thus *mirieth* (**1, 19**, 1), *miriest* (**1, 27**, 64), *many a* (**1, 32**, 2), *Miri it* (**1, 36**, 1), *body and* (**1, 54**, 38), *buried* (**1, 60**, 84), etc., are pronounced as two syllables as 'mir-yeth', 'mir-yest', 'man-ya', 'mir-yit', and so on.

---

[3] See Brown XIII, p. 44, line 34 for this form in MS Cambridge, Trinity College B.14.39.

[4] See Brown XIII, p. 80, line 49 for this form in MS BL Arundel 248.

[5] See **1, 60**, 24 and 134.

[6] Spelt *þeite* in MS BL Arundel 248, but *þe eykte* in MS Oxford, Bodl. Rawlinson G.18.

(4) *Syncope*   This involves a reduction of syllables by the loss of an unstressed syllable either within a word or in a sequence of words. Thus, *comely, lovely* and *every* may be pronounced as three syllables, but may also (as in present-day English) be pronounced as two, with the loss of the medial syllable, and are sometimes spelt as two syllables. Likewise, *stevenyng* (**1, 19,** 33), *soveraigne* (**1, 30,** 29), *recoverer* (**1, 33,** 3), *wakenëth* (**1, 52,** 1), *thrivenë* (**1, 54,** 21), *gamenës* (**1, 54,** 41 and 51), *merveilëth* (**1, 60,** 97), are pronounced 'stev'nyng', 'sov'raigne', 'recov'rer', 'wak'neth', 'thriv'ne', 'gam'nes', 'merv'leth'. Syncope occurs frequently where words ending in '-el', '-en' or '-er' are followed by a word beginning with a vowel (or 'h' plus vowel). Thus, in the following examples, the first word is reduced by the loss of the 'e' of the final syllable in each case: *girdel of* (**1, 25,** 61), *athel is* (**1, 27,** 67), *litel a* (**1, 49,** 6), *evel and* (**1, 51,** 46 and 47), *sutel as* (**1, 54,** 12); *thriven and* (**1, 2,** 34), *chosen and* (**1, 25,** 34), *driven away* (**1, 28,** 3), *y-loren is* (**1, 26,** 2), *gamen and* (**1, 40,** 23), *gamen y-lad* (**1, 47,** 8), *thriven and* (**1, 54,** 24), *biforen I* (**1, 54,** 48); *other a* (**1, 2,** 56), *power of* (**1, 3,** 66), *Ever and* (**1, 4,** 7), *water in* (**1, 18,** 32), *Beter is* (**1, 18,** 35), *fader and* (**1, 24,** 36), *never a* (**1, 24,** 53), *moder and* (**1, 24,** 69), *ever in* (**1, 27,** 54), *ever at* (**1, 27,** 55), *sumer i-last* (**1, 36,** 1), *water of* (**1, 37,** 43), *siker hit* (**1, 51,** 72), *another is* (**1, 60,** 64), *over himself* (**1, 62,** 14), etc. Likewise, the '-ed' of *y-loved* and the '-es' of *sterres* are probably reduced by syncope in *y-loved and* (**1, 13,** 3) and *sterres in* (**1, 4,** 43). What looks like a combination of elision and syncope is seen in *Hevene I* (**1, 1,** 39), *hevene hath* (**1, 62,** 69), and *folowe his* (**1, 64,** 3) which have two syllables each.

(5) *Apocope*   This is usually defined as the suppression of a final unaccented vowel before a following consonant. Frequently, where necessary to preserve the rhythmic pattern of a single weak syllable between two accented syllables, a final '-e' is silent before a following consonant. Thus, in **1, 53,** 2, the final '-e' of *swete* is silent in *that swete savòur* before the initial unstressed syllable of *savòur* to preserve the rhythm as / × /, whereas the same final '-e' is retained in *that swetë tide* in the following line, as required by the same rhythm. In such cases, however, what is involved is not the suppression of a vowel but the selection of a variant pronunciation without final '-e'.[7]

(6) *Alternative forms*   It is clear from Chaucer's verse that words with alternative forms (e.g. *never* and *ner*, *ever* and *er*) were sometimes, even though spelt as full forms, pronounced as reduced forms as required by the metre.

---

[7] See Smithers (1983), p. 213.

Select Bibliography

Alexander, M., and F. Riddy, eds, *The Middle Ages, 700–1550*, Macmillan Anthologies of English Literature 1 (Basingstoke, 1989).

Anderson, J. J., 'Two Difficulties in *The Meeting in The Wood*', *Medium Ævum* 49 (1980), 258–9.

Arn, M.-J., *Fortunes Stabilnes: Charles of Orleans's English Book of Love*, Medieval and Renaissance Texts and Studies 138 (Binghamton, New York, 1994).

Bartsch, K., ed., *Altfranzösische Romanzen und Pastourellen* (Leipzig, 1870).

Bawcutt, P., and F. Riddy, eds, *Selected Poems of Henryson and Dunbar* (Edinburgh, 1992).

Beadle, R., and A. E. B. Owen, introduction and facsimile, *The Findern Manuscript: Cambridge University Library, MS Ff.1.6* (London, 1977).

Benson, L. D., ed., *The Riverside Chaucer*, 3rd edn (Oxford, 1988).

Boffey, J., '"Loke on þis wrytyng, man, for þi devocion!": Focal Texts in Some Later Middle English Religious Lyrics', in *Individuality and Achievement in Middle English Poetry*, ed. O. S. Pickering (Cambridge, 1997), 129–46.

Boffey, J., and A. S. G. Edwards, eds, *A New Index of Middle English Verse* (London, 2005).

Brandl, A., and O. Zippel, *Mittelenglische Sprach- und Literaturproben* (Berlin, 1917).

Brewer, D. S., 'The Ideal of Feminine Beauty in Medieval Literature, especially "Harley Lyrics", Chaucer, and Some Elizabethans', *Modern Language Review* 50 (1955), 257–69.

Brook, G. L., ed., *The Harley Lyrics*, 4th edn (Manchester, 1968).

Brown, C., ed., *English Lyrics of the XIIIth Century* (Oxford, 1932).

—— ed., *Religious Lyrics of the XVth Century* (Oxford, 1939).

—— ed., *Religious Lyrics of the XIVth Century*, 2nd edn rev. G. V. Smithers (Oxford, 1952).

Bühler, C. F., 'Lydgate's *Horse, Sheep and Goose* and the Huntington MS. HM 144', *Modern Language Notes* 55 (1940), 563–9.

Bukofzer, M., 'The First Motet with English Words', *Music and Letters* 17 (1936), 225–33.

Burrow, J. A., ed., *English Verse, 1300–1500* (London, 1977).

—— *Essays on Medieval Literature* (Oxford, 1984).

Burrow, J. A., and T. Turville-Petre, eds, *A Book of Middle English* (Oxford, 1992).

Chambers, E. K., and F. Sidgwick, eds, *Early English Lyrics* (London, 1907, repr. 1926).

Champion, P., ed., *Charles D'Orléans: Poésies*, vol. 1 (Paris, 1923).

Connolly, M., *John Shirley: Book Production and the Noble Household in Fifteenth-Century England* (Aldershot, 1998).

Craig, H., ed., *Two Coventry Corpus Christi Plays*, EETS ES 87 (London, 1957).

Croft, P. J., 'The "Friar of Order Gray" and the Nun', *Review of English Studies* ns 32 (1981), 1–16.

Curtius, E. R., *European Literature and the Latin Middle Ages*, trans. from German edn (1948) by W. R. Trask (New York, 1953).

Cutler, J. L., 'A Middle English Acrostic', *Modern Language Notes* 70 (1955), 87–9.

Davies, R. T., ed., *Medieval English Lyrics* (London, 1963).

Dearmer, P., R. Vaughan Williams and M. Shaw, eds, *The Oxford Book of Carols* (London, 1928).

Dobson, E. J., and F. Ll. Harrison, eds, *Medieval English Songs* (London, 1979).

Doyle, A. I., 'More Light on John Shirley', *Medium Ævum* 30 (1961), 93–101.

Dronke, P., 'The Rawlinson Lyrics', *Notes & Queries* ns 8 (1961), 245–6.

—— *The Medieval Lyric* (London, 1968).

—— 'Two Thirteenth-Century Religious Lyrics', in *Chaucer and Middle English Studies in Honour of Rossel Hope Robbins*, ed. B. Rowland (Kent, OH, 1974), 392–406.

Duncan, T. G., review of Dobson and Harrison, *Medieval English Songs*, *Medium Ævum* 50 (1981), 338–41.

—— 'The Text and Verse-Form of "Adam lay i-bowndyn"', *Review of English Studies* ns 38 (1987), 215–21.

—— 'Textual Notes on Two Early Middle English Lyrics', *Neuphilologische Mitteilungen* 93 (1992), 109–20.

—— 'Two Middle English Penitential Lyrics: Sound and Scansion', in *Late-Medieval Religious Texts and Their Transmission*, ed. A. J. Minnis (Cambridge, 1994), 55–65.

—— ed., *Medieval English Lyrics, 1200–1400* (Harmondsworth, 1995).

—— 'The Maid in the Moor and the Rawlinson Text', *Review of English Studies* ns 47 (1996 [a]), 151–62.

—— 'Poetry by Accident? Middle English Lyrics from Latin Sources', in *The Medieval Translator*, vol. 5, ed. R. Ellis and R. Tixier (Turnhout, 1996 [b]), 225–35.

—— ed., *Late Medieval English Lyrics and Carols, 1400–1530* (Harmondsworth, 2000).

—— ed., *A Companion to the Middle English Lyric* (Cambridge, 2005).

Duncan, T. G., and M. Connolly, eds, *The Middle English Mirror: Sermons from Advent to Lent*, ed. from MS Hunterian 250, Glasgow University Library (Heidelberg, 2003).

Dyce, A., ed., *The Poetical Works of John Skelton*, 2 vols (London, 1843).

Eliot, T. S., *On Poetry and Poets* (London, 1957; 6th impression, 1971).

Ellis, F. S., ed., *The Golden Legend or Lives of the Saints as Englished by William Caxton*, 7 vols (London, 1900).

Erbe, T., ed., *Mirk's Festial*, EETS ES 96 (London, 1905).

Faral, E., ed., *Les Arts poétiques du XIIe et du XIIIe siècle* (Paris, 1962).

Fein, S., 'Good Ends in the Audelay Manuscript', *Yearbook of English Studies* 33 (2003), 97–119.

Förster, M., 'Kleinere mittelenglische Texte', *Anglia* 42 (1918), 145–224.

Furnivall, F. J., 'Chaucer and Lydgate Fragments', *Notes and Queries* 5th series 9 (1878), 342–3.

—— ed., *The Pilgrimage of the Life of Man, Englisht by John Lydgate, a.d. 1426, from the French of Guillaume de Deguileville, a.d. 1335*, Part 1, EETS ES 77 (London, 1899).

—— ed., *Political, Religious, and Love Poems*, EETS OS 15, re-edited (London, 1903).

Gardner, H., *Religion and Literature* (London, 1971).

Gillington, A. E., ed., *Old Christmas Carols of the Southern Counties* (London, 1910).

Godefroy, F., *Dictionnaire de l'ancienne langue française*, 10 vols (Paris, 1880–1902).

Goldin, F., ed., *Lyrics of the Troubadours and Trouvères* (New York, 1973).

Gordon, E. V., ed., *Pearl* (Oxford, 1953).

Gray, D., 'A Middle English Epitaph', *Notes and Queries* 206 (1961), 132–5.

—— review of R. L. Greene, ed., *A Selection of English Carols* (Oxford, 1962) and R. H. Robbins, ed., *Early English Christmas Carols* (New York, 1961), *Notes and Queries* 208 (1963), 431–2.

—— *Themes and Images in the Medieval English Religious Lyric* (London, 1972).

—— ed., *A Selection of Religious Lyrics* (Oxford, 1975).

—— 'Songs and Lyrics', in *Literature in Fourteenth-Century England*, ed. P. Boitani and A. Torti (Cambridge, 1983), 83–98.

—— 'Lyrics', in J. A. W. Bennett, *Middle English Literature*, ed. and completed by D. Gray (Oxford, 1986), 364–406.

—— ed., *The Oxford Book of Late Medieval Verse and Prose*, paperback edn (Oxford, 1988).

—— ed., *Robert Henryson and William Dunbar* (Harmondsworth, 1998).

Greene, R. L., *The Lyrics of The Red Book of Ossory*, Medium Ævum Monographs ns 5 (Oxford, 1974).

—— ed., *The Early English Carols*, 2nd edn (Oxford, 1977).

Hamer, R., ed., *A Choice of Anglo-Saxon Verse* (London, 1970; repr. 1972).

Harris, K., 'The Origins and Make-Up of Cambridge University Library MS Ff.1.6', *Transactions of the Cambridge Bibliographical Society* 8 (1983), 299–333.

Jeffrey, D. L., *The Early English Lyric and Franciscan Spirituality* (Lincoln, NE, 1975).

Kane, G., *Middle English Literature* (London, 1951).

Kean, P. M., *Chaucer and the Making of English Poetry*, 2 vols (London, 1972).

Ker, N. R., ed., *Facsimile of B.M. MS. Harley 2253*, EETS 255 (London, 1965).

Kinsley, J., ed., *The Oxford Book of Ballads* (Oxford, 1969).

—— ed., *The Poems of William Dunbar* (Oxford, 1979).

Luick, K., *Historische Grammatik der englischen Sprache* (Leipzig, 1914–40; repr. 1964).

Macaulay, G. C., ed., *The English Works of John Gower*, 2 vols, EETS ES 81 and 82 (London, 1900–1901; repr. 1957, 1969, 1979).

Male, E., *The Gothic Image*, English trans. (1913) of French edn (1910), Fontana Library (London, 1961).

Manning, S., *Wisdom and Number* (Lincoln, NE, 1962).

Mason, H. A., *Humanism and Poetry in the Early Tudor Period* (London, 1959).

Matsuda, T., *Death and Purgatory in Middle English Didactic Poetry* (Cambridge, 1997).

Matthew, F. D., ed., *The English Works of Wyclif Hitherto Unprinted*, EETS OS 74 (London, 1880).

Meech, S. B., and H. E. Allen, eds, *The Book of Margery Kempe*, EETS OS 212 (London, 1940; repr. 1997).

Menner, R. J., 'The Man in the Moon and Hedging', *Journal of English and Germanic Philology* 48 (1949), 1–14.

Migne, J. P., ed., *Patrologiae cursus completus ... series latina*, 221 vols (Paris, 1844–64).

Muir, K., and P. Thomson, eds, *Collected Poems of Sir Thomas Wyatt* (Liverpool, 1969).

Murphy, J. J., ed., *Three Medieval Rhetorical Arts* (Berkeley, CA, 1971).

Mustanoja, T. F., *A Middle English Syntax* (Helsinki, 1960).

Niermeyer, J. F., *Mediae Latinitatis Lexicon Minus* (Leiden, 1976).

Oliver, R., *Poems without Names* (Berkeley, CA, 1970).

Osberg, R. H., 'The Alliterative Lyric and 13th-century Devotional Prose', *Journal of English and Germanic Philology* 76 (1977), 40–54.

Panum, H., *The Stringed Instruments of the Middle Ages*, rev. J. Pulver (London, 1941).

Patterson, F. A., *The Middle English Penitential Lyric* (New York, 1911).

Perkins, G., 'A Medieval Carol Survival: "The Fox and the Goose"', *Journal of American Folklore* 74 (1961), 235–44, and 77 (1964), 263–5.

Person, H. A., ed., *Cambridge Middle English Lyrics* (Seattle, 1953; rev. edn, 1962).

Pike, L. J., *Hexachords in Late-Renaissance Music* (Aldershot, 1998).

Putter, A. D., 'The French of English Letters: Two Trilingual Verse Epistles in Context', in *Language and Culture in Medieval Britain: The French of England, c. 1100–c. 1500*, ed. J. Wogan-Browne *et al.* (York, 2009), 397–408.

Raby, F. J. E., *A History of Christian-Latin Poetry from the Beginnings to the Close of the Middle Ages*, 2nd edn (Oxford, 1953).

Ragusa, I., and R. B. Green, *Meditations on the Life of Christ* (Princeton, 1961; repr. 1977).

Ransom, D. J., *Poets at Play: Irony and Parody in the Harley Lyrics* (Norman, OK, 1985).

Reese, G., *Music in the Middle Ages* (London, 1941).

Reiss, E., *The Art of the Middle English Lyric* (Athens, GA, 1972).

Rigg, A. G., *A Glastonbury Miscellany of the Fifteenth Century* (Oxford, 1968).

Robbins, H. W., 'An English Version of St. Edmond's *Speculum*, ascribed to Richard Rolle', *Publications of the Modern Language Association* 40 (1925), 240–51.

——, trans., *The Romance of the Rose* (New York, 1962).

Robbins, R. H., 'The Earliest Carols and the Franciscans', *Modern Language Notes* 53 (1938), 239–45.

—— 'The Authors of the ME Religious Lyrics', *Journal of English and Germanic Philology* 34 (1940), 230–38.

—— 'The Poems of Humfrey Newton, Esquire, 1466–1536', *Publications of the Modern Language Association of America* 65 (1950), 249–81.

—— 'The Findern Anthology', *Publications of the Modern Language Association of America* 69 (1954), 610–42.

—— ed., *Secular Lyrics of the XIVth and XVth Centuries*, rev. edn (Oxford, 1955).

—— ed., *Historical Poems of the XIVth and XVth Centuries* (Oxford, 1959).

—— 'Middle English Lyrics: Handlist of New Texts', *Anglia* 83 (1965), 35–47.

Robinson, F. N., ed., *The Works of Geoffrey Chaucer*, 2nd edn (London, 1957).

Saintsbury, G., 'The Prosody of Old and Middle English', in *The Cambridge History of English Literature*, vol. 1, ed. A. W. Ward and A. R. Waller (Cambridge, 1907), 372–78.

Saltmarsh, J., 'Two Medieval Love-Songs set to Music', *The Antiquaries Journal* 15 (1935), 1–21, including 'The Music of *Bryd one Brere*' by F. McD. C. Turner, M.A., pp. 19–21.

Salu, M. B., *The Ancrene Riwle* (Welwyn Garden City, 1955).

Sandison, H. E., *The 'Chanson d'Aventure' in Middle English* (Bryn Mawr, 1913).

Schoeck, R. J., review of R. H. Robbins, *Secular Lyrics of the XIVth and XVth Centuries*, *Anglia* 71 (1953), 355–6.

Silverstein, T., ed., *Medieval English Lyrics* (London, 1971).

Sisam, C., 'Ne Saltou Neuer Leuedi', *Notes and Queries* ns 12 (1965), 245–6.

Sisam, C., and K. Sisam, eds, *The Oxford Book of Medieval English Verse* (Oxford, 1970).

Sitwell, G., 'A Fourteenth-Century English Poem on Ecclesiastes', *Dominican Studies* 3 (1950), 285–90.

Skeat, W. W., ed., *The Vision of William concerning Piers The Plowman, etc.* (Oxford, 1886).

—— *Twelve Facsimiles of Old English Manuscripts* (Oxford, 1892).

—— ed., *The Complete Works of Geoffrey Chaucer*, 7 vols (Oxford, 1894 and 1897).

Smithers, G. V., 'The Scansion of *Havelok* and the Use of ME *-en* and *-e* in *Havelok* and by Chaucer', in *Middle English Studies Presented to Norman Davis in Honour of his Seventieth Birthday*, ed. D. Gray and E. G. Stanley (Oxford, 1983), 195–234.

South, H. P., 'The Question of Halsam', *Publications of the Modern Language Association* 50 (1935), 362–71.

Southern, R. W., *The Making of the Middle Ages* (London, 1953; Grey Arrow edn, 1959).

Spitzer, L., 'Emendations Proposed to *De Amico ad Amicam* and *Responcio*', *Modern Language Notes* 67 (1952), 150–55.

Steele, R., ed., *The English Poems of Charles of Orleans*, EETS OS 215 (London, 1941), and (with M. Day) EETS OS 220 (London, 1946).

Stemmler, T., *Die englischen Liebesgedichte des MS. Harley 2253* (Bonn, 1962).

—— *Medieval English Love-Lyrics* (Tübingen, 1970).

Stevens, J., ed., *Medieval Carols*, Musica Britannica 4 (London, 1952).

—— *Music and Poetry in the Early Tudor Court* (London, 1961).

—— ed., *Music at the Court of Henry VIII*, Musica Britannica 18 (London, 1962).

—— *The Old Sound and the New: An Inaugural Lecture* (Cambridge, 1982).

—— *Words and Music in the Middle Ages: Song, Narrative, Dance and Drama, 1050–1350* (Cambridge, 1986).

Stevick, R. D., 'The Criticism of ME Lyrics', *Modern Philology* 64 (1966), 103–17.

Thomson, S. H., 'The Date of the Early English Translation of the *Candet Nudatum Pectus*', *Medium Ævum* 6 (1935), 100–105.

Tolkien, J. R. R., and E. V. Gordon, eds, *Sir Gawain and the Green Knight*, 2nd edn, rev. N. Davis (Oxford, 1967).

Tupper, F., ed., *The Riddles of the Exeter Book* (Boston, 1910).

Utley, F. L., 'How Judicare Came in the Creed', *Mediaeval Studies* 8 (1946), 303–9.

Waddell, H., *Medieval Latin Lyrics*, 4th edn (London, 1933).

Weber, S. A., *Theology and Poetry in the Middle English Lyric* (Columbus, OH, 1969).

Weever, J. de, *Chaucer Name Dictionary*, Garland Reference Library of the Humanities 709 (New York & London, 1996).

Wenzel, S., 'The "Gay" Carol and Exemplum', *Neuphilologische Mitteilungen* 77 (1976), 85–91.

—— *Preachers, Poets, and the Early English Lyric* (Princeton, 1986).

—— ed., *Fasciculus Morum* (University Park, PA, 1989).

Whiting, B. J., and H. W. Whiting, eds, *Proverbs, Sentences and Proverbial Phrases from English Writings mainly before 1500* (Cambridge, MA, 1968).

Whiting, E. K., ed., *The Poems of John Audelay*, EETS OS 184 (London, 1931).

Wilkins, N., 'The Post-Machaut Generation of Poet-Musicians', *Nottingham Mediaeval Studies* 12 (1968), 40–84.

Wilson, R. M., *The Lost Literature of Medieval England*, 2nd edn (London, 1970).

Wolpers, T., 'Geschichte der englischen Marienlyrik im Mittelalter', *Anglia* 69 (1950), 3–88.

—— 'Zum Andachtsbild in der mittelenglischen religiösen Lyrik', in *Chaucer und seine Zeit: Symposion für Walter Schirmer*, ed. A. Esch (Tübingen, 1968), 293–336.

Wooldridge, H. E., *Early English Harmony*, vol. 1 (London, 1897).

Woolf, R., *The English Religious Lyric in the Middle Ages* (Oxford, 1968).

—— 'The Construction of *In a fryht as y con fare fremede*', *Medium Ævum* 38 (1969), 55–9.

—— 'Later Poetry: The Popular Tradition', in *Sphere History of Literature in the English Language*, vol. 1, ed. W. F. Bolton (London, 1970), 263–311.

Wright, T., ed., *Songs and Carols* (London, 1856).

—— ed., *The Book of the Knight of La Tour-Landry*, EETS OS 33 (London, 1868; rev. edn, 1906).

Wyatt, A. J., ed., *Old English Riddles* (London, 1912).

Index of Lyrics

The lyrics are listed by first line and number. The first lines of the burdens of the carols and the titles of Chaucer's lyrics are also listed, printed in italics.